CONSTITUTION

LEGISLATIVE

THE CONGRESS

Senate   House of Representatives

Architect of the Capitol
Cost Accounting Standards Board
General Accounting Office
Government Printing Office
Library of Congress
Office of Technology Assessment
United States Botanic Garden

JUDICIAL

THE SUPREME COURT OF THE UNITED STATES

United States Courts of Appeals—Circuit Courts
United States District Courts
The Judicial Panel on Multidistrict Litigation
Temporary Emergency Court of Appeals
United States Court of Claims
United States Court of Customs and Patent Appeals
United States Customs Court
Territorial Courts
United States Court of Military Appeals
United States Tax Court
Administrative Office of the United States Courts
Federal Judicial Center

DYNAMICS
OF
AMERICAN POLITICS

DYNAMICS
OF
AMERICAN POLITICS

RAYMOND E. WOLFINGER
MARTIN SHAPIRO
FRED I. GREENSTEIN

PRENTICE-HALL, INC.
ENGLEWOOD CLIFFS, NEW JERSEY

Library of Congress Cataloging in Publication Data

WOLFINGER, RAYMOND E.
    Dynamics of American politics.

    Bibliography: p. 615
    Includes index.
    1. United States—Politics and government—
Handbooks, manuals, etc.   I. Shapiro, Martin M.,
joint author.   II. Greenstein, Fred I., joint
author.   III. Title.
JK274.W72   320.4'73   76-2645
ISBN   0-13-221168-8

Printed in the United States of America

10 9 8 7 6 5 4 3 2 1

Design by Ben Kann
Photo research by Mira Schachne
Illustrations by Vantage Art, Inc.
Cover photograph by Glenn Heller

Part and chapter opening photo credits:

Elinor S. Beckwith: Pages 517, 519

Culver Pictures: Page 57

Monkmeyer Photos: Page 437

The National Archives: Page 37

Paul Sequeira, Photo Researchers, Rapho Division: Page 167

Katrina Thomas, Photo Researchers, Rapho Division: Pages 1, 3

Wide World Photos: Pages 19, 85, 87, 123, 213, 247, 295, 297, 345, 389, 477, 561, 585

PRENTICE-HALL INTERNATIONAL, INC., *London*
PRENTICE-HALL OF AUSTRALIA PTY. LIMITED, *Sydney*
PRENTICE-HALL OF CANADA, LTD., *Toronto*
PRENTICE-HALL OF INDIA PRIVATE LIMITED, *New Delhi*
PRENTICE-HALL OF JAPAN, INC., *Tokyo*
PRENTICE-HALL OF SOUTHEAST ASIA PTE. LTD., *Singapore*

TO BARBARA,
WITH LOVE FROM ALL OF US

OUTLINE

CONTENTS

PREFACE

B Y the mid 1970s, the American political system had passed through one of the periods of domestic turmoil that occur from time to time in our history: the Vietnam war, campus unrest, ghetto uprising, followed by the unprecedented scandals associated with the Watergate case. These events were resolved by the forced resignation of a Vice President under threat of criminal prosecution, and by President Nixon's decision to quit the White House rather than be impeached. As a result, Gerald Ford became the only President who had never been elected.

This series of crises tested our traditional notions of how the political system works. At the same time, the political science profession experienced unusually sharp disagreements about what to study, how to study it, and how to interpret the results. By now, we can go beyond the disputes over elitism versus pluralism or behaviorism versus institutionism, and apply a *variety* of approaches to the complex reality of American politics. Political scientists *have* learned a great deal about how the American political system works, and our purpose in this book is to convey this knowledge in a clear, decisive, and hopefully interesting manner.

Dynamics of American Politics describes and explains the main elements of the American political system. The book is organized into four parts: it moves from the *place* where politics is done (Part One); to *individual political behavior* and to the *groups* that link individuals to government (Part Two); then to government itself—the *institutions* of government (Part Three); and finally to the chapters describing policy making, change, and evaluation of government (Part Four).

We begin talking about why politics is a necessity in civilized society. The next three chapters then set the context of American politics: social and economic cleavages in contemporary society, the constitutional context, and an outline of the enduring themes and contradictions in American ideology.

In Part Two, the focus shifts first to individual political behavior in chapters on public opinion, voting behavior, and political participation. We consider how Americans see the political world, what they know about it, how they form and organize their political attitudes, what factors affect their voting, how elections function as mechanisms of choice. We go on to consider what kinds of people participate in politics and for what reasons, the influence of money, and the role of political activists. This discussion of individual political behavior sets the stage for consideration of the organizations—interest groups and political parties—that link individuals to government.

The next step, in Part Three, is to the national governmental institutions themselves: Congress, the presidency, the bureaucracy, the courts. In discussing each institution, we are concerned with its roots in the political processes discussed previously, with the motivations of the people who are its officials, and with the interplay of conflict and cooperation among these institutions.

In Part Four, we move from the structure of government to the functioning of government as a political entity—from anatomy to physiology. We analyze the process by which public policy is made, and then examine change, as well as violent and other extralegal political tactics. We conclude with a chapter that provides students the tools to evaluate our political system for themselves.

The title of the book—**Dynamics** *of American Politics*—reflects an approach we have tried to follow consistently throughout the book. First, rather than treat the political system as firmly fixed forever, we view American politics as a system in a state of continual evolution. The dual themes of change and continuity are intertwined throughout. Second, not only do we describe the "nuts and bolts" of each element in the political system, we also show the interaction and interdependence among its many components. Third, we believe that demonstrating how the system actually works is just as important as teaching how it ought to work. Fourth, we are concerned with how government works or fails to work, not with what government policy should be. We do not see politics in terms of good guys versus bad guys. We have set out to describe and explain, not to praise or condemn. Describing American politics without either apology or denunciation has been a key goal in this textbook.

ACKNOWLEDGMENTS

Much of the research done for this book reflects the work of our talented assistants, particularly Robert B. Arseneau, Steven J. Rosenstone, G. C. Mackenzie, and Paul Quirk. Among the many people who have transformed our drafts into a manuscript, we are particularly indebted to Marian Adams, Phyllis Dexter, Helen Petit, Bojana Ristich, and Sheila Saxby.

Professors Allan P. Sindler, Richard W. Boyd, and Francis E. Rourke read the bulk of the manuscript and made innumerable helpful criticisms and suggestions. Professor Richard F. Fenno, Jr., and Matthew Pinkus of *Congressional Quarterly* improved our treatment of Congress. Michael A. Rappaport of the Opinion Research Corporation generously advised us on the design and political use of public opinion polls. Herbert E. Alexander of the Citizen's Research Foundation shared his matchless knowledge of campaign finance with us.

Anyone who has written a book knows that a vast chasm lies between the authors' manuscript and the finished product in the readers' hands. Philip Rosenberg's strong, sensible, and literate editing improved our work immeasurably. Ann Torbert supervised every aspect of the book's production with skill and patience, both of which were sorely needed. Most of all, we are indebted to Edward H. Stanford, the master architect of the bridge between what we wrote and what you will read.

R. E. W.
M. S.
F. I. G.

DYNAMICS
OF
AMERICAN POLITICS

PART ONE
THE GENERAL SETTING OF AMERICAN POLITICS

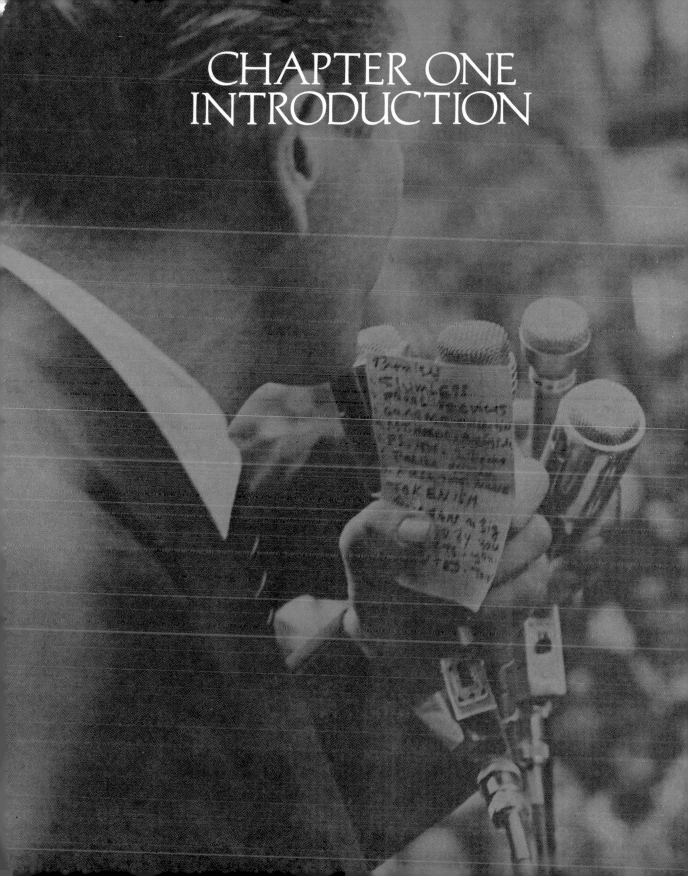

CHAPTER ONE
INTRODUCTION

P OLITICS exists because people live together and seek to act collectively. When people live together, conflicts arise among them because they have differing interests. When they seek to act collectively, their individual actions must be coordinated in order to get things done. Politics faces two ways. On the one hand, it is the ultimate means to reduce or resolve conflict. On the other, it is one way to organize numbers of persons to do things together that they could not have done separately.

POLITICS

CONFLICT

Much of this book is about ways to resolve conflict. A great deal of politics consists of bargaining and compromise designed to give each of two or more conflicting interests enough of what they want so that they can continue to cooperate with each other. The farmer wants a new irrigation project but will not be able to get it without the support of the environmentalist, who wants to use the same land for a new park. Without the farmer's support, the environmentalist will not get his park. So they cooperate. Each side supports the other and they both settle for less than they originally wanted but more than they could have had if they did not join forces. The farmer gets a less extensive irrigation project than he could have had if there were no park to share the land with—but it's still more than he could have gotten without the environmentalist's support. And the environmentalist is better off with the small park than with nothing at all.

Sometimes a course of action can be found that, instead of merely compromising conflicting interests, actually ends the conflict. Two groups, each strongly backing its own candidate for office, may discover a third possible candidate whom they can both support with more enthusiasm than the two they started with.

How successful politics can be at compromising conflict or at ending it altogether frequently depends on whether the conflict comes in little or big pieces. Let us imagine a society composed solely and in equal parts of fishermen and farmers. Let us also suppose that this society was one in which all the fishermen were poor, black, Protestant, city-dwelling, uneducated, and diseased while all the farmers were wealthy, white, Catholic, country-dwelling, educated, and healthy. Nearly any issue in the society would pit 50 percent of the people against the other 50 percent. More important, each and every issue would pit the *same* 50 percent against the same other 50 percent. Whether the issue was urban renewal or farm subsidies or aid to parochial schools, all of the farmers would always be opposed by all of the fishermen.

To a large extent, whether or not a political system works depends on whether or not conflicts can be broken down into small enough parts so that everyone can have a little something. If so, everyone will win sometimes and lose other times. Everyone will sometimes be a political ally of some people and sometimes of other people. In the United States, for example, if a farm subsidy bill passes, all of our farmers may be happy. But only some of our rich and some of our poor, some of our Protestants and some of our Catholics, some of our well-educated and some of our uneducated will be happy, because we have rich and poor, Protestant and Catholic, educated and uneducated farmers. When a law to aid parochial schools is proposed, the Catholic and Protestant farmers who fought together on farm subsidies may find themselves on opposite sides. The Catholic farmers will find themselves allied with Catholic factory workers who fought against the farm subsidy law. The saying that "politics makes strange bedfellows" reflects this pattern of coalition building.

Sometimes, but not often, conflict can be resolved by giving everyone what they want. We can have Mother's Day and Father's Day, and St. Patrick's Day and National Eat More Peanuts Day and Support Your Local Police Day and so on forever because any one of our three hundred and sixty-five days can be two or three different ceremonial days at once. But we cannot resolve most of our political conflicts this way because a basic fact of politics is scarcity.

SCARCITY

The problem of *scarcity* arises because many of the things people want do not exist in sufficient quantity to satisfy everybody. The case of the irrigation project and the park is an excellent example. There simply was not enough land to give both the farmers and the environmentalists as much as they wanted. There probably was not enough money, either. Time is also one of the commodities in scarce supply. For example, most politicians probably would not find it possible to spend as much time listening to the problems of their constituents as some of the constituents might want. Most politics involves the attempt to reduce conflicts about who gets how much of something when there is not enough of that something for everyone.

Indeed, politics at its best may be the art of finding compromises where none seems to exist. For example, liquor prohibition would seem to be an all-or-nothing proposition. If the prohibitionists get what they want, the drinkers get nothing to drink. And if the drinkers get their drink, then the prohibitionists do not get prohibition. But it is possible to allow the sale of liquor and still give the prohibitionists *something* of what they want. Thus, some states where prohibitionist sentiment is strong do not allow the sale of alcoholic beverages in bars or restaurants and confine retail sale to a few state-run stores.

IDEOLOGICAL CONFLICT

There remains, however, one type of difference that is virtually immune to compromise. Some people have intense, complete, and all-encompassing beliefs about what the whole of society must be like to satisfy them. These complete belief systems, called *ideologies,* may leave those who subscribe to them with little room to maneuver in the political arena. Thus, radical socialists, extreme right-wing conservatives, and militant ethnic separatists may refuse to compromise with their ideological principles. The socialist may reject as "capitalist hypocrisy" every small government policy that aids the poor but does not help bring about government ownership of industry, which is an essential feature of the ideal socialist state. The black militant may similarly reject government programs that aid poor blacks but do not contribute to the creation of the militant's ideal of totally independent, totally self-sufficient black communities. Some ideologies may not be concerned with reorganizing the whole of society, but nevertheless they may be so intense that they dominate everything else. Before the Civil War, the most fervid Abolitionist may have had no vision of an ideal society, but he was certain that it was better to have a bloody civil war than to allow the country to continue half-slave and half-free.

When an issue taps wide and deep emotions among at least some of the people, the secret of conflict resolution sometimes lies in confining the issue in such a way as to keep it from becoming dominant. Or it may lie in coercing the militant into keeping quiet. Or, finally, such conflicts may require that we undertake major changes in the political, social, and economic structure to meet the demands of those who feel most deeply.

POLITICS AS A SOURCE OF CONFLICT

In speaking of politics as conflict resolution, we must not forget that politics is itself a major *source* of conflict. One of the things politics is about is who shall govern. Individuals, groups, and political parties seek political power both for its own sake and to use that power to pursue their other interests. Obviously, there is not enough political power to go around. There never can be, for if one person or group gets to govern, then other people and groups must be governed. For instance, there are two major political parties, but there is only one presidency. Only one party at a time can win a presidential election. Just as scarcity of other things leads to conflict, so scarcity of political power leads to conflict.

To be successful in the realm of conflict resolution, the political arrangements of a nation must be capable of holding the level of conflict created by politics itself at an acceptable level. In the United States there are many devices for accomplishing this task. The best known of these is the creation of a great number of governing bodies, political offices, and places of political power in nongovernmental organizations. There are three branches of the central government, fifty state governments, and thousands of county, city, and town governments. We have one President, nine Supreme Court Justices, 535 members of Congress, several thousand high-level federal executives, and hundreds of thousands of state and local officials ranging from governors to members of local school boards. In addition, there are millions of officers of political parties and private organizations ranging from the secretary-treasurer of a local PTA to the president of the American Bar Association. Thus, while not everyone who wishes to hold a position of power can do so, a great many can. And while only one party can hold the presidency at a given time, the others can hold many congressional seats, governorships, judgeships, and so on.

Perhaps even more important than the large number of political offices is the American consensus on the rules of the political game. One of the things that reduces the tension in American politics is the fact that the losing party knows it will get another chance in the next election. As we can see from reading newspaper accounts of events in less stable parts of the world, politics can be a bloody business in nations where the winning party proceeds to outlaw the losing party and execute its leaders as traitors. In the United States, our commitment to a democratic electoral process and to rotation of political offices among large numbers of politicians according to changing electoral fortunes is a major way of reducing the conflict that arises from politics itself.

COLLECTIVE EFFORT

So far we have emphasized the negative role of politics, its role in reducing or avoiding conflict. But politics also has a positive side. One of the major functions of politics is to *organize collective effort* in order to achieve social goals that individuals or private groups find it difficult to achieve by themselves. Governments build dams, maintain fire departments, create parks, aid the needy, provide national defense forces, and so on. There are no natural or required activities for government. At various times in history there have been private rather than government-owned armies and private fire departments. In the contemporary world we often see government-owned hospitals and schools operating alongside privately-owned institutions providing the same services. Government is one means of operating collective enterprises or of focusing large and diverse social resources to deal with a problem or to provide a new benefit for mankind. But it is not the only means. For instance, in the United States we pay for the planes and warships that defend us through politically imposed and governmenally collected taxes, but we make most of them in private factories. Other arrangements are of course possible, with the government engaging in many activities or in few.

Just how much the government should own, operate, regulate, or plan, and just which and how many new collective enterprises it should undertake are themselves political questions giving rise to political conflict. But no major American school of thought has ever maintained that the government ought to do nothing at all. Even those who believe in the old maxim "That government which governs least governs best," nevertheless favor certain government enterprises—for instance, government-operated armies, diplomatic activities, and penitentiaries. Purposive activity of government directed at improving the quality of life need not necessarily involve government ownership or operation. It may involve governmental subsidies, such as grants or loans of money to keep symphony orchestras or railroads going when they are in financial trouble. Other government activity may involve regulation, such as requiring smog control devices to improve air quality.

The political and governmental process must expend a great deal of energy on its own internal processes — that is, on making government work. Campaigns must be organized, elections conducted, legislation deliberated, passed, and administered, court cases heard, and so on. But all this is secondary, for the government's first job is to decide what it is going to do for whom. Politics does not exist simply to maintain itself or to resolve conflict. It also exists to call into being, organize, and coordinate diverse human and material resources in order to make things and provide services that people want.

NEGATIVE CONNOTATIONS OF POLITICS

For all the positive benefits that result from political government, Americans frequently think of politics negatively. One of the ways the *Random House Dictionary* illustrates the word *politics* is with the sentence "The advocated reforms have become embroiled in politics." Or we say of someone we believe to be insincere or without principles that "he's just a politician." To label something "just politics" means that it is without real content, without any purpose other than to get someone reelected or to gain him some other advantage.

Throughout American history we have honored individual politicians such as Lincoln or Jefferson while at the same time expressing our contempt for politicians in general. Not all politicians are good public servants. Some of politics *is* self-serving, designed to save a politician rather than to serve the people. But the reader must guard against unconsciously importing negative connotations whenever he or she sees the word *politics*. In each instance, whether the politics is good or bad — nation-serving or self-serving — is an open question to be decided after a good look. Usually one finds that events in the political world contain a mixture of selfish and other-regarding motives. The self-interest of politicians is one of the basic fuels of politics. It provides much of the energy that keeps politics going. But that does not mean that the sole purpose or product of politics is to improve the lot of politicians.

Much of our negative feelings about politics come from our vision of politics as the self-serving manipulation of some people by others. On the other hand, whatever sympathy we have for political leadership and good government comes from our vision of politics as getting people to work together to solve their problems. Often these two visions are simply different ways of looking at the same thing.

POLITICAL SKILLS

Politics is, among other things, a set of skills through which people seek to increase their influence over others in order to achieve their goals. As such, *politics* means far more than government and the selection of people to govern. At work we speak of the "office politician," and at home we have become increasingly aware of the "politics" that governs the relationships between husbands and wives or parents and children. As these usages indicate, one aspect of politics is gaining control over others or reaching a position of leadership or command. A person may seek such a position either for its own sake of for some substantive purpose, like making the family buy a new car or making the business more profitable. Here again, as in governmental politics, we usually encounter a mixture of desire for self-advancement and desire to achieve a better state of affairs.

Although we can often tell when political skills are being used, it is not easy to specify exactly what they are. A whole range of skills may be useful at various times and in various settings to get others to reduce their conflicts and to work together. Anything from bursting into tears to proposing a new solution no one else has thought of may turn the trick in a given instance. The same technique that has worked in one situation may utterly fail in another. Thus, when we speak of someone as being "a good politician," we usually mean someone who knows which tool to pick and how to use it at exactly the right moment.

Politics is often called the "art of the possible." As in all arts, the political artist must seek to create, to form new things within the limitations imposed by tradition and the materials with which he works. As we have seen already, the art of politics often involves the fashioning of compromise. But political compromise is not necessarily built on giving everybody part of what he wants or treating everyone equally. Political skill is skill at risking and channeling conflict, at accepting some risk and hostility in order to achieve goals. As an artist, the politician must know when and whom to fight, when and in which direction to run, and how to make people happy.

AMERICAN NATIONAL POLITICS

Although we make occasional forays into family, business, religious, and other kinds of politics, this book is largely about politics in the narrower sense. Primarily, we will be examining the activities of government and the processes by which the nation decides who shall govern. We also will be more concerned with national than state and local politics. But, because much of American *national* politics occurs at the state, local, and nongovernmental levels, we must pay close attention to these "lower" levels of political activity. For example, the mayor of Chicago has enormous power within the city of Chicago. His actions have significant consequences for the lives of all Chicago citizens. To the degree that the mayor is simply a political actor within Chicago, we shall not be interested in him. But he is also an actor on the national political level. In this capacity, he influences the behavior of Illinois delegates to the national nominating convention of his political party. He also influences the way the eight members of Congress from Chicago act and vote in the House of Representatives in Washington. And he may have a vital say in the way certain national programs, such as federal urban renewal, affect Chicago.

Similarly, we shall see that many policies of the national government are implemented or even initiated by state governments, or by private firms or groups to whom the central government "contracts out" its work. For example, the government in Washington may tell a state that it will give it a certain amount of money if the state will repair a federal highway to meet federal standards; or it may pay an aerospace firm in Oregon to design a new missile for the Defense Department. To the extent that state and local governments and private organizations do the national government's business, they will concern us in this book.

More is known about American politics than about the politics of any other nation, simply because the great bulk of the world's political scientists are in the United States and many of them have devoted themselves to analyzing the nearest available political facts. They are aided in their study by the fact that the American government is enormously less secretive than most other governments. What is more, because the United States is the largest democratic nation in the world, the study of American politics is probably the best path to an understanding of democracy.

THE DYNAMICS OF POLITICS

There are two ways in which political science can approach the study of government. On the one hand, there is a *static* approach, which is concerned with describing how a political system is designed to operate. In essence, the static approach gives us an "idealized" account of politics, for it tells us how the system *ought* to work. For example, by studying the Constitution, we can learn what powers are supposed to belong to the President, what powers are supposed to belong to Congress, and so forth. Similarly, a study of the laws regulating interstate commerce can tell us what economic activities are allowed and which ones are prohibited.

In real life, though, things seldom work out exactly as their designers intended. Over the years, the living institutions of government grow and evolve. Thus, American politics is always changing. Fortunately, so is the state of knowledge about American politics. For this reason, we cannot hope to present a *final* account of our political system. If it is to stay in touch with reality, political inquiry must always be a matter of continuing investigation, clarification, and revision. This is why an understanding of the way our political system was designed to operate must be supplemented by an understanding of the *dynamic* elements of politics. The *dynamic approach* to politics provides an account of how the system *really* works, which is surely as important as the official formulas about how it ought to work.

Although our focus, therefore, will be largely on what we *know* about how American politics *actually works,* the ideal or "ought" elements of politics will not be overlooked. For instance, in Chapter 3 we will treat the Constitution as part of the political context of American politics. The Constitution is one of the many factors setting the outer limits of political action. It tells politicians that although they can choose to do many different things, there are some they cannot do at all. Yet the Constitution is more than merely a set of limits. Most American politicians, like most other Americans, have "internalized" the Constitution. Their sense of political right and wrong is largely shaped by it—or, rather, by their understanding of it. For many people, the Constitution is the cornerstone of their faith in American politics. Although a document written in 1789 says nothing specific about many of the specific issues facing us today, our sense of the spirit of the Constitution serves as a guide to action. Because we believe in a living Constitution, it does live. If it were not for this belief, the Constitution would be little more than a historical document on display at the National Archives. Of course, we cannot grasp the dynamics of twentieth-century government in its entirety by reading an eighteenth-century document like the Constitution. But on the other hand, we cannot really understand those dynamics without paying attention to beliefs and expectations about how American politics ought to be organized.

POLITICAL EVALUATION

In political analysis, a distinction is often made between *description* and *evaluation*, and we are often warned about the danger of confusing the two. We must try to distinguish those accounts of a political system that show us how the system works from those accounts that pass judgment on it. Yet some kinds of political evaluation are very closely related to description of the dynamics of politics. For instance, we may ask "What is the impact of the seniority system in Congress?" This is not really a question of opinion or value, of whether the seniority system works in a way we approve. Various observers may give different answers. Some may say it helps conservatives control Congress. Others may say it doesn't. But the disagreement is about how the thing works in fact, not about whether it is a good or bad thing. Indeed, we can't tell whether it is a good or bad thing until we know how it works in fact.

A little farther from factual description is evaluation in terms of specific criteria. For instance, does the seniority system increase or decrease citizen control over political leaders? We need not agree on whether citizen control is a good or bad thing in order to ask and answer this question. Basically, the question remains one of fact—how does the seniority system really work? But now it is a question of fact focused on a specific criterion of evaluation. It asks us to analyze how seniority works in terms of whether it turns out well or badly in terms of a specific value—citizen control.

Finally, farthest away from dynamic description is evaluation in the sense of broad judgments of intrinsic value. Is citizen control over leaders a good thing? Social scientists usually offer "if . . . then" answers to these ultimate value questions. They say: "Our knowledge of how the world actually works leads us to the conclusion that *if* you want more citizen control of politicians, *then* you should reform the seniority system in such and such a way." In some cases, though, such if-then answers are not possible. We often don't know enough about how politics really works to predict accurately whether a particular value will actually be fostered if we make a given change in our political process.

Of course, political scientists, including the writers of this book, do have their own ultimate political values. No doubt these values color some of what we say. But on the whole, the evaluations offered in this book are most concerned with assessing the impact of a given political arrangement in terms of specific criteria. We will attempt to make "if . . . then" statements where we have the knowledge to do so. We are not concerned with assigning intrinsic values. The basic questions as to what is ultimately good and bad are left to the reader. We have sought to provide him or her with the kind of analysis of actual political dynamics that will help in answering these questions.

PLAN OF THE BOOK

So far we have spoken about politics, political dynamics, and political evaluation without defining the word *politics*. Dictionary definitions of complex phenomena like politics are either circular or so abstract as to be of little use, particularly to beginning students. Speaking in an obscenity case, a judge once said "I can't define it, but I know it when I see it." The same is true of politics. When our readers have completed this book, they still may not know how to define American politics, but they should know it when they see it. At this point the reader will get less help from definitions than from a brief outline or roadmap of how this book describes the workings of American politics.

We begin with a description of the environment or context within which American politics operates (Chapters 2, 3, 4). Then we move to the level of individual political behavior (Chapters 5, 6, 7). Next come the ways people join together in groups and parties to do politics (Chapters 8, 9). We then move on to an account of the government (Chapters 10, 11, 12, 13, 14). In Chapters 15 and 16 we describe the dynamic process of policymaking and change through which politics actually has its effect on society. Finally, in Chapter 17, we offer some thoughts on evaluating the system we have described. In other words, the book moves from the place where politics is done to individual political action, then to ways individuals organize into groups in order to choose and influence governments, then to government itself, and finally to the processes of government.

THE CONTEXT OF AMERICAN POLITICS

We start with the context or environment of politics because it provides both the resources for politics and the limitations on how much politics can do. Chapter 2 is devoted to the socio-economic context of American politics. It describes the physical and economic resources available to the United States as well as its human resources, the people. Obviously, the physical and economic side of American life is important for its politics. For example, if there were no deserts in the United States, there would be no political action directed at getting the government to build irrigation projects. Conversely, if the land were all desert, rather than a rich industrial and agricultural society, the government could not raise the tax dollars to build irrigation projects. Indeed, the economic and physical resources of a country influence its foreign policy as well as its domestic policies. A small, poor country could not have won World War II and would not have been tempted to try to win a war in Vietnam.

The human context of politics may be even more important. Some Americans belong to the upper class and a great many more to the middle class. Some have much more education than others. Some live in poverty, others in plenty. Some are black and some are white. In politics people are not merely faceless votes. They are also individuals. Perhaps even more important is the fact that those individuals fall into such larger categories as poor urban blacks, or Catholics, or white-collar suburbanites. Often a politican thinks about how people in one or another of these groups will react to some political action he is about to take. Obviously, all of the human characteristics of a person influence how he or she feels about politics and what he or she wants out of politics.

In Chapter 3, we deal with the constitutional context of American politics. We examine the written Constitution and our beliefs about it as well as the general structure of government that it establishes. One of the most confusing things about politics is the fact that it acts and reacts on itself. In a sense, politics creates its own environment because what politicians do helps shape the world in which they operate. Thus, the constitutional context is both a product of political actions and a major influence on them. For example, American politicians at the Constitutional Convention of 1789 made the political decision to create a federal system of government. Out of the original thirteen states and one nation have grown fifty states and one nation. Today's politicians must operate within this context, which was created by politicians almost two hundred years ago. In our federal system the states are not as strong as the central government. But the central government finds it hard to impose on the states its decisions in certain areas, such as the control of crime, because most policemen work for city and state governments, not the government in Washington. These are some of the facts of life politicians today must deal with. But these facts are themselves the products of political acts in the past.

Chapter 4 is about the ideological context of American politics. Here we will examine the broad and general ideas held by Americans about how politics should be done and what its goals ought to be. Because many of these ideas are expressed in terms of what Americans think is constitutional and unconstitutional, Chapter 4 flows rather naturally out of Chapter 3. Clearly, the ideological context provides both restraints and resources for political action. For example, if most Americans think that everyone should be allowed to speak freely, then the President is going to have a hard time getting Congress to pass a censorship statute. On the other hand, if Americans have a basic commitment to human dignity and equality, this commitment can be harnessed to get Congress to support government food programs designed to end malnutrition among the poor.

INDIVIDUAL POLITICAL ACTION

From the environment or context of politics we turn to the individual level of political action. Chapters 5 and 6, on public opinion and voting behavior, form a natural pair. Public opinion is the total of individual opinions, just as election outcomes are the total of individual votes. Moreover, data from public opinion polls and elections give us most of the knowledge we have about how individuals think and act in politics. Indeed, expressing their opinions and voting are the only political actions that most individual Americans undertake.

Although both opinion polls and elections give citizens an opportunity to express their political preferences, there are important differences between them. Public opinion is expressed continuously, not simply at election time. It is far more issue-oriented and fragmented than voting. There are usually only two or three candidates for an office and the voter can choose only one of these. But there are hundreds of issues—farm subsidies, social security, gas rationing, school integration, and so forth. Each individual can have an opinion on each issue. What is more, there are many positions on each issue. A person need not simply be for or against school integration, the way he must vote either for or against a candidate. He may be partly in favor of integration and partly opposed. For instance, he may be for changing school boundaries but against busing to achieve integration.

VOTING IS THE
FOUNDATION FOR
ALL LINKAGES BE-
TWEEN PUBLIC
OPINION AND
GOVERNMENT
POLICY.
Wide World Photos

Chapter 5 examines how people learn about politics and how they form their political opinions. It also examines the changing strengths and distributions of the countless public opinions on various issues that compose what we refer to for short as "public opinion." Chapter 6 examines voting as the form of political action most common to all Americans. It describes who votes and examines why they vote the way they do.

The voting described in Chapter 6 is the most widespread form of political activity, but some citizens do more than vote. Chapter 7, on political participation, forms a bridge between the chapter on voting and those on collective political action. In exploring forms of political participation other than voting, it addresses itself to the question of why some Americans move beyond voting to more active involvement in politics and what forms that involvement takes.

COLLECTIVE POLITICAL ACTION

Many Americans do not confine their political activity to the individual level. They also act collectively through the formation of *interest groups* and *parties*. Interest groups seek to organize and focus the political desires of their constituents. Parties seek votes. Chapters 8 and 9 on interest groups and parties, examine the ways in which individual political preferences are brought together and organized so that they can more effectively influence government.

Earlier, we stressed that politics came about because people of differing and sometimes conflicting interests sought to live and work together. People sometimes can express their interests through their votes and through other individual acts such as writing public officials. They also can band together with others who share the same interests. Chapter 8, on interest groups, examines the organized political effort of various interests to achieve their goals and adjust their relations with other interests. Interest groups are a more collective, more organized expression of interests than are individually expressed opinions or votes. They are a smaller-scale, more specialized form of interest expression than are the political parties, which seek to collect or cut across numerous interests. Thus, the chapter on interest groups appears between the chapters on individual political activity and the chapter on parties.

Chapter 9 examines political parties in America. The American party system is one of the principal means we have of collecting, compromising, and integrating large numbers of the individual and group interests in the society so that they can work together to win elections. We choose who will govern through the system of parties and elections. In this sense, parties serve as a transmission belt between all the individual and group politics discussed earlier in the book and the government, which will be discussed later. Because they must get many people together to wage electoral campaigns, and then must get even more voters together to win elections, parties are, like government itself, among the basic American mechanisms for channeling and consolidating conflict among various interests and organizing diverse people for collaborative action.

GOVERNMENT

Chapters 10, 11, 12, 13, and 14 examine the institutions of the national government. Chapter 10 is closely linked to Chapter 9 because it begins with a discussion of how Congressmen are elected, and how Congress is organized. Chapter 11 examines how these factors produce legislation.

Chapter 12 is on the presidency. Within the government, the President faces in three directions. He must deal with Congress in the passage of new laws; he heads the federal bureaucracy which does the day-to-day work of the Executive Branch of government; and he must be concerned with how the judiciary interprets the laws made by Congress and the actions of the Executive Branch, including his own actions. Thus, the chapter on the President occurs after those on Congress and before the chapters on the bureaucracy and the federal courts.

In its examination of the administration of the federal government, Chapter 13 goes considerably beyond the civil servants who sit in Washington. Today the business of the federal government is done not only in government offices in Washington, but in federal field offices scattered across the country, in state and local government agencies which do the local administration of many federal programs, and in private organizations which are paid to do all sorts of research, development, and administrative chores for the government.

Chapter 14 on the judiciary is especially attentive to the courts' relations to the other parts of government described in Chapters 10, 11, 12, and 13.

Each part of government acts on all the others, and, in turn, is acted on by them. No one can fully understand Congress until he has studied the presidency because the President is an important source of the legislation Congress considers. And no one can fully understand the presidency without studying Congress, because a President who is not on friendly terms with Congress leads a very different political life from one who has the support of the legislators on Capitol Hill. Nor can we understand the President unless we understand his relation to the vast federal bureaucracy. The bureaucracy, in turn, sits at the intersection between the power of the President, who is theoretically its boss, and the Congress, which provides it with its money and its new programs. Nor can the Supreme Court be understood in isolation. The nature of the Court is fundamentally shaped by the President who nominates its members and the Senate which must confirm them. Yet this influence, too, runs in both directions, for one of the basic jobs of the Supreme Court is to review the laws enacted by Congress as well as the decisions and actions of the President and the federal bureaucracy. Thus the Court, rather than being nine wise men operating in isolation, is constantly engaged in close relations with the rest of government.

For this reason, some patience is required in reading Chapters 10 through 14. It is not possible to say everything all at once. Yet until everything is said about the government, nothing is complete or even completely clear. Because the flow of change runs through many interconnected parts, it is necessary to grasp the whole pattern of interconnections. But the beginner who does not look at one part at a time will become hopelessly confused. Thus we take up the parts of government one at a time. But as we do so, we try from the beginning to stress the interconnections. When the student has finished these chapters, he or she should have a distinct feel for each of the parts of the government and some sense of their interactions.

THE CENTERS OF
NATIONAL GOVERN-
MENT IN WASHING-
TON: THE SUPREME
COURT *(top)*; THE
CAPITOL *(center)*;
THE WHITE HOUSE
(bottom).
American Airlines

POLICY AND CHANGE

One of the major purposes of Chapter 15, which is devoted to policy-making, is to further assist the student in putting the parts of government back together again. This chapter describes how public opinion, interest groups, parties, and the various parts of government combine to make policy. In this sense, it is a review of the whole book.

Another way of looking at Chapter 15 is to say that Chapters 2 through 9 describe what goes into government. They describe the support people give to government—by believing in its legitimacy and participating in politics—the demands they make upon government to satisfy their particular interests, and the efforts of parties to put their candidates into governmental offices. Chapters 10 through 14 describe what happens to individual opinions, group and party interests, and party politicians in each institution of government. They are about what goes on inside the government. Chapter 15 considers features of decision-making that transcend each individual institution of American government.

Policy-making is essentially change making. Every call for a new policy is a call to change the way the government does something, or to get it to do something it hasn't done before. Of course, most governmental policies involve only small changes. Chapter 15 assumes that very few government policies change the basic way that the government itself or the political process works. Chapter 16, on the other hand, confronts directly the potential for major, radical, violent, and even revolutionary change in American politics. It discusses the costs and benefits of employing the tactics of confrontation, limited violence, war, and revolution. It treats efforts to substantially change politics, including approaches to changing the entire structure and dynamics of the political system. It also deals with changes that would radically alter the whole political scene.

EVALUATION

Chapter 17 is about political evaluation. In one sense, it is closely linked to Chapter 16, because demands for major change are usually linked with beliefs that current arrangements are very bad. In another sense, however, Chapter 17 seeks to provide a new perspective on everything that the reader has seen earlier in the book. The person who is absolutely sure that something is "totally" good or bad often is the person with superficial knowledge of the thing being evaluated. By the time readers reach Chapter 17, we hope that they will know enough about American politics to make them hesitant to accept the easy slogans of the right or of the left. Chapter 17 does not offer the author's own evaluations. It does point out the various modes of arriving at political evaluations and the advantages and pitfalls of each. It is about asking political questions, and about how to answer them. But it does not *give* the answers. It provides what we hope is an appropriate non-conclusion to an introductory text, because political evaluation does not end with one book or one course.

SUMMARY

People engage in politics in order to resolve conflicts and organize themselves for collective activities under conditions in which scarcity of resources means that everyone cannot have everything he or she wants. This book describes how and why American national politics works as it does. After examining the social, economic, constitutional, and ideological contexts of American politics, it moves on to individual political activity, collective political action, and governmental institutions. Then it examines the policy-making process and the modes for achieving change in the political system. It concludes by providing intellectual tools for evaluating American politics.

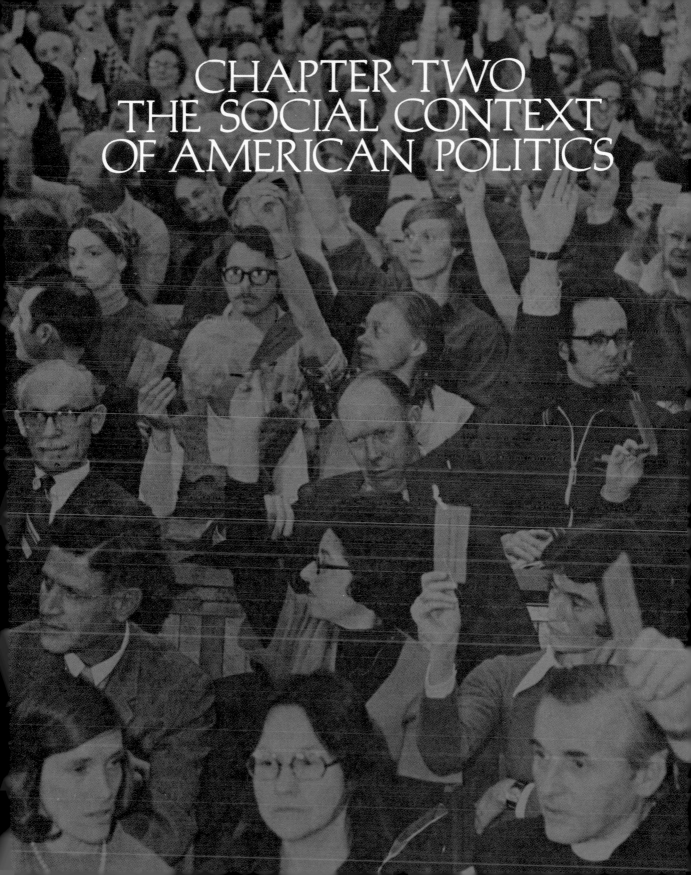

CHAPTER TWO
THE SOCIAL CONTEXT
OF AMERICAN POLITICS

W HO are the American people? Where did they come from? What do they do for a living? How well are they succeeding at it? Where do they live? There are literally millions of answers to these questions, for the United States is one of the most heterogeneous nations in the world. Its people can trace their origins to every corner of the planet, and there is also constant migration within the country — from east to west, from south to north, from rural areas to cities and suburbs. Its occupations run the gamut from cowboy to astronaut, and incomes range from virtually nothing to millions of dollars a year. Obviously, ethnic, social, and economic differences of this magnitude must have an enormous impact on American politics. They are major sources of political interests. They are bases of political conflicts and alliances, and they provide the resources of political influence.

Of course, political conflict is not simply an extension of social differences. Nevertheless, these differences do condition politics in important ways. Rich and poor often have dissimilar interests and frequently vote differently, as do people of different ethnic backgrounds, different educational levels, and different occupations.

In order to provide some sense of the sources and divisions of American politics, we present the following broad-brush portrait of the United States and the American people.

GEOGRAPHY

The United States is located in a massive, resource-rich land bounded on the east and west by wide oceans.[1] These physical features fostered development of an independent nation with a culture that was not merely a reproduction of the parent civilizations in Europe. Although the ocean permitted direct contact with Europe in the early days of the nation's history, it was a formidable enough barrier to keep that contact to a minimum. This gave the early colonists access to European goods and ideas but prevented them from being overwhelmed by the Old World's ways of thinking and doing things. The ocean barrier also reduced the possibility of foreign military threats and minimized the need for a large standing army.

When Europeans first arrived on this continent, the American land mass was sparsely populated by native tribes. Over the course of centuries of struggle, the original Americans were overwhelmed by the technology, manpower, and organization the European settlers brought to their campaign of westward expansion. The existence of ice-free ports on both coasts and an abundance of coal and iron — the two basic raw materials of the Industrial Revolution — also contributed to the growth of a uniquely wealthy and powerful nation. Yet these physical circumstances of the United States cannot tell the whole story. They may have made the development of modern

---

[1] The United States has the fourth largest amount of land among the world's nations, ranking after the Soviet Union, the People's Republic of China, and Canada. It is seventy-third in population density.

America possible, but they are not what made modern America. They have been influential only because human beings *made* them important.

WEALTH

Discussion of American geography leads naturally to consideration of the uses to which these physical advantages have been put. Some countries with modest natural endowment, such as Denmark, Switzerland, and Israel, nevertheless enjoy considerable economic well-being. Other nations blessed with ample resources seem unable to exploit them and remain mired in desperate poverty. The United States, which combines remarkable natural resources with the impulse and capacity to develop them, has made economic achievements unparalleled in human history. Although Americans comprise only 6 percent of the world's population, they account for almost 40 percent of the world's total production of goods and services — gross national product (GNP).

It does not follow that we have achieved 40 percent of all human satisfaction! Leaving aside considerations about the shortcomings of materialism, we recognize that some aspects of GNP obviously do not correspond to personal satisfaction. For example, if industrial production in a wealthy country forces its residents to move to the suburbs to escape air pollution and then to buy second cars to commute to work, all this endeavor increases the GNP but reduces total human satisfaction. In the last chapter, we will consider some alternative ways to measure socially beneficial output. Here we will stick to money, not because it is the most important measure of social well-being, but because it is the most convenient for comparative purposes.

How is America's unprecedented wealth manifested at the level of the individual family? The most common measure is *median family income,* which was $12,051 in 1973.[2] The median, a highly useful statistical concept, is the midpoint in a distribution of some attribute among people who have that attribute. Here we mean that in 1973 half of all American families had incomes of more than $12,051, and half had less than this amount. Prosperity has increased steadily in the United States since the Great Depression of the 1930s. In 1950, for example, median family income was $3,300. Of course, a dollar is worth less today than in 1950, but in spite of inflation, Americans are still much better off than they were then. Real income has almost doubled in twenty-five years. Indeed, during this period Americans came to accept annual increases in real income as natural and inevitable. The 1970s, however, brought a decline in the real income of many segments of the population. National income figures cover wide variations from one region to another. In the Northeast, the most prosperous part of the country, the 1973 median was $12,850. In the poorest region, the South, the 1973 median was only $10,627.

[2] Unless otherwise indicated, the social and economic information in this chapter is taken from *Statistical Abstract of the United States 1974* (Washington, D.C.: U.S. Government Printing Office, 1974).

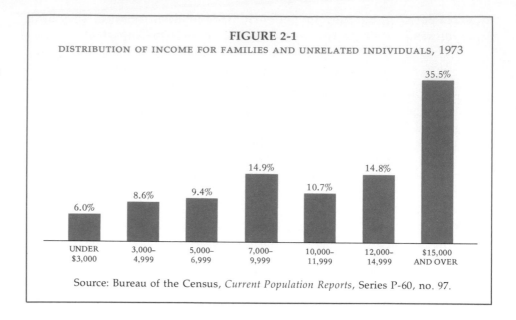

FIGURE 2-1

DISTRIBUTION OF INCOME FOR FAMILIES AND UNRELATED INDIVIDUALS, 1973

Source: Bureau of the Census, *Current Population Reports*, Series P-60, no. 97.

To fully understand the significance of these statistics, we must look beyond the median income figures. Focusing entirely on median income tends
to hide the great inequality of family incomes. The poorest fifth of all American families in 1973 had incomes under $6,081 and received only 5.5 percent
of the total income received that year. The poorest two-fifths of the population, with incomes ranging up to $10,034, got only 17.4 percent of all income.
On the other hand, the top 20 percent of all families, with incomes at $19,-
254 and above, took in a whopping 41.1 percent of all income.

In 1973, over a third of all American families had incomes of more than
$15,000, as Figure 2–1 shows. Only 11 percent received less than $4,540 that
year. This means that one family out of every nine was below the federal
government's official poverty line. (The poverty line is calculated for an
urban family of four. The government revises it each year to reflect changes
in the cost of living.) These figures point out an important aspect of the poverty problem in the America of the 1970s: the poor are a minority who lack
the traditional political weapon of the underprivileged—numbers. In the not
too distant past—and at present in most other countries—the poor are "the
masses." In America, the achievement of prosperity for the masses means
that those who continue to be deprived cannot rely only on their voting
power to bring their problems to the attention of government.

ETHNICITY AND RACE

The nation has grown from a population of 3.9 million at the time of the
first census in 1790 to 203 million in the 1970 census. It continues to add

over 2 million residents each year.[3] The most significant historic cause of this growth is immigration. One of the great clichés about the United States is that it is a "nation of immigrants." Like many clichés, this one is true. With the exception of less than a million American Indians, everyone in this country can trace his or her ancestry to relatively recent migrants from Europe, Africa, Latin America, or the Far East.

Over 45 million people immigrated to the United States between 1820 and 1970. About 80 percent of them came from Europe.[4] In addition, several million blacks were brought here forcibly as slaves, almost all before 1820. The peak of immigration was reached in the first decade of the twentieth century, when our population was swollen by almost 9 million migrants, mostly Catholics and Jews from southern and eastern Europe. In 1920, 40 percent of the population consisted of immigrants and their children.

In the early 1920s, the tide of culturally different newcomers led to the passage of laws that sharply limited both the number of immigrants and the countries from which they could come. This quota system gave the most

[3] The Census Bureau estimates that it "missed" about 5.3 million people in 1970, of whom 1.8 million were black. We will stick with the official census figures because they provide the best comparative measure of population characteristics.

[4] Reliable records on immigration were not kept until the 1820 census. Since then, 6.9 million people have come here from Germany and about 5 million each from Great Britain, Italy, and Ireland.

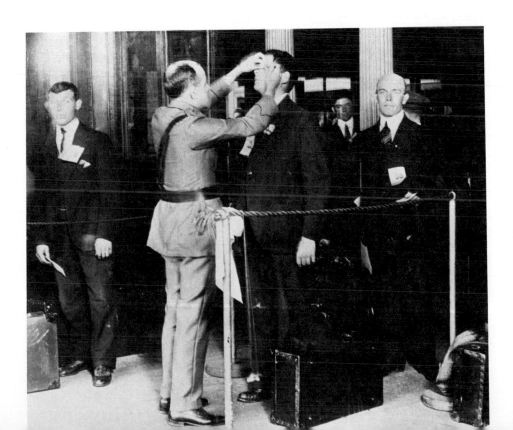

IMMIGRANTS BEFORE WORLD WAR I GOT THEIR FIRST VIEW OF AMERICA ON ELLIS ISLAND, NEW YORK CITY. HERE, NEW ARRIVALS ARE LINED UP FOR EXAMINATION BY PHYSICIANS.
Wide World Photos

generous allowance to northern European countries, where there was little interest in emigration, and the smallest quotas to those nations whose citizens were most anxious to cross the Atlantic. Asians were almost wholly excluded. Contrary to popular belief, however, this legislation did not put an end to all significant immigration. Today one American in six was born abroad or has at least one foreign-born parent. Almost 6 million people immigrated in the twenty years between 1950 and 1970. Most of them, however, were not Europeans. The largest contributions came from Canada and Mexico. A major reform of the immigration laws in 1965 paved the way for a large increase in immigration from Asian countries. At present, over 100,000 people from the Far East immigrate to the United States each year. In 1973, for the first time in American history, more Asian than European immigrants entered the United States.

These trends will slowly alter the ethnic makeup of the American population, further mixing an already disparate citizenry. Intermarriage already has resulted in many millions of Americans who cannot easily identify themselves as belonging to a single nationality group. Of those Americans whose ancestry is not too confused, we can identify the major components of the current population, as shown in Figure 2–2.

During the first half century of nationhood, free Americans were mostly English-speaking Protestants. This homogeneity made it easy to maintain the assumption that the United States would be a "melting pot" in which people from any part of the world would lose their original identities and

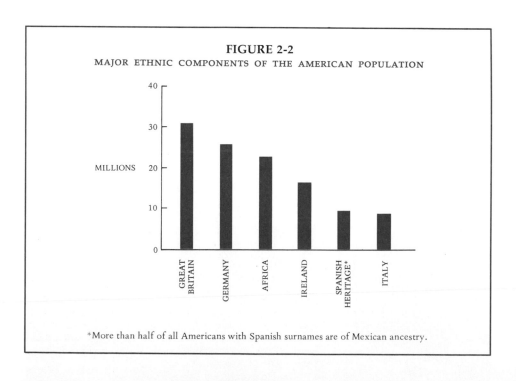

FIGURE 2-2

MAJOR ETHNIC COMPONENTS OF THE AMERICAN POPULATION

*More than half of all Americans with Spanish surnames are of Mexican ancestry.

become simply "Americans."[5] This ideology was severely strained in the 1840s, when America began to get a new kind of immigrant, who was neither Protestant nor English-speaking. Arriving just as America was beginning to industrialize, the masses of Irish Catholics who came here in this period encountered harsh religious bigotry and economic exploitation. Rebuffed in their attempts to become Americans, the Irish retreated into the solace of their own ethnic identity. They lived in Irish neighborhoods, attended Irish churches, joined Irish social and civic associations, and so forth. In urban areas the same pattern was repeated with successive waves of immigrants from Germany, Italy, Poland, and other countries. The immigrants who settled outside the industrial areas of the Northeast and Midwest experienced less discrimination and were more easily assimilated. The same was true of those who became farmers.

The first generation of immigrants usually was desperately poor. But even when their children went to school and attained some measure of prosperity, they often continued to experience discrimination from Americans of English-speaking Protestant stock. In many instances these children retained ancestral memories of their rejection, and in turn passed these memories on to their children. The consequence of these experiences has been to maintain to this day a strong sense of nationality-group consciousness among many millions of Americans. Their national ancestry is what psychologists call a *reference group*—that is, a collectivity with which people identify and whose existence helps its members define themselves, at least in some circumstances. We all belong to various reference groups. Depending on the context, we may think of ourselves as Americans, students, professors, radicals, conservatives, blacks, whites, and so on. Different reference groups are important in different contexts.

There is good reason to believe that the impact of ethnic groups on American politics increases as immigrant groups attain some measure of prosperity. Usually a group does not produce political leaders until it has developed a middle class. These leaders then symbolize the aspirations of the nationality group and make group membership politically relevant. Millions of nationality group members vote for candidates of "their own kind" in preference to other candidates, crossing party lines if necessary to manifest their continuing ethnic solidarity. As we will see in Chapter 6, moreover, there are strong tendencies for members of particular nationality groups to identify with one party or the other.

ETHNIC STEREOTYPES

In the last few years, European nationality groups have been "rediscovered," and there has been widespread speculation about their social and political

POLITICIANS
TRADITIONALLY
INCLUDE ETHNIC
ACTIVITIES IN THEIR
CAMPAIGNING.
HERE, PRESIDENTIAL
NOMINEE GEORGE
MCGOVERN TRIES
HIS HAND AT
BOCCIE IN AN
ITALIAN NEIGH-
BORHOOD.
Wide World Photos

[5] The "melting pot" notion is not inevitable in any country populated by immigrants. In Canada, for instance, it is widely assumed that immigrants will maintain their cultural identities and not become merged into a general Canadian national identity. Canadians speak proudly of the "mosaic" character of their society and believe that it leads to a rich diversity of cultures flourishing in amicable proximity. Canada, however, has paid political costs for ethnic separatism, particularly in the cleavage between Canadians of English and French extraction.

characteristics. Perhaps the most conspicuous beliefs about ethnics are that they are predominantly blue-collar workers, always on the point of abandoning their traditional loyalty to the Democratic party, prejudiced against blacks, and belligerently patriotic in foreign policy. Sociologist Andrew M. Greeley has shown that all these beliefs about European nationality groups are *not true*. They are no more than myths, although they are among the most prominent myths of our times. For example, European ethnics are *not* the core of the blue-collar working class. On the contrary, they are relatively prosperous. Of the three most numerous relatively unassimilated nationality groups, Irish Catholics are *more* likely than the average American to hold white-collar jobs, Italo-Americans are at about the national average in this respect, and Polish-Americans are only slightly below the average. All three of these groups are well above the national mean on income. The most prosperous ethnic groups in the country are Jews, Irish Catholics, and "British Protestants." The three least prosperous groups are blacks, people of Spanish heritage, and Irish Protestants.

Members of almost all European ethnic groups have attained extraordinary progress in the last twenty years. If we look at people aged sixty or more, we see that Americans of Italian, Polish, and other Slavic ancestry are well below the national average in income and education. But members of the same ethnic groups below the age of thirty rank above the national averages in these categories.

Greeley has also shown that, far from being "hard hats," Irish Catholics, Italians, and Poles were no more likely than Protestants to be hawks on the Vietnam war. By the same token, members of these groups are just as favorable to racial equality, generous welfare payments, the eighteen-year-old vote, conservation, and other liberal policies.[6]

BLACK AMERICANS

Americans of British and German descent no longer maintain a strong sense of their own separate national identity. Blacks are now the largest self-conscious ethnic group in America. About one American in nine is black. Blacks have fared less well than any of the other ethnic groups we have discussed so far. They have less education, worse jobs, and lower income. In 1973, for example, blacks had a median family income of $7,596 compared to $12,595 for whites. Since 1968, black per capita income has been about 60 percent of white per capita income. In 1973, about 7.4 million blacks—one third of all those in this country—were below the poverty line. More than twice as many whites — 15.1 million — were below the poverty line, but they comprised only 8 percent of the white population. For the last twenty years,

[6] Andrew M. Greeley, "The Demography of Ethnic Identification," unpublished paper, National Opinion Research Center, University of Chicago, 1973; and "Political Attitudes Among American White Ethnics," *Public Opinion Quarterly,* 36 (Summer 1972), 213–20.

the unemployment rate for blacks has been about twice that of whites.[7] Almost a quarter of all black families get some kind of public assistance, compared to only one white family in twenty. (In 1972, 15 million Americans were on welfare.)

PERSONS OF SPANISH HERITAGE

Along with the blacks, another major ethnic group that does not seem to be getting its share of the blessings of American society consists of what the census calls "persons of Spanish heritage." This includes about 5.25 million Americans of Mexican descent, living mostly in the Southwest and California, and about 1.5 million Puerto Ricans, most of whom live in or near New York City. All in all, more than 9 million Americans are of Spanish heritage. Of these, 2.4 million—more than 25 percent—are below the poverty line. Their median family income in 1971 was $7,550, which is slightly better than the figure for blacks but well below that of white families. Along with the European nationality groups and blacks, people of Spanish heritage have become more conscious of their own ethnic identity in the last few years. Like blacks, they also have become far more active and articulate in pressing their claims upon the majority of society.

RELIGION

Turning from the racial and ethnic analysis of the American people, let us examine the way the population breaks down in terms of religion. Sixty percent of the American people are Protestants, 27 percent are Catholics, 2 percent are Jews, and the remainder either profess no religion or affiliate with minor denominations. About 16 percent of Protestants and 6 percent of Catholics are nonwhite. Although the original settlers were almost wholly Protestants, and most of the Catholics and Jews arrived in the United States within the past century, comparisons of the three religious groups on education, income, and occupations show that the Protestants have lost the superior position they once enjoyed in these respects, the Catholics have caught up, and Jews have forged ahead.

Jews are the most prosperous and best educated of any major religious or ethnic group. In 1975, 41 percent were employed as managers, administrators, or professionals—twice the proportion of Protestants and Catholics. Similar proportions held for college education; about one out of two Jews had attended college, compared to one of four for Protestants and Catholics. Sixty-eight percent of all Jewish families enjoyed incomes of $15,000 or more, compared to 27 percent for Protestants and 31 percent for Catholics.

The various religious groups are distributed quite unevenly around the country. About half the Jews live in and around New York City and almost all live in cities and suburbs. The East is the least Protestant part of the

[7] Herman P. Miller, *Rich Man, Poor Man* (New York: Thomas Y. Crowell, 1971), pp. 68–69.

country—42 percent of its residents are Protestant, 42 percent Catholic, and 5 percent Jewish. The South is almost wholly Protestant—80 percent.[8]

Our brief examination of racial, ethnic, and religious divisions in American society should be enough to indicate that, for the most part, the lines of ethnic division do *not* coincide with lines of social class. Blacks and people of Spanish heritage are the two major exceptions to this generalization. Political theorists point out that discontent is likely to be greatest when all of the lines that divide a population are drawn in the same places.[9] That is, when people who are bound together by religion are also united in poverty or plenty, they are more likely to find a base for political action than when the lines that separate them on one issue bind them together on another. As we have seen, blacks and persons of Spanish heritage find that all the major lines of cleavage coincide. Thus, it should come as no surprise that they have begun to make increasingly strong demands to remedy the situation. At present, middle-class elements are emerging in both these groups, and it is from these middle classes that political leadership is drawn. Some observers, however, speculate that the continued development of a middle class ultimately will mute black and brown militants. This is a question that only the future can answer.

AGE

We all have heard innumerable discussions about "the youth generation." The middle years of this century witnessed a dramatic increase in the number of young people as the low birth rates during the Depression and World War II were followed by a release of pent-up reproductive energy. This produced the famous postwar "baby boom." But the youth generation already is becoming the young married generation, as the unglamorous and inexorable processes of aging continue. Indeed, the proportion of school-age children actually has been shrinking for the past few years.

Nevertheless, young people constitute a mighty political army, at least in potential. At the time of the 1972 election, there were 25 million Americans aged eighteen through twenty-four. They accounted for 18 percent of the potential electorate. But because of the well-known tendency for young people not to vote, the potentially vast political power of the "youth bloc" has not been realized. Thus, although the median age of the voting-age population was forty-three in 1972, the median age of those who actually turned out at the polls was a couple of years higher.

[8] Because the Census Bureau has been forbidden to ask questions about religious affiliation for more than thirty years, information on this subject can be obtained only from polls or "informed estimates." Almost all the information reported here is from *Religion in America: 1975, Gallup Opinion Index,* Report No. 114. The estimate about the location of Jews is from the *American Jewish Year Book,* published by the American Jewish Committee and cited in *Congressional Quarterly Weekly Report,* February 5, 1971, p. 245.

[9] See Robert A. Dahl, ed., *Political Oppositions in Western Democracies* (New Haven: Yale University Press, 1966).

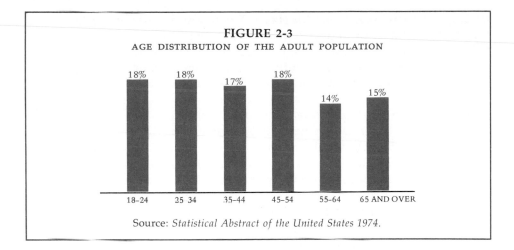

FIGURE 2-3

AGE DISTRIBUTION OF THE ADULT POPULATION

Source: *Statistical Abstract of the United States 1974.*

Often overlooked because of the emphasis on youth is the fact that 21 million Americans were over the age of sixty-five in 1972. The elderly account for 15 percent of the potential electorate. In certain respects, the interests of the elderly are rather special. Because many of them live on fixed incomes, inflation hits them with particular severity. They are also concerned with increasing social security benefits and protecting the market value of stocks, which provide income for many retired people. Their economic plight is summarized by the fact that 27 percent of Americans over the age of sixty-five had incomes below the poverty line in 1972.

The number and proportion of elderly voters will increase because of advances in medical science and the aging of a population produced when birthrates were higher. Conversely, the young share of the electorate will decline owing to the dwindling of the postwar baby boom and perhaps also to a growing belief in the virtues of minimal population growth.

OCCUPATIONS

At the beginning of this century, 38 percent of the American labor force worked on farms and in other "primary industries" such as mining and forestry. An additional 35 percent were blue-collar workers, chiefly in factories. Thus, almost three-quarters of the population could be called "workers and farmers." By 1970, on the other hand, only 3 percent of the labor force worked on farms and in other primary industries, 37 percent were engaged in various kinds of manual occupations, ranging from skilled craftsmen and foremen to factory workers, and 48 percent of the population had various kinds of white-collar jobs—professional and technical, managerial and administrative, sales, and clerical. The remainder of the labor force was in various kinds of service occupations. From these figures we can see one reason why the United States is sometimes called a "post-industrial society." Only about two-fifths of the labor force actually produce things; the other three-fifths are engaged in providing one or another kind of service. This trend toward an increase in the service sector of the economy is sure to continue.

Not all the people with white-collar jobs are executives or professionals. Indeed, the biggest proportion of them are salespeople or clerks. Nevertheless, partially because they work with well-educated, prosperous associates, such people have a very different outlook on social and political questions from blue-collar workers. Moreover, something near a fifth of all employed people in this country are professionals or executives—"the bosses." These changes in the occupational structure of our society explain why political theories such as Marxism, which assign a special historical role to "the workers," are becoming increasingly irrelevant to modern American society.

What is more, important shifts are occurring within the working-class section of the labor force. Only about 6 percent now are unskilled workers, down by more than half from what it was at the beginning of the century. The continuing reduction in the market for unskilled labor is a gloomy portent for the uneducated parts of the population. Half a century ago, the economy demanded large numbers of people whose only qualification was their muscles. Now the economy needs fewer such people, with the result that the uneducated find it increasingly difficult to get work.

Another trend in employment is the enormous expansion in the number of government employees. Out of a labor force of 89.5 million in 1974, 14.7 million were government employees. This means that one out of every six American workers is employed by the government. In just 14 years, the number of government employees went up by nearly 6 million, almost en-

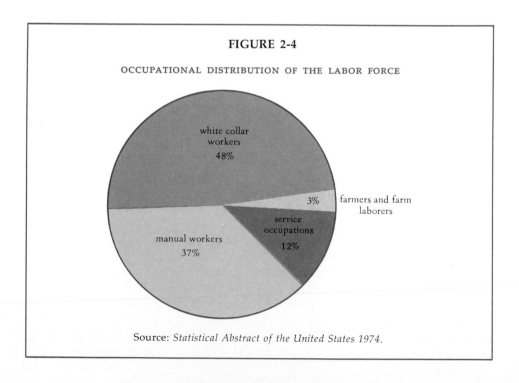

FIGURE 2-4

OCCUPATIONAL DISTRIBUTION OF THE LABOR FORCE

white collar
workers
48%

3% farmers and farm
laborers

service
occupations
12%

manual workers
37%

Source: *Statistical Abstract of the United States 1974.*

tirely at the state and local levels, which now account for 11.8 million of the 14.7 million public employees. (These figures do not include over 2 million men and women in the armed forces. Although the number of federal civilian employees increases slowly and steadily, the number of uniformed military personnel fluctuates, depending upon American military and foreign policy. At the height of the war in Vietnam, over 3.5 million men were in the armed forces.)

It is estimated that during the 1970s one new job in four will be at some level of government. One important implication of this continuing trend is that governmental budgets will go up at all levels in order to pay the salaries of this growing population of public servants. (Generally, pay for government jobs is higher than in corresponding civilian employment, except at the top levels, where compensation in private employment is much higher. Few public officials receive more than $50,000 a year, but salaries reaching above this level are commonplace at the higher levels of private employment.)

Another trend of considerable importance is the increasing tendency for women to work. In 1973, 35 percent of the total labor force was female, and this figure is expected to rise continuously in the years ahead. Among full-time workers, women's earnings were only 62 percent of men's earnings. To a small extent, this inequality results from the fact that women have less work experience. Mostly, though, it can be traced to discriminatory practices against women, such as not giving them equal pay for equal work and not providing them with equal job opportunities.

About a quarter of the labor force—over 20 million people—belong to labor unions. In a later chapter we will explore more aspects of the union movement; here we wish only to note that the kinds of jobs that traditionally have been least likely to be unionized—public employment, professional and managerial work, and so on—are growing rapidly, while factory and skilled labor jobs are not. Thus, the outlook for the continued expansion of the labor movement seems to be quite limited, unless the unions can achieve major breakthroughs in organizing government employees and clerical workers.

INCREASING NUMBERS OF WOMEN ARE WORKING IN ALL SORTS OF OCCUPATIONS. *Wide World Photos*

SOCIAL CLASS

If we look at the distribution of occupations in terms of the class structure of American society, we find the following. The upper class and the upper middle class, consisting of professionals, executives, and administrators, makes up 20 percent of the working population. The lower middle class, consisting of sales and clerical workers, accounts for another 30 percent. And the working class, including foremen, craftsmen, factory workers, service workers, and farmers, weighs in with 50 percent.[10]

Looked at in this way, social classes are *categorical groups*. That is, they are regarded as groups by virtue of the fact that the people in them are con-

[10] Farmers present a thorny problem in this respect, for they include millionaire ranchers and impoverished sharecroppers. But since the total of all those engaged in agriculture accounts for only 3 percent of the population, this difficulty need not give us too much concern.

sidered to share certain characteristics. In this case, however, the characteristics are exceptionally vague. They include such factors as the status or prestige attached to an occupation as well as the income it produces. For many occupations, high status tends to coincide with high income, and vice versa. But there are numerous exceptions. For example, teachers are classified as middle-class professionals despite the fact that most of them earn less than skilled workers. Similarly, a physician with a general practice in a poor community might have a very high status but a modest income. Because of such disparities, only the most stubborn of orthodox social theorists would insist that categorical groups like this really constitute bases for political action.

For this reason, most modern class theorists would argue that what is important is not the category to which people "belong," but how they identify themselves. It is not their class but their *class consciousness* that matters. For example, we cannot tell how the low-income doctor will vote simply on the basis of the fact that we consider him a member of the professional middle class. We would have to know whether he identified primarily with his more affluent colleagues or with his impoverished patients. Indeed, on some issues he might identify with one group while on others he might see that he shares the same interests as the other group. This means that it is more useful to regard social class as a *reference group* than as a categorical group. When Americans are asked if they think of themselves as members of one social class or another, about a third of them say that *they do not think of themselves in these terms at all,* and the remainder sort themselves fairly evenly into the "middle class" and the "working class." Moreover, these two ways of identifying class membership do not coincide very neatly. About 31 percent of the people who think of themselves as being in the working class are, by objective standards, in the middle class; that is, they hold white-collar jobs. And about 32 percent of those who call themselves members of the middle class have blue-collar jobs.

Even more to the point for the purposes of political analysis is the fact that class consciousness does not seem to be an important factor in determining how Americans think about political issues. In one survey, 40 percent of the people interviewed did not seem to believe that the working class and middle class have different views about political issues. Only 7 percent felt that the two classes always agreed and less than 2 percent thought that they were consistently in disagreement.[11]

In short, we can speak of differing levels of wealth, education, political power, and social prominence in the United States. These levels are real and they have real political consequences. But we cannot easily lump those differing levels into two or three neat, distinct, and definite classes whose identity determines political behavior and attitudes. In this sense, there is no clear class structure or class conflict in the United States, although there is a great deal of political, social, and economic inequality and conflict over that inequality.

[11] The findings here and in the preceding paragraph are based on data from the 1972 Presidential Election Study of the University of Michigan Center for Political Studies.

TABLE 2-1
DO WORKINGMEN AND THE MIDDLE CLASS USUALLY AGREE
OR DISAGREE ON IMPORTANT ISSUES?

RESPONSE	PERCENT
Always agree	7%
Usually agree	11
Sometimes agree	15
Neither agree nor disagree	40
Sometimes disagree	12
Usually disagree	3
Always disagree	2
Don't know	11
Total	101%

Source: Data from the 1972 National Election Study of the University of Michigan Center for Political Studies.

WHERE DO AMERICANS LIVE?

Half of the population of the United States resides in only eight states: California, Illinois, Michigan, New Jersey, New York, Ohio, Pennsylvania, and Texas. About 140 million Americans live in 243 different standard metropolitan areas.[12] Of these, the largest portion, 76 million, live in the suburbs. This represents an increase of 20 percent over the suburban population just ten years earlier, continuing a trend that has seen the suburban share of the national population almost double since 1940. Another 64 million people live in central cities, which grew by just 1 percent from 1960 to 1970.[13] About an equal number—63 million—live in smaller cities, towns, and in the country. These nonmetropolitan places account for a decreasing share of the population. Half the counties in the country lost population from 1960 to 1970. In 1970, only one American in twenty-two lived on a farm.

As the suburbs grow, the nation's central cities are becoming poorer and blacker. In 1970, blacks comprised over a quarter of the population of central cities in large metropolitan areas. New York City, for example, lost a million white residents between 1960 and 1970 and gained half a million blacks, who made up more than a fifth of its population. Washington, Newark, and Atlanta all have black majorities, and more than 40 percent of the residents of Baltimore, New Orleans, Detroit, and St. Louis are black. Several of these cities already have elected black mayors, and in the years ahead more cities will be led by black politicians.

[12] The Census Bureau defines a "standard metropolitan statistical area" as a city and its surrounding suburbs. This includes such relatively non-cosmopolitan areas as Omaha and Grand Rapids. One hundred million Americans live *outside* standard metropolitan areas of 500,000 or more people.

[13] Although central cities in the aggregate have held their own in population, the older core cities of the North have been losing significant numbers of residents. These losses are offset in the national totals by the growth of newer cities in the South and West.

THE MOVEMENT OF
WHITE AMERICANS
TO THE SUBURBS
HAS LEFT MANY OF
THE NATION'S
CENTRAL CITIES
WITH INCREASINGLY
NONWHITE POPU-
LATIONS.
Stan Wakefield (top);
Bob Combs, Photo
Researchers, Rapho
Division (bottom)

What is the impact of population shifts on politics? At first glance, it might seem to be slight. Most people who move to the suburbs do not seem to change their political outlook along with their address. That is, a person from, say, a small predominantly Republican town tends to remain a Republican when he moves to the city; a central city Democrat keeps his party loyalty when he moves to the Republican suburbs. There is, however, a different kind of political result from these population shifts. As the nation's cities are drained of much of their middle-class population, they also lose much of their Republican voting strength and become Democratic strongholds. This has increased the number of safe Democratic seats in the House of Representatives — safe seats that represent crowded urban neighborhoods rather than rural southern backwaters. This means that the congressmen with the most seniority increasingly will be liberals representing working-class constituencies, whether black or white. This is a marked change from the recent past, when the overwhelming bulk of safe seats tended to be in placid, conservative rural areas. Thus, the consequence of suburban growth is to enhance the power of liberal Democrats in Congress and to reduce the power of conservative southerners. Concurrent social and economic changes in the South are hastening this process by affecting the other side of the equation. Increasingly, Republicans are being elected in what used to be called the "solid South." This reduces the number of conservative southern Democrats who come from "safe" districts and easily build up impressive amounts of seniority.

THE BASES OF FACTION

Much of this chapter is or can be cast into a discussion of the *bases of faction* in the United States, as well as a body of information that any student should have before plunging into study of the political system. We have seen that the United States is large. It is geographically, ethnically, and racially diverse. There are great disparities of wealth. What is more, all of these differences and inequalities are distributed irregularly through the population. There is a higher proportion of poor among blacks than among whites. There is a higher proportion of poor people in the South than in the Northeast. There are proportionally more blacks in the cities than in the suburbs. Catholics and Protestants have about the same educational levels, but Jews are more highly educated. Jews live predominantly in the Northeast, Chicanos almost entirely in the Southwest. If we had painted a more elaborate picture of our economic geography, we could have shown that there are no tuna fishermen but a lot of steelworkers in Gary, Indiana. And there are no steelworkers but a lot of tuna fishermen in San Diego, California.

In a nation of 210 million people and such diversity, there must be a great diversity of political interests, goals, and values. And there must be many groups or factions — that is, sets of persons who have in common one or more of those interests, goals, or values. There are, of course, some overreaching commonalities that stretch across the lines of faction. All of the unemployed have something in common. All of the nonwhites have something in common. All of the poor have something in common. But the unemployed tuna fisherman may want something different than the unemployed steelworker. The fisherman might be hoping for a ban on the importation of foreign tuna while the steelworker may want policies that encourage the use of more steel. Similarly, although all nonwhites may feel themselves to be the victims of discrimination, this does not necessarily mean that blacks, Chicanos, and American Indians want the same things or would be happy if treated the same way by the government. Nor do all the poor view all issues the same way, despite the fact that they have many interests in common. The working poor may seek a higher minimum wage, but that means little to the unemployed poor.

At times, our critical faculties may be sharpened by viewing American politics as a conflict between the haves and the have-nots, the whites and the nonwhites, the elites and the masses, the bourgeoisie and the proletariat, the North and the South, or the old stock and the immigrants. However, for everyday working purposes it is most useful to examine American politics as a vehicle for expressing and satisfying a very wide range of very unevenly distributed human needs and desires. We should not assume in advance that American politics does a good job of satisfying the totality of these needs and desires. Nor should we be surprised if it does a better job at serving some of them than at serving others. Most importantly, we should not be taken aback to learn that a political process reflecting such diversity is composed of countless different parts interacting in countless different ways. Therefore we may discover that any two parts may interact very differently with one another at different times, depending upon what needs and desires come to the fore at any given moment.

The remainder of this book necessarily introduces a great number of political people, processes, and institutions which act in a variety of ways to meet the diverse demands of thousands of factions. At the same time, it provides some insight into the common aspirations of the American people as a whole. Precisely because of the diversity of American life, we can rarely offer a clear, simple rule or law of politics that specifies exactly how any part of the political process will invariably act. A tolerance for complexity is necessary if one is to learn about American politics because American life is complex.

SUMMARY

This chapter has portrayed a large, wealthy, highly industrialized nation, whose population is marked by great differences in income, ethnicity, race, religion, age, occupation, and place of residence. The U.S. does not have a few clearly defined social classes acting in political opposition to one another. Instead, its great range of differences tends to create a very large variety of political interests which are mirrored in our very diverse and complex political system.

CHAPTER THREE
THE CONSTITUTIONAL CONTEXT OF AMERICAN POLITICS

THE United States Constitution ought to be an easy thing to describe. It is a relatively short document. Indeed, it is printed at the back of this book and the student ought to read it now. We know who wrote it and why and a good deal about what went on at the Constitutional Convention.[1] Yet when we try to relate the actual document, which now lies under glass in the National Archives, to what actually goes on in American politics, it is not so simple.

THE IDEAS BEHIND THE CONSTITUTION

In one sense, the Constitution is interesting because it records much of the political ideology current in 1789. It was this ideology that stamped the character of the new nation. From England, the colonists imported the liberal philosophy of John Locke, which taught that government was essentially the result of a contract freely entered into by individual citizens. The framing and ratification of the American Constitution was a literal, historical enactment of Locke's theory. The Constitution was and is viewed as a contract between the people and their government. It specifies what powers the government shall have and what limits are placed on those powers. When we say an act of government is *unconstitutional,* we say it is legally null and void, because anything the government does that violates its contract has no legal force.

The philosophy of Locke and the other English liberals drew not only on the notion of contract but also on the idea of "natural law." At least since Roman times, some philosophers had argued that there was a "higher law" than man's law. This higher law, which ultimately derived from God, was inherent in nature. Men could understand it through the exercise of human reason. According to this philosophic tradition, any man-made law that violated the natural law was not law at all, for no human law could stand against the will of God and the natural order of the universe. Americans have always viewed the Constitution as an embodiment of this higher law. This line of argument provides American legal thinkers with yet another reason for their conviction that an unconstitutional law is no law at all. It is no law both because it violates the contract represented by the Constitution and also because it violates the higher law.

A third English heritage behind our Constitution is the tradition of English common law. The common law was a mass of court decisions, old statutes, legal maxims, and lawyers' lore passed on from generation to generation. By the seventeenth century, most Englishmen believed that the common law embodied the collective, traditional wisdom—the "right reason"—

[1] Much material on the Convention, as well as other information bearing on the background of the Constitution, is summarized in Broadus Mitchell and Louise Pearson Mitchell, *A Biography of the Constitution of the United States* (New York: Oxford University Press, 1961). One of the most important collections of original documents relating to the Constitution is Max Farrand, ed., *The Records of the Federal Convention of 1787,* 4 vols. (New Haven: Yale University Press, 1911).

of the English people. Indeed, many Englishmen saw it as a kind of higher law against which new government actions should be measured. Adapting this tradition to the situation in the United States, most Americans came to see the Constitution as our equivalent of the common law, embodying the wisdom and right reason of our people. Here again it follows that a law that violates the Constitution is not a law at all—this time because it runs against the collective, historical, legal wisdom of Americans.

Notice how all three conceptions of the Constitution—contract, natural law, and common law—came together to give us two overriding ideas. *First, the Constitution is higher law.*[2] Whenever there is a conflict between the Constitution and a law passed by Congress or a state or city government, the new law must be wrong and the Constitution must be right. *Second, the Constitution is an ordinance of reason,* so that any government act that is unreasonable must be unconstitutional.

THE LIVING CONSTITUTION

These powerful traditions behind the American Constitution make it more than simply a document written at a particular moment by particular men. It is a symbol or code word for whatever our current ideas are about what the government ought and ought not do, about what is or is not reasonable public policy. It is in this sense that we speak of "the living Constitution." For example, Americans do not find it peculiar to debate the "constitutionality" of the government's licensing television stations, even though the men who wrote the Constitution could not even have imagined television.

We often use the term *constitution* to mean the whole structure of something—as when we say a person has "a strong constitution." The British speak of their constitution even though they have no specific written document like ours. By "constitution," the British simply mean their basic arrangements and procedures of government. In this sense of the term "constitution," Americans encounter a peculiar problem, for as we shall see, our basic governmental arrangements and procedures do not really match our written Constitution. In many ways, the *constitution* of American government does not square with what is described in the *Constitution.* For example, two of the most fundamental features of our living, political constitution—parties and the bureaucracy—are not really contemplated in our written Constitution. Parties are not mentioned in the document at all, and although the "executive departments" are mentioned a few times, the Founding Fathers clearly did not anticipate the huge bureaucracy that has become a central feature of American government. (Parties will be discussed in Chapter 9 and the bureaucracy in Chapter 13.)

Nor does the document itself mention the Supreme Court's power to declare laws unconstitutional, which is discussed in Chapter 14. Even more

[2] Edward S. Corwin, *The Higher Law Backgrounds of the Constitution* (Ithaca: Cornell University Press, 1956).

important, it does not precisely define the relation of President to Congress, discussed in Chapters 11 and 12. Indeed, throughout our history, the balance of power between Congress and the President has shifted back and forth. Each change in this balance has been greeted by critics who denounced it as "unconstitutional." But who can say which of the many balances is the truly constitutional one? Was President Jefferson behaving constitutionally when he totally dominated the House of Representatives? Or was the Senate within its constitutional rights when it sternly blocked President Wilson's dreams of international cooperation by frustrating American participation in the League of Nations?

THE INTENT OF THE FRAMERS

Our written Constitution is not a detailed and specific blueprint for government. Even if it were far more detailed than it is, there would still be countless government activities that it does not deal with, simply because life has grown far more complex in the centuries since it was written. Hence there are bound to be discrepancies between our written Constitution and our living constitution. How can these discrepancies be resolved? How can one tell whether an act of government is constitutional or unconstitutional when the situations covered by the act could never have arisen in the eighteenth century, when the framers of the Constitution met to draft the document?

One of the ways for dealing with such questions is to try to ascertain the "intent of the framers." By analyzing their ideas about government, we can make some educated guesses about how they would have looked at the constitutional issues that arise today. In this way, we can keep our contemporary constitutional interpretations more or less consistent with the principles upon which the nation was founded.

What do we know about the intent of those who wrote the Constitution? The men who met in Philadelphia in 1789 were representatives of the wealthier and better educated segments of colonial society. For a number of reasons, they were dissatisfied with the weak central government established by the Articles of Confederation and headed by the Continental Congress. First, the Confederation government did not have sufficient economic power to prevent the states from erecting trade barriers along their boundaries, which would inhibit the flow of business across state lines and prevent the growth of a flourishing national economy. Second, a confederation of separate states could not establish a single, firmly backed currency that would cover all the former colonies. A sound dollar, acceptable everywhere, was a key to the expansion of interstate and international trade. And third, the confederation could not speak with sufficient unity in vital international affairs.

Moreover, several of the state governments were subject to strong pressure, perhaps even capture, by small farmers who were heavily in debt and desired new laws favoring debtors over creditors. A national government would be far less likely to come under the control of these local agrarian interests than some of the states in which this radical sentiment was concentrated. A relatively strong central government also might help ensure that the big states, like Massachusetts and Virginia, did not dominate the smaller ones. Above all, a stronger central government might ensure that the political experiment initiated by the Revolution would prosper rather than disintegrate in the squabbling of thirteen small states.

There was substantial agreement among the framers on a moderately strong central government. But most of them were loyal to their states as well as to the ideas of Locke and other liberals. They wanted a national government strong enough to ensure international security, national economic and political development, and the security of traditional property rights. But they also wanted to create a government that would not be able to tyrannize its citizens.

Numerous political thinkers, from Locke all the way back to the ancient Greek philosopher Aristotle, had preached *mixed government* as a solution to this problem. A mixed government was one in which power was divided among a number of governing institutions, and both the masses of people and the wealthier and better educated had some say. Thus, one branch of government would check the others and prevent them from abusing their powers, just as one segment of the population would balance the other to keep the interests of one group from dominating. The framers embodied these ideas in the Constitution, but they were not content with mixing as the sole guarantee against tyrannical government. Again, borrowing from Locke's ideas about contract, as well as from revolutionary experience in England and the colonies, they sought to impose specific limitations on the powers of even a mixed government.

As we read the Constitution, this pattern of granting limited powers to a mixed government becomes clear.[3] It is reflected in the very structure of the Constitution. Articles, I, II, and III establish the basic framework of government, dividing it into three parts: the Congress (Article I), the Executive (Article II) and the Courts (Article III).

ARTICLE I: ALL LEGISLATIVE POWERS HEREIN GRANTED SHALL BE VESTED IN A CONGRESS OF THE UNITED STATES, WHICH SHALL CONSIST OF A SENATE AND A HOUSE OF REPRESENTATIVES.

The framers were more concerned about the legislature than the other two branches because they felt it had the most potential for undue expansion. Thus, they not only provided for a division of power between the three branches, but also divided the legislative branch into two parts, the House of Representatives and the Senate. Each part was supposed to check the other,

---

[3] An extremely valuable guide to reading the Constitution is Edward S. Corwin, ed., *The Constitution of the United States of America: Analysis and Interpretation* (Washington, D.C.: Government Printing Office, 1953). See also the latest edition of *The Constitution and What It Means Today* (Princeton: Princeton University Press, 1954), originally written by Corwin and periodically brought up to date by other authors.

THE CAPITOL BUILDING WENT THROUGH SEVERAL DESIGNS BEFORE IT WAS COMPLETED IN THE FORM FAMILIAR TO MOST AMERICANS. CONSTRUCTION OF THE CAPITOL BEGAN IN 1793; THE FIRST DOME, SHOWN HERE, WAS FINISHED IN 1827.
Culver Pictures

for a bill could become a law only with the assent of both. The House of Representatives was to be the "popular" wing of the legislature, directly elected by the people and representing their interests. The House alone was to have the power to initiate *revenue* (tax) bills, although such bills would also have to be passed by the Senate, which was allowed to amend them. By custom, this House priority has been extended to appropriations bills — that is, the laws that allow the government to spend the money raised by tax laws. This special role for the House with regard to money matters was based on British tradition. In England, the principal control that the people had over the Crown was the ability of the House of Commons to withhold new taxes needed by the king until he had responded to their grievances.

The very name of the Senate suggests age. The Latin *sen* is the stem of the English word senate, and the senate of the ancient Roman Republic was intended as a body of wise elders. This usage reflects the framers' intention that the Senate of the United States of America serve as a mature, rather aristocratic check on the popular enthusiasms of the House. The number of House seats assigned to each state is geared to the population, so that the more populous states have larger delegations. But in the Senate all states are equal, for each has two senators. House members had to be at least twenty-five years old, but the minimum age for senators was set at thirty. (Both minimum ages may seem rather young today, but given the lower life expectancies in colonial America, and the fact that revolutionary governments are usually staffed by very young men, thirty seemed old at the time.) The House was to be elected every two years, so that it would reflect the opinion of the moment, but senators were to have six-year terms. One-third of their number was to be elected every two years. This arrangement of staggered terms meant that at most only a third of the Senate could be turned out at any one time. This was further insurance against the Senate's yielding to sudden bursts of popular sentiment. Most important, senators were not to be chosen directly by the people as were members of the House. Instead, they were elected by the state legislators — an arrangement that remained in effect until 1913, when ratification of the Seventeenth Amendment provided for direct, popular election of senators.

REPRESENTATIVE DEMOCRACY

This contrast between House and Senate should not be allowed to obscure a more basic fact about both bodies, however. The framers believed that representation, as opposed to direct rule by the mass of people, was itself a device for mixing aristocratic with popular government. They were confident that the people would elect the most responsible, the most educated, the most qualified among them as their representatives. Representative government would serve as a filter and elevator of mass sentiment. It would place the actual power of day-to-day governing in the hands of the better sort. Thus, the name *House of Representatives* had a nondemocratic connotation that we tend to forget today. Indeed, one of the basic motives for founding a large central government with its capital far away from where most citizens lived was that such a government necessitated representation. It could not be run like town meetings or local assemblies of the people. This nondemocratic strain in the thinking of the framers was further emphasized by the fact that the less popular of the two parts of the legislature, the Senate, was not only given an equal share in lawmaking with the House, but also was assigned special responsibility to advise and consent to grave matters of executive government, including the appointment of Cabinet members, Supreme Court Justices, and other high officers, and the concluding of treaties with foreign powers.

THE INDEPENDENCE OF CONGRESS

Following English experience in the struggle to preserve parliamentary freedom from the encroachment of the king, Article I also gives the Congress power to regulate its own elections, make its own internal rules, elect its own officers, and set the pay of its members.[4] Members of both houses also were given special protection from arrest, libel suits, and other forms of harassment. They were forbidden to hold executive office while in Congress or even to resign in order to accept an executive office that had been created or whose salary had been increased while they were in Congress. These measures obviously were intended to maintain a free and independent legislature not subject to either threat or bribery by the executive. But these provisions also rendered impossible the evolution of the sort of Parliament-Cabinet government that was developing in England at that same time. This form of government is based on the fact that members of the cabinet — that is, the executive branch of government — are simultaneously members of the legislative branch.

POWERS OF CONGRESS

The core of Article I of the Constitution is to be found in Section 8. It specifies the powers of Congress. It begins by enumerating a series of taxing, spending, borrowing, commerce, bankruptcy, monetary, postal, patent, and copyright powers designed to allow the new government to foster and encourage a prosperous national economy. Then comes a series of law enforcement and war powers designed to make the new government powerful enough to ensure our national security against foreign powers and domestic insurrection. This is followed by a clause providing for a national capital.

The long list of enumerated powers in Article I, Section 8 reflects still another division of powers intended by the framers — the division between the central government and the states. The central government was to have only those powers specifically enumerated in the Constitution. All other powers were to be retained by the states — although, as we shall see in a moment, there are constitutional grounds for arguing that the central gov-

[4] Although Congress was empowered to regulate its own elections, election procedures for the House were left to the states unless Congress chose to intervene.

ernment should have very broad powers. Nevertheless, the notion that all powers not specified in the Constitution are reserved for the states is one of the central reasons the Constitution has loomed so large in our history. Most governments in the world can introduce a new program on the assumption that they have the general power to govern. When the United States government seeks to introduce a new program, no such general assumption exists. Instead, the government must find some specific mandate in the Constitution for what it proposes to do.

To some extent, the notion that the government is limited to the powers strictly enumerated in the Constitution is offset by the last clause in Section 8. This is the famous "necessary and proper clause," which says that in exercising the enumerated powers, Congress is permitted to "make all laws . . . necessary and proper" for carrying out these powers. This is one of the central creative ambiguities of the Constitution. Two other key ambiguities in Section 8 are the power to "lay and collect taxes . . . to . . . provide for the . . . general welfare" and the power to "regulate commerce . . . among the several states." The broad and rather vague wording of these passages, combined with the general implication of the "necessary and proper" clause, means that the powers of the central government are far less narrowly enumerated and far more capable of step by step expansion, than the strictest theory of constitutional enumeration would imply. Over the years, the central government has managed to amass many powers not mentioned in the Constitution, on the grounds that these powers involved interstate commerce, were aimed at the "general welfare," or were "necessary and proper" for exercising those powers that the framers did enumerate.

LIMITATIONS

We have noted that the Constitution was designed not only to divide and mix powers but also to limit them. Article I is full of specific limitations. Most of the limitations on Congress are to be found in Section 9, although others are included in Sections 2 and 8. The bulk of them serve to ensure that Congress will not discriminate for or against any particular state in its tax and commerce laws. Section 9 also contains three important protections for individuals against government repression. The first prohibits *bills of attainder*, which are laws explicitly directed at a particular individual and at his family. The second prohibits *ex post facto laws*—laws making an act criminal after it has been done, so that a man could be punished for doing something that had not been criminal when he did it. The third makes it illegal for the government to suspend the *writ of habeas corpus*. The writ of habeas corpus allows an imprisoned person to demand that he be brought before a judge so that the judge can determine whether his imprisonment is legal. Other specific limitations on government are included in Article III, Section 2, which provides for the right to trial by jury, and Article VI, which forbids a religious test as a condition of holding public office.

Section 8 also creates a number of prohibitions growing out of the English struggle between king and Parliament. The executive is forbidden to draw money from the treasury except on the basis of an appropriation law. And no titles of nobility are to be allowed. This is to ensure that politicians will not be bribed with special honors into betraying the people.

Section 10 of Article I contains a host of limits on the states designed to ensure that the new central government will have unrivaled control over the national economy and the national defense. A key phrase forbids the states from "impairing the obligation of contracts" — that is, from tampering with debtor-creditor agreements to favor the debtors.

IMPEACHMENT

Article I contains two of the most famous constitutional "checks and balances" between the Congress and the President. Although the impeachment power was certainly not intended to be used as a routine device for checking the President, the provisions establishing this power are broadly worded to allow the Congress plenty of leeway. Although the House may *impeach* (that is, indict or accuse) the President on a simple majority vote, the impeachment trial takes place in the Senate, where a two-thirds vote of the members present is required to convict the President and remove him from office. Article II, Section 4 specifies that impeachment shall be for "treason, bribery or other high crimes and misdemeanors."

The impeachment provisions jumped into sudden prominence during the Watergate scandal in the early 1970s. In the entire history of the nation, they had been employed only once against a President. Abraham Lincoln's successor, Andrew Johnson, was impeached by the House but not convicted in the Senate. Despite the fact that the impeachment provisions had not been employed in over one hundred years, no one questioned the right of Congress to proceed with the Nixon impeachment. The words of the framers endowed this almost unprecedented course of political action with great legitimacy. But here, as in many other spheres of political action, the words of the framers gave little specific guidance. For one thing, they do not specify what procedures the House and Senate are to use. For another, the phrase "high crimes and misdemeanors" can be interpreted in various ways. It may mean only legal crimes for which an ordinary citizen could be sent to jail. Or it may be interpreted to include presidential abuse of the powers of office or failure to enforce the laws as well as crimes in the narrow legal sense. It is widely believed that the framers meant something more than crimes in the narrow sense.[5] It is reasonable to assume that they intended that impeachment could be used against a President who clearly violated some specific provision of the Constitution. For instance, a President who signed a treaty without the advice and consent of the Senate could be impeached for such an act even though it is not a crime for which a private citizen could be tried and sent to prison. On the other hand, it is not clear just when a President has abused his vast discretionary powers so much that

[5] See Raoul Berger, *Impeachment* (Cambridge: Harvard University Press, 1974).

he is guilty of a "high crime." In any case, Nixon's resignation in 1974 ended the impeachment proceedings that had begun in the House. Nearly all commentators agreed that the President's resignation was better for the nation than a lengthy impeachment trial would have been.

VETO

A second major check in Article I is the veto power provided in Section 7. The President can veto a bill by returning it to Congress. In this case it does not become a law unless the veto is overridden by a two-thirds vote in each house. Section 7 also provides for the "pocket veto." If the President neither signs nor vetoes a bill within ten days of its passage by Congress, it becomes law without his signature unless Congress adjourns within the ten days. Thus, at the end of a congressional session, when bills normally pile up for presidential signature, the President may veto simply by not signing.

The veto power of the President is appropriately introduced in Article I rather than Article II. It is a lawmaking, not an executive power, and fits with the Article I description of the legislative process, for when one man's "no" vote on a bill is worth more than the "yes" votes of two-thirds minus one of the House and Senate, he is certainly a very powerful legislator. In all, only about 4 percent of the roughly 2250 vetoes cast by Presidents since George Washington have been overridden by Congress. Bills successfully vetoed must be brought up again and go through all of the complexities of the legislative process.

THREE PARTS OF GOVERNMENT WITH OVERLAPPING POWERS

The placement of the veto power in Article I is an important clue to the much misunderstood intentions of the framers with regard to the "separation of powers" among the three branches. It shows that the framers quite deliberately gave the President a very important share of the lawmaking power. They intended to make it extremely difficult for Congress to pass laws unless it gained the cooperation of the President. The idea that American government is based on a system of "separation of powers" with "checks and balances" does *not* mean that the Constitution gives all lawmaking power and nothing but lawmaking power to Congress, all executive power and nothing but executive power to the President, and all judicial power and nothing but judicial power to the courts. Power is separated into three branches of government. But each branch checks and balances the others because each *shares* the lawmaking, administrative, and judicial powers with the other two. Separation of powers really means *sharing of powers*.

All three branches share judicial power. Articles I and III give the Congress power to establish the lower federal courts and to determine what the appellate jurisdiction and rules of the Supreme Court shall be. Article II gives the President the power to appoint the Justices with the advice and consent of the Senate. By the same token, all three branches share executive power. Article II, Section 2 gives Congress the power to set the basic executive

FACED WITH A CHALLENGE TO HIS CLAIMS OF EXECUTIVE PRIVILEGE, PRESIDENT NIXON ANNOUNCED THAT HE WOULD TURN OVER TRANSCRIPTS OF THE WATERGATE TAPES. *Wide World Photos*

structure of the United States when it specifies that executive departments shall be established "by law" — that is, by act of Congress. It is Congress that determines whether there shall be a Defense Department or a Commerce Department at all. Although Article III is not specific in assigning legislative or administrative powers to the Supreme Court, the Court's power to declare statutes and acts of administrative officers unconstitutional gives it the power to "veto" statutes and to block actions of the executive branch. Judicial lawmaking and administration are discussed at length in Chapter 14. And, as we already have seen, all three branches share legislative power. The Court's ability to declare laws unconstitutional makes it a factor in the legislative process, just as the President's veto power gives him a key role as a legislator. Article I is *roughly* about Congress, Article II the President, and Article III the Supreme Court. But lawmaking, executing, and judging are scattered throughout the Constitution just as they are divided and shared by the three branches.

ARTICLE II: THE EXECUTIVE POWER SHALL BE VESTED IN A PRESIDENT OF THE
UNITED STATES OF AMERICA. HE SHALL HOLD HIS OFFICE DURING THE
TERM OF FOUR YEARS . . .

Article II, Section 1 begins with one of the broad ambiguities for which the Constitution is famous. It says that "The executive power shall be vested in a President of the United States," but it does not define "executive." It then goes on to describe the procedures for electing the President. We know that the framers saw the presidency as a dangerous institution. They had just fought the Revolution to overthrow the king and become a republic, and they realized that a President was a potential king. Yet they saw that the absence of a strong executive was a key factor in the failure of the government established by the Articles of Confederation, and they desired to replace the Articles with something better. They were somewhat comforted by the knowledge that George Washington would certainly be the first President, for Washington was not a man who would grasp excessive political power. Nevertheless, they were afraid that in the future a popular demogogue would become a tyrant. This was the fate that many philosophers predicted for a democratic government, because they believed that the masses, being easily swayed, would turn a popular hero into a dictator.

Therefore, the framers designed the elaborate electoral college mode of electing the President. The electoral college is another variation on the notion of using the principle of representation to preserve democracy. According to this system, the people would not choose the President directly. Instead, they would choose the best among them to be *electors,* and these electors would then choose a President. As we shall see in Chapter 9, the growth of political parties, which was not anticipated by the framers, has meant that this electoral mechanism has worked far differently than the framers originally thought it would.

Article II, Section 2, which designates the powers of the President, consists of only three short paragraphs. Yet the vast, complex powers of the modern executive branch have grown from these few words. Read them and you will see how little the general language of the Constitution tells us about the actual operations of modern government.

Chiefly, Sections 2 and 3 give the President four broad kinds of power. (1) He is the commander-in-chief of the armed forces and the chief of our relations with foreign nations. (2) He appoints the principal officers of government. (3) He gathers and disseminates information about the "state of the nation"—that is, what the government is doing and what it ought to do. (4) "He shall take care that the laws be faithfully executed"—that is, he has some sort of general administrative power.

Article II also includes many checks and balances on the power of the President. Although the President is commander-in-chief of the armed forces, the power to declare war is vested in Congress. Although the President is charged with responsibility for foreign policy, the Senate must advise and consent to treaties negotiated by the President or they do not become lawful. Similarly, the fact that the departments of the executive branch are to be created by congressional statute means that the organization of the branch headed by the President is to be dictated by Congress. Indeed, the President's principal power is defined as carrying out the laws passed by Congress rather than pursuing his own policies.

Nevertheless, the commander-in-chief, chief diplomat, and chief executive roles are potentially very powerful ones. The framers did not take nearly so many precautions in limiting the President as they did in limiting Congress. In part, this was because the framers did not foresee the rise of an international situation in which defense and diplomacy, and thus the President, became the central concerns of government. Also, the framers saw the lawmaking power as the central power of government, and therefore the power most in need of limitation. Chapters 11 and 12 describe the shifting modern balance of lawmaking power between Congress and President and the growth of the President's foreign affairs powers. Chapter 13 describes the growth of the executive branch bureaucracy, which has played a fundamental role in shifting a great deal of the lawmaking power from Congress to the executive branch.

PRESIDENT ROOSE-VELT APPEARED BEFORE CONGRESS ON DECEMBER 8, 1941, TO ASK FOR DECLARATION OF WAR IN RESPONSE TO JAPAN'S ATTACK ON PEARL HARBOR. *Wide World Photos*

ARTICLE III: THE JUDICIAL POWER OF THE UNITED STATES
SHALL BE VESTED IN ONE SUPREME COURT, AND IN SUCH INFERIOR COURTS
AS THE CONGRESS MAY FROM TIME TO TIME ORDAIN AND ESTABLISH.

Article III vests "the judicial power of the United States" in "one supreme court" and whatever lower federal courts Congress chooses to establish. This latter provision is one of the compromises for which the framers are famous. Many of the Founding Fathers were concerned about states' rights. They feared that a network of lower courts spread throughout the states would interfere in the legal affairs of the states. For this reason, they preferred to limit federal judicial power to one court in the capital. Those who desired strong central government wanted a full system of federal courts to spread federal law throughout the states. They compromised by leaving to

Congress the authority to establish or not establish lower federal courts. Indeed, so much of the judicial system is *not* specified in the Constitution that the Judiciary Act of 1789 is considered almost a part of the Constitution itself. It was passed by the First Congress to fill in the constitutional gaps. Eventually, a full system of lower federal courts was established. This system is described in Chapter 14.

Much of Article III is devoted to spelling out the jurisdiction of the Supreme Court and lower federal courts. The Constitution goes into considerable detail about what kinds of cases the courts can and cannot take. In spite of these details, however, the power of *judicial review* — that is, the power of the Supreme Court to declare laws unconstitutional — is not mentioned in the Constitution at all. Nevertheless, it has become one of the important checks and balances of the Constitution and a major factor in determining the division of powers between the federal government and the states. We know from various debates, documents, and letters that most of the framers probably favored some sort of judicial review, but it is not clear how much of this power they wanted the Supreme Court to have. In Chapter 14 we will see how this power gradually evolved out of Supreme Court interpretations of the Constitution.

ARTICLES IV-VII

Article IV is largely devoted to adjusting the relations of the new federal government to the states. It is one of the several places in the Constitution where specific concessions are made to the institution of slavery in the southern states. Article V sets out the procedures for amending the Constitution. If we study the wording of the Constitution carefully, we can see that the framers made the wording broad and flexible enough to allow for changing interpretations as circumstances changed. But Article V does make it difficult to amend the Constitution.

Article VI contains a number of important miscellaneous provisions. One, designed to improve the international credit of a struggling new nation, guarantees that the new national government will take over the debts owed by the old. Here, again, we see the special concern for the rights of creditors to be found in several places in the Constitution.[6] Most importantly, Article VI contains the *supremacy clause*, which provides that the "constitution . . . the laws . . . and treaties . . . of the United States, shall be the supreme Law of the Land." It is this provision that changes the former colonies from a confederation of thirteen equal, sovereign states into a federal system in which the central government is supreme within the sphere assigned it by the Constitution. In practice, the supremacy clause means that the Supreme Court can strike down state laws that conflict with valid federal laws.

Article VII, which provides for the ratification of the Constitution, is not of much relevance today. But it does provide us with a good insight into the thinking of the framers, for it contains a truly revolutionary maneuver. Arti-

[6] See Robert E. Brown, *Charles Beard and the Constitution* (Princeton: Princeton University Press, 1956); Forrest McDonald, *We the People: The Economic Origins of the Constitution* (Chicago: University of Chicago Press, 1958).

cle VII stipulates that the new government will come into existence as soon as any nine of the thirteen members of the old confederation ratifies the document. In short, it would have been possible for four of the former colonies to reject the Constitution, and to have been compelled, nevertheless, to enter the new federal union.

THE AMENDMENTS

At the time of the Constitutional Convention, one of the great arguments against ratification was that the Constitution did not contain a sufficient number of specific limitations on the powers of government. Nevertheless, the Constitution was ratified. Three years later, in 1791, these objections were answered when the first ten amendments to the Constitution were adopted.[7] Known collectively as the Bill of Rights, these amendments guarantee a variety of individual rights ranging from freedom of speech through a prohibition on excessive bail. They have been interpreted and reinterpreted in hundreds of Supreme Court decisions. What they mean in practice today often can barely be guessed from reading their original wording.[8]

After the adoption of the Bill of Rights, subsequent amendments have been rare, with the exception of the outburst that followed the Civil War, when a number of amendments were adopted in order to end slavery and to protect those newly freed. In all, only fifteen amendments have been adopted since 1791. Except for the Bill of Rights and the Civil War amendments, most of the others are designed to cure omissions in the original document or to reverse particular Supreme Court interpretations of specific constitutional provisions.

CONSTITUTIONAL LEGITIMACY

Upon reading the Constitution, it becomes clear that the effort to discover the "intent of the framers" is in some respects a false search. The Constitution is the product of a large body of men with differing intents. It was written in broad, general language and frequently embodies compromises that were designed to bridge conflicting viewpoints. What is more, on many issues that are important to us now, the framers had no intentions at all or deliberately sought to avoid commitment. Where the language of the document is not clear, the debates of the Convention of 1787 usually reveal differing intents from various speakers. No single clear intent emerges.

On most of the specific questions of constitutional interpretation that arise

[7] See Robert Rutland, *The Birth of the Bill of Rights* (Chapel Hill: University of North Carolina Press, 1955).

[8] The current meaning of the Bill of Rights and the Civil War amendments is discussed at greater length in Chapter 14. See also Henry J. Abraham, *Freedom and the Court*, 2nd ed. (New York: Oxford University Press, 1972); Samuel Krislov, *The Supreme Court and Political Freedom* (New York: The Free Press, 1968); and Richard E. Morgan, *The Supreme Court and Religion* (New York: The Free Press, 1975).

today, appeals to the "intent of the framers" or the "true meaning" of the Constitution can be somewhat misleading. Often, they are little more than attempts to clothe a particular set of contemporary policy views in the mantle of legitimacy that Americans reserve for the Founding Fathers and the great contract of government. From the words of the document itself, it is impossible to tell precisely what kinds of laws the framers thought might be "necessary and proper." We have no way of knowing whether "commerce among the several states" was intended to include manufacturing as well as transportation. Nor can anyone tell whether the framers, in conferring the commander-in-chief power on the President, intended to authorize operations such as the undeclared wars in Korea and Vietnam.

Nevertheless, it is easy to understand why contemporary politicians want to enlist the framers on their side and why they try to couch modern political preferences in old constitutional language. They are responding to the fact that the Constitution is perhaps the central aspect of the political context of American political life. Americans believe that the Constitution does and ought to set the rules by which politics is played. In this sense, it is the Constitution that confers *legitimacy* on the American government. By this we mean that when political decisions are reached by following the constitutional rules, the American people feel that these decisions deserve respect and obedience. We feel this way as a people not because we are forced to go along with the decisions, and not necessarily because we agree with the decisions, but because we support the constitutional rules and procedures that produced them.

THE FEDERAL CONTEXT

The various branches of American government—Congress, President, Supreme Court—have persisted as outlined in the Constitution. They con-

PRESIDENT FORD ADDRESSES A JOINT SESSION OF CONGRESS. THE POWER OF THE CONSTITUTION IS SUCH THAT IT CAN CONFER LEGITIMACY ON AN ADMINISTRATION NOT ELECTED BY THE PEOPLE.
Wide World Photos

tinue to provide the basic setting in which American politicians must work. Another basic constitutional outline, the division of the nation into states, also persists as a major part of the institutional setting of American politics. This system of *federalism*, in which each separate state retains a degree of autonomy and sovereignty even while it is subordinate to the sovereignty of the central government, is one of the most distinctive features of the American political system. Just as it was in 1787, federalism remains a key phenomenon in contemporary policy making and implementation.[9]

As we shall see in Chapter 4, the principle of federalism is a major ingredient in the American ideology. It is also an extremely important aspect of the workaday world of American politics. It would be impossible to understand the operation of the national parties, congressional voting patterns, the organization of the executive branch, the construction of the federal budget, the pattern of policy outcomes, and many other features of national politics without some understanding of the various levels of local government. To a large extent, local political units are the building blocks out of which the national parties are built and the operating agencies through which a substantial share of national programs are carried out.

Technically, federalism is defined as the *division of political powers between a number of governments sharing the same territory.* The essential legal characteristic of federalism is that both the federal and state governments enjoy independent legal powers derived directly from the Constitution and the people. We often speak of the *sovereign* states to stress the fact that their fundamental legal authority is as complete and as clearly and directly derived from the people as is that of the central government.

MANY GOVERNMENTS, MANY OFFICES, MANY POLICIES

The constitutional division of governing authority between nation and states has had a profound effect on the political system. A political party that has fallen very far from national majority status, for instance, may continue to flourish on the power, offices, and patronage of local governments in areas where it continues to enjoy local majorities. This is how the Federalist party managed to postpone its final departure from the political scene for many years while the Jeffersonians and the Jacksonians dominated national politics. Similarly, although the Democratic party went through many lean years after the Civil War, its dominance in the South kept it alive and played a major role in the party's eventual recovery.

As these examples illustrate, federalism provides an enormous number of chances for small victories in state and local affairs. The geographic division of power in the United States underlies and accentuates the American political tendency to settle for "half a loaf." Because small local victories are possible under our system, politics in America is not a desperate all-or-nothing game for control of the national government. Each party can hope to

---

[9] See Richard H. Leach, *American Federalism* (New York: W.W. Norton & Company, 1970); and William Riker, *Federalism* (Boston: Little, Brown, 1964).

win something somewhere. This may be federalism's greatest contribution to American political moderation.

Many of the other advantages of federalism have what could be described as a negative character. That is to say, the system is good at preventing things we don't want but not quite as efficient at providing things we do want. For example, the division of powers among a number of governments allows each to act as a barrier against the potential excesses of the others. If one state adopts insane policies, they need not be adopted by the others. If a tyrannical majority seizes control of the national government, at least it does not gain total control of the lives of the people, for most of the everyday facets of life are subject to state rather than national law. There is little doubt that at various times the existence of the federal system has acted to check the will of either local or national majorities on specific issues, particularly in the spheres of business and labor regulation. To cite one instance, for many years there was a fairly clear national majority in favor of laws regulating child labor. Yet the will of this majority was thwarted by a constitutional interpretation that assigned labor regulation to the states. During that period state laws varied widely. Some sharply limited the hours and working conditions of children while others permitted almost unlimited employment.

Despite such examples, however, federalism ought not to be seen solely in terms of its capacity to block new action. Locally based interest groups may be able to use the resources of local government to lead national sentiment. At a crucial period, groups concerned about the environment managed to get anti-smog measures through the California legislature. The California laws then were used as a lever to prod a lagging Congress into action. Such instances are not the only examples of the dynamic potential of our federal system. The fact that our major parties are organized along federal lines allows new candidates to use the state primaries in order to challenge old-line leaders who are committed to the *status quo*.

The federal system not only provides local opinion with a testing ground where it can develop until it is strong enough to have an impact on national policy. It also can work the other way around, providing national sentiment with an opportunity to influence recalcitrant states. For example, southern blacks repeatedly found themselves politically overwhelmed in their own states. Eventually, however, they were able to recruit national majorities who were willing to use the instruments of the federal government to get them better treatment in voting, education, employment, and housing from their own states. And in many instances federal conservation practices have saved natural beauties when the state governments would have given in to pressure groups favoring economic exploitation of these resources.

EVALUATION OF FEDERALISM

Federalism has certainly provided for flexibility and variation in government policies, which would seem to be an advantage in a nation as large and diverse as the United States. Yet aside from an act of faith in favor of diversity, it is not easy to draw up an accurate balance sheet of the advantages and disadvantages of federalism in terms of the quality of government policy. It is often argued that the states are "little laboratories" in which new policies can be tried out on a small scale and the successful ones then transferred to the whole country. On the whole, however, at least since the turn of the century, we have been much more accustomed to seeing the federal government engage in innovations while the reluctant states have to be dragged along, often with a fair degree of resistance. This has been particularly true in many areas, including social security, transportation, resource planning, labor regulation, health, education, and criminal law. Some states may be well in advance of the federal government, but the remainder follow along only as a result of federal pressure.[10]

This being the case, it seems impossible to avoid the conclusion that federalism has worked roughly as the Founding Fathers expected it to—as a constraint on national majorities. Some observers have applauded this constraint, arguing that it protects the freedom of individuals by giving them, through their state governments, the power to resist national sentiments to which they are opposed. Others have condemned federalism on the grounds that it fosters sluggishness in the central government and makes it difficult to provide national solutions to such national problems as the plight of the cities, health care, and poverty. We will leave it to the reader to decide which of these two sides has the better arguments.

THE MANY FEDERALISMS

As opinions have shifted on these questions, the nature of American federalism also has changed. There is no single, correct, constitutional version of American federalism. From the earliest days of the Republic, each faction has remolded its ideal federalism to meet its current needs. The South was for strong central government and the Abolitionists were states-righters when the Federal Fugitive Slave Laws returned escaped blacks from Massachusetts to the South. Ten years later, the Abolitionists were for saving the union while the slave owners championed states' rights. Pro-business forces favored a strong federal government in the early days of the nation's history and then again in the late nineteenth century, when Progressivism and Populism swept a number of states into major economic and social experimentation. But when Wilson, Roosevelt, and other Presidents put the central government at the head of the reform movement, the business interests rediscovered the glories of the states.

In effect, then, American federalism is actually a series of very open devices used by the states and the central government for mutual control. These devices do not exactly specify who has just how much authority over whom. There are so many of these devices that the alert reader will find them scattered throughout this book, from the chapter on parties to those on Congress and the Supreme Court. Let us look at just three examples here.

[10] Aaron Wildavsky, *American Federalism* (Boston: Little, Brown, 1967).

1. The federal government has almost unlimited taxing powers. It can offer to dispense huge sums of money to the states if they will spend the money according to policies established by the federal government. The states either do what the central government wants or they do not get the money.
2. The Fourteenth Amendment gives Congress power to ensure that no man is sent to jail without due process of law. But the vast bulk of the criminal law enforcement machinery remains in the hands of the states. Congress could fulfill its duties under the Fourteenth Amendment only if it were willing to establish a large federal apparatus to police the hundreds of thousands of judges, jailers, court officials, and police employed by state and local governments. It has not done so.
3. The states retain the vast residual police powers of government over health, safety, morals, and welfare. Yet, under the enumerated powers of the federal government, federal laws and regulations may dictate the most minute details of everything from the number of windows in the bedrooms of new houses to the size of the lettering on no-left-turn signs.

As these examples illustrate, the quantity and quality of controls that each level of government wields over the other are subtle and constantly changing. In general, the federal government has the advantage of preponderant resources. It has dominant authority in the realm of foreign and defense policy. It has the ability to dramatize whatever issues it chooses. The states, however, perform the bulk of government services immediately visible to the citizens. They retain their traditional role as spokesmen for local interests. Above all, they retain the strong voice within the central government that is generated by a system of elections, party organization, and congressional representation that continues to use the states as basic building blocks.

SUMMARY

The constitutional context of American politics is complex. There are many parts. Each part is sometimes more, sometimes less important with regard to getting things done. There is always the danger that some part will block the others and slow the nation to a standstill. And there is no guarantee that at certain times the President, Congress, the Supreme Court, the bureaucracy, or one of the parties may not become so powerful as to sweep all the parts before it. Whether we consider such a sweep bold leadership or tyranny often depends upon where we are being swept. It may be called leadership if it moves us into a war on poverty, and tyranny if the war is on Vietnam. States' rights may appear to be a bulwark of liberties or a bulwark against the will of national majorities.

That is why we have spoken of the "constitutional context" rather than the "Constitution." The written Constitution may be vague on many specifics, but it is clear enough in its general outlines. A bill passed by the Federal Trade Commission and signed by the Chief Justice cannot be treated as a law. Nor would the Army respond to a message from the Council of Economic Advisers ordering it into battle. Nor can the House of Representatives enter into a treaty with Bolivia. The Constitution typically leaves open a number of paths that are arguably constitutional. But it also firmly closes off many other avenues. The President may nominate anyone he pleases to the Supreme Court, but no matter how much he yearns to, he simply cannot appoint a Supreme Court Justice without Senate consent. If he did, no one would believe that the person was really a Justice.

In this sense, the Constitution does not mean whatever we want it to mean. It sets the context and establishes definite outer limits within which politicians must operate. The written Constitution does not tell us how American politics and government actually work. But it is an important element in establishing the context, the political geography, within which politics and government operate.

CHAPTER FOUR
THE IDEOLOGICAL CONTEXT
OF AMERICAN POLITICS

By *ideology* we mean the set of basic ideas that Americans use when they seek to understand and evaluate American politics. The word *ideology* frequently is used in a negative way. Thus, to a Communist, Marxist ideas are regarded as scientific truth while capitalist ideas are criticized as "bourgeois ideology." The word is also used in another way. Sometimes students of comparative politics speak of one nation as having *ideological politics* and another nation as having *pragmatic* or *interest group politics*. What they are saying is that in some nations voters and politicians compete about which set of ideas should be adopted by the government. Perhaps communist, socialist, and free enterprise parties strive against one another, or perhaps it is the monarchists versus the republicans, or the totalitarians versus the liberal democrats. In other nations, however, politics seems to be less concerned with ideas and more involved with everyday and immediate considerations of who gets what. Should a new law favor the interests of the dairy farmers or the consumers, the unions or the corporations? In such countries, people seem either to share a common ideology or to have agreed that they will not bring up fundamental ideological questions in their political campaigns.

In this book we want to stick to the simplest view of ideology. This chapter is about the fundamental ideas—such as *equality, freedom,* and *democracy*—that Americans use when they think about their own politics. The question of whether a nation engages in ideological politics or pragmatic politics is always one of degree. All nations mix ultimate ideals with concerns about immediate problems, although some may be more consciously concerned with political theories than others. This chapter is devoted to American ideology because the ideas Americans have about what politics is and ought to be affect their actual behavior in politics.

American ideas about politics tend to be loosely interconnected. They cannot be neatly separated into a series of clearly bounded building blocks because that is not the way people really think. This chapter is organized into seven main parts, each of which examines a number of overlapping ideas. The first is about American ideas of *democracy,* and the second about *individual rights.* The third is about our *constitutional ideas* because this is where our notions of democratic majority rule are combined with our concern for individual rights. Then follow sections on *equality* and *justice,* two of the basic values of most Americans. Then comes a section on the various combinations of ideas that Americans label *liberal, conservative,* and *radical.* Finally, there is a concluding section on the vision Americans have of their country as a unique political achievement.

In examining the ideological context of American politics, we will be concerned with the values and loyalties of individuals, with the pictures in their minds of what is good, bad, desirable, undesirable, possible, and impossible in their political relations with one another. In the end, we will find that there is no such thing as *the* American political ideology. The best we can do is to identify the dominant features of a mass of differing and often contradictory ideas.

Just as Chapter 2 presented a picture of the social, economic, and organizational resources currently available to the American people, so this chapter describes the fund of political ideas that Americans have ready at hand as a result of their historical experience. In painting this picture, we have relied heavily on historical and literary sources. It is important to remember that such an analysis only can tell us what ideas are in the air. To find out how many people believe how much of which ones, we must turn from the study of ideology to the study of public opinion—the subject of Chapter 5.

DEMOCRACY

REPRESENTATION AND THE CONSENT OF THE GOVERNED

In a phrase which every schoolchild knows, Abraham Lincoln characterized our political system as a "government of the people, by the people, for the people." We all know what "of the people" and "for the people" mean, but it is not so clear what "by the people" means. It does not seem to mean actual popular participation in government, in the manner of a town meeting, for that obviously is not the way the American system works. Yet our political system is nevertheless a government *by* the people in the sense that our government depends upon the *consent of the governed*. Although the people do not actually make the government's decisions, they do consent to the decisions made by those who do govern.

How do they express this consent? They do it by electing representatives to run the government. This is the central democratic feature of the Constitution, which provides for the election of Congress and the President. Most Americans identify these elections as the most important guarantee of rule by the people. The basic rationale for representative government is that most individuals do not have the time or the desire to run the government themselves. What is more, in a large country such as ours, it would be physically impossible for all the people to come together often enough to run the government themselves. So the people elect some of their number to represent them in governing.

What do we mean, though, when we say that we elect certain individuals to *represent* us in government? Actually, there are at least two distinct theories of representation, and most Americans subscribe more or less to both of them. The first is the simplest and the most democratic theory. According to this view, the representative's job is simply to express the wishes of those who sent him or her to Washington. In this sense, the representative is merely the *means* through which the people govern. This theory of representation seems to have an undeniable validity. For example, when an election campaign is dominated by one issue, it is tempting to claim that the people are voting on the issue rather than the candidates. They are saying that they favor school busing or oppose it, that they favor abortion law reform or oppose it, and so forth. Thus the voters should have every reason to expect that the person they send to Washington will work to carry out the wishes they expressed when they voted for him.

In fact, voters do not behave this way, as we will see in Chapter 6. Furthermore, elections rarely fit this theory of representation, because campaigns seldom are devoted to a single issue that overrides all other present and past concerns. So the winner goes off to Congress without anything that could be regarded as a specific set of instructions from his or her constituents. When casting their ballots, the voters simply said, "We think candidate X will do a better job of looking after our interests than candidate Y." If they cast their ballots on this basis, they were subscribing to the second theory of representation. According to this theory, the representative does not merely carry out the wishes of the voters. Rather, the voters choose a representative in whom they have confidence, and the representative is then supposed to decide for himself what is best for his constituents and for the nation as a whole.[1]

One way of comparing these two theories of representation is to say that in the first, the wisdom that goes into political decision making is assumed to reside in the people themselves. In the second, however, political wisdom is assumed to reside in the legislators. As the English political philosopher John Stuart Mill explained about a hundred years ago, according to this theory of representative government, it is the people's job simply "to make in general a good choice of persons to represent them, and having done so, to leave to those whom they had chosen a liberal discretion."[2]

Most of the men who wrote the United States Constitution generally thought of representative government in this second way. They saw representation as a device designed deliberately to filter and elevate public sentiment rather than simply to express it. They hoped that the common people would choose the best minds among them as their representatives. A glance at the data in Chapter 10 will show that in general our representatives have been chosen from among the higher status segments of the community, and they clearly have a higher level of education than the population as a whole. The degree to which we subscribe to the second theory of representation is indicated by the fact that most congressmen and Presidents who hold our esteem did not always follow the moods of the voters. We sometimes praise politicians because they "rose above" mere "politics" and seemed genuinely to pursue what they thought was best for the nation, even at the cost of popular support.

To the extent that we ask our politicians to rise above politics, to resist pressure, to solve problems, to do what is best, we seem to be endorsing this second theory of representation. Under this theory, the election of representatives becomes essentially a means of popular consent. By electing one set of people rather than another, we give our consent in advance to what they will do in office. Then, if we do not like what they do in office, we can withdraw our consent from them at the next election and give it to another set of people. Although Americans do not adopt consent of the governed as their sole democratic theory, we shall see shortly that one of the central

[1] Hanna Pitkin, *The Concept of Representation* (Berkeley: University of California Press, 1967).
[2] John Stuart Mill, *Autobiography* (New York: Columbia University Press, 1924), p. 74.

interpretations of American elections rests in part on such notions. American elections usually do not present the people with a clear choice between alternative future policies. Instead, they permit the people to choose leaders in whom they have confidence and also to throw out leaders whose past policies have not met with their approval.

POPULAR SOVEREIGNTY

Closely related to the idea of the consent of the governed, but perhaps moving a little closer to pure democracy, is our notion of *popular sovereignty*. Americans tend to believe that all political power comes from the people and ultimately "belongs" to them. In the sixteenth and seventeenth centuries, the idea became prevalent that each nation possessed some ultimate, absolute, complete ruling power called *sovereignty*. This sovereignty usually was held to reside in the king, who was often called the sovereign.

The men who set down the words "We, the People . . ." in the preamble to the Constitution specifically meant them as a declaration that in the United States the people were the sovereign. The people replace the king as the source of all the powers wielded by the government. They retain the ultimate political power.

It is clearer now than it was in the seventeenth century that power is not a thing like a rock or a horse that can belong to someone. Neither the king nor the people can be sovereign in the sense of owning all the power. Power is a relationship, not an entity—a relationship in which one individual or group is influenced by another. Thus the power wielders are the individuals who actually make the decisions about what the government does and does not do. As the idea of sovereignty becomes less convincing, *popular sovereignty* becomes merely a slogan. However, it can be an effective slogan when it is used by those who seek more political power. Such persons try to justify their demands for greater participation in the making of government decisions by identifying themselves with "the people." When we hear that the candidate is a "man of the people" or that a party is the "people's party," we are hearing echoes of the old idea of popular sovereignty.

Another way of looking at the question of popular sovereignty is to analyze it in terms of the theories of representation we have already discussed. To the extent that representatives act as direct reflections of the desires of the people who elected them, we come close to rule by the people. To the extent that our elected representatives act on their own, the link between "the people" and the government becomes less direct. After the reader has read more about political parties, voting, and Congress, he or she will be in a better position to decide to what extent the United States can or should achieve the old ideal of government by the people.

DIRECT DEMOCRACY AND THE FEAR OF BIG GOVERNMENT

A belief in the value of popular participation in government is one of the major strands in the American ideology. The New England town meeting,

IN THE TRADITION OF JACKSONIAN DEMOCRACY, HARRY S. TRUMAN
PROVED THAT THE "FOLKSY" POLITICIAN CAN BE A POPULAR FIGURE
ON THE AMERICAN POLITICAL SCENE.
Wide World Photos

63

THE IDEOLOGICAL
CONTEXT OF
AMERICAN POLITICS

in which the citizens debated and decided every major question of government, is an old reality and a continuing dream. This style of government is often described as *direct* as opposed to *representative democracy*. Recent provisions for the participation of the poor in the management of poverty programs reflect this ideal of the people governing themselves rather than having government imposed upon them from above. Much of the recurrent denunciation of big government, bureaucracy, Washington, and the military industrial complex is based on this loyalty to the principle of direct democracy. So is the insistence on maintaining the strength of local government. The appeal of keeping government "close to the people," which is a slogan widely used by local government enthusiasts, rests on the assumption that the citizens can participate more directly in the government of their own town and state than in a government way off in Washington. Such an assumption may no longer be correct, given the large size of the local communities in which the majority of Americans live. Indeed, most Americans seem to pay more attention to national than to local politics.

Although for many years the call for local government was associated with what we tend to call "conservative" political thinking, in recent years direct participation has also become an aim of the so-called New Left. (These ideological labels will be discussed later in this chapter.) The hope that big government can wither away, that men can live a simpler political life of face-to-face cooperation, is a recurrent theme of Western civilization. The commune, the town meeting, and the self-sufficient utopian community, all of which were popular among nineteenth-century socialists, reflect a rebellion against large and complex political structures that inhibit significant participation by the mass of citizens.

JACKSONIAN DEMOCRACY

This rebellious side of American democratic ideology is not new. It was made explicit during the period of Jacksonian democracy which stretched from about 1820 to the Civil War.[3] The Jacksonians subscribed to the theory of representation which holds that the representative should accurately reflect and faithfully follow the views of his constituents rather than seek to purify and elevate them. They sought to implement this theory by electing common people rather than gentlemen to office. Even today, the "folksy" politician can still be a popular figure on the American political scene. Nowadays, however, the appeal to the idea of popular control of government is

---

[3] Arthur Schlesinger, Jr., *The Age of Jackson* (Boston: Little, Brown, 1953).

more likely to be made by vague allusions to the "silent majority" or "the people" than by wearing a straw hat.

The Jacksonians were not content simply with putting common people in the legislature. They also wanted to achieve direct popular participation in the administrative aspects of government. They argued that the tasks of the bureaucracy were simple, so that in their view public employment was basically a way of taking money *from* the government, not working *for* it. Not only was every citizen qualified to do what little had to be done, but everyone was entitled to a turn at the public trough. To the victorious party at each election, then, should go the spoils. Whenever the party in power was voted out of office, incumbent government workers should be turned out to be replaced by the party faithful on the winner's side. This philosophy of public service was known as the *spoils system*. It enabled a large number of citizens to be rotated through office. In a fully developed spoils system there would be no such thing as a corps of government officials separate from the people. Both the legislative and administrative branches would literally embody the principle of government by the people.

DEMOCRACY AND EFFICIENCY

After the Civil War, as government tasks became larger and more complicated, the ideal of democratic public administration began to come into conflict with another element in the American ideology—the desire for efficiency and technological excellence. In industrial and technical areas, the traditional American solution to an increase in the scale and complexity of the task to be done has been the division of labor, specialization, and the upgrading of professional and technical qualifications. All of these approaches run directly counter to the philosophy behind the spoils system, which assumes that any citizen can do any government job for a short time and then rotate back to private life. In the late nineteenth century, the ideology of efficiency began to replace the ideology of participation. The result was the *merit,* or *civil service* system, which will be described in Chapter 13. This system stressed technical qualification for each of thousands of specific and permanent government jobs. The goal of the Civil Service Reform movement was to take public employment out of politics and create a highly professional force of career administrators who would do the business of government effectively and efficiently. Admirable as these reforms may have been in ending the corruption and inefficiencies of the spoils system, they also spelled the end of direct democracy. Government administration was to be done largely by professional employees whose special, full-time, lifelong business was governmental service.

American ideology has never successfully resolved this conflict between the demand for efficient government service and the yearning for direct democracy. Most of today's talk about alienation, the "establishment," and peoples' participation echoes an earlier generation's derision of bureaucratic red tape. Yet the notion of democratic participation is itself a screen for an even deeper ambiguity in American thought.

Just how much participation by how many and what kind of citizens do we want? Chapter 7 will show that political participation is in fact very unevenly distributed in this country.

Although the United States was established on democratic principles, the Founding Fathers distrusted democratic participation even in elections. Of all the elected officials of the national government, only members of the House of Representatives were chosen by popular vote, according to the scheme originally set forth in the Constitution. And even House elections were conducted under state laws, many of which limited voting to those owning a certain amount of property. The growing American allegiance to democracy can be seen in the step-by-step broadening of the electorate. This broadening began with the early elimination of property qualifications in the states. It continued in the post-Civil War amendments barring slavery and, at least formally, barring racial restrictions on voting. The Seventeenth Amendment, ratified in 1913, provided for the popular election of senators, and there has been considerable recent agitation to abolish the electoral college. The Nineteenth and Twenty-sixth Amendments extended suffrage to women and to eighteen- through twenty-year-olds. In the mid-twentieth century, Supreme Court decisions and voting rights legislation put teeth in the Constitutional barrier against racial restrictions in voting. As we shall see in Chapter 14, even the Supreme Court has been strongly affected by the view that only elected officials should make policy. In addition, many of the states provide for direct voting on proposed legislation through the initiative and referendum.

Even in the electoral realm, however, our enchantment with democracy is not complete. We continue to use the word *demagogue* as a pejorative term to characterize candidates who court popularity by appealing to the baser sentiments of the masses. Thus, we temper our belief in democracy with a fear that the people can be easily misled or converted into an ugly mob. Similarly, our belief in the value of strong presidential leadership may be taken as an indication that we think the people are not always capable of choosing the best policies spontaneously.

MAJORITY RULE

The concept of majority rule is probably the most widely shared and deeply held element of the American ideology. We see it at work from the smallest informal group trying to decide what movie to see to the Supreme Court of the United States deciding the most solemn constitutional questions. Having voted eight yea and five nay, it is hardly conceivable that a group of Americans would then say, "The nays have it," except under such specialized circumstances as the two-thirds majorities required in the Senate for treaty ratification and conviction of an impeached official, or in a wholly advisory body like the President's Cabinet.

Yet Americans continue to doubt that the will of the majority is always what is best for the country. Long ago, the French philosopher Jean-Jacques

Rousseau, who was much read by some of the Founding Fathers, drew a sharp distinction between the will of the people, which he called the *general will,* and the will of the majority. The will of the majority, he said, is often merely the sum of the selfish desires of the individual voters. It does not necessarily coincide with what would be best for the people as a whole. Rousseau's thinking is echoed in the widely held suspicion that there can be good majority decisions and others that are not so good. We see it expressed when Americans distinguish between whether or not a decision is popular and whether or not it is in the *public interest.* Americans tend to reserve special praise for politicians who stand up for the public interest in the face of hostile public opinion. Whenever we do so, we are acknowledging that some particular policy would be good for the people even though a majority of them did not particularly want it.

AMERICAN THOUGHTS ON DEMOCRACY

As we have just seen, Americans have a number of different ideas about democracy. They believe that no government is legitimate that does not enjoy the consent of the governed. They believe that the people are in some vague way the ultimate source of political power. They want the people to participate in government both directly and through their elected representatives. They believe in majority rule. But at the same time, they acknowledge that the mass of citizens cannot themselves directly run large and complex governments if those governments are to be run well. And they suspect that what the majority of the people may want at any given moment is not always what would be best in the long run for the country as a whole.

INDIVIDUAL RIGHTS

Even before establishing in the Constitution that "We, the People" are the source of government, the Founding Fathers had proclaimed in the Declaration of Independence the "self-evident" truth that all men had been endowed with "certain inalienable rights." Our continued allegiance to the concept of *rights* is a major ideological check on the equally self-evident truth of majority rule.

THE LIBERAL TRADITION

The dominant school of American historiography argues that our country, at its inception, was so steeped in the political ideas associated with the English Whig, or liberal, philosophy that to this day American thought is almost exclusively liberal.[4] Near the end of this chapter, we shall look briefly at the normal, everyday political usage of the terms *liberal* and *conservative.*

[4] Daniel Boorstin, *The Genius of American Politics* (Chicago: University of Chicago Press, 1953); and Louis Hartz, *The Liberal Tradition in America* (New York: Harcourt, Brace, Jovanovich, 1955).

The point here is that both those who think of themselves as liberals and those who think of themselves as conservative share a basic common ideology. This ideology derives from a specific historical body of thought that is commonly described as *liberal* because it emphasizes the rights of the individual against the powers of government.

Echoing earlier Greek and Roman writers, the thirteenth-century philosopher and theologian St. Thomas Aquinas taught that there was a hierarchy of law, with the Divine Law at the top and positive law—the laws men made and wrote down in their statute books—at the bottom. The Divine Law was beyond mere human comprehension, except with the aid of the revelations in the Bible. However, some portion of God's scheme for man and the universe was directly available to man through the exercise of his reason, a faculty that God had implanted in every individual. This *natural law,* which could be discovered by human reason, was a reflection of the Divine Law. It followed that positive law ought to be a reflection of natural law. In this way, a criterion quite apart from the general will of the sovereign was created for determining which laws were good and which bad. God-fearing persons should obey the real laws. They need not obey false laws. Only reasonable laws—that is, laws in accord with natural law—were real laws. Human laws not in accord with natural law were not really laws at all. We inherit this notion in our concept of *unconstitutionality.* As we saw in Chapter 3, the Constitution is assumed to embody the principles of natural law. Thus, a law that is not in accord with the higher law of the Constitution is null and void, not a real law at all, so that a man cannot be punished for refusing to obey it, assuming that the Supreme Court accepts his view of constitutionality.

In seventeenth-century England, the philosophy of natural law underwent a significant change. The emphasis now fell on the idea of *natural rights.* Since God had given every person reason, each individual had the right to make his own decisions and to live his own life freely, according to the dictates of his own reason. The thinkers who defended the idea of natural rights did not believe that their ideas would lead to anarchy or lawlessness. As they saw it, if society were governed by the principle of natural rights, all people would live under the natural law, the law of reason. Even under the rule of natural law, government would not be abolished completely. Statutes would have to be passed governing some aspects of human behavior because people were not so totally rational as to be able to live in absolute harmony under the natural law alone. The purpose of government, then, was to provide certain added protections to the natural rights of the individual that he or she could not fully protect unaided. But a government that infringed on the rights of the individual had violated its very reason for being.

THE DOCTRINE OF *LAISSEZ FAIRE*

The philosophy of natural rights which the founders of the nation so strongly believed was essentially a philosophy of individual autonomy. It stressed the limitations that should be placed upon the government. The Founding

Fathers were committed to individual rule with occasional assistance and protection from government. In most things, people should rule themselves, not be ruled by government. In late nineteenth-century America, this individualism was expressed in the doctrine of *laissez faire,* a French term meaning "leave alone." Essentially, the *laissez faire* doctrine was based on the principle that the government should interfere with the "natural" workings of society as little as possible. In the economic realm, for example, it was believed that if the government would only "leave things alone," the system of free competition in the open market and the laws of supply and demand would automatically correct any temporary imbalances. The role of government should be limited to providing basic police services to ensure the safety of the individual and the security of his property.[5]

As the champions of *laissez faire* saw it, the main threat to the rights of the individual came from the state. In their view, the idea that a person has a right to do something meant chiefly that the government should not be allowed to hinder him from doing it. It did not mean that the government should take positive steps to assist him. For example, today many people believe that each citizen has a right to earn a decent living. Many of us take this to mean that the government should set minimum wage standards, that it should take steps to correct the economy when there are not enough jobs for the people, and so on. In the heyday of *laissez faire*, however, the right to earn a living meant the right to be free from government legislation requiring that a person work only so many hours for a certain wage. The right to work was the right to decide for oneself where, when, and for how much one would work. *Laissez faire* doctrine was used to justify the "right" of financially pressed people to work long hours at low wages under hazardous conditions and to permit their children to be subjected to similar practices.

In other words, the *laissez faire* thinkers defined rights essentially in negative terms. To say that a citizen had a right to do something was chiefly a way to indicate what the government should not be allowed to do. In many areas we still think of rights in this negative way. Freedom of speech and religion, our First Amendment rights, mean that we may speak and worship where, when, and how we please, free from government interference. The First Amendment reads "Congress shall make *no* law abridging freedom of speech." This is a *laissez faire* right—a right to be "let alone" by the government.

PRIVATE PROPERTY AND *LAISSEZ FAIRE*

From the time of the Founding Fathers, one of the most fundamental individual rights has been the right to hold private property. The Declaration of Independence substituted "pursuit of happiness" for "property" in the traditional English slogan, "Life, liberty and property." For the founders,

---

[5] Robert McCloskey, *American Conservatism in the Age of Enterprise* (Cambridge: Harvard University Press, 1951).

the advantage of the new phrase was only that it covered a little more ground than "property" alone. They certainly conceived of the accumulation of wealth through the institution of private property as the central vehicle for the pursuit of happiness. The old phrase reappears in the Fourteenth Amendment: "Nor shall any State deprive any person of life, liberty, or property, without the due process of law."

The American ideological commitment to private property and individual economic initiative has been so strong that Marxist ideologies, which swept so much of the world, hardly have made a dent here. The highest vote ever achieved by a socialist party in a presidential election was 926,000 in 1912. To be sure, there have been socialist presidential candidates at nearly every election in the twentieth century, and local socialist parties have had some success in a few areas. By and large, however, being labeled "socialistic" is the kiss of death for any politician or policy. Although our anti-Communism is no longer as intense as it was in the 1950s, it is still a fundamental part of American political opinion.

All this is not to say that the American commitment to property rights is complete and unquestioning. In the first place, an unlimited right to private property conflicts with the American commitment to equality, which we will examine later in this chapter. Glaring disparities in the distribution of property have always been an issue in American politics. Fear of the "money power," the "trusts," the "big corporations," "Wall Street," and the "banks" has been a constant theme of American life. Indeed, one of the most interesting features of the American ideology is the way it reconciles the belief in private property with the belief in equality. Often, the people who push programs of business regulation and progressive taxation are staunch believers in private property. They want programs of social reform in order to ensure that major concentrations of family and corporate wealth cannot economically enslave "the little man," and that everyone has at least the minimum economic base that makes the acquisition of property possible. Most Americans are so deeply committed to the value of private property-holding that this issue rarely even rises to the level of political consciousness. But arguments over what distribution and regulation of property are desirable are the very stuff of day-to-day politics. In a sense, then, the American economic ideology consists of a series of constantly readjusted compromises between our commitment to private property and our commitment to equality.

ECONOMIC INTERESTS

Laissez faire never became the exclusive ideology of the United States. In the period after the Civil War, which was the heyday of the *laissez faire* philosophy, strong political movements arose which we usually lump together under the title *Populism*.[6] These movements were aimed at preserving the individual freedom of the small farmer, businessman, and worker. As

[6] Richard Hofstadter, *The Age of Reform* (New York: Alfred A. Knopf, 1966).

the Populists saw it, the freedom of these people was being threatened by the trusts, the banks, and the railroads. For them, freedom did not mean freedom from government interference. On the contrary, they wanted the government to play an active role in protecting their rights. They demanded legislation to preserve their individual autonomy from enterprises that had become so large and powerful that their exercise of complete freedom threatened the freedom of others.

Thus, by the early twentieth century, the idea of liberal government took on a new meaning. The government would secure the liberty of the people not by leaving them alone, but by settling the clashes that arose between the rights claimed by various individuals and collectivities. We began to speak less of rights and more of *interests,* each of which was entitled to government protection to assure it its place in the sun. Gradually, we came to see rights less as negative protections *against* government interference and more as positive claims that individuals and groups were entitled to make for governmental services that would protect and foster their individual freedom. Particularly during the New Deal and World War II, the concept of rights took on more and more positive connotations. The right to employment was no longer the right to be free from government interference in deciding how and at what wages one would work. Under the terms of the Employment Act of 1946, the government acquired a moral obligation to foster the highest feasible levels of employment.

NEGATIVE VERSUS POSITIVE RIGHTS

Obviously, all of these different concepts of rights can come into conflict with one another, even though they are all grounded in the same ideas about the fundamental worth of the individual and the desirability of personal autonomy. If the government is to prevent some people from infringing on the rights of others, it is going to have to reduce the right of the infringer to be free from government intervention. Thus, the government may ensure a right to pure air by prohibiting smoking. But in doing so, it interferes with the freedom of the smoker. If the government is going to assure its citizens the positive right to a job, the right to eat, the right to medical care, the right to education, it must of necessity direct a larger and larger share of their lives and increasingly reduce their negative rights to be free of government interference. For example, an increase in the worker's right to a job means a decrease in the employer's right to hire or not hire whomever he wishes. Similarly, we cannot guarantee all our citizens the right to medical care without curtailing the medical profession's right to dispense its services as it sees fit.

Quite obviously, negative and positive concepts of rights coexist uneasily in contemporary American ideology. Nevertheless, we retain a strong commitment to preserving our negative rights. We continue to believe that there are certain fundamental individual rights that ought to be absolutely inviolable. And we continue to look to the Constitution and the working political system to protect these rights, even if we do not know exactly how to draw the boundaries between one person's rights and those of another.

IDEAS OF THE CONSTITUTION

As we already have noted, one of the basic ingredients in the American ideology is the belief that ours is a government "by the people." This idea has many complex meanings, but central to them all is the conviction that our democratic government works on the principle of *majority rule*. We also have observed that a second important element in the American ideology is our belief that every individual enjoys certain *inalienable rights*. These two beliefs—the belief in majority rule and the belief in individual rights—are the bedrock on which the American ideology rests.

It is easy to see that, in the abstract, these two principles provide admirable guidelines for government action. They are why Americans can take a justifiable pride in our free, democratic system. Yet it is also easy to see that these two principles can readily come into conflict. In any given time or place, the majority may not want to respect the rights of the minority. In that case, one of the two principles must suffer. Either the belief in individual rights will triumph and the majority will not have its way, or the principle of majority rule will triumph and the minority will lose its rights. Nazi Germany has provided a tragic example of what can happen when a majority of the people feels it is entitled to disregard the rights of a minority. Throughout much of American history, the treatment of blacks, American Indians, and a number of other racial and ethnic minorities serves as a sad reminder that a government based on the principle of majority rule does not *guarantee* that the rights of all persons will be respected.

The American political system was designed to keep such abuses to a minimum. In part, this is why our commitment to the principles of the Constitution is such a fundamental part of the American ideology. For the Constitution is the point of intersection between belief in rule by the people and belief in individual rights. In the next few pages, let us briefly examine some of the ways in which the Constitution reconciles these two potentially conflicting strains in the American ideology.

RECENT INDIAN OCCUPATIONS OF ABANDONED GOVERNMENT PROPERTY ARE BELATED CLAIMS TO MINORITY RIGHTS TAKEN AWAY BY WHITE MAJORITY RULE. *Wide World Photos*

Americans are frequently confronted with the following paradox: If you believe in majority rule, then you must believe that the majority can do what it pleases, including taking away the rights of minorities. If you believe in minority rights, then you must believe that the minority may sometimes block the majority. If, however, the minority can block the majority, then you have minority rule. But if the majority can always win, why should minorities continue to play? Why should they remain loyal to the government?

The standard answer, and one that continues to satisfy most Americans, is based on our faith in the Constitution. The majority rules, we believe, but its rule is not absolute. The majority may not deprive individuals of their constitutional rights. Indeed, many of the rights embodied in the Constitution are designed specifically as minority rights. Freedom of speech and the right to vote, for instance, are guarantees of the rights of minorities to participate in the political process. They assure minorities a fair chance to work toward building majority support for their views. Much of the political power of the Supreme Court rests on this principle, for the Court traditionally has been visualized as a major means of protecting individual rights from excited majorities. In this sense, then, minority rights do not mean that the minority has the right to block the majority. It means that the minority has the right to participate in the democratic process. The only thing the majority may not do is block the access of minorities to the process. Thus minority rights do not contradict the principle of majority rule. They simply allow everyone a fair chance at becoming part of a winning majority.

FACTIONS

So far, we have been discussing ways in which the Constitution protects the rights of minorities against the will of *the* majority. In a sense, this is an oversimplification, for the Constitution was actually designed to produce a political system in which there was no such thing as *the* majority.[7] James Madison, one of the Founding Fathers, expressed this idea most clearly in *The Federalist Papers*, and his thinking has continued to be one of the major strands in the American ideology.[8]

As Madison saw it, the nation was divided into a number of *factions*, each of which would pursue its own interests. Farmers had somewhat different interests than merchants, creditors than debtors, shipowners than manufacturers, northerners than southerners, gentlemen than common men. So long as none of these factions was politically dominant, the government would necessarily have to operate on the principle of compromise. In the long run, no single faction could dominate by itself, each faction would get some of what it wanted, and no faction would ever have its way entirely.

[7] Max Farrand, *The Framing of the Constitution of the United States* (New Haven: Yale University Press, 1965).

[8] Alexander Hamilton, John Jay, and James Madison, *The Federalist* (Cambridge, Mass: Belknap Press, 1966).

The problem, of course, is how to put Madison's principles into practice. How can a government be set up in such a way as to keep any single faction from ever becoming a majority, and thus dominating the political process?

GEOGRAPHICAL DIVERSITY. The first part of the answer to this question lies in the tremendous geographic diversity of the United States. Today, the nation spans the entire continent, but even the original thirteen states were immense by European standards. When the United States of America first came into being, it was almost twice the size of France, two and a third times the size of Germany, three times the size of Italy, and almost four times the size of Great Britain. Moreover, the state of transportation was so primitive and weapons were so widely distributed among the citizens that the sparsely settled land mass constituting the United States was less subject to control from Washington than it is today. And this huge area contained many different sorts of people in many different occupations. Madison recognized that in this diversity lay the key to the type of government he wanted. With so many widely divergent factions, it was improbable that enough of them could ever find enough in common to form a permanent ruling majority.

ELECTIONS. To assure that this would be the case, the Founding Fathers designed an electoral system that would take maximum advantage of the natural diversity of American society. For example, the framers of the Constitution permitted the states to set their own rules for House elections because they knew that most states would choose representatives in ways that made them responsive to a diversity of interests. The provision of two Senators per state, regardless of size, although based on a compromise in the Constitutional Convention, also became justified as a device for ensuring diversity. What is more, different terms of office were established for representatives, senators, and presidents. Representatives served for two years, the President for four years, and senators for six years, with a third of the senators coming due for election every two years rather than all at one time. The Supreme Court was not elected at all, but appointed for lifetime terms. Thus, it seemed highly unlikely that the strength of a single faction would accidentally be so nicely distributed over space and time as to control a majority of House seats, a majority of states, and the electoral college.

How does this system serve to prevent the emergence of a dominant majority? First, although states varied in their arrangements for choosing members of the House of Representatives, by the middle of the nineteenth century, virtually all Representatives were being chosen in small, single-member districts. This means that minorities are going to stand a pretty good chance of electing some representatives who will support their interests. For example, a state may be largely rural, with only a few sizable towns. If representatives were elected on a statewide basis, obviously the rural vote would predominate. But with small districts, the chances are that the people in the towns will be the majority in a few districts, so that they can control a small number of House seats. Similarly, none of the various ethnic minorities is numerous enough in any state to be able to assure themselves of representation in statewide elections. But in a number of House districts various ethnic minorities actually make up a majority.

Similarly, the staggered terms of senators also serve to blunt the force of temporary majority opinion. For example, imagine that the majority of Americans became very excited during the oil crisis of the early 1970s. Imagine that they decided that war with the oil producing nations was the only way to solve the crisis. Wherever they could, they would vote for senators and representatives who were pledged to a militant oil policy. As a result, the House would tend to support these militant views. (Even here, though, the victory of the militants would not be complete, thanks to the geographic diversity we have just discussed. Farm states, for example, might not feel the oil crisis very acutely, and so they would not side with the nationwide majority. Or farm communities within industrial states might vote for representatives who did not agree with the militant opinions expressed by the statewide majority.) But even granting that the House would come to be dominated by representatives who were swept along with the majority opinion, we can readily see that the Senate would be relatively immune to such short-term passions. Only a third of the Senators are up for election in any election year. Even if the hawks swept twenty-five of the thirty-three senate seats up for election, this would give them only a quarter of the votes in the Senate. Two years later, when the next third of the Senate stands for election, the passions raised by the issue may have calmed down, and four years later, when the final third runs for office, the issue may be totally dead. In other words, just as the small size of House districts keeps national or state majorities from totally dominating local minorities, so the staggered terms of senators prevent temporary majorities from controlling the political process.

CHECKS AND BALANCES

In addition to designing an electoral system which takes maximum advantage of the diversity of American society in order to protect minority rights, the Constitution also has provided other devices to serve the same purpose. Indeed, for Madison and some of the other Founding Fathers, the most crucial check on the rise of a dominant majority was what is commonly called the system of *checks and balances*.

As we saw in Chapter 3, the Constitution is designed so that each branch will do some legislating, some administering, and some judging. It is because their functions overlap that the branches can check and balance one another. For instance, for a new law to come into effect, the Congress must pass it. The President must then sign it rather than veto it. And the Supreme Court must declare it constitutional rather than unconstitutional if its constitutionality is challenged in court. The three branches can check one another because no law can come into existence or remain in existence unless all three cooperate in using the lawmaking or legislative power they *share*. Because it was unlikely that all three would be in the hands of the same faction for any length of time, no single faction—no matter what its numerical strength—could use the government to its sole advantage. Any operation of government would require cooperation and compromise between the various factions holding strategic points.

Faith in the separation of powers remains a major element of American political ideology.[9] Few Americans would be willing to concentrate all the powers of government in any one of the branches.

MAJORITIES OF THE MOMENT

We have just examined a number of ways in which the Constitution protects minority rights from the will of the majority. From all this, it might be surmised that Madison and other Founding Fathers of similar persuasion did not believe in the principle of majority rule. Nothing could be further from the truth. The Constitution does contain a long series of devices for avoiding the dominance of a single faction or interest that actually became a majority. But it also presupposes majority voting in the House and Senate as well as the majority principle throughout the election process. The Founding Fathers were afraid of what would happen if the government fell into the hands of a dominant majority. Instead, they wanted a system in which decisions would be made by what have been called *majorities of the moment*.[10] Such a majority is not a permanent, homogeneous one capable of turning government into the servant of a single interest. It is a coalition of a number of factions that find themselves in momentary agreement on a single specific issue. Having combined to form a voting majority in Congress and gained the cooperation or at least neutrality of the President, this coalition will dissolve again as soon as what it wants becomes law. Having achieved the single purpose that the member groups or factions shared, there is nothing further to hold the coalition together. As new issues arise, new coalitions will form. A group that happened to be in the winning coalition one time may be among the losers the next time.

The American tendency to government by compromise and coalition is enhanced by the fact that the Constitution, as well as various political practices that have gradually evolved over the years, provides many points in the political process where a small group can block government action. The theory is that in this way a prospective majority will have to court each of these groups and win the support of a good number of them in order to get what it wants. In this way, the chance of every group frequently being a member of the winning majority coalition is maximized. There is a risk, however, in excessively strengthening the position of small groups in order to ensure that they will be courted. Some disgruntled group may then always be strong enough to block the majority of the moment. If this happens, we will have what amounts to minority rule. This danger is a very real one

[9] Ralph Gabriel, *The Course of American Democratic Thought* (New York: Ronald Press, 1956).
[10] Arthur Holcombe, *Our More Perfect Union* (Cambridge: Harvard University Press, 1950).

since the power to thwart a majority is the power of a minority to rule in favor of the status quo. And at any given time there is bound to be a fairly large number of Americans who are convinced that one minority faction or another is obstructing the political process and thwarting the majority. The continuous American concern with election rules, congressional reform, and administrative reorganization (all of which will be discussed later) stems largely from this sort of dissatisfaction with whatever the current balance may be between the strength of minorities and majorities.

The existence of majorities of the moment helps explain why minorities generally remain loyal to the American political process. Because the United States contains so many minorities with so many overlapping interests, most minorities can be relatively confident that they will sometimes find enough others willing to cooperate with them to form a majority of the moment. It is this confidence that encourages a minority that loses a vote to calmly abide by the majority decision.

What would happen, however, if there were a permanent minority, one that loses every vote, that is never in a winning coalition? Who would be fool enough to believe that he has a stake in democracy if he never gets what he wants out of his right to participate? This is not merely a hypothetical question. Racial minorities have always provided American democracy with its most significant failures, including a Civil War. For long periods of time, they have been permanent minorities who were not admitted to the political process. Or, once admitted, they found themselves or imagined themselves still to be permanent minorities who always lost. Those who see themselves as members of a permanent minority that always loses may interpret their condition as a case of majority tyranny and may look to revolution as the only way out. It is for this reason that both the most self-satisfied white and the most militant black are equally products of American ideology. In Chapter 16 we will further explore the role of violence and revolution in the American political system.

THE TOWN MEETING FORM OF GOVERN-MENT THAT EXISTS IN SOME PARTS OF THE COUNTRY IS BASED ON FUNDA-MENTAL BELIEF IN POLITICAL EQUALITY AND INDIVIDUAL RIGHTS.
Wide World Photos

EQUALITY

POLITICAL EQUALITY

The idea of equality is one of the great traditional themes of American ideology. The Declaration of Independence announces that "all men are created equal" even before it explains that they are endowed by their creator with "certain inalienable rights." This close association between belief in equality and commitment to individual rights has continued throughout American history. Indeed, ideas about equality and ideas about individual rights are really two sides of the same coin. If all men are equal, then each man is equal to every other. If each is equal to every other, then each has rights all others are bound to respect.[11] Equality in the American setting

[11] Sanford A. Lakoff, *Equality in Political Philosophy* (Cambridge: Harvard University Press, 1964).

implies individual autonomy, the freedom of each person to make his or her own decisions.

When the Declaration of Independence says that "all men are created equal," it is talking about *political equality*. This idea is echoed in the Constitution, which says that every citizen has a right to "the equal protection of the laws."

SOCIAL EQUALITY

Legal political equality, as protected in the right-to-vote guarantee of the Fifteenth Amendment, is actually the only type of equality that the Constitution specifically acknowledges. Nevertheless, other types of equality are prominently featured in the American ideology. For example, most Americans believe in the principle of *social equality*. Of course, America is not immune to snobbism; there are many people in this country who think quite highly of themselves and look down at their social "inferiors." Nevertheless, judged by Old World standards, America is a remarkably unsnobbish nation. For centuries, European visitors have been impressed by the extent to which the principle of social equality permeates American society. In the 1830s, the great French social commentator Alexis de Tocqueville commented on the fact that in America the lordly owner of a factory and his hired hands treat each other as equals when they met after working hours. In Europe, this type of relationship would have been unthinkable.

There is, however, a negative side to the American commitment to social equality. This manifests itself in a marked tendency toward *conformism*. We sometimes look at differences between people with great suspicion. It is as though Americans confuse equality with sameness. Thus, when an individual wants to do things differently or to live differently, he may well run into hostile critics who say, in effect, "The way we do things is good enough for us. What makes you think you're any better than we are?" Indeed, nearly every acute observer of democracy has warned that there is a grave danger to the human spirit inherent in democratic systems. Emphasis on political equality may gradually transform itself into the demand that everyone demonstrate his equality by conforming to the dead level of thought and action set by the "common man."

EQUALITY OF OPPORTUNITY

In twentieth-century America, one of the major manifestations of the drive for equality has been the growing concern about still another kind of equality. Increasingly, the government takes on the task of guaranteeing a certain minimum of food, housing, education, and health care to every American, as well as seeing that guarantees of political equality actually are enforced. Questions of how much, how fast, and how soon have been the standard fare of American political debate for at least the last fifty years. Nevertheless, what is most striking about these debates is the almost universal agreement that there must be equality—at least in the sense that everyone must be assured the bare necessities of life and some chance for their children to better themselves. This type of equality is known as *equality of opportunity*. Although most Americans believe in equality, they are willing to tolerate enormous disparities in wealth between the richest and the poorest segments of the population. Americans often explain this seeming contradiction in terms of equality of opportunity. Believing in equality of opportunity does not necessarily mean believing that all people should be equally well off. It does not even mean believing that some day, when everyone has been given a fair chance, the inequalities will even out and the wealth of the nation will be equally distributed. Equality of opportunity simply means that every individual should have an equal chance to become wealthy. In other words, *we all are entitled to an equal opportunity to become unequal.*

By applying the principle of equality of opportunity, Americans in the second half of the twentieth century have taken some steps toward eliminating inequalities in our society. For example, the Supreme Court's famous school desegregation decision of 1954 struck down laws that denied black students an opportunity to attend the same schools attended by whites. Similarly, the Civil Rights Act of 1964 prohibited forms of discrimination that denied blacks an equal opportunity to get jobs, education, and access to public facilities.

Nevertheless, in many respects the idea of equal opportunity rests on a naive misunderstanding of social and political reality. Even if we could eliminate all the formal and legal barriers that deny some people an equal opportunity, the poor would still stand less of a chance for success than the middle-class and wealthy members of society. To mention just a few factors, the middle-class child lives in an environment which places a high value on education and encourages ambition; he is probably surrounded by successful adults who can serve as role models for him as he grows up. The poor child may have none of these advantages. To say, then, that these two children have equal opportunities simply because there are no formal, legal barriers blocking the poor child's way is obviously a fallacy. Today, a major issue of American politics is the extent to which government should give additional assistance to the poor in order to level out some of the grave inequalities that must exist in a nation with such disparities of wealth and family background.

RACIAL EQUALITY

The most troubling aspects of the American commitment to equality are related to racial equality. Indeed, it is the depth of our attachment to equality that makes American racism such a deeply frustrating phenomenon to its opponents. Contemporary American racism rarely rests on an open, conscious, and deliberate assertion of racial superiority. It is accompanied by massive doses of guilt generated by the knowledge that the plight of racial minorities does violate our basic belief in equality. Our allegiance to equality is clearest on the political level. Deprivation of the vote on racial grounds, for instance, was the most unpopular form of prejudice. And official government social discrimination by law, such as racially segregated public facilities, was the second. But when some white Americans confront the unofficial social and economic consequences of racism, their enthusiasm for racial equality generally begins to fade. The greatest problem of American politics today is whether the admission of racial minorities to a greater degree of legal equality will, in turn, produce enough social and economic gains to satisfy them. If such equality is not achieved, they may come to see themselves as the kind of embittered permanent minority we mentioned a little earlier.

JUSTICE AND THE RULE OF LAW

The idea of justice is very closely related to the idea of equality. One of the oldest definitions of justice is giving equality to equals.[12] We also think of justice as being intimately connected with the rule of law. Perhaps the connection between equality and law can be seen most easily by imagining a state in which disputes between individuals were settled by the unguided personal wisdom of some government official. Few of us would have enough confidence in such a system willingly to entrust our fate to it in any important matter. We would prefer that a law be announced in advance, detailing how all people in the same situation would be treated. This is because we feel that uniform, equal treatment will yield better results across the board for all individuals than would special treatment for each individual.

Thus, one component of the idea of justice is equal treatment. A second component is fair procedure. If two people are having a dispute and go before a judge, we expect that both will get a chance to tell their side of the story. If the court used rules and procedures that prevented one side from talking, we would say that the court was not giving both sides a fair hearing and thus not doing justice. Before we are ready to say that a law or a decision is just, we want to know whether it provides for fair rules and procedures that allow everyone concerned a chance to have his say.

We also think of justice as having an ideal component. Justice should be not only equal and procedurally fair, but good. Let us suppose that a nation proposed a new law for the extermination of all the mentally retarded. It might provide for equal treatment in the sense that it would treat all of the mentally retarded exactly alike. It might be fair in the sense that it set up fair procedures, complete with lawyers, expert witnesses, and scientific tests, to determine who was and who was not mentally retarded, giving everyone a fair chance to prove that he was not retarded. But we would not call such a law *just*. We would deny that it was just because we believe that killing people because they are handicapped violates their fundamental human rights. Or to put it another way, such a law violates our fundamental beliefs about how a good society would treat its citizens.

[12] Carl J. Friedrich and John W. Chapman, eds., *Justice* (New York: Atherton, 1963).

Americans on the whole place a great deal of confidence in the ability of our legal system to provide fair and equal treatment for all who come before it. What is more, Americans generally believe that the surest way of attaining justice is through the legal system. But this does not mean that we believe that law and justice are synonymous. On the contrary, the idea that justice is a higher value than law has long been a feature of the American ideology. We use the concept of justice as a critical check on our faith in law. Americans often criticize laws on the grounds that they are unjust.

In sum, Americans tend to see justice as a higher ideal than law. But they also tend to see law as the surest and safest way of achieving justice. Even where they disagree with particular laws, they remain deeply committed to the principle of *the rule of law*. This is why theories of civil disobedience, violence, resistance, and rebellion have never played a dominant role in the American ideology.[13] Instead of resisting or rebelling against unjust laws, Americans traditionally direct their efforts toward changing them. They try to use the law to correct whatever injustices the law has created.

LIBERALS AND CONSERVATIVES

As we come to the end of this brief survey of ideology, let us examine two of our most popular ideological labels, *liberal* and *conservative*. Later in this book, you will discover how little of the political thinking of many Americans is shaped by strings of interrelated political attitudes. That is to say, most people do not exhibit a consistent pattern in the way they feel on various issues, one pattern roughly labeled *liberal*, and the other *conservative*. Data will also be presented that show a very rough correspondence between the Democratic party and liberalism and the Republican party and conservatism. Most Americans do not exhibit either of these attitude patterns, however. Both for citizens in general and for the most attentive and informed observers of American politics, the terms *liberal* and *conservative* have always been a source of confusion. For example, a "conservative" Republican favors big business and the free enterprise system; he is opposed to big government and welfare legislation. He feels strongly that individual freedom has to be protected from government encroachments. Yet he may be a "law and order" advocate, singularly insensitive to the rights of the accused. In short, he may be strongly opposed to government limitations on the freedom of businessmen but in favor of a great deal of government limitation on the activities of alleged criminals. Conversely, the liberal Democrat generally favors programs such as medicare and other such policies that lead to greater government involvement in the daily affairs of the people. On the one hand, the liberal worries about F.B.I. or C.I.A. snooping, but on the other hand he may propose programs that give environmental and public health officials almost unlimited powers to dictate the terms and conditions under which individuals must earn their daily bread, use their own property, and engage in recreational pursuits.

[13] See Henry David Thoreau, *Civil Disobedience* (Boston: Houghton Mifflin, 1960).

As you can see, both the liberal and the conservative believe in individual rights. This is why we remarked earlier that Americans are fundamentally liberal regardless of their political persuasion. Both sides want to protect the liberties of the individual citizen. But each sees the threats to individual liberties as coming from a different direction, and therefore each adopts a different strategy aimed at what is essentially the same end. Those we call liberals typically wish the government to aid the needy, control the powerful, and leave free the critics and nonconformists. Those we call conservatives typically want the government to aid business enterprise, control those who threaten the good order of society, and leave free the business and professional leaders whom they see as contributing most to our prosperity.[14]

RADICALISM IN AMERICA

In addition to liberals and conservatives, there is also a third ideological grouping that has achieved a certain level of significance in recent years. The contemporary American political scene contains a fairly small but highly visible number of people who are commonly identified as *radicals*.[15] As far as ideology is concerned, American radicalism generally shares a common set of values with liberalism and conservatism. Here, too, the ideals of equality, democracy, and justice are prominent aspects of the ideology. Except for the small core of Marxist radicals who conscientiously opposed the whole American socio-economic system, most of the so-called radicals who received headline attention in the 1960s differed from the mainstream of American political thought chiefly in the vehemence with which they pressed their claims. For example, radicals who denounce the power of the government in Washington and demand "power to the people" are not really asking for anything very different from what conservative Republicans have been wanting for a long time—the dismantling of the huge federal bureaucracy. Similarly, the thrust of black radicalism in the sixties and seventies has been aimed at winning for blacks the right to participate in the American dream—of equality, prosperity, and freedom—if necessary even at the cost of seceding from American society.

On the whole, then, it seems fair to conclude that there is no such thing as a significant independent radical ideology in America today. The various radical movements use violent rhetoric, threats, and occasional outbursts of actual violence in order to recruit and energize support. But this rhetoric does not amount to a coherent alternative to the ideology we have been describing throughout this chapter. Rather, it is a denunciation of America for failing to live up to the ideals proclaimed in the dominant ideology.[16] It is a vehement protest against the enormous discrepancies between our values and our behavior. And sometimes it is an impassioned assertion that a nation with the political, social, and economic system one finds in America

[14] Henry Steele Commager, *The American Mind* (New Haven: Yale University Press, 1959).

[15] William P. Gerberding and Duane Smith, eds., *The Radical Left* (Boston: Houghton Mifflin, 1970).

[16] See Daniel Bell, *The End of Ideology* (New York: The Free Press, 1966).

cannot possibly achieve its own ideals of true democracy, equality, freedom, and justice.

Nevertheless, the radicals have not been able to offer any clear vision of how the political, social, and economic systems of the country should be organized in order to achieve these venerable American values. Because it lacks this independent ideological base, it seems probable that the "New Left" will be bled off into various programs of social improvement and liberal reform. Even now, it is little more than the left end of the continuum of contemporary America ideology.

CONSENSUS

It is often argued that a nation cannot have democratic politics unless it enjoys a strong consensus on basic political ideas. For if the majority and minority of the moment had fundamentally different ideas about political good and evil, the minority would not yield gracefully to the majority. It would fight for its basic principles rather than let evil triumph until the next election.

Sometimes the consensus argument is put a little differently. Perhaps the citizens of a democracy need not agree on all fundamentals. Some may be Catholic and some atheist. Some may be socialists and some capitalists. But they still can operate a democracy if they all believe in the same *rules of the game*. If there is a consensus across all groups on free elections, majority rule, freedom of speech, and the preservation of the individual's right to participate in politics, then democratic politics is possible. In other words, if people can agree on the procedures or ways of doing politics, then they can cooperate democratically even if they disagree on what goals politics should be seeking to achieve. For example, socialists have a fundamental belief in government ownership of the means of production. Capitalists have a fundamental belief in private ownership. But so long as both share the belief that the people should decide the issue through free elections, then socialists and capitalists can live together in a democracy.

This argument can be related very specifically to the United States. The people of the United States come from different ethnic, religious, racial, linguistic, political, and economic backgrounds. We might expect them to be in conflict over many major and fundamental issues. Yet so long as most of them subscribe to the fundamental rules of the game, it is possible for the United States to maintain a democratic political system.

In the final analysis, however, we do not know how correct this argument is. In public opinion surveys, many Americans do not express very great support for such democratic rules of the game as allowing freedom of speech to people with unpopular opinions. There does seem to be a greater consensus on the rules of the game among the better-educated, and since this population category is more active in politics and in leading public opinion, perhaps their consensus is the crucial one for the functioning of democratic government.[17]

There is a kind of chicken and egg situation here. A democratic nation which avoids projecting fundamental conflicts into politics can continuously proclaim and foster the consensus on the rules of the game found in its historic documents and political writings. It can do so because it never has to test very hard just how deeply that consensus runs in the hearts of its people. And a nation which enjoys a fairly high consensus on the constitutional democratic rules of the game can use that consensus to help keep basic conflicts out of politics. On the whole, except for the Civil War, the United States has done quite well at fostering and proclaiming a liberal democratic political ideology and avoiding the kind of crises that would put that ideology to ultimate tests.

SUMMARY

We have seen that basic American ideas about politics do not fall into a very neat pattern. Americans believe in rule by the people. But they also believe in representative and efficient government. They want government decisions to be right as well as popular. Americans believe in majority rule, but they also believe that minorities have rights the majority must respect. They see rights both as positive claims by needy individuals for government help toward living a better life and negative commands telling government that it must not interfere with individual freedom. American constitutional ideas combine a desire to give governing power to majorities of the moment and a fear that a too powerful and too permanent majority will destroy minority interests. Americans believe in political equality and equality of opportunity but are willing to tolerate great disparities of economic well-being. Americans believe in the rule of law, but they frequently attack laws that they consider unjust. "Liberal" and "conservative" belief patterns overlap one another greatly in their basic values and special attitudes, and each contains internal contradictions of its own.

Most people do not have ideologies that are precisely stated or logically consistent. Human beings are quite capable of deeply believing a number of overlapping and conflicting things at the same time. They possess a number of psychological mechanisms for helping them not notice contradictions. And even when they do notice them, people in politics often resolve the dilemma by pursuing a little of each of the contradictory things they want.

One of the basic ways people deal with the complex problems of political ideology is not to think about them much. For most Americans, political

[17] Herbert McClosky, "Consensus and Ideology in American Politics," *American Political Science Review,* 58 (June 1964), 361–82; and Robert W. Jackman, "Political Elites, Mass Publics, and Support for Democratic Principles," *Journal of Politics,* 34 (August 1972), 753–73.

ideology tends to be a series of felt assumptions and vaguely held beliefs. Our ideology is not a fully articulated set of premises rationally debated day by day. For this very reason, the basic impact of ideology on politics cannot be determined very exactly.

PART TWO
THE EFFECTIVE SETTING: LEVELS OF PARTICIPATION AND MODES OF INFLUENCE

CHAPTER FIVE
PUBLIC OPINION

OUR purpose in this chapter is to give more precise meaning to the vague term *the people*. We begin by describing how Americans perceive the national government and form attitudes about public affairs. Then we examine *political socialization,* the process by which children first learn about the world of politics. From there we go on to discuss the role of ideology in America and the distribution of political opinions in the population. Finally, we look at the *mass media* and *public opinion polls.*

In a general sense, public opinion can be considered the foundation of any government. All organized social systems depend to some extent on the sufferance of their populations. The most unstructured commune must have some system of rules which its members accept and with which they cooperate. Otherwise it could not exist. Conversely, the most rigorously disciplined police state must be accepted by some of its members to some extent if it is to survive. Even a brutally repressive regime could not impose its will for long over the strenuous objections of its whole population. At the very least, a police state has to be able to count on the loyalty of the police.

Discussions of public opinion are often confusing because we naturally assume that since ours is a government "by the people," there should be some specific, visible entity that can be identified as the "public" and that has an opinion. We assume that the government does what it does because the people somehow express their opinions about what it should do. But who are the people, and how do they express their opinions?

It would be easy to say that "the people" are all the people who live in the country, but this is obviously too simple. If, for example, 65 percent of the voters in an election vote in favor of a bond issue, then the issue passes. In that case we say that "public opinion" favored the issue and this is why it became law. But what about the other 35 percent? Aren't they part of the public? And what about all those who couldn't vote or didn't? Aren't they part of the public, too? Of course they are.

Perhaps, then, we should forget about definitions for the time being and approach the question factually. Instead of asking what public opinion is, we could ask how it reaches and influences public officials. The simplest answers to this question are based on a model of democracy as the more or less automatic conversion of public opinion into public policy—in short, the direct democracy model discussed in the previous chapter. For example, the public can communicate directly with the government by letters, telephone calls, and the like. Or it can express its views through opinion surveys, which tell government officials where the public stands on various issues and thus serve as a vehicle for translating public opinion into policy. Finally, the public can express its opinion on public policy through election campaigns. When candidates run for office, they explain their differing views about public issues. The voters then consider the alternative views and cast their votes in accordance with the view they prefer. The candidate who gets the most votes is declared the winner and proceeds to carry out the "mandate" that brought him into office.

Notice that in all the activities just described, the initiative for political action is from the public to their leaders. This model explains how the public communicates with officials, but it allows no room for leadership as a positive component of democracy. That is to say, it does not take into account the fact that the communication of opinion between people and political leaders is a two-way street. In fact, while the people inform the government about what they want, competing leaders also inform the people about what they offer, and in doing so they help to shape public opinion.

Furthermore, the direct democracy model also ignores representative institutions, such as interest groups and political parties, that mediate between citizens and leaders. Clearly, then, this portrait is a caricature—although a surprisingly large number of people seem to accept it uncritically as an accurate account of the role of public opinion in a democracy. This chapter presents a more realistic view of public opinion, beginning with how politics figures in the perspectives of most citizens. The following four chapters will then examine the linkages between public opinion and the government— voting, political participation, interest groups, and political parties.

HOW THE POLITICAL WORLD LOOKS

In 1972, as American military operations in Vietnam were coming to a close, and after a quarter century of deep disagreement about our national policies in the Far East, 37 percent of adult Americans did not know that mainland China had a Communist government. In that year the voters elected a Democratic Congress; at the same time the incumbent Republican President, Richard M. Nixon, won a landslide re-election. Yet scarcely more than half the people knew that the Democrats had maintained control of Congress in the 1972 election. Less than half the population can name their representative in Congress, and only 59 percent know the name of even one of their U.S. senators. Such examples, which can be multiplied endlessly, demonstrate the scanty political information possessed by citizens who nevertheless go to the polls and cast their votes for the people who then run Congress and occupy the White House.[1]

This level of ignorance exists because the workings of the national government usually are remote from the day-to-day lives of most citizens, are complex and abstract, and therefore seem irrelevant to their concerns. Supreme Court decisions, China, foreign aid, and the like are not immediate issues for most people.

Occasionally, though, events in the political arena are so sensational or hit so close to home that almost everyone becomes acutely aware of them.

[1] We computed these findings from data gathered in the 1972 National Election Study of the University of Michigan's Center for Political Studies. All unattributed findings on public opinion in this chapter are based on CPS data obtained through the Inter-University Consortium for Political Research. We are solely responsible for the analysis of these data. The statistics on familiarity with the names of House and Senate members are based on a Harris poll reported in the *New York Times*, December 3, 1973.

It should be noted that Americans are better informed about politics than the citizens of England, Germany, and Italy. See Gabriel A. Almond and Sidney Verba, *The Civic Culture* (Princeton, N.J.: Princeton University Press, 1963), p. 96.

For example, during a single week at the height of the Watergate scandal, almost nine out of every ten adults watched the televised Senate Watergate hearings.[2] And in a general way, "everyone" is aware of, concerned about, but also puzzled by such issues as the Vietnam and Korean wars and severe economic dislocations such as those of the 1930s and the beginning of the Ford Administration. Thus it would be false to imply that public attention and opinion are nonexistent, although it is true that most people do not have much detailed knowledge about even these attention-getting events.

In the final analysis, no single generalization can sum up the state of public opinion in our society. At one extreme, there is a largely uneducated hard-core group of about 20 percent of the population who are chronic political know-nothings and who seldom think at all about politics. Near the other extreme is the college-educated segment of the population, which makes up the most politically informed part of American society. In 1974, however, only 13 percent of all Americans over the age of twenty-four had completed four or more years of college. In contrast, 39 percent of the same population had not graduated from high school, and 23 percent had not gone beyond the eighth grade.[3] Figure 5-1 presents the complete educational profile of the adult population.

In other words, most Americans do not have the educational experience

---

[2] *Gallup Opinion Index,* September 1973. The Gallup organization publishes the monthly *Gallup Opinion Index,* which is available in most college libraries and contains interesting compilations of public opinion data.

[3] These figures on educational level are from U.S. Bureau of the Census, *Current Population Reports,* Series P–20, no. 274.

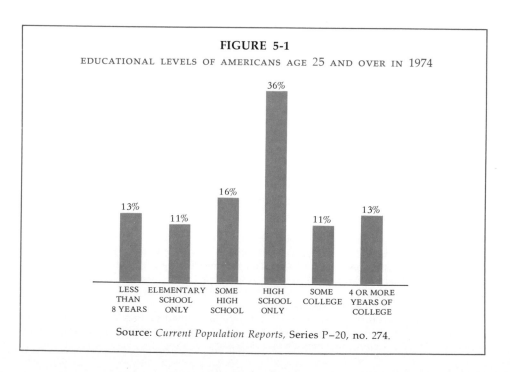

FIGURE 5-1

EDUCATIONAL LEVELS OF AMERICANS AGE 25 AND OVER IN 1974

Source: *Current Population Reports,* Series P–20, no. 274.

of the typical reader of an American government textbook such as this. As a result, their view of the world naturally tends to be somewhat different from the view of those who have had these experiences. Like everything else we acquire, information has costs. Learning something requires giving up time that can be spent doing other things. Naturally, the cost of information is higher for people who have little experience in reading the complex and often abstract books and articles that contain political information.

The bulk of the electorate falls between the two extremes. They could not be described as informed about or interested in politics, but on the other hand they are not irreversibly apathetic. These people are the majority of those who usually vote in presidential elections and are at least intermittently attentive to political affairs.

Although, as we have just seen, most people *do not* have much *knowledge* of political events, they *do* have or at least are willing to express political *opinions* of one sort or another. Political opinions may be weak and likely to change in response to superficial stimuli, or they may be so solid as to be bedrock features of an individual's political outlook. How are these opinions formed and altered? Perhaps the best way to begin is at the very beginning —with the process by which children first come to think about the political world and to form their earliest impressions of it.

THE POLITICAL SOCIALIZATION OF AMERICAN CHILDREN

The human species is unique in its dependence on learning for survival. No other form of life on this planet relies less on direct genetic inheritance—that is, instinct—and more on patient care and instruction by the older generation to produce the fundamentals of successful behavior. Instinct helps the young tiger or duck learn to feed and care for itself, but the young human must be taught how to make a living. What is more, the importance of learning—what students of human development call *socialization*—goes well beyond the physical aspects of existence. Every society has countless rules of conduct that must be learned. There are rules about how to address older people, younger people, or strangers; rules about appropriate behavior in stores, playgrounds, and other people's houses. In addition, every society has some sort of political system. This means that all citizens must acquire some sort of mental map that tells them where they fit into the political system, what they may and may not do as political actors.

From the time of Plato to the present, commentators on the political condition have recognized the importance of the learning of citizenship by each new generation. Nevertheless, it has remained for recent social science to begin systematic studies of the actual course of political learning. Such studies reveal that a remarkable amount of political learning becomes "fixed" in childhood. Courses in civics, American government, or "problems of democracy" are required of public school students in almost every American state. This is one manifestation of official recognition of the importance of pre-adult learning. But the schools are only one small component in the larger process known as *political socialization*. Indeed, much of the basic psychology that activates the political behavior of both leaders and citizens begins in early childhood, long before the child's first "civics" course.

Let us examine some of the steps through which most Americans, in the course of growing up, are introduced to the political world. No single individual follows all these steps, and there are differences in the style and content of political learning from group to group, as well as changes over the years. Nevertheless, the account that follows gives us a generally valid picture of how American children develop their first political attitudes and beliefs.

THE ETHOS OF POLITICAL AND SOCIAL EQUALITY

Observers of American life are often astounded at the readiness with which young children argue with their parents, choose their own food, and conduct their own lives. Most people assume that the remarkable openness and reciprocity of American parent-child relations are relatively recent developments. In fact, foreign visitors to the United States were making the same observation over a century and a half ago. An English visitor of that period, for example, recorded what happened when a young boy refused to obey his mother: "The father instead of punishing him smiled and commented, 'A sturdy republican, sir.' "

The father's little witticism in this case points to an important truth. In a very real sense, the family is the first political system to which we belong. Often our political ideas about equality and authority were first formed in the little social system in which we grew up. Thus it is no surprise that the same visitors who commented on the nonauthoritarian nature of American families were also struck by the extraordinary sense of social and political equality that Americans expressed. It is well established that there were extensive social and economic inequalities in early American society, but they were slight compared to the situation in nineteenth-century Europe. Later, especially after the Civil War, the social and economic inequalities in the United States increased markedly. Nevertheless, the *subjective* reality —what people *believe* to be true—is as consequential in many respects as the objective situation. And Americans, from post-Revolutionary times to the 1970s, seem to have retained an unusually tenacious belief in the principle of equality. This belief was one of the persistent themes that ran through the court and congressional proceedings which led in 1974 to the resignation of President Nixon.

The pervasive ethos of American egalitarianism can be illustrated by parallel quotations from two interviews, one with an American child and the other with a French child. Both children were studied in a comparative inquiry into political socialization that explored spontaneous expectations about political behavior by asking children to imagine the conclusions of incomplete stories designed to pose standard dilemmas of social and political existence. Compare the following pair of grade-school students: Michelle, the daughter of a French businessman, and Debbie, the daughter of an American doctor. First, their answers to a question about how an everyday problem of equality would come out.

INTERVIEWER: Michael, Susan, and their parents often watch television together. One evening they disagree over what to watch. Imagine an end to the story.

Michelle

M: Usually in families the parents make the decisions. The children haven't any right to dictate what they want to see. If they want to watch a war movie, the parents certainly won't say they [can] see it, because they're not usually suitable for children. So they'll choose a program which they think the children will like.

I: Yes, so the parents choose a program which the children will like?

M: Yes, yes, because sometimes the children insist on seeing war movies and the parents think they'll be frightened. . . .

I: If there aren't any war films on that evening, how do they decide?

M: They sometimes *let* the children choose.

Debbie

D: How many TVs are there in the house?

I: One.

D: Well, they finally agree on a schedule. They have their favorite programs and there's two programs on one night. So each one gets their choice every other week. So one week they'll get it and one week they won't

I: Let's suppose that on this particular night there are two special shows on at the same time and there's some people in the family that want to watch one . . . and . . . some . . . that want to watch the other.

[Debbie proposes that one of the children see her preferred program with a friend and the interviewer counters by supposing that they are on a farm, far away from any other television sets, and cannot manage this. How then would they decide?]

D: *Take a vote.*

I: Would everyone be happy with that way of doing it?

D: Yeah. If there were five in the family [and] two wanted one show and three wanted to see the other, you know, [voting would be] better because then three people would be enjoying while if it was the other way, only two people.

The striking thing about Debbie's response is not that she imagines the children triumphing over the parents but that she is reluctant to imagine conflict at all. Her basic assumption is that all the family members are equal— at least on the matter of television viewing. Now consider how each of these children responded to an explicitly political question—another story they were asked to complete.

INTERVIEWER: One day the President was driving his car to a meeting. Because he was late, he was driving very fast. The police stopped the car. Finish the story.

Michelle

M: First of all, it isn't true that General de Gaulle drives his own car. He has a chauffeur and can tell him to go very fast. If he is stopped by a policeman, the policeman will have to let him go because General de Gaulle commands everyone, because they all must serve France and they are there to see that order is maintained in France. They release him immediately, because General de Gaulle has a very important meeting, so they are forced to let him go.

I: What will the policeman say?

M: "I apologize, *mon Général,* for stopping you, but I didn't recognize your car."

Debbie

D: The President asks him why he's stopping him and the policeman says, "You're going too fast." And he says, "Well, I'm going to be late for a meeting." And the policeman says, "I don't really care if you're President or anything, you've got to obey the rules of the country and if you don't you shouldn't be President." And then, of course, the President agrees, if he's smart enough to agree, so he believes him. And so he slows down. He's late for the meeting, but it was worth it.

The investigators responsible for the study in which Michelle and Debbie were interviewed were struck by the many references by children like Debbie to the equality of all Americans — references like the following:

It doesn't make a difference who you are in this country, you still have to obey the laws.

And the policeman says, "I don't really care if you're the President or anything, you've got to obey the rules of the country and if you don't you shouldn't be President."

The President is an American. He's just like anybody else, only he's got a high office.

Such ideas about equality were not expressed by all American children, however. The study found that although *white* American children were considerably more likely than French children to refer to the equality of all citizens, the *black* American children interviewed were *less* likely than any other group to employ this theme. Coming from a deprived segment of the population, which hasn't participated fully in "The American Dream," these children have adopted a more cynical attitude than their white counterparts. Understandably, they find it hard to believe that all Americans are equal.

This points to one of the important lessons learned by political socialization researchers. *What is true of one group and one individual at a particular time may not be true of others at other times.* American political culture and socialization are *not* composed of a single fabric, even though there *are* certain overall patterns.

ACQUISITION OF NATIONAL LOYALTY

Early in elementary school, American children first begin to think of themselves as Americans. In one study in which children were shown pictures of the flags of different nations and asked which they liked most, kindergarten children most often preferred the Thai flag, which at the time of the research pictured an elephant. But first graders rejected the flag of Thailand in favor of the American flag—a triumph of patriotism over a childish love for zoological wonders.[4] Apparently the kindergarten children saw the flags simply as pictures or patterns, whereas the first graders understood that the flag was a symbol of America, that they were Americans, and that being American is *good.* Like much other political learning, of course, the formation of national loyalty proceeds with feelings running ahead of facts. But gradually various facts, symbols, and rationalizations will be added to provide the flesh that adheres to this skeleton of political loyalty.

AWARENESS OF THE INSTITUTIONS OF NATIONAL GOVERNMENT

Studies of early political socialization reveal that the President is by far the first political object to come to the child's attention. The young child typically has a highly *positive* view of the President of the United States. During the Kennedy and early Johnson years, even black children had benign conceptions of the President. But as ethnic assertiveness grew in the late 1960s, black children and children from some other minority groups did not share in the tendency to consider the President a "benevolent leader." Then, in the early 1970s, when President Nixon's popularity hit bottom during the Watergate episode, children of all descriptions began to express more negative views of the President. Unpublished research on the early Ford administration showed a rapid return of juvenile idealization of the Chief Executive, at least by white children.

Most commonly, the response of American children is to praise the President. When asked simply to *describe* the job of the President, youngsters often answer with praise. A typical response came from the child who said, "To make people happy. . . . He helps other people in other countries too, and tries to make things better for everyone." (And this was during the Watergate hearings in 1973, when Nixon's popularity among adults was very low.)

A PRESIDENCY CENTERED VIEW. It may be a number of years before the child knows very much about national politics apart from his or her awareness of

NATIONAL LOYALTY IS ACQUIRED EARLY IN ONE'S LIFE. THIS PRESCHOOLER, WHOSE FATHER IS IN THE AUSTRALIAN DIPLOMATIC CORPS, TOLD HIS SCHOOL PRINCIPAL THAT HE COULD NOT PLEDGE ALLEGIANCE TO THE U.S. FLAG, BUT MUST PLEDGE TO THE QUEEN. *Wide World Photos*

[4] Edwin D. Lawson, "The Development of Patriotism in Children: A Second Look," *Journal of Psychology,* 55 (1963), 279–86.

TABLE 5-1

POLITICAL INFORMATION OF CHILDREN AND YOUNG ADULTS

	PERCENTAGE WHO KNOW THE NAME OF EACH OFFICIAL		
	13-YEAR-OLDS	17-YEAR-OLDS	YOUNG ADULTS
President	94	98	98
Vice President	60	79	87
Secretary of State	2	9	16
Secretary of Defense	6	16	24
Speaker of the House of Representatives	2	25	32
Senate Majority Leader	4	14	23
At least one Senator from own state	16	44	57
U. S. Representative from own district	11	35	39

Source: *National Assessment of Educational Progress*, Report 2: Citizenship: National Results—Partial (Denver and Ann Arbor, July 1970), p. 37.

the President. Indeed, this presidency-centered view of American politics carries over into adult life, as we can see in Table 5-1, which is based on a 1970 national survey of teenage children and young adults. In fact, most adults do not know individual political leaders other than the President by name, except for certain temporary political celebrities such as Henry Kissinger and, at the time of the 1970 survey, Vice President Spiro Agnew, who was then a highly publicized spokesman for conservative Republicanism.

As we shall see, in many significant ways the American political system is in fact presidency-centered. Thus, the prominence both children and adults assign to the President is actually a somewhat realistic way of looking at things. As a result, belief and reality tend to reinforce one another. The fact that our system is actually presidency-centered reinforces our beliefs, and our beliefs in turn enhance our tendency to look to the President to establish the basic agenda of politics. We also tend to look to the President with a somewhat exaggerated view of the goodness and the power of the office and its occupant. At times, this can lead to severe disillusionment when the government obviously is not performing well. Thus, the prolonged and unsuccessful war in Vietnam, the Watergate scandals, and the economic distress of the 1970s may lead to more despondency than would have resulted if many Americans did not have such high expectations of the President in the first place.

PARTY PREFERENCES. As we have seen, children tend to develop political feelings before they learn the relevant facts. Patriotism is one example of this pattern. Another is identification with a political party. Many children consider themselves "Republicans" or "Democrats" at an early age, well in advance of any knowledge of what the parties do or of differences between them. Like sports fans, they support a team because it is "theirs."

These precocious loyalties are learned from parents and from sharing the same political and social environment with one's parents. Few children depart from their parents' party loyalties. What is more, the great bulk of those young people who do not share their parents' choice of party do not develop any partisan loyalties of their own. That is, they are independents. In fact, since the mid-1960s there has been an increase in the tendency of children *not* to form any political party attachments. This will be examined in more detail in Chapter 6.

HOW POLITICAL ATTITUDES ARE SHAPED

As we have noted already, the general public may not possess much detailed political information, but most people have *some* interest in politics and do have opinions on various specific issues. Where do these political opinions come from?

One of the most important sources of political opinion already has been discussed in Chapter 2 in connection with *reference groups*. Any group to which a person feels he belongs qualifies as a reference group if the person's sense of common identity with other group members tends to define his view of himself. A Jew might assess a foreign policy issue in terms of its impact on Israel, a traveling salesman might be concerned about how it would affect the price of gasoline, a farmer might think about its consequences for foreign demand for American wheat, and a black might think about its impact on employment in the ghettos. Although group identifications play a significant part in opinion formation, reference groups have clear limits as guides to belief. In the first place, most people belong to numerous reference groups. A Jewish traveling salesman, for example, might favor aid to Israel, despite the fact that it might antagonize the Arab states and thus raise the price of gasoline. The fact that he is also a salesman would not influence his opinion. Knowing what reference group a person belongs to will not help us predict his opinions unless we know *all* the groups with which he identifies, and which are most important to him. What is more, many issues are not group relevant, and often groups are divided on issues.

Major historical changes can be a spur to shifting political beliefs. These include periods of depression and war, domestic unrest and tranquility—indeed, all the possible trends that may affect the life circumstances of an individual. Such events by themselves are not a clear signpost for individual beliefs. Usually, it is political leaders or academic and journalistic commentators who provide the "interpretations" that link societal earthquakes to personal seismographs. For example, large numbers of people may be dissatisfied with the economy. They find it hard to get jobs and notice that prices are rising. But on their own, they may not see this as a political issue.

Generally, it will not become an issue until political leaders and the press interpret it as such. A senator may give a speech in which he denounces the President's economic policies, or a newspaper editorial or syndicated column may lay the blame on Congress. Such interpretations serve to transform actual events into political issues.

DISSONANCE REDUCTION

Various psychological mechanisms affect this process of translating changes in circumstances into changes in opinion. One of the most interesting of these is the process referred to by psychologists as *dissonance reduction*. Dissonance occurs when two elements of experience seem to contradict each other, thus creating emotional discomfort that the individual tries unconsciously to eliminate. For example, say you are elected to a school honor society. Shortly after your election, you run into a close friend who fails to congratulate you on your achievement. This bothers you because it creates a dissonance between two of your beliefs. On the one hand, you believe that this person is a friend who cares about you; on the other hand, you believe that a friend wouldn't pass over such an accomplishment in silence. Almost automatically, you will take mental steps to reduce the dissonance. You may change one of your beliefs—"I guess he isn't really a friend after all"—or the other—"It's not necessary for a real friend to say anything; after all, he knows I know how he feels about it." Or you may change your perception of the situation—"He must have been preoccupied with something else. Yes, come to think of it, he did seem distracted, like his mind was somewhere else."

This process of dissonance reduction goes on all the time in politics. It is one of the reasons why the United States has only two major parties even though the possible combinations of opinion are endless. No party can ever satisfy many voters on all the issues, but people still remain loyal to the party of their choice. A voter may like the position a candidate takes on, say, ecology, the Middle East, and taxes, but may disapprove of the candidate's stand on abortion and relations with China. This produces a dissonance that Americans tend to handle by adjusting either their beliefs or their priorities—or by misperceiving what the candidate said. Perhaps the voter will change his mind about abortion and China in order to get rid of the dissonance. Or he may decide that it's more important to have a good tax policy than a good abortion law. Probably the most common way of eliminating dissonance is by getting the message wrong, or by failing to note and remember the discordant fact.

In other countries, it should be noted, dissonance is handled in other ways. In France, for example, there is a great proliferation of political parties, sometimes running into the dozens. This makes it possible to shop around for a candidate who agrees with you on all, or at least most, of the major issues.

Dissonance reduction is one of the chief mechanisms that make political leadership work. When an admired political figure makes a pronouncement that conflicts with the beliefs of some of his followers, they must take steps to reduce the dissonance between their admiration of the leader and their opinion on the issue. Some of them will do this by ceasing to support the politician, but others will change their opinion on the issue to bring it into conformity with his.

A good example of this occurred in early 1970 when, after more than twenty years of diplomatic isolation of China by the United States, majority sentiment continued to be opposed to admitting China to the United Nations. Yet seven months later, after President Nixon's visit to China and the identification of his administration with a policy of *détente,* surveys showed majority support in favor of admitting China to the UN. The movement of opinion in these few months was greatest among Republicans, and by the spring of 1971 Republicans were somewhat more likely to support warmer relations with China than were Democrats—a striking reversal of previous partisan attitudes.[5]

We can safely assume that China was not a major object of concern to most Americans, that few people ever thought about it, and thus that there was (and is) little public emotional investment in the subject one way or the other. This is not true about loyalty to one's party, nor about attitudes toward the President. With the double advantage of his office and his position as party leader, Nixon's actions produced dramatic changes in public opinion. In this situation, attitudes toward China were the "weak link" most vulnerable to change as conditions changed. As this example suggests, officials usually have more freedom in foreign than domestic policy, since public opinion about almost all international issues is weakly held and thus amenable to political leadership.

The war in Vietnam was vastly more prominent and emotion-laden than any other foreign policy issue of the past generation. Nevertheless, attitudes toward the war reflected not only the ups and downs of the war itself but also the influence of more durable points of reference. There were three general sources of attitudes toward the war. One group consisted of *followers* who supported the President and what he was doing because he was the President. A second category consisted of *partisans* who supported or opposed Vietnam policy depending on the party of the man in the White House. During the Johnson administration, Republicans were most likely to think that the war had been a mistake. But by the time Nixon had been President for eight months, Republicans were more favorable to the war than Democrats. "Johnson's war" thus became "Nixon's war." Finally, there were *believers,* people who were moved chiefly by the substance of what was going on. These people made up their minds on the merits of the policy as they understood it, rather than on the basis of what party was in power or what the President was doing.[6]

Because *believers* are a small minority on most issues, a great deal of public opinion is determined not by perceptions of the issue itself, but by various factors associated with it, such as the people who are seen to be for and

---

[5] *Gallup Opinion Index,* June 1971.

[6] These categories and the evidence for them are from John E. Mueller, *War, Presidents, and Public Opinion* (New York: John Wiley, 1973), Chapter 5.

against it and the party positions of those concerned. People seek guidelines for evaluating the political world and for determining their own positions on issues. Often these guidelines are provided by personal and party loyalties that really have little to do with the issue itself.

IDEOLOGY IN AMERICA

An *ideology* is an internally consistent pattern of general beliefs that leads to specific perceptions and attitudes about political issues. Ideology simplifies the problems of political thought by providing an overarching key for opinion formation in specific contexts. For example, the *conservative* ideology generally maintains that the government should interfere as little as possible with the "natural" workings of the national economy. If a person who subscribes to this ideology is asked to form an opinion on a piece of price control legislation, he does not have to assess all the facts and implications before making up his mind. Unless he can be shown some overriding reason why his general opposition to economic controls is not valid in this particular case, he will oppose the proposed legislation.

What role does ideology play in the formation of political opinions in America? If most Americans had developed ideological outlooks and took them seriously, then liberals would always adopt the liberal position and conservatives would always embrace the conservative solution whenever a new issue arose. Indeed, ideology would be a substitute for information in opinion formation. If this were the case, the widespread lack of information about current events would be politically unimportant because people would make their political decisions on the basis of their ideologies. But even at the doctrinal level, as we saw in the previous chapter, the United States does not have internally consistent, fully coherent political ideologies.

Liberal and *conservative* are handy labels that many people use in talking about politics. These terms are used far beyond our ability to define them. Commentators often talk about public opinion and election results in ideological terms. Assertions are made such as "America is moving to the right" or "The outcome of the election revealed a pronounced liberal shift among the voters." As we shall see, most such interpretations are out of touch with the real world of political opinion patterns.

Of course, some people *do* have a general political philosophy that could properly be called ideological. These people base their conclusions about particular issues and candidates on their ideologies. By knowing the attitudes of such people on one issue, one can predict how they will respond on other issues. It is also true that any individual's attitude on any specific issue could be labeled radical, liberal, conservative, reactionary, or what have you. *But the vast majority of Americans do not have ideological perspectives, or even internally consistent clusters of attitudes.*

Let us examine this conclusion more fully by asking three specific questions about the role of ideology in American politics. How many Americans identify themselves in ideological terms? How many Americans actually think about politics in such general, abstract categories as *left* and *right,* or *liberal, conservative* and *radical?* To what extent are the opinions people hold on a single issue related to the opinions they hold on other issues?

IDEOLOGICAL SELF-IDENTIFICATION

When Americans are asked the forced-choice question, "How would you describe yourself—as very conservative, fairly conservative, middle-of-the-road, fairly liberal, or very liberal?" almost all will readily use one of these terms.[7] But a different picture emerges if a more sensitive question is asked, enabling citizens to use their own thought categories. In some studies, instead of pushing citizens to give themselves ideological labels, researchers ask questions such as these: "We hear a lot of talk these days about liberals and conservatives. I'm going to show you a seven-point scale on which the political views that people might hold are arranged from extremely liberal to extremely conservative. Where would you place yourself on this scale, or haven't you thought much about this?"

We have arranged answers to this question in Figure 5–2, which shows that less than 3 percent of the population call themselves either extremely liberal or extremely conservative; about 7 percent call themselves liberal, another 10 percent slightly liberal, 15 percent slightly conservative, and 10 percent conservative. Counting the number of people on the liberal and conservative sides of the midpoint in Figure 5–2, we can see that about 19 percent of the population put themselves on the left, compared to 26 percent on the right. More significant is the fact that 28 percent of the population say that they really have not thought much about locating themselves ideologically, or they just plain do not know. Another 27 percent call themselves moderates or middle-of-the-road, which may be another way of ducking the problem altogether. Thus 55 percent of Americans either do not define themselves ideologically or make the wishy-washy statement that they are moderates.

These findings about self-identification lead us to conclude that most Americans have a very low level of ideological consciousness. But even this conclusion may overestimate the importance of ideology in American political life. Only about half the adults in this country even know what the words *liberal* and *conservative* mean.[8] What is more, people who call themselves conservatives often do not take the conservative position on specific issues, just as many self-professed liberals stray from the liberal side of many issues. For example, in one study, 28 percent of the people who called themselves liberals were opposed to national health care, while 46 percent of the self-identified conservatives did not oppose plans for federally financed medical

[7] *Gallup Opinion Index,* December 1970, p. 7.

[8] Philip E. Converse, "The Nature of Belief Systems in Mass Publics," in David E. Apter, ed., *Ideology and Discontent* (New York: Free Press, 1964), p. 223; and John G. Pierce, "Party Identification and the Changing Role of Ideology in American Politics," *Midwest Journal of Political Science,* 14 (February 1970), 25–42.

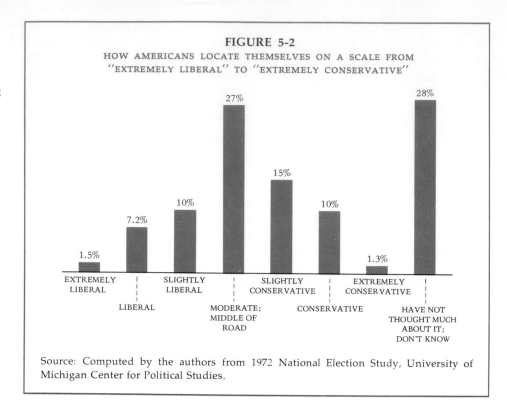

FIGURE 5-2

HOW AMERICANS LOCATE THEMSELVES ON A SCALE FROM
"EXTREMELY LIBERAL" TO "EXTREMELY CONSERVATIVE"

Source: Computed by the authors from 1972 National Election Study, University of Michigan Center for Political Studies.

care.[9] Thus although self-labeled conservatives are more numerous than self-labeled liberals, the number of people in favor of liberal policies designed to equalize the distribution of wealth and to provide minimum levels of well-being to all Americans often is greater than the number opposed.[10] In other words, the American people tend to see themselves as more conservative than liberal, but their opinions on many specific issues are more liberal than conservative.

DO AMERICANS THINK IN IDEOLOGICAL TERMS?

Another way to analyze the role of ideology in American politics is to ask how many people *spontaneously* use ideological labels in describing the two major political parties and their presidential candidates. The authoritative University of Michigan political pollsters have asked questions designed to elicit this kind of information in every one of their national election surveys since 1952. Respondents are asked to mention the good and bad points of the Republican party, the Democratic party, and the two presidential con-

[9] Norman H. Nie, "Mass Belief Systems Revisited: Political Change and Attitude Structure," *Journal of Politics*, 36 (August 1974), 556.

[10] John G. Stewart, *One Last Chance: The Democratic Party, 1974–76* (New York: Praeger, 1974), p. 107.

tenders. The answers they give reflect the role of ideology in their political evaluations.

In the relatively quiet elections of the 1950s, only about one-eighth of the population used any kind of ideological frame of reference in expressing opinions about the parties and candidates. But in 1964 the Republican candidate, Senator Barry Goldwater, based his campaign on the claim that he was offering the voters a significant philosophical alternative to the liberalism of the Democratic party. "A choice, not an echo" was his campaign slogan. It seems likely that Goldwater's candidacy, coupled with the heated political atmosphere produced by the Vietnam war and heightened racial tensions in the late 1960s, brought about a higher level of popular political consciousness and a heightened sensitivity to ideology. Thus, by 1968 the proportion of Americans who saw politics in ideological terms reached 23 percent, almost double the figure for the placid 1950s.[11] But although twenty-three percent is quite a jump from 13 percent, it still constitutes less than a quarter of the population

INTERRELATION OF OPINIONS

It might be argued that we are being too demanding, that it is not fair to test for ideology by asking people to apply an abstract label either to themselves or to a political party or presidential candidate. Perhaps the American people do not feel comfortable with abstractions, but they may have a kind of folk wisdom that serves to distinguish left and right. The best way to test for this sort of *inarticulate ideology* is to establish whether the position a person takes on one issue is related to his positions on other issues. If his opinions actually were derived from some general political outlook—that is, from some ideology—we would expect them to be related to each other in a consistent pattern.

We can discuss this question at two levels. First, let us divide political issues into four rough categories: (1) economic issues, (2) civil rights issues, (3) foreign policy issues, and (4) what we will loosely call the "new politics." Now let us ask, to what extent are liberals or conservatives in any one of these issue areas also liberal or conservative in others? That is, if a person has liberal opinions about foreign policy, will he also be liberal on civil rights? On economic policy? Will he be in favor of the so-called "new politics"? Second, let us directly examine each of these clusters of opinion to see how internally consistent people are *within* each of the issue areas. That is, if a person takes a conservative view of an economic issue such as deficit spending, how likely is he to take a conservative position on other economic issues?

Over the past half-century, one of the enduring disputes in American politics has been the extent to which the government should take responsibility for meeting the essential human needs of every citizen. Among the

[11] Angus Campbell et al., *The American Voter* (New York: John Wiley, 1960), Chap. 10; and Warren E. Miller and Arthur H. Miller, *Political Realignment in 1972, Party Loyalties and Issue Preferences* (Ann Arbor: University of Michigan Center for Political Studies, n.d.), p. 26.

most important of these needs are a job, a decent standard of living, and good health. The liberal position on these issues is that "the government in Washington should see to it that every person has a job and a good standard of living" and that "the government in Washington ought to help people get doctors and hospital care at low cost." By the same token, conservatives argue that individuals, rather than the government, should be responsible for getting their own jobs and obtaining their own medical care.[12] On civil rights, the liberal position is that the government in Washington should take steps to integrate schools, while the more conservative position is that the federal government should not involve itself in such questions.

Do economic liberals tend to be liberals on civil rights? We find that 54 percent of people who took a liberal position on medical care were also liberals on school integration. Conversely, 39 percent of liberals on medical care were opposed to the federal government's involving itself with the question of racial balance in the schools.

Almost identical results appear for the conservatives on the issue of medical care. About a third of them (35 percent) were liberal on the school issue, and about 55 percent were conservative. In other words, there is some tendency toward consistency on these two issues, with slightly more than half the people expressing consistent views but more than a third of the population being inconsistent.

As we go beyond domestic politics and look at attitudes toward foreign policy, we see even less consistency. A fifth of the people who are liberal on medical care oppose foreign aid, as do a fifth of those who are conservative on medical care. In short, knowing someone's position on this important domestic welfare issue does virtually nothing to predict his or her position on aid to other countries. Many similar examples could be given.

If we examine in greater detail the way people think about particular policy questions *within* the major issue areas, we also fail to find cohesive, ideologically consistent belief systems. For example, of those people who expressed opinions about whether the government in Washington should help provide medical care and whether it should help provide every person with a job and a good standard of living, only 31 percent took the liberal position on both these matters. Another 26 percent took the conservative position on both questions. Thus, 57 percent were consistent on this pair of attitudes toward government responsibility for health and employment. The other 43 percent were either liberals on one issue and conservative on the other, or could not give two clear, unqualified answers.

There is somewhat more attitudinal consistency on some aspects of foreign policy—at least on the conservative side. People who are opposed to foreign aid also tend to be opposed to increased American trade with Communist countries by a ratio of about three to one. On the other hand, liberals on the issue of foreign aid are fairly evenly split on the question of increased imports and exports with Communist countries. There is, however, a much greater tendency for people to say that they "don't know" when

---

[12] These questions are from the Michigan Center for Political Studies research on presidential elections, which is the source of the findings cited in footnotes 13 and 15.

asked about foreign policy—a reminder of how remote most aspects of foreign affairs are to the great bulk of the population.

Civil rights is the area of greatest belief consistency. Seventy percent of one group surveyed were either in favor both of school integration and federal enforcement of fair employment practices or opposed to both policies. In general, attitudes about various aspects of race relations seem to be more strongly and consistently held than other kinds of political attitudes. Consistent with this is the small number of people who answer "don't know" in this area. In this respect, civil rights attitudes are the very opposite of foreign policy attitudes. In the foreign policy area, many people do not have opinions one way or the other. Those who do have opinions tend to be rather inconsistent. In the civil rights area, however, most people have opinions and these opinions tend to be consistent on the various civil right issues.[13]

Nevertheless, we must be careful about what we mean when we talk about liberal and conservative consistency with regard to civil rights. Views about different aspects of race relations can be ranked in descending order of popularity. For example, by the 1970s very few white Americans were opposed to blacks voting, but most whites were still opposed to racial intermarriage. Thus, whether someone is a liberal or conservative with regard to race relations is a matter of where one chooses to draw the line between these two opposing tendencies. Interestingly, despite all the talk about "white backlash" over the past ten years, there has been a steady and consistent trend toward more liberal, integrationist attitudes by whites with regard to every aspect of relations between the races.[14]

Finally, we come to the fourth of our major issue areas, which we have called the "new politics." We use this term to refer to those issues that are said to be a departure from the past, to represent a new consciousness, the cutting edge of political concerns in the 1970s. Among the major themes in the new politics are attitudes toward:

"law and order"
the police and the military
various "countercultural" trends that became conspicuous in the 1960s, ranging from rock festivals to the use of drugs
protests and demonstrations

In 1970, less than a third of the adult population took consistent positions on these four topics. A mere 14 percent were uniformly in favor of "law and order," sympathetic to the police, hostile to "contercultural" mores, and opposed to protests and demonstrations. Another 17 percent exhibited the mirror image—consistent sympathy to demonstrations and countercultural life styles, and hostility to "law and order," the police, and the

---

[13] These findings about attitude consistency are from Charles A. Bann, "Interrelations of Opinions: 1964 and 1968," unpublished paper, University of California, Berkeley, 1973.

[14] Andrew M. Greeley and Paul B. Sheatsley, "Attitudes toward Racial Integration," *Scientific American*, December 1971, pp. 13–19.

military. The other two-thirds were inconsistent, taking a liberal position on some of these issues and a conservative position on others.[15] Thus, although many prophets of revolution or repression proclaim that these issues have "polarized" American society, we see no evidence of polarization. America is not divided into two hostile camps, one in favor of the "new politics" and the other opposed. Instead, there is the same mixture of views that one finds in other issue areas.

Although these interrelationships among attitudes are weak, they represent more patterning of political beliefs than existed before 1964. The greater connectedness of attitudes seems to be a product of the 1964 presidential election campaign, which was something of a watershed. Political attitudes seem to have become more structured during Goldwater's campaign, and since then they have been stabilized at the 1964 plateau.[16]

There are, of course, variations among the population with respect to ideological thinking. Better educated people have more structured attitudes, are more likely to think of themselves as liberal or conservative, and are more likely to have opinions consistent with such self-identifications. Even among college graduates, however, ideological awareness and coherence are far from overwhelming.[17]

These findings about the failure of the population to coalesce into two neatly defined groups remind us of our discussion in Chapter 2 about *cross-cutting social cleavages.* These cleavages, you will recall, mean that lines of ethnicity, religion, and social class in the United States tend to run *across* each other rather than to build into a series of cumulative antagonisms. The political consequences of this mixture of attitudes are nicely described by V. O. Key:

> People do not divide into two camps, with members of one group in agreement on one side of all domestic economic issues and united to oppose the other group united within itself in opposition on the same issues. . . . Instead, the liberal-conservative cleavage divides the population along different lines, depending on the matter at issue.

Key then goes on to describe the consequences for the general character of the political system and the level of political conflict:

> Enemies on the burning issues of today may be allies on the foremost questions of tomorrow. Antagonists will, in short, have com-

---

[15] The findings in this paragraph are from Teresa E. Levitin and Warren E. Miller, "The New Politics and Partisan Realignment," paper delivered at the 1972 annual meeting of the American Political Science Association.

[16] Nie, "Mass Belief Systems Revisited."

[17] *Ibid.;* William Schneider, "Public Opinion: The Beginning of Ideology?" *Foreign Policy,* Winter 1974–75, p. 96; and Arthur H. Miller et al., "A Majority Party in Disarray: Policy Polarization in the 1972 Election," *American Political Science Review,* 70 (June 1976).

mon interests, and the mixture of antagonism and alliance may induce restraint in conflict.[18]

Although the existence of overlapping, inconsistent belief systems tends to restrain bitter political conflict in American politics, it also makes it difficult for people to form alliances based on common attitudes. Thus the low level of ideology in our political system helps to explain why the government often finds it difficult to reach decisions about policy.

Looking at all the different possible combinations of attitudes, one might wonder why the United States has a two-party system rather than a number of parties, each one representing one of the major constellations of political opinion. The answer is complicated, as we shall see in the following chapters, but one reason is that the weakness of ideological perspectives on many issues means that party allegiance must play a dominant role in our political thought processes. Because we do not rely on ideology to help us sort our opinions into meaningful patterns, we must rely on "brand label" political loyalties of the type we shall examine in Chapter 6.

WHO HAS WHAT OPINIONS?

As we have just seen, most Americans cannot be simply described as either liberal or conservative. But on an opinion-by-opinion basis, it is possible to make certain generalizations about what kinds of people have what sorts of opinions. The two personal characteristics that seem most strongly related to differences in political opinion are *occupation* and *education*. This is not to say that these two factors are the *only* lines along which political differences occur, but they are by far the most important. Moreover, most other relationships merely reflect these two prime factors. In reading about the connections between, say, education and racial tolerance, it is important to remember that these are *tendencies*, not hard-and-fast "laws." The conclusion that educated people are less prejudiced against racial minorities (which consistently emerges from studies of this topic) does not mean that all college graduates are tolerant and all unschooled people are bigots. It means only that the proportion of tolerant people is higher among the better educated. Schooling is also the background factor most associated with liberal attitudes on such foreign policy issues as economic aid, trading with Communist countries, support for the United Nations, and international cooperation.

On domestic economic issues, in contrast, the most important determinant of attitudes is occupation rather than education. Business and professional people are most conservative about government action to provide security and to regulate business. Clerical and salespeople are somewhat more liberal on such issues, and blue-collar workers are most liberal of all.

[18] V. O. Key, Jr., *Public Opinion and American Democracy* (New York: Alfred A. Knopf, 1961), p. 164.

On "new politics" issues like marijuana, abortions, demonstrations, and the like, education is by far the most important consideration. College graduates are the most permissive on such questions, and uneducated people the least permissive. Since education and income are closely related, the pattern of liberalism on these life style issues runs counter to that on economic issues. For example, 62 percent of those making more than $15,000 a year favor legalizing abortion, compared to only 27 percent of people with annual incomes under $5,000. Over half of the poorer group and a fourth of the richer one say they would turn in their own child if they caught him or her smoking marijuana.[19]

One fundamentally important kind of attitude is concerned not with government policy so much as with the ground rules of democracy. These attitudes emerge in issues concerning free speech and a willingness to extend to advocates of unpopular and "immoral" points of view the same freedoms that are claimed for people in the mainstream of politics. At the abstract level, virtually all Americans are in favor of civil liberties. Almost everyone agrees that "no matter what a person's political beliefs are, he is entitled to the same legal rights and protections as anyone else."[20] But once we turn from broadly stated attitudes to concrete examples, a considerable decline in support for civil liberties is evident. A great many people who are in favor of freedom of speech as a general proposition are not, when it comes down to cases, willing to say that Communists or atheists should be allowed to express their opinions in public. Half the population would not let "an admitted Communist" make a speech. A third would deny this right to someone who wanted to speak "against churches and religion." Although these figures about willingness to grant basic rights to unpopular minorities may be depressing, they represent considerable increases in support for civil liberties in less than twenty years. When these same questions were asked in the 1950s, a far greater proportion of the population was in favor of denying civil liberties to atheists and to Communists, and less than three Americans in five were in favor of letting someone make a speech "favoring government ownership of all the railroads and big industries."[21]

What kinds of people are likely to support the democratic creed, and who are most opposed to it? Again, level of education is the key factor. The more education people have, the more willing they are to extend the Bill of Rights to everyone. In Table 5–2, we present answers to questions about tolerance from different educational categories. This shows that there is almost unanimous support for civil liberties among college graduates, but that as the level of education declines, so does the extent of tolerance. People with less than a high-school education are overwhelmingly hostile to letting Communists and atheists speak, and are evenly split on the relatively innocuous topic of government ownership of industries. Further-

---

[19] "Who Opposes Social Change?" *The Public Interest,* Spring 1974, pp. 126–27.

[20] Herbert McClosky, "Consensus and Ideology in American Politics," *American Political Science Review,* 54 (June 1964), 366.

[21] Samuel A. Stouffer, *Communism, Conformity, and Civil Liberties* (Garden City, N.Y.: Doubleday, 1955), pp. 29–42.

TABLE 5–2

EDUCATION AND SUPPORT FOR FREEDOM OF SPEECH

PERCENTAGE WILLING TO ALLOW VARIOUS
TYPES OF INDIVIDUAL TO SPEAK

	GENERAL PUBLIC	COLLEGE GRADUATES	SOME COLLEGE	HIGH SCHOOL GRADUATES	SOME HIGH SCHOOL	GRADE SCHOOL OR LESS
An advocate of government ownership of industry	77	95	85	83	72	55
An opponent of churches & religion	65	90	81	74	54	33
An admitted Communist	52	84	71	56	39	22

Source: National Opinion Research Center, General Social Survey, 1972.

more, the better educated are tolerant without concern for the content of the particular unorthodoxy, as shown by the small differences in their responses about the three different unpopular opinions. But the uneducated are more inclined to consider the substance of a person's views in deciding whether he should be allowed to speak. Note the large gap between the number who would give freedom of speech to a socialist and to an "admitted Communist."

Educated people are more tolerant of free speech because they are more likely to understand the importance of civil liberties to the functioning of democratic government. Furthermore, since they have the highest levels of political activity, they have a vested interest in free speech. The greater political influence of such people helps explain why we continue to have a fairly high degree of political freedom despite the large number of people who are not committed to civil liberties. Since the educated are more influential, their political views have a greater chance of success than the views of the poor, disorganized, apathetic, and uninformed.

WHAT KINDS OF OPINION COUNT?

One can easily produce examples of the government's steadfastly ignoring overwhelming public sentiment on particular measures. One can also muster evidence that politicians do indeed respond to public opinion. Presenting an inventory of such episodes would be useful only if we could draw from them some general conclusions about the ultimate question of "who rules?"

Given the present state of knowledge in this area, we cannot be very precise about distinguishing between those areas where the government is responsive to popular pressure and those where it is not. We can, however, offer a few generalizations about the effectiveness of public opinion in influencing government policy.

In most cases it is difficult to get one's way politically unless one knows what public officials have done already on the topic under consideration. Outrage—whether by the average citizen, a union leader, or a millionaire—is not useful unless one knows how to direct it. Thus, one fundamental prerequisite to having influence is knowing how one's elected representatives have behaved. We have already seen that such knowledge is not widespread. In Figure 5–3 we have charted the relationship between a citizen's wealth and his or her knowledge of Congress. The figure shows that people who make more than $15,000 a year tend to be well informed about who represents them and have a fairly good chance of knowing how that representative has voted. But as income declines, so does information. Less than half the people making under $7,000 a year know who represents them in Congress, and at this income level only about one person in eight knows how the representative has voted. As we shall see, people and groups who do not have this kind of knowledge can exert a certain amount of indirect influence over how the parties behave, but more specific and precise exercises of influence are possible only if one knows who the players are.

Although knowledge of the political process increases with wealth and education, even the most highly educated stratum of the population is not

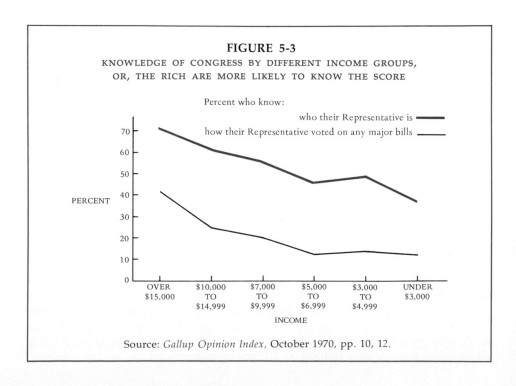

FIGURE 5-3

KNOWLEDGE OF CONGRESS BY DIFFERENT INCOME GROUPS, OR, THE RICH ARE MORE LIKELY TO KNOW THE SCORE

Source: *Gallup Opinion Index*, October 1970, pp. 10, 12.

informed about the complex specifics of government personnel and policy alternatives to the degree prescribed by textbook theories of democracy. Who, for example, knows the provisions of the President's annual legislative program, which committees in Congress consider which bills, and the countless other crucial details of policy making? Obviously, the answer is: Not very many people. A Washington lobbyist or correspondent might be informed about such matters, but the average American does not have the time or the resources required for keeping track of the day-to-day activities of the government. Whatever else it may be, democracy simply cannot be the direct enactment by the government of the detailed policies that the majority wants, because in fact the majority virtually never knows what precise alternatives are available, much less which ones it prefers.

Even when the people do have clear preferences, however, there is no guarantee that their opinions will be effective. Public opinion is largely irrelevant when people do not care very much about an issue. One of the most striking examples of public opinion favoring reform that does not seem likely to come about concerns the electoral college. Four out of five Americans would approve a constitutional amendment "which would do away with the Electoral College and base the election of a President on the total vote cast throughout the nation."[22] Yet Congress has consistently failed to adopt such an amendment, and the chances of abolishing the electoral college do not seem bright. Such a resolution once passed the House of Representatives but was stalled in the Senate. There was no public outcry about this flouting of popular will. The failure of the American public to manifest active concern about abolishing the electoral college is undoubtedly explained by the fact that while almost everyone expresses an opinion about the electoral college, only 35 percent of the public actually know what it is.[23] On the other hand, when people *do* care about an issue, or only *seem* to care about it, then politicians are often quite responsive. The politician's problem is to find out what the public really wants. Here there is something of a dilemma, for most politicians know that people who write letters, demonstrate, or in some other way make their opinions known may not be representative of the public as a whole. A politician who favors a policy simply because his mail runs strongly in favor of it may find that he is supporting a vociferous minority and displeasing the majority of his constituents, who dislike the policy but are not vocal about it. On the other hand, articulate people who speak out strongly on an issue, even though they are only a minority, may be the very ones who care enough to change their votes if their congressman displeases them, or even may contribute their time and money to defeat him.

THE MEDIA OF MASS COMMUNICATION

Most of what Americans know about national politics comes to them, directly or indirectly, through the mass media. Newspapers and television are the

POPULAR MAYOR FIORELLO LAGUARDIA ONCE USED THE RADIO TO READ COMIC STRIPS TO NEW YORKERS DURING A NEWSPAPER STRIKE IN THE 1930s—A MOVE THAT GAINED HIM MANY LISTENERS AND MUCH GOODWILL.
Culver Pictures

[22] *Gallup Opinion Index*, October 1969, p. 22.
[23] Hazel Gaudet Erskine, "The Polls: Textbook Knowledge," *Public Opinion Quarterly*, 28 (Spring 1963), 139.

primary sources of information, radio and magazines are less important. Although magazine circulation is tiny compared to the other three media, magazine readership is heavily concentrated among educated, interested people. As a result, magazines have an impact out of proportion to their numerical readership.

The mass media are a perennial political whipping boy. Almost all losing candidates complain that the press is against them. Even some winners do not seem happy about the media. Long before Watergate, President Nixon and other members of his administration felt that the press had a distinct bias to the left. On the other side of the ideological spectrum, radicals consider the media part of the "establishment" that hoodwinks and oppresses "the people." Since one can find newspapers and magazines to satisfy any conceivable political taste, from Maoist to Nazi, anyone complaining about press bias can make a plausible case based on a careful selection of the evidence.

Although television and radio stations are prohibited by licensing laws and the supervision of the Federal Communications Commission from advocating political viewpoints, no such restrictions apply to the print media. At election time, most newspapers publish editorials endorsing the candidates of their choice. It is the owners of the newspapers who decide which candidates to recommend, and most newspaper owners have a conservative outlook. This becomes evident when one tabulates their endorsement of candidates. Republicans are always favored over Democrats by a wide margin. In 1968, Richard Nixon got the editorial support of 80 percent of the nation's newspapers; this figure went up to 90 percent in 1972. Independent voters who read papers that endorsed Nixon were more likely to vote for him than were independents who read papers backing Humphrey in 1968 or McGovern in 1972. This could have accounted for as much as 3 percent of the total vote—a crucial margin in 1968, but trivial in the 1972 landslide.[24]

The conservative bias of most owners is only part of the story, however. There are major limits to the ability or willingness of owners to transfer their political opinions from the editorial page to the news columns. As businessmen, their first interest is in selling their product. If they are too offensive politically, some of their audience may not buy their product. Moreover, most reporters and lesser editors are sympathetic to liberal—and sometimes radical—causes. Thus the conservatism of the owners is often counterbalanced by the liberalism of the working press. In their actual news coverage of presidential campaigns (in contrast to the editorial page commentary, which is not widely read) the nationwide press services, electronic media, and most newspapers seem even-handed in their treatment of the Democratic and Republican presidential nominees'.

An important factor is the influence of a handful of important publications. Much of the content and emphasis of national political news coverage

[24] *Institute of Social Relations Newsletter*, Winter 1974, p. 8.

is guided by a few influential publications. The most important journalistic pace-setters are the *New York Times,* the *Washington Post,* the *Wall Street Journal, Time,* and *Newsweek.* The *New York Times* and the *Washington Post* (in partnership with the *Los Angeles Times*) each has its own news service, which is received daily by hundreds of newspapers. In addition, the *Post* owns *Newsweek.* The relatively detailed and sophisticated coverage provided by these organs helps set the tone for the rest of the mass media, including television news. Directly or indirectly, these strategic publications provide a major share of the stories read in local papers and seen on television. They are read by most national politicians, television network executives, and newspaper editors. In short, their influence is far greater than their circulation figures would suggest. Conventional views of American politics usually underestimate the degree to which these major media are a central component of the governmental system. Except for the *Wall Street Journal,* the owners and editors of these crucial organs are moderates and liberals.

These publications are the core of the "elitist eastern liberal press" that was on the receiving end of so much criticism and harassment from the Nixon administration. Shortly before he resigned, Nixon complained that "90 percent" of the Washington reporters were fundamentally opposed to him:

> Basically, they're ultra-liberal and I am conservative. . . . The reasons for their attitudes toward the President go back many years, but they're basically ideological, and I respect that. If I would pander to their liberal views, I could be infinitely popular with some of our friends out there, and a lot of the heat would go out of Watergate.

Nixon thought that the Washington press corps not only disagreed with him politically but was out to get him. His counterattacks on real and imagined enemies in the press included wiretapping, auditing tax returns, and seeking subpoenas to force reporters to divulge the sources of their information. One newspaper got over four hundred subpoenas in a four-year period. Discussing the *Washington Post,* which was probably the most influential newspaper in the country in its coverage of the Watergate scandal, Nixon observed that "The *Post* is going to have damnable, damnable problems out of this one. They have a television station . . . and they're going to have to get [its license] renewed." Speaking of one of the *Post*'s lawyers, he said, "I think we are going to fix the son of a bitch."[25]

Although most Presidents have done better than Nixon both in tolerating criticism and in coping with reporters, they all complained about the press and had mixed relations with it. Lyndon Johnson, who was quite accessible to reporters in the early days of his administration, grew increasingly

WHEN GERALD FORD ASSUMED THE PRESIDENCY IN 1974, PRESS CONFERENCES BECAME MORE FREQUENT AND MUCH LESS HOSTILE THAN THEY HAD BEEN DURING THE NIXON ADMINISTRATION.
Wide World Photos

[25] Nixon's complaint about press bias is from an interview with James J. Kilpatrick, *San Francisco Chronicle,* May 23, 1974, p. 41. The threats against the *Post* were revealed on the famous White House tapes; see the Kilpatrick interview and *Newsweek,* May 27, 1974, p. 29. The figures on subpoenas are from Paul Weaver, "The New Journalism and the Old—Thoughts After Watergate," *The Public Interest* (Spring 1974), p. 84.

withdrawn and suspicious of the press, which he blamed for his declining popularity. Kennedy canceled the White House subscriptions of one paper that offended him and tried to get the *New York Times* to transfer its Vietnam correspondent after the correspondent filed a story that displeased him. Eisenhower brought a Republican convention audience to its feet with a famous denunciation of "sensation-seeking columnists and commentators."

Far from indicating that something is wrong, such complaints are a sign that the press is functioning as it should. The fact of the matter is that *all* politicians have a natural adversary relationship with the press because they have different interests. Politicians want to maintain their own power and get their programs enacted. Media owners want to sell more papers or attract more viewers. They do this by looking for new material. The ambitions of individual reporters lead them in the same direction. They want to present new facts. They are, indeed, seeking after sensations. Among other things, this means that bad news is more interesting than good news. But bad news, of course, is unwelcome to politicians in power, no matter how much it may be greeted by the opposition.

LEAKS TO THE PRESS

The desire of the press to tell what's happening day after day tends to irritate officials, but it also makes the press dependent on them for information. One expert described the reporter's dilemma this way:

> Journalists are rarely, if ever, in a position to establish the truth about an issue for themselves, and they are therefore almost entirely dependent on self-interested "sources" for the version of reality that they report.[26]

At first glance, this seems to give the party in power an enormous advantage, since officials can release only as much information as they want. The facts that make the President and his policy look good can be announced with great fanfare, while the facts that point in the opposite direction can be passed over. In reality, however, the President does not have as much of an advantage as it may at first appear, because he cannot prevent members of his administration from "leaking" information to the press. Indeed, the American governmental system is exceptionally leaky. Secret information often finds its way into print, unless national security is involved. This is because the vast majority of government employees do not owe their jobs to the administration in power at any given time. They are career civil servants. Civil servants are supposed to carry out the policies adopted by the President, who represents the will of the people as manifested in elections. Although they cannot openly defy their political superiors, they can subvert them by leaking embarrassing information.

---

[26] Edward Jay Epstein, "Journalism and Truth," *Commentary*, April 1974, p. 36.

Political reporters devote a good deal of time to cultivating sources who can provide them with information that the President wants to keep confidential. Columnists specializing in exposés are particularly adept at developing networks of inside informants. The best known reporter of this kind, Jack Anderson, describes his methods:

> The most reliable sources are the professional, nonpolitical public servants whom the public never sees. Their first loyalty is to the citizens who pay them, not to their political superiors.
>
> I have been cultivating informers for twenty-five years; I know something about the psychology of one who has a dark secret and is teetering on the awful brink of disclosing it. His motive may be noble or base or just human; he may seek to protect the public from fraud, to advance a good cause, to discredit a rival, or to avenge a personal grievance.[27]

There is an obvious conflict between the public's right to know what the government is doing and the government's need to keep secrets for purposes of national security. The problem is complicated by an official tendency to classify material secret when disclosure will simply embarrass the administration but will not endanger the national interest. For this reason, some reporters argue that the government has no right to keep secrets, or that the decision to respect official secrecy should be a matter of individual conscience.

[27] Jack Anderson, with George Clifford, *The Anderson Papers* (New York: Random House, Inc., 1973), pp. 7–8, 17.

"THIS IS TURNING OUT TO BE SUCH A HIGH-MINDED MEETING IT WOULD BE A SHAME IF SOMEONE DIDN'T LEAK IT TO THE PRESS."
Drawing by Ed Fisher; © *1975 The New Yorker Magazine, Inc.*

In addition to leaks emanating from civil servants, and, for that matter, from officials who owe their appointments directly to the President, but who have come to differ with the President or among themselves, there are also "official leaks." These leaks consist of material given deliberately by Administration representatives to a friendly reporter for use without attributing it to the actual source. This technique is used to get an idea or a fact or an accusation into the media without taking responsibility for it. Reporters differ in their willingness to cooperate with politicians this way, depending on the nature of the material and the journalist's relations with the politician. Often, when one reads that "Sources close to the President revealed . . . ," the source may be the President himself. A leak attributed to "a high State Department official" may actually come straight from the Secretary of State. In fact, for many years this phrase was virtually a code word for Henry Kissinger to the politically knowledgeable.

Leaks are a peculiarly American practice. In almost all other democratic countries, it is a crime for government employees to reveal any official information. The American belief that one of the government's jobs is to provide information to the public strikingly differs from the European conception that government business is not to be shared with the public. Complaints about excessive secrecy in Washington should be evaluated in light of the fact that political observers in the rest of the world are astounded at what seems to be the American practice of conducting government business in a goldfish bowl.

The press is not as influential as some of its critics think. This is largely because most people have developed the habit of selective perception. They see and hear what is comfortable and convenient and congenial. This is particularly the case with political material, which, as we have seen, is inherently uninteresting to most people. Obviously, the media carry far more information than most citizens want or can retain. Indeed, a number of commentators on the media argue that the press should be less concerned with being "topical" and interesting to a large audience, and more concerned with presenting detailed coverage to that fraction of its audience that wants and could make good use of it.

THE POLLS

In this book we already have made ample use of findings from survey research—more popularly called *public opinion polls*—and we will be using this kind of material even more in subsequent chapters. Polls have come to be a major topic of news coverage, particularly in election campaigns. They are used heavily by social scientists and perhaps even more heavily by market research firms and political candidates. Polls can be vastly more enlightening if a few simple but important points about them are understood.

Although scientific survey research did not begin until the 1930s, there is nothing new about querying citizens to learn their opinions and voting intentions. This was done by newspaper reporters as early as the election of 1824. *Straw polls,* as they were then called, were commonplace throughout the nineteenth and early twentieth centuries. The most famous one was conducted by the *Literary Digest,* a magazine that for many years had accurately predicted the outcome of presidential elections. But in 1936 the *Literary Digest* predicted that Alfred M. Landon would decisively defeat the incumbent Democratic President, Franklin D. Roosevelt. Roosevelt's record-breaking majority buried both Landon and the *Literary Digest.* But that election also served to make the reputation of scientific survey research secure, because a young pollster named George Gallup had accurately predicted the winner.

HOW POLLS ARE CONDUCTED

Laymen commonly wonder how pollsters can claim to know what 210 million people are thinking after asking questions of only 1,200 to 2,000—the normal size of a national sample. The size of the sample, though, is not what determines the accuracy of the poll. The *Literary Digest* based its disastrous prediction that Landon would defeat Roosevelt in 1936 on replies from 2,376,000 people. Unfortunately, these people were *not representative of the whole electorate,* for the lists from which they were drawn were limited to people who had telephones and automobiles—a highly unrepresentative group of Americans in the Depression years. By polling the relatively prosperous, the *Literary Digest* vastly overrepresented the Republican vote.

What is important about a survey is less the *size* of the sample than how it is chosen. The most rigorous technique is one used by academic survey analysts and many commercial pollsters. It is called *probability sampling.* In such a sample, everyone in the population being surveyed has a known chance of being chosen to be in the sample. A national probability sample is drawn by establishing several hundred *primary sampling units,* which may be electoral precincts or similar small areas chosen randomly throughout the United States. Within each sampling unit, a specified number of respondents is chosen by pre-established procedures that do not give the interviewer any discretion as to whom he will interview. This rules out one potential source of bias in polling—the tendency of interviewers to underrepresent hard-to-find or "unattractive" respondents. And the use of strict, mathematical respondent selection procedures makes it possible for a sample to be an adequate cross-section of the population. Such a cross-section faithfully represents the group from which it is drawn within a narrow range of what is technically called *sampling error,* namely the extent to which the answers given by the sample are likely to differ from the responses that would be given by the entire population. The sampling error in most of the polls reported in newspapers, and conducted by academics, is plus or minus 3 percent. In other words, a Gallup or Harris poll news release asserting that a candidate is favored by 43 percent of the population should be interpreted as meaning that the candidate's "real" support is almost certainly somewhere between 40 and 46 percent. The nature of statistical probability theory is such that increasing the size of a sample would not markedly reduce the sampling error, unless the sample were expanded enormously, and therefore pollsters have settled on the customary sample of 1,200 to 2,000 respondents to estimate attitudes in the entire nation.

An important key to interpreting survey findings is the effect that differences in question wording have on responses. For example, if the question used in a poll forces a "Yes-No" or "Approve-Disapprove" response, the results may be quite different than if a gradation of responses is permitted, including "Don't know," or if the question is open-ended, leaving the respondent free to provide his or her own answer. What is more, questions that assume public familiarity with candidates or issues are likely to produce misleading results. An enterprising researcher demonstrated this point dramatically some years ago by asking people what they thought of the "Metallic Metals Act." Many people were willing to produce favorable and unfavorable opinions about this wholly imaginary piece of legislation.

Even apparently trivial changes in the way a question is phrased may produce dramatic shifts in public responses. For this reason, answers to a question that has only been asked once are particularly hard to interpret. Sophisticated students of public opinion pay particular attention to shifts in answers to different versions of the same basic question and to answers to the same question asked at different times as well as to differences among different groups in the population in their answers to a question.

In spite of the complexity of effective public opinion surveying, carefully designed and evaluated polls are a priceless source of information about public opinion. The validity of polls is indicated by the great consistency over the years in survey responses on various topics.[28] Another source of reassurance is the resemblance poll results bear to those of the national Census, which consists of a full inventory of the population. Finally, especially since pollsters improved their techniques after their failure to predict the 1948 Truman-Dewey election outcome, the correspondence between the polls and the election results over the years provides highly convincing evidence that when polls are used intelligently they furnish a reliable indication of what the public is thinking.

Although election prediction success is a spectacular demonstration of the utility of polls, a number of problems about such predictions should be noted:

1. The rate of people who decline to be interviewed has increased in the last decade from about 3 percent to 10 percent or more. Pollsters believe that this reflects, in large measure, an increasing amount of generalized distrust in American society. It certainly means that pollsters must do without the information that can be gathered from these people. They can

"WHICH CANDIDATE
ARE YOU MOST
APATHETIC ABOUT?"
© 1972 by the Chicago
Tribune

---

[28] For a particularly extensive demonstration of this consistency, see Mueller, *War, Presidents, and Public Opinion*, pp. 4–7.

only hope that refusals distribute their opinions and votes more or less like those people who consent to be interviewed.

2. The only votes that count are those cast by people who appear at the election booths when the time comes to vote. A substantial fraction of citizens polled in a random sample either do not vote or may not even have registered to vote. Merely asking someone whether he is going to vote is not terribly reliable, because people are embarrassed about not performing their civic duty and often say they will vote when they won't. Once again, it is possible that those people who do not vote have somewhat different political preferences from those who do. Pollsters have developed ways to predict with reasonable accuracy who will vote in general elections, but they still have considerable difficulty with primary elections, where the voting turnout is much lower.

3. During election campaigns people change their minds in response either to the campaign itself or to the pressure of events. A poll can only measure intentions at the time the interview is conducted. Presidential campaigns see less vote shifting than campaigns for any other elected office, because the candidates are fairly well known and party loyalties determine most votes. But in primary elections, or in other circumstances when the candidates have not attracted much attention and the turnout level is lower and less stable, predictions are particularly hazardous.

The survey data used in this book are drawn largely from academic survey organizations, particularly the Center for Political Studies of the University of Michigan, which has conducted careful national studies of every presidential election since 1948 and every midterm national election since 1954. The Michigan CPS data collections are the basis for much of what is known about public opinion and voting in this country. We also have made some use of findings from the principal commercial polling organizations, particularly George Gallup's American Institute of Public Opinion and Louis Harris and Associates.

HOW POLITICIANS USE POLLS

In addition to Gallup and Harris, there are dozens of commercial research firms, most of which concentrate in the areas of advertising and market research. But increasingly in the last twenty-five years politicians have been using polls for their own purposes. In order to stay in touch with public opinion, friends and supporters of Presidents Eisenhower, Kennedy, Johnson, and Nixon frequently financed "weathervane" polls on particular issues or events.[29] But polls serve their most important political function during campaigns. It is estimated that around $6 million was spent for this

---

[29] Both Gallup and Harris provide poll results to the mass media (for a sizable fee) every week or two. Neither organization now accepts political clients. See also Andrew J. Glass, "Pollsters Prowl Nation as Candidates Use Opinion Surveys to Plan '72 Campaign," *National Journal,* August 14, 1971, p. 1693.

purpose in the 1968 campaign. Of this amount, Richard Nixon and the Republican National Committee spent about $1 million, Hubert Humphrey spent considerably less, and the rest was spent by candidates for state and local offices.

Politicians are interested in polling not only to find out whether they are winning or losing, but also because:

1. In order to build a winning coalition of voters, they need to find out what groups in the population support them and which present problems. Learning that he is unpopular in a particular part of the state or among a particular economic or ethnic group will enable a politician to make special appeals in that direction.

2. Polls can help politicians find out about their public images. Strange as it may seem, it is not always easy for political candidates to understand how they are perceived by voters. Particularly in primary elections, where issues are submerged and party loyalties are irrelevant, most votes are thought to turn on personal appeal. Before a candidate can campaign on this basis, he or she has to know what his or her personal strengths and weaknesses are in the eyes of the voters. (Candidates usually overestimate their visibility to the electorate. Most contenders for public office cannot believe how few voters know or care who they are, what they have done, and what they propose to do if elected.) The same is true in the general election, where the personal qualities of the candidates present by far the most important dynamic element from one election to the next.

3. Polls can tell candidates what issues are troubling voters, how particular groups in the electorate feel about particular problems, and how these groups assess the performance of the party in power in these respects. Sometimes one party so thoroughly "owns" an issue that the other side has no way to exploit it and so must talk about other issues. For example, a President running for reelection when the country is prosperous but crime is increasing would stress material blessings and the horrors of the depression that would be likely if his policies were changed. The other candidate would give short shrift to economic issues in favor of an emphasis on morality and the virtues of law and order.

The predictive value of polls is important at the level of campaign organization. Unfavorable showings can discourage campaign workers and potential contributors. In September 1968, when the polls showed Hubert Humphrey 16 percentage points behind Richard Nixon, Humphrey's fund-raising efforts were seriously handicapped, particularly among big contributors who "buy insurance" by giving to both candidates in order to be sure of a friendly reception by the winner. If Humphrey was a sure loser, many potential contributors felt no need to buy insurance from him by giving to his campaign. Because of his feeble showing in the polls, Humphrey could not raise enough money to confirm long-range television advertising schedules.[30]

---

[30] *San Francisco Chronicle*, September 5, 1972, p. 17.

As it turned out, Humphrey rapidly closed the gap on Nixon in late September and October, and the election ended in a photo finish. Humphrey felt that if he had had more money to spend on television, he would have beaten Nixon.

Candidates particularly prize favorable polls before the nominations have occurred, because they can use the optimistic findings to impress potential contributors. But research is costly. A competent statewide survey costs at least $10,000 and a careful survey in a single congressional district is not much cheaper.

Despite their limitations, polls seem to be the best way to find out about public opinion. They are certainly far superior to the reporter's favorite tactic of talking to half a dozen bartenders, cabdrivers, and barbers to form conclusions about "public opinion." A profound problem about polling and democratic politics lies in how the opinions of the public can be translated into public policy, and the degree to which they should be. The American people have an enormous, disorganized diversity of opinions and non-opinions about public issues. A survey conducted in July might reveal that the problem bothering most Americans was urban unrest and ghetto riots, a poll just after Christmas might show that inflation was of greatest concern, and a third study in the springtime could well indicate apparent preoccupation with campus disorders. Such findings do not suggest that polls cannot measure what people really think. What they do show is that public attention fluctuates drastically in response to events in the real world. Further, relying on polls as a source of public policy ignores the creative role to be played by democratic leaders in shaping public opinion.

In this chapter we have presented the raw material of individual political action—how Americans perceive the political world. In the following chapters, we will see how this raw material is mobilized and focused on the government, through the linkages provided by elections, participation, interest groups, and political parties. These mechanisms all simplify and otherwise distort the diversity of individual opinions, rendering them more intelligible to the government. They also have considerable impact on what people think. Thus public opinion is not formed in a vacuum. It both feeds and is shaped by the institutions that link it to the government.

SUMMARY

Politics and politicians seldom are very interesting to most Americans. Popular information about politics therefore is astonishingly sparse. But people often have opinions on subjects about which they know and care very little. Since many political opinions are weakly grounded in prior thought and commitment, they may change as admired political leaders change their policies.

Ideally, political ideologies could help people form opinions about specific issues without knowing much about them. In fact, most Americans do not think about politics in ideological terms, do not think of themselves in such terms, and do not have well-related or "consistent" opinions.

The key question then becomes *who* has *what* opinion on each of hundreds of different political issues. On economic questions, people with better occupations tend to have more conservative opinions. But on most other issues, education is the prime factor. Liberalism is greatest among the better-educated. Given the diffuseness of public opinion, an issue tends to be *least* politically important when most people know little and care little about it, and *most* politically important when a substantial number of people know enough and care enough to impress their opinions on politicians.

People get their information about politics from the mass media. The media are under constant attack from the left for serving "the establishment" and from officials for being hostile to the current government. The media are unpopular with politicians in power because they manage to expose most of what happens in Washington to public scrutiny.

Polls provide us with our information about public opinion. Politicians may use polls to guide their campaign efforts. However, polls frequently show that public opinion fluctuates dramatically in response to events, many of which are created by political leaders. Thus politicians cannot simply follow public opinion as shown in the polls because what politicians do one day is a key factor in determining what the public wants them to do the next day.

CHAPTER SIX
VOTING BEHAVIOR

AMERICANS can influence what their government does in several ways: They can participate in politics as individuals, through interest groups, and through the political parties. These three forms of interaction between citizen and government will be described in Chapters 7, 8, and 9. Here we will concentrate on *voting,* the only act of influence that most citizens perform and the foundation for all other linkages between public opinion and government policy.

Voting is the mechanism by which government leaders are chosen. Almost 3 million civilians are on the federal payroll. Only 537 of them reach and hold their jobs through elections. The President and Vice President are elected every four years and limited to two terms; 435 members of the House of Representatives are elected every two years; and 100 senators are elected to six-year terms, a third of them being elected every two years. These 537 men and women are connections between "the people" and "the government." The processes that put them in and out of office are, therefore, not only fundamental to the functioning of the government but also a major basis for calling the United States a democracy.

In this chapter we will concentrate on the core of this process, the voting behavior of individuals. We shall begin by examining voter *turnout*—the number of people who actually vote in elections. Then we shall look into the question of how Americans decide to vote as they do. This will lead us into a consideration of the lines of political cleavage in America, how the outcome of elections can be interpreted, and what can reasonably be expected of elections as mechanisms for popular control of government. The study of voting behavior is a relatively advanced field. We can talk about it with a good deal more confidence than we can bring to topics where data are less accessible, such as the presidency or the decision processes of Supreme Court justices.

TURNOUT

How many Americans vote, what kinds of people vote, and under what circumstances? There are essentially two kinds of answers to these questions. The first involves various *situational variables,* such as the voting laws and different types of election. The second is concerned with the personal characteristics of citizens. Analysis of the voting laws and their effects yields important insights about the personal meaning of voting and also shows how such seemingly neutral principles can have important political consequences.

THE IMPACT OF VOTING LAWS

Originally, the Constitution left the individual states free to determine the crucial question of who could vote. At first, qualifications and procedures for voting differed considerably from state to state, but by the Civil War the franchise everywhere had been extended to all adult white male citizens. Since then, the power of the states to set eligibility standards for voting has been restricted by a series of constitutional amendments that have forbidden them to deny the right to vote on various grounds:

1. The Fifteenth Amendment, adopted in 1870, forbade the states to deny or limit the franchise because of "race, religion and previous condition of servitude."
2. The Nineteenth Amendment (1920) extended the vote to women;
3. The Twenty-fourth Amendment (1964) prohibited states from requiring voters to pay a special tax (poll taxes had been used in the South to discourage voting by poor people);
4. The Twenty-sixth Amendment (1971) forbade the states to deny the vote to anyone over seventeen years old on the basis of age.

Despite the Fifteenth Amendment, by 1900 the southern states had prevented almost all blacks from voting. Indeed, they continued to deny black citizens this basic right until quite recently. In 1940 a mere 5 percent of southern blacks were registered to vote, and even those who could vote in general elections often were not allowed to participate in the Democratic primaries, which at that time were the only meaningful elections in the southern states. This changed in the 1940s, when court decisions outlawed the "white primary." In the following years, a combination of social change and legal and political pressure brought southern black registration to 27 percent by 1962. Nevertheless, some states still held out almost completely against democracy for blacks. In Mississippi only 5 percent of the black voting-age population was registered, and in Alabama only 13 percent. In 1965 the Voting Rights Act provided for replacement of local election officials by federal registrars in areas where denial of the right to vote was most blatant. The result was a dramatic expansion of black registration, which rose to 65 percent between 1964 and 1974. The proportion of blacks registered to vote in Mississippi increased tenfold. Throughout the South, black registration and voting rates now approach those of whites.[1]

[1] See Neal R. Peirce, *The Deep South States of America* (New York: W. W. Norton & Company, Inc., 1974). Informal pressures against black voting remain in some rural southern counties, but they are merely a vestige of the former ruthlessness.

DR. ANNA SHAW AND MRS. CARRIE CHAPMAN CATT LEADING THE 20,000 WOMEN WHO MARCHED FOR SUFFRAGE ALONG NEW YORK'S FIFTH AVENUE IN 1918.
Wide World Photos

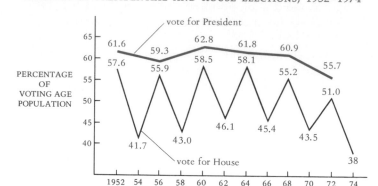

FIGURE 6–1

TURNOUT IN PRESIDENTIAL AND HOUSE ELECTIONS, 1952–1974

Source: *Statistical Abstract of the United States 1973*, p. 379; and *Congressional Quarterly Monthly Report*, February 1, 1975, p. 246.

Paradoxically, while these measures have removed legal restrictions and also have effectively prevented extralegal denial of the franchise, other developments in twentieth-century America have served to *reduce* the proportion of the population which turns out on election day. In recent decades the proportion of voting-age citizens who actually cast a ballot for President has never been as high as 65 percent. In off-year congressional elections the average turnout is 44 percent, and no off-year election has seen as much as half the population at the polls. Figure 6–1 shows the turnout in presidential and congressional elections since 1952.

This voting rate compares badly with most other democracies, where 80 to 90 percent of the population go to the polls. Why so many Americans stay home on election day is a subject of some controversy. One school of thought, noting that turnout during the last century was as high as that in Europe, argues that around the turn of the century both American parties were captured by big business; many voters, discouraged and confused by the lack of real alternatives, responded by staying home.[2]

Many scholars now think that a simpler, more mechanical explanation is more convincing. In the days when Americans voted as freely as Europeans, there were no laws requiring voters to register. This permitted a great deal of fraud, including repeat voting and voting by noncitizens. Around the turn of the century most states adopted laws requiring potential voters to register before the election, thereby establishing that they were citizens, residents of the voting locality, and of voting age.

Registration is an extra step, often requiring a visit to a governmental

---

[2] Walter Dean Burnham, *Critical Elections and the Mainsprings of American Politics* (New York: W. W. Norton & Co., Inc., 1970); and "Theory and Voting Research: Some Reflections on Converse's 'Change in the American Electorate,'" *American Political Science Review*, 68 (September 1974), 1000–27 and 1050–57.

office. Usually, people are required to register some weeks or months before the election, when political interest is generally low. Originally adopted to discourage fraud, registration laws have had the effect of discouraging many marginally interested Americans from voting. Comparative studies show that although Europeans are more likely to vote than Americans, they are *less* interested in politics. The higher voter turnouts reflect the fact that all European countries have automatic national permanent registration. Political scientists who have studied this problem have concluded that the lower turnout in America is due largely to the requirement that people who want to vote must register in advance of the election.[3]

Although observers often comment on the low turnout in American elections, in fact nationwide generalizations are not very accurate. There are enormous differences in turnout from one state to the next. These variations reflect the impact of different state election laws. Generally speaking, registration is lowest in the South. In 1960, for example, 32 percent of eligible citizens were registered in Columbus, Georgia, and 34 percent in Atlanta. In Detroit and Seattle, however, 92 percent of all eligible residents were registered. Most of these differences are explained by the variations in the laws concerning registration, including the closing date for registration, the convenience of places to register, the hours when one can register, and

[3] Stanley Kelley, Jr., et al., "Registration and Voting: Putting First Things First," *American Political Science Review*, 61 (June 1967), 359–77; Philip E. Converse, "Change in the American Electorate," in Angus Campbell and Philip E. Converse, eds., *The Human Meaning of Social Change* (New York: Russell Sage Foundation, 1972), pp. 284–92; and the "Comments" by Converse and Jerrold G. Rusk in the *American Political Science Review*, 68 (September 1974), 1024–49. One attempt to account for ill, ineligible, and other involuntary nonvoters produced an estimate that about 82 percent of the "legal, able electorate" voted in the 1960 election. William G. Andrews, "American Voting Participation," *Western Political Quarterly*, 19 (December 1966) 639–52.

REGISTRATION LAWS
HAVE HAD THE
EFFECT OF
DISCOURAGING
SOME AMERICANS
FROM VOTING.
Wide World Photos

whether registration is temporary or permanent. When the closing date in California was moved from fifty-four days before the election to thirty days, an additional 413,000 people registered in the extra twenty-four days. A Supreme Court decision in 1972 imposed a maximum thirty-day residence requirement for voting in any election.[4] Legislation to establish nation-wide voter registration by mail has been introduced in Congress, but has not passed either house. Chances for some sort of national registration are growing brighter, however. This may be an idea whose time is coming.

Registration laws are a prime example of a *situational variable* affecting turnout. Another situational variable is the *kind* of election. Presidential contests, which are the most glamorous, exciting, and publicized elections on the American political scene, attract considerably more voters than congressional elections, as Figure 6–1 shows. Primary elections, held by each party to choose its nominees for the general election, are even less appealing to many voters. The turnout in primaries usually is about half as great as in the following general election.

WHO VOTES?

What kinds of people are most likely to vote? One answer, not quite so simple-minded as it might seem, is that people who are very interested in the campaign are most likely to vote. As Table 6–1 shows, those people who said that they were "very much interested" in the 1968 or 1972 presidential election were very likely indeed to go to the polls, whereas people who said that they were "not much interested" had only a fifty-fifty chance of voting. It seems reasonable to assume that the 12 to 15 percent of the very interested who did not vote were deterred by ineligibility or inescapable circumstances such as illness.

Turnout rates can be analyzed according to many personal characteristics, but the two most important factors related to voting are *age* and *education*.

[4] *Dunn* v. *Blumstein*, 405 US 330.

TABLE 6-1

INTEREST IN THE CAMPAIGN AND VOTING TURNOUT IN 1968 AND 1972

	NOT MUCH INTERESTED		SOMEWHAT INTERESTED		VERY MUCH INTERESTED	
	1968	1972	1968	1972	1968	1972
Voted	52%	48%	76%	74%	88%	85%
Did not vote	48	52	24	26	12	15
	100%	100%	100%	100%	100%	100%
Number of cases	272	573	566	961	545	746

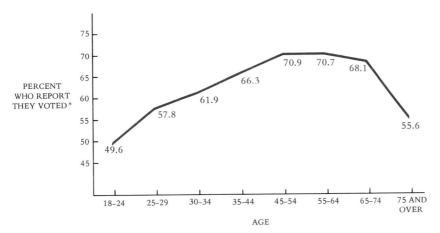

FIGURE 6–2

AGE AND TURNOUT IN THE 1972 PRESIDENTIAL ELECTION

PERCENT WHO REPORT THEY VOTED*

Data points: 49.6, 57.8, 61.9, 66.3, 70.9, 70.7, 68.1, 55.6

Age: 18–24, 25–29, 30–34, 35–44, 45–54, 55–64, 65–74, 75 AND OVER

AGE

*These figures are about 7 percent too high because of a persistent tendency for exaggeration when reporting voting.

Source: Bureau of the Census, *Voter Participation in November 1972,* Series P-20, No. 44 (December 1972).

Figure 6–2 charts the voting level of different age groups. It shows that people up to the age of twenty-four are least likely to vote. (The constitutional extension of voting rights to eighteen- to twenty-year-old youths thus has reduced overall national voting turnout somewhat.) As age increases, so does turnout, reaching its peak in the middle years from forty-five to sixty-four, when just over 70 percent report that they go to the polls. Thereafter, voting slacks off slightly, and then falls sharply for the oldest group.

There is no difference in turnout rates between men and women until the age of sixty-five, although it took this equalization of turnout many years to come, following the passage of the Nineteenth Amendment. After age sixty-five, men are more than 10 percentage points likelier to vote than women. Indeed, the drastically lower figure for elderly women accounts for most of the decrease in voting for people over the age of sixty-four. This difference between the sexes may simply reflect the fact that the people involved belong to an older generation whose political perspectives were formed before women had the right to vote. If so, the voting rates of the elderly should increase within the next fifteen years.

The low turnout of young people may come as a surprise. In fact, research down through the years has consistently shown that the young vote less than their elders. Perhaps this reflects an uncertain, unsettled state of mind, which reduces political interest and participation except for a handful of highly motivated political activists. As people marry, have families, begin

MODELS DISPLAY SOME OF THE PRODUCTS AIMED AT THE ESTIMATED 25 MILLION YOUNG VOTERS MADE ELIGIBLE TO VOTE BY THE TWENTY-SIXTH AMENDMENT. *Wide World Photos*

long-term jobs, and put down roots in their communities, they are likely to develop the interests and habits that lead to registration and voting.

The other key factor affecting turnout is education. The more education one has, the more likely to vote one is. Only 38 percent of people with less than five years of school voted in 1968, compared to 86 percent of those with five or more years of college. Although the young are less likely to vote than their elders, they are also, as a group, better educated than older people. Obviously, then, these two major factors push in opposite directions. We can see that the least likely voters are the unschooled young. Those most likely to vote are middle-aged college graduates. Indeed, except for recent college graduates, virtually everyone with a college education votes, unless prevented by illness or ineligibility. Better educated people have more confidence in dealing with intangible subjects like politics and more experience in overcoming the minimal bureaucratic hurdles involved in registering. They are also more likely to be interested in politics.

Income, occupation, and race are other factors relating to voting. The richer someone is, or the better job one has, the more likely that person is to vote. By the same token, whites are somewhat more likely than blacks to vote, and both groups have a vastly higher turnout level than Spanish-heritage citizens. But none of these differences is nearly so great as the difference between better and less educated people. In fact, the other factors largely reflect differences in education, for the rich are better educated than the poor, whites better educated than blacks, and so on.

Like the data on public familiarity with politics in Chapter 5, these findings reveal one of the major explanations for differences in political influence. Groups that have very high rates of turnout are better able to use the ballot box to get what they want from government than are groups with very low rates of turnout. Spanish-heritage citizens are by far the most disadvantaged in this respect, since they comprise almost 5 percent of the population but only 2½ percent of the electorate.[5]

We have examined the act of voting from two standpoints — the situation and the individual. What if we combine these explanations? It is an easy logical step to see that the more intense an individual's involvement, the greater his or her chance of participating when the election is not exciting or where the laws make registration relatively inconvenient.[6] Registration laws are barriers to participation. The higher the barriers, the greater the discouragement to those with less interest and skill at coping with

[5] These figures on the turnout of different groups are taken from: U. S. Bureau of Census, Current Population Reports, Series P-20, No. 192, *Voting and Registration in the Election of November 1968* (Washington: U. S. Government Printing Office, 1969); and from similar, preliminary figures issued by the Bureau of the Census for the 1970 and 1972 elections.

[6] Robert B. Arseneau and Raymond E. Wolfinger, "Voting Behavior in Congressional Elections," paper delivered at the 1973 meeting of the American Political Science Association; and Austin Ranney, "Turnout and Representation in Presidential Primary Elections," *American Political Science Review,* 66 (March 1972), 21–37. For a general discussion of the interplay of psychological and situational determinants of political behavior, see Fred I. Greenstein, *Personality and Politics* (New York: W. W. Norton & Company, Inc., 1969), Chap. 1.

bureaucratic requirements—the uneducated, the poor, and minorities. Making registration and voting easier and more interesting, by the same token, increases the participation of these groups, and therefore their power. Indeed, politicians have long been aware of the connection between registration laws and voting by marginally interested citizens. Although controlling fraud was the major justification for registration laws, conservative politicians often took advantage of the opportunity to discourage voting by some groups, usually by making registration difficult. This was particularly true in the South, where registration by both blacks and poor whites was impeded by long residency requirements, frequent re-registration, and awkward closing dates, as well as taxes on the right to vote that discouraged the poor from voting. Beyond this, black registration was discouraged in some localities by physical or economic sanctions and threats.

ABSTENTION: A PLAGUE ON BOTH YOUR HOUSES?

We have explained individual nonvoting as a consequence of ignorance, confusion, and apathy. What about *principled abstention,* a refusal to vote because all candidates are distasteful or because there seem to be no meaningful differences between them? Could it be, as some commentators have suggested, that our distressingly low levels of turnout reflect popular revulsion at the available candidates?

The argument that nonvoting was a product of dissatisfaction with the alternatives was most commonly heard in the 1968 campaign, when the overriding issue was the war in Vietnam. Voters could choose among George Wallace, who took a hard line on the war; Richard Nixon, who avoided a clear statement of his position; and Hubert Humphrey, who, as Vice President in the Johnson administration, was saddled with the legacy of Johnson's war policy. Some observers claimed that because there was no clear peace candidate, millions of Americans who wanted nothing more than an end to the war stayed home on election day.

At first glance, these claims seem to be backed up by the fact that "doves" were a few percentage points less likely to vote than "hawks" or supporters of the status quo. But the same was true in 1964, when the election offered a seemingly clear choice between Goldwater's hawkish stand and Johnson's apparently peaceful policy. It turns out that doves voted less in both elections because opposition to the war was commonest among less educated people, who are less likely to vote under any circumstances. Furthermore, almost half of the people who reported that they disliked all three candidates and could see no differences between them still voted in 1968.[7]

In 1972, when there were clear differences between Nixon and McGovern on almost every major issue, turnout was substantially less than in 1968. And the lowest turnout in the past half-century (51.5%) was in the 1948 elec-

[7] E. M. Schreiber, "Vietnam Policy Preferences and Withheld 1968 Presidential Votes," *Public Opinion Quarterly,* 37 (Spring 1973), 91–98; and Richard A. Brody and Benjamin I. Page, "Indifference, Alienation, and Rational Decisions," *Public Choice,* 15 (Summer 1973), 1–17.

tion, when voters had their choice of four major candidates representing a range of opinion from Henry Wallace's radicalism to Strom Thurmond's ultraconservative segregationist platform. In short, it seems clear that the public's ability to distinguish differences between the candidates has little or no relation to voter turnout. Nevertheless, there undoubtedly are *some* principled abstainers, although their numbers are far from significant.

In any presidential election the ballot includes a variety of candidates expressing unorthodox points of view—vegetarians, ultraconservatives, and an assortment of socialists—all of whom offer alternatives to the two major parties. These candidates seldom attract more than a few thousand votes and never affect the outcome of the election. (Major third-party candidates are another matter. They will be discussed in Chapter 9.) The failure of these fringe candidates is further evidence that the causes of election day apathy do not include popular rejection of the narrowness of the choices offered by the major parties.

There are millions of "alienated" citizens who say they are suspicious of politicians and mistrustful of the government. These self-proclaimed cynics vote at the same rate as people who express faith in the system.[8] Either their cynicism is merely lip service to current fashion or their voting is more a habit than anything else. Perhaps the truth includes a bit of both explanations.

So far we have discussed what kind of people vote, and in what circumstances, without saying anything about *how* they vote. We will devote the remainder of this chapter to trying to unravel this crucial, fascinating, and elusive topic.

PARTY IDENTIFICATION

Choosing among candidates is the most important political decision that the average person makes. It is part of our national mythology that Americans "vote for the man, not the party." Fully 84 percent of the population say that this is how they decide on election day.[9] If you ask friends and relatives how they made up their minds, they will probably talk about the personal qualities of the candidates or the issues that seemed most important. This may be accurate in some cases, but for most of us, the man (or woman) we like most is the one who belongs to our own party. In 1972, two-thirds of the voters admitted they had made up their minds about the presidential race by the time the nominating conventions chose the candidates, and fully 85 percent decided before the campaign got under way.[10]

[8] Jack Citrin, "Comment: The Political Relevance of Trust in Government," *American Political Science Review*, 68 (September 1974), 984.

[9] This Gallup Poll finding is reported in Richard M. Scammon and Ben J. Wattenberg, *The Real Majority* (New York: Coward, McCann & Geoghegan, Inc., 1971), p. 172.

[10] The source for these findings and all other unattributed data used in this chapter is the national election studies of the Center for Political Studies (CPS) of the University of Michigan, obtained through the Inter-University Consortium for Political Research. We computed these data and are solely responsible for their analysis.

Thus voting choice usually is not made anew in each contest, but instead reflects a standing partisan decision. This decision is based on a lasting identification with the Democratic or Republican party. Of the three major guidelines to voter choice—party, issues, and candidates—the first is especially potent. Party preferences are enduring, whereas the issues and candidates change from one election to the next. This is true even during a period when many commentators are speaking of the declining importance of political parties.

The two parties have so many different functions that party "membership" has several meanings. In its tangible form, being a Republican or Democrat has a specific legal meaning. In many states an individual cannot vote or seek nomination in a party's primary election without registering as a member of that party.

Here we are concerned not with legality, but with intangible affiliation; not with formal membership in an organization, but with personal identification. This intangible, psychological meaning of party membership is more important than the explicit legal meaning. Although American political parties are organizationally weak, they are a major force on the political scene because they have a powerful influence on voter psychology.

It is useful to think of the parties as *reference groups*—sources of identification and self-definition for their "members." Political scientists commonly measure party identification by this simple question: "Generally speaking, do you usually think of yourself as a Republican, a Democrat, an Independent, or what?"[11] Almost two-thirds of the population say that they consider themselves Republicans or Democrats. So few people identify with third parties that minor party identifiers are insignificant in national samples. Among those who call themselves Independents, most say that they think of themselves as "closer to" one party or the other. These people are sometimes called "Independent Democrats" and "Independent Republicans," but they are usually far more partisan than Independent. Thus, only one American in seven is a "pure Independent," devoid of any partisan attachment.

The partisan division of the electorate has been remarkably stable since 1952, as Figure 6–3 shows. The proportion of Republicans has never been lower than 22 percent nor higher than 29 percent during these years. Democratic strength has fluctuated a bit more, but still has remained within fairly narrow bounds. Although there is a growing number of Independents (a trend we discuss later in the chapter), party identification resists the assaults of time, changing personal circumstances, and historical developments. It is vastly more stable than any other kind of political outlook, including attitudes on issues, evaluations of politicians, or general political

"ME, I VOTE THE MAN, NOT THE PARTY. HOOVER, LANDON, DEWEY, EISENHOWER, NIXON, GOLDWATER, NIXON . . ."

© *1956 Crowell Collier Publishing Company; reproduced by courtesy of Bill Mauldin.*

[11] This question has been used since 1952 in the biennial national election studies of the Michigan CPS and is the standard measure of party identification used in hundreds of books and articles. For an early discussion, see Angus Campbell et al., *The American Voter* (New York: John Wiley & Sons, Inc., 1960), Chaps. 6 and 7. The Gallup Poll uses a similar question.

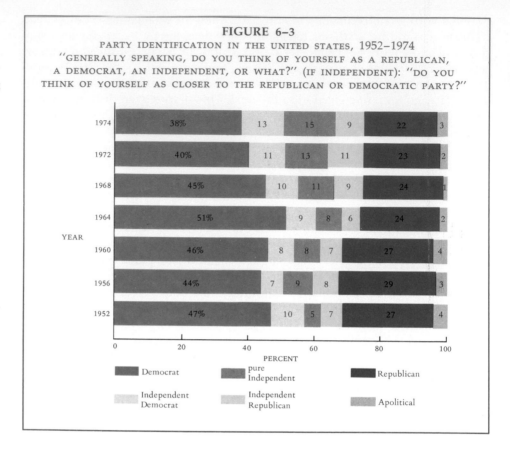

FIGURE 6–3

PARTY IDENTIFICATION IN THE UNITED STATES, 1952–1974
"GENERALLY SPEAKING, DO YOU THINK OF YOURSELF AS A REPUBLICAN,
A DEMOCRAT, AN INDEPENDENT, OR WHAT?" (IF INDEPENDENT): "DO YOU
THINK OF YOURSELF AS CLOSER TO THE REPUBLICAN OR DEMOCRATIC PARTY?"

philosophy.[12] It is also by far the best single predictor of an individual's vote. People who identify with the Republican party tend to vote for Republican candidates, usually by overwhelming margins. The same is true for Democratic identifiers.

Identifying with a party should not be confused with voting for its candidates in a particular election. Identification is a durable affiliation that usually lasts a lifetime—in effect, a permanent "brand label" preference. Voting is a short-term act that usually reflects party identification, but not always. Republicans and Democrats can and do vote for the other party's candidate without changing their subjective attachment to their own party. Crossing party lines typically is a temporary aberration, not a permanent conversion. Most defectors return to their party in subsequent elections. Defection is much more common for presidential candidates than in House and Senate elections. In 1972, for example, less than a third of the Democrats who defected to Nixon also voted for a Republican House candidate.[13] The

[12] Philip E. Converse, "Public Opinion and Voting Behavior," in Fred I. Greenstein and Nelson W. Polsby, eds., *The Handbook of Political Science*, Vol. 6 (Reading, Mass.: Addison-Wesley Publishing Company, 1975), pp. 75–169.

[13] Arthur H. Miller et al., "A Majority Party in Disarray: Policy Polarization in the 1972 Election," *American Political Science Review*, 70 (June 1976).

bulk of the Democrats who voted *against* McGovern voted *for* their party's candidates for other offices—that is, they "split their tickets."

Consequently, a massive presidential victory by one party does not mean that the other party has suffered a *permanent* loss of support. There have been four major presidential landslides since World War II—in 1952 and 1956 when the Republican candidate Dwight Eisenhower beat Adlai Stevenson; in 1964 when Lyndon Johnson overwhelmed Barry Goldwater; and again in 1972 when Richard Nixon crushed George McGovern by a margin of almost two to one. Each of these elections was followed by a flood of journalistic predictions that the losing party was on the verge of dissolution.

These predictions were premature, because even though a substantial fraction of one party's identifiers defected in each case, those individuals rarely abandoned their party loyalties. For this reason, such contests are sometimes called *deviating elections*. The outcomes of these elections reveal *temporary* departures from the ordinary party alignments as a result of such short-term forces as the striking popularity of Eisenhower, the unpopularity of Goldwater and McGovern, or widespread disapproval of the incumbent party's performance, as in 1952. The continued congressional majorities of the party with the most identifiers, the Democrats, in the face of Republican landslides in 1956 and again in 1972, demonstrate that winning an election for one party or the other is not the same thing as winning long-term converts.

As important as party loyalty is, however, it should not be overemphasized. If voting resulted *only* from party identification, the Democrats would always control the White House and would invariably be guaranteed congressional majorities. Since election results are nowhere near this consistent, it follows that party loyalty is sometimes weaker than at other times. When is party-line voting most common, and when does party have a weaker hold on the voter?

Table 6–2 provides a quick answer to this question by showing the proportion of the vote cast in presidential and House elections by Independents, defectors, and party identifiers voting for their party's candidate. The last category is always the lion's share of the electorate. Party-line voting is particularly common in congressional elections; voters are far more likely to cross party lines in voting for president. This is because virtually everyone knows who both candidates are in presidential elections. The intense publicity given to the campaign increases the likelihood that voters will identify one or the other candidate with something they like or dislike about the performance of the government. In congressional elections, however, the personal qualities of candidates are far less important. As we noted in Chapter 5, less than half the electorate can even name their representative. This means that party labels are the main tools voters use in choosing among congressional candidates. Consequently, there is less fluctuation in party support in congressional elections, and voters tend "automatically" to vote their standing party preferences. After all, the party labels are often the only information that they have about the candidates.

Table 6–2 also reveals a gradual increase in defection by party identifiers from the 1950s through 1972. This probably results from the electorate's

TABLE 6-2

THE COMPOSITION OF THE VOTE IN PRESIDENTIAL AND HOUSE ELECTIONS:
PARTY-LINE VOTERS, DEFECTORS, AND PURE INDEPENDENTS, 1956-72

HOUSE ELECTIONS

	1956	1958	1960	1962	1964	1966	1968	1970	1972
Party-line votes[a]	82%	84%	80%	83%	79%	76%	74%	76%	75%
Defection[b]	9	11	12	12	15	16	19	16	17
Pure Independents	9	5	8	6	5	8	7	8	8
	100%	100%	100%	101%	99%	100%	100%	100%	100%

PRESIDENTIAL ELECTIONS

	1956	1960	1964	1968	1972
Party-line votes[a]	76%	79%	79%	69%	67%
Defection[b]	15	13	15	23	25
Pure Independents	9	8	5	9	8
	100%	100%	99%	101%	100%

[a]Votes by party identifiers (including partisan independents) for the candidate of their party.
[b]Votes by party identifiers for another party's candidate.

rising educational level. The better educated a voter, the greater the chance that he or she will cross party lines to vote for a particular candidate. In a sense, then, party identification is a substitute for other kinds of information. People who are well informed about the issues and candidates are in a better position to defect, since they have more to take into consideration than party loyalty.

Party identification also has the effect of bringing to the polls people who might otherwise stay home on election day. It makes much more difference for poor people than for the wealthy. Among the poor, people who are strongly partisan vote at about the same rate as all Americans, while poor Independents are very unlikely to vote. Members of the middle and upper classes vote almost as much whether or not they are identified with a party.[14] Thus, party identification is something of a substitute political stimulus for the poor, who "need" it to motivate them to vote more than the well-off do.

Party labels make it easier for voters to evaluate candidates by providing them with a simple, familiar, and meaningful guideline. Abolishing party labels and party identification would make it necessary for voters to have a higher level of interest and knowledge to make sense of the election, as indeed seems to be the case in primary elections and in localities that bar the party label from the ballot in local or state elections. "Information costs" are less for better educated people. The party label helps many uninformed and uninterested citizens relate their inadequate knowledge to the political process and to the choices they can make in the voting booth.

[14] Sidney Verba and Norman H. Nie, *Participation in America* (New York: Harper & Row, 1972), p. 219.

Party identification helps explain the continued monopoly of the Democratic and Republican parties in the face of numerous protest movements and attempts to found other parties. With so large a proportion of the population committed to the major parties, would-be new parties have an almost insuperable obstacle to overcome. This contributes to the stability of American political institutions and processes. The other side of stability, of course, is unresponsiveness.

ROOTS OF PARTY IDENTIFICATION

Searching for the causes of individual and group loyalty to the Republicans or Democrats sheds light on a variety of important aspects of American politics, ranging from the private, personal meanings of politics to the public, historical convulsions that have shaped the course of American life for the past century. In tracing the roots of party identification, we gain insight into contemporary political behavior, and this helps us understand the potential for future changes.

At the individual level, a fundamental explanation for party loyalties is that the vast majority of Republicans come from Republican families, while Democrats have Democratic parents. As we saw in Chapter 5, children call themselves Democrats or Republicans at an age when these labels and the name of the President virtually exhaust their fund of political information. In the mid 1960s, when the last systematic survey of the political views of children and their parents was conducted, only about 8 percent of high school students identified with a party different from that of their parents. A somewhat larger number of students from partisan families call themselves Independents.[15] For most citizens in most historical periods, not only is party identification largely "inherited," but it persists long after any objective justification.

American society is highly mobile, both economically and physically. Education, better jobs, prosperity, economic decline, moving from one place to another—all these changes alter life styles; but life styles change more rapidly than party loyalties. Perhaps this is because politics is not a fundamental and continuing preoccupation for most Americans, and therefore "inertia" helps stabilize party preferences. Only about one person in eight has ever changed from one subjective party identification to the other. The most commonplace cause for individual party change is marriage, when one spouse converts to the other's party. The only exception comes during the very rare periods of social upheaval and party realignment.[16]

SOCIAL AND ECONOMIC BASES OF FACTION

What kinds of people are Democrats, and what kinds Republicans? How do the lines of partisan affiliation fit with economic, religious, ethnic, and ideological divisions? To put the question in the language used by James Madison, what are the "bases of faction" in modern America? This is one

[15] M. Kent Jennings and Richard G. Niemi, "The Transmission of Political Values from Parent to Child," *American Political Science Review*, 62 (March 1968), 172–73.

[16] Converse, "Public Opinion and Voting Behavior."

of the most important questions to be asked about any country. The answers help explain the strengths and weaknesses not only of the parties themselves, but of the political system in which the parties play such a major role. We will consider two kinds of answer, first looking at how party identification is related to social groupings, and then examining the ways that the parties reflect the political beliefs of Americans.

In some nations the parties so closely reflect societal cleavages (rich versus poor, farmers versus workers, workers versus businessmen, Catholics versus Protestants) that they have virtually no meaning independent of the social categories they represent. The closer partisan lines correspond to economic and social divisions, the greater the chance that political conflict will be bitter and unrestrained. In other nations, however, political divisions cut across social alignments. In these countries, the parties tend to be coalitions of different interests, less capable of unity and singleness of purpose, but also more conducive to compromise and reconciliation.

American parties generally fall in the second category. Both Republicans and Democrats are coalitions embracing a variety of interests. Although each party is more popular than the other among certain social and economic groups, in virtually no case does one party enjoy a complete monopoly of support from a major American social group.

In considering the political loyalties of various groups in the population, three questions need to be answered:

1. How does the group divide among the two parties—evenly, slightly favoring one party, or strongly favoring one party?
2. How big is each group? Is it a small fraction of the population, a substantial proportion, or a vast majority?
3. What is the group's turnout? Do most of its members vote, or do many of them stay home on election day?[17]

Since the most important lines of division in any political system are generally economic, regional, religious, and racial, we will examine the American electorate in terms of each of these categories, and then look at the political loyalties of different age groups.

ECONOMIC DIFFERENCES. The richer an American is, or the better job he holds, the more likely he is to be a Republican. As one goes down the status ladder, Democrats become increasingly more common. About 44 percent of business and professional people consider themselves Democrats, compared to 53 percent of clerks and salespeople, and fully 57 percent of manual workers. Democrats are especially scarce at the highest reaches of big business. A mere 13 percent of the heads of major corporations are Democrats. Compared to the leaders of big business, independently wealthy people are somewhat more sympathetic to the Democrats. Democrats outnumber Republicans among two other elite groups—high-ranking civil servants and executives

[17] For an interesting application, see Robert Axelrod, "Where the Votes Come From: An Analysis of Electoral Coalitions, 1952–1968," *American Political Science Review*, 66 (March 1972), 11–20.

and commentators in the mass media. Among the latter groups, however, the largest fraction consider themselves Independents.[18]

Whether social class is measured by income, by self-identification, or by occupation, the same results emerge. Republican sympathies are more common in the upper classes than in the lower classes. As you can see from Figure 6–4, the greater the sympathy for the Republican party, the smaller the social grouping. At the same time, the Democrats' popularity among the largest social classes is offset to some degree by their lower turnout. According to one careful estimate, if Democrats had gone to the polls in 1968 at the same rate as Republicans, Humphrey would have defeated Nixon.[19]

As Figure 6–4 makes clear, no party even approaches having a monopoly on any economic group. Moreover, these socioeconomic categories are quite large and overlap with other significant divisions of the population, thus retarding the kind of deep social and political division found in many European countries.

[18] Carol H. Weiss, "What America's Leaders Read," *Public Opinion Quarterly*, 38 (Spring 1974), 3–4.

[19] Arthur C. Wolfe, "Challenge from the Right: The Basis of Voter Support for Wallace in 1968," paper presented at the 1969 annual meeting of the American Political Science Association, p. 2.

FIGURE 6–4

THE SOCIOECONOMIC SOURCES OF DEMOCRATIC IDENTIFICATION

	% Democrat	% who voted in 1972[†]	% of the population*
Business & professionals	44	82	28
Clerks & sales people	53	75	12
Blue collar workers	57	65	14
College-educated	47	86	29
High school-educated	51	73	32
Grade school only	57	58	39
Protestants	47	68	66
Catholics	64	77	24
Jews	77	88	3
Whites	49	72	89
Blacks	77	64	10

*These figures do not always add up to 100% because certain categories are excluded. For example, farmers and people not in the labor force are not included in the "occupation" categories.

[†] Remember that some people being interviewed falsely claim that they have voted, and that such reports of turnout are about 7 percent too high.

The relationship between social class and party preference (or voting choice) has weakened since the 1950s, and support for the two parties is less polarized along class lines than it used to be. This reflects the Democratic inclinations of younger members of the middle class. The descendants of poor immigrants have retained their ancestral Democratic allegiances as they have risen in the world. This trend portends a further weakening of the links between class and partisanship as the older, more polarized generation passes from the scene.[20]

REGIONAL DIFFERENCES. Among the most important cross-cutting cleavages in American history have been the lines separating one geographical area from another. At times in our past, the most pressing issues have pitted section against section in disputes that muffled, diverted, or submerged conflict between haves and have-nots. The most important sectional antagonism was, of course, the Civil War. This bloody confrontation took the lives of almost a tenth of the adult male population and left a political legacy that survives memories of the war and its causes. Because the Union was successfully defended by the first Republican President, the defeated South became almost entirely Democratic. The small-town, Protestant, middle-class conservatives who elsewhere formed the backbone of the Republican party were, in the South, fervent Democrats. The overwhelming Democratic loyalty of white southerners was even stronger in the middle class than among workers. Until the 1950s the South was safely Democratic, with the single exception of the 1928 election, when Democratic candidate Al Smith's membership in the Catholic Church drove many southerners temporarily into the Republican camp.

In 1952, Republican presidential candidates began to win southern votes in substantial numbers. By 1964 the Republican share of the presidential vote in the South was *greater* than their nationwide percentage. Aside from presidential voting, however, southern political loyalties still reflect the Civil War heritage. Republicans have made substantial gains in southern congressional elections since 1961, but in 1975 they had only six of twenty-two southern Senate seats and twenty-seven of 108 House seats. Figure 6-5 compares the proportions of Democrats, Republicans, and Independents in the North and the South in 1952 and 1972. It shows that while the Democrats no longer enjoy a virtual monopoly on southern party affiliation, southerners are still more Democratic than their counterparts in the North.[21]

[20] Paul R. Abramson, "Generational Change in American Electoral Behavior," *American Political Science Review,* 68 (March 1974), 93–105.

[21] Raymond E. Wolfinger and Robert B. Arseneau, "Partisan Change in the South, 1952–1972," paper presented at the 1974 annual meeting of the American Political Science Association. It should be noted that although the South in general has been solidly Democratic since the Civil War, there have been isolated areas of Republican strength in the South. Interestingly, these also reflect Civil War passions. For example, the mountaineers of eastern Tennessee are doggedly loyal to the Republican party because their ancestors did not have slaves, opposed secession, and had no interest in fighting for the wealthy plantation owners who led their state out of the Union.

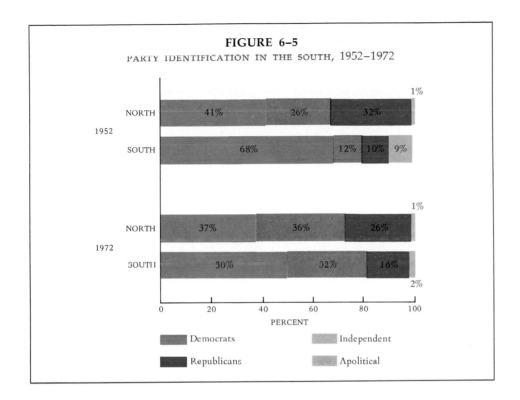

FIGURE 6–5

PARTY IDENTIFICATION IN THE SOUTH, 1952–1972

Not only in the South, but throughout the United States, political alignments based on regional considerations often result from a historical "legacy" of past experience that has lost tangible relevance to contemporary political events but still leaves its mark on voting patterns. For example, the contrasting Democratic and Republican inclinations of many areas in the Midwest can be traced to historically distant antecedents. Those parts of Ohio and Indiana settled by New Englanders are still a good deal more Republican than the otherwise socially identical areas in the same states that were first occupied by southerners. Such regional divisions are fading somewhat, but other legacies remain as strong today as they ever were, notably differences in party affiliation based on religion.

RELIGIOUS DIFFERENCES. Cutting across the class division of the electorate is a network of religious alignments. Catholics are more likely than Protestants to identify with the Democratic party and to vote for Democratic candidates. And Jews are vastly more Democratic than Catholics. In 1972, 47 percent of Protestants identified with the Democratic party, compared to 64 percent of all Catholics and fully 77 percent of Jews. These differences are not due to religious disparities in income. As we saw in Chapter 2, Catholics and Protestants are about equally prosperous, while Jews are somewhat better off.

The differences in party identification among the three major religious groups are reflected in their voting behavior. In 1972, for example, McGovern got 31 percent of the presidential vote cast by Protestants, 40 percent of the Catholic vote, and 69 percent of the Jewish vote.[22]

Party loyalties based on religion, like loyalties based on regional considerations, often can be traced to historical causes. Before 1928, Catholics were not nearly as prone to vote Democratic as they have been since. In that year Governor Al Smith of New York was the Democratic presidential nominee. This was the first time a major party had nominated a Catholic as its presidential candidate. The resulting campaign, which featured intense anti-Catholic sentiments, had a "backlash" effect that cost the Republican party millions of Catholic voters. These conversions proved to be quite durable. In 1960, when John F. Kennedy, the nation's second Catholic presidential candidate, was nominated by the Democrats, political-religious cleavages were reactivated. Catholics generally are 10 to 15 percent more Democratic than Protestants, but in 1960 fully 80 percent of the Catholic vote went to Kennedy, a sharp increase from the 50 percent who voted for Adlai Stevenson in 1956.[23]

Party loyalties based on nationality are quite similar to religious cleavages. Consciousness of national origins is high and politically relevant in much of the Northeast and Midwest. In New England, for example, appeals to Irish and Italian sentiments often are a prominent feature of election campaigns. Even where national origins are not so conspicuous a feature of the political scene, the two parties often have very different appeal to voters according to the European roots of their ancestors. Generally speaking, people of Irish Catholic, Italian, and Slavic descent are a good deal more likely to identify with the Democratic party and to vote for Democratic candidates than are Americans whose ancestors came from Scandinavia, Great Britain, or Germany. In 1968, for example, when Hubert Humphrey got 43 percent of all votes cast, he won almost two-thirds of the votes in predominantly Slavic and Irish neighborhoods and was an easy winner in Italian districts also.[24]

Ethnic and religious voting is not a function of underlying economic differences. In fact, it cuts across economic lines. Jews are the most prosperous ethnic group in the country, and are also, next to the blacks, the most strongly Democratic. Indeed, Jews voted more heavily for McGovern than any other group of white voters, and McGovern apparently did better among richer Jews than poorer ones.[25] Further, ethnic and religious loyalties do not appear to be fading, even though the disappearance of ethnic voting has been predicted for generations. Consciousness of national origins

---

[22] Miller et al., "A Majority Party in Disarray;" and Milton Himmelfarb, "The Jewish Vote (Again)," *Commentary,* June 1973, 81–85.

[23] V. O. Key, Jr., "A Theory of Critical Elections," *Journal of Politics,* 17 (February 1955), 3–18; and Angus Campbell et al., *Elections and the Political Order* (New York: John Wiley & Sons, Inc., 1966), pp. 87–88.

[24] *Congressional Quarterly Weekly Report,* March 11, 1972, p. 533.

[25] Himmelfarb, "The Jewish Vote (Again)."

seems to be important for many voters. Even when this consciousness itself fades, its political effects remain.[26]

RACIAL DIFFERENCES. The history of the political loyalties of black Americans in the twentieth century is interesting and complex. As recently as 1956, about a third of all black adults did not identify with either party. Half of them called themselves Independents and the other half professed to be apolitical, to have no interest in politics at all. But the civil rights movement, rising black political awareness, and federal action to protect the rights of southern blacks produced a dramatic change. By 1964, only one black in twenty-five claimed to be apolitical, and by 1970 this dwindled to a mere 2 percent.

Before the Roosevelt administration, blacks tended to vote Republican, largely out of gratitude to "the party of Lincoln." Since the New Deal, they have voted Democratic, although the extent of black support for the Democrats has varied considerably. These shifts reflect the course of events and the images of the two parties on civil rights, which changed from ambiguity to clear-cut differentiation in the mid-1960s. Adlai Stevenson, the Democratic presidential candidate in 1952 and 1956, seemed less than enthusiastic about proposed civil rights laws. Although President Eisenhower was not responsible for the momentous Supreme Court school desegregation decision issued in 1954, he and his party benefited from it. In 1956, almost one black in five was a Republican and Eisenhower got 39 percent of the black vote. Four years later, when Eisenhower's Vice President, Richard Nixon, ran for the presidency, he received a quarter of the votes cast by blacks.

In 1964, Republican nominee Barry Goldwater appealed to white southerners. In the Senate he conspicuously voted against the Civil Rights Act of 1964, a historic piece of legislation which had been the most prominent item in the legislative programs of Presidents Kennedy and Johnson. One result was a sharp divergence in the popular images of the two parties. For the first time, the Democrats were widely perceived as more liberal than the Republicans on civil rights. As a consequence, there was a conspicuous change in black support of Democrats from a strong advantage to a near monopoly. Black identification with the Republican party fell to 6 percent in 1964 and has remained near this level ever since. Republican presidential candidates in 1964 and 1968 got only a handful of black votes, perhaps 5 percent at most. At the same time, black Democratic affiliation rose from around 50 percent in the 1950s to a high of 83 percent in 1968. It held at a still impressive 77 percent in 1972, when blacks were overwhelmingly for McGovern. Although McGovern's personal unpopularity was evident even in the black community, he did receive 87 percent of the black vote.[27]

[26] Raymond E. Wolfinger, *The Politics of Progress* (Englewood Cliffs, N.J.: Prentice-Hall, Inc., 1974), Chap. 3.

[27] *Gallup Opinion Index*, December 1972, p. 10.

Black loyalty to the Democratic party is clearly not a matter of blind commitment. In Baltimore, black wards that went 93 percent Democratic in the 1964 presidential election voted a mere 13 percent Democratic in the 1966 race for Governor of Maryland, in which the Democratic candidate based his campaign on opposition to civil rights legislation.[28] This is a particularly good example of rational voting. The issue was clear, of paramount importance to the group, and not obscured by other concerns. An ironic historical footnote is the fact that the Republican gubernatorial candidate who benefited from his opponent's racism was Spiro Agnew. His meteoric political career ended in 1973 with his resignation from the vice presidency in order to avoid having to face trial for corruption.

AGE DIFFERENCES. Although Democrats outnumber Republicans in every age group, the elderly are more likely to be Republicans than are younger people. This is not because people become Republicans as they grow older, but because many Americans who were in their late sixties or older in the 1970s had always been Republican. They grew up before the New Deal, when the Republicans were the majority party. Having reached the age of political consciousness when Republicans dominated American politics, they were more likely to adopt and maintain what was then the prevailing partisan loyalty.

The Great Depression that began in 1929 and extended through the 1930s was the most durable source of political realignment in twentieth-century America. At the depth of the Depression, a quarter of the labor force was unemployed. Millions more worked part-time or worried that they might lose their jobs. This momentous catastrophe came during the Republican administration of Herbert Hoover. Hoover had been in office only a few months when the Depression began and could hardly have been responsible for it, although his relatively limited attempts to deal with the crisis earned him severe criticism. The Republican party was blamed for the disaster that overtook the country during its time in power.

In 1932 Hoover was decisively defeated by Franklin D. Roosevelt, the dominant political figure of mid-twentieth century America. Among other things, Roosevelt established the idea that the government was responsible for the economic well-being of all citizens. This proposition, embodied in a mass of New Deal legislation during the 1930s, firmly established the Democrats as the party of social welfare legislation and government intervention in the economy. By the end of Roosevelt's administration, the Democrats were the nation's new majority party, with a three-to-two advantage in number of party identifiers.

The great increase in Democratic affiliation that came with the New Deal was not chiefly the result of wholesale conversion of former Republicans. Indeed, except among blacks and Jews, switches of party were not especially common. What happened was a change in the climate of opinion that brought the Democrats the lion's share of those entering political conscious-

[28] Walter Dean Burnham, "American Voting Behavior and the 1964 Election," *Midwest Journal of Political Science*, 12 (February 1968), 37.

ness. We can see this by comparing the party identification of various age groups. In 1945, people aged sixty or over were Republicans by a ratio of about three to two, people in their fifties were about evenly split, and younger Americans were strongly Democratic. The declining proportion of Republicans since then primarily reflects the death of a political generation that was predominantly Republican.[29]

Young people seldom differ very much from the rest of the population on political issues, except for "life style" topics such as legalizing marijuana. But in one area a significant generation gap has developed since the early 1960s. Young people have become much likelier to call themselves Independents. By 1972 more than half of all whites under the age of thirty were Independents. (As we have seen, blacks have moved in the opposite direction, toward greater identification with the Democratic party.) Most of these young, white Independents, however, concede that they lean to one party or the other. In fact, only about one out of six young people were *pure* Independents, devoid of any attachment to a party.[30]

Contrary to popular belief, young voters are not ordinarily heavy supporters of Democratic candidates. In four of the six presidential elections between 1952 and 1972, the young gave the Democratic presidential candidate virtually the same proportion of their vote as the whole country did.[31] But in 1972, when the nation as a whole turned sharply away from McGovern, he actually won a majority from voters aged eighteen to twenty-four and captured 43 percent of the vote from those aged twenty-five to twenty-nine.[32]

AN IDEOLOGICAL PORTRAIT OF THE TWO PARTIES

Scholars and journalists commonly consider the Democrats the liberal party and the Republicans the conservative party. Is this picture reflected in the way rank-and-file Republicans and Democrats think about themselves, about the issues, and about their parties? In other words, do ordinary Democrats and Republicans have sharply divergent opinions about policy and philosophy, or are the ideological roots of the two parties as mixed as their socioeconomic sources of support?

For the most part, the answer is that the differences between identifiers with the two parties are *distinct but moderate*. As can be seen from Figure 6–6, when members of the two parties are asked to locate themselves on a spectrum running from "extremely liberal" to "extremely conservative," the most popular label for both Republicans and Democrats is "moderate," or "mid-

[29] See Campbell et al., *The American Voter*, pp. 153–60; and Norval D. Glenn and Ted Hefner, "Further Evidence on Aging and Party Identification," *Public Opinion Quarterly*, 36 (Spring 1972), 35–36. In addition to showing that people do not become more Republican as they grow older, Glenn and Hefner also report that their "findings cast strong doubt upon the belief that aging individuals tend to become more conservative in their political attitudes and values" (p. 47).

[30] Bruce Keith, David Magebly, Candice Nelson, Elizabeth Orr, Mark Westlye, and Raymond E. Wolfinger, *The Independent Phenomenon* (forthcoming).

[31] Axelrod, "Where the Votes Come From," pp. 16–17.

[32] Miller et al., "A Majority Party in Disarray."

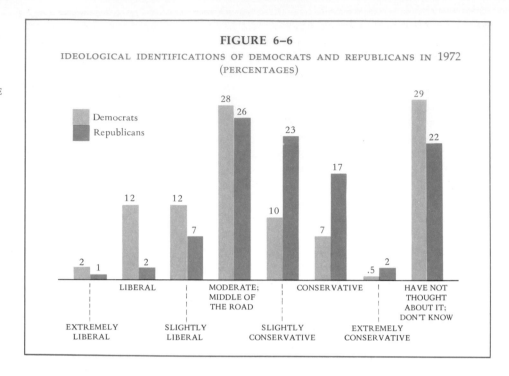

FIGURE 6–6

IDEOLOGICAL IDENTIFICATIONS OF DEMOCRATS AND REPUBLICANS IN 1972
(PERCENTAGES)

dle of the road." While there is some tendency for Republicans to place themselves on the right side of the spectrum and for Democrats to be more toward
the left, one could hardly say that the two parties are sharply divided by the
ideological self-identifications of their followers.

When specific issues are examined, the same blurring of differences is
found. On almost any controversial issue, many Republicans take the liberal
position and many Democrats the conservative one. Indeed, on numerous
issues there are virtually no differences between followers of the two parties.

Partisan differences are strongest on issues involving the economic role of
the federal government. This is evident in Figure 6–7, which charts the
relationship between party identification and attitudes about medical care,
school integration, federal aid to education, and foreign aid. Democrats are
more liberal on each of the three domestic issues. About 55 percent of those
who identified themselves as "strong Democrats" favor federal aid to
education, compared to 15 percent of the strong Republicans. Government
financing of medical care shows a similar relationship to party identification,
although here almost two-fifths of the Republicans take the more liberal
view. Federal intervention in support of local school integration is favored by
about 60 percent of strong Democrats, and by only half as many strong Republicans. There are virtually no differences on this issue between Independents and weak partisans of the two parties, all of whom oppose "busing."
Republicans and Democrats have almost identical views on the question of
American aid for other countries. In fact, Republicans and Democrats rarely
differ much on foreign policy *unless* the issue is posed in terms of approving

the performance of a particular President. Then, Republicans tend to support what a Republican President has done while Democrats support Democratic Presidents.

These tendencies for Democrats to be more liberal may seem rather modest, but in fact they represent a considerable *increase* in polarization between followers of the two parties. During the 1950s and early 1960s, Republicans and Democrats were not very far apart on most questions of public policy and did not see differences between the parties.[33]

It seems reasonable to expect that the way people look at the two parties depends on the character of contemporary political competition and particularly on the appeals of the presidential candidates. When the two parties have nominated moderates who display few areas of disagreement, we would expect less polarization between their supporters. In the 1950s, both parties' candidates—Eisenhower and Stevenson—projected moderate images. In 1960, Nixon was Eisenhower's heir-apparent and continued the Republican middle-of-the-road presidential tradition. On the Democratic side, although John Kennedy presented himself as a man who wanted America to start moving toward a "New Frontier," he was not very specific about what policies would be found on that frontier. In other words, both parties continued the pattern of the 1950s by nominating non-ideological, middle-of-the-road candidates.

This pattern changed drastically in 1964 when Senator Barry Goldwater

[33] Campbell et al., *The American Voter*, Chaps. 8, 9; and Herbert McClosky et al., "Issue Conflict and Consensus among Party Leaders and Followers," *American Political Science Review* 54 (June 1960), 406–27.

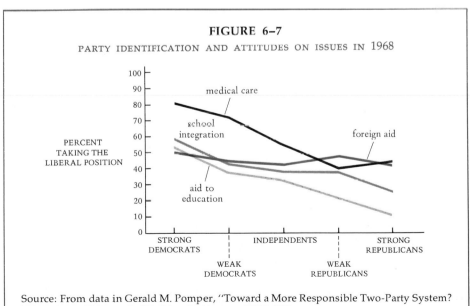

FIGURE 6–7

PARTY IDENTIFICATION AND ATTITUDES ON ISSUES IN 1968

Source: From data in Gerald M. Pomper, "Toward a More Responsible Two-Party System? What, Again?" *Journal of Politics*, 33 (August 1971), 926.

captured the Republican nomination. Goldwater was the hero of his party's ultraconservative enthusiasts and had attacked Republican moderates for their acceptance of the New Deal. Promising to give the American people a clear-cut alternative to Democratic programs, Goldwater launched a challenge to the consensus ideology that had dominated presidential campaigns since the end of World War II. Although the electorate is not very well attuned to ideological nuances, Goldwater succeeded in communicating his dissent to millions of voters. The immediate result was an overwhelming victory for Lyndon Johnson. The longer-run consequence included a heightened public sense of policy differences between the two parties that endured beyond the 1964 election.

The increased perception of party differences on major issues was most conspicuous on civil rights. Prior to 1964, most voters had not seen differences between the parties on this issue, and in fact the followers of the two parties had similar attitudes. Less than half the population thought that Republicans and Democrats differed on civil rights, and less than half of those who did see a difference considered the Democrats the more liberal party.[34] But as the 1964 election approached, civil rights came to the center of public attention and became, in the eyes of most citizens, the most important problem facing the country.

The legislative focus of this concern was the Civil Rights Act of 1964, approved by bipartisan congressional majorities and signed into law by Lyndon Johnson shortly after Goldwater won the Republican nomination. Declaring his intention to appeal to the South, Goldwater said, "We're not going to get the Negro vote as a bloc in 1964 or 1968, and we ought to go hunting where the ducks are." His vote against the Civil Rights Act was the most notable symbol of his determination to go "where the ducks are." Goldwater's hunt for southern votes was not lost on the public. More than three-quarters of the electorate knew about the Civil Rights Act and of these, 84 percent knew that Goldwater had been against it. Almost everyone knew that Johnson was for it.[35] Goldwater's clear opposition to civil rights legislation was an important step in identifying the Republicans as the more conservative party on racial issues. In the election, Goldwater carried only six states, but five of them were in the deep South and had been consistently Democratic since the end of Reconstruction.

Even during an era of relative party polarization on issues, however, many voters do not perceive differences between the parties. This is the case with the issues of medical care, aid to education, government control of the economy, and other highly controversial subjects that sharply divide Democratic and Republican politicians. Only on the issue of medical care do as many as two-thirds of those people who have opinions think that the Republicans and Democrats are on different sides. After decades of highly

[34] Gerald M. Pomper, "From Confusion to Clarity: Issues and American Voters, 1956–68," *American Political Science Review*, 66 (June 1972), 418–19; and Philip E. Converse et al., "Electoral Myth and Reality: The 1964 Election," *American Political Science Review*, 59 (June 1965), 329.

[35] Richard W. Boyd, "Popular Control of Public Policy: A Normal Vote Analysis of the 1968 Election," *American Political Science Review*, 66 (June 1972), 444.

partisan wrangling among leaders about federal aid to education, 40 percent of the public did not think that the two parties differed on this question.[36]

Many voters are equally unclear about how the two parties differ in terms of broad ideology. In 1972, spokesmen of both parties identified McGovern as the champion of numerous liberal positions and claimed that a vast gulf separated his approach from Nixon's. But only 58 percent of the public thought that one of the two parties was "more conservative" or "more liberal" than the other. Among those who claimed to see an ideological difference, about one in five regarded the Democrats as the more conservative party. People who did not perceive a difference between the parties were then asked which party was *generally considered* more conservative. Only a quarter of these people thought that the Republicans were publically perceived as more conservative.

In short, many Americans have strong party loyalties but weak, confused, or inconsistent ideas about what policies their parties actually stand for. For this reason, party identification is an important factor in its own right, quite apart from opinions about what the government should do.

THE END OF THE AMERICAN PARTY SYSTEM?

Although the United States has had the same two major parties for 110 years, almost every national election breeds a rash of speculation that this state of affairs is about to end. Such claims reach new peaks whenever one party loses an election by more than a small margin. Since these claims have been with us for so long, there is a tendency for sophisticated observers to discount them, for much the same reason that the boy who cried "wolf" was ignored. But the wolf eventually did come, and in fact there have been significant shifts in the sources of support for each party in the past. Moreover, we can reasonably expect more realignments in the future. Therefore, some alternatives to our present party alignment need to be considered.

THIRD PARTIES. Democrats and Republicans have totally dominated elections in the twentieth century. The only serious threat to their monopoly on voter attention has come from occasional "third party" presidential candidates. In 1912 Theodore Roosevelt, disappointed at his failure to take the Republican nomination away from his successor in the White House, William Howard Taft, ran as the Progressive party candidate. Roosevelt outpolled Taft, but by splitting the Republican vote he put Woodrow Wilson in the White House, the only Democratic president between 1897 and 1933.

In 1924, disappointed by conservative candidates on both major party ballots, Senator Robert La Follette won almost 5 million votes on the Independent Progressive ticket. In 1948 there were two "third parties." Infuriated by the Democratic convention's adoption of a liberal civil rights platform, southern segregationists walked out and formed the States' Rights Democratic party, with J. Strom Thurmond, then Governor of South Carolina, as their candidate. Nicknamed the "Dixiecrats," Thurmond's party got a little

---

[36] Pomper, "From Confusion to Clarity," p. 418.

over a million votes and carried four southern states, where they appeared on the ballot as the official Democratic party. On the other side of the 1948 ideological spectrum was Henry Wallace, a former Vice President, who won about as many votes as Thurmond and cost Truman victory in New York. The most successful third party movement in more than fifty years was headed by Governor George Wallace of Alabama in 1968. He gathered over 10 million votes—13 percent—and carried five southern states.

Theodore Roosevelt was the only third party candidate to outpoll one of the major party candidates. On only two other occasions, in 1924 and 1968, did a third party win as much as a tenth of the vote, and in neither case was the election outcome affected by the presence of the third party. Each of these movements was the personal vehicle for the political ambitions of a single leader. No third party ever ran many candidates for offices other than the presidency, and none have tried to build grass roots organizations.

The main significance of this outline of past third parties is to emphasize the probability that the Republicans and Democrats are here to stay. Their common response to the threat of serious competition from a third party is to adopt enough of the upstart party's program to steal its thunder. As we will see, there *are* elements of ideological rigidity in the two major parties, but their instinct for survival provides the flexibility needed to adjust to popular sentiment.

PARTY REALIGNMENT. If it is true that our two-party system probably will not be significantly altered by the rise of third parties, what about the possibility that the two parties will acquire different bases of support—either sociological or ideological—than they presently have? Some commentators have advocated a particular realignment for the past half century. These observers would like to see southern conservatives leave the Democrats for a more comfortable doctrinal home in the Republican party, while liberal Republicans make a similar transfer to the Democrats. This development has been very slow in coming. As we have seen, it now appears that some realignment is occurring, but only as a one-way street. Many southerners are leaving their traditional Democratic allegiance, but the traffic in the opposite direction, from the Republican party to the Democratic, is very light. In 1952, fully 74 percent of all whites in the South were Democrats. This dwindled to 46 percent twenty years later—still more than for northern whites, but quite a decline nevertheless.

While actual realignments are scarce, predictions about coming realignments are commonplace. After the 1972 election, one often read verdicts like this one: "The Democratic coalition—forged in New Deal days and composed of the big city vote, manual workers, Catholics, labor union members and non-whites—fell into disarray in this year's presidential campaign."[37] Indeed, every time the Democrats lose a national election, political pundits talk about the "collapse of the old New Deal coalition" and predict an imminent realignment of the two parties. In fact, however, every one of the groups mentioned in this quotation gave a considerably larger share of its

[37] *Gallup Opinion Index*, December 1972, p. 8.

vote to McGovern than did the national electorate. The Democratic presidential candidate lost support from *every* segment of society, but he still did better among the traditional backers of the Democratic party than among other groups.

Similarly, every time the Republicans lose, the same kinds of writers announce that the two-party system is collapsing because the minority party is fading into oblivion. Predictions about the imminent extinction of one of the major parties have been a fact of journalistic life since the Democrats lost the midterm congressional election of 1946. One unchanging political fixture is that one or the other of these two pronouncements will appear after every national election.

ARE PARTIES BECOMING IRRELEVANT? The weakening of party ties is another one of those predictions that have been heard for at least a generation. Almost everyone has read about the phenomenal growth of Independents, a trend that is regarded as potentially lethal to the party system. But as we have noted already, there are two kinds of Independents: those who reject any affinity for one party or the other, and those who admit that they are "closer" to the Democrats or the Republicans. The "pure Independents" are only about a third of the total, around 13 percent of the population. (They were 9 percent in 1956.) The other two-thirds are Independent Democrats or Independent Republicans. Their political behavior does *not* support the notion that they are free from affiliation with one or the other party. Most important, they are very much inclined to vote for the candidates of the party toward which they lean. In fact, other than their initial preference for being called "Independents," there is very little reason to separate them from ordinary Democrats and Republicans.

Social scientists have been unable to identify the causes of the increase in either type of Independent. It is clearly not due to alienation from the American political system or cynicism about contemporary politicians. Although expressions of political disillusionment became quite popular in the late 1960s and early 1970s, this growing disenchantment had nothing to do with the parallel growth in Independents. People who identify with a party are no less cynical than those who decline any partisan identification. The most alienated group in the country is blacks, who have the most reason to be dissatisfied with the status quo and distrustful of existing political institutions. Yet in 1972 less than a quarter of all blacks considered themselves Independents, compared to 36 percent of all whites.[38]

Another sign of weakening party ties is *defection* — voting for the other party's candidate. Although the percentage of defecting party identifiers has risen, the trend is a moderate one. Defection in House elections has increased from 10 to 12 percent in the 1950s and early 1960s to 17 to 19 percent in more recent elections. In 1972, a year of massive crossing of party lines, three-fourths of all votes cast in House elections were by Democrats and Republicans voting for the candidate of their party, only one out of eight votes was across party lines, and the rest were cast by pure Inde-

[38] Our discussion of Independents is based on Keith et al., *The Independent Phenomenon.*

pendents. The pure Independents' share of the total vote for House candidates in 1972 was the same as in 1956, 1960 and 1966. (See Table 6–2.) As the number of Independents has risen, they have become less inclined to vote. Thus, they account for the same proportion of the voters as they always have.

CANDIDATE APPEAL

Elections are won and lost by a combination of long-term forces, such as party identification, and short-term forces, such as the issues and the popularity of the candidates. Of the two short-term factors, the attraction of the other party's candidate or distaste for one's own party's candidate is more influential than issues in causing people to cross party lines.[39]

With the exception of Barry Goldwater in 1964, the Republican candidate has been substantially more appealing to the public than his Democratic opponent in every election from 1952 through 1972.[40] Candidate popularity usually is measured by asking people what they like about each candidate, and then what they dislike about him. The questions are "open-ended" — that is, the respondents are free to give any answer they wish. One explanation for Republican success in the face of the Democratic advantage as the majority party is their ability to nominate more appealing candidates.

Although answers to questions about candidates are influenced by the individual's party and his opinions on particular issues, candidate image is somewhat independent of either of these considerations. Dwight Eisenhower was unquestionably the most popular presidential candidate since World War II. His enormous personal appeal brought the Republicans back to the White House after twenty years in opposition. In addition to winning the votes of almost all Republicans, Eisenhower got most of the Independent vote and a substantial fraction of Democratic support.

His popularity was not simply a result of his positions on issues. Indeed, as a career soldier Eisenhower had not taken positions on most issues. Part of his appeal belonged to the past, to his role as the man who led the Allies to victory in Europe in World War II. But being a military hero alone was hardly enough for political success, as was shown by General Douglas MacArthur's futile attempts to get a presidential nomination. Other aspects of Eisenhower's appeal were his enormously ingratiating, "unmilitary" manner. Liking Ike was a result of liking his personal public image, not a matter of agreement with him on political issues. To be sure, liberal Republicans were somewhat more favorably inclined toward him than conservative ones; and in the general election, Republicans were more favorable than Democrats. But Eisenhower's appeal transcended partisan and ideological considerations to a remarkable extent. Liberals who liked him thought he

[39] Richard W. Boyd, "Presidential Elections: An Explanation of Voting Defection," *American Political Science Review*, 63 (June 1969), 498–514; and Donald E. Stokes, "Some Dynamic Elements of Contests for the Presidency," *American Political Science Review*, 60 (March 1966), 19–28.

[40] Miller et al., "A Majority Party in Disarray."

was a liberal, conservatives who liked him thought he was a conservative, and people in the middle of the road thought that Eisenhower was right there with them.[41] Of course, the fact that Eisenhower was new to politics was a great help in this respect. Never having held–or even run for–elective office, he had no record upon which voters could base an assessment of his political position. Indeed, he *himself* did not even decide whether he was a Republican or a Democrat until a year or two before he won the Republican nomination.

A candidate's appeal may be based on his nonpolitical record and experience, as Eisenhower's was. It may be based on his political abilities, as in the case of Lyndon Johnson, who was widely reputed to be a politician who could get things done. Or it may be based on his personal qualities, whether positive or negative, such as Goldwater's allegedly impetuous manner or Kennedy's perceived vigor. Many of these characteristics do not have any particular ideological coloring, yet as one political scientist

[41] Herbert H. Hyman and Paul B. Sheatsley, "The Political Appeal of President Eisenhower," *Public Opinion Quarterly*, 17 (Winter 1954–55), 443–60.

EISENHOWER'S POP-
ULARITY AS A PRESI-
DENTIAL CANDIDATE
REFLECTED HIS
RECORD AS A FULL
MILITARY LEADER.
Wide World Photos

has observed, the voters' impressions of the candidates as human beings "do not fall on wholly unprepared ground."[42] For one thing, Democrats always take a much more favorable view of the personal qualities of Democratic candidates than Republicans do, and vice versa.

When a candidate has some particular feature which seems to be politically relevant, in all likelihood it will be more important to some voters than to others. A particularly important aspect of John Kennedy's personal image in 1960 was his religion. Its significance was apparent even among people who did not mention Kennedy's Catholicism when asked "Is there anything in particular about Kennedy that might make you want to vote for (against) him?" While Democrats were more likely to have a favorable impression of Kennedy than Republicans or Independents, Catholics also tended to see him in a more favorable light. Catholic Republicans were more favorable to Kennedy than Protestant Republicans, and the same went for Democrats. Democratic Protestants who never went to church voted loyally for Kennedy. But Protestant Democrats who were regular churchgoers were a good deal more uneasy, and almost 40 percent of them defected to Nixon.[43]

In 1964, Goldwater managed to create an exceptionally unfavorable personal impression of himself. Although voters are inclined to have positive personal impressions of presidential candidates, only one out of three

[42] Stokes, "Some Dynamic Elements," p. 23.
[43] Campbell et al., *Elections and the Political Order*, pp. 87–89.

"FRANKLY, AL, WE
FEEL IT WASN'T
YOUR STYLE, YOUR
PLATFORM, OR THE
PEOPLE AROUND YOU
THE VOTERS
WOULDN'T BUY.
WHAT THEY
WOULDN'T BUY WAS
YOU."
Drawing by Lorenz;
© *1974 The New
Yorker Magazine, Inc.*

references to Goldwater was favorable. As one student of that election has written, "The detailed references to Goldwater are an impressive amalgam of doubts—a wild and erratic campaigner, muddled and unclear, unstable, poorly educated, and so on."[44]

The next most unpopular candidate in the post World War II era was Senator McGovern in 1972, whose candidacy was similar to Goldwater's in various respects. Initially a decided underdog for the nomination, he successfully seized control of his party's convention through the dedicated work of hundreds of thousands of enthusiastic activists, many of whom regarded the political process as an arena for expressing moral values rather than as a stage for compromise. Like Goldwater, McGovern often took the unpopular side of issues. He was unfortunate in being perceived by many Americans as an advocate of abortion, amnesty for draft resisters, legalization of marijuana, and other positions rejected by most citizens.[45] Moreover, there were many voters whom McGovern was unable to convince of his stability, integrity, judgment, and intelligence. In part this was due to impressions received from watching the Democratic National Convention, which seemed to be dominated by young countercultural radicals, and in part it reflected McGovern's mode of handling the controversy that arose when it was discovered that his vice presidential candidate, Senator Thomas Eagleton, had been hospitalized three times for nervous disorders.

By the end of the summer, McGovern found himself hopelessly saddled with a reputation for indecision, weakness, and bad judgment. In August a Gallup poll revealed that more than twice as many people thought that phrases like "sticks to principles" and "good judgment" described President Nixon than McGovern. Fully 20 percent of the electorate considered McGovern "an extremist," compared to only 3 percent who put this label on Nixon.[46]

Table 6 3 illustrates how far McGovern's image was from the American people's conception of their own ideological position. It contrasts the proportion of people who rated themselves at each ideological category from "extremely liberal" to "extremely conservative," with the proportion of people who put Nixon and McGovern in each of these categories. Fully 41 percent considered McGovern "liberal" or "extremely liberal," but only 8 percent applied this label to themselves. Nixon's image, on the other hand, much more closely resembled the public's own ideological profile. (Notice also how much disagreement there is about how to classify each candidate.)

The voters became so distrustful of McGovern that they did not even consider him preferable to Nixon on those issues that traditionally had been the Democrats' strongest suits. Although McGovern campaigned heavily against "the entrenchment of special privilege," Nixon was far more suc-

[44] Converse et al., "Electoral Myth and Reality," 330–31; and Stokes, "Some Dynamic Elements," 22.

[45] Miller et al., "A Majority Party in Disarray."

[46] John G. Stewart, *One Last Chance: The Democratic Party, 1974–76* (New York: Praeger Publishers, 1974), pp. 20–21.

TABLE 6-3

HOW THE AMERICAN PUBLIC CLASSIFIED THEMSELVES,
NIXON, AND MCGOVERN AS TO IDEOLOGY IN 1972

	SELF-IDENTIFICATION (%)	IMAGE OF NIXON (%)	IMAGE OF MCGOVERN (%)
Extremely liberal	1	1	15
Liberal	7	3	26
Slightly liberal	10	5	11
Moderate, middle of road	27	15	6
Slightly conservative	15	19	3
Conservative	10	20	2
Extremely conservative	1	4	1
Don't know and haven't thought about it	28	33	36
	99%	100%	100%

cessful in convincing the voters that he would keep "the big interests from having too much influence over the government" and would make "the government pay more attention to the problems of the working man and his family." Indeed, both Nixon and George Wallace were more popular than McGovern among people who agreed that special interests were too powerful. Although Nixon demonstrably had failed to reduce unemployment during his first term as President, even on this issue most people considered him superior to McGovern.[47]

As crucial as candidate appeal may be in presidential elections, it is far less important in congressional elections, where most voters are unlikely to know the name of either candidate. When a voter *does* know the name of the other party's candidate, the chances of defection increase markedly. But because such knowledge is not widespread, party-line voting is more frequent in House elections than in presidential races. For this reason, congressional elections exhibit much more partisan stability than presidential contests do. Figure 6–8 shows the Democratic proportion of the vote in every House and presidential election since 1952. The Democratic share of the presidential vote has fluctuated from a high of 61.1 percent in 1964 to a low of 37.5 percent in 1972, a gap of 23.6 percentage points. During the same period the spread was only 10.3 percent in House voting, from 49.7 percent in 1952 to 60 percent in 1974.

Much of a candidate's personal popularity is not based on the policies he advocates, but on his imagined personality or character, or his past achievements. The same is true of unpopularity, which often has nothing to do with issues. It follows, then, that a vote for a candidate is not neces-

[47] Stewart, *One Last Chance*, pp. 25–26.

sarily a vote for some or all of the positions he takes. In order to explore directly what an electoral victory "means," we must turn to the most difficult problem in election research: To what extent are voting decisions determined by issues?

ISSUE VOTING

How close to reality is the idealistic textbook image of an electorate that judges candidates solely in terms of the policies the candidates stand for? Many politicians and political scientists think that "issues are not important." Instead, they stress candidate image, party loyalty, and get-out-the-vote drives. Other scholars and politicians concede the potency of all these factors but nevertheless argue that in recent years more and more people have come to base their choices on the closeness of fit between their own issue positions and the candidates' stand on policy.

We have already seen evidence for both points of view. The drastic switch of Baltimore blacks from 93 percent support of Lyndon Johnson in 1964 to 13 percent for the Democratic gubernatorial candidate in 1966 was based on their correct impression that George Mahoney's campaign for the governorship was based on racist appeals. The other side of the coin is exhibited by repeated findings that many voters do not have opinions, or have only weak and unstable opinions, about most issues. Moreover, voters often are ignorant of the candidates' positions on issues. During the 1950s only 18 to 36 percent of the American public had an opinion on major issues, knew what government policy had been on these issues, and saw differences

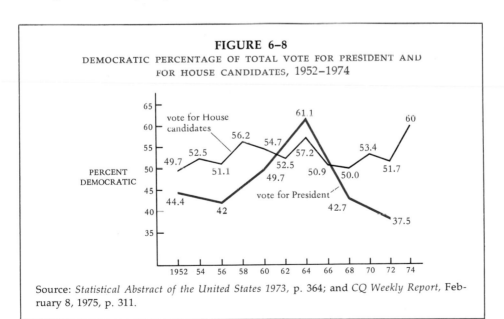

FIGURE 6–8

DEMOCRATIC PERCENTAGE OF TOTAL VOTE FOR PRESIDENT AND FOR HOUSE CANDIDATES, 1952–1974

Source: *Statistical Abstract of the United States 1973*, p. 364; and *CQ Weekly Report*, February 8, 1975, p. 311.

between the two parties on them.[48] What of the 1970s, when, as we have seen, there has been increasing awareness of party differences?

At first glance, this question seems easy to answer. Why not simply ask the voters their positions on the issues and what they think the candidates' positions are? One drawback to this approach is a widespread tendency for voters to rationalize their choice of candidate by misperceiving where the candidates stand. Many will "pull" their favored candidate toward them by thinking mistakenly that he agrees with their policy preferences. At the same time they "push" the other candidate away by imagining that he disagrees with them even when he does not. Furthermore, many voters will change their minds on issues so as to be consistent with the candidate they prefer. In other words, the candidate may be more important than the issue. Thus, it is difficult to tell if one's vote is caused by one's position on an issue, or whether the position on the issue is caused by the vote intention. What is more, there are many issues in each election and only one vote. The voter must reconcile his possibly divergent issue positions with the need to make a single either/or decision about the two candidates.

Voters' perceptions on the issues are further clouded by the common desire of politicians to sit on the fence. For example, although the war in Vietnam was by far the biggest issue on voters' minds in 1968, neither Humphrey nor Nixon spent much time on the subject. Each made it difficult for voters to understand his position. Not surprisingly, then, more than half the 1968 electorate could see no difference between Humphrey and Nixon on Vietnam. Those voters who did see a difference were likely to think that the candidate they favored shared their own positions:

> Those who saw a big difference between Humphrey and Nixon—a difference in either direction—were generally perceiving each candidate as standing wherever they wanted him to stand. They projected their own opinions onto their favored candidate. Among Republicans, who mostly favored Nixon, extreme hawks thought that Nixon was an extreme hawk; extreme doves thought he was an extreme dove; and those in the middle thought that Nixon stood in the middle! . . . Similarly, among Democrats, extreme hawks tended to think Humphrey was an extreme hawk; extreme doves thought Humphrey an extreme dove; and those in the middle thought he stood in the middle.[49]

Thus in 1968 many voters fervently committed to an antiwar position were frustrated by the absence of a clear peace candidate in the general election. In 1972, however, the picture seemed to change.

Unlike Humphrey and Nixon in 1968, George McGovern impressed the electorate as a man of very pronounced views on many issues, particularly those that dominated public concern, such as the war in Vietnam, amnesty

[48] Campbell et al., *The American Voter*, p. 182.

[49] Benjamin I. Page and Richard A. Brody, "Policy Voting and the Electoral Process: The Vietnam War Issue," *American Political Science Review*, 66 (September 1972), 987.

for war resisters, unrest in urban ghettos, and student demonstrations. In the public's eye, McGovern's positions on most issues were somewhat to the left of the Democratic party and well to the left of Nixon. As we saw in Table 6–3, Nixon managed to create an image that nicely coincided with the modal opinions of the electorate. On almost all issues, the position he was thought to have was in fact near the midpoint of what the public thought on the issue.

Many scholars and journalists interpreted the 1972 election as the dawn of a new era in which "issue politics" would replace the older party-line voting. This verdict is an exaggeration, however. Concern about issues did not affect Republicans, who remained loyal to Nixon irrespective of their ideas about government policy. Similarly, the old habits of party loyalty were as strong as ever in voting for congressional candidates.

Like Goldwater eight years earlier, McGovern claimed to be offering a meaningful choice instead of the lack of alternatives that usually confronts the electorate. Indeed, it is true that the people who voted for them had, in the aggregate, somewhat different opinions than those held by supporters of Johnson and Nixon. The Republicans who defected from Goldwater were more liberal than those who remained loyal, and the Democrats who abandoned McGovern were more conservative than the loyalists. But attempts to relate attitudes on particular issues to individual voting decisions have not been very successful. Knowing that some liberal Republicans deserted Goldwater is a far cry from being able to show which of his policy positions did the trick. Some Democrats shared Goldwater's philosophy that "the government should just let each person get ahead on his own," and some Republicans agreed with the Democratic philosophy that it was the responsibility of the federal government to "see to it that every person has a good job and a good standard of living." Yet the Democrats who agreed with Goldwater's position on this point nevertheless voted overwhelmingly for Johnson, while the Republicans who had adopted the welfare state philosophy still voted strongly for Goldwater. In other words, party loyalties were more important than philosophical affinities.[50]

LOOKING BACKWARD

We have defined issue voting as a choice of candidates based on the voter's preference for one policy alternative rather than another. In other words, *issue voting is concerned with what the government is going to do in the future.* This definition requires that the voter have opinions about future policy, know the candidates' positions on them, and vote accordingly. Now let us relax the definition and consider as *issue voting an occasion when a citizen votes to express his estimate of the past performance of a candidate or party.* This does not require having a preference about policy for the future and knowing which candidate is closer to that policy. All it requires is a judgment on the past. It is a verdict, not a prescription.

[50] Angus Campbell, "The Meaning of the Election," in Milton C. Cummings, Jr., ed., *The National Election of 1964* (Washington: The Brookings Institution, 1966), p. 271.

Looked at this way, voters *did* exercise some judgment in 1968. A vote for Nixon was not necessarily a demand for more or less force in Vietnam. It was an unfavorable verdict on the Johnson administration's performance. For just this reason, Nixon left the door open for support by both hawks and doves by refusing to state his own intentions about the war. In a similar situation in 1952, Eisenhower avoided specific policy commitments and attracted both hawks and doves on the Korean war by making his famous pledge: "If elected, I will go to Korea." This committed him to nothing but a long trip.

Humphrey lost millions of votes in 1968 both from those who wanted to pull out of Vietnam altogether and those who wanted to "take a stronger stand even if it means invading North Vietnam." He did not lose votes from Democrats who agreed with administration policy. Thus, it was less important that most voters saw little difference between the two candidates than that they were predominantly disenchanted with existing American policy. Humphrey's greatest problem was his identification with Johnson. As Richard Boyd put it, "Politically, people saw them as a single person." Since almost two-thirds of the public disapproved of LBJ's handling of the war, this meant that Humphrey, as Johnson's Vice President, was tied to an unpopular leader and a disliked policy.[51]

In any presidential campaign, a variety of issues is available for discussion by the candidates. Major attention inevitably goes to the current performance of the party in power. That party's candidate will dwell on areas of success. A President running for re-election in a time of prosperity will talk about how he has brought good times. His challenger naturally will emphasize issues where the administration has been less successful. The candidates seldom engage in genuine debate. Instead, they talk past each other, each stressing those subjects where he thinks he has the more appealing side of the argument.

With so many genuine issues confronting the electorate, and with the two candidates talking about different sets of problems, it is reasonable to expect that the most influential issues will be those that the voters consider most important. To some extent, the priority of different issues will reflect events in the real world—wars, racial unrest, oil shortages, inflation, unemployment, and so on. But to some extent also, the public's view of what is most important will reflect the different candidates and the campaign appeals they make. Neither rhetoric nor reality is necessarily dominant, however, and what the voters think are the most important issues depends on a blend of the two. The actual mix more or less reflects the extent to which the campaigners have accurately assessed the mood of the public. Sometimes, as McGovern found in 1972, this assessment is far wide of the mark. Sometimes, as with Lyndon Johnson in 1964, or Nixon in 1968 and 1972, campaign strategy meshes with popular moods.

Since there are so many issues, one way to establish their influence on the

[51] Richard W. Boyd, "Popular Control of Public Policy," 440; and *Gallup Opinion Index* (April 1968), p. 3.

outcome of the election is to ask people what they consider the most important problem facing the government. Research on this subject reveals considerable fluctuation from one election to the next, as shown in Figure 6–9. In the Kennedy-Nixon election of 1960, for example, foreign policy issues had first priority with three-fifths of the electorate, while domestic issues were more important to the remainder. Only 6 percent of the population considered race relations the top issue in 1960. Four years later, at the height of the civil rights movement, over 20 percent thought that racial problems were the foremost issue confronting the government; all domestic issues combined were at the top of the agenda for more than 60 percent of the population. Vietnam was most important to only one out of eight Americans. By 1968, fully 43 percent thought that Vietnam was the most important problem facing the country. Indeed, Vietnam almost totally occupied the attention of people who considered foreign policy most important. Half the public still thought that domestic issues were most important, but civil rights had dwindled away to being most important to only 9 percent of the population, most of them black.

Unfortunately for Humphrey, the issue that was at the forefront of attention in 1968 was not one where most people had confidence in the Democratic party. Of the 43 percent who thought that Vietnam was the most

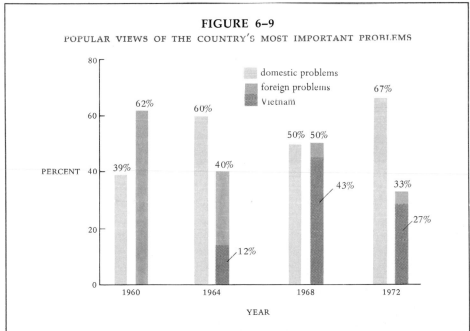

FIGURE 6–9

POPULAR VIEWS OF THE COUNTRY'S MOST IMPORTANT PROBLEMS

Sources: For 1960 and 1964, David E. RePass, "Issue Salience and Party Choice," *American Political Science Review,* 65 (June 1971), 392; for 1968, Alan A. Oldall, "Salient Issue Preferences and Voting Defection, 1964–1968," unpublished paper, University of California, Berkeley, 1973; for 1972, Mark Westlye, "The Role of Issues in Presidential Voting in 1972," unpublished paper, University of California, Berkeley, 1975.

important issue facing the government, only one out of five thought the Democratic party was likely to do a better job on the issue. Over a third thought that the Republicans could do better, and most of the rest thought there was no difference between the parties. The Democrats fared even worse on another major problem in 1968, public order and crime. Eleven percent of the people who considered this issue most important thought the Democrats would do a better job, but more than three times as many thought the Republicans were likely to outperform the Democrats.[52]

In 1964, the Democrats had enjoyed the advantage in public confidence as the party most likely to perform well on the issue most important to Americans. Whatever issue they chose, 43 percent of the people thought that the Democrats would do a better job on the issue most important to them, compared to 23 percent who chose the Republicans and 25 percent who said there was no difference between the parties. But in 1968, the proportion of people having confidence in the Democrats fell to 21 percent, whereas 31 percent thought the Republicans would do a better job. The greatest share of the voters—39 percent—thought that there was no difference between the parties. These figures are shown in Table 6–4.

One index of the erosion of confidence in the Democratic party between 1964 and 1968 is the fact that about one Democrat in six thought that the Republicans were the better party on the crucial Vietnam issue. Only a quarter of these Democrats voted for Humphrey. A similar situation occurred with other issues, and as a result, many Democrats voted for Nixon because they thought the Republicans could do a better job on the issue that was most important to them. These Democratic defectors were not necessarily embracing the Republican solution to the problem. But they had lost confidence in the Democratic party's ability to solve it. In voting for Nixon they

[52] Alan A. Oldall, "Salient Issue Preferences and Voting Defection, 1964–68," unpublished paper, University of California, Berkeley, 1973.

TABLE 6-4
PREFERRED PARTY TO DEAL WITH THE MOST IMPORTANT PROBLEM

	1964	1968	1972
Democrats best	43%	21%	24%
Republicans best	23	31	25
No difference	25	39	42
Don't know	9	10	9
	100%	101%	100%

Source: For 1960 and 1964, David E. RePass, "Issue Salience and Party Choice," *American Political Science Review*, 65 (June 1971), 392; for 1968, Alan A. Oldall, "Salient Issue Preference and Voting Defection, 1964–68," unpublished paper, University of California, Berkeley, 1973; for 1972, Mark Westlye, "The Role of Issues in Presidential Voting in 1972," unpublished paper, University of California, Berkeley, 1975.

were not voting for his position. They were passing an unfavorable judgment on the Johnson administration's performance.[53]

We have looked at the Vietnam issue in the 1968 election in two different ways in order to illustrate how issues affect voting. The 1968 election clearly was not a referendum where the voters chose which policy to follow in Vietnam. But it was an opportunity to pass judgment on the Johnson administration's performance in Vietnam and on other issues as well. Johnson did not rate highly in the eyes of the many voters who thought Vietnam was of paramount importance, including millions of Democrats and Independents. A substantial fraction of these disappointed Democrats deserted Humphrey because they associated him with an administration they judged to be a failure.

In short, "A party will be known more for its deeds in office than for its words out of office."[54] Verbiage is easily ignored, but an unpopular war, racial unrest, inflation, unemployment, scandal, and the like do have an impact. The opinions with the greatest influence on voting decisions are not individual preferences for one policy as opposed to another, but individual judgments about the performance of governments and political parties. "The public does not necessarily *prescribe* a particular policy, but it can *proscribe* a policy. . . ."[55]

If we think about issue voting in this way, there is less reason to be preoccupied about the accuracy of voters' perceptions, their ability to use political philosophies, or the internal consistencies of their beliefs. Even if the outcome of an election is not a choice by the voters among conflicting proposals about what the government should do in the future, it may well express a verdict on the adequacy of past performance. When an incumbent is running for re-election, it is his performance that is likely to be evaluated. If incumbents are not candidates for re-election, the candidate of the incumbent's party is likely to be the beneficiary — or the victim — of the reputation that his party has established.

ELECTIONS AS MANDATES

After the votes have been counted, what does the outcome mean? People who win elections customarily claim that their victory means that they have a "mandate" to carry out the policies that they have advocated during the campaign. But is this true? In voting for a candidate, do the people vote for everything he has said? Clearly the answer is no, even though politicians and journalists alike persist in reading such mandates into election outcomes.

It is particularly tempting to regard a candidate's victory as popular affirmation of his most conspicuous campaign theme. Sometimes interpretations of this sort are grotesquely wrong. The first presidential primary in 1968 was in New Hampshire, where the only Democrat on the ballot was Senator Eugene McCarthy, running as a peace candidate opposed to John-

---

[53] Oldall, "Salient Issue Preferences and Voting Defection."

[54] Campbell et al., *The American Voter*, p. 61.

[55] Boyd, "Popular Control of Public Policy," p. 443.

son's war in Vietnam. A write-in campaign brought Johnson more votes than McCarthy, but McCarthy still got over 40 percent. This was interpreted as a moral victory for him and a remarkable setback not only for Johnson but for his policy in Vietnam. Shortly thereafter, Johnson announced that he would not be a candidate for re-election. Closer analysis revealed that McCarthy had gotten more votes from hawks than doves. New Hampshire Democrats choosing McCarthy were voting not *for* his policy, but *against* Johnson's. Johnson was opposed from both sides—by hawks as well as doves—and McCarthy's candidacy presented an opportunity to register discontent with Johnson from all points of view. Indeed, many voters in New Hampshire did not seem as concerned about the war as about other issues. When they were dissatisfied with Johnson's performance, for any reason, they voted for McCarthy.[56] Thus, to the voters in the New Hampshire primary, the most important thing about McCarthy was not what he stood for, but the stark fact that he was an alternative to Johnson.

Elections do provide some sort of a mandate when the question is not a choice among policies, but rather confidence in the administration or in a party. This could be seen in the six special elections held during the spring of 1974 to fill empty seats in the House of Representatives. As it happened, all six seats had been strongly Republican for long periods. Democrats won five of the six special elections, in many cases for the first time in more than half a century. Political observers attributed the Democratic triumphs to popular disgust with Watergate, as well as high prices and the energy crisis.

A famous political scientist wrote some years ago that "The vocabulary of the people consists mainly of the words 'yes' and 'no'; and at times one cannot be certain which word is being uttered."[57] This is so because each voter is limited to a single "yes" or "no" although the issues debated in the campaign are invariably numerous and each is susceptible to far more than two possible answers. As a result, different voters use their votes to answer "yes" or "no" to different questions in the very same election. For example, although blacks were much more strongly opposed to the Vietnam war than whites, they voted 97 percent for Humphrey in 1968. In doing so, they were not expressing their opinion about the war. Rather, they were indicating which candidate they considered most sympathetic to racial justice. An inherent limitation of our elections is that they permit only one answer, no matter how many questions emerge in the campaign.

SUMMARY

Voting is the mechanism by which government leaders are chosen. Voter turnout is determined in part by election laws and by the relative importance of elections. In addition, some kinds of people are more likely to vote than others. People in their middle years are more likely to vote than the very young and very old. The more education one has, the more likely to vote one

[56] Converse et al., "Continuity and Change."

[57] V. O. Key, Jr., *Politics, Parties, and Pressure Groups*, 5th ed. (New York: Thomas Y. Crowell & Co., 1964), p. 544.

is. Very little nonvoting occurs as an expression of hostility to the political system or to the choices available in an election.

Party identification is a key factor in determining for whom the voter votes, but those who identify with one party nevertheless will sometimes vote for a candidate of the other. The more an individual knows and cares about particular candidates and their attachments to particular issues, the less he will rely on party identification alone in deciding how to vote. Neither the Democratic nor Republican party appeals exclusively to any particular segment of the society. In general, the higher the socioeconomic status of an American, the more likely he or she is to vote Republican. Although the "solid South" is breaking down, southerners still are more likely to be Democrats than are northerners. Jews are more likely to be Democrats than Catholics, and Catholics are more likely to be Democrats than Protestants. Persons of Irish-Catholic, Italian, or Slavic descent are more likely to vote Democratic than are those of Scandinavian, British, or German descent. Blacks are more likely to be Democrats than whites.

The ideological differences between identifiers with the two parties are distinct but quite moderate. With much overlapping, Republicans as a whole are somewhat more conservative than Democrats. These differences are clearest on issues involving the economic role of the federal government. Only on the issue of government-financed medical care do as many as two-thirds of those people who have opinions think that the Republicans and the Democrats are on different sides.

Despite constant predictions of party realignment, the present pattern is quite durable. Third parties occasionally arise—and disappear. Some southern conservatives are finding the Republican party more congenial than their traditional Democratic allegiance. A few more people—mostly young adults—consider themselves Independents. Party-identifiers are voting for the other party's candidate a bit more frequently. None of these phenomena is massive enough, however, to indicate the immediate demise of the traditional two-party system.

Elections are won and lost by a combination of long-term forces, such as party identification, and of short-term forces, such as candidate appeal and the issues. The appeal of presidential candidates is in part a purely personal matter and rests in part on the candidate's identification with issues or segments of the population. To the extent that people do base their votes on the issues, the crucial question is which party is thought to have the "right" position on the issues that are the most important to particular voters. Votes cast on the basis of promises about future policies are difficult to identify. More marked is the tendency for citizens to use their votes to express their estimate of the past performance of a candidate or party. Many people who think the party in power has done a bad job will vote for the presidential candidate of the other party. Some of them also will vote for the other party's congressional candidate.

Because people who vote for one candidate may be doing so because of party identification or personal appeal, or to punish the rival candidate for bad past performance, elections are not mandates for the policies exposed by the winning candidate. There will be many issues raised in the campaign.

On some issues each voter may agree with one candidate and on some with the other candidate. Yet he can vote for only one of them. Thus, a vote for a candidate does not mean that the voter agrees with all or even most of the candidate's policy stands.

The purpose of voting is to aggregate individual choices into a collective decision about which men and women shall hold elective office. For most citizens, voting is the only political activity in which they engage. This effort determines who will occupy public office. The preferences of voters play a role in determining who the candidates will be and what positions they will take, for politicians try to pay attention to what the public will "buy."

Nevertheless, the voters themselves clearly do not produce the alternatives from which they will be asked to choose. Where do these alternatives come from? Up to this time we have said nothing about the processes that must take place before a candidate is presented to the voters at a general election. In the following three chapters we shall examine parts of the political scene that are more specialized than the voting public. In these chapters we shall look into the role of activists, interest groups, and the parties themselves.

CHAPTER SEVEN
POLITICAL PARTICIPATION

E LECTIONS are the basic instrument for popular control of government in any democratic society. But they are an exceedingly blunt instrument because national elections occur only once every two years, only a minority of the adult population votes in off-year congressional elections, and vote choices are confined to only the candidates of the two major parties, running for at most three national offices—representative, President, and senator. Although a citizen may have opinions on many issues, his vote is limited to one choice, between only two candidates for each of two or three national offices.

Are there other ways in which "government by the people" can be achieved? Yes. One such way is through *interest groups*, which "represent" most of us, usually several times over. Another way is through *direct participation* in politics. Private citizens can engage in political activities other than voting. For example, they can participate in the selection of candidates for elected office and in the formulation of public policy. Participation is important to an understanding of politics for three reasons:

1. It is a form of political behavior engaged in by millions of Americans.
2. It is an essential part of the process by which candidates are nominated and elected.
3. It is one of the most important ways in which politicians learn what the public wants.

No area of political life has more conflicting moral overtones and offers more ambiguities for students. Consider the different labels commonly applied to private citizens who are active in politics. Sometimes they are called concerned citizens, and sometimes they are called vested interests, ward heelers, hacks, fat cats, or lobbyists. As we will see, the motivations for political participation, the characteristics of the participants, and the resources they bring to the political struggle all shape the nature of the political system.

By participating in politics, individuals can expand their influence beyond their own votes. Of course, some people are more likely than others to participate. As with voting, the more education or money someone has, the greater the chances he will be politically active. People with money, time, energy, and political skill can extend their influence by using these resources to affect the outcome of elections and the decisions of officials. Does the fact that such resources are unequally distributed in the population mean that the rich and the articulate are able to impose their rule on the rest of the people? There is no doubt about the value of money, energy, and ability in politics—as in any other area of life. But no group or political faction in America has a monopoly on any of these resources. And the amount of time and money expended for political purposes is only a tiny fraction of what could be spent. This is because the amount of time and money devoted to politics really depends more on motivation than on the absolute amount of these resources one possesses. The crucial thing is not how much money is available, but how much and how effectively it is used. In politics, potential power is far less important than the ability and will to mobilize that power.

Apathy is a universal and enduring characteristic of political life. From the Greek city-states to the present, most citizens have refrained from active involvement in public affairs. Even in such widely acclaimed models of civic virtue as ancient Athens and New England town meetings, penalties often had to be assessed for absenteeism in order to produce attendance at meetings.[1] In contemporary America, people who are *interested* in politics are a minority. As we might expect, those who are *active* in politics are an even smaller minority.

What do we mean by *active participation?* Specifically, participation consists of giving any sort of help to an election campaign or attempting to influence what the government does. It includes campaign contributions, licking envelopes, registering voters, going to conventions, writing speeches, raising money, and all the other actions connected with nominating and electing any of the more than 500,000 elected government officials in the United States. Influencing the government might involve many of the same sorts of behavior, as well as communicating with officials and trying to get other people to do the same. It also includes litigation, which is discussed separately on pages 238–39. The types of participation discussed in this chapter are limited to legal activity. They exclude arson, murder, violations of free speech, refusal to pay taxes as a form of protest, ideologically based shoplifting, and other varieties of coercion. These tactics are discussed in Chapter 16, where we examine the use of extra-legal political weapons.

The most common forms of political activity are listed in Figure 7–1. The bars on the right side of the figure show how many adult Americans engaged in each type of activity in 1972 or in their lifetimes. Figure 7–1 illustrates how political activity is the province of a minority. The most common form of participation in 1972 — as in past campaigns — was giving money. Ten percent of the population supplied financial aid to at least one candidate or party in 1972. Almost as large a proportion went to some sort of campaign meeting or rally, and about half as many did something else to help out. The total number of campaign workers is somewhat greater than the number who perform any single task, but there is a good deal of overlap because the most active workers are likely to do a variety of things for their candidate or party. All told, 17 percent of the sample worked in the 1972 campaign in one way or another.

The level of activity has been remarkably stable over the years, at least since 1952. Every presidential election year, about one American in six works in a campaign in one way or another, although not necessarily in the campaign for the presidency. This is an interesting contrast to recent

[1] Robert A. Dahl, *Modern Political Analysis,* 2nd ed. (Englewood Cliffs, N. J.: Prentice-Hall, Inc., 1970), pp. 78–79. Although Americans vote less than citizens of other countries, they participate in politics at a much higher rate. For example, 16 percent report that they have tried to influence a decision of the federal government, compared to only 6 percent of Englishmen and even smaller proportions in other European countries. Americans more frequently say that ordinary citizens should be active in politics. See Kenneth Prewitt and Sidney Verba, *An Introduction to American Government* (New York: Harper & Row, 1974), pp. 164–65.

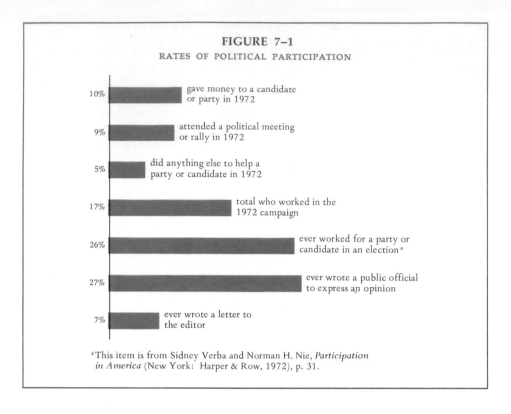

FIGURE 7–1

RATES OF POLITICAL PARTICIPATION

10% — gave money to a candidate or party in 1972

9% — attended a political meeting or rally in 1972

5% — did anything else to help a party or candidate in 1972

17% — total who worked in the 1972 campaign

26% — ever worked for a party or candidate in an election*

27% — ever wrote a public official to express an opinion

7% — ever wrote a letter to the editor

*This item is from Sidney Verba and Norman H. Nie, *Participation in America* (New York: Harper & Row, 1972), p. 31.

trends in turnout. In Chapter 6 we saw that the percentage of eligible Americans who vote has declined since the mid 1960s. But behavior that requires a higher level of involvement has not slackened. Indeed, letter writing to public officials has increased considerably, from about a sixth of the population in the 1960s to the present level of 27 percent.

This suggests that the impulses leading to participation are not necessarily the same ones that lead to voting. The considerations that induce a minority of citizens to work for a candidate or a cause often differ from what brings the majority of citizens to the polls on election day. We find support for this theory if we divide the campaign activists into Democrats and Republicans. For the past twenty years, we have statistics that enable us to see whether the number of campaign workers a party has is related to the total number of votes the party's presidential candidate gets. This computation reveals that there is *no relationship between a candidate's share of the popular vote and the number of activists working in his campaign.*[2] In fact, the peak year for grassroots campaign participation by Republicans was 1964, which was a disastrous electoral year for Republicans. Although Senator Goldwater, the Republican candidate, was a flop with the general public, he was an enormously appealing hero to Republican activists. The 1956 election presented the same picture for the Democrats. Adlai Steven-

[2] These calculations are from Carolyn K. Ban, "The Party Activist: 1956–68" (unpublished Ph.D. dissertation, Stanford University, 1975).

son, the Democratic candidate, did not make a good personal impression on the mass electorate, but he was an inspiration to millions of Democratic activists. The point is not that campaign work is worthless, for there is plenty of evidence to the contrary. Our point, rather, is that activists and voters do not always march to the same drummer. Causes and candidates that attract activist support may be unpopular with the general public. Conversely, candidates who get massive popular backing may not be able to inspire the support of those who go in for active participation.

Figure 7-1 provides one other important clue for understanding political participation. We can see from the graph that the proportion of people who worked in one campaign or another in 1972 is considerably smaller (17 percent) than the number who say they have ever worked in an election (26 percent). In fact, the amount of turnover is probably even greater than these figures indicate. A study that interviewed the same people in two consecutive elections found that half of the people who participated in the 1956 campaign were inactive in 1960, and that half of the 1960 activists did nothing in 1956.[3] In other words, although activists are always a minority, they are not always the same minority. They are not a closed elite. Instead, there is a good deal of circulation into and out of their ranks.

The substantial turnover in participation illustrates our earlier observation that the important thing about participation is not the total amount of available resources, but the extent to which those resources are mobilized. As political conditions change and new leaders, issues, and organizations emerge, the composition of the activist population changes. It also changes in response to the political skills of the candidates. The Kennedy brothers have all been known for their ability to recruit and organize campaign workers. Hubert Humphrey, another well-known presidential candidate, is noted for his lack of success in this area.

MOTIVES FOR PARTICIPATION

Why do people participate? This is an important question because differences in motivation are directly related to differences in the consequences of participation. People drawn to politics by, say, personal friendship for the candidate will make very different claims on him than those who are moved by a desire to raise the oil import quota or the minimum wage. We assume that all human behavior is motivated by expectations of some sort of reward. The anticipated reward may be in heaven or on earth. It may be tangible or intangible, noble or base, sacred or profane. By looking at the motivations, we can learn a great deal about the consequences of participation. In this section we will describe four major categories of incentive for participation in politics.[4] As you read this material, try to remember

[3] Ban, "The Party Activist."

[4] This typology and the material on New Haven are from Raymond E. Wolfinger, *The Politics of Progress* (Englewood Cliffs, N. J.: Prentice-Hall, Inc., 1974), Chap. 4.

that individuals do not fit neatly into any of these boxes. The same person may have many motivations and consequently may belong in more than one category.

POLICY-ORIENTED PARTICIPATION

More than 40,000 dairy farmers belong to the American Milk Producers, Inc. (AMPI), a national dairy cooperative. In 1970, they contributed $535,422 to AMPI to be spent on political campaigns. This "milk money" was donated to the campaign funds of a number of Democratic and Republican congressmen. Together with another giant dairy co-op, AMPI gave a total of $50,000 to four members of the Dairy and Poultry Subcommittee of the House Committee on Agriculture, and almost as much to four men on the counterpart subcommittee in the Senate.[5] All this money was spent to influence policy on two areas that attract little attention from anyone but dairy farmers: the federal support prices for domestic dairy products and import controls on foreign dairy products. In 1971, the Nixon administration raised the support price, thus increasing the American public's expenditure on milk by many million dollars.

In 1970, labor unions gave $1,767,044 to candidates for the Senate. All but a few thousand went to Democrats, six of whom got over $100,000 each. In the same year, labor gave over $10,000 to each of forty-two candidates for the House. Thirty-two of them won their elections. An additional forty-eight winners got between $5,000 and $10,000 apiece.[6] These expenditures are puny compared to what organized labor did for Humphrey in the 1968 presidential election, as described by Theodore H. White:

> the ultimate registration, by labor's efforts, of 4.6 million voters; the printing and distribution of 55 million pamphlets and leaflets out of Washington and 60 million more from local unions; telephone banks in 638 localities, using 8,055 telephones, manned by 24,611 union men and women and their families; some 72,225 house-to-house canvassers; and on Election Day, 94,457 volunteers serving as car-poolers, materials-distributors, baby-sitters, poll-watchers, telephoners.[7]

Although the goals of the unions were different from those of the milk producers, they, too, wanted to influence government policy. They were interested in such things as federal medical insurance, higher minimum wage laws, and amendment of the laws regulating unions.

Policy-motivated participation is by far the easiest kind of participation to understand. Millions of people want the government to enact laws or

---

[5] These contributions were made between the end of the 1972 election and the spring of 1974. *Congressional Quarterly Weekly Report,* October 5, 1974, pp. 2678–79.

[6] The figures on labor spending in 1970 were compiled by Americans for Constitutional Action from official reports and were released on May 17, 1971, and June 4, 1971, by ACA.

[7] Theodore H. White, *The Making of the President, 1968* (New York: Atheneum, 1969), p. 365.

regulations to do all sorts of things: register guns, build freeways, limit grazing in national forests, include farmworkers under the National Labor Relations Act, prohibit abortions, give aid to Israel, and so on. All these goals—and thousands more—are supported by interest groups, which we will discuss explicitly in Chapter 8. Individuals who want the same goals, acting on their own or through organizations, also contribute vast amounts of money and time to political campaigns. The purpose behind these contributions, of course, is to put sympathetic officials in office and to create an obligation toward the contributor. In this way the contributors hope to achieve some particular policy or collection of policies.

It is important to remember that the goals of political contributors are not necessarily related to economic benefits, as many of the examples in the preceding paragraph indicate. Political activity of this type is aimed at influencing government policy. By its very nature, government policy usually affects all members of a particular category. For example, tax laws affect all taxpayers, price supports for wheat affect all wheat farmers, a ban on certain chemical additives to foods may affect all producers of diet drinks, and so on. We call these decisions *indivisible,* because, as Robert Dahl observes, they lead to benefits (or penalties) that "cannot be or ordinarily are not allocated by dividing the benefits piecemeal and allocating various pieces to specific individuals" or firms or places.[8]

PATRONAGE-BASED PARTICIPATION

All government activity is not indivisible, in the sense just defined. Much of it concerns only a particular person, firm, organization, or place. Shall Jones be hired? Shall Smith be promoted? Shall a contract for building the new freeway be given to the X Construction Company or the Y Construction Company? Shall a new post office be built in Tucson now or in the indefinite future? Shall the post office be designed by this architect or that one? Shall the Gulf Oil Company be investigated for possible violation of any of the 417 laws, regulations, and guidelines that affect its operations? Of all the factories that are polluting the air, shall the Wonder Widget Company be fined?

Decisions of this sort are different from policy decisions in three important respects: (1) They are divisible; (2) they concern the routine operations of government; and (3) they depend on the discretion of individuals. That is, such decisions are not mandated by laws or regulations. Human beings make them by choosing one course of action rather than another. Official discretion can be based entirely on objective or even scientific criteria. But when such considerations do not provide a clear basis of decision—and sometimes even when they do—the official who has to make the decision may look for other criteria. Given a choice of two people to hire, he may pick the one who has worked for the winning political party. Confronted with four insurance brokers, each offering the same premium to insure pub-

---

[8] Robert A. Dahl, *Who Governs?* (New Haven: Yale University Press, 1961), p. 52.

TOP 10 POLITICAL CAMPAIGN COMMITTEES, 1974

(Rank based on the sum of expenditures and cash on hand for each committee)

COMMITTEE	EXPENDITURES	CASH ON HAND	TOTAL (EXPENDITURES PLUS CASH ON HAND)
1. Committee for Thorough Agricultural Political Education, C-TAPE (*Associated Milk Producers Inc.*)	$193,969	$1,682,708	$1,876,678
2. American Medical Political Action Committee (*national, American Medical Association*)	1,775,531	−15,816	1,759,715
3. MEBA Retirees' Group Fund (national, Marine Engineers' Beneficial Association, *AFL-CIO*)	982,532	272,124	1,254,656
4. National Education Association (national and state groups)	421,863	672,986	1,094,849
5. *AFL-CIO COPE* Political Contributions Committee (national, AFL-CIO)	960,393	102,697	1,063,090
6. *UAW-V-CAP, United Auto Workers Voluntary Community Action Program* (International Union of Automobile			

lic property, he may pick the broker who contributed to the ruling party's campaign fund. These are examples of *patronage,* which is the practice of rewarding or stimulating political activity by the exercise of discretion on divisible matters of governmental routine. A few examples will make clear the range of patronage and its relevance to the national political system.

• A typist employed by the City of Chicago is assessed 2 percent of her salary by the Democratic organization in her ward. When a fund-raising dinner is held, she is expected to buy a fifty-dollar ticket. She explains her position:

> You can't tell the organization "no." If they say pay, you pay. Sure, there's a lot I don't like. But the organization got me the job

COMMITTEE	EXPENDITURES	CASH ON HAND	TOTAL (EXPENDITURES PLUS CASH ON HAND)
Aerospace and Agricultural Implement Workers of America)	402,268	519,103	921,371
7. Laborers Political League (Laborers' International Union of North America, AFL-CIO)	360,451	263,628	624,079
8. United Steelworkers of America Political Action Fund (United Steelworkers of America, AFL-CIO)	146,794	366,267	513,081
9. Trust for Special Political Agricultural Community Education, SPACE (Dairymen Inc.)	161,703	349,635	511,338
10. Machinists Nonpartisan Political League (national, International Association of Machinists, AFL-CIO)	334,915	171,873	506,788

Source: National Information Center on Political Finance, Congressional Quarterly Service, *Dollar Politics* (Washington, D.C.: Congressional Quarterly Inc., 1974) p. 56.

when I couldn't find work anywhere else. I'm not exactly a great typist.[9]

The Democratic organization in Chicago has about 35,000 patronage jobs at its disposal. The head of the organization, Mayor Richard Daley, personally reviews every application for these jobs.[10] Daley controls the nomination of eight Democratic congressmen from Chicago, has a good deal to say about who the Democratic senatorial nominee will be, and ordinarily picks much of the Illinois delegation to the Democratic National Convention. When a Democrat is in the White House, residents of Illinois considered for federal

[9] Quoted in Martin and Susan Tolchin, *To the Victor . . .* (New York: Random House, 1972), p. 39.
[10] *Newsweek,* April 5, 1971, p. 82.

appointments are cleared with Daley. The patronage at his disposal extends far beyond municipal jobs, but these positions alone give him ten campaign workers for every one of Chicago's 3,421 voting precincts.

• The chairman of the Democratic party in New Haven solicits a campaign contribution from a local businessman: "Look, you son-of-a-bitch, do you want a snow removal contract or don't you?" This is no idle threat, for the chairman is also director of the municipal Department of Public Works, which is responsible for keeping the streets free of snow. The chairman also complains that some of the municipal employees in his department have not worked hard enough in the current presidential campaign:

> All of you came to me prior to your employment telling me of your great political activity in behalf of the Democratic party. It appears as though that activity ceased when you received your share of the so-called "spoils." . . .
>
> I intend to be there [at the next campaign meeting] and check off the names of those present.
>
> It is my intention in the future to deal with those who are missing, as I feel they should be dealt with.

When the Connecticut Democratic party holds a convention to nominate a senatorial candidate, all forty-three New Haven delegates vote the same way. This is not surprising, since most of them work for the city or do business with it.

• John V. Lindsay is elected Mayor of New York in 1965 as an opponent of machine politics. His campaign stresses his dedication to good government and the merit system. Within five years, the number of "temporary" municipal jobs, which are exempt from civil service, expands tenfold. Lindsay also finds that contracts with outside private consultants can be used for patronage. The city's expenditures on consultants increase 900 percent in Lindsay's first term. Consultants study traffic on the Queensboro Bridge five times in two years. New York City has a Neighborhood Youth Corps with 43,000 people on the payroll. Forty percent of the names on the payroll cannot be traced to actual human beings, although paychecks have been issued to these names and cashed.[11] In 1971, Lindsay switches from the Republican to the Democratic party and tries for its presidential nomination. New York municipal employees turn up as far away as Arizona to help his campaign.

• Congressman Morris K. Udall, a high-ranking member of the House Committee on Post Office and Civil Service and a liberal candidate for the 1976 Democratic presidential nomination, explains how the patronage system works:

> When a Post Office building was to be located in my district, I was notified that I could pick the architect. The congressman is always

[11] Tolchin and Tolchin, *To the Victor*, pp. 24, 61–64, 84.

asked which architect he would like. One of the local Democrats was asked which architect he would like, and got a $2,000 campaign contribution from the architect he eventually selected. Now that Nixon is in power, I doubt that I'd have much to say.[12]

• Claude C. Wild, Jr., a vice president of the Gulf Oil Corporation — the eleventh largest company in the United States — explains his firm's $100,000 contribution to the 1972 Nixon re-election campaign. He was told by Maurice Stans, Nixon's Secretary of Commerce, that a contribution of this size was expected from every large company. Wild said that he feared Gulf Oil could "be on a blacklist" if he didn't contribute, that sixty-one different federal agencies had jurisdiction over some aspect of his company's operations, and that "I just wanted someone [in the government] to answer my telephone calls once in a while." In other words, he felt he had no alternative, even though the contribution was from company funds and therefore illegal.[13] In any case, the legality of this particular contribution is beside the point. Most of the uses of patronage we have discussed do *not* involve illegal behavior. Even if all illegal practices were eliminated, the patronage system would remain virtually unchanged.

FACT AND FICTION ABOUT PATRONAGE. When most people think of patronage, they commonly think of big cities and the Democratic party. This association is wrong on both counts, as some of our examples indicate. The *New York Times* says that "the most effective political machine east of Chicago" is the suburban Nassau County (New York) Republican organization. It gets much of its income from 17,000 public employees in Nassau County who pay it 1 percent of their annual salary.[14] Patronage seems to flourish in some parts of the country and to be far less common and less popular in other regions. The Governor of New York, for example, can make 39,000 political appointments when he takes office. The Governor of Pennsylvania can make 50,000, and the chief executives of Illinois, Indiana, and some other states are not far behind. In contrast, the Governor of Oregon has less than a dozen patronage jobs, the Governor of Wisconsin has about twice as many, and the Governor of California has only a few hundred.[15]

Public opinion with regard to patronage also seems to vary regionally. Eastern politicians believe that it is essential to the proper functioning of the party system. The Democratic leader in the Bronx told a reporter that he believed in patronage because, "How can you ask a man to go out and give the time and energy [to politics] without any reward. . . . Lindsay would be ungrateful if he didn't reward the people who helped elect him."[16] In contrast, however, people in the West and in parts of the Midwest regard this attitude as an immoral perversion of civic virtue. In California, paying precinct workers is considered scandalous. Nobody really knows the reason

[12] Tolchin and Tolchin, *To the Victor*, pp. 219–20.
[13] *San Francisco Chronicle*, November 15, 1973, pp. 1, 6.
[14] *New York Times*, July 7, 1974, Sec. E, p. 5.
[15] Tolchin and Tolchin, *To the Victor*, p. 96.
[16] *New York Times*, June 1, 1970, p. 30.

for such striking regional variations in the prevalence of patronage. The old idea that patronage flourished in communities made up largely of immigrants and poor people can hardly hold water in view of ample evidence that political machines are going strong in the suburbs and in rural areas as well as in big cities.

PATRONAGE IN THE FEDERAL GOVERNMENT. Many Americans assume that federal patronage is something that vanished with the civil service reforms of the late nineteenth century. This view is largely correct so far as job patronage is concerned. An incoming President can make fewer than seven thousand appointments (see pp. 414–17). Some of these are used to reward supporters, but the President also must worry about appointing able lieutenants who can help him grasp control of the immense federal bureaucracy. His success in office may depend on the quality of the people he appoints to some of these key positions, so he naturally will be reluctant to use these jobs simply to pay off political debts. As a result, the patronage value of federal jobs, although far from trivial, is far less than what can be found in many city halls and state capitols.

As we have seen, however, patronage is not limited to jobs. The cases of the Gulf Oil executive and the congressman who could choose the architect to build a post office in his district suggest some of the other possibilities. The federal government is engaged in a vast number of regulatory activities and contractual relationships. Usually, decisions in these areas are not made on political grounds. But if political officials in Washington want to, they can use their discretionary powers to extract campaign contributions from businessmen who fear retribution if they do not contribute, or who expect rewards if they do. In 1970, the chairman of the Federal Maritime Commission, which regulates the shipping industry, asked executives of ten shipping firms to contribute to the Republican candidate for Governor of Maryland. Many of the executives interpreted the calls as implicit threats.[17] Such interpretations are often not far from the mark. *Fortune,* the well-known business magazine, declared in an editorial: "The fund-raising tactics used in the Nixon campaign smacked of a Mafia-style shakedown of the nation's leading business enterprises." The chairman of the board of directors of American Airlines, who made an illegal $55,000 contribution, admitted to *Fortune:* "A large part of the money raised from the business community for political purposes is given in fear of what would happen if it were not given."[18]

Not all contributions are made because of fear of reprisals, however. Many contributions come from people who want to increase their chances of favorable treatment by federal agencies. Among the contributors mixed up in the Watergate scandal was Dwayne Andreas, a Minneapolis businessman who gave $25,000 to the Nixon campaign even though he had been a major Humphrey supporter in 1968. Andreas was a director of a bank which

"WE'RE IN THE
PROTECTION BUSI-
NESS. YOUR FOUR-
YEAR-POLICY WILL
BE $100,000."
© 1973 Herblock

---

[17] *San Francisco Sunday Examiner and Chronicle,* October 4, 1970, Section A, pp. 1, 8.
[18] Quoted in *San Francisco Sunday Examiner and Chronicle,* August 19, 1973, Section B, p. 3.

got a federal charter in an unusually short time a few months after his contribution to Nixon's re-election.[19]

It is more difficult to use the federal government for patronage. The civil service is professionalized and thus has a strong sense of autonomy and commitment. While this often impedes a President's attempts to control his administration, it also restrains improprieties, as Nixon learned to his sorrow. Since there is more public attention to national politics, civil servants can easily leak information about attempts to use the government for patronage. Subordinates also can simply refuse to follow improper orders from the White House. For example, the Internal Revenue Service often refused or dragged its feet when directed to audit the tax returns of Nixon's "enemies."

MACHINE POLITICS AND THE GROWTH OF PATRONAGE. By now it should be apparent that a vast array of governmental decisions can be used as patronage if the people involved want to do so. Among the most common types of patronage are: jobs, deposits of government funds, insurance, contracts, franchises, bankruptcy receiverships, guardianships of the estates of minors, and zoning variances. In the past, when patronage seemed to consist largely of city jobs passed out by local bosses, patronage was widely regarded as something for poor people, a sort of unofficial welfare system. Today, however, many of the spoils of government go to the middle classes. Poor people are not in the bidding for cable television franchises, or to be court-appointed referees for bankrupt businesses.

As government services have proliferated since the New Deal, the number of opportunities for the exercise of favoritism also has expanded. The essence of *machine politics* is that every government decision is treated not as a matter of routine but as a favor. Naturally, the recipient of the "favor" is obligated to repay it by contributing money or work. As its part of the bargain, the machine performs such services as interceding to speed the bureaucratic process along, to get special treatment for its favorites, or to cut through red tape. New federal welfare programs can be used as a source of patronage to supplement or compete with the established political powers. This is one of the reasons why local politicians have been so eager to put control of antipoverty agencies in city hall. In recent years, a number of candidates have built their campaign organizations with the patronage provided by the federal Office of Economic Opportunity (OEO). Shirley Chisholm, the first black woman elected to the House of Representatives, had her political base in the antipoverty agency in the Bedford-Stuyvesant ghetto in Brooklyn.[20] Some OEO officials wanted to encourage the rise of new political leaders, like Ms. Chisholm.

When political contributions are motivated by policy considerations, we assume that the contributor has bought influence with his gift, that he has the upper hand. But with patronage, the opposite is the case. As we have seen, activity based on patronage is seldom voluntary. Patronage employees

[19] *CQ Weekly Report,* September 2, 1972, p. 2273.
[20] Tolchin and Tolchin, *To the Victor,* pp. 78–79.

are assessed a percentage of their salary; they do not give because they want to. They work in the campaign for the same reason. Sometimes people who do business with the city, county, or state are told bluntly that they must contribute. Usually, though, this reminder is not necessary. This sort of contribution does not buy influence. It is simply a business expense that has to be paid if one wants to do business with the government. For example, Richard Cohen and Jules Witcover observed that "In Maryland, and especially in Baltimore, political contributions were considered part of the overhead, like the monthly bill from Baltimore Gas and Electric."[21] In other words, patronage is participation without influence.

Machine politicians take quite a dim view of participation based on any consideration other than financial gain: "You can't keep an organization together without patronage. Men ain't in politics for nothin'. They want to get somethin' out of it."[22] "Enthusiasm for causes is short-lived, but the necessity of making a living is permanent."[23] These judgments are just as inaccurate as all the premature predictions about the end of patronage. As we shall see, among the various incentives for participation, "enthusiasm for causes" is at least as important as "the necessity of making a living."

IDEOLOGICAL PARTICIPATION

So far we have discussed incentives to political participation that involve expectations of a tangible reward. These include both divisible returns like a paving contract and indivisible ones like defeat of gun control legislation or an increase in the price of milk. Now, let us turn to people who are not motivated by hopes of getting something tangible for themselves or achieving a particular policy goal. Instead, they are idealists, moved to action by their vision of the good, true, and beautiful. They are interested not so much in particular issues as in pursuing through political action their vision of a better society. Occasionally, such a passion may find its momentary focus on a particular issue. This was the case in 1968 and 1972, when the peace issue drew many activists to the McCarthy, Robert Kennedy, and McGovern campaigns. In cases like this, the dividing line between ideologues and policy-oriented activists is dim and fuzzy. The difference might be stated this way: the policy-motivated activists have finite goals. Achieving those goals provides their gratifications. The ideologues may mention specific goals, but in fact they will never be satisfied until they achieve the ideal society they envision.

Of course, ideologues are not limited to one party, one cause, or one side of the ideological spectrum. They are not limited to one social class, either, although they do tend to come largely from the middle and upper

---

[21] Richard M. Cohen and Jules Witcover, *A Heartbeat Away* (New York: Bantam Books, 1974), p. 41.

[22] William L. Riordan, *Plunkitt of Tammany Hall* (New York: McClure, Phillips & Co., 1905), p. 51.

[23] Quoted in Martin Meyerson and Edward C. Banfield, *Politics, Planning and the Public Interest* (New York: The Free Press, 1955), p. 71.

classes. Regardless of whether they are left-wing or right-wing ideologues, political idealists are likely to be well educated and well-to-do. They have the capacity to give both time and money to the causes and candidates they favor. Because they are people who feel strongly about politics, they are capable of sustained attention to detailed and obscure tasks. Like patronage-motivated activists, ideologues are the kind of people who turn out to vote in primaries, attend caucuses in large numbers, pack meetings, go from door to door to register new voters, and perform all the humdrum tasks that generate political power in those obscure aspects of election campaigns that do not get on television or in the headlines.

Although ideologues generally are deeply committed to their ideals, their attention to politics tends to be somewhat sporadic. They are intensely active when a candidate or cause captures their fancy, but at other times they just fade away. The machine politicians, on the other hand, always can count on a high level of activity from their followers because the supporters know that they will lose their jobs, contracts, or whatever if the candidate loses his election.

Ideologues are interested chiefly in national politics, particularly presidential elections. Even House and Senate contests often do not seem important enough to draw the attention of many ideologues. Thus, their influence is greatest when the office at stake is most conspicuous. National politics, on the other hand, is not usually of great concern to machine politicians. The stakes for them are control of patronage, which is located in city hall or the state capitol. Congress is particularly unpromising as a source of patronage, so most machine politicians have little interest in it (see page 312). Although the White House does have some patronage possibilities, these do not loom very high in the calculations of people accustomed to dealing with local concerns. For most machine politicians, national politics is very much a sideshow. This means that the ideologues are left a somewhat clearer field than they would have if they were in competition with the patronage dispensers for control of national offices.

Ideological activists are particularly susceptible to the appeal of candidates who seem to embody ideals. Adlai Stevenson, who ran for the presidency against Eisenhower in 1952 and 1956, was the first of these candidates in the postwar era. His eloquence and ability to articulate sophisticated commitment to civic virtue drew many thousands of eager volunteers into active participation in the Democratic party. Stevenson was a rather moderate Democrat, but his most conspicuous followers were to be found on the "intellectual" liberal wing of the party. In 1960, when Kennedy ran against Nixon, neither candidate seemed to ignite the same sort of intense ideologically-based adulation. But in 1964, ideological politics came to the fore again. This time the active ideologues were on the far right of the Republican party rather than on the left of the Democratic party. Hundreds of thousands of political newcomers actively supported Barry Goldwater's challenge to the bipartisan consensus about the welfare state and coexistence with the Soviet Union. In 1968, the idealistic "amateur" politicians were to be found once again on the left wing of the Democratic party. Legions of mostly youthful supporters labored on behalf of Eugene McCarthy's unsuccessful campaign for the Democratic nomination. The left wing of the Democratic party was the scene of amateur activity again in 1972, when George McGovern captured the Democratic nomination on the crest of a wave of idealistic enthusiasm. McGovern's nomination was a stunning upset, but his landslide defeat by Nixon was quite predictable. Indeed, from Stevenson through Goldwater to McCarthy and McGovern, ideological candidates have compiled a track record that shows they can mobilize intense support among activists but are unable to achieve broad enough appeal to the electorate as a whole to win office.

Apparently so unlike, all of these candidates appealed to their supporters in ways that were very similar in style, if not in content. Political scientists who studied Goldwater and McCarthy delegates at their respective nominating conventions were struck by their similar approaches to politics, which they label "purist." Compare the following descriptions of Goldwater's and McCarthy's appeal:

> It was not so much his [Goldwater's] principles (though these were undoubtedly important) but the belief that he stuck to them that counted most with his supporters. "He can be trusted." "He is straightforward." "He does not compromise." "He doesn't pander to the public; he's against expediency." . . . The purists manifested amazingly little interest in specific issues. In our interviews at the convention, we simply could not get them to talk about anything concrete. . . . The purists did express strong belief in the importance of being interested in issues, but this is not equivalent to being interested in specific issues.[24]

> These political purists consider . . . compromise and bargaining, conciliating the opposition, bending a little to capture public support—to be hypocritical; their style relies on the announcement of principles and on moral crusades. Since it is difficult to make public policy or to win elections without compromising one's self in some way, there is an understandable tendency for purist political leaders to adopt a highly critical view of the main activities of American politics. . . .

> Since McCarthy's integrity was his stock in trade, his supporters were concerned that he remain pure at all times. Many of his supporters eagerly assured us that "McCarthy wouldn't sell out. He wouldn't compromise. He won't accept the Vice Presidency with Humphrey." On hearing McCarthy say that he would support neither Humphrey or Nixon, a delegate leaped up and cried out, "What a man! What a man! What guts he has!" Telling established powers where to go was dear to the hearts of McCarthy men.[25]

THE NERVE CENTER
OF THE MCGOVERN
CAMPAIGN AT THE
DEMOCRATIC NA-
TIONAL CONVEN-
TION, MIAMI, 1972.
Wide World Photos

[24] Aaron B. Wildavsky, "The Goldwater Phenomenon: Purists, Politicians, and the Two-Party System," *The Review of Politics*, 27 (July 1965), 393–94, 402.

[25] Nelson W. Polsby and Aaron B. Wildavsky, *Presidential Elections*, 3rd ed. (New York: Charles Scribner's Sons, 1971), pp. 36–37, 41–42.

Criticizing "established powers" and "the establishment" is something that purists of all kinds seem fond of. The Goldwater enthusiasts of the 1960s and the Ronald Reagan fans of the 1960s and 1970s condemn "politics as usual" and depict themselves as outsiders trying to clean up a political system hopelessly corrupted by compromise. Indeed, when Reagan first ran for public office in 1966, he called himself a "citizen candidate" to differentiate himself from "ordinary politicians." Even after eight years as Governor of California and one unsuccessful try for the Republican presidential nomination, he still insisted that he was not a politician as he tried again for the nomination. By the same token, the purists of the left challenge the evils of "the establishment" and rival their ultraconservative counterparts in vilifying "politicians."

All this talk about being outsiders should not lead one to think that purists are actually outside the mainstream of American society. As we have said, purism is largely a middle-class phenomenon. And there are even plenty of purist millionaires, with all varieties of ideological persuasions. The late H. L. Hunt, an ultraconservative billionaire, was one of the best known purist fat cats, but there have been many others who spent immense sums of money out of ideological sympathy for conservative, moderate, liberal, and radical candidates of both major parties and some minor parties as well. The notion that the "big money" contributors are all on the conservative and Republican side needs re-examination. The left wing and the right wing both have their own financial angels. Consider the case of Nicholas H. Noyes, an heir to the Eli Lilly pharmaceutical fortune, who gave $7,000 to the Nixon campaign in 1972 while two of his grandsons furnished McGovern $400,000.[26]

A striking illustration of the ideological commitment of many large contributors is provided by an extraordinary letter written in 1968 by Stewart Mott, the son of one of the founders of General Motors, a multimillionaire in his own right, and a very generous contributor to liberal and radical causes. Mott was probably the most important contributor to the McCarthy campaign and wanted to continue his role in Democratic politics after McCarthy failed to win the nomination. Yet, because his motivation was largely ideological, he was unwilling to contribute to the campaign of Hubert Humphrey, the Democratic nominee, unless he was satisfied with Humphrey on ideological grounds. The following excerpts from a letter he wrote to Humphrey in October of 1968 make clear the ideological nature of his commitment:

> I've spent over $325,000 this year in politics. . . . Yet I am still not convinced that I should give money and time to your campaign. . . . The least we on the McCarthy Finance Committee could do for you would be to give you a hearing—a personal private interview of an hour's length—in order to question you about our own view of the nation's future and what it ought to be. We will be meeting

[26] *CQ Weekly Report*, October 6, 1973, p. 2658.

you next Wednesday evening with an open mind and a sense of fair-play. . . . We realize that you would like to have us contribute towards your campaign, but you should not expect an immediate decision from any of us, checkbook-in-hand. . . . We have the capacity to give $1,000,000 or more to your campaign—and raise twice or three times that amount. But we will each make our own individual judgements on the basis of how you answer our several questions and how you conduct your campaign in the coming weeks.[27]

SOCIABILITY, PRESTIGE, AND FRIENDSHIP

Many organizations formed for a particular purpose produce social by-products for their members. Companies, schools, churches, unions, and military units are not only purposive organizations but also social groups. That is, they provide a social environment in which people interact and from which they derive the gratifications that come from a sense of belonging and the pleasures of friendship. Political groups are no exception to this rule. Although some are "membership organizations" which involve no face-to-face interaction, others provide opportunities for social relationships. This is true both of the so-called "old-fashioned" clubhouses based on patronage and the ultramodern "amateur" clubs of trendy young ideologues.

Amateur clubs in California stage dances, parties, boat trips, and a variety of other social activities. Like many college extracurricular activities, they provide a way for men to meet women, and vice versa. One of the most powerful of such ideological clubs is the Democratic group in New York City's Greenwich Village. The political clout of this group is indicated by the fact that it overthrew Carmine DeSapio, the last really famous boss of Tammany Hall. Yet the club is not all business. One of its subcommittees is devoted to planning charter flights to Europe for club members.

For some of their members, political organizations provide an important social environment. They become special "worlds," with their own sources of prestige and gratification. Consider the case of one particular party activist in New Haven who aspired to greater acceptance and prestige in the special world of the Democratic machine. To make himself seem more important, he told his friends that he could fix their parking tickets. In fact, he lacked the influence to do this. Instead, he paid his friends' tickets with his own money and bathed in his reputation as a fixer. This man is like many people who fill unremunerative political positions out of a need for recognition or status. There are many thousands of such honorific posts at every level of American government. These posts do not confer money or power on the people who hold them. But they do confer status.

The most elevated of these positions in the federal government are ambassadorships. Ambassadors are treated with great deference on ceremonial and social occasions. They are in demand as dinner guests, live in ornate

---

[27] Quoted in Herbert E. Alexander, *Financing the 1968 Election* (Lexington, Mass.: D. C. Heath & Company, 1971), pp. 263–64.

houses, and can, if they wish, spend most of their time being adulated by social-climbing residents wherever they happen to be. It has been a tradition in the United States to appoint campaign contributors to these posts, thus rewarding their monetary help with positions providing unique ceremonial rewards. In the nineteenth century, when both American foreign policy and American public opinion were isolationist, this practice was not as damaging as might be thought. Although we have abandoned isolationism in recent years, this old tradition is still very much alive. Indeed, the exchange of ambassadorships for political contributions is an important source of financial support to the president's party. This practice is tacitly accepted by both parties. Although the President's nominees must be confirmed by the Senate, there seldom is any partisan conflict about this, even when one party has the White House and the other controls Congress.[28]

Fortunately, even though this practice puts individuals who are not particularly qualified in charge of some of our foreign embassies, a number of modern developments have reduced the importance of ambassadors, with the result that this practice is hardly more dangerous than it was in the past. Instantaneous global communications and jet travel have drastically limited the discretion of the person on the spot, who often is little more than a mouthpiece for instructions sent from the State Department. What is more, the development of a career Foreign Service means that a politically appointed ambassador can turn his serious diplomatic duties over to the professionals, leaving him free to concentrate on such non-sensitive duties as attending social affairs, participating in various ceremonies, and "meeting the ordinary citizens" of the host country.

[28] See the *San Francisco Chronicle*, February 26, 1974, p. 1, and June 28, 1974, p. 13.

AMBASSADORS AND MONEY

A list of eight American ambassadors and their contributions to Nixon's 1972 re-election campaign:

COUNTRY	AMBASSADOR	CONTRIBUTION
Great Britain	Walter H. Annenberg	$250,000
Switzerland	Shelby Davis	$100,000
Luxembourg	Ruth L. Farkas	$300,000
Belgium	Leonard K. Firestone	$112,600
Netherlands	Kingdon Gould	$100,900
Austria	John F. Humes	$100,000
France	John N. Irwin II	$50,500
France	Arthur K. Watson	$300,000
Ireland	John D. Moore	$10,442
TOTAL		$1,324,442

Source: Congressional Quarterly Service, *Dollar Politics*, Vol. 2 (Washington, D.C.: Congressional Quarterly Inc., 1974), p. 15.

As elsewhere in the netherworld of politics, the Nixon administration was more explicit, thoroughgoing, and organized about trading ambassadorships for money than previous administrations. After his re-election, Nixon appointed eight noncareer envoys who had given over $700,000 to his campaign. All told, noncareer ambassadors gave over $1.8 million to Nixon in 1972, and six more people, who contributed over $3 million, were actively seeking such posts. In 1974, Herbert Kalmbach, Nixon's personal attorney and one of his major fund-raisers, was convicted of selling ambassadorships. It is a violation of federal law to offer public employment as a reward for anything done to help a party in an election campaign. This law is generally ignored. Kalmbach was a victim of the heightened sense of public morality that followed Watergate. In a sense, too, his downfall is attributable to the systematic way that he and other Nixonites expanded on traditional political practices.

Americans seem to be of two minds about public life. On the one hand, "politics" and "politicians" have very unfavorable connotations to most people. On the other hand, Presidents, senators, representatives, governors, and mayors all find that their offices convey enormous prestige. The prestige of these public officials is so great that many people want very much to cultivate their friendship for reasons that have nothing to do with getting special treatment from the government. It is a genuine status symbol to have personal contact with a major political official, to call him by his first name, to be invited to a dinner or reception where other famous people will be present, to feel able to invite the official to one's own social affairs. There are people who value such symbols enough to pay for them by contributing money.

Some wealthy people like to cultivate the friendship of artists, to spend time with artists, and to be accepted by them as patrons of the arts. Others have the same feelings about actors, baseball players, authors, or even gangsters. And some rich people like to hang around with politicians, to be able to feel that they are "on the inside." Politicians know this, of course, and exploit these ambitions in order to raise funds, using their own time and presence for promotional purposes much as movie stars do.

Most major political figures have backers of this sort, who ask for little more than a chance to bask in their hero's reflected glory. The most famous contemporary hero-worshiper is probably W. Clement Stone, an enormously wealthy insurance man whose hero was Richard Nixon, to whose presidential campaigns he contributed about $5 million. There are no indications that Stone was trying to influence government policy or that he made demands on Nixon in return for his gifts. The motivation behind Stone's generosity seems to have been just what he said it was: "Simply by issuing a check you become a part of a great man's life."[29]

Each party has its traditional fat cats, who seem to contribute out of a sense of civic duty, rather like helping support a local ballet company, repertory theater, university, or orphanage. Such "checkbook Democrats"

---

[29] Quoted in *National Journal*, January 22, 1972, p. 133.

and "checkbook Republicans" usually can be counted on in the general election. In primary struggles to get the nomination, they are one of the major targets of prenomination strategy, just like major population blocs and interest groups.

The glamor and excitement of political life and the ties of friendship often combine to provide political candidates with surprisingly loyal organizations. Indeed, the personal loyalties directed at political figures are often strong enough to survive fundamental changes in ideological direction by the candidate. Representative Paul N. McCloskey, a maverick Republican from California, entrusted much of his fund raising and constituency organizing to friends and neighbors with quite conservative beliefs. As McCloskey moved farther and farther to the left—even going so far as to run against Nixon for the 1972 Republican nomination—many of these backers stayed loyal to him, thus choosing friendship over ideology.

MONEY IN POLITICS

As we observed earlier, the giving of financial contributions is the most common form of political activity. In 1968, 8.7 million people, or 11 percent of the electorate, gave a total of $300 million to assorted parties and candidates. By 1972, the level of election spending had risen to $425 million. How can we appraise the significance of this fact? From one point of view, it is a symptom of corruption and moral bankruptcy. We often read that "the cost of elections is escalating out of sight," and there can be no doubt that election expenditures in the United States are increasing. No one can deny that $300 million is a great deal of money. But is it too much? Three hundred million dollars was merely one one-thousandth of the cost of government in 1967, or about $1.50 for every adult American. Is this too much to spend on electing over 500,000 officials? One way to answer this question is to look at election costs in other democratic countries. From this point of view, American campaigns are not terribly expensive. The cost per capita in the United States is rather low compared to expenses in most countries with free elections.[30]

The most important questions about campaign contributions are: How important are they? What limitations does the need for money impose on candidates? To what extent does the importance of contributions pervert the constitutional guarantee of political equality? If money were very important, but relatively freely available, then we would be less concerned about the problem. If money were far more available to some kinds of candidates than to others, but not very important in deciding elections, we still would not be so concerned about it. But to the extent that money is both important and restricted, it becomes a threat to the health of the American political system.

[30] The information in this paragraph is from Herbert E. Alexander, *Political Financing* (Minneapolis: Burgess Publishing Co., 1972), pp. 33, 38–39.

Let us explore both of these problems, to see the extent to which money is important in determining the outcome of political campaigns and the extent to which its availability is limited. Throughout this discussion, the reader should bear in mind that legislation enacted in 1974 imposes limits on campaign spending and provides federal funding for presidential candidates. Although we shall describe these new laws shortly, we must realize that at present there is no way to predict how they will work out in practice. In reading any discussion of campaign financing, one should also remember that until passage of the Federal Election Campaign Act of 1971, which took effect on April 7, 1972, the laws requiring reporting of campaign contributions were easily evaded. This means that reliable information is often scarce.[31] The most authoritative source in this murky area is the Citizens' Research Foundation, a private nonprofit institution whose director, Herbert E. Alexander, is acknowledged as the country's leading expert on campaign funding.

HOW THE LAWS WERE EVADED

For generations, various laws limited the amounts of money that could be received by candidates, required that contributions be reported, and prohibited donations from corporations and labor unions in federal elections. As a practical matter, these laws did not seriously interfere with anyone's desire either to get or to give campaign contributions. The limits on donations, for example, applied to individual campaign committees and were commonly evaded by establishing dozens of committees for a single candidate, each of which could accept the legal maximum contribution.

The prohibition on contributions by corporations was evaded in several ways. Many firms have programs to solicit contributions from their executives, collect their checks into substantial bundles, ranging over the $100,000 level, and then bestow them on a candidate with a clear message about what firm all the contributors work for. One variation on this technique is to combine the bundles from several firms. By means of this technique, the Bankers' Political Action Committee raised more than $200,000 in 1970. In all fairness, it should be added that a few corporations have impartial plans to encourage their employees to help support the party of the employee's choice.

The second way to get around the law is to give executives inflated bonuses or expense account payments with the understanding that the extra money will be given to a designated candidate. Once paid to the executive, the money becomes part of his own private resources rather than corporate funds. A vice president of the International Telephone

---

[31] We have some information on 1972 as a result of a lawsuit by Common Cause, an interest group concerned with governmental reform. The Common Cause suit forced revelation of the contributions that were made to the Nixon campaign prior to April 7, 1972. A total of $19.9 million was given before then, in many cases by people who believed that their donations would remain secret. These early payments included eleven separate contributions of $40,000 or more *in cash*. See *CQ Weekly Report*, October 6, 1973, pp. 2659–60.

and Telegraph Corporation reported that he was told by another executive that ITT was giving to both parties "to butter both sides so we'll be in a good position whoever wins." Therefore, the vice president was told,

> [The chairman of the board] has given me a selected list of top executives to contribute to the election campaign. You are down for $1,200. This can be financed for you by the company if necessary. . . . You will be expected to recover the amount by covering it up in your travel expense account.[32]

These evasions are so commonplace a part of American political practice that it would seem quite unnecessary for any company to break the law by giving its own money directly, rather than "laundering" it as we have described. Yet strange as it might seem, some firms do manage to avoid the gaping loopholes in the Corrupt Practices Act. Eighteen corporations were prosecuted for giving a total of $832,500 in corporate funds to the Nixon campaign in 1972. One of these illegal gifts, $150,000 from the Northrop Corporation, also broke another law forbidding contributions from government contractors. Northrop and its chairman of the board, Thomas V. Jones, were each fined $5,000. The judge explained that Jones might have been sent to jail, but for the fact that the law under which he was convicted had never been enforced before.[33]

Corporations also get around the Corrupt Practices Act by donating goods and services to campaigners. For example, a company can contribute indirectly by paying its own public relations consultant, advertising agency, or law firm for services performed for a candidate.

This sort of "in-kind" contribution is, however, more commonly the practice of labor unions. Like corporations, they have not found the laws a serious impediment to their political activity. As we have seen earlier in this chapter, unions can mobilize thousands of people for campaign work. Many unions train some of their members as campaign organizers and dispatch these people around the country to help—or even take over—the campaign of a favored candidate. The unions also can give money through their "education committees." The most important of these is the AFL-CIO's Committee on Political Education (COPE), which is a formidable political instrument and a major power center in the Democratic party. Such committees are supported by what are politely called "voluntary contributions" from union members. These are not always free-will offerings, even though the unions, unlike the corporations, cannot offset the contributions with padded expense accounts. Money can be spent directly from union coffers for such supposedly nonpolitical purposes as voter registration campaigns,

---

[32] Quoted in Jack Anderson, with George Clifford, *The Anderson Papers* (New York: Random House, 1973), p. 21.

[33] *San Francisco Sunday Examiner and Chronicle*, July 14, 1974, Section A, p. 15; *San Francisco Chronicle*, May 2, 1974, p. 10, and May 14, 1974, p. 1. Part of the Northrop contribution was a $50,000 cash payment used to reimburse the seven men convicted of breaking into the Democratic National Committee offices in the Watergate building.

get-out-the-vote drives on election day, and publicizing the voting records of members of Congress. In 1972, total campaign spending by labor was almost identical to the amount given by business and professional groups. Each gave about $9.4 million.[34]

WHO GIVES MONEY AND WHO GETS IT?

Three reliable generalizations can be made about the types of candidates who do best in getting contributions. (1) Republicans get more than Democrats. (2) Incumbents get more than challengers. (3) Expected winners get more than people who are expected to lose.

Of course, these criteria are not necessarily consistent with each other; there are no hard and fast guidelines enabling us to predict who will get more money when an incumbent Democrat faces a Republican challenger. We can readily see, however, that generalizations 2 and 3 are closely related to each other. Incumbents do better than challengers because, having been in office, they have had an opportunity to form alliances with potential contributors. The executive secretary of one powerful interest group explained why his organization would support friendly incumbents no matter how attractive their opponents looked: "We have no choice but to support those showing loyal service rather than those who show promise. A high seniority friend is better than a low seniority one."[35] Incumbents also have an advantage in fund raising because, as we shall see in Chapter 10, the statistical probability that an incumbent congressman will be re-elected is very high. Thus the incumbent is usually favored to win simply because he is the incumbent. Quite naturally, many potential contributors feel that money given to a loser is money wasted. The incumbent, in short, can count on a high level of support both because he has had years in which to make himself useful to potential contributors and because he is likely to win. The challenger, on the other hand, suffers from being less well known and less likely to win.

As helpful as our three generalizations are in explaining the give and take of political fund raising, there are some other significant factors which must be considered. One of these, obviously, is the personal wealth of the candidate and his or her immediate family. Clearly, a Kennedy or Rockefeller is better off than, say, a Humphrey. Nor do our three rules take account of the candidate's skill at fund raising. Contributions do not just happen. Like anything else, they are the result of work and organization. And some people are a great deal more skilled at the kinds of work involved than others. The Kennedy-Humphrey contest for the Democratic presidential nomination in 1960 is instructive. Not only was Humphrey contending against a family worth hundreds of millions of dollars, but he also was badly outmatched on the nuts-and-bolts business of raising money.

---

[34] Herbert E. Alexander, *Financing the 1972 Election* (Lexington, Mass: Heath-Lexington Books, 1975).

[35] Quoted in *CQ Weekly Report*, June 1, 1974, p. 1415.

Figure 7–2 shows the expenditures by each party on presidential campaigns from 1932 through 1972. With one exception, Republicans have always spent more than Democrats on presidential campaigns. The size of the Republican financial advantage has fluctuated enormously, from a slight margin in some years to an overwhelming lead in others. In recent congressional elections, however, Democrats have actually spent more money than Republicans. In 1974, for example, in all contested House and Senate races combined, Democrats spent a total of $38.4 million compared to $32.5 million for Republicans.

It seems likely that the higher level of Democratic spending in 1974 reflects our second and third generalizations: incumbents and expected

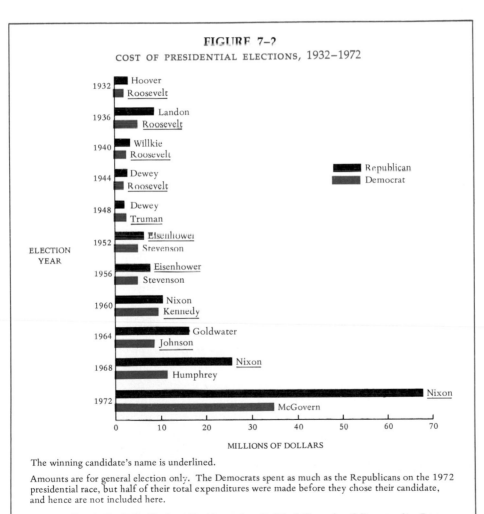

FIGURE 7–2
COST OF PRESIDENTIAL ELECTIONS, 1932–1972

The winning candidate's name is underlined.

Amounts are for general election only. The Democrats spent as much as the Republicans on the 1972 presidential race, but half of their total expenditures were made before they chose their candidate, and hence are not included here.

Sources: For 1932–1968, Herbert E. Alexander, *Political Financing* (Minneapolis: Burgess Publishing Co., 1972), p. 6; for 1972, Herbert E. Alexander, *Financing the 1972 Election* (Lexington, Mass.: Heath-Lexington Books, 1975).

winners do better. The Democrats had a healthy majority in both houses of Congress before the election, and 1974 was widely and accurately considered a Democratic year. The average Democratic incumbent spent more than twice as much as his Republican challenger. Republican incumbents, on the other hand, had about a three-to-two financial advantage over their Democratic opponents. Two years earlier, incumbents of both parties likewise had almost twice as much money as their challengers. Republicans were a bit further ahead of their challengers than Democrats in 1972, perhaps because that was a Republican year.[36]

Most complaints about the role of money in politics assume that conservative candidates have an enormous advantage because most wealthy people tend to be conservative. Although this accusation contains a germ of truth, it misses so much of the reality of American politics as to be more misleading than helpful. The best way to make our argument is by example.

The two top spenders in the 1974 congressional elections were both incumbent liberal Democratic senators. Alan Cranston, a Democrat from California, the largest state in the country, spent $1,336,000 as he took 60 percent of the vote. This works out to about 33 cents for every vote Cranston received. The next biggest spender was George McGovern of South Dakota. Coming from one of the smallest states in the nation, McGovern spent $1,173,000 as he squeaked to a third term with 53 percent of the vote. McGovern spent $7.93 for every vote he got, by far the highest ratio in 1974. In all probability, the bulk of his contributions came from outside South Dakota, motivated by the same ideological fervor that had made McGovern his party's presidential nominee in 1972.

The most heavily financed House election was in the Chicago suburbs, where a liberal Democrat named Abner Mikva spent $286,000 to defeat a Republican incumbent, Samuel Young, whose campaign cost $215,000. Only one Republican representative spent more than Young and he, too, lost. Two Democrats spent more than Mikva. Both are independently wealthy liberals and both won.[37]

These cases suggest an important generalization about money in politics. *There is no necessary connection between a candidate's ideological inclination, the size of the contributions he receives, or the total amount of his financial backing.* Rightwingers do not invariably enjoy huge campaign budgets, nor do liberals or radicals have to limp along with nickels and dimes contributed by "ordinary people." Barry Goldwater was unquestionably the most conservative politician to win a major party's presidential nomination in the modern era. His opponent, Lyndon Johnson, was responsible for the greatest increase in social welfare legislation in a generation. Yet Goldwater was the first candidate to develop broadly based financial backing. Scarcely a fourth of his money was from donations of $500 or more, while 69 percent of Johnson's campaign funds came in such substantial chunks.[38]

[36] *San Francisco Chronicle,* September 14, 1973, p. 7, and April 11, 1975, p. 16.

[37] The data on expenditures in House and Senate races in 1974 are reported in the *San Francisco Chronicle,* April 11, 1975, p. 16.

[38] Herbert E. Alexander, *Financing the 1964 Election* (Princeton, N. J.: Citizens Research Foundation, 1966), pp. 70, 84.

In 1968, there were two major challenges by political outsiders, Eugene McCarthy from the left and George C. Wallace from the right. McCarthy's campaign for the Democratic presidential nomination was inspired and carried along by an articulate minority's profound opposition to the Viet-

---

QUESTIONS WITHOUT ANSWERS

The difference between a campaign contribution and a bribe is often very dim. Trying to explore the difference illustrates the ethical ambiguities that surround this subject. The legal distinction is clear. If a politician uses a contribution for professional expenses—either in his campaign or to supplement his office budget—he does not have to declare it as income and pay tax on it. If a politician takes money and uses it for personal expenses, he has to declare it as income. To most people, taking money to cover political expenses seems innocent enough, but taking money for personal use smacks of corruption. But if a politician's career is the most important thing in the world to him, money for his campaign is much more important than money for fast cars or fancy houses. Thus, despite the tax laws, should not a campaign contribution be considered another form of bribery?

On the other hand, don't citizens have the right to help elect the candidate of their choice? One form of help is giving money. Can we condemn a congressman who votes a certain way because he expects to get a campaign contribution if he does? To be consistent, wouldn't we also have to condemn the person or group that gave the contribution? But if we do, aren't we denying the potential contributor his right to help the candidate of his choice?

What is the morality of contributions motivated by ethnic solidarity? Senator Abraham Ribicoff, a liberal Democrat from Connecticut, explained that he could sponsor legislation opposed by Connecticut interests because "My money comes from what I call emotional money, wealthy Jewish liberals from New York who like to see a good Jewish boy in the Senate."* Can we then say that the Jewish contributors from New York have bribed a senator whose primary concern should be the interests of Connecticut? James Abourezk of South Dakota is the first Senator of Arab descent. In his first year in the Senate, he received $49,425 in speaking fees, largely from Lebanese-American groups. Just four speeches to such bodies earned him a total of $29,335.47. He used $30,000 of the proceeds of his lecturing for office expenses.** Was he being bribed to take a pro-Arab position on issues involving Middle Eastern affairs?

* Quoted in Tolchin & Tolchin, *To the Victor*, p. 241.
**Congressional Quarterly, *Financial Disclosures by Members of Congress* (Washington: Congressional Quarterly, Inc., 1974), pp. 1, 4, 32.

nam war. His active supporters came almost wholly from the liberal-to-radical side of the political spectrum. McCarthy raised $11 million in his futile pursuit of the nomination—almost as much as Humphrey spent in the general election campaign against Nixon. What is more, a significant share of this backing came from a few very large contributors, most of whom were new to bigtime political giving. For example, $2.5 million came from only fifty people. Indeed, liberal members of the Wall Street legal and financial community were particularly prominent in McCarthy's fund raising. Herbert Alexander concluded, "It is probably fair to say that because most McCarthy money was contributed for ideological or Vietnam-policy-related reasons, it represented probably more money less touched with vested interest than in most other campaigns."[39]

The McCarthy case discredits the myth that liberal and left-wing candidates cannot hope to receive large campaign contributions. Let us now look briefly at the Wallace campaign to see whether the counterpart myth holds true on the conservative side. Although Wallace was certainly as far to the right as any recent presidential candidate, his financial backing was much more broadly based than any other candidate's. He raised about $7 million, far less than the liberal McCarthy, and he got it from five times as many contributors. Less than 15 percent of Wallace's financial backing came in contributions of $100 or more. The same pattern of broad-based support could be seen in Wallace's fund raising for the 1976 presidential campaign. Fully 90 percent of the money he received in 1974 was in amounts of $100 or less.[40] In other words, the notion that conservative candidates can count on large contributions from wealthy donors is as erroneous as the belief that liberals cannot get that kind of money from that kind of contributor.

THE DIRECT MAIL REVOLUTION

For generations, some politicians deplored their reliance on the rich and tried to broaden their financial base by appealing to small contributors. These efforts invariably failed. Indeed, they often were losing propositions. The cost of raising political money in small amounts sometimes exceeded the return. Thus, one of the conventional political maxims was that appealing to small donors was a will-o'-the-wisp—probably a nice idea, but impractical.

This maxim was scrapped in 1964, when the Goldwater campaign reaped a golden harvest of small contributions from hundred of thousands of people. Goldwater got a third of his funds from direct mail and an additional 14 percent from televised appeals.[41] In fact, Ronald Reagan's political career was launched by his extraordinarily effective television appearance on Goldwater's behalf.

---

[39] Alexander, *Financing the 1968 Election*, pp. 43–44, 45. It should be noted that McCarthy also received about 150,000 small contributions.

[40] Alexander, *Financing the 1968 Election*, pp. 158–60; and *CQ Weekly Report*, February 2, 1975, p. 403.

[41] Herbert E. Alexander, "Financing the Parties and Campaigns," in Milton C. Cummings, ed., *The National Election of 1964* (Washington: The Brookings Institution, 1966), pp. 178–79.

HOUSE OF REPRESENTATIVES
WASHINGTON, D.C.

MORRIS K. UDALL
ARIZONA

Dear Friend:

Do you <u>really</u> mean it when you tell elected officials, like me, that you want to be told the truth?

Do you <u>really</u> want us to give you the cold, uncompromising facts without sugar coating?

Because... if I become President, I'm going to tell it exactly like it is. And for starters, I'll tell you right now that the only way you and I and all America will ever overcome our current economic and energy crises is to acknowledge the painful truth that <u>we must change our way of life</u>.

Dear Congressman Udall...

Enclosed is my investment in your campaign for the Presidency.

☐ $10   ☐ $25   ☐ $50   ☐ $100   ☐ $250   Other $_____

Name_____

Address_____   Make checks payable to:
UDALL '76 COMMITTEE

City_____ State_____ Zip_____

Occupation and Employer's Name (This information is needed to comply with the Federal Election Campaign Act.)

☐ I would also like to volunteer some time for the campaign; call me at_____

Help Us Double Your Contribution.

When you fill in the above information, your contribution—up to the first $250—will qualify for matching funds from the federal government under the new election reform laws.

Your Tax Benefit Is Now Doubled.

You can now deduct your contribution to the Udall '76 Campaign from your federal income tax in either of two ways:

1. You can subtract one-half of your contribution (up to a maximum of $50 on a joint return; $25 if you file separately) directly from your federal tax. This means you get back $1 for every $2 contributed regardless of your tax bracket because this is a credit to your final tax bill.

2. You can declare your contribution (up to a maximum of $200 on a joint return; $100 if you file separately) just as you would a charitable gift.

A copy of our report is filed with the Federal Election Commission and is available for purchase from the Federal Commission, Washington, D.C.

Goldwater's fund raisers succeeded by transferring to politics techniques that had been developed in advertising. Commercial advertisers had vastly expanded their use of direct mail advertisements mailed to selected prospects. The key to this explosion was the computer, which makes possible the storage and retrieval of information about potential customers. The raw material of computerized mailings is provided by magazine subscription lists, records of donors to particular charities, organization membership rosters, and the like. Magazines, charities, book clubs, and many other organizations sell their membership lists to direct mail advertisers or to "list brokers." Even the United Nations International Childrens Emergency Fund (UNICEF) sells its lists of Christmas card purchasers. Such lists permit an advertiser to direct his appeal at a tailor-made audience of people whose interest in a particular subject, product, or activity has been demonstrated by their previous purchases, contributions, or affiliations. The computer breakthrough led to enormously increased sophistication in preparing the messages used in direct mail advertising.

These skills, developed for commercial purposes, were now applied to political fund raising. Politicians have always kept and jealously guarded their mailing lists, which contain the names of people who have given money in the past, have written a letter of complaint or praise, are known to be sympathetic, have gotten a favor, are related to a patronage employee, and so on. Computerizing these lists makes them infinitely more usable, and also lets the politician add, delete, and classify the names on his list far more easily.

Nixon's 1968 campaign followed up on Goldwater's success by raising almost $9 million by direct mail. The Democrats were slower to catch on to this new technique. In 1972, however, they far exceeded the Republicans in their use of this newfangled medium. One of McGovern's greatest resources in his presidential campaign came from a chance encounter in 1971 with an Alabama lawyer named Morris Dees. Having just sold his direct mail advertising business for several million dollars, Dees had a good deal of time on his hands. Deeply impressed by McGovern's positions on the issues, Dees joined the McGovern campaign and took charge of direct mail fund raising. Thanks in good measure to Dees, McGovern's campaign escaped the financial anemia that had plagued Humphrey in 1968. He received $20 million from direct mail appeals.[42]

Direct mail has no ideological boundaries. Any serious candidate will have a base of support from which substantial financial backing can be raised by this technique. From the politician's standpoint, direct mail has the advantage of providing money without commitments to the contributors. The average donation is only ten to twenty-five dollars, and there is no continuing interaction between the candidate and the contributor.

If direct mail fund raising has been successful in the past, we can expect it to be even more successful in the future. Changes in the tax laws to encourage campaign contributions are likely to enhance the return from direct mail appeals to small donors. Contributors receive a tax credit for half

[42] This figure was revealed by Dees in a letter to *Newsweek,* December 23, 1974, p. 4.

the amount of campaign contributions, up to a maximum credit of fifty dollars for a joint return or twenty-five dollars for a single return. Thus a married couple who contribute $100 can deduct half this amount from the tax they owe the government. Or the entire amount of the contribution can be deducted from income, just like a charitable contribution. In this case there is a $200 limit on a joint return.

DOES MONEY BUY ELECTIONS?

The most obvious way to answer this question is to see whether better financed candidates are more likely to win. The difficulty with this approach is separating cause and effect. Did Jones win because he had more money, or did he have more money because he was expected to win? Or did both his victory and his success at fund raising result from some third factor, such as better organization or more vigorous campaigning? We have seen already that some sorts of contributors like to invest in winners. Thus it is not surprising to find that often a candidate is a fund-raising success because he is a winner, not the other way around. Indeed, candidates who win unexpectedly usually get a flood of checks dated before election day, often with lame explanations like, "My secretary forgot to mail this to you last week."

Even taking this into account, however, a glance at Figure 7–2 will reveal that the bigger spender does not necessarily win presidential elections. Of the eleven elections from 1932 through 1972, the candidate who spent the most won five times and lost six. Except for 1948, Republicans always spent more. If money could buy victory, Harry Truman would be the only Democratic President since Woodrow Wilson, and Franklin Roosevelt, John F. Kennedy, and Lyndon Johnson would have been losers.

Furthermore, it does not appear that most of the Republican victories were a result of bigger campaign budgets. Eisenhower's popularity and his promise to end the Korean War could not have been overcome in 1952 by any conceivable Democratic campaign spending. And McGovern's loss in 1972 was hardly a consequence of poverty. The only modern presidential election where money may have made a difference was in 1968. Nixon outspent Humphrey by more than two to one, and won the election by a scant half million votes. It is unusual for a candidate to lack the irreducible minimum of money, but it appears that Humphrey was in this plight several times in 1968. His advertising campaign was far behind schedule because he could not make even a down payment to an advertising agency to begin reserving space in the mass media. In October, at the peak of the campaign, the Democrats had to cancel much of their scheduled radio and television advertising because they lacked the money to pay for it. In fact, Humphrey's organizers could not even buy lapel buttons and bumper stickers until the end of September.[43] Despite these handicaps, Humphrey

[43] Alexander, *Financing the 1968 Eelction*, pp. 64, 85, 101.

MARGARET CHASE
SMITH, INCUMBENT
SENATOR FROM
MAINE, WAS DE-
FEATED IN 1972 BY
AN OPPONENT WHO
OUTSPENT HER IN
HIS CAMPAIGN BY A
RATIO OF MORE
THAN 13 TO 1.
Wide World Photos

staged a last-minute rush that almost wiped out the enormous lead that Nixon had enjoyed since the early summer. The bitter fight within the Democratic party kept many wealthy purists from contributing, as Stewart Mott's letter indicates (see pp. 183–184). Even in this case it is difficult to say with certainty that finances determined the election outcome. Humphrey may have suffered on election day because of his lack of money. To some extent, however, his financial straits were the *result* of his dim prospects of victory. The public opinion polls showing Nixon's immense early lead discouraged many potential contributors from investing in Humphrey's campaign.

Efforts to unravel the effects of campaign spending in congressional elections are obscured by the tendency for incumbents to be re-elected and to get greater contributions than their challengers. Many incumbents feel so secure that they spend virtually nothing. Margaret Chase Smith was re-elected to the Senate from Maine several times on little more than the $10,000 she received from the Republican Senate Campaign Committee. In 1972, running for her fifth term at the age of seventy-four, she spent only $14,950. She was upset by a vigorous young Democratic candidate who spent $202,208.[44] Although her age may have had something to do with her defeat, it is also hard to escape the suspicion that being outspent by a ratio of more than thirteen to one helped insure her loss.

Money is more important in primaries than in general elections. These contests are more obscure and party identification—the major guideline in general elections—is not relevant. When several candidates contend for their party's nomination, none is likely to be known to most of the voters. The candidates with ample treasuries can afford extensive publicity campaigns to bring their names to everyone's attention. In the 1970 Democratic primary in New York, four major candidates battled for the senatorial nomination. The winner was Representative Richard Ottinger, who spent around $2 million on his primary campaign, compared to a total of $353,200 spent by his three opponents. Although Ottinger may have bought the primary, he was unsuccessful in the general election, where he spent another $2 million. If he did not get to the Senate, he at least had the distinction of having waged the most expensive Senate campaign in history. Ottinger could afford it, however. Most of his budget came from his family, the heirs to the U.S. Plywood Corporation fortune.[45]

Of course, not all candidates have such splendid backing. Fortunately, there are substitutes for money. One is fame. Someone who is already well known does not have as much need for lavish advertising and mass media expenditures. And no matter how famous a candidate is or how much money he has, he cannot buy a political organization that registers voters and then gets them to the polls on election day. For these tasks he needs a dedicated army of supporters. Interpersonal campaigning of this kind has long been a favorite tactic of patronage-based machines and of labor

---

[44] Alexander, *Political Financing*, p. 1; *CQ Weekly Report*, December 1, 1973, p. 3130.

[45] Congressional Quarterly Service, *Dollar Politics* (Washington: Congressional Quarterly, Inc., 1971), p. 28; *Newsweek*, May 1, 1972, p. 33; and Herbert E. Alexander, *Money in Politics* (Washington: Public Affairs Press, 1972), pp. 26–27.

unions. It is also one of the hallmarks of the "new politics" associated with ideological candidates ranging from Goldwater to McCarthy and McGovern.

DOES MONEY BUY POLITICAL INFLUENCE?

Sometimes it does and sometimes it does not. Some sorts of contribution do not provide much opportunity for influence. Money raised by direct mail, squeezed from patronage employees, or extracted from contractors as a condition of doing business with the government clearly does not earn any control over policy. Large contributions by policy-oriented groups are another matter. Obviously, such groups are looking to gain influence over policy. Nevertheless, the purpose of the contribution is not so much to buy a friend as it is to elect one. Sometimes the two processes are difficult to separate, as Senator Biden's testimony on the next page illustrates. But as a general rule it is safe to say that the candidate who gets the group's money is the one who would be most likely to be sympathetic to the group's aims anyway.

Politicians seem to be forever disappointing their contributors. One of Theodore Roosevelt's major financial backers was Henry C. Frick, the president of the United States Steel Corporation. Frick was not very happy with his investment in Roosevelt's presidential campaign, however. He felt that Roosevelt's progressive policies were a betrayal of the principles that led Frick to give his support. "He got down on his knees to us," Frick complained. "We bought the son of a bitch and then he did not stay bought."[46]

Perhaps the fundamental wisdom about money and politics is summed up in advice that Jess Unruh, the former Speaker of the California Assembly, gave some members of the state legislature: "If you can't eat their [the lobbyists'] food, drink their booze, . . . and then vote against them, you have no business being up here."[47]

THE CAMPAIGN FINANCE REFORM ACT OF 1974

After a legislative struggle lasting nearly two years, in the fall of 1974 Congress passed a bill concerned with almost every aspect of campaign finance. Signed into law by a reluctant President Ford, this law takes effect in time for the 1976 congressional and presidential elections. Only time will tell the extent of the changes it will produce in the conduct of election campaigns. Nor can anyone tell at present whether these procedural reforms will substantially alter the pressures on federal officials and the kinds of policies they pursue. All we can do here is list the new law's major provisions and discuss some of the questions and dilemmas brought into focus by its passage.[48]

[46] Quoted in Alexander, *Political Financing*, p. 21.

[47] Quoted in Lou Cannon, *Ronnie and Jesse* (Garden City, N. Y.: Doubleday & Co., Inc., 1969), p. 101.

[48] Our description of the law's provisions is based largely on *CQ Weekly Report*, October 12, 1974, pp. 2865–70.

A few months after his surprising election to the Senate in 1972, Joseph R. Biden, Jr., a Democrat from Delaware, testified in favor of public financing of election expenses before a Senate subcommittee:

. . . we all know how tough it is to raise money and we all know what we have to do to raise that money.

Let me give you a couple of examples. . . . I can recall in one instance going to a labor union who I knew was contributing $5,000 to a Senate campaign—to anyone they endorse—all above board, all honest, you know, by the numbers and it was a check, the full works. And we walk in and we sit down and start off the discussion very polite. He said, "Mr. Biden, would you like a cup of coffee?" We go through that routine, we have a cup of coffee . . . and then you really get down to it. Then, no one asks you to buy your vote or to promise a vote but they say things like this to me anyway . . . , "Well, Joe, had you been in the 92nd Congress how would you have voted on the SST and while you're at it how would you have voted on bailing out Lockheed?" Now, I may be a naive young feller, but I knew the right answer for $5,000. I knew what had to be said to get that money.

The same thing occurred again when it looked like the polls started to narrow and Joe Biden is going to win . . . 13 multi-millionaires invite me out to cocktails. . . . We sit down and we start off, only the only difference is they offer me a Bloody Mary instead of a Coke or a cup of coffee, and they're a little more frank about it. The spokesman for the group said, "Well, Joe, let's get right to it, looks like you may win this damn thing and we underestimated it. Now, Joe, I'd like to ask you a few questions. We know everybody running for public office has to talk about tax reform, Joe, and it's particularly capital gains. . . ." One fellow leans over and sort of pats me on the knee in a fatherly fashion and says to me, "Joe, you really don't mean what you say about capital gains, do you?" Now I knew the right answer to that one for $20,000 and quite frankly, were it not for the fact that I had a Scotch Presbyterian wife who had a backbone like a ramrod . . . and who I was more afraid of than those people I was talking to, I would have said on both occasions, "No, I didn't mean what I said about capital gains and yep I would have gone for the SST." Only because of her I didn't and I thought I lost it.*

* Quoted in *National Journal Reports,* November 10, 1973, pp. 1678–79.

LIMITS ON CONTRIBUTIONS. Each individual is permitted to contribute only $1,000 for each primary or general election, with a total maximum contribution of $25,000 per year for all federal candidates combined. Candidates and their families are limited to $50,000 for the presidential election, $35,000 for the Senate, and $25,000 for the House. No organization may contribute more than $5,000 in any election. Cash contributions of over $100 are prohibited.

LIMITS ON SPENDING BY CANDIDATES. Presidential primaries: $10 million is the maximum that can be spent by each candidate in all primaries combined.

Presidential general election: a $20 million limit per candidate.

Senate primaries: $100,000 or eight cents for each state resident of voting age, whichever is greater.

Senate general elections: $150,000 or twelve cents for each resident of voting age.

House primary and general elections: $70,000 maximum in each.

LIMITS ON NATIONAL PARTY SPENDING. The two major parties have a $2 million spending limit for presidential nominating conventions. Minor parties have a lower limit, but this is not a major restriction because, in fact, minor parties rarely have conventions. Their candidates are not so much nominated as annointed.

Spending by the national party on behalf of its candidates is limited to $10,000 per candidate in each House general election; $20,000 or two cents per voting age citizen in Senate elections; and two cents per voting age citizen in presidential elections.

PUBLIC FINANCING OF CAMPAIGN EXPENSES. The provisions on public funding apply only to presidential elections and are optional. If he wishes, a presidential candidate can raise his money privately. But if he opts for public funding, he cannot accept private contributions. Public funding covers all general election expenses for major party candidates up to the $20 million limit. Funding for minor candidates is proportional to votes received. It is available after the election to candidates who get at least 5 percent of the vote. A minor party can get public funding before election day only if its presidential candidate won 5 percent of the vote four years earlier.

Presidential primary funding is on a matching basis. A dollar of public money is paid for every dollar raised privately by the candidate. But to qualify for public support in a primary, each candidate must first raise on his own at least $5,000 in each of twenty states, in contributions of $250 or less. This provision is intended to screen out frivolous or hopeless candidates, so that public support is provided only to serious contenders.

The money for public financing comes from the Presidential Election Campaign Fund, which is supplied by a check-off on the federal income tax form. Any taxpayer who chooses can assign one dollar of his or her federal tax (or two dollars in the case of a joint return) to this fund.

REPORTING AND DISCLOSURE. Each candidate is required to form a single committee through which all expenditures and contributions on his or her behalf are reported.

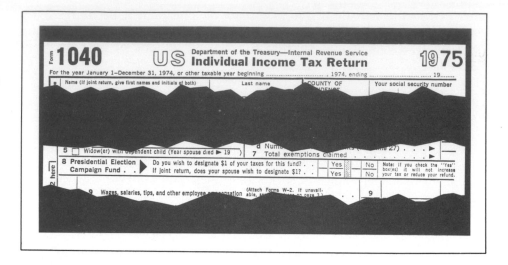

Any organization that does anything to influence an election must file reports as a political committee. This provision of the law was aimed at "public interest" organizations like Common Cause that publicize voting records and in other ways try to influence legislation or elections. (The U. S. Court of Appeals ruled in 1975 that this provision was unconstitutional. The Supreme Court probably will sustain this ruling when it decides the legal challenge to the entire law in 1976.)

Corporations, unions, and government contractors are permitted to maintain separate funds for political action.

ENFORCEMENT. A bipartisan Federal Election Commission will make rules to implement the law, receive reports, and oversee compliance with the law. It can subpoena witnesses and documents and can seek injunctions. It will refer actual prosecution to the Department of Justice.

One of the weaknesses of previous election finance laws was the Justice Department's extreme reluctance to do anything about violations. This meant that for all practical purposes these laws were meaningless. The hope behind the Federal Election Commission is that a public agency formed and staffed for the express purpose of regulating campaign finance will be motivated to take action, if only so its members can justify their positions. This hope is further supported by the fact that newly created federal agencies generally tend to reflect the political interests and emotions that lay behind the establishment of the agency.

THE OUTLOOK FOR THE NEW LAW. Very little about the 1974 act is a sure thing. It seems likely to increase the importance of direct mail fund raising, which draws on thousands of smaller contributions rather than the big gifts that are now outlawed. It may make it difficult for last-minute presidential candidates, because of the time it takes to raise $5,000 in each of twenty states. The limits on financial aid to candidates may shift influence to interests with disproportionate amounts of other resources that can affect election outcomes. These include the mass media, with their control of publicity, and unions and other organizations that can mobilize manpower (and woman-power)—highly potent resources that are not counted as money. Otherwise, few observers can agree on the law's ultimate impact.

Even its survival is in doubt. A lawsuit challenging its constitutionality was brought by a coalition of left-wing and right-wing-ideologues, joined by the New York Civil Liberties Union and a few other groups. These and other critics of the law make three fundamental criticisms.

1. They argue that it is an "incumbent protection law, an insurance policy to keep people in office," because challengers are not allowed to spend more than the incumbents to whom they are opposed. Since incumbents have the additional resources provided by their staffs and all the campaigning advantages of public office, it is felt that challengers need to be able to spend more money in order to make the odds fairer. Although this criticism is indisputably correct, it is difficult to see how the problem can be solved without sky-high limits on non-incumbents.

2. Many observers are concerned about the implications of the campaign reform movement for freedom of speech. The rationale behind the disclosure provisions of the law is that they enable the electorate to be fully informed about the sources of support for each candidate. But there is no evidence that many voters will ever know or care about such matters. In fact, the main beneficiaries of full disclosure may be political scientists. On the negative side, though, full disclosure may expose some contributors to various forms of retaliation. Customers, bosses, and colleagues who dislike an individual's choice of candidates might well express their dislike by punishing him in some way. For example, a businessman in a conservative community might lose customers if it were known that he supported a liberal candidate. Critics point out that full disclosure might "chill" free expression of unpop-ular political views. As these critics see it, the right to contribute in secret is an important safeguard of political freedom, just like the right to vote in secret.

There are, of course, merits to both sides of the argument on this issue. The goal of campaign reform is to equalize access to money and thus free candidates from restrictions based on their ability to attract contributions. Equality in this sense may conflict with the goal of freedom of speech. Moreover, it can be argued that enforcing financial equality discriminates against people who have money to give to politics but no time, and favors people who have time but no money.[49] Restricting the political use of money

[49] This argument is not as far-fetched as it may seem. In June 1974 the voters of Berkeley, California, approved a referendum measure that prohibited corporations or labor unions from spending money in municipal elections. The forces behind this measure then put on the November ballot a proposal for the city government to take over the local gas and electric company. The proponents had no trouble publicizing their point of view but the utility could not present its side of the case because of the law forbidding it to spend money in a local elec-tion. With the help of the American Civil Liberties Union, the utility went to court and won an injunction nullifying the no-spending provision as an unconstitutional restriction on free speech. *San Francisco Chronicle,* October 16, 1974, p. 4, and October 17, 1974, p. 6.

while allowing full exploitation of nonmonetary resources gives advantages to some political interests at the expense of others. As is so often the case, "reform" is not neutral. Whether these particular reforms infringe on constitutional rights is a question to be decided by the courts. And whether the new law will actually equalize access to money is a question that can be answered only by experience. It is possible that some parts of the law will be overturned in the courts, but in late-1975 we have no way of predicting the outcome of the Supreme Court's decision in this case.

3. By limiting the ability of individuals to publicize their views, the law limits free speech in another way. A candidate, interest group, or concerned citizen who cannot spend money is silenced for all practical purposes, since the right of free expression is meaningless without the ability to communicate that expression.

WHO PARTICIPATES IN POLITICS?

In the final analysis, we are interested in political participation because the people who engage in such activities are more influential than those who do not. Even after making allowances for types of participation that do not provide any power over government decisions, we cannot escape the conclusion that activists are "more equal" than other people. This is true for two reasons. First, candidates need money and campaign workers. Anyone running for office must attract at least a core of backers in order to be taken seriously. Unless some activists can be won over, a candidate cannot even get his or her name on the ballot, so the opinion of the electorate is irrelevant. Thus activists are a constituency that must be wooed, just like the electorate as a whole. In places where one party's dominance makes its nomination tantamount to election, the minority that picks its party's nominee is all that matters. Second, activists are powerfully overrepresented among those people with whom politicians have contact and who provide them with many of their impressions of public opinion. It is the activists who write letters, go to meetings, ask officials for favorable consideration. In short, they are more visible to the politicians and thus count for more in political decisions.

ACTIVISTS ARE BETTER OFF

As we noted in Chapter 6, educated people are more likely to vote because they are more interested in politics, more self-confident, more comfortable with abstract issues, and more experienced in the minor administrative hurdles required in registering to vote. Participation is a more "demanding" activity than voting, and thus we would expect that the educated and wealthy would be even more overrepresented in the ranks of the activists than they are among voters. The more education someone has, the greater the probability that he or she will participate in politics. Since education is so strongly related to income, this means that rich people are more likely to participate

Although poor people participate in politics less than rich people, blacks are *not* less active than whites. Beginning in the late 1950s, black political activity increased sharply. Within ten years, blacks were participating in politics at the same rate as whites. In fact, blacks participate *more* than whites at equivalent levels of income. That is, well-off blacks are more active than well-off whites, middle-class blacks more active than middle-class whites, and poor blacks more active than poor whites. Since blacks are more likely to be poor, averaging out the activity level of all blacks brings it to the same point as for all whites.

Blacks who are particularly race conscious are also more likely than other blacks to engage in politics. Thus, racial awareness is a source of motivations for political action. It is likely that this is true for other groups, but we have no evidence to support this assumption. Still, it seems reasonable to suppose that awareness of a common interest and perception that the interest is politically relevant lead to heightened political involvement in order to achieve the group's goals.

The authors of a study of political participation provided this explanation for the high level of black activism:

> There are a number of reasons why one would expect that opportunities for political participation would be more open than opportunities for jobs, income, or education. Equalitarian values are probably more generally held in relation to politics than in relation to other areas, and such values are more easily enforced in the political than in the social and economic arenas. Furthermore, the advantages the deprived groups have in terms of numbers and potential organization are particularly relevant to politics.
>
> . . . When blacks break through the barrier that separates the totally inactive from those who engage in at least some activity, they are likely to move to quite high levels of such activity.

Source: Verba and Nie, *Participation in America,* Chap. 10; the quoted passages are on pp. 152 and 155.

than poor people. Like voting, participation is also related to age. One reason for the feebler participation of the young is their shorter length of residence in any given locality. As people settle down, they start to participate more.[50]

Table 7–1 shows the disproportionate extent to which campaign activists are drawn from the educated and prosperous portion of society. College

[50] Sidney Verba and Norman H. Nie, *Participation in America* (New York: Harper & Row, 1972), Chap. 9.

TABLE 7-1
THE SOCIOECONOMIC COMPOSITION OF PARTY ACTIVISTS IN 1972

	ALL DEMOCRATS (%)	DEMOCRATIC ACTIVISTS (%)	ALL REPUBLICANS (%)	REPUBLICAN ACTIVISTS (%)
Make over $15,000 per year	18	35	28	47
Attended college	27	52	36	55
Have business or professional jobs	23	40	37	58

Activists are people who did anything to help a candidate get elected.

educated people comprise 27 percent of all Democrats but more than half of all Democratic activists. People who have been to college also account for over half the Republican activists but only 36 percent of all Republicans. The same relationships hold for occupation and income. The percentage of activists who are well-off and have business or professional jobs (or who are married to people who do) is vastly greater than the percentage of such people in the voting population as a whole.

THE IDEOLOGY GAP

The fact that activists are richer than other people has led some observers to the conclusion that this imbalance favors conservative interests. We think that this conclusion is badly mistaken and overlooks other, and more interesting, differences between activists and non-activists. The most important of these differences concern the political awareness of activists and non-activists. As we would expect, campaign participants are far more interested in and informed about public affairs than the average American. At either end of the ideological spectrum, they are much more consistent in their opinions about political issues, in contrast to the rather unstructured pattern displayed by most citizens. By the same token, they are far more ideologically aware than other citizens. In past years, this was mostly true of Republican activists, who were considerably more attuned to ideology than rank-and-file members of their party. Republican activists were also much more conservative on almost every issue than Republican non-activists. Neither of these gaps was very noticeable in the Democratic party—at least until the 1972 election. Up until then, Democratic activists were no more ideologically conscious and only faintly more liberal than other Democrats.[51]

[51] Verba and Nie, *Participation in America*, p. 88, Chap. 12; Ban, "The Party Activist"; Herbert McClosky et al., "Issue Conflict and Consensus Among Party Leaders and Followers," *American Political Science Review*, 54 (June 1960), 406–27; and David Nexon, "Assymetry in the Political System: Occasional Activists in the Republican and Democratic Parties, 1956–64," *American Political Science Review*, 65 (September 1971), 716–30.

In the 1972 election, activists of both parties were more conscious of ideology than non-activists. They were also much less likely to have moderate opinions and much more likely to be at one end of the ideological spectrum or the other. As we saw in Chapter 5, a majority of Americans either refuse to identify themselves as conservatives or liberals, or locate themselves right in the middle of the road. In contrast, activists take a stand, generally not in the middle. These findings are shown in Figure 7–3, which compares the proportion of activists and non-activists who accept ideological labels in describing themselves. For example, 16 percent of the activists call themselves liberal or extremely liberal. Only 7 percent of those who did not participate in the campaign were willing to describe themselves in these terms. Similarly, 16 percent of the activists called themselves conservative or extremely conservative, compared to 11 percent of the less active.

As we noted a moment ago, before 1972 only the Republicans had an "ideology gap" between activists and ordinary voters. In 1972, however, a similar gap manifested itself in the Democratic party. Indeed, liberals and extreme liberals were much more active on the Democratic side than conservatives and extreme conservatives were on the Republican side. Liberal and extremely liberal activists outnumbered conservative and extremely conservative activists by a ratio of about three-to-two. In fact, the conservatives were only slightly more active than people who claimed to be in the middle of the road. This increase in liberal participation probably reflected George McGovern's ability to mobilize millions of ideologically committed liberals, many of whom had sat out previous campaigns because of distaste for the Democratic presidential candidates.

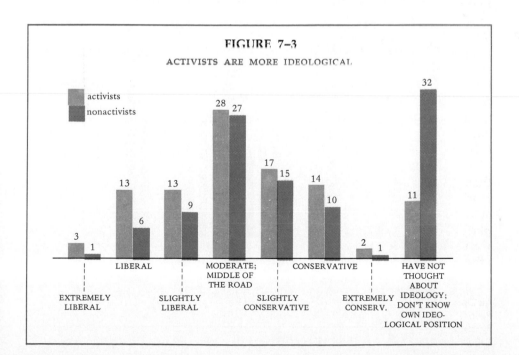

FIGURE 7–3

ACTIVISTS ARE MORE IDEOLOGICAL

Our argument up to this point can be summarized briefly. People who participate in politics are richer and better educated than the general public. But the fact that activists are richer than non-activists is not by itself adequate evidence that they are necessarily more conservative. On the contrary, activists are much more attuned to politics than the average voter and tend to be more polarized. While ordinary Republicans and Democrats do not usually differ very much in their opinions about political issues, the gap between the activists in the two parties is much larger.

These conclusions can be illustrated by the results of a study of delegates to the Republican and Democratic presidential nominating conventions in 1972. The *Washington Post* succeeded in getting the great majority of delegates to each convention to fill out a questionnaire that yields some fascinating insights into both the 1972 election and the dynamics of political participation.[52]

The Democratic party had placed great emphasis on making the convention delegates representative of the party's mass membership. By using a quota system, the Democrats succeeded in opening up the convention to women, blacks, and young people. Almost half the delegates were under forty, two-fifths were women, and 15 percent were black. Achieving representation for these three categories did not mean achieving it for other

[52] The *Washington Post* findings used here were reported in the *San Francisco Chronicle,* August 21, 1972, p. 12.

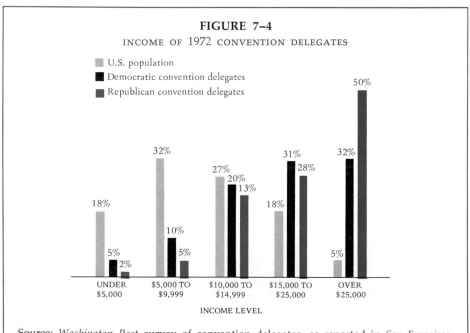

FIGURE 7–4

INCOME OF 1972 CONVENTION DELEGATES

- U.S. population
- Democratic convention delegates
- Republican convention delegates

Source: *Washington Post* survey of convention delegates, as reported in *San Francisco Chronicle,* August 21, 1972, p. 12.

categories of people, however. In many respects, the Democratic delegates were quite unrepresentative of the American people. For example, 39 percent of them had gone to graduate school and a total of 58 percent were college graduates. The "new politics" Democratic delegates were also an elite in terms of income. Fully 63 percent of them had family incomes over $15,000 — which is far ahead of the general population and not too far behind the Republicans, who had 78 percent of their delegates in this income bracket. The income distribution of the Democratic delegates, Republican delegates, and the entire population is shown in Figure 7–4.

Although the delegates to the two conventions were similarly prosperous and well educated, they were worlds apart in terms of their political outlook. More than half the Democratic delegates called themselves liberals. Only 7 percent identified themselves as conservatives. The Republicans inclined strongly in the opposite direction, with only 5 percent liberals and 32 percent conservatives. What is more, each set of delegates was considerably further to the left and right, respectively, than the rank-and-file identifiers with their parties. For example, the Democratic delegates were strongly in favor of school busing and amnesty for Vietnam war resisters, two positions rejected by massive majorities of the general public.[53]

These findings are enough to refute the notion that the American political system is in the hands of an elite corps of prosperous *and* conservative activists. The activists *are* more prosperous than the population as a whole, but their ideological commitments run in both directions. Republican activists are indeed more conservative than the average Republican, but Democratic activists are more liberal than the average Democrat. What emerges, then, is *not* a picture of a system tipped toward one end of the ideological spectrum. Instead, we have a situation in which many activists in each party exert pressure to pull their party away from the center and toward the left or right. But neither party's activists are a monolithic elite. Within each party, the ideologues are resisted by moderates and by politicians willing to compromise to appeal to the broader electorate. These struggles reach a climax every four years, when the parties select their presidential candidates, as we will see in Chapter 9.

IMPLICATIONS AND CONSEQUENCES

We have seen that differences between Republicans and Democrats are much sharper among activists than among ordinary voters. Activists are as important a constituency for candidates as the total electorate. Indeed, the candidate's need for contributors and workers comes before his need for mass appeal because he must be nominated before he can even get to the general election. Activists are extremely important in the nominating phase because of the small turnout in primaries and the tremendous leverage that money and precinct workers can exert in low visibility elections. More-

[53] Denis G. Sullivan et al., *The Politics of Representation* (New York: St. Martin's Press, 1974), p. 107.

over, the voters in primaries are more polarized by party than the people who vote in general elections. That is, Republican primary voters are likely to be more conservative and Democratic primary voters to be more liberal than Republicans and Democrats in general elections. As a result, Democratic candidates generally are more liberal than the average Democratic voter while Republican candidates are even more conservative than their voters. The candidates are pushed to the left and right, respectively, by the activists in their parties. And the fact that candidates are almost always recruited from the ranks of the activists further increases the likelihood that the people running for office will be somewhere toward the "extremes" of their parties.

Another factor that tends to push the parties apart is the unrepresentative character of the people who communicate with candidates and officials. Politicians need to get information about what the public thinks. The people with whom they come in contact are one obvious and important source of information. For example, during campaigns, candidates use the people they see at meetings as samples of the public. But the individuals who come to meetings and rallies are much more opinionated than the vast majority who refrain from such involvement.[54] By the same token, the most common form of contact with politicians is through letter writing. This is something that over a quarter of the population has done. But here again, the people who write letters to public officials are not a representative selection of the public. Like the campaign activists, they are not only better educated and richer but also far more ideologically oriented. Their opinions are likely to be located more on the left and right, and less in the middle of the road, than general opinion. Thus politicians who rely on the mail for their impressions of public sentiment may be grievously misled.

The 1964 election presents a dramatic example of this. Barry Goldwater won the Republican presidential nomination despite the fact that most Republicans preferred other candidates. However, Goldwater had the support of a majority of that fraction of Republicans who cared enough about politics to have written a letter to an official or newspaper. The letter writers were not only far more conservative than other Republicans but also more active. If the general election had been restricted to people who had written letters, Goldwater would have beaten Johnson by a comfortable margin. Unfortunately for him, his popularity among this select group was not matched by his appeal to the mass electorate. Goldwater's support among activists may explain why he persisted in ignoring the polls, which showed that his favorite ideas were highly unpopular. The very policies rejected by the mass public were the ones most ardently embraced by the people who wrote letters. As a result, Goldwater may have been misled into overestimating his own strength because he relied on letters as an indication of public opinion.[55]

[54] John W. Kingdon, *Candidates for Office: Beliefs and Strategies* (New York: Random House, 1966), pp. 91–101.

[55] Philip E. Converse et al., "Electoral Myth and Reality: The 1964 Election," *American Political Science Review*, 59 (June 1965), 333–36.

McGovern's nomination in 1972 was achieved much the same way as Goldwater's. A year before the convention that nominated him, McGovern was the choice of less than 5 percent of all Democrats. He was the first choice of only 6 percent of Democratic county chairmen, but these same leaders reported that McGovern's supporters were working harder than any other candidate's backers to win convention delegates.[56] By the time the convention rolled around, McGovern's popularity had risen dramatically, but he was still far from having a majority among all Democrats. He succeeded in winning the nomination because he was the overwhelming favorite of activist Democrats, just as Goldwater had been the favorite of activist Republicans eight years earlier.

Goldwater and McGovern illustrate a dilemma of the American party system that may be growing in importance. Each won his party's nomination by appealing to a dedicated and relatively extreme wing of the party. (Although "extreme" is perhaps too strong a word to describe the positions that either man took, we should emphasize that Goldwater was clearly the most conservative serious Republican contender in decades while McGovern likewise was far more liberal than any other figure who had a realistic chance of winning the Democratic nomination.) But extremism is not really the issue. The point to be borne in mind is that the way in which each man won the nomination doomed his chances of winning the general election. Their activist constituencies were too far away from the political mainstream. Both men were easily defeated by incumbent Presidents who moved to the center and thus won the votes of millions of defecting moderates. At present, these two examples are anomalies. Most presidential candidates, after all, do not have such close ties to eccentric minorities. Nevertheless, the fact that such instances occurred in two of the last three presidential elections may be significant. It indicates that a wide gap between a party's activists and its rank-and-file voters can have dire consequences for the party's chances of electoral success.

Perhaps the best way to conclude our discussion of political participation is to consider an even broader implication of these findings about the gap between activists and the general public. There has been a great deal of rhetoric since the mid 1960s about the need to "increase popular participation" in every aspect of political and civic life. The evidence about who actually engages in political action should make it clear that efforts at "increasing participation" usually end simply by increasing the influence of people who are not representative of the general public, although they customarily claim to speak in the name of the public. Who goes to meetings? Who can write and speak effectively? Who knows how to raise money? Who is experienced in organization and in dealing with legal requirements? Obviously, not everybody. Nor does everybody care enough about politics to invest the time and energy to participate. Therefore, most methods of "increasing participation in decision making" will in fact increase the influence of the committed believers, those who are middle-class enough

---

[56] *Gallup Opinion Index*, July 1971, p.16.

to be comfortable with political organization and committed enough to invest the requisite energy.

SUMMARY

Only a minority of Americans participate in parties through such activities as working in a campaign, making political contributions, or writing to public officials. Some are motivated by a desire to influence government policy in ways favorable to themselves. Some want government jobs or similar forms of patronage. Others strive to gain success in national politics for their particular ideals and ideologies. Some people find that participating in politics brings them personal satisfaction in terms of pleasant social gatherings, increased prestige, and demonstrations of friendship.

Contributing money is a major mode of political participation engaged in by both individuals and organizations such as corporations and labor unions. In general, Republicans get more contributions than Democrats, and incumbents and expected winners get more than challengers and expected losers. Conservative candidates do not necessarily get more campaign money than liberal ones. In recent years candidates have raised a great deal of money by direct mail advertising, thus increasing the importance of the small donor.

It is difficult to say just how important money is in winning elections. It is more important in primaries than general elections. Big donors may hope to have increased influence over the policies of those whom they have helped to elect. These hopes frequently are disappointed, however.

The Campaign Finance Reform Act of 1974 limits the size of contributions and the amount of campaign spending by candidates and also provides public financing of presidential campaigns. It is too soon to know how much of the law actually can be enforced or what its effects will be.

Those who participate in politics are likely to be more influential than those who do not, because candidates need money and campaign workers. Those who participate are older, better educated, wealthier, and better informed than those who do not participate. They are likely to be more ideologically committed than others in their party. Participating Democrats are more liberal than other Democrats. Participating Republicans are more conservative than other Republicans. Thus, the Republican and Democratic parties, in the sense of those who actively participate in party affairs, are likely to be further apart than are rank-and-file Republican and Democratic voters. As a result, presidential candidates who win their party's nomination by appealing to party activists may find themselves "too liberal" or "too conservative" for a majority of the voters.

CHAPTER EIGHT
INTEREST GROUPS

ONE commonplace vision of the political world sees it as composed of two main elements. First, there are *the people*. Second, there are *interest groups*. The people are regarded as good and unselfish while the interest groups are selfish and bad. The goal of all right-thinking Americans, therefore, should be to help "the people" at the expense of the interest groups. Stated this baldly, we can all recognize that this is nothing but a burlesque. Why? Because "the people" is not an organic whole with a common point of view. Instead, "the people" consists of individuals with widely varying points of view. In other words, "the people" consists of numerous individuals with numerous interests, some of which they share with other individuals. The people, in short, are a collection of interest groups.

Our purpose in this chapter is to elaborate on this approach to interest groups. We will do so primarily by describing a series of groups, after which we will draw conclusions about some of the properties of interest groups. Finally, we will examine the principal methods used by groups to get what they want from the government.

WHAT IS AN INTEREST GROUP?

In the first instance, we must distinguish between *categorical groups* and *real groups*. Categorical groups are classifications of individuals, called "groups" by virtue of a characteristic they have in common. Blacks, Irish-Americans, women, people with blue eyes, doctors, cheese importers, candy manufacturers, conservationists, and fat people are all categorical groups. As this list suggests, however, all categorical groups are not politically relevant. For political purposes, some of them are not *real groups*. What does it take for a categorical group to become a real group?

First, it must be a *reference group*. That is, it must provide a basis of identity for its members. It must be a source of some common feelings among its members. And it must give its members some cues about the appropriate types of behavior and thought for members of the group. In Chapter 2 we pointed out that many categorical groups are reference groups for only some of the people who "belong to" them, and some categorical groups are not reference groups at all. For example, left-handed people constitute a categorical group but not a reference group. They do not derive any sense of identity from being left-handed, they do not share a pool of common feelings with other lefties, and they do not act in some consistent and appropriate way. Of course, it is possible for a categorical group to become a reference group. Under some circumstances, collections of people with some common characteristic may become aware of their common identity, or their previous awareness may become dramatically heightened. We sometimes call this process *consciousness raising*. Any individual "belongs to" a great many categorical groups. Some of these are also reference groups, but most are not.

Second, there must be some perceived connection between group membership and the political world. That is, the group members must have a political interest, some calculation of how they will gain or lose as a result of political decisions. Postal workers, dairy farmers, civil libertarians, oil producers, auto workers, rifle shooters, Catholics, aerospace manufacturers, blacks, and so on, all have political interests. This does not mean that all members of the group have to see the political significance of the group. Many reference group members do not see any connection between their interests and politics. Even people who are directly affected by what the government does are not always politicized. Nevertheless, if the connection is perceived by some members, then the group meets our second criterion for *real groups.*

Third, there is the question of *organization.* All the interests just mentioned have organizations that state their goals and make claims on the government in their behalf. The level of organization of different interests varies enormously from time to time and from interest to interest. Very large interest groups may be represented by organizations with rather small memberships. This does not mean that we should consider that the group consists only of the organized members. Rather, it consists of all the people who consider themselves members of the group and who evaluate political decisions (chiefly their vote) on the basis of that membership.

Members of categorical groups may or may not be conscious of their common identity. They may or may not see the political relevance of their group membership. Different identities may come to the fore in different circumstances. When neighbors organize to get a stop sign on a dangerous corner, they take action on the basis of their common identity as members of the neighborhood. But this identity may not be relevant to any other political action. Each of the neighbors has a variety of other interests based on his or her occupation, places of employment, political beliefs, sex, age, family situation, and so on. When he is involved in activities related to the stop sign, a person whose favorite hobby is rifle shooting will not think of himself as a gun fancier. But when he is writing his congressman to oppose gun control legislation, he will not think about himself as a member of a particular community that happens to be concerned about a stop sign. As we will see, groups can become politicized as they begin to see a political relevance in their common situation where they did not do so before. At this point, such groups often organize. For example, neighborhood residents might hold meetings and form a committee to press their demand for a stop sign on the city government. Sometimes such organizations take on a life of their own and become permanent features of the political landscape. The neighborhood committee may not dissolve after the stop sign is installed. Pleased with its success, it may continue to meet in order to press for other benefits the community wants. In this way, the neighborhood becomes not only a place where people live, but also an *interest group.*

We can define an *interest group,* then, as a collection of people making claims on the government on the basis of shared attitudes. It is not necessary that they share all political attitudes, only that they share the one that is the basis of their claim.

THE EFFECTIVE
SETTING: LEVELS OF
PARTICIPATION AND
MODES OF INFLUENCE

Americans seem to be particularly inclined to form organizations in order to pursue a common interest. This readiness to organize to achieve joint goals is far more common in the United States than in other nations. The classic statement of the importance of associations in American society was made by the most famous of all foreign commentators on America, Alexis de Tocqueville. Written in the 1830s, Tocqueville's portrait of the American proclivity for forming groups still rings true:

INTEREST GROUPS
HEADQUARTERS IN
WASHINGTON
OFTEN ARE LARGE
AND IMPRESSIVE.
HERE, HEADQUAR-
TERS OF THE AFL-
CIO (TOP); B'NAI
B'RITH (MIDDLE);
THE NATIONAL
ASSOCIATION OF
HOME BUILDERS
(BOTTOM).
*Ransdell Inc. (top);
B'nai B'rith (middle);
Del Ankers Photo-
graphers (bottom)*

> Americans of all ages, all conditions, and all dispositions, con-stantly form associations. They have not only commercial and manu-facturing companies, in which all take part, but associations of a thousand other kinds,—religious, moral, serious, futile, extensive or restricted, enormous or diminutive. The Americans make asso-ciations to give entertainments, to found establishments for educa-tion, to build inns, to construct churches, to diffuse books, to send missionaries to the antipodes; and in this manner they found hospi-tals, prisons, and schools.[1]

In 1968, there were 10,933 national associations in the United States, devoted to everything from sports to religion to education to science to business. Sixty-two percent of all American adults belong to at least one organization (not necessarily a nationwide one), and 40 percent of all Americans say they are active in at least one organization.[2] Predictably, there is a strong relationship between education and belonging to and participating in organizations. As Figure 8–1 shows, only half the people who have not graduated from high school belong to an organization, and only a quarter are active in a group to which they belong. The proportion of members increases to two-thirds among high school graduates and almost four-fifths among those who have attended college. Active engagement in an organization increases even more drastically with education, so that fully three-fifths of those who have been to college report that they are active in at least one group to which they belong.

As striking as these figures are, they still underestimate the representa-tional reach of organized groups. It would be difficult to imagine anybody whose interests are not represented by organized groups, usually many times over. Even a hermit living in a cave would find his craving for solitude supported by innumerable conservationist groups, his interest in pure food taken care of by dozens of public interest lobbies, and his concern about pure air guarded likewise by environmental advocates.

The vast number and the diverse character of interest groups in America make it difficult to generalize about the subject. The answer to almost any

[1] Alexis de Tocqueville, *Democracy in America,* trans. Henry Reeve (New York: Schocken Books, 1961), Vol. II, p. 128.

[2] Sidney Verba and Norman H. Nie, *Participation in America* (New York: Harper & Row, 1972), p. 176.

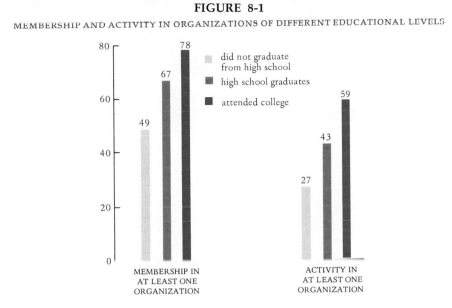

FIGURE 8-1

MEMBERSHIP AND ACTIVITY IN ORGANIZATIONS OF DIFFERENT EDUCATIONAL LEVELS

Source: Sidney Verba and Norman H. Nie, *Participation in America* (New York: Harper & Row, 1972), p. 181.

question about interest groups is "it all depends." The best that we can do to untangle this situation is to describe some examples of the most important types of groups and to use these capsule portraits as a basis for stating a few important generalizations about the subject. On pages 218–19 of this chapter, the reader will find a selective list illustrating the extraordinary number and range of national associations in the United States.

By emphasizing the diversity of groups, we do not mean to say that all Americans have an equal chance at being represented by interest groups. It is true that the group struggle is a game that anyone can play, but it is not true that everyone enters the game with the same partners, the same number of chips, and the same skill. It is true that the number of organized interests in this country is absolutely stupendous. But it is not true that everyone is equally taken care of by this multiplicity of groups. In Chapter 17 we will suggest some ways to look at the problem of equality. Here, we wish only to describe the intricate mosaic of group life in America.

ECONOMIC INTEREST GROUPS

BUSINESS ORGANIZATIONS

Business interests of every description have three advantages in dealing with the government. First, they have a pre-existing organization. It is not necessary to form a group for political purposes, since one exists

Trade, business, and commercial organizations:
American Association of Attorney-Certified Public Accountants
Automotive Advertisers Council
Television Bureau of Advertising
Air Traffic Control Association
National Aeronautic Association
American Apparel Manufacturers Association
Bow Tie Manufacturers Association
Woolen Hosiery Institute of America
American Society of Appraisers
National Armored Car Association
Art Dealers' Association of America
American Automobile Association
National Association of Baby-Sitter Registries
Paper Bag Institute
American Bakers Association
National Pretzel Bakers Association
National Ballroom Operators Association
National Association of Mutual Savings Banks
American Bankers Association
Associated Master Barbers and Beauticians of America
Barn Equipment Association
National Better Business Bureau
Carbonated Beverage Institute
National Association of Wine Bottlers
Root Beer Institute
United States Brewers Association
Bicycle Institute of America
Box Association of America
National Association of Broadcasters
American Butter Institute
Casket Manufacturers Association of America
Cheese Importers Association of America
National Association of Chewing Gum Manufacturers
Chocolate Manufacturers Association of the United States
National Institute of Dry Cleaning

Brazilian Coffee Institute
National Association of Home Builders
Council on Consumer Information, National Consumers League
National Association of Credit Management
Dairy Industry Committee
Data Processing Management Association
World Association of Detectives
Maine Sardine Council
Grocery Manufacturers of America
National Association of Greeting Card Publishers
American Hotel and Motel Management Association
Insurance Rating Board
Rain and Hail Insurance Bureau
American Ladder Institute
National Macaroni Manufacturers Association
Monument Builders of America
Academy of Motion Picture Arts and Sciences
New York Board of Trade
American Newspaper Publishers Association
White House Correspondents Association
American Association for Public Opinion Research
National Association of the Pet Industries
American Petroleum Institute
White House News Photographers Association
Public Relations Society of America
American Association of Railroads
National Restaurant Association
National Secretaries Association
National Association of Stevedores
National Sporting Goods Association
Association of Stock Exchange Firms
Federal Excise Tax Council
Tea Council of the United States of America
Denim Council
Vinegar Institute
National Association of Gag Writers

Agricultural organizations of commodity exchanges:
Artichoke Advisory Board
American Breeders' Association
American Conservation Association
Orangutan Recovery Service
Future Farmers of America
4-H Program
Arabian Horse Club Registry of America
National Maple Syrup Council
National Egg Council

Chicago Mercantile Exchange
National Pork Producers Council

Governmental, public administration, military, and legal organizations:
National League of Cities
International City Managers' Association
National Association of Counties
Institute for Defense Analyses
National Association of Federal Career Employees
International Association of Arson Investigators
American Bar Association
American College of Trial Lawyers
Federal Bar Association
National Institute of Municipal Law Officers
Air Force Association
Association of the United States Army
Marine Corps League
Navy League of the United States
United States Coast Guard Auxiliary
International Narcotic Enforcement Officers
National Parks Association
American Institute of Planners
International Association of Chiefs of Police
International Association of Postmasters of the United States
Association of Unclaimed Property Administrators

Scientific, engineering, and technical organizations:
American Institute of Architects
American Society of Golf Course Architects
Association of Universities for Research in Astronomy
Society of Automotive Engineers
Users of Automatic Information Display Equipment
American Nuclear Society
American Society for Oceanography
Northeastern Bird-Banding Association
Radiation Research Society
American Statistical Association
Weather Modification Association
American Society of Zoologists

Educational and cultural organizations:
American Alumni Council
American Institute of Arts and Letters
Authors League of America
Council on Interracial Books for Children
Future Business Leaders of America
American Association of Teachers of the Chinese Language

Association of American Colleges
American Education Association
Modern Language Association of America
Public Library Association
Linguistic Society of America
American Institute for Marxist Studies
American Montessori Society
United Negro College Fund
National Science Teachers Association
Council for Advancement of Secondary Education
American Sociological Association
Association of Urban Universities
Society of Scribes and Illuminators
International Christian Youth Exchange

Social welfare organizations:
National Committee for the Prevention of Alcoholism
American Society for the Prevention of Cruelty to Animals
National Anti-Vivisection Society
Boy Scouts of America
Boys Clubs of America
Campfire Girls
National Conference of Christians and Jews
Jewish Family Service
Foster Parents Plan
Indian Community Action Program
Automotive Safety Foundation
Citizens Committee for UNICEF
American Youth Hostels
Young Women's Christian Association of the United States of America

Health and medical organizations:
American Society of Abdominal Surgery
Fraternity of the Wooden Leg
American Society of Anesthesiologists
Braille Institute of America
Eye-Bank for Sight Restoration
Guide Dog Foundation for the Blind
Cancer Care, Inc.
Institute for Cancer Research
Childbirth Without Pain Education Association
American Dental Association
American Diabetes Association
American Heart Association
American Association of Hospital Consultants
American Board of Internal Medicine
American College of Physicians
American Medical Association
American Psychiatric Association
American Psychoanalytic Association
Association of American State Board of Examiners in Veterinary Medicine

Public affairs organizations:
African Affairs Society of America
Anti-Communist League of America
National Committee on United States-China Relations
National Association for the Advancement of Colored People
Communist Party of the United States of America
Church League of America
American Council for Emigrés in the Professions
National Indian Youth Council
Organization of American States
Pan-American Highway Conference
American Political Science Association
Public Affairs Council
Republican National Committee
Students for a Democratic Society
United Nations Association of America

Fraternal, foreign interest, nationality, and ethnic organizations:
American Arab Relief Agency
Catholic Workmen
Danish Brotherhood in America
American-Hungarian Federation
American Italian Congress
Knights of Columbus
National Association of Polish-Americans

Religious organizations:
Fellowship of Christian Athletes
Society of Biblical Literature
Society of Descendants of Colonial Clergy
Joint Commission on Church Music
American Jewish Congress
United Jewish Appeal
Americans United for Separation of Church and State
World Council of Churches
First Zen Institute of America

Veterans', hereditary, and patriotic organizations:
American Legion
Bay of Pigs Veterans' Association
United States Flag Foundation
World War Tank Corps Association
Wives of the Armed Forces

Hobby and advocational organizations:
Man-Will-Never-Fly Memorial Society International
American Bottle Collectors' Association

Clown Club of America
World Pen Pals
American Beagle Club
National Goldfish Society
International Brotherhood of Magicians
National Mahjongg League
Collectors of Numismatic Errors

General organizations:
Amalgamated Flying Saucer Clubs of America
National Federation of Grandmother Clubs of America
Kiwanis International
Little People of America
National Nudist Council
Optimist International
Rotary International
Vacation Exchange Club
American Vegetarian Union
World Association for Celebrating the Year 2000

Labor unions:
Negro Labor Committee
Actors' Equity Association
Airline Stewards and Stewardesses Association
International Brotherhood of Bookbinders
United Brotherhood of Carpenters and Joiners of America
International Brotherhood of Electrical Workers
International Association of Fire Fighters
International Longshoremen's and Warehousemen's Union
Brotherhood of Painters, Decorators, and Paperhangers of America
National Rural Letter Carriers Association
United Steel Workers of America
United Telegraph Workers
Transport Workers Union of America
American Watchmakers Union

already—the firm itself. Moreover, businessmen form associations for a number of reasons that have nothing to do with their relations with the government. There are business associations to provide information to their members, to conduct advertising, to deal with labor unions, and to handle relations with suppliers and customers. All these groups give businessmen ready-made instruments for the pursuit of political goals.

Second, when businessmen deal with the government they are dealing with a subject about which they are knowledgeable—their own businesses. This is not quite the same thing as being knowledgeable about politics, but it does give them an advantage not always shared by other elements in society.

Third, business organizations, whether they are individual firms or trade associations, generally have an ample supply of money.

Of course, there are enormous variations in the importance of politics to business firms. There are also enormous variations from company to company and industry to industry in the amount of energy expended on politics. Finally, there are considerable variations in the success that different firms have in their dealings with the government.

The business community generates the largest number of active interest groups. There are almost three thousand nationwide trade and business associations, ranging from the Associated Corset and Brassiere Manufacturers to the Latex Foam Rubber Council. Many of these organizations are quite specialized. For example, there is a Paper Bag Institute, a Box Association of America, and an Envelope Manufacturers Association. Trade associations often find themselves on opposite sides of the fence from each other. The Farmers and Manufacturers Beet Sugar Association is interested in the highest possible prices for sugar. But high sugar prices are not in the interests of big users like the National Association of Chewing Gum Manufacturers, the Chocolate Manufacturers Association of the United States, or the Flavor and Extract Manufacturers Association.

As some of these examples indicate, there are many issues which pit different business groups against each other. But there are also some concerns that they all have in common. The closest thing to an overall lobby for American business is the Chamber of Commerce of the United States. The Chamber's membership includes over one thousand trade associations, about 2500 local, state, and regional chambers of commerce, and around 4600 firms and individuals. It employs 400 people in its Washington headquarters and engages in a great variety of activities. Indeed, its production of reports, magazines, memoranda, newsletters, and so on is so prolific that many of its members confess that they find it difficult to read much of the Chamber's output. The Chamber lobbies Congress and the executive branch on a variety of issues of general concern to the business community. Generally, it speaks only on issues with very broad relevance and remains silent on matters that are interesting mainly to a particular industry. Its flexibility is severely limited by its federal structure. The staff may not take action on a matter until a formal "policy" has been adopted by the Chamber. This is a laborious and complicated process involving study by committees and adoption by the Chamber's annual meeting. For this reason, the Chamber is not very fast on its feet.

Of equal prominence, but with somewhat more limited scope, is the National Association of Manufacturers. Even more than the Chamber, this organization represents big business. In most respects, the NAM's activities and limitations resemble those of the Chamber. It, too, is constrained by the need for formal policies adopted by the membership before it can take action. Since the membership consists of industries that frequently have conflicting interests—for example, liberal versus restrictive import tariff levels—"peak groups" like the NAM often are neutralized by their membership and unable to take positions on significant economic issues.

Although some government policy is so broad in its application as to apply to "business in general," most of the affairs of government are more limited in focus. Matters of concern to particular categories of business are commonly dealt with by trade associations. An example is the Grocery Manufacturers of America, Inc. The GMA is the Washington representative of the massive supermarket industry. The range of its interests can be suggested by identifying some of its board members in 1971. The chairman and president represented Pepsi-Cola; the vice-chairman represented the H. J. Heinz Co.; the secretary was the president of The Quaker Oats Company; the treasurer was the chairman of General Mills. Board members included representatives of Coca-Cola, Lever Brothers, and other manufacturers of products sold in grocery stores. GMA gives members of the grocery industry a way to mobilize pressure on the government at many levels, from regulatory agencies like the Federal Trade Commission and the Food and Drug Administration through the Commerce Department to individual members of Congress. The corporations that make up GMA include among their executives and directors men with contacts in many, if not all, congressional districts. Therefore, the GMA can draw on a widespread network of personal connections and political contributors—particularly to the Republican party—in attempting to make its case to the government on any issue. But an organization that represents all food interests cannot attain the unity to act in all areas. What is good for butter may be bad for margarine, and what is good for frozen foods may be bad for canned goods. Thus, conflicting interests often make agreement impossible. In these cases the GMA is paralyzed.[3]

An even more powerful and well-financed interest group is the American Petroleum Institute, whose members include seven of the twenty largest corporations in the United States. It is an association of 350 oil and gas companies and associations, plus seven thousand individual members. Like most such groups, it is dominated by the major firms among its members. The API had a budget in 1974 of $15.7 million. It was successful in leading the fight to enact a bill to permit construction of an oil pipeline

[3] The Grocery Manufacturers of America and many other specialized groups represented in Washington are described in the set of case studies collected in *The Pressure Groups* (Washington, D.C.: National Journal, 1971).

across Alaska. It also succeeded in fighting off an excess profits tax on the oil industry. It failed to prevent the repeal of the depletion allowance, the oil industry's most controversial and widely attacked tax "loophole." The well-known tax advantages that oil companies have enjoyed for generations are the result in part of the lobbying power of the API. Like other broadly based organizations, the API is paralyzed whenever its component firms are not agreed on an issue. It is easy to achieve agreement on taxes or on an Alaskan pipeline, but not on issues like the oil import quota, which pits domestic against international oil firms. On issues like this, the API takes no action.[4]

Some economic organizations have no trouble at all expressing their political interests, because they are united on what they want. An example is the American Milk Producers, Inc., a dairy cooperative with more than 40,000 individual farmers as members. AMPI is quite singleminded about what it most wants from government—a higher federal support price for milk. It succeeded in getting this in 1971. Other organizations of dairymen share this devotion to limited and specific goals. Their members are united, and they are therefore able to act with extraordinary determination and sense of purpose.

Even individual corporations sometimes suffer from the divided counsels that often paralyze or delay trade associations. Some firms are well known for their effective lobbying activities. They watch carefully to see where their interests lie in regard to various government policies, and then they pursue those interests with vigor. On the other hand, many companies cannot reach an internal consensus on their political priorities and do not invest much energy in lobbying. The General Motors Corporation, the biggest manufacturing firm in the world, has a tiny Washington lobby, does not work hard at government relations, and often loses struggles in Congress. For example, General Motors was unsuccessful in its fight against air pollution control devices and higher auto safety standards. Unlike its Detroit counterpart, the Ford Motor Company, General Motors historically has not considered the government important to its basic concerns—making automobiles and trucks at a profit. One Michigan congressman observed about General Motors:

> GM probably has the worst lobby on Capitol Hill. It ranks at the bottom in terms of effectiveness. Its Washington operation is the most inept and ineffectual I've seen here. . . . Management has this disdain for relations in Washington. . . .

> GM is constantly getting hit in the back of the head because they don't pay enough attention to Washington. They get more bad surprises than any other major firm in the nation, and it doesn't have to be that way.[5]

[4] *Congressional Quarterly Weekly Report,* February 16, 1975, pp. 359–64.
[5] Quoted in Frank V. Fowlkes, "Washington Pressures," *National Journal,* November 14, 1970, p. 2504.

American workers traditionally were not highly organized. Labor unions grew slowly in the United States, in part because government policy was not hospitable to their growth. The first major union, the American Federation of Labor (AFL), was organized to represent skilled workers in what were called *craft unions*. Samuel Gompers, the long-time president of the AFL, took the view that labor should be politically nonpartisan, rewarding its friends and punishing its enemies regardless of party affiliation.

In fact, very little rewarding or punishing occurred during the days when only highly skilled workers were organized. The AFL was dedicated to the principle that progress would occur through collective bargaining with employers. Labor, it was felt, had little to gain by political involvement. The AFL leaders attacked the notion that unions should take sides in election campaigns or support candidates on an individual basis. In fact, they were so dedicated to keeping the government out of union affairs that in the 1930s the AFL objected to legislation to establish the social security system and a federal minimum wage.

A very different kind of union developed in the sympathetic climate of the New Deal. The new idea was to organize workers by the industry in which they worked rather than by their skills. In the AFL, all welders were in one union, regardless of whether they worked in shipbuilding or construction; all carpenters were in one union, and so forth. The new principle of organization gave birth to the Congress of Industrial Organizations (CIO). In the CIO, all auto workers were grouped together, regardless of the craft they practiced. Similarly, all steel workers would be grouped together, and so forth. This meant that, for the first time, unskilled and assembly line workers had unions representing them. By the end of the 1930s, the CIO had established itself as a rival group to the AFL. In contrast to the AFL's principle of non-involvement, a number of prominent CIO leaders believed that labor should not ignore politics. Otherwise, as one of their spokesmen often observed, what labor gained at the bargaining table could be lost in Washington. Moreover, the CIO leaders believed that labor could be a major force to bring about policies that would help not only union members but also working people in general.

When the AFL and the CIO merged in 1955, the CIO concept of political action quickly became dominant. The combined AFL-CIO has about 13.5 million members. There are about a million members each in two important independent unions, the Teamsters and the United Automobile, Aerospace, and Agricultural Implement Workers (UAW). Altogether, about a quarter of the total working force in America belongs to unions.

Unions are a good deal more centralized as pressure groups at the national level than are businesses. The AFL-CIO is, of course, the most important. Each of the constituent unions in the AFL-CIO, called *internationals*, maintains its own Washington headquarters and its own lobbyists, campaign workers, and campaign fund. So do the independent unions such as the Teamsters and the UAW. But there are only 110 internationals and a handful of independent unions, compared to the thousands of trade associations and hundreds of thousands of independent economic units, ranging from corporations to large cooperatives. Thus, the points of contact between labor unions and the government are fewer than those between business and the government. The labor movement also tends to concentrate on major issues, whereas the business associations are able to exert pressure on a broad range of topics. There is no counterpart in the labor movement to the thousands of minor, specialized decisions that occupy a great deal of the political activity of individual trade associations and corporations.

To be sure, some individual unions do pursue their own specialized aims. For example, the primary goal of the American Postal Workers Union is federal legislation that would give postal workers the right to strike. In 1973, they reported spending $393,399 on Washington lobbying. This was the third highest amount officially reported by any lobby that year.[6] Sometimes the union in a particular industry will find itself allied with the employers. For example, the UAW has joined with auto manufacturers to lobby for repeal of the excise tax on automobiles. Such practices are especially common in industries that are heavily regulated by the federal government. Thus, the chairman of the Subcommittee on the Merchant Marine of the House Committee on Merchant Marine and Fisheries received very substantial financial support from both management and labor, including a $15,000 contribution from the Marine Engineers Union in 1974.[7]

LABOR'S POLITICAL GOALS. The AFL-CIO itself, as well as many of its constituent internationals, is concerned with a far wider range of issues than any business group. The unions are interested not merely in laws regulating their activities, but also in matters that affect what they consider to be the well-being of workers, whether or not they belong to unions. *The labor movement is active on more issues and influential on more issues than any other single interest group.*

Labor representatives are generally the most active and influential lobbyists on tax reform, medical insurance, school aid, most consumer issues, and many other proposals that would result in redistribution of income from the wealthy to the working classes. The labor movement is also the strongest source of pressure for enactment of legislation to guarantee racial equality in employment, voting, public facilities, and other areas where discrimination was previously a way of life in the South.

The unions were not particularly interested in many of the issues which seemed most important in the late 1960s, including the war in Vietnam, environmental affairs, defense spending, and "lifestyle" concerns in general. When they did take positions on these issues, the union lobbyists were often opposed to the liberal side. Thus the unions, which at one time seemed to be on the left wing of the Democratic party, increasingly have found themselves cast as "conservatives" on many controversial issues. But, as the so-called "new politics" issues that were so prominent in the sixties fade with the

GEORGE MEANY,
PRESIDENT OF THE
AFL-CIO, EMBODIES
UNION INFLUENCE IN
NATIONAL POLITICS
Wide World Photos

[6] *CQ Weekly Report,* July 27, 1974, p. 1948.
[7] *New York Times,* November 10, 1974, p. 57.

depression, inflation, and energy shortages of the seventies, the unions may once again move back to the position they formerly occupied as the liberal stimulus in Washington.

At present, however, the unions are still locked in the struggle within the Democratic party over party rules and presidential nominees. This was particularly notable in the 1972 election, when the unions were almost wholly excluded from participation in the Democratic convention that nominated George McGovern. McGovern had never been particularly friendly to the unions, and his enthusiastic young supporters felt that the labor movement's traditional economic concerns were old-fashioned. One prominent labor leader expressed the union's side of the dispute as follows:

> We're going to talk bread and butter to our people, and we think by the time November 3 comes around this will have an impact. [Democrats should] stay away from esoteric issues that seem to involve liberals — unlimited busing, unlimited abortions, legalized homosexuality, legalized marijuana, paying reparations to Hanoi When the influence of this kind of people gets dominant, we lose. I look upon myself as a political pragmatist. I want to win. I am not interested in winning arguments and losing elections.[8]

The AFL-CIO's highly publicized abstention from McGovern's campaign surely was a heavy blow to his chances, although it was hardly responsible for his defeat.

Working through its principal political arm, the Committee on Political Education (COPE), the labor movement has come a long way from the days when it followed a nonpartisan policy. Today it is, in fact, the single most important element within the Democratic party. In 1972, organized labor gave more money to congressional candidates than any other interest group. Unions contributed $45,000 or more to each of twelve Senate candidates and $21,000 or more to each of thirteen candidates for the House. In the series of special elections to fill vacancies in the House of Representatives in 1974, labor was particularly active. As one labor leader put it, "The Democratic National Committee didn't give a thing—it was almost entirely a labor effort. We don't need the DNC; they need us."[9] COPE gave $5,000 or more to forty-one freshmen Democrats elected to the House of Representatives for the first time in 1974.[10]

In addition to giving money, many unions also train campaign organizers. In fact, several unions have the capacity to assume most of the specialized work in a congressional campaign. Moreover, unions typically expend a great deal of effort registering sympathetically inclined citizens and then getting them to polls on election day. Unions are probably the only interest group which can mobilize enough manpower to conduct precinct work in

[8] Quoted in "Bread and Butter Man," *The Pressure Groups*, p. 79.
[9] *CQ Weekly Report*, June 8, 1974, pp. 1476–78.
[10] *New York Times*, November 10, 1974, p. 57.

the same style as political machines or the "new politics" ideologues. Although a substantial minority of union members are Republicans, the campaign actitivies of the unions are conducted almost entirely on behalf of Democratic candidates. It is unusual for a Republican to receive substantial support from unions other than the handful of Republican-inclined unions such as the Teamsters and some of the building trade unions.

PROFESSIONAL ASSOCIATIONS

As we have seen, the labor movement became a formidable political force as a result of a change in its leaders' perceptions of the economic relevance of politics. The traditionally nonpartisan, politically cautious trade union leaders were replaced by a newer generation who believed that unions should engage in the political struggle. A similar process is occurring in some professional organizations, which traditionally have remained aloof from politics. The most interesting example is the National Education Association (NEA). The NEA has long been the major professional organization representing schoolteachers. Until recently, it eschewed political involvement. In 1972, it formally decided to abandon this policy and plunge into politics. As its aggressive new executive secretary remarked, "The united teaching profession is on the brink of an unprecedented professional offensive. Its aim is to give teachers the decision-making authority, the public esteem, and the economic remuneration they deserve and must have." The NEA has an annual budget of $34.5 million and a Washington staff of 670. When it decided to enter politics in 1972, it formed NEA-PAC, its own political action committee, along the lines of similar committees founded by the unions, business organizations, and such other professional groups as bankers and doctors. The NEA and its state political affiliates spent $3.74 million on election campaigns in 1974[11]

The NEA's wealth and extensive membership give it the potential for considerable political influence. One of its first projects was to help the re-election campaign of Senator Claiborne Pell, the chairman of the Education Subcommittee of the Senate Committee on Labor and Public Welfare. The NEA's major long-term goal is increased federal funding for education. Because Senator Pell favors this aim, the teachers felt it important to keep him in office. Pell explained the result this way:

> My election is a victory for teacher power. Before the teachers began to help me, I was a two-to-one underdog. Now, thanks to an army of teachers who knocked on thousands of doors and made thousands of phone calls, I have won by more than 33,000 votes. This victory is a victory for education.[12]

---

[11] CQ Weekly Report, June 1, 1974, p. 1414; National Journal Reports, August 30, 1975, p. 1246.
[12] CQ Weekly Report, June 1, 1974, p. 1415.

One of the NEA's allies in its struggle for such goals as higher federal educational aid and winning the right to strike for public employees is its rival, the American Federation of Teachers (AFT), an AFL-CIO union. The AFT has 400,000 members and competes with the NEA to represent teachers. Its more aggressive attitude toward political action may have been partly responsible for pushing the NEA into its new politically active role. Although the NEA and the AFT are allies on some issues, they are opposed on others, such as the sales tax, which the NEA supports and the AFT opposes.

The NEA manages to engage in political action even though its members are evenly divided between Democrats and Republicans. Here, as with the unions, a strong organization seems able to overcome divided political sentiments among its members.

The NEA illustrates two important generalizations: (1) Changes in political consciousness can induce previously quiet groups to enter the political scene. (2) Like many other interest groups, it is capable of forming alliances for particular purposes, and then of opposing its former allies on other issues.

POLITICAL INTEREST GROUPS

The groups that we have discussed up to now have one extremely important characteristic in common. Political action is *incidental* to their principal purposes. None of them was formed specifically for the purpose of engaging in politics. The bulk of their services is to their members. One of the most influential students of interest groups has described them this way:

> The common characteristic which distinguishes all of the large economic groups with significant lobbying organizations is that these groups are also organized for some other purpose. Large and powerful economic lobbies are in fact the byproducts of organizations that obtain their strength and support because they perform some function in addition to lobbying for collective goods.[13]

ALBERT SHANKER OF THE AMERICAN FEDERATION OF TEACHERS.
Wide World Photos

This is true of all organizations that represent the economic interests of their members. Politics is a byproduct of their activities. The American Medical Association, for example, provides its members with such benefits as journals, educational conventions, defense in malpractice suits, and admission to hospitals. All of these are nonpolitical benefits that make the association attractive to its members for reasons that have nothing to do with politics. It is these benefits that give corporations, trade associations, professional organizations, and unions the basis of their organizational strength.

There are, however, organizations whose *primary* purposes are political. These organizations are not sustained by a desire to provide their mem-

[13] Mancur Olson, Jr., *The Logic of Collective Action* (Cambridge: Harvard University Press, 1965), p. 132.

bers with individual benefits. Instead, they aim directly, via politics, at what economists call "collective goods." These organizations are a good deal smaller in size than those for which politics is a byproduct. Whether, for this reason, they are less politically effective has never been demonstrated.

ETHNIC GROUPS

As we saw in Chapter 7, increasing numbers of black Americans are acutely alert to their political interests. Blacks vote for and against candidates on the basis of the candidate's perceived position on racial issues. The reason is that blacks increasingly have become a politically self-conscious reference group. With the expansion of racial consciousness in the 1960s, political participation by blacks increased sharply and is now at a level similar to whites, despite the lower educational level of blacks. Since the mid-1950s, blacks have won a series of important victories at the federal government level, beginning with the landmark Supreme Court decision in 1954 outlawing school segregation and extending through a series of historic acts of Congress. Although the record of White House commitment to civil rights measures has been somewhat more uneven, the effect of federal involvement on the racial front has been persistently in the direction of greater equality and opportunity. There is no doubt that these victories by blacks reflect in large measure increasing black political awareness, the ability of blacks to hurt their enemies and help their friends, as well as the development in Washington of a powerful network of alliances that link blacks to the labor movement, to organized religion, and to an assortment of ideological liberal organizations.

In other words, American blacks in the 1970s are a powerful interest group in every sense of the word. This is so even though the stable, solidly established organizations devoted exclusively to black interests are neither nu-

SINCE THE MID-
1950s, TACTICS OF
LITIGATION, POLIT-
ICAL ACTION, AND
LOBBYING HAVE
MADE BLACKS A
SIGNIFICANT INTER-
EST GROUP.
Wide World Photos

merous nor very large. By far the most important of these has been the National Association for the Advancement of Colored People. The NAACP has been the organizational spearhead of black attempts for racial equality for more than half a century. Together with its legal fund, a separate but allied organization, the NAACP has symbolized black aspirations and has lobbied for them in the halls of Congress and in the White House. Yet the NAACP has a membership of only 440,000, many of whom are white. Its gross income in 1974 was less than $2 million.[14] Other black organizations are much smaller than the NAACP, in terms both of membership and of financial resources.

Clearly, the political influence of blacks cannot be measured by the sparse membership and budgets of black organizations. This leads us to an important generalization. *The power of an interest group cannot be measured by the size of its formal organizations.* Few politicians doubt the power of black voters. But at the same time, few people think that the power of blacks is contained *in their organizations.*

Another point about black political action is a negative one. Blacks are one of the few major ethnic groups in this country to have virtually no influence on American foreign policy toward their homeland. In fact, there is virtually no effort by blacks to influence American foreign policy toward either Africa in general or toward specific issues involving individual African countries.[15]

In this respect, blacks contrast strikingly with American Jews. Although Jews are exceptionally active in politics as voters, campaign workers, and contributors, there is very little Jewish interest in domestic politics on issues that pertain explicitly to Jews. In all their varied political engagements, Jews do not make demands on the government as Jews, insofar as domestic policy is concerned. But the picture is very different on foreign policy. There Jews are a self-conscious interest group concerned, of course, with securing favorable American policy toward Israel. The American Israel Public Affairs Committee (AIPAC) is an umbrella organization for over thirty individual Jewish groups that represent every segment of the American Jewish community. It has a staff of 20, an annual budget of $400,000, and about 15,000 members.[16] When Congress takes up an issue that concerns Israel, the AIPAC can mobilize a network of activists around the country, each of whom in turn can bring into action a corps of influential citizens.

Jewish influence on American policy toward Israel is partly a result of the concentration of Jews in large states and partly a result of generalized American support for Israel vis à vis the Arab nations, as shown in numerous public opinion polls. But that influence also derives from the fact that Jews are an important source of financial contributions to the Democratic party, out of all proportion to their percentage of the population. A

AMERICAN JEWS ARE A SELF-CONSCIOUS INTEREST GROUP WITH RESPECT TO FOREIGN POLICY. HERE, COSTUMED PRO-ISRAEL MARCHERS PASS A PRO-ARAB GROUP IN A PARADE MARKING ISRAEL'S 27TH ANNIVERSAY. *Wide World Photos*

[14] *The Crisis,* March 1975, p. 99.

[15] For a discussion of the lack of black political pressure on African policy, see Roger Wilkins, "What Africa Means to Blacks," *Foreign Policy,* Summer 1974, p. 133.

[16] *CQ Weekly Report,* August 30, 1975, p. 1871.

number of important politicians from areas with virtually no Jewish residents are active champions of Israel. As we observed earlier, most wealthy Americans are Republicans. But most Jews are Democrats, and a good number are financially well-off. Therefore, it turns out that a substantial proportion of well-to-do Democrats are Jewish, a source of strength for the pro-Israel lobby.

Other ethnic groups also have a good deal of influence on American foreign policy or are capable of being influential if their reference group attachments are brought to the fore politically. For example, the congressional vote in 1974 to cut off aid to Turkey was a response to pressure from Greek-Americans outraged by the Turkish invasion of Cyprus.

IDEOLOGICAL AND PUBLIC INTEREST GROUPS

One thing that the Chamber of Commerce, the NAACP, and the NEA have in common is their devotion to looking after the interests of their members and constituents. Other groups, which have grown vastly in importance in the last few years, do not claim to speak for a particular interest or a particular group, or even for those of a particular point of view. One of these new groups describes itself as a "non-partisan people's lobby." As we shall see, there is room for doubt about whether these groups do indeed speak for "the people." But there can be no doubt at all that they do not appeal to economic self-interest in recruiting supporters and financial support. They rely instead on idealism and ideological commitment. Their members tend to resemble the "purists" we discussed in Chapter 7.

For many years a variety of economically "unselfish" groups have operated in politics. They have represented ideological inclinations ranging from far left to far right, and have been active on issues ranging from prayer in the schools to preservation of wilderness areas. In the last few years, however, a new kind of group of this sort has grown up, based on the power of publicity, direct mail fund-raising techniques, and the use of litigation as a means of political action.

It once was an axiom of interest group studies that associations are effective when they pursue issues that involve the *productive interests* of individuals. When a person's livelihood is threatened or when opportunities to improve his or her position come up, it is easy and logical to form associations to deal with these situations and to pressure the government. Under most circumstances, it is harder to bring together the broad mass of individuals who buy things, pay taxes, and breathe air. People who make something or supply a service tend to focus their attention on that process since it is the core of their livelihood. But everyone is at once a consumer, a user of the environment, and a taxpayer. There is no similar intense individual focus for issues involving these aspects of life. It is this imbalance in determination and attention that, more than anything else, accounts for the weak enforcement of many laws concerned with protection of consumer interests, such as the Pure Food and Drug Act and the Meat Inspection Act.

THE CONSUMER MOVEMENT AND RALPH NADER. The political power of consumers has been increasing markedly since the mid 1960s. The public career of Ralph Nader is a landmark to this development. In 1965, Nader's book *Unsafe at Any Speed* created a sensation. In it, Nader launched an attack on the Corvair, a compact car made by General Motors. He argued that the car had such fundamental safety defects that it was prone to fatal accidents even at low speeds. Trying to discredit its annoying critic, General Motors hired a private detective to investigate him. Among other things, illegal efforts were made to pry into his private life and to trap him in a sexual adventure. In the course of seeking to smite David, Goliath instead made him a king. The General Motors sleuthing was uncovered in the course of a congressional investigation into auto safety. The president of General Motors apologized to Nader publicly. The resulting publicity aided the passage of the National Traffic and Motor Vehicle Safety Act and the Highway Safety Act, two major laws which brought federal control into the area of automobile design. Nader brought a multimillion dollar suit against General Motors for invasion of privacy and settled out of court for $280,000, which he promptly used to help develop his extensive program on consumer protection activities.

Nader went on to build a remarkable career as a political activist. A gifted writer and speaker, he earned hundreds of thousands of dollars annually in royalties and speaking fees. This income helped finance a burgeoning empire of organizations devoted to reforming various aspects of American life. Nader became a hero on college campuses. Together with his organizational talents, this reputation helped him enlist thousands of recent college and law school graduates in his various organizations. Working at low salaries, or

Cartoon strip by Hank Ketcham; © 1975 Field Newspaper Syndicate

even as unpaid volunteers, people associated with Nader soon began to investigate, expose, and report on a wide variety of government agencies and private corporations, ranging from the Food and Drug Administration to the nursing home industry. By the early 1970s, at least nineteen organizations were associated directly or indirectly with Nader, on an annual budget of over $2.5 million. This far-flung network was supported by Nader's book royalties and lecture fees, by grants from foundations, and finally, in the 1970s, by a national organization called Public Citizen, Inc., which used sophisticated direct mail techniques to raise more than a million dollars in its first year of operation.[17]

Nader's initial impact on government was the result of his extraordinary ability as a publicist. The numerous projects conducted under his sponsorship often succeeded because the magic of Nader's name induced cooperation from officials who might otherwise have been reluctant to provide information. Recently, the emphasis of Nader's work has shifted from sensational exposés to litigation. The power to sue is a formidable political instrument. As many political observers have learned over the years, passing a law is only the first battle in a continuing struggle. It is something of a cliché among reformers that many problems do not need new laws; they could be solved if the laws already on the books were adequately enforced. Recognizing the truth of this insight, Nader's organization and other groups unconnected with Nader have turned to suing the government to compel it to enforce the law, or to suing private interests that may be violating the law.

For the private citizen, litigation is usually a prohibitively expensive way to get what one wants out of the government. This is primarily because lawyers are expensive. But if a lawyer does not charge for his time, or if he is employed by a public interest law firm, or even by a conventional firm that releases its members to work part-time in the public interest, then litigation changes from an expensive luxury into one of the cheapest forms of political action. This elementary fact, combined with the availability of hundreds of young law school graduates eager to use their training for idealistic purposes, has led to the development of nearly one hundred "public interest" organizations in Washington alone. One of the most important of these is the Center for Law and Social Policy (CLASP). It has a board of directors of eminent citizens, a million-dollar budget provided largely by foundations, eighteen staff lawyers, and sixteen law student interns.[18] CLASP is only one of dozens of similar organizations that attract young, idealistic people who work very long hours for relatively low salaries.

COMMON CAUSE. Low-paid or volunteer workers are one solution to the problem of financing public interest lobbies. The most important source of

[17] Theodore Jacqueney, "Nader's Focus," *National Journal Reports,* June 9, 1973, pp. 840–49.
[18] Theodore Jacqueney, "Public Interest," *National Journal Reports,* February 23, 1974, pp. 267–77.

funds for these organizations, however, is direct mail advertising. Common Cause, the best-known of all the public interest groups, depends almost entirely on direct mail membership drives and fund-raising campaigns. Founded in 1970 by John Gardner, a Secretary of Health, Education, and Welfare in the Johnson administration, Common Cause grew in four years to an organization with 325,000 members and an income of $6.5 million. Unlike other public interest groups, which are composed almost entirely of politically inexperienced young lawyers and scientists, Common Cause is well staffed with seasoned veterans of the Washington scene. After Gardner, its two most important figures are Jack T. Conway, a former labor leader and head of the federal antipoverty program, and David Cohen, a protégé of Conway's and a former lobbyist for the labor movement and for Americans for Democratic Action, a traditional liberal organization.

Common Cause has had as many as thirty-five professional employees in its Washington office and has generated over 2 million pieces of mail each month. Its "Washington Connection," a telephone network connecting headquarters in Washington and volunteer members in hundreds of congressional districts, is used to pressure individual congressmen. At peak effectiveness, the connection could mobilize as many as three thousand members for this purpose. Common Cause regularly sends press releases to every radio and television station in the country and to every newspaper with a circulation of more than ten thousand. It supplies a daily five-minute radio show to 125 stations.[19]

Common Cause's principal focus is on lobbying Congress. Originally, it concentrated on such "structural" issues as campaign financing, lobby registration, and reforming congressional procedures. It has since become involved in substantive questions such as tax policy. Like other public interest groups, Common Cause's lobbying allies include the trade unions and such explicitly liberal ideological organizations as Americans for Democratic Action.

BY THE PUBLIC OR FOR THE PUBLIC? Common Cause and the Nader direct mail operation, Public Citizen, Inc., are the two most widespread fund-raising efforts in this field. Each asks for an annual contribution of fifteen dollars. Their fund-raising letters paint a dire picture of the country's condition (see box), but also claim spectacular successes for their respective organizations. Nader's letters say that "our society is not best left in the custody of the powerful few. So the citizen movement must take action." Without passing judgment on the policies advocated by these groups, it is possible to be skeptical of their claims that they are a "citizen movement" and that they substantially increase the number of people who actively participate in politics.

[19] Theodore Jacqueney, "Common Cause," *National Journal Reports,* September 1, 1973, pp. 1294–1304.

EXCERPTS FROM COMMON CAUSE'S DIRECT-MAIL APPEALS

And do you really feel safe and comfortable in the privacy of your own home (as guaranteed by the Constitution) when the U.S. Department of Justice continues to be a political office?

Remember . . . only the tip of the iceberg of political corruption and the misuse of power was revealed in the Watergate scandal. The cancer of corruption in government still has not been removed. And it is up to you to see that our government is restored to full health.

Our name tells our story. Common Cause is a dynamic citizens' movement, a non-partisan people's lobby. We are Democrats, Republicans and Independents who have joined forces in our fight for the rights we all share. We are a common cause. We came together in Common Cause because we found that everybody was organized except the people! We stand in answer to the small voice of the solitary citizen crying, "What good does any single voice do? Who can hear it?" When 325,000 voices are joined, they can be heard loud and clear.

Remember: Your government is your business. Common Cause was born of a dire need to return to all citizens their constitutionally guaranteed right of having their voices heard in their own government.

In the first place, the number of people who contribute, while large in absolute numbers, is an infinitesimal fraction of the total public. Second, these groups make it clear that what they want from their contributors is money, not any other kind of participation. Third, they are a long way from representing all major elements of American public opinion. Common Cause describes itself as a "non-partisan people's lobby." In fact, like virtually all the other public interest organizations, it is decidedly on the liberal side of the political spectrum. The "public interest" field seems at present to be a monopoly of the left. Perhaps some day the pendulum will swing in the other direction here, as it does in so many areas of political life, and the techniques of direct mail fund-raising, publicity, and litigation will be more broadly used across the political spectrum. (They already have been used by Alabama Governor George Wallace for conservative electoral campaign fund raising.) But for the present at least, the mantle of the "citizens' lobby" seems firmly settled on activists who represent the views of only one segment of the population.

INTERNAL DEMOCRACY AND EXTERNAL EFFECTIVENESS

The inner life of interest groups is a subject that has fascinated many political scientists. The way in which a group is organized is determined largely by its nature. If its principal purpose is *not* politics, then one can expect that it will be organized in accordance with that purpose. For example, business firms are not organized democratically and are not responsive to anyone other than their management and, ultimately, their stockholders.

Trade associations that represent groups of businesses are based, however, on the consent and support of their members. The staffs of such organizations are acutely sensitive to what constituent individuals and firms want. That such groups have to touch base with so many members before they can take action is one reason why they are sometimes rather cumbersome in their lobbying.

Most other sorts of organized interest groups have at least the facade of democratic organization. Often, however, as in the case of labor unions, the facade conceals a reality that is fundamentally different. But whether a group is officially democratic is of less significance than the fact that virtually all groups are controlled by the minority of members who are interested enough to be active. Most people do not care enough about their associations to vote, much less come to meetings or otherwise take part. This means that the leadership does not need the support of the bulk of the members and must maintain the support only of the *active minority* if it is to remain in power. This control of voluntary associations by the active minority of their members has been called the "iron law of oligarchy." This phrase was coined by the sociologist Robert Michels, who argued that any organization is bound to be dominated by its active minority, because the inactive members delegate to the leaders not only the conduct of affairs, but also policy decisions about what to do.[20]

Some mass membership groups do not even make a pretense of consulting their members. Nader's direct mail fund-raising organization, Public Citizen, Inc., is in this category. The literature produced by Public Citizen makes clear that the function of a member is to contribute fifteen dollars a year. Nader and his associates make the decisions about how to spend the money. The only way in which members can indicate their disapproval of the group's activities is to stop contributing. In contrast, Common Cause from time to time does poll its members to find out their views about what priorities the organization should follow. Only about 10 percent of the membership responds, however. One conclusion to be drawn is that even in this "citizens' lobby," members are not very influential. Indeed, Common Cause policy is made, from start to finish, by the professional staff, who have no trouble getting rubber stamp approval from the board of directors.[21] Another conclusion from these facts is equally valid, however. Most members of Common Cause in fact do not *want* to be influential in deciding what the organization should do. Their willingness to give money in what they consider a good cause is not matched by their willingness to make any other

[20] See Robert Michels, *Political Parties: A Sociological Study of the Oligarchical Tendencies of Modern Democracy*, trans. Eden and Cedar Paul (New York: The Free Press, 1966, originally published in 1911).

[21] Jacqueney, "Common Cause," p. 1296.

effort. They may be fully willing to contribute to "democracy" without themselves participating democratically in the organization they fund.

This attitude is not particularly surprising. Why *should* the member of Common Cause—or of the Teamsters Union or any other group, for that matter—care much about internal democracy as long as the organization provides what he wants from it? If a member of the union gets higher wages and better working conditions as a result of the leaders' activities, is it important to him that the leaders are really not democratically elected? If a member of Common Cause or Public Citizen, Inc., is pleased by the lobbying efforts of John Gardner or Ralph Nader, what is lost by failing to have a say in what they do? These are, after all, voluntary associations. People who are dissatisfied with them are at liberty to fail to renew their membership, thus voting with their checkbooks. Indeed, a substantial minority of such organizations exercises this liberty every year. Thus direct mail organizations must devote a good deal of money to "cleaning their lists" and otherwise maintaining an adequate financial base.

PRESSURE GROUPS OR CONCERNED CITIZENS?

For such reasons as those just indicated, it is fundamentally misleading to see politics as a contest between "selfish interests" and "the people." For one thing, who has the right to decide which demands made by different people are selfish and which are not? It is easy and comfortable to view a corporation seeking a favorable tax law as "selfish." But in what way are the poor less "selfish" for wanting higher welfare payments, minimum wage laws, day care centers, and public housing? Are they any more or less selfish than coal miners who want to impose a quota on the import of foreign oil, or doctors who wish to limit the licensing of new medical schools? It is a truism that most people want what they can get from the government. Indeed, our political tradition insists that one of the reasons why government exists, and one of the reasons why people consent to be governed, is because the government can provide its citizens with some of the things they want.

Moreover, any given proposal is likely to be supported by a coalition made up of people with very different motivations, some of which may seem selfish and some of which may seem altruistic. Doctors calling for higher federal funding of cancer research may have very different motives from laymen who are determined to find a cure for the nation's second most important cause of death. Similarly, one of the annual goals of the milk industry's six fulltime lobbyists on Capitol Hill is being sure that the federal school milk program is not excluded from the budget. Their allies in this connection are some of the most liberal, public-spirited groups in Washington. The milk industry lobbyists may be selfishly concerned with the money the dairymen will get from the government, while the liberal groups are concerned with the nutrition the children will get from the milk. But both are pulling in the same direction.

Few policies do not bring tangible and immediate economic benefits to some particular individuals or groups. Thus, it is usually quite artificial to begin with the premise that politics consists simply of conflict between good guys and bad guys. A few years ago, a controversy arose over a canal that the Army Corps of Engineers was building across the width of Florida. Intense pressure by alarmed conservationists finally created so much public opposition to the project that President Nixon ordered the engineers to stop building the canal. This was a victory for groups concerned about the quality of the environment and the protection of endangered species. But it was also a triumph for the railroad interests, whose business was threatened by the possiblity of barge traffic across Florida. Indeed, the railroads contributed generously to the conservation organizations that conducted the publicity campaign. In short, it is not uncommon for idealists to find themselves linked in uneasy alliance with vested interests.

We tend to define selfishness in limited and material terms. If someone wants a law passed because it will raise his income, we consider that selfish. But there are many other motivations in politics, including power, self-righteousness, and other aspects of the murkier depths of the human psyche. Often the most intense political struggles involve intangible values, such as religion, racial prejudice, moral standards, and other things that have little to do with money. The desire to fulfill these motivations may be just as deeply based in private, self-centered psychological needs as desires to enhance one's economic well-being.

For all these reasons, it is important to realize that interest groups do not clearly divide between "selfish" vested interests and selfless paragons of virtue. Interest groups, as defined analytically, enormously vary in motivation. A group in favor of better health care for poor families is just as much an interest group as one seeking to have the government purchase silver. That one of these policies is an uneconomical use of public money for no useful purpose and the other will bring health and happiness to people deprived of basic human needs does not alter the fact that both groups are trying to influence economic conditions through government action.

THE POWER OF ANTICIPATED REACTIONS

Sometimes an interest group can gain a major victory without any organized pressure at all. One striking example of this came during the passage of the Civil Rights Act of 1964. Among other provisions, this law prohibits discrimination in employment on grounds of race or sex. The bill was aimed at discrimination against blacks. As originally drafted, it had nothing to say about women. Women's rights were not a conspicuous political issue in 1963 and 1964. But when the measure was being debated in the House of Representatives, it was amended to cover discrimination on grounds of sex as well as race. This change was introduced by the leader of the bill's opponents, who calculated that his "sex amendment" would muddy the waters, provoke stronger opposition to the bill, and dilute its eventual impact on racial equality by smothering the enforcement agency in complaints from women. As it turned out, he was right, but his stratagem did not affect the bill's passage.

After being passed by the House, the bill came before the Senate. Officials of the National Association of Manufacturers were alarmed at the sex amendment. They expressed their opposition to Everett Dirksen, the Republican leader in the Senate and a pivotal figure in the bill's consideration there. Dirksen told the NAM that many of his fellow Republican senators shared its dislike of the sex amendment, but that not one of them would introduce an amendment to strike it from the bill. None of them wanted to chance the retribution from women that might result from publicly opposing a provision to outlaw sex discrimination. The result was the survival of the sex amendment, which has become the principal legal instrument against sex discrimination.[22]

One of the interesting features in the history of this law is the fact that there was no lobbying of consequence by women's groups in favor of the sex amendment. Indeed, in those years there was hardly any women's groups taking active political positions. The sex amendment was not a hard-won victory by advocates of women's rights, but the inadvertent outcome of an unsuccessful strategy to defeat the bill. Yet it stayed in the bill because politicians feared female outrage if attempts were made to remove it. Two conclusions, then, can be drawn from this episode.

1. Under certain circumstances, interest groups need not be organized or even politically conscious to be important in policy making.
2. Interest groups often are influential not because of anything they do but because of what they are thought capable of doing. In other words, *anticipated reactions* can be as potent as direct pressure. As in poker, sometimes the cards you hold matter less than the cards the other players think you hold.

INTEREST GROUP TACTICS

The three principal ways that interest groups try to get what they want are *litigation, political action,* and *lobbying.* Each of these is discussed to some extent in another chapter. Here we will examine these techniques specifically as they relate to the goals of interest groups.

LITIGATION

Interest groups traditionally have turned to the courts to get what they could not obtain from Congress or the executive branch, or to overturn

[22] See David B. Filvaroff and Raymond E. Wolfinger, *The Civil Rights Act of 1964* (forthcoming).

laws and executive regulations that they found distasteful. For the first third of the twentieth century, business organizations were quite successful in using the process of judicial review to frustrate various attempts to regulate their activities. This was most notable during the early New Deal, much of which was foiled by Supreme Court decisions declaring progressive legislation unconstitutional. In the 1950s, the courts became the principal source of relief for black organizations that wanted enforcement of the Constitution's guarantees of equality. These organizations often mustered high-powered voluntary legal talent, including law professors. More recently, public interest groups have turned to the courts to force thorough administration of the laws.

The antipoverty program initiated in the mid 1960s provided a powerful legal resource that vastly expanded these efforts. Part of the original antipoverty program was the legal services program, initially conceived as a way to provide lawyers to people too poor to afford them. Many of the neighborhood legal groups funded by this program quickly evolved into sources of legal help for various reformist and radical organizations. For example, the San Francisco Neighborhood Legal Assistance Foundation, financed by the Office of Economic Opportunity, "serves as the chief law office for the entire California Welfare Rights Organization." In this capacity, the poverty lawyers won important cases, including one that removed California's residence requirements for welfare recipients and another that increased the total welfare payments in California by $155 million a year.[23]

The principle of using litigation as a means of pressure group activity was affirmed by the Supreme Court in 1963 in the case of *NAACP* v. *Button:*

> . . . In the context of NAACP objectives, litigation is not a technique of resolving private differences; . . . it is thus a form of political expression. Groups which find themselves unable to achieve their objectives through the ballot frequently turn to the courts. Just as it was true of the opponents of New Deal legislation during the 1930s, for example, no less is it true of the Negro minority today. . . . For such a group, association for litigation may be the most effective form of political association.[24]

POLITICAL ACTION

Defeating disliked candidates or trying to elect sympathetic ones is unquestionably the most widespread form of interest group activity. Any citizen whose vote is based upon anything other than simple party loyalty or the sheer attractiveness of a candidate's personality is engaging in a form of pressure politics. He or she is helping a friend or hurting an enemy. Starting with the simplest kind of political reward and punishment, political action

[23] *San Francisco Chronicle,* August 7, 1972, p. 10.
[24] *N.A.A.C.P. v. Button,* 371 U.S. 415 (1963).

runs the gamut of activity up to electioneering and campaign contributions, as we saw in Chapter 7. Even before the fall election campaigns got under way in 1974, a total of 526 different special interest groups had raised $16.7 million to give to candidates. Labor unions had by far the largest share of this kitty—$6.1 million. Doctors and other members of the health professions were second with $3.9 million.[25]

For the most part, as we indicated in Chapter 7, such contributions are motivated by a generalized desire to put sympathetic candidates in office. It is usually difficult to trace a direct cause and effect between such donations and actual decisions in the government. Occasionally, however, the connections do become exceedingly clear. In 1968, the American Medical Association's Political Action Committee gave $681,965 to the Nixon campaign. According to a well-informed pair of Washington reporters, this was a crucial factor in the White House's 1969 decision to oppose the appointment of an outspoken reforming doctor as Assistant Secretary of Health, Education and Welfare.[26]

The decision that President Nixon made in 1971 to overrule his Secretary of Agriculture and increase the federal milk support price closely followed a series of contributions to Nixon's 1972 campaign by the American Milk Producers, Inc., that eventually amounted to over $600,000. There is no way to prove that the contributions produced the price increase, but the decision by the President was so well synchronized with the contributions by AMPI that suspicions were inevitable. The entire episode produced such a taint on "milk money" that some candidates to whom the milk producers contributed in 1974 returned their checks rather than take the risk of guilt by association. This does not mean that contributions are the only way in which interest groups can influence candidates. Simple endorsement of a candidate by a popular interest group leader may be just as effective as money and is usually a good deal less subject to moral judgments.

LOBBYING

Lobbying, a term that has widespread sinister connotations, is nothing more than trying to induce Congress to introduce, modify, pass, or kill legislation. A lobbyist is someone who spends much or all of his time in this pursuit. Some lobbyists are part-time or temporary Washington representatives for their employers or clients. Others represent several interests simultaneously or in succession. Lobbyists of this sort tend to be lawyers and public relations specialists. Most of them have worked on Capitol Hill or in the executive branch, and some are former members of Congress. The District of Columbia bar has its share of attorneys with conventional practices, but it also includes a host of lawyers who specialize in government work, a type of practice that inevitably shades into lobbying.

Many important national interest groups retain Washington law firms and

[25] *CQ Weekly Report,* September 28, 1974.
[26] Rowland Evans, Jr., and Robert D. Novak, *Nixon in the White House* (New York: Random House, 1972), pp. 61–65.

also employ lobbyists who serve as long-term advocates for the organization or cause. The most influential lobbyists in this category are significant figures on the Washington scene. They are on a first-name basis with hundreds of politicians and reporters and are major spokesmen for the interests they represent.

One of the lobbyist's important activities is providing sympathetically inclined members of Congress with information favorable to the lobbyist's clients. Although this is done primarily to alert congressional allies to a threat or an opportunity, it can benefit the members of Congress by supplying them with useful information. Of course, such information always must be weighed carefully, since it obviously does not come from a disinterested source. On the other hand, only the most short-sighted group representative would deliberately misinform a congressman in order to get support on a particular issue. Like a salesman, a group advocate must have credibility to enjoy long-run success. Occasionally, a lobby scores a coup by being the only source of relevant information. When Congress convened in 1975, the seventy-five new Democratic representatives held the balance of power in the fight about maintaining the seniority system for appointing committee chairmen. Common Cause prepared a detailed "bill of particulars" that criticized several chairmen for violating party rules and other arbitrary behavior. This material was very influential with the freshmen, who had no personal experience with the chairmen and no other detailed sources of information about them.[27]

In addition to supplying congressmen with information beneficial to their clients, lobbyists also keep their clients informed about developments in Congress that may affect their interests. Major lobbying campaigns rely mainly on constituent pressures. Before these can be mobilized, the constituents must be informed that they are necessary. Rallying public support for a particular measure may involve stimulating mail and personal contact from constituents and inducing campaign contributors to call strategic congressmen. Sometimes a lobbyist may bluntly remind a congressman of past favors or the possibility of future help or opposition. Tactics this

---

[27] Michael J. Malbin, "House Upheaval," *National Journal Reports,* January 25, 1975, pp. 131–32.

PERHAPS THE MOST PRESTIGIOUS LOBBYIST IN WASHINGTON IS ANDREW BIEMILLER (CENTER BACKGROUND), THE CHIEF LEGISLATIVE REPRESENTATIVE OF THE AFL-CIO SINCE 1959. HE AND NEARLY 50 OTHER LABOR LOBBYISTS MEET WEEKLY TO COORDINATE THEIR EFFORTS ON CAPITOL HILL.
Wide World Photos

25 TOP SPENDERS AMONG LOBBYISTS IN 1973

The top 25 spenders of the organizations that filed lobby spending reports for 1973 are listed below with the amounts they reported spending in 1973 and 1972

ORGANIZATION	1973	1972
Common Cause	$934,835	$558,839
International Union, United Automobile, Aerospace and Agricultural Implement Workers	460,992	no spending record
American Postal Workers Union (AFL-CIO)	393,399	208,767
American Federation of Labor-Congress of Industrial Organizations (AFL-CIO)	240,800	216,294
American Trucking Associations, Inc.	226,157	137,804
American Nurses Association, Inc.	218,354	109,642
United States Savings and Loan League	204,221	191,726
Gas Supply Committee	195,537	11,263
Disabled American Veterans	193,168	159,431
The Committee of Publicly Owned Companies	180,493	no spending record
American Farm Bureau Federation	170,472	180,678
National Education Association	162,755	no spending record
National Association of Letter Carriers	160,597	154,187
National Association of Home Builders of the United States	152,177	99,031
Recording Industry Association of America, Inc.	141,111	88,396
National Council of Farmer Cooperatives	140,560	184,346
American Insurance Association	139,395	82,395
The Farmers' Educational and Co-operative Union of America	138,403	113,156
Committee of Copyright Owners	135,095	no spending record
National Housing Conference, Inc.	125,726	77,906
American Petroleum Institute	121,276	38,656
American Medical Association	114,859	96,145
Citizens for Control of Federal Spending	113,659	no spending record
American Civil Liberties Union	102,595	73,131
National Association of Insurance Agents, Inc.	87,422	50,924

Source: Congressional Quarterly Service, *The Washington Lobby* (Washington, D.C.: Congressional Quarterly Inc., 1974), 2nd ed., p. 38.

crude are unusual and can easily backfire. Usually it is enough to speak the key phrase, "We're very interested in this bill." In political code, this conveys an adequately urgent message.

A third kind of lobbying uses publicity either to make a public argument on the merits of a particular bill or simply to put direct pressure on Congress or administrators. When the Senate Finance Committee seemed reluctant to end special tax breaks for oil companies in 1975, Common Cause issued a press release claiming that members of the committee had received over $350,000 in campaign contributions from people in the oil industry. As much as the senators disliked this move, it did force them to worry about seeming too sympathetic to the oil business. This pressure undoubtedly played a role in getting the committee to report a bill that ended the oil depletion allowance.

REGULATING LOBBYING

The Federal Regulation of Lobbying Act, passed in 1946, requires lobbyists to register and report their expenses. At the beginning of 1975 there were 1,773 registered lobbyists. The total reported spending for lobbying in 1973 was $9.5 million. These figures represent only a fraction of the total lobbying effort. In part, this inadequate reporting reflects the government's failure to enforce the law. A study by the General Accounting Office found that almost half of all lobbyists' reports were incomplete and 61 percent were filed late. Yet no violation of the lobbying law has ever resulted in an indictment by the Justice Department.[28]

Lack of legal enforcement is not the most fundamental explanation for the inaccuracy of official reports. The basic problem lies in the vague language of the original law and subsequent interpretations by the Supreme Court. The gaps in the lobby registration law are obvious. But how they should be closed raises fundamental questions about whether lobbying can be effectively regulated without restraining free speech.

The 1946 law requires anyone to register and report if he or she obtains money "to be used *principally* to . . . influence, directly or indirectly, the passage or defeat of any legislation" (emphasis added). Eight years after the law went into effect, the Supreme Court used this "principal purpose" language to open a giant loophole in the law. The Court ruled that the law did not apply to organizations whose lobbying was *incidental* to their principal purpose, and that fund raising for lobbying should be covered only where "a substantial part is to be used to influence legislation." Moreover, the Court defined lobbying as "*direct* communication with Members of Congress on pending or proposed federal legislation."[29]

The result of this interpretation was to exempt organizations whose main purpose is *not* direct lobbying, that is, most groups that lobby. It also excluded "grass-roots lobbying," i.e., attempts to sway congressmen through their constituents, or by publicizing their voting records. Yet this is one of the principal techniques used by many organizations to lobby Congress. In one year, for example, the National Association of Manufacturers spent over

---

[28] Richard E. Cohen, "Lobbying Report," *National Journal Reports,* April 19, 1975, pp. 571–73.
[29] *United States v. Harriss,* 347 U.S. 612 (1954); emphasis added.

$2.5 million for activities related to grass-roots lobbying, which it did not need to report.[30]

The consequence is that very few organizations disclose what they really spend on lobbying. Common Cause is one exception. It reports every penny spent: $1.6 million in 1974 alone. In contrast, the Chamber of Commerce of the United States reported less than $1,000.[31] Since dozens of organizations do as much lobbying as Common Cause, hundreds more maintain full-time lobbyists, and innumerable more have part-time legislative representatives, one can scarcely imagine how big the hidden part of the iceberg is.

The heightened concern for precedural reform that followed the Watergate scandals has focused attention on the failure of the 1946 act to achieve its purposes. A number of bills have been introduced in Congress to close the loopholes in the law. Among the provisions in these proposals are the following:

1. Expand the definition of lobbying to include grass-roots efforts like stimulating letter writing campaigns.
2. Relax the "principal purpose" criterion so as to apply the law to all organizations that seek to influence legislation.
3. Require lobbyists to keep records of all officials whom they see and the specific measures they are trying to influence.
4. Expand the law to cover lobbying the executive branch as well as lobbying Congress, a form of group representation that many political scientists consider more important than attempts to influence legislation. (Whether lobbying via litigation could be controlled is a very complex question, and one that reformers have not seriously attempted to explore.)
5. Require members of the executive branch to keep logs of all contacts with private citizens. The idea here is to discourage "secret meetings" with people looking for favors.[32]

None of these proposals had been enacted into law by the end of 1975. Although they seem like good ideas, they also call into question the wisdom of trying to regulate contacts between the people and their government. For example, what about someone who comes to Washington on business once a year and drops by to see if his congressman can help him with a problem? Should he register and file reports? And what of informal contacts with congressmen that run the gamut from attempts to affect pending legislation to "maintaining a useful contact" to sheer sociability? If reports were required in such cases, the red tape would be massive and constituents would be discouraged from the democratic practice of keeping in touch with their legislators. Presumably, everyone wants to encourage popular participation in government, citizen action, and so on. But there is no practical way to draw a hard and fast line between a "concerned citizen" and a

---

[30] *CQ Weekly Report,* July 27, 1974, p. 1949.

[31] Cohen, "Lobbying Report," p. 573.

[32] Since 1973, the federal Consumer Product Safety Commission has required that any meeting between a staff member and a private citizen be recorded, announced a week in advance, and opened to the public.

"lobbyist." Each wants something from the government and will be better off (materially or psychologically) if he or she gets it. This is not an argument against amendments to the 1946 law. It *is* an argument that one could easily "cure" one "abuse" by going so far in the other direction as to chill direct access to the government and accountability of officials to their constituents. In the final analysis, interest groups are not something opposed to "the people." They *are* "the people," with all the selfishness, idealism, and diversity that exists in a country of 210 million individuals.

SUMMARY

An interest group is a collection of people making claims on the government on the basis of shared attitudes, usually through an organization. Such associations have always been an important feature of American political and social life. Corporations, labor unions, professional organizations, racial minorities, ideologically motivated organizations, and many other groups all seek to influence public policy. Sometimes more and sometimes less politically active, they form shifting political alliances depending upon their changing perceptions of how government can help or hurt them. Although every American is not equally represented by interest groups, most people's interests are represented by a number of organizations.

For most economic interest groups, politics is one of many activities, and often only an incidental one. Other interest groups, however, have primarily political purposes. They are designed to act politically in the cause of ethnic minorities or to pursue various causes, such as consumer protection, conservation, and conservatism and liberalism in the abstract. Such groups frequently portray themselves as fighters for justice or for "the public interest," as opposed to the selfish special interests supposedly represented by economic interest groups. Nevertheless, most public interest groups seem to represent relatively narrow segments of political opinion rather than "the public as a whole."

It is a mistake, however, to assume automatically that organized interest groups always pursue "selfish" goals opposed to "the public interest." Organized interest groups are *directed* by a relatively small number of persons rather than fully enlisting the participation of their entire memberships.

Sometimes politicians give groups things they want even before they ask for them. If this does not happen, groups may seek to influence public opinion, take direct action to elect their friends and defeat their enemies, seek to lobby government officials, or resort to lawsuits designed to force officials to act in ways favorable to their group's interests.

CHAPTER NINE
POLITICAL PARTIES

THE political parties play so many roles in the national political system that discussion of them cannot be confined to a single chapter. Already we have seen how the parties function as reference groups, molding the political identity of American voters, providing them with a way to understand elections, and guiding their voting choices. We also have looked at some of the motives that induce individuals to give their money and time to the parties. Our discussion of Congress and the President in later chapters also will reveal the influence of the parties on those institutions. Here we want to look at the parties as organizations. We want to consider how they perform their most important function—selecting the candidates from whom the voters make their final choices on election day. In doing so, we will examine the entire process of selecting the President, from the nomination stage to the election campaign and the electoral college. The mechanisms involved in this process both shape and reflect the American party system. Finally, we will analyze the dynamics of party competition. We will try to understand what factors make the parties similar, and what forces drive them apart.

More than thirty years ago an influential political scientist wrote that:

> . . . the political parties created democracy and that modern democracy is unthinkable save in terms of the parties. . . . The parties are not therefore merely appendages of modern government; they are in the center of it and play a determinative and creative role in it.[1]

Few serious political observers would disagree fundamentally with this view. But no one seems to like parties as much as scholars do. From the Founding Fathers to the present, parties as institutions have been distasteful to very large numbers of Americans. In 1972, when asked, "Which part of the government has done the worst job in the past couple of years?" more Americans named the political parties than Congress, the Supreme Court, and the President combined.[2] The parties are something of a stepchild, unloved but unavoidable.

Why are the parties so unpopular? One reason may have to do with the fact that in some parts of the country one or both parties is represented by machines that take graft, collaborate with gangsters, corrupt law enforcement, and pervert government by the people. How seriously such considerations contribute to the dislike of parties is questionable, however, because parties are not more popular where local government is clean. The fundamental explanation for the unpopularity of parties seems to be that most Americans believe that the parties stir up and inflame political conflict, and that conflict is undesirable. In the most detailed study of the public image of the political parties, almost two-thirds of the people interviewed agreed that

[1] E. E. Schattschneider, *Party Government* (New York: Farrar & Rinehart, 1942), p. 1.

[2] Unattributed findings on public opinion are from data gathered by the University of Michigan Center for Political Studies and analyzed by the authors, who are solely responsible for the analysis and interpretation.

"The political parties more often than not create conflicts where none really exists"; and 53 percent thought that "Our system of government would work a lot more efficiently if we could get rid of conflicts between the parties altogether."[3]

In contrast to the broad public, which seems to want politics to be more placid, ideologues of both left and right (as well as many people in between) believe that the parties betray the public interest by failing to generate *enough* conflict. These critics assert that the major parties confuse the voters by failing to present them with two clearly opposed alternative programs. To some extent, these criticisms refer to matters of degree and political preference. How much conflict is "enough"? How big must a difference be to become significant? This debate is not wholly a matter of taste, however, and in the concluding section of this chapter we will explore the causes and dimensions of differences between the two parties. But first, let us examine some of the contributions the parties make to the operation of the political system.

FUNCTIONS OF THE POLITICAL PARTIES

The party system organizes political conflict by providing channels for competition for public office. This does not mean that all political conflict is partisan — that is, all issues are not primarily conflicts between Republicans and Democrats. It does mean that competition to occupy public office at the national level occurs in the framework of the two parties. Indeed, a political party could be defined simply as *an organized attempt to win electoral office.* How do parties go about achieving this aim? Essentially, the answer lies in the five principal functions the parties perform.

1. *Parties organize individual perceptions of the political world.* One aspect of this perceptual organization is party identification, which we discussed at length in Chapter 6. In addition, the parties provide a way to link events and candidates so the voters can fix responsibility. Party labels help the public identify officials and would-be officials. They make it possible for voters to blame one ticket for failure and/or to reward the other ticket for success. Although parties often cannot deliver what they promise, they can be and are held responsible by the public for what they appear to have done. No Republican congressman had any part in the Watergate scandal, President Ford's pardon of Nixon, or the combination of inflation and recession that plagued the country in 1974. But thirty-six of them were defeated in the 1974 election primarily because of what the public saw as Republican failures. By the same token, Hubert Humphrey had no part in Lyndon Johnson's disastrous Vietnam policy, but the fact that both men were Democrats cost Humphrey the 1968 election. If a presidential candidate is very popular, he may carry into office other candidates on his party's ticket. In this case, we talk of the strength of his "coattails." Again, this

[3] Jack Dennis, "Support for the Party System by the Mass Public," *American Political Science Review*, 60 (September 1966), 605.

is an example of the party as perceptual link. People tend to see all candidates from the same party as a group. We will have occasion to observe the same phenomenon again in examining the relations between President and Congress. It can be summed up simply: What is good for one Republican candidate is good for all of them, and vice versa. Depending on the situation, candidates try to embrace or put distance between themselves and the rest of the ticket. They do this because the party affiliation shared by all candidates on the same ticket is the only way most of the electorate can allocate blame and credit.

2. *The parties organize electoral competition.* They simplify the problem of choice for the voters by presenting them two alternatives instead of an infinite variety of possible candidates.

3. Because of these two functions, *the parties are a major way of coordinating decisions both within and between the executive and legislative branches,* as we will see in Chapters 10, 11, and 12.

4. *The parties select general election candidates through the nomination process.* We will examine presidential nominations later in this chapter and congressional nominations in Chapter 10.

5. *The parties restrain social conflict and unite people with different interests and characteristics.* Each party contains members from all races, social classes, regions, religions, occupations, and so on. Neither party can assemble a majority out of the diversity of American society without appealing to a variety of groups. Both parties try to win votes from Catholics, Protestants, Jews, farmers, city dwellers, rich, and poor. Although, as we saw in Chapter 6, they have varying levels of success in these appeals, it is uncommon for a party to write off any major social group. When a group cannot vote, as was true of southern blacks until quite recently, politicians may feel free to attack it. But when blacks got the vote in the South, race-baiting by southern politicians faded away. Political observers differ on the desirability of the parties' tendency to muffle conflict. Some people think that more conflict is needed, either to make better public policy or simply to abolish the ambiguity that characterizes the party struggle. They feel that firm lines should be drawn between the parties. Other commentators celebrate the way the American parties restrain direct confrontation; they feel that the horrors of civil war illustrate the penalty of wholly unfettered political conflict.

WHY TWO PARTIES?

The five functions of the parties we have just described are not inherent in the notion of a political party as such. Many countries have political parties which do not fulfill some of these functions. American parties work the way they do, not just because they are parties, but because there are only two of them. If, for example, there were eight parties, there would be much less incentive for any party to appeal to a broad constituency. As a result, the level of political conflict would rise. It is not difficult to imagine a multi-party system in a country as diverse as the United States. There might be a party of labor, of southern whites, of blacks, of western agriculture, and so on. The contrast between the vast complexity of American interest groups and the presence throughout our history of only two parties is striking. The parties have an extraordinary heritage. The Democrats descend from the party Thomas Jefferson founded for the election of 1800. The Republican party has its roots in the time of Abraham Lincoln.

Why they have survived without significant challenge to their monopoly is a matter of some dispute, but several reasons seem to be important. The first political battle after the Revolutionary War was fought over a simple and clear issue—whether or not to adopt the Constitution. Subsequent struggles between the Federalists and the Jeffersonian Democrats followed the same line. Debtors—usually farmers—were pitted against creditors —usually merchants, bankers, professional men, and shippers. Thus there

---

THIRD PARTIES

There are two sorts of parties other than the Democrats and Republicans. One, by far the more common but less important, consists of sectarian groups founded to express a particular ideological, ethnic, or issue orientation. There are a surprising number of these in any election year, although it is exceptionally rare for one of them to get enough votes to affect the outcome of any election. Some of these parties have a good deal of continuity; others are one-time affairs. Among them are the Communist, Prohibition, and Vegetarian parties. These sectarian parties use the electoral process as a publicity device for airing their respective points of view. Table 9-1 lists the various parties on the ballot in the 1972 election, showing the variety of sectarian third parties and the miniscule fraction of the popular vote they garnered.

The other type of "third party" is essentially a "breakaway movement" from one of the major parties. Such parties are a vehicle for the personal career of a leader whose ambitions have been frustrated in the major party to which he belonged. The possibility of a third-party candidacy is an important weapon in factional conflict within the Democratic and Republican parties. A popular figure like Ronald Reagan or George Wallace often can exert influence within his own party by threatening to run for President outside the party. Many McGovern delegates at the 1972 Democratic convention hinted that their man would take this route if he lost the nomination.

Table 9-2 shows the presidential votes won by all significant third parties in the twentieth century. Except for the Socialists in 1912, these were all "breakaway movements."

POPULAR CANDI-DATES LIKE GEORGE WALLACE AND RON-ALD REAGAN CAN EXERT INFLUENCE WITHIN THEIR PAR-TIES BY RAISING THE POSSIBILITY OF RUN-NING AS THIRD-PARTY CANDIDATES. *Wide World Photos*

TABLE 9-1

POPULAR VOTES CAST IN THE
1972 PRESIDENTIAL ELECTION

PARTY	CANDIDATES	NUMBER OF VOTES	PERCENT OF TOTAL VOTES
Republican	Richard M. Nixon and Spiro T. Agnew	47,169,911	60.7
Democratic	George S. McGovern and R. Sargent Shriver	29,170,383	37.5
American	John G. Schmitz and Thomas J. Anderson	1,099,482	1.4
People's	Benjamin Spock and Julius Hobson	78,756	.1
Socialist Workers	Linda Jenness and Andrew Pulley	66,677	*
Socialist Labor	Louis Fisher and Genevieve Gunderson	53,814	*
Communist	Gus Hall and Jarvis Tyner	25,595	*
Prohibition	E. Harold Munn and Marshall E. Uncapher	13,505	*
Libertarian	John Hospers and Theodora Nathan	3,673	*
America First	John V. Mahalchik and Irving Homer	1,743	*
Universal	Gabriel Green and Daniel Fry	220	*
In addition to the above, scattered votes from various states		34,795	*

*less than 1/10 of 1 percent of the total popular vote.

Source: Richard M. Scammon, ed., *America Votes* (Washington, D.C.: Governmental Affairs Institute, 1973), Vol. 10, 1972, p. 14.

were essentially two main political groupings. American politics in the early days was undistracted by ethnic conflicts, an established church, or an aristocracy—all factors that shaped the political history of most democratic nations with more than two major parties. First experiences are very influential on subsequent behavior. In the American instance, the initial dualism of political conflict seems to have set a mold which shaped later political struggles.

The early politicians found the new nation's governmental institutions powerfully conducive to two-party politics. One key institutional feature was the single-member legislative district. In each district, only one individual was elected to the legislature. The candidate who got the most votes in the district won the legislative seat. This system discourages lasting third-party movements, because it gives nothing at all to anybody but the winner. Thus only a party that has a chance of getting the most votes has any reason for existence. To make their voices effective, potential third-party voters are apt to switch to one of the major parties. Their desire not to waste their votes by voting for a party that has no chance of getting the most votes strengthens the two major parties.

Countries with more than two major parties usually use a system based on *proportional representation*. This is a method of allocating legislative seats to each party in accordance with its share of the total number of votes *throughout the country*. Under proportional representation, a party that received only 5 percent of the vote would still get five percent of the seats in the legislature. Under a single-member district plurality system, a party that won 5 percent of the votes in each district would get no seats in the legislature. Clearly, proportional representation provides an incentive for even very small splinter groups to persevere, whereas our system based on plurality voting and single-member districts does not.

The second major institutional incentive to a two-party system is the fact that the President in our system is a *unitary executive* elected in a winner-take-all contest. The presidency has the same effect on the number of parties as the single-member district. Since only one party can win the presidency in any given election, there is little point in voting for the presidential candidate of a party that has no chance of winning. In contrast to the United States, nations with multiparty systems usually have some form of *cabinet government*. In cabinet government, executive power is wielded by a group of cabinet members, each of whom has control of one government department. This arrangement encourages many parties since a large number of parties can each win one or more cabinet positions. In our presidential system, in contrast, executive power is wielded by one person. The Cabinet in the United States has little other than the name in common with the system we

TABLE 9-2

SIGNIFICANT THIRD PARTIES IN PRESIDENTIAL
ELECTIONS IN THE TWENTIETH CENTURY

PARTY	YEAR	PERCENT OF TOTAL POPULAR VOTES	NUMBER OF ELECTORAL VOTES
Progressive	1912	27.4	88
Socialist	1912	6.0	0
Progressive	1924	17.1	13
States' Rights	1948	2.4	39
Progressive	1948	2.4	0
American Independent	1968	13.5	46

have just described as cabinet government. Cabinet officers in this country are appointed by the President. Although their nominations must be confirmed by the Senate, they are the President's subordinates and may be discharged by him. In short, the party that wins the White House wins a monopoly of executive power.

Thus three factors set the United States on the road to two-party politics: the initial dualism of conflict dating from the nation's earliest days, the adoption of single-member districts, and the unitary executive. To this list a further factor should be added. Once a political system takes on a particular form, politicians have a vested interest in maintaining the existing ways of doing business. They pass laws and regulations designed to perpetuate those forms—the ease of third parties getting on the ballot, laws making it simpler for voters to back the entire slate of a party, and so forth. Similarly, once the two-party system is established, voters tend automatically to see political conflict as a matter of Republicans versus Democrats. The psychological habits of the people also serve to reinforce the existing pattern. We have already noted the extraordinary persistence and strength of party identification in the United States. This makes it difficult for contenders to challenge candidates running as Republicans or Democrats.

Finally, the two parties keep their monopoly by *ideological opportunism.* Both parties have been threatened from time to time by the prospect of defection by a substantial number of supporters. Usually, these efforts have been reactions against the middle-of-the-road policies of the Republicans or Democrats. The prospective defectors want something, such as old age pensions or an end to school busing, that their party has not strongly supported. The party threatened with such desertions usually tries to bring the bolters back into the fold by offering to incorporate some of what they want into the party's goals. The same thing occurs when a third party seems likely to attract a significant vote. Candidates from one or the other major party—and sometimes both—will shamelessly steal its thunder.

PARTY MEMBERSHIP

We often hear it said that someone is "a member of the Republican (or Democratic) party." Yet generations of scholars, lawyers, judges, and politicians have been unable to agree on a satisfactory definition of what it means to be a "member" of a party in the United States. The question is far from academic, because presumably only "members" should participate in each party's principal organized activity—nominating its candidates for office. Moreover, all the talk about making party conventions "representative" of the party assumes that it is possible to define just what it is they should be representative of.[4]

Some possible meanings of "membership" can be dismissed fairly

[4] This subject is discussed at length in Austin Ranney, *Curing the Mischiefs of Faction* (Berkeley: University of California Press, 1975), Chap. 5.

easily. Psychological membership—party identification—is probably the most commonly used definition of party membership. Almost 90 percent of the adult population of the country identifies to some extent with one party or the other. Although it is terribly useful to social scientists, however, the concept of party identification is wholly without legal meaning. It is difficult to see how it could be given such meaning, since it is an entirely subjective condition.

A second definition of "membership" depends on stricter standards, such as belonging to a formal organization that has a formal process for joining, a set of criteria for membership, perhaps dues, a roster of members, and so on. In Europe, for instance, many people are members of the Socialist or Christian Democratic party in the sense that they have formally applied for membership, have been accepted, pay dues, and carry a membership card. In the United States, 3 to 4 percent of the adult population belong to some sort of political club or organization. Some of these are not party groups, so the total of formal members of party organizations is somewhat less than that. Clearly, this is not what party membership means in this country. At its 1974 midterm conference, the Democratic party voted overwhelmingly against a proposal that might have been a start to formalizing membership in the party, with cards, dues, formal application, and the like.

A third possible definition of membership involves legal registration as a Democrat or Republican. State laws vary enormously in this field, however. In some states there is no registration by party. Elsewhere, voters register in a party only if they wish to. And in some states, a party member is anyone who declares that he is a member when he votes in that party's primary. This lack of uniformity makes registration useless as a criterion for party membership.

The main purpose of registration by party is to prevent adherents of one party from voting in the other party's primary. A party primary in which the only citizens allowed to vote are those registered in the party is called a *closed primary*. In contrast, an *open primary* is not restricted to adherents of any party. The Supreme Court has weakened the ability of the states to limit access to primaries. In 1973 it struck down an Illinois law that prohibited a voter from participating in one party's primary within twenty-three months of his voting in another party's primary. On the other hand, the Court did sustain a New York law that required a delay of eight to eleven months before switching.[5] Austin Ranney sums up the present political reality this way:

> You are a Democrat if you say you are; no one can effectively say you are not; and you can become a Republican any time the spirit moves you simply by saying that you have become one. You accept no obligations by such a declaration; you receive only a privilege —the privilege of taking an equal part in the making of the party's

[5] *Kusper* v. *Pontikers*, 94 SC 303 (1973); and *Rosario* v. *Rockefeller*, 93 SC 1245 (1973).

most important decision, the nomination of its candidates for public office.[6]

In short, one "joins" a party by engaging in its activities, with or without benefit of formal admission procedures. A party consists of all those people who participate in any of the following activities: running for office under its label, trying for its nomination, contributing money, working for a candidate, attending a caucus or other meeting, or voting in its primary. This conception of membership does not satisfy people who would like a more stringent definition. Some scholars, such as Ranney, argue that the parties need to be protected from episodic involvement by activists who care only for some particular cause or candidate and are cheerfully willing to sacrifice the party if they don't get what they want.[7] On the other side of the fence, some doctrinal purists in both parties crave stricter criteria for party membership so that they can keep out people who do not meet their ideological standards. One regular Republican politician described this attitude among the members of the American Conservative Union (ACU):

> The ACU is looked upon by moderates as the quasi-fringe. They're zealots. They have a purge mentality. They're more interested in maintaining purity than in winning. They want to keep liberals out of the Republican party.[8]

REGULARS AND PURISTS

As we saw in Chapter 7, political participation is not the province of a closed elite. Rather, there is a great deal of circulation into and out of the ranks of the activists. This is partcularly noticeable in the composition of the parties, which are exceptionally open institutions. Because they are so open, the parties are vulnerable to sudden influxes of activists who have never previously taken an interest in party affairs and who suddenly arrive in great numbers to win a nomination for their favorite. This was the complaint of regular Republicans against both the liberal supporters of Eisenhower in 1952 and the conservative supporters of Goldwater in 1964. Veteran Democrats successfully resisted the McCarthy newcomers in 1968 but were overwhelmed by McGovern's skillfully organized "outsider" campaign in 1972.

As these examples indicate, party activists can be divided into two types. On the one hand, there are the *regulars,* who are sometimes called *professionals,* although this does not necessarily mean that they earn their living at politics. On the other hand, there are the *purists,* whose commitment is basically to a particular cause or candidate. Obviously, there are important differences in how these two sorts of activists regard the party in which they

---

[6] Ranney, *Curing the Mischiefs of Faction,* p. 166.
[7] Ranney, *Curing the Mischiefs of Faction,* p. 166.
[8] Quoted in *Congressional Quarterly Weekly Report,* September 7, 1974, p. 2440.

are working. To the regulars, the party is the most important consideration. Its success has the first claim on their loyalties and efforts. They look back on past achievements of their party and consider its survival essential for future success. Purists, in contrast, see the party only as a means to the policy they favor. They do not look at things in the same long perspective as the professionals. They tend to be in a hurry, to think that this year's favored candidate is the country's last hope. These two opposed tendencies are nicely summarized in the following passages. The first is by Arthur Miller, the noted playwright and a purist delegate at the 1968 Democratic convention:

> The professionals . . . see politics as a sort of game in which you win sometimes and sometimes you lose. Issues are not something you feel, like morality, like good and evil, but something you succeed or fail to make use of. To these men an issue is a segment of public opinion which you either capitalize on or attempt to assuage according to the present interests of the party. To the amateurs . . . an issue is first of all moral, and embodies a vision of the country, even of man, and is not a counter in a game.[9]

The professional outlook is described by Ranney, a political scientist sympathetic to this viewpoint:

> The professionals are people who have a substantial commitment to the party itself. They have served it before the nomination contest and expect to serve it after the election. . . . The professionals seek a candidate whose style they think will appeal to the voters they need to win, not necessarily to party leaders. They judge a candidate by how well or badly he runs in the election and by how much he has helped or hurt the rest of the ticket. And they see negotiation, compromise, and accommodation not as hypocrisy or immorality but as the very essence of what keeps parties—and nations—from disintegrating.[10]

Few people are unreserved purists or professionals. Purists have been known to compromise to get what they wanted, and professionals are not amoral calculators. But purists whose motivations are centered in a cause or a hero are not likely to be concerned about the party's other candidates and long-term prospects. Conversely, professionals are likely to see issues as a means to the end of victory rather than as go-for-broke goals. Both parties always have both points of view represented in them. Candidates themselves generally try to exploit both approaches in order to attract enough support to win the nomination.

Political parties are not coherent, stable entities. They are complex organisms whose component parts are in a constant and changing state of tension.

---

[9] Arthur Miller, "The Battle of Chicago: From the Delegates' Side," *New York Times Magazine,* September 15, 1968, p. 29.

[10] Ranney, *Curing the Mischiefs of Faction,* pp. 140–41.

Issue-oriented activists (and candidates who hope to exploit them), Presidents hoping to go down in history, and congressmen hoping to make their reputations all contribute to the state of flux in which both parties exist.

HOW THE PARTIES ARE ORGANIZED

One impediment to understanding the parties is our tendency to describe them in language that conveys an exaggerated impression of the reality beneath the verbiage. In talking about "the national Republican (or Democratic) organization," we are using a term that suggests vastly more coherence and discipline than exists. The same is true in most states and localities, where "the party organization" is a welter of activities and officials, candidates' personal campaign apparatuses, and past and future participants. If the right candidate comes along, with the right combination of popularity, organizational ability, and probability of success, some of these elements can be mobilized in a network that actually works together for a common purpose. More often, though, the "party organization" is little more than a figure of speech. In a few states and localities, on the other hand, there really is a stable and ongoing party organization. Let us look briefly at the most common patterns of organization at each level.

In doing so, two points should be remembered. The first is *decentralization*. As Schattschneider observed, "Decentralization is by all odds the most important single characteristic of the American major party."[11] No common chain of command holds together the diverse networks that make up our major parties. No one can give orders to the many localized centers of power in either party. In the party that occupies the White House, the President is nominally the party leader. But this does not prevent other party members, either in Congress or in the localities, from going their own way. The President simply does not have enough patronage and other sinews of organizational strength to impose discipline on his party. The key to party discipline is centralized control over nominations. No such control exists in the United States. As we shall see in Chapter 10, the President has very little ability to help or hinder congressional hopefuls in his own party once they are nominated. He has even less ability to dictate to the local parties whom they will nominate for national offices such as congressman and senator, and virtually no control over the nomination process for state and local office. Thus he has no decisive way of imposing his own will on local and state officials in his party should they choose to defy or ignore him. It almost goes without saying that the party that does not control the presidency has even less hierarchy, because it is headless—or it has dozens of would-be leaders, which amounts to the same thing.

The second important point about party organization is a paradoxical one. Side by side with the fact that the parties have virtually no centralized organization we must set the fact that, *in terms of popular perceptions, the*

---

[11] Schattschneider, *Party Government*, p. 129.

parties appear to be quite centralized indeed. Party identification is not a matter of local loyalties. It is a national phenomenon. No matter where they live, people see the party with which they identify as a national entity, not a state or local group. By the same token, something that is good for one of the parties in one part of the country is almost always good for it everywhere, although perhaps not to the same degree. As we saw in Chapter 6, changes in voting patterns are related to shifting party images, which in turn are associated with the popularity of the presidential candidates and the public's assessment of the current administration's performance. These popular verdicts are reflected in the tendency for party fortunes in congressional elections to move generally in the same direction. The common observation that "1974 was a good year for the Democrats" or "1966 was a Republican year" captures this important truth about the parties. Their fortunes move in national tides. Thus *the parties are national without being hierarchical*.

NATIONAL PARTY STRUCTURES

In theory, each party's presidential nominating convention is that party's highest governing body. The delegates at the conventions pass resolutions on the mechanics of future conventions and delegate selection. What is more, they also create committees, commissions, and task forces to meet during the inter-election period. These groups often are empowered to adopt and enforce rules that can have important consequences. But it is plain that conventions cannot serve as stable sources of leadership. Massive, confused assemblages of several thousand strangers who meet for five days every four years to choose the party's presidential candidate can hardly be expected to give much serious attention to anything else.

The ongoing national party leadership rests formally in each party's national committees. These groups consist of varying numbers of national committeemen from each of the fifty states, plus the District of Columbia, Puerto Rico, the Virgin Islands, and, in the case of the Democrats, the Canal Zone. Normally, the national committee meets as a group two or three times a year. The best academic study of the national committees has a title that reveals its authors' conclusions about their topic: *Politics Without Power*.[12] This judgment may be a bit harsh, but it is not wide of the mark.

One of the few important tasks of the national committees is the selection of the national party chairman. In the case of the party in the White House, this involves little more than rubber-stamping the President's choice. In the opposition party, the choice falls to the presidential nominee, and then is automatically ratified by the committee. After the presidential election, however, the chairman of the party that lost usually resigns and the national committee then picks a new national chairman. In such instances, the defeated presidential candidate may exert considerable influence but he obviously is in no position to dictate a choice to the committee.

---

[12] Cornelius P. Cotter and Bernard C. Hennessy, *Politics Without Power* (New York: Atherton, 1964).

The chairmanship can vary in influence and significance. At most, the head of the in-party is one of the President's political operatives. He is little more than the mouthpiece through which the President speaks on national party matters, and sometimes he is not even that. Some Presidents, such as Nixon and Johnson, have chosen to run national party affairs directly from the White House, thus even further reducing the role of the chairman. In the out-party, the chairman usually is more conspicuous and significant, simply because the out-party has no President to speak for it. It is the party chairman who makes statements, appears on the Sunday afternoon television public affairs programs, and generally "represents" his party. Yet he must do so without stealing the thunder from any of its potential presidential candidates. An exceptionally able national chairman also can exercise his political skills in raising funds, encouraging strong candidates to run for office, and performing miscellaneous tasks that fall somewhere between those of the coach of a football team and a mere Monday morning quarterback.

Under the leadership of its national chairman, each party maintains a national committee headquarters with substantial staffs and budgets. In a recent non-election year, for example, the Republican National Committee had about 160 employees. These include researchers, writers, and specialists in polling, public relations, campaign organization, and fund raising. They provide a variety of technical services to all their party's primary and general election candidates, including position papers on issues and advice on campaign organization. For example, the Democratic National Committee has begun to hold four-day regional "campaign institutes" to help candidates and their staffs deal with the issues. The DNC also holds regional "clinics" to advise local campaigners on topics such as direct mail, fund raising, media, advertising, research, and other nuts-and-bolts aspects of running for office. (A sample of this how-to-do-it material is on page 261.)

STATE AND LOCAL PARTIES

Variety is the hallmark of any comparative study of American parties below the national level. Generally speaking, parties are organized around elections and candidates — and around patronage, where it exists in quantity. As we saw in Chapter 7, patronage consists of government jobs, contracts, and other benefits given by the party to those who work for it. If substantial patronage is available, there are likely to be party organizations that have some continuity between elections and are more than the personal creations of individual office holders.

In some places, one can still find thriving specimens of so-called "old fashioned" political *machines*. A political machine is a close-knit hierarchy of politicians, beginning with the "captain" of the individual precinct (a precinct is the area covered by a single polling place) and ascending up to the city or county boss. The party structure includes leadership positions at every level — ward, assembly district, state senatorial district, city, and county. These official posts often convey a good deal of power over patronage and thus are eagerly sought after. Machines of this sort are fueled by patron-

ADVANCING, RALLIES, AND MASS MEETINGS

INTRODUCTION
PLANNING
MUSIC, DECORATIONS AND SIGNS
PRESS
ADDITIONAL SUGGESTIONS
PLANNING A RALLY
TIPS FOR A SUCCESSFUL RALLY
RALLY CHECK LIST

INTRODUCTION

Advance work in a Congressional campaign, particularly for an incumbent, is a relatively simple routine if some basic rules are strictly followed by those working for the candidate.

Overall, good advance work is common sense. It is the type of work cut out for persons with a great deal of diplomacy and with great administrative abilities. There are many factors, such as the height of the microphone, proper seating at head tables and in motorcades, which might seem unimportant in the overall picture, but which have greatly contributed to winning or losing an election. It is the responsibility of the advance man to make sure that no one is inadvertently snubbed in the rush of the campaign. He must make it an unbroken rule never to speak unkindly of any person, even one who has tried his patience. To do so would reflect adversely on the candidate.

Since Congressional Districts vary in size, advance men are confronted with problems such as determining a tight airplane and helicopter schedule, as well as perhaps deciding which traffic-congested city streets should be avoided in order to move his candidate from place to place on time.

In most cases, particularly with an incumbent, the candidate will know almost everyone attending the rally. However, it is always a good idea to prepare 3x5 cards with the names of special people, and a line or two of briefing for the candidate.

For example, if a Congressman helped a constituent with a case involving a Federal agency, this could be noted on the card. It will give the candidate the opportunity to mention a few specifics, such as names and circumstances, to his constituent. This is always helpful.

An advance man is also responsible for all follow-up work after the candidate's appearance. A good advance man will obtain the names and addresses of persons who were particularly helpful and see that they are passed on to Headquarters. Many Congressmen purchase ashtrays with the Congressional Seal through the Stationery Room and send them to those who have made a particular contribution to the campaign. It is an impressive but relatively inexpensive gift, and the thoughtful gesture is always appreciated.

Names of individuals who were helpful in advancing should be sent back to Headquarters, where letters of appreciation from the candidate should be sent promptly.

PLANNING

1. In advancing a dinner or banquet appearance, it is wise to leave some extra room at the head table and have at least two extra chairs available in case someone has been overlooked or a dignitary unexpectedly arrives.

2. When in doubt as to the size of crowd to anticipate, it is best to select the smallest hall or auditorium available. Far better to have people standing in the aisles — or on the outside of a hall listening to a speech over an outside loudspeaker — than to have a large hall or auditorium half empty. The press invariably refers to the size of the crowd in terms of a "jam packed hall" or a "sparsely attended" rally.

3. The advance man should have extra copies of speeches and press releases available. While several members of the press may travel with a Congressional candidate, there are always local reporters who are covering only one stop. Copies of speeches and press releases should be available to them.

4. Bios and glossies (black and white) should be included with copies of the speech, particularly if the candidate is an incumbent.

5. Whenever possible, arrangements should be made for the candidate to stop in at the local newspaper office to meet with its executives.

Source: Democratic National Committee, *Democratic Campaign Manual* (Washington: Democratic National Committee, n.d.), p. 90.

age and therefore are focused on state and local politics. Where patronage is common, it usually provides the motivation for a corps of activists who pack nominating caucuses and conventions, get out the votes in the more obscure primaries, and maintain the organization in power. Contrary to popular belief, machine politics is not necessarily monolithic, with all power emanating from one center. If patronage comes from more than one source — say, both city and county government — the result may be two competing machines.[13] In some cities, such as New York, the machine leaders are more likely to be at each other's throats than each other's sides.

Although machine politicians are most interested in the local elections that provide them with the spoils of office, their command of those spoils often makes them the most influential figures in national party affairs in their areas. This is especially true in places where the local leaders speak with one voice. Chicago traditionally is a prime example because of the regular machine's control of thousands of government jobs and other benefits. In New York, on the other hand, a vigorous amateur reform movement invariably contests primaries with the divided regular leaders.

A more common situation than either of these is found in places where other incentives than patronage animate most of the political activists. In such places there may be no stable political organizations with continuity of membership, substantial influence over nominations, and a hierarchical chain of command. Official party positions may be unfilled or held by people who do nothing. In these cases, the most meaningful manifestations of party organization are the structures built by individual candidates for the purpose of winning their own personal nomination and election. We will examine this process as it concerns congressmen in Chapter 10 and as it concerns presidential candidates in the next few pages.

First, though, let us sum up what we have said so far about national party politics. The Democratic and Republican parties consist of a diffuse, fluctuating, and loosely affiliated rank-and-file membership, weak national party organizations, and disparate local organizations. These local organiations range from highly disciplined, tightly knit local machines exhibiting great continuity to sporadic, undisciplined amateur efforts that pop up only at election time. Most typically, the local party will consist of a number of elements. There may be several party leaders and regular organizations built around various sources of patronage. There will be a number of separate campaign organizations built up by individual politicians to work for their own election or re-election. And there will be sporadic activities by reform movements or amateur clubs. These movements come into existence around election time because a particular candidate or issue is so important to some people at that moment that they will take time out of their daily lives to become temporarily active in politics.

This diffuse organization of American parties is both a cause and an effect of the scattered flow of campaign contributions. Only a small proportion of all political contributions is given to the national committees and the congressional campaign committees of the two parties. Candidates for most offices, both national and local, must raise most of their own money. The national parties cannot discipline their candidates by giving or withholding money because the national parties have almost no money to give. Indeed, fund raising by individual candidates may undercut national party efforts. For example, when the Democratic National Committee tried to schedule

---

[13] For a discussion of the difference between centralized party organizations and patronage incentives, see Raymond E. Wolfinger, *The Politics of Progress* (Englewood Cliffs, N.J.: Prentice-Hall, Inc., 1974), Chap. 4.

fund-raising dinners to help erase an $8 million debt left over from the 1968 campaign, local Democrats objected to its plans because they did not want the national party to tap their contributors. The local candidates did not want to find themselves hearing potential contributors say, "I'm sorry, but I gave already." Under pressure from the local Democrats, the DNC backed down—a clear indication of where the power lay.[14]

PRESIDENTIAL NOMINATIONS

Choosing their respective presidential and vice presidential candidates is the most important single action that the parties perform. It is significant for two different reasons. First, nomination constitutes a far greater part of the process of political choice than does the general election. In the election, voters have their choice of two serious candidates. It is the nominating process that reduces the alternatives to two by eliminating all other contenders, of whom there may be as many as a dozen or more before the selection ritual begins. In some years, the choice of candidates virtually predetermines the outcome of the election, as with Goldwater in 1964 or McGovern in 1972, neither of whom stood much of a chance in the general election. But even when the general election is a genuine contest, it is still limited to two people—those who have most successfully dealt with their parties' candidate selection procedures.

The second significance of the nominating process is that it determines who will have control of the party itself. Control of the nomination is control of the party. The nominee is the legitimate user of the one thing of great value the party has to give—its name. In winning the nomination, he inherits the party's habitual voters as well as its campaign machinery. If he then wins the election, he is indisputably the party leader. And even if he loses, he still may retain influence within the party so long as he loses in a way that indicates that he might win the next time. Either way, he has put his brand on his party for at least a season. His image has powerfully affected his party's image. The degree of his success affects the fortunes of those supporters who stake their reputations on his ability. And his drawing power at the polls—his coattails—affects the chances of thousands of other candidates on his party's ticket, running for every office from the United States Senate to the state legislature.

The parties choose their presidential candidates in national conventions held in the summer of the election year. Whether the conventions are actual decision-making bodies or merely occasions for crowning a winner is an issue we will take up later. Irrespective of the answer, the most important parts of the nominating cycle occur before the convention, in the tortuous process of delegate selection.

The number of delegates at the convention varies from year to year as well as from one party to the other. It ranges anywhere from around 1,400 to more than 3,000. Both parties follow a policy of apportioning delegates to states on

[14] *New York Times*, February 6, 1970, p. 14.

a basis both of population and past support for the party. How these two factors are weighted has consequences that do not fall evenly on all factions. Delegate apportionment is a perennial controversy, with the losing faction occasionally challenging the formula in court.

The method of choosing delegates is determined by the election laws of each state. Thus both parties in a state choose their delegates by the same method. In the recent past, "reform" efforts in the national parties have imposed certain guidelines on the state parties, particularly among the Democrats, who have led the way in this respect. These efforts often take the form of lobbying state legislatures for changes in the election laws.

In some countries it is assumed that the political parties are private associations that should be free to conduct their affairs without interference from the government. The process of choosing candidates for public office is not regulated by law in any other democratic country except West Germany.[15] The United States is unique in the intricacy and extent of the legal system controlling the "internal" business of its political parties.

It is also unique in entrusting the choice of candidates to voters in primary elections. Elsewhere in the democratic world, the party leadership picks the candidates so as to obtain the most appealing candidates and the most loyal and effective legislators. But in the United States, virtually all congressional candidates are now nominated by primaries, as are about 80 percent of the delegates to the presidential conventions. The rest are chosen by the caucus-convention method. We will describe each of these procedures in turn.

At present, both parties are engaged in a great round of reform that began in 1968 when a large group of liberal Democrats voiced their dissatisfaction with the existing procedures for selecting national convention delegates. A year before the 1976 nominating conventions, many of the rules in both parties for choosing delegates were still undecided. We have no doubt that one aftermath of the 1976 election will be further changes in these procedures, with the party that loses the election taking the lead. This level of uncertainty further complicates a nominating process that is already exceptionally intricate. As one expert on the subject has written:

> The United States must have the most elaborate, complex, and prolonged formal system of nominating candidates for chief executive in the world. The selection of delegates to the national party conventions is spread over approximately six months. The states decide when and how this is to be done. . . . The result is mind-blowing complexity and variety in delegate selection methods and the extent to which delegates are mandated to support specific presidential candidates at the convention. The winning candidates must somehow attract the votes of 50 percent plus one of these delegates, chosen under 50 different sets of laws and political arrangements.[16]

[15] Ranney, *Curing the Mischiefs of Faction*, pp. 75–79.
[16] Donald R. Matthews, "Presidential Nominations: Process and Outcomes," in James David Barber, ed., *Choosing the President* (Englewood Cliffs, N.J.: Prentice-Hall, Inc., 1974), p. 56.

One of the most conspicuous trends in American politics has been the growth of presidential primaries. Less than half of the delegates to the 1968 conventions were chosen in primaries. By 1972, almost two-thirds of the delegates were from primary states, and in 1976 over three-quarters of the delegates, from at least thirty-three states, were picked in primary elections.

It is generally believed that primaries are the most "democratic" way to nominate candidates, since they involve many more people than the handful who participate in conventions and caucuses. Yet the voters in primary elections are far from a simple cross-section of the population. Considerably older, richer, and better educated, they are more politically aware and ideologically conscious than the people who vote only in general elections. They are usually more intensely concerned with the issues, and often take more extreme stands.[17] The Democrats who vote in their party's primary are likely to be more liberal than the larger numbers of Democrats who vote in general elections. Conversely, voters in Republican primaries tend to be more conservative than Republican voters as a whole.

Each state has its own rules for presidential primaries. The variations are considerable and can have extraordinary consequences for the fortunes of the presidential candidates. This is one of the least-known and most important illustrations of the fact that obscure rules can have momentous results. The two most important dimensions of primary rules are the complexity of the ballot and the formula for relating votes to delegates.

PRIMARY BALLOT COMPLEXITY. States like New York, New Jersey, and Pennsylvania, which have been dominated by patronage-oriented political machines for generations, use very complicated presidential primary ballots. In New York and New Jersey, state law forbids mentioning the names of the presidential candidates on the primary ballot. Only the names of the candidates for delegate running in each congressional district may appear on the ballot. Needless to say, few voters know the names of the delegates pledged to their preferred presidential candidate. As a result, only those people who are exceptionally knowledgeable, or who are "helped" by a strong campaign organization, are likely to know what they are doing in these primaries. Thus it comes as no surprise that only 20 percent of the eligible Democrats in New York voted in the 1972 presidential primary. This was par for the course in New York. Contrast the situation in the California primary, where the turnout rate was three times as high as New York's. California has never had political machines worthy of the name, and its primary ballot simply presents the voter with a choice among the candidates for the nomination.

[17] Austin Ranney, "Turnout and Representation in Presidential Primary Elections," *American Political Science Review*, 66 (March 1972), 21–37; and James I. Lengle, "Representativeness in Presidential Primary Elections," unpublished doctoral dissertation, University of California, Berkeley, 1976.

A naive observer looking at the situation in New York might wonder why a party would tolerate a system that effectively discourages participation. In fact, political machines actually *want* low voter turnout, because a larger number of voters is generally harder to influence with the traditional electioneering technique of door-to-door precinct work. Ironically, Senator McGovern managed to turn the tables on the machine politicians in the 1972 New York primary. McGovern was the only one of the contenders for the Democratic nomination that year who had organized for an intensive interpersonal campaign. His work paid off in New York, where he won 263 of the state's 279 convention delegates. He was able to pull off this coup because he was the only candidate prepared to distribute sample ballots and otherwise help his supporters decipher the maze of unfamiliar delegate names on the ballot. In short, ballot complexity favors the candidate with the best organization. Usually this will be the machine candidate, with his army of patronage employees. Occasionally, though, it may be an outsider who can mobilize a crusade of issue-oriented idealists.

The absence of candidates' names from primary ballots is not the only oddity of primary voting that can affect the outcome. In Pennsylvania, for example, primary voters must mark their ballots several times—once at the top to indicate their candidate preference, and then several more times at the bottom of the ballot to choose their candidate's delegates in their congressional district. This required a degree of persistence in the face of bureaucratic complexity that was much more difficult for Humphrey's working-class supporters in the 1972 primary than for McGovern's better-educated backers. Humphrey lost twenty delegates in Pennsylvania because people who voted for him in the preference part of the ballot did not follow through and mark their ballots completely at the bottom, where the delegates were actually selected.[18] In this and similar cases, "voter fatigue" favors the candidate with the best organization and with the richest and best educated supporters.

THE VOTE/DELEGATE RATIO. When several candidates run against each other in a primary, various things can happen after the votes are tabulated. In some states, all the state's delegates will be given to the winner. In others the delegates are divided among the candidates in proportion to their share of the popular vote. And in still others the delegates are elected by congressional districts, so that the presidential candidate who gets the most votes in each district will get that district's delegates. At first glance, all three plans seem reasonable and "democratic." They probably are. But this does not mean that each plan doesn't have its own type of bias that will favor one candidate or another. Each candidate has his own peculiar pattern of support. Some are about equally popular throughout the state while others are very strong in some areas but not in others. Some candidates may enter only a few primaries. Others may enter all or most, but may give very little attention to some states while concentrating on others. Thus

[18] James I. Lengle and Byron Shafer, "Primary Rules, Political Power, and Social Change," *American Political Science Review*, 70 (March 1976).

the three ways of relating votes to delegates can have very different consequences for the different candidates. The same plan may not be equally beneficial for a candidate in every state, since his pattern of support may vary from state to state. Obviously, a candidate is best off if the states where he is strong use the winner-take-all method while the states where he is weak use one of the other systems. Similarly, he benefits if the states where his support is concentrated in a few areas use the districted system. In this way he can capture all the delegates from those districts where his supporters are numerous. On the other hand, if his supporters are thinly scattered throughout the state, he will do best with the straight proportional system, because even though he may not have a majority anywhere, he can still pick up some delegates.

These arguments are not merely hypothetical. Table 9-3 shows them dramatically in operation in a real case. The table allows us to compare what actually happened in the first fifteen Democratic primaries in 1972 with what would have happened if all fifteen states had used the same system. We can readily see that McGovern was exceptionally fortunate in that the pattern of his support in these fifteen states was such as to take maximum advantage of the system being used in each state. As a result, he won 401.5 delegates, putting him handily ahead of Wallace's 291 and Humphrey's 284. If the winner-take-all system had been used in all fifteen states, however, Humphrey would have come out ahead and McGovern would have placed third, well behind Wallace. If the proportional system had been used, Wallace would have been the winner, with McGovern second, a scant five delegates ahead of Humphrey. And if all the states had used the districted method, Wallace again would have been the winner, closely followed by McGovern and Humphrey.

McGovern's luck in the first fifteen primaries continued in the sixteenth—California. Although he won only 44 percent of the vote there, he collected

TABLE 9-3

DELEGATES WON BY DEMOCRATIC CANDIDATES IN 1972 AND THE NUMBER EACH WOULD HAVE WON IF ALL PRIMARIES HAD BEEN OF THE SAME TYPE

	ACTUAL DELEGATES[a]	WINNER TAKE-ALL	PROPORTIONAL	DISTRICTED
Humphrey	284	446	314	324
Wallace	291	379	350	367
McGovern	401.5	249	319	343
Muskie	56.5	18	82	52
Others	59	0	27	6

[a]For fifteen primaries before the California primary.

Source: James I. Lengle and Byron Shafer, "Primary Rules, Political Power, and Social Change," *American Political Science Review* 70 (March 1976).

all of the state's 271 delegates. Ironically, McGovern had urged California Democrats to abandon their traditional winner-take-all plan the previous winter, when neither he nor they expected him to do so well there. After the primary, it was his opponents' turn to complain about the evils of a plan that would give 100 percent of the delegates to a candidate with a minority of the votes, and no delegates at all to 56 percent of the state's Democrats. The anti-McGovern forces challenged his capture of all the California delegates and carried the issue to the floor of the convention in Miami Beach. There the delegates voted to reject the "California challenge," a decision that signaled McGovern's grip on the nomination.

In the aftermath, the Democrats decided to do away with *statewide* winner-take-all primaries.[19] The party's new rules—at least as they will apply to the 1976 election—require that if a state selects its convention delegates in a primary, at least 75 percent of the delegates must be chosen at the congressional district level. Up to 25 percent of the delegates may be chosen by the state party committee, but even these handpicked delegates must be proportional to the candidate preference pattern revealed in the primary voting. A candidate must receive at least 15 percent of the primary vote to qualify for a share of the delegates. This latter rule is designed to avoid dispersing delegate strength among a great many marginal candidates with little support. States can still choose whether the winning candidate in each district will get all the district's delegates or only a fraction of them, with the remaining delegates given to the other candidates in proportion to their share of the vote. In 1976, the most common method was that the winner in each congressional district would get all the district's delegates.

THE CAUCUS-CONVENTION SYSTEM

The caucus-convention method is an alternative to primaries as a way of selecting convention delegates. This is a complex, multi-tiered system of choosing delegates who choose other delegates, and so on until a state party convention picks the delegates to the national convention. The caucus-convention method used to be quite popular, but it has lost ground rapidly as states have switched to the primary system rather than try to adapt the caucus-convention method to the new rules the national parties have enacted.

This method begins with precinct caucuses, which are open to all party members. At these caucuses delegates are chosen to a convention at the next level, usually the county. The county convention may then pick delegates to the state convention, or there may be yet another intermediate tier of meetings before the final statewide gathering at which the national delegates are chosen.

The initial caucus is the most crucial meeting in the series, because it is here that the basic political alignment is set. Because these meetings are

---

[19] Actually, the convention does not have the authority to change state primary laws. Instead, it voted to refuse to seat any delegation that was not proportional to the popular vote. This rule exerts sufficient pressure to cause the states to alter their own laws.

so little publicized, they tend to be limited to people who either are strongly committed to a candidate or strongly encouraged by the local political machine. As a result, this method favors the candidates with the best organization. Such candidates usually are those who can inspire great enthusiasm among purist activists or those who can mobilize the support of machine politicians. Because few persons other than party activists will even know when and where the precinct caucus is being held, let alone bother to show up for it, small numbers of activists can—and do—pack neighborhood caucuses. The local caucus is thus one of the sources of the continued power of "old-fashioned" political machines.

Some caucus-convention states used to have an equivalent of the winner-take-all provision found in some primary states. This was the *unit rule*, which bound all delegates chosen by the state convention to go to the national convention pledged to support the candidate favored by a majority of the state delegation. Like the winner-take-all primary, the unit rule also has been a casualty of the wave of reform. Indeed, the Democratic party's new rules require that at every level the distribution of delegates be proportional to the support given each candidate by the party members from whom the delegates to the next level are chosen. Proportional representation now begins at the precinct caucus level and continues right up to the state convention.

PROLONGED AGONY OR CAREFUL TESTING?

The formal process of delegate selection begins in January of each presidential election year when Iowa selects its national convention delegates by the caucus method. Four more caucus-convention states make their

THOMAS E. DEWEY ON A 1948 TOUR OF OREGON TO CAPTURE THE VOTES OF THE STATE'S DELEGATES TO THE REPUBLICAN CONVENTION. *Wide World Photos*

picks before the first spring primaries, traditionally held in New England, begin to focus public attention on the nominating season. Then follows a string of primaries in one state after another. The process continues until mid-June, when the final delegates are picked for the national conventions, which are held in July or August. The entire process takes seven or eight months. (The candidates, of course, have been planning, organizing, and fund-raising for months or years before the first caucus.) It also consumes millions of dollars, an extraordinary amount of human energy, and, usually, some political reputations. There is no doubt that the numerous primaries that have been added to the schedule since 1968 have made the nomination procedure even more exhausting then before.

One result has been the proposal that this protracted and complicated system be replaced by a single nationwide presidential primary in which each party chooses its candidate for the general election. If the first round did not produce a clear majority for any one candidate, a run-off primary involving the top vote-getters in the first primary could be held a short time later. The advantage would be to shorten drastically the distraction of our year-long presidential selection process and conserve the energy of the candidates, who must spend so much time running from one primary to the next, from the snows of New Hampshire in March to the heat of California in June.

The disadvantages of the proposal are quite clear. It would favor the candidates with the greatest initial popularity and financial support. It also would exclude "outsiders" who can use the present system to work their way into public attention. The sequence of primaries strung out over several months favors underdogs and challengers. A candidate near the bottom of the polls has a chance to show his appeal in the primaries in small states, where he does not need a large campaign budget. A good showing in these first attempts can help him accumulate the backers, money, and attention that are necessary if he is to have a chance in the bigger primaries that come later. To take a case in point, in 1960, the protracted, staggered primaries let John Kennedy demonstrate that he could win elections in wholly Protestant states, thus convincing dubious party leaders that his Catholicism was not an insuperable obstacle. As 1972 began, McGovern was the favored candidate of less than 5 percent of all Democrats. His early primary victories brought him more attention from the press and higher name recognition from the public. Support from the most liberal wing of the party, concerned with Vietnam and other noneconomic issues, crystallized around him. Instead of competing with other candidates for liberal support, he quickly monopolized it. This gave him the advantage of being the champion of one wing of the party, rather than being merely one of several contenders for "peace money" and the backing of ideological activists. Figure 9-1 shows the dramatic increases in support that McGovern and some other candidates have achieved.

The early primaries also provide a mechanism for pushing unpopular incumbent Presidents aside. Truman in 1952 and Johnson in 1968 surely could have won national primaries against scattered opposition, but both

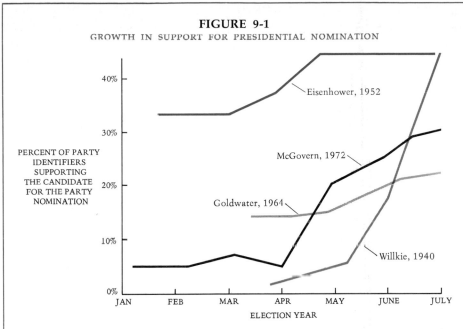

FIGURE 9-1
GROWTH IN SUPPORT FOR PRESIDENTIAL NOMINATION

PERCENT OF PARTY
IDENTIFIERS
SUPPORTING
THE CANDIDATE
FOR THE PARTY
NOMINATION

Eisenhower, 1952

McGovern, 1972

Goldwater, 1964

Willkie, 1940

ELECTION YEAR

Source: Based on data from George Gallup, *The Gallup Poll* (New York: Random House, 1972), and from *Gallup Opinion Index.*

men decided not to run again after their humiliating showings in the New Hampshire primary, in which the total Democratic turnout was less than 100,000. A national primary would reduce the present system's capability of drastically elevating challengers and bringing the mighty down.

A compromise solution that will preserve the advantages of the present system while minimizing its bad effects is the regional primary, in which adjoining states agree to hold their primaries on the same day. Oregon, Idaho, and Nevada have arrived at such a compact. The New England states may move in the same direction, but New Hampshire is resisting this idea, since it wants to keep the attention and economic boost that come from having the first primary of the election season.

STRATEGIES FOR THE NOMINATION

How a presidential hopeful goes about his nomination campaign depends on his circumstances. If he is already President, his renomination usually can be taken for granted—unless he seems to be presiding over a disastrous policy, as was the case with the Korean war for Truman in 1952 and Vietnam for Johnson sixteen years later. Both men chose to quit, thus depriving political observers of an opportunity to see how easily a sitting President could withstand a challenge to his renomination. Ronald Reagan's challenge of President Ford finally provided this test in 1976.

Sometimes a politician is so clearly the heir apparent to his party's nomination that there is no point in resisting fate. This was the case with Nixon in 1960. As Eisenhower's Vice President, he moved almost inevitably to the top of the ticket when Ike had to step down after completing two terms. More often, one figure is the clear favorite of his party's voters, although his nomination is not quite a foregone conclusion. As a general rule, such a frontrunner chooses to play a cautious strategy, on the assumption that he should not change a winning policy. Thus the leading candidate often will not enter primaries that he is not assured of winning—unless they are in states that he calculates he must have. By the same token, frontrunners generally try to avoid giving offense to significant factions within the party. Whether or not they have been moderates in the past, they minimize risks by avoiding strong positions about controversial issues on the assumption that they should make it easy for people on both sides of the fence to support them.

Underdogs, on the other hand, must be more venturesome. They have to take risks on uncertain primaries because they have little to lose. If they have a conspicuous liability, such as Kennedy's religion, they must seek opportunities to show that their apparent handicap is not serious. They must build a national organization, which is not an easy task because potential backers are not eager to support someone who seems to have little chance of winning. Underdogs often meet this challenge by trying to establish themselves as the symbol of strong political emotions. McGovern's campaign was a textbook example. His basic strategic problem in the preconvention period was how to establish himself as the leading liberal candidate in a crowded field that included at least two other formidable liberal spokesmen. One of these, Eugene McCarthy, had a much higher rating in the polls than McGovern. McGovern's strategists figured that if their man could win the early primaries, he would begin to look like the strongest of the liberal Democratic candidates. Thus, he would attract the support of liberal activists, who would rally to the candidate with the best chance of winning for the liberal cause.[20]

STRATEGIES THAT
WIN NOMINATIONS
SOMETIMES UNDER-
MINE SUCCESS IN
THE GENERAL ELEC-
TION, AS GEORGE
MCGOVERN DISCOV-
ERED IN 1972.
Wide World Photos

Like Goldwater eight years earlier, McGovern could win only by differentiating himself from the field and appealing to an existing ideological constituency. Yet this strategy, which was essential if he was to capture the nomination, contained the seeds of his defeat in the general election. By dramatizing his sympathy with ultraliberal causes, McGovern won the nomination but lost the election. The following account by a sympathetic observer describes McGovern's prenomination strategy and his subsequent attempts to move back to the middle of the road after that strategy had played its part in his successful challenge to the mainstream Democrats:

> Throughout 1971 McGovern had toured the college campuses, enlisting recruits for his "new politics" campaign. In those appearances,

[20] William Cavala, "Changing the Rules Changes the Game," *American Political Science Review*, 68 (March 1974), 34–35.

he allowed students to believe (while generally using careful language) that he agreed with them, that he wanted to legalize marijuana, to get out of Vietnam at once, to declare an amnesty for draft dodgers and deserters, and to liberalize abortion laws. . . . The young signed aboard the campaign, organized key primary states, canvassed door-to-door, packed local caucuses, and attended state conventions. . . .

As he prospered in the primaries, McGovern first tried to broaden his appeal beyond Vietnam and the student issues . . . he began to move toward the center. . . . All this was done artfully while loudly denying any change.[21]

THE NATIONAL CONVENTIONS

The conventions are the "supreme governing body" of their respective parties. They nominate candidates, make rules for the party, and write the platform. All this is done in five days by several thousand people, the vast majority of whom do not know each other, have never been at a convention before, and do not know the rules.[22] The tasks that must be performed by the convention delegates are not as staggering as this might suggest, however. For one thing, the major criterion for all convention decisions is what will hurt or help one's own candidate. Since almost all important decisions are made with an eye on the favored candidate's chances, it is not difficult for the individual delegate to figure out what to do. He does what his candidate's representative tells him to. Moreover, in recent years the conventions have not really been where the actual choice of candidates was made. *In every national convention from 1956 through 1972, the presidential nomination was settled on the first ballot.* Even before the convention met, the leading candidate already had enough delegate votes to remove any doubts about the outcome. The convention was merely a ceremony to crown the candidate who had the nomination locked up, not a meeting at which a choice was to be made. In fact, in only four of the twenty conventions from 1928 through 1972 was more than one ballot needed to pick the nominee.

For a long time, then, all the talk about "smoke-filled rooms" and secret bosses manipulating conventions to put across their own sinister designs has been nonsense, not because the conventions have been purer than the cynics like to think, but because there has been nothing for the bosses to manipulate. It is likely, however, that these misconceptions about the conventions will become increasingly true in the future.

---

[21] Denis G. Sullivan et al., *The Politics of Representation* (New York: St. Martin's Press, 1974), pp. 108–9.

[22] In 1972, 81 percent of the Democratic delegates and 72 percent of the Republicans were at their first convention. (*San Francisco Chronicle*, August 12, 1972, p. 12.) In the period from 1944 through 1968, an average of just under two-thirds of the delegates to both parties' conventions were newcomers. See Loch K. Johnson and Harlan Hahn, "Delegate Turnover at National Party Conventions, 1944–68," in Donald R. Matthews, ed., *Perspectives on Presidential Selection* (Washington: The Brookings Institution, 1973), p. 148.

Ironically, this prediction stems from the wave of reforms in the early 1970s. One of the main goals of these changes was to make the convention delegates more faithfully representative of the sentiments of the grassroots party faithful. The unit rule and winner-take-all primaries sacrificed representativeness for decisiveness. Replacing them with proportional representation of each candidate's strength will produce situations in which several candidates each will have a substantial number of committed delegates. This diminishes the chance of there being a leading candidate who comes to the convention with a majority. The result then becomes a "brokered convention," in which the nomination is worked out by negotiations among a handful of leaders.

To understand how such negotiations work, one must realize that under most state laws, delegates who are pledged to a certain candidate need vote for him only on the first ballot at the convention. This rule is necessary or else a convention that started out deadlocked would remain deadlocked forever. If the first ballot does not produce a candidate with a majority of delegate support, there must be a second and then a third ballot, and so on until one candidate does receive a majority. As the balloting proceeds, therefore, the various candidates, their friends, and the delegates begin to bargain with one another. Eventually, as a result of these negotiations, enough

delegates switch their votes from whomever they supported on the first ballot to give one candidate a majority on the fifth or tenth or one hundredth ballot. The fact that conventions increasingly will have real decisions to make also means an increase in the possibility of backroom wheeling and dealing.

One student of parties describes the delegate reforms as a triumph for people who think that the parties should be "expressive" of all points of view, rather than "effective" agencies for winning elections.[23] Another political scientist thinks that the reformers have created a serious dilemma:

> The contemporary convention problem is that recent demands for fairness and democracy in procedures may clash headlong with the convention's traditional objective of efficiency, legitimacy, reasonableness, and unity as a means to victory. For example, it may be difficult to reconcile fairness to every faction with the rapid choice of a nominee and approval of a platform and the rallying of a broad

[23] Austin Ranney, "Changing the Rules of the Nominating Game," in Barber, ed., *Choosing the President*, pp. 79–82.

THE DEMOCRATIC NATIONAL CONVENTION, 1972. *Jan Lukas, Photo Researchers, Rapho Division*

party consensus. And a party that bares its internal struggles to public scrutiny may find it difficult to win elections.[24]

EVALUATING THE RESULTS

At least three criteria can be used in evaluating the nominating procedures of the two parties. (1) Are they fair? (2) Do they pick the candidate most popular with his party's members? (3) Do they pick the strongest candidate for the general election? These are all apparently reasonable standards, but they are not necessarily consistent with each other.

The most difficult criterion is the first one. What is fairness? Does it mean giving every party member a chance to participate? If so, how is membership defined? Should the privilege of participating in the presidential selection process be limited to people who have assumed certain minimal responsibilities to their party, or should anyone who calls himself a party member be allowed to participate equally?

The second criterion is more easily discussed. The leading candidate in the public opinion polls almost always becomes his party's nominee. Thus, it does not seem that a national primary is necessary to nominate the most popular candidates. The convention system, *in recent years,* has already done that. But neither a national primary system nor a convention system can guarantee that the party's candidate will be the choice of a majority of party members. There may be no candidate on whom a majority agree. Twice in recent years the leading candidate received the nomination but had much less than a majority of grassroots support. In 1964, Goldwater was the choice of 22 percent of all Republicans, compared to the same proportion for Nixon, 21 percent for a third candidate, and 20 percent for a fourth. In 1972, McGovern led all other candidates but still had the support of only 30 percent of rank-and-file Democrats.[25]

The third criterion poses a great problem for any nominating system. With the examples of Goldwater and McGovern before us, it is not difficult to see that the candidate who is most popular in his own party may not have the most appeal to Independents and members of the other party. What is more, Goldwater and McGovern are not the only such cases. In 1968, Humphrey, the preferred candidate of Democrats, was less attractive to Republicans and Independents than Eugene McCarthy, who was a poor third in his own party.[26] This, then, is the ultimate dilemma of the presidential nominating process: *If the party's goal is to win the election, increasing participation may be counterproductive.* The more the candidate reflects the rank-and-file preferences of his own party faithful, the less he may appeal to independent voters and those who identify with the other party.

[24] Judith H. Parris, *The Convention Problem* (Washington: The Brookings Institution, 1972), pp. 14–15.

[25] Matthews, "Presidential Nominations," p. 63.

[26] Arthur C. Wolfe, "Challenge from the Right: The Basis of Voter Support for Wallace in 1968," paper presented at the 1969 annual meeting of the American Political Science Association, p. 15.

He may need some of their votes to win the general election. The more liberal candidate is more likely to appeal to the majority of Democratic primary voters. The more conservative candidate probably will be preferred by a majority of Republicans who vote in their primary. But a candidate who must demonstrate in a very open nominating process that he is liberal enough or conservative enough to win his own party's nomination may be demonstrating simultaneously that he is too liberal or too conservative to appeal to a majority of the entire electorate. And it is the majority of the entire electorate that decides who actually gets to be President. This is one reason why party leaders sometimes oppose openness and total democracy in their own party's nominating process. They feel that if they can avoid excessive pressure from their own activists, they can come up with candidates who have a better chance of actually winning the election although they are less popular within the party.

PARTY REFORM

The Democratic activists who deposed President Johnson in 1968 and came close to denying the nomination to his successor, Hubert Humphrey, felt that they had been cheated by rules and procedures that could not be defended on any rational ground. Their complaints led to the formation of the Commission on Party Structure and Delegate Selection, popularly known as the McGovern Commission after its first chairman. After extensive research and deliberation, the Commission formulated eighteen guidelines that were adopted by the Democratic National Committee in 1971. Members of the Commission's staff were chiefly responsible for an organized campaign to bring all state Democratic parties into compliance with the guidelines in time for the 1972 election.

Some of the reforms were eminently sensible and aroused little public opposition. For example, the new rules required that all delegates be selected in the year of the election, that any meetings to choose delegates be publicized, and that rules governing each state party's selection procedures be written down and available on request. Some of the other reforms did not receive such unanimous support. By far the most famous and controversial guidelines were those requiring "affirmative action":

> . . . including representation of minority groups on the national convention delegation in reasonable relationship to the group's presence in the state.
> . . . the Commission requires State Parties to overcome the effects of past discrimination by affirmative steps to encourage representation on the national convention delegation of young people—defined as people of not more than thirty nor less than eighteen years of age—and women in reasonable relationship to their presence in the population of the State.[27]

[27] Commission on Party Structure and Delegate Selection, *Mandate for Reform* (Washington: Democratic National Committee, 1970), p. 40.

This passage was accompanied by a footnote: "It is the understanding of the Commission that this is not to be accomplished by the mandatory imposition of quotas." Despite the footnote, the language of the report did effectively impose quotas in 1972.

The issues involved are clearly stated by Ranney, a member of the McGovern Commission, who originally proposed a quota for blacks and then changed his mind and argued unsuccessfully against the idea. He describes the debate in the Commission:

> . . . The party could provide for a fair fight or it could provide for a guaranteed result, we said, but it could not provide for both.
>
> In the end the commission voted, by 10 to 9, to require representation of women, young people, and members of minority groups. Many people have asked since, why only *those* groups? Why not also guaranteed representation for, say, people over sixty-five, or labor union members, or poor people? The answer is simple, if not edifying: the commissioners who believed in [quotas] spoke only for the special interests of women, youth, and minority ethnic groups; and those of us who sought a different kind of representation did not counter by pressing for the special interests of other groups.[28]

These observations suggest one of the drawbacks to quotas. They do succeed in altering the demographic composition of the delegates, but only in the most literal sense and only with respect to the specified characteristics. As we saw in Chapter 7, although the Democratic delegates in 1972 included ample numbers of blacks, women, and young people, they also were enormously richer and better educated than the American public. In some respects, their unrepresentativeness was grotesque. For example, fully 22 percent of them were teachers or professors and another 8 percent were students.[29]

As we write, it is not clear if quotas will be enforced at the 1976 Democratic convention. The position taken by the party's midterm charter conference in 1974 was highly ambiguous. It called for affirmative action, opposed *mandatory* quotas, and then deleted a provision stating that demographic imbalance on a delegation should not be taken as a presumption of discrimination. All candidates will probably play it safe by making sure that their delegate slates have the proper proportion of blacks, women, and young people.

In some respects, it does not matter greatly where the party finally comes down on this issue, for the great debate over quotas is actually more symbolic than real. Convention delegates are not important in themselves. They are not free agents who can act as they please. If a convention becomes deadlocked and bargaining determines the result, then age, sex, or race will have little to do with the likelihood that a delegate pledged to one candidate will be delivered to another. Usually, the candidate to whom they are

[28] Ranney, *Curing the Mischiefs of Faction*, p. 114.
[29] Sullivan et al., *The Politics of Representation*, pp. 23–24.

pledged will be able to deliver all his delegates as a single bloc to whichever candidate he favors in the later ballots. Moreover, candidates do not seem to have trouble finding people of the appropriate race, sex, and age to be on their delegate slates. George Wallace, for example, had black delegates, just like the other candidates.

While the Democrats have led the way in reforming delegate selection procedures, the Republicans have not failed to take many of the same steps, albeit somewhat more haltingly.

The foregoing considerations should not be taken as an indication that the reform movement is meaningless. One of the major long-term consequences of the party reform movement is to impose a certain measure of centralized control on state and local parties insofar as presidential nominations are concerned. Because compliance with the guidelines is a condition of being seated at the national convention, the state parties are under a good deal of pressure to march to the national party's tune. Even before the McGovern Commission, the Democratic convention voted to refuse seats to any state party that did not extend equal treatment to all Democrats. The Mississippi delegation was excluded from the 1968 convention for this reason. Since then, it has allowed blacks to participate — quite a departure from its previous custom.

However, the major impact of recent party reforms is not going to be in the racial, sexual, and age compositions of the delegations. Instead, it will be in the distribution of delegates *among the various candidates,* particularly to the extent that proportional representation replaces winner-take-all caucuses and primaries. This change may create many situations in which three or four prospective candidates go into the convention with substantial delegate strength. Moreover, if the reforms do generate a greater degree of rank-and-file participation, each party may find itself more frequently faced with the Goldwater-McGovern dilemma. The candidate it chooses may be so popular with his own party rank-and-file that he is too unpopular with Independents and moderates of his own party to pick up the votes necessary to win the presidential election. Thus the gap between the parties is likely to widen and victory will go to the party least affected by the reforms.

CAMPAIGNING FOR OFFICE

Once nominated, a presidential candidate must face the problem of uniting his party behind his campaign. One route to unity depends on lining up the active support of the candidates whom he defeated for the nomination. This support is not always easy to request or give, however. The wounds of recent combat may be too painful to permit reconciliation. The losing candidate may be willing to cooperate, but his key staff may find peacemaking more difficult. The problem is worse if the winner is an "outsider" who has won by overwhelming the regulars with hosts of political newcomers. This situation exacerbates the normal tension between the candidate's own staff and activists whose loyalty is to the party. It is even more difficult when the candidate is someone like McGovern, who based his campaign on criticism of party regulars. Relationships were so bad in 1972 that some major Democratic leaders would not talk to the McGovern campaign chairmen in their states.

Even when there is a history of ill-feeling between a nominee and other influential members of his party, cooperation may still be possible, however. For example, Governor Nelson Rockefeller of New York scarcely lifted a finger to help Richard Nixon when Nixon ran for the presidency unsuccessfully in 1960 and successfully in 1968. But in 1972 Rockefeller's entire political apparatus was mobilized for Nixon. Rockefeller supplied the Republican standard-bearer with more than three hundred specialists on every aspect of campaigning. How did Nixon induce Rockefeller to cooperate? In essence, he offered a simple exchange: if Rockefeller would help Nixon, Nixon would not have to create his own organization in New York, an organization that could threaten Rockefeller's control of Republican politics in that state.

In the broad sense, "the campaign" includes innumerable endeavors ranging from registration campaigns aimed at voters likely to support a candidate to carefully planned symbolic actions addressed to key groups. This latter category includes face-to-face attempts to obtain sizable campaign contributions from rich people and endorsements from influential newspapers. (One ritual of every presidential campaign is a meeting between each major candidate and the editorial board of the *New York Times*.) A famous example of campaigning-by-deed was John Kennedy's 1960 telephone call to the wife of Reverend Martin Luther King, Jr. King had been jailed on a trumped-up charge and Kennedy's highly publicized gesture of support for him was widely considered a masterstroke of publicity.

As this incident indicates, appeals to ethnic groups are a staple element of American campaigns. In 1972 the "Nationalities Division" of the Committee for the Re-election of the President had a budget of more than $1 million and a repertoire of activities directed at blacks, Jews, and Spanish-heritage voters. Nixon's campaign distributed bumper stickers in nine languages. In addition, the Republican National Committee had a "Heritage Division" that worked with thirty-two different nationality groups. Not to be outdone, Citizens for McGovern also had a nationalities branch and the Democratic National Committee had twenty-three different nationality organizations coordinated by an "All Americans Council." McGovern spoke at such ethnic gatherings as Von Steuben Day and Columbus Day parades.[30] In an effort to offset a belief that McGovern was cool to Israel, Senator Abraham Ribicoff of Connecticut, one of his most influential Jewish supporters, assured a group of uneasy rabbis that McGovern would make no decisions about the Middle East without first consulting Ribicoff.

The oldest and most basic element of "old politics" campaigning involved direct personal contacts with voters. To secure these contacts, the candidate traditionally relied on the memory of the precinct captain, who knew his

"THE BIG GUY IN FRONT IS JOSEPH T. COCHRANE. CALL HIM JOE. YOU MET HIM IN MARYSVILLE THREE WEEKS AGO. TALK ABOUT HUNTING. HE GOES AFTER DEER EVERY FALL. MAN ON LEFT IS LEO BROWN. SIXTEENTH DISTRICT IN HIS POCKET. DON'T ASK HIM ABOUT HIS WIFE. SHE'S DITCHED HIM. FELLOW WITH MUSTACHE IS JIM CRONIN. WATCH YOUR STEP WITH HIM. HE'S COCHRANE'S BROTHER-IN-LAW, AND . . ."
Drawing by Peter Arno; copyright © 1946, 1974 The New Yorker Magazine, Inc.

---

[30] *Congressional Quarterly Weekly Report,* October 28, 1972, pp. 2795–97.

neighbors intimately and could count on a sure reservoir of votes by mobilizing patronage job-holders and other citizens beholden to the party organization. Today the box of file cards and the computer have supplemented the precinct captain's memory, but the traditional techniques are still very much in use, especially by the ideologically motivated activists of the so-called "new politics." The Democratic boss of Buffalo commented on this marriage of old and new:

> If the new politics teaches anything at all, it's that the old politics was pretty good. The McCarthy kids in New Hampshire rang doorbells, made telephone calls and made the personal contact that people associate with the old-style machines.[31]

In 1972, fully 29 percent of the public was contacted by a worker for one party or the other. A substantial fraction of them were reached by both parties.

---

[31] Quoted in Martin and Susan Tolchin, *To the Victor* . . . (New York: Random House, 1972), p. 23.

THE FRANTIC PACE OF CAMPAIGNS

To the major participants in a campaign the pace is constant and frantic. Authority in a campaign tends to be fluid rather than rigid, based on persuasion rather than command, and enforced rather through a sense of legitimacy than through sanction. Because most activists are involved in a campaign at least as much for the pleasure they derive from the activity as for a concern with the hope of eventual gain should victory be theirs, compliance with campaign decisions is best obtained primarily through discussion. The smallest decision may involve a campaign staff person in hours of such discussion. But to neglect this form of "involvement" often means making the campaign less enjoyable to the participant, thus diminishing one of the prime motives for his or her participation in the first place. Further, the need for money is infinite and the supply is always less than needed. Endless hours must be spent on fund-raising. Events must be planned. Contributors have a somewhat annoying wish to be talked with on matters other than money. "Leaders" of every group, no matter how small, must be courted courteously. All such activities take time—leaving precious little time for reflective thought. Moreover, the best minds of a campaign will usually be put to work on the most serious problems— which are always the most immediate problems.*

*William Cavala, "Changing the Rules Changes the Game," p. 33n.

Along with the survival of old-time personal politics there has been a simultaneous introduction of new techniques and technology. Artfully designed commercials for radio and television typify the wholesale expansion of advertising techniques into the political arena. These commercials are designed, produced, packaged, and disseminated by teams of specialists on scenario writing, photography, media space buying, and television direction. The total spent on radio and television by all political candidates in 1972 was $59.6 million.

Every few years journalists seem to be struck by the fact that candidates spend a lot of money on television advertising. One result of this attention is a proliferation of stories expressing concern that the political process is on the verge of being taken over by specialists in the art of manipulating images. This charge was widely heard during the 1970 election campaign, but when the returns came in they showed that the advertising geniuses lost as many campaigns as they won. This was also the success ratio of candidates who spent more for radio and television advertising than their opponents.[32] By the same token, some pundits used to worry that the influence of television would lead to the rise of candidates who could offer the public nothing but personal glamor. After looking at such distinctly unglamorous figures as Gerald Ford, Richard Nixon, Lyndon Johnson, and George McGovern, it is safe to conclude that the ranks of successful politicians include about the same proportion of movie star personalities as the general public.

THE ELECTORAL COLLEGE

By election day, each voter decides which presidential candidate he prefers. But he does not vote directly for the candidate of his choice, even though he probably thinks he does. Technically, he votes for a slate of *electors* pledged to his candidate. A state has one electoral vote for each senator and representative. The candidate who gets the most popular votes in the state receives all the state's electoral votes. The electoral college meets early in December, at which time the chosen electors gather in Washington to cast their ballots for the candidate to whom they are pledged.

This method was devised by the framers of the Constitution because they wanted the President chosen by a body of distinguished men who would draw on their own experience and knowledge and would exercise independent judgment. The emergence of popular candidates and political parties quickly put an end to the electors' independence. Since 1820, only five electors (out of a total of 15,783) have been "faithless" by failing to vote for the candidate to whom they were pledged.[33]

If no candidate receives a majority of electoral votes, the House of Representatives chooses the President from among the top three candidates, with each state delegation having a single vote. This has happened twice in our

OKLAHOMA'S EIGHT
ELECTORS CAST
THEIR BALLOTS.
Wide World Photos

[32] *New York Times*, June 18, 1971, p. 47.
[33] Lawrence D. Longley and Alan G. Braun, *The Politics of Electoral College Reform* (New Haven: Yale University Press, 1972), p. 29.

A SAMPLE
SPOT TELEVISION COMMERCIAL

Video	*Audio*
1. *Opening network disclaimer:* "A POLITICAL ANNOUNCEMENT."	
2. DOLLY DOWN LS EMPTY ROAD ACROSS WESTERN AREA. DISSOLVE TO MATCH MOVEMENT PAY—TILT IN ON DEJECTED MAN ASLEEP ON PARK BENCH. THEN INTO SCENES OF BOTH URBAN AND RURAL DECAY.	MUSIC UP AND UNDER. *Richard Nixon:* For the past five years we've been deluged by programs for the unemployed—programs for the cities—programs for the poor. And we have reaped from these programs an ugly harvest of frustrations, violence and failure across the land.
3. . . . SEQUENCE OF FACES OF AMERICA—ALL RACES, ALL BACKGROUNDS. THERE IS A QUALITY OF DETERMINATION TO THEM, BUT THEY APPEAR SORELY TIRED. THEY ARE THE HUNGRY OF APPALACHIA—THE POOR OF AN URBAN GHETTO—THE ILL-HOUSED MEMBERS OF A FAMILY ON AN INDIAN RESERVATION. SLOWLY BUT FIRMLY THE PICTURE LEADS TOWARD A SCENE OF FRUSTRATED ANGER, WHICH IS EXPRESSED IN THEIR FACES.	*Richard Nixon:* Now our opponents will be offering more of the same. But I say we are on the wrong road. It is time to quit pouring billions of dollars into programs that have failed.
SIGN ON STREET WHICH SAYS, "GOVERNMENT CHECKS CASHED HERE."	*Richard Nixon:* What we need are not more millions on welfare rolls—but more people on payrolls in the United States. I believe we should enlist private enterprise, which will produce, not promises in solving the problems of America.
4. SERIES OF QUICK, EFFECTIVE CUTS OF CONSTRUCTIVE WORK SCENES—A SHIP UNLOADING—A TOWER BEING RAISED—A FACTORY LINE—A BUILDING ERECTED.	
5. DISSOLVE TO SHOT OF CHILDREN STANDING IN THE MUD OF APPALACHIA. THEY STARE AT THE CAMERA. TILT DOWN FOR MATCH MOVEMENT DISSOLVE TO SILO OF LITTLE BOY (BACK TO CAMERA) AS HE LOOKS OUT WINDOW. HOLD. FADEOUT.	MUSIC UP AND OUT.

Source: Joe McGinniss, *The Selling of the President 1968* (New York: Trident Press, 1969), pp. 244–45.

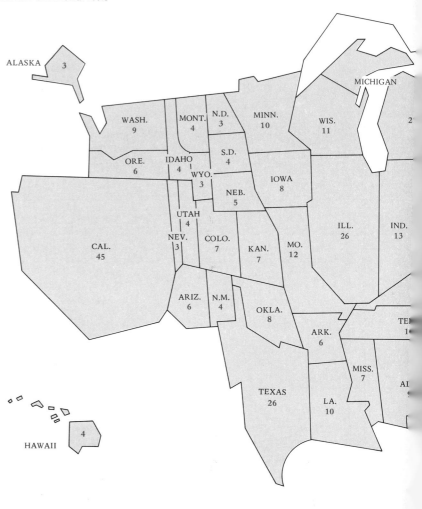

FIGURE 9-2
ELECTORAL VOTES PER STATE

THE UNITED STATES
A Political Map

States drawn in proportion to
number of electoral votes

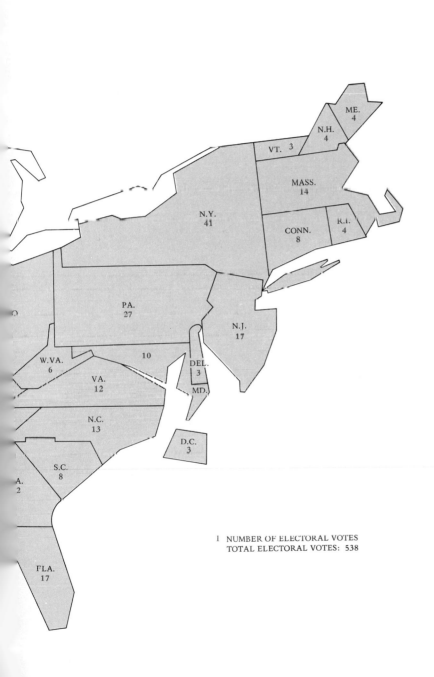

1 NUMBER OF ELECTORAL VOTES
TOTAL ELECTORAL VOTES: 538

history, most recently in 1824. Neither was a very happy occasion. Accusations of betrayal and corruption seriously eroded the legitimacy of the outcome. It is generally believed that throwing an election into the House is a bad thing. Nevertheless, as we shall see in a moment, there seems to be no sense of urgency about changing the law to eliminate this possibility, even though the contingency almost came to pass in 1968 as a result of Wallace's third-party candidacy. It is also possible for the electoral college to give the election to a candidate who did not receive the most popular votes. This has happened three times, although in each case the disparity in popular vote was not at all substantial.

The real significance of the electoral college derives from the way it structures the presidential campaign and the calculations of politicians. Because a candidate who gets a plurality of popular votes in a state gets all the state's electoral votes, there is no reason for him to pay any attention to states where he is sure to win or lose. In such states, picking up or losing a few votes makes no difference to the final outcome of the election. For instance, let us say that the popular vote in a state ran 3,200,000 for a Democrat and 2,000,000 for a Republican. The Democrat will receive all the electoral votes of that state. If he campaigned hard and got 4,000,000 votes, he still would win all the electoral votes. Conversely, if the Republican waged a vigorous campaign and closed the margin to 2,700,000 for his opponent and 2,500,000 for himself, it wouldn't do him a bit of good. He still would get none of the state's electoral votes. Thus, the campaign efforts of both candidates are always concentrated on the doubtful states. This encourages the candidates to compete for the same common ground, rather than leading them to maximize votes by appealing to their supporters in the states they are sure of winning.

To put this matter another way, the candidates seek to please voters in doubtful states more than voters in sure Democratic or Republican states. One more popular vote for a Democratic candidate in a state that is already going Democratic by a two to one margin makes no difference. But one more popular vote in a close state may give the Democrats a plurality of popular votes in that state, and thus all the state's electoral votes. This means that the most important voters, as far as presidential candidates are concerned, are those in large states with many electoral votes which are closely balanced between Democrats and Republicans. Campaigns tend to be pitched particularly to those voters.

An even more important effect of the electoral college is the way it discourages most third parties. Since a plurality is enough to bring in all of a state's electoral votes, only a party with a chance of winning has any motivation to run at all. There is little opportunity for third parties to play a "spoiler" role or to use this possibility as a way to blackmail a major party into making concessions. The electoral college does not completely eliminate this threat, since a regionally based third-party candidate can deliberately seek to throw the election into the House, but it does make the threat considerably less credible under normal circumstances. As a consequence, the two parties are the main arenas for political struggle. Only when a prospective third party is large enough to actually win a plurality of popular votes in a substantial number of states does a vote for that party really count—and then only in those states where it has a chance of winning. Thus, the electoral college has two basic results. It tends to preserve the stability of the two-party system and it focuses the attention of presidential candidates on swing voters in close states rather than on piling up bigger and bigger leads in states already favorable to them.

Wallace's third-party candidacy in the 1968 election almost succeeded in throwing the election to the House of Representatives and therefore revived interest in replacing the electoral college with direct popular election of the President. As we observed in Chapter 5, the polls showed a healthy popular majority against the electoral college. But they also showed that few people really knew what the controversy was all about. There seems to be little public pressure behind direct election proposals. Barring a continuation of Wallace-like threats, change to direct popular election does not seem a likely short-run prospect.

Most political scientists agree that the public's indifference to these proposals is not a bad thing. A few scholars object to the electoral college. Since its advantages are well understood, whereas the uncertainties of direct popular election are substantial, the status quo seems preferable here.

HOW DIFFERENT ARE THE PARTIES?

It is easy enough to provide deductive reasons why the Republican and Democratic parties should be similar, or why they should be different. We will do just this shortly. But first let us explore some of the numerous dimensions along which the gap between the two parties can be measured. Differences and similarities between Republicans and Democrats can be measured along any or all of the following lines:

1. *The parts of society from which they draw supporters.* As we saw in Chapter 6, Republicans and Democrats are not quite the same kind of people. The Democratic party includes more blacks, Jews, Catholics, poor people, and southerners; the Republican party includes more wealthy people. Except for blacks and Jews, however, the Democrats do not have anything even approaching an exclusive hold on any group, and the Republicans do not have a corner on millionaires.
2. *The opinions of their rank-and-file members.* Here again, we saw in Chapter 6 some issues where there were distinct but moderate differences between the parties, and other issues where their followers had virtually identical patterns of belief.
3. *The attitudes of their activists and primary voters.* The partisan gap is considerably greater among convention delegates and participants in campaign activities than among rank-and-file voters. It is even wider among congressional candidates, as Table 9–4 shows.

TABLE 9-4

HOW REPUBLICAN AND DEMOCRATIC
CONGRESSIONAL CANDIDATES DIFFER ON ISSUES

	PERCENT WHO AGREE	
	DEMOCRATS	REPUBLICANS
"Defense spending should be substantially reduced and the funds diverted to domestic social needs."	73%	21%
"Would you favor a Federally financed national health insurance plan covering all medical expenses?"	77%	21%
"Any licensed physician should be allowed to perform an abortion for any woman who wants one."	61%	31%
"Civil rights laws enacted in the past decade should be significantly expanded in the years ahead."	57%	19%

Source: *Congressional Quarterly Weekly Report*, October 16, 1970, pp. 2567–69.

4. *The behavior of their officials.* As we will see in Chapter 11, party is the best predictor of voting patterns in the House and Senate.
5. *Their party platforms.* It is generally believed that platforms are meaningless. Sometimes even the presidential candidate does not seem to care much about the platform on which he is to run. At other times, however, the platform is a subject of hot dispute. But even at the ideologically aware 1972 Democratic convention, few delegates had actually read the platform that they fought about and finally approved. The authors of a study on the convention report their findings about delegate familiarity with the platform:

> When asked about the platform, one old-line leader from Connecticut replied with an incredulous stare and finally growled, "Have *you* ever read a platform?" (The questioner had not.) A veteran Missouri labor leader said, "It means nothing. There's only twelve people that read it. The candidate is the platform."[34]

One political scientist decided to test what "everyone knows" about party platforms by actually reading and comparing them for every election year from 1944 through 1964. He found that more than half the planks in the platform were specific enough to enable him to see if they had been carried out. *Fully 72 percent of the promises made in the party platforms had indeed*

[34] Sullivan et al., *The Politics of Representation*, p. 73.

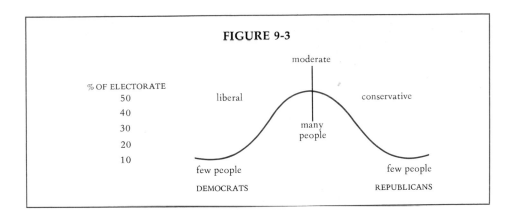

FIGURE 9-3

been kept by 1966. He also found that the platforms differed considerably, partly in emphasizing different issues, partly in making opposing promises. Over half the promises were made by one party only, a third were made by both, and the rest were in conflict.[35] It appears, then, that the platforms are not meaningless. They represent an accumulation of what each party has been pushing for in Congress and what its more issue-oriented activists would like to see enacted.

Perhaps the most fundamental source of disagreement between the parties does not come from real differences in policies but from the fact that their leaders feel that there is a difference. Even when they favor the same policies, politicians see politics as an us-against-them business. What is good for Republicans must be bad for Democrats, and thus what Republicans propose should be opposed by Democrats on grounds of simple self-interest. Opposition to what the President does is expressed by members of the other party with presidential ambitions of their own, as well as by any other party figure looking for publicity and knowing that it is available by criticizing the administration.

One long-standing belief about the American electorate is that it is composed of some extreme liberals, a lot of moderate liberals, a lot of mod-

[35] Gerald Pomper, *Elections in America* (New York: Dodd, Mead, 1970), pp. 149–70.

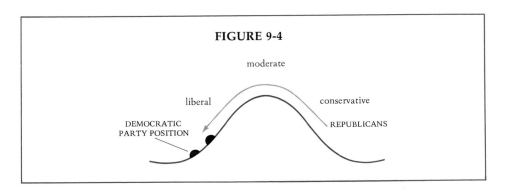

FIGURE 9-4

erate conservatives, and some extreme conservatives. Figure 9–3 shows this view of the electorate graphically. According to this view, if the Democratic party adopted a quite liberal stance, it would allow the Republican party to move over the hump and capture more than half the votes, as shown in Figure 9-4. Conversely, if the Republicans adopted a very conservative position, then the Democrats might get all the liberal votes plus most moderate votes. Thus the desire to capture the high ground where most of the voters are supposed to be pushes both parties toward the same intermediate policy positions.

At times this may be a true picture, but there are also a number of major forces pushing the parties apart. First, public opinion on an issue often does not resemble this bell-shaped curve. On some individual issues there may be two humps. For instance, a substantial share of the population may be in favor of government aid to parochial schools while another substantial portion is opposed. (See Figure 9–5.) In such instances, each party could climb to the top of one of the humps without giving much advantage to the other. They would then have distinctly different positions.

Another factor keeping the parties apart is the fact that voters often split differently on different issues, as we saw in Chapter 5. The voters oppose school busing and favor government-subsidized medical care. The Republican party might seek to win their votes by denouncing school busing while the Democrats concentrated on advocating socialized medicine to woo the same voters. As long as we have only two parties, it is not possible for each to be ideologically distinct and coherent, because there is no corresponding ideological clarity and polarization among the population.

In short, our one-hump model with the two parties elbowing one another in the middle assumes that all Americans are arranged along a single all-encompassing liberal-to-conservative dimension. In reality, however, presidential elections involve many overlapping and conflicting issue dimensions with differing distributions of voter attitudes. The two candidates may choose to emphasize different issues. Both parties can occupy several humps, each of which contains the majority opinion on one issue. In this way the two parties may present different images to the public even while both are taking individual issue positions that a majority of the voters want.

Another reason why the parties remain apart is the fact that their leaders

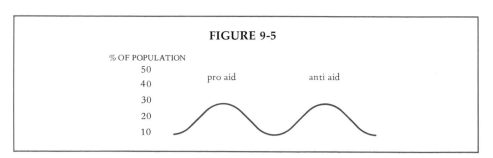

FIGURE 9-5

% OF POPULATION

50
40
30
20
10

pro aid   anti aid

have differing estimates as to which of the many current issues will be most important to the voters. Not surprisingly, Republican politicians will tend to believe that their party's favored positions are more popular with the public, while Democratic leaders will justify their own preferences by rationalizing that these positions will enable them to win favor with more voters. (In point of fact, of course, politicians of all varieties are likely to overestimate the electorate's knowledge, interest, and decisiveness about issues. As we saw in Chapter 6, few voters base their decisions on the issues. Party identification and candidate image account for the vast bulk of voting decisions in any election.)

The differences between parties created by different estimates as to what positions will win is reinforced by yet another factor. We have seen that Republican and Democratic activists have quite different attitudes. Moreover, the two parties traditionally have relied on somewhat different bases of support. The Democrats have been more popular with labor, blacks, city dwellers, and certain farm groups. The Republicans have had more support from business and other farm groups. These associations have been sources of votes, campaign workers, and campaign funds. Now, let us suppose that the Democrats believe that a majority of Americans are strongly opposed to school busing and that this issue will be an important one in the election. Nevertheless, they still may not rush toward the same anti-school-busing positions that Republicans may take. There are a number of reasons for this. First, the active members of the party may be strongly in favor of school integration; and second, an anti-busing position might lead to wholesale black defections from the party. Similarly, the Republicans may not come out for government-subsidized medical care, even if a majority of Americans want it, because a majority of Republican leaders and a majority of Republican campaign contributors do not want it.

In short, a party may not move to a position occupied by the majority of voters on a particular issue because the party's more active members strongly support the minority position on the issue. Or the leadership may feel that adopting the most popular position on a given issue might favorably influence the majority of voters concerned with that issue, but only at the cost of causing terrible splits in the party that would reduce its chances of winning the election. Frequently, then, one party may not seek to get next to the other on an issue. Instead, it may take a less popular stand or no stand at all in order to avoid a split in the party or a policy stance which some key supporters dislike.

The combination of different tactical notions, rival candidates, and opinionated activists introduces powerful dynamic elements into party competition. We have seen that sometimes the gap between the two presidential candidates is relatively narrow, as was the case in the 1950s. And sometimes the partisan gap is substantial, as it was in 1964 and 1972. When this happens, the more moderate candidate generally exploits the situation by holding out a hand of welcome to voters from the other party. The Democrats responded in this way to Goldwater's nomination in 1964.

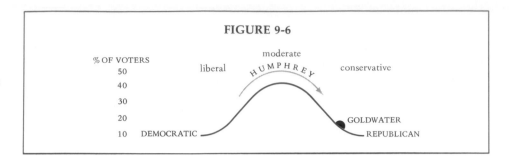

FIGURE 9-6

In his convention speech accepting the Democratic vice presidential nomination, Hubert Humphrey said:

> Yes, yes my fellow Americans, it is a fact that the temporary Republican spokesman is not in the mainstream of his party, in fact he has not even touched the shore. . . . I say to those responsible and forward-looking Republicans—and there are thousands of them—we welcome you to the banner of Lyndon B. Johnson. . . .

Humphrey was trying to move over the top of the hump and pick up votes on the Republican side because Goldwater appeared to be far down toward the right end of the liberal-conservative spectrum. (See Figure 9–6.) Nevertheless, the Goldwater nomination indicates that political parties often move far away from the center in choosing their candidates. This is not because a stable entity called "the party" has made a policy decision to do so, but because the party label has been captured temporarily by one of the contending factions that comprise each party.

When the winner is someone like Goldwater or McGovern, the party's congressional candidates hastily try to disassociate themselves from what they consider a symbol of disaster. The other party's campaigners, of course, gleefully try to hang the unpopular presidential nominee around the neck of every candidate running on his party's ticket. In 1972, the director of the Fair Campaign Practices Committee reported that the "one specific complaint received more than any other was from Democrats claiming they were unfairly identified with George McGovern."[36] Nothing could illustrate more clearly the fragmented character of American political parties.

The gap between the parties is like an accordion. Sometimes it is narrow as moderate candidates lead both parties in search of the golden mean. Then each party tries to appeal to the same body of popular opinion. But sometimes the parties diverge sharply, under the influence of leaders in pursuit of the ideal society, their own place in history, or the campaign contributions and workers they need to win. We will learn more about these motivations in the next three chapters, as we look directly at the political calculations of congressmen and the President.

[36] Quoted in *San Francisco Sunday Examiner & Chronicle,* November 19, 1972, Section A, p. 28.

Political parties select candidates and seek to influence people to vote for those candidates. They provide orderly channels for political competition among those seeking public office; they organize various political ideas and personalities into two large packages designed to compromise and coordinate the diverse political strivings that we find on the American scene.

A number of factors, including the debate over adoption of the Constitution, the initial duality of political conflict, the prevalence of single-member electoral districts, the winner-take-all presidency, and the tactics of the major parties themselves, have tended to create and maintain a two-party system in the United States.

American political parties do not have specifically defined memberships. An American is a Democrat or a Republican if he says he is. Some people are more active in party affairs than others. Even among the activists, only some are party regulars who work election after election irrespective of the candidates and the issues. Others are purists who only work for the party when they feel that the party can become the means of gaining victory for persons or policies that they identify as particularly good.

Basically, American parties are decentralized. Most of their workers and money are found and used by local party organizations in behalf of individual candidates. Although the voters perceive the Democratic and Republican parties as national parties with national programs, there is little national organization. The President serves as national spokesman for his party but usually has little control over the affairs of the state and local branches of the party. State and local parties exist in a wide variety of forms, from disciplined patronage-based machines to informal working groups put together by a particular candidate for a particular election.

The greatest single task of each party is nominating a presidential candidate at its national convention held every four years. The delegates to these conventions are chosen either in state primary elections or in state caucuses or conventions. Both methods of delegate selection involve a number of complex problems that revolve about the issue of whether presidential nominations ought to be controlled by party regulars or by purists who are more concerned with issues of the moment than with long-term questions of organizational success.

Presidential nominating politics today is dominated by the long string of state primaries beginning in the New England states in early spring and running into mid-June. In the last forty years the outcomes of most national conventions have been determined before the conventions went into session because one candidate already captured enough delegates to win on the first ballot. However, recent changes in the rules for delegate selection may lead to more conventions in which no one has a clear majority on the first ballot. Then the convention's eventual choice must be determined by bargaining among candidates and their delegate supporters.

The convention method has been successful in that it usually has chosen the candidate who was most popular among rank-and-file party members.

However, this is not necessarily the person who would have the most appeal to Independents and members of the other party.

The early 1970s saw a great wave of reform in delegate selection procedures, particularly in the Democratic party. These reforms were aimed at allowing fuller minority participation and increasing rank-and-file participation in general. It is not yet clear what the actual outcome of these reforms will be.

Once nominated, the candidate and his party wage a general election campaign involving all sorts of activities from voter registration drives to television appearances by the candidates. A peculiar feature of the election itself is the electoral college system in which the candidate winning a plurality of popular votes in a state wins all of its electoral votes.

The two major parties are substantially different from one another along a number of important dimensions. Nevertheless, they will not necessarily present opposite or even clearly different positions on each of the policy issues of the day. Both may or may not offer presidential candidates who strive to occupy the middle ground of American politics, depending on the outcome of the complex struggle for their presidential nominations.

PART THREE
THE NATIONAL POLITICAL PROCESS

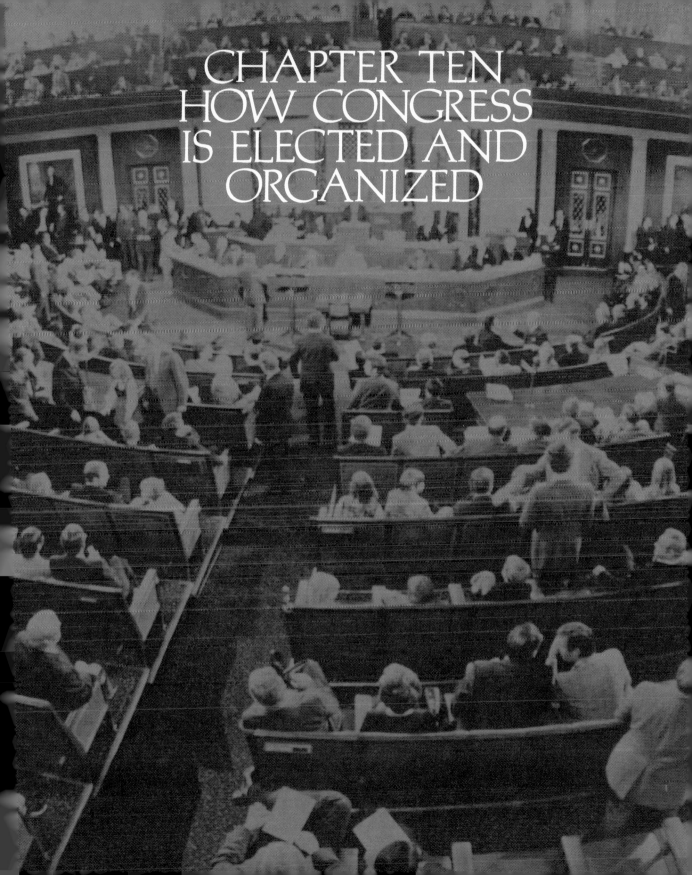

CHAPTER TEN
HOW CONGRESS
IS ELECTED AND
ORGANIZED

WHEN Arizona became a state in 1912, its voters elected to the House of Representatives a young man named Carl Hayden. Fifty-seven years later, Hayden finally retired from Congress at the age of ninety-one. William Howard Taft was in the White House when Hayden first went to Congress, and Richard M. Nixon had been elected President by the time he retired. In between, nine other Presidents came and went, but Hayden served on, first in the House and then, for forty-two years, in the Senate.

Carl Hayden was not an ordinary senator. No one else has been in Congress for fifty-seven years, few others served until the age of ninety, and not many attained as much power as he amassed before his retirement. Yet Hayden might be considered the ideal—an ideal that is approached by a surprising number of representatives and senators. In the course of this chapter, we will see why congressmen serve so long and the consequences of this long tenure.

Compared with other national legislatures, the United States Congress is unique, or very nearly unique, in two important respects. It is genuinely an independent legislature, not a mere appendage of the executive branch, as in Britain, France, Germany, and other democratic countries. Although members of Congress are in many ways responsive to the executive, they are not dominated by it. The Congress is, as the Founding Fathers intended, a co-equal branch of government. Congress is also one of the very few effectively *bicameral* legislatures, which simply means that it has two houses rather than one. The two houses are also rather different, both formally and informally, as we will see from time to time.

Congress is the most unpopular and consistently criticized of the three branches of government. There seldom has been a time in the twentieth century when calls of "reform" have not been heard. Congressmen themselves join in this chorus. Richard F. Fenno, a political scientist who has accompanied a number of congressmen running for re-election, reported that "they often seek support and trust for themselves by encouraging a lack of support and trust in the Congress. . . . each portrays himself as a fighter against its manifest shortcomings. . . . Congress is not 'we'; it is 'they.' And Congressmen run *for* Congress by running *against* Congress."[1]

Congress is criticized for being unresponsive, dishonest, old-fashioned, and so on. It is denounced for not doing what "the people" want, for not doing what the President wants, for not doing what is obviously just and true. Congress does not do what the President wants because it is genuinely independent of the President, both by constitutional prescription and in political reality. It does not do what "the people" want because it is not a clear lens, reflecting public opinion directly into laws, but rather a series of distorting lenses resembling prescription eyeglasses. And Congress does not do what its critics think is obviously just and proper because congressmen themselves have their own ideas about what is just and proper.

We will explore the reasons for this behavior in this chapter and in Chapter 11. This chapter describes how congressmen (a term that means both

[1] Richard F. Fenno, Jr., "Congressmen in Their Constituencies: An Exploration," paper presented at the 1975 annual meeting of the American Political Science Association, pp. 52, 43.

representatives and senators unless the context suggests otherwise) reach office and how Congress is organized. As we will see, these topics are intertwined; for if the legislature were elected by different means it would have a very different structure. Chapter 11 is about "Congress in Action." It will be concerned with how the mechanism described in this chapter operates.

BASES OF REPRESENTATION

The division of Congress into two bodies came about because the Founding Fathers were faced with a dilemma. On the one hand, they believed that the legislature should reflect popular opinion through elected representatives. On the other hand, they feared "the people," who were widely thought by eighteenth-century elite opinion to be incapable of complete responsibility for self-government.[2] Because the House of Representatives was elected by popular vote, it was expected to be a direct expression of the people's will. The Senate, in contrast, was originally designed to serve as a check on the popular will. For this reason, it was to be elected by a method that would prevent its being a direct expression of public opinion. For a century and a quarter, senators were chosen by state legislatures. It was thought that this would provide more distinguished, judicious, and deliberate legislators who would also tend to be more sympathetic to the interests of the wealthy.

The Sixteenth Amendment to the Constitution, ratified in 1913, changed this arrangement to provide that senators would be elected by the people. This change, together with various other developments, produced an ironic reversal of the original conception of the relationship between the House and the Senate. Now, rather than being the more conservative body, the Senate is generally thought to be the more liberal of the two houses.

Having decided on two branches, the Founding Fathers had next to decide how to apportion membership in the Senate. They easily agreed that the House, "the popular body," would be based on population; the more citizens each state had, the more representatives it would be allowed in the House. (In tabulating population each slave counted as three-fifths of a free man.) The small states, however, feared that they would be dominated by the larger ones if Senate seats were determined in the same way. They felt so strongly about this issue that the Constitutional Convention almost broke up. That disaster was avoided by the Great Compromise, which provided that each state would elect two senators. This decision has since come to be regarded as a basic principle of American political theory, rather than as the completely pragmatic compromise that it was.

From that day to this, small states have been grossly overrepresented in Congress. An American citizen living in Nevada or Wyoming has forty times the Senate voting power that a Californian or New Yorker does.

---

[2] Alexander Hamilton once remarked, "Your people, sir, is a great beast."

Fortunately, there have not been many issues in American politics that found small states on one side and large states on the other, so it is not clear that this imbalance has actually damaged the interests of California and helped those of Wyoming.

The constitutional differences between the House and the Senate are important but limited. The Senate ratifies treaties with other nations and confirms presidential nominees to the Cabinet, the Supreme Court, ambassadorships, and certain regulatory commissions. Bills for taxation originate in the House. One other difference is generally irrelevant—but occasionally crucial: the House has the power to impeach the President or other high officials by majority vote. Impeachment is comparable to indictment. The impeached official is then tried by the Senate, where a two-thirds majority is required for conviction.

The size of the Senate is determined by the number of states and has never been an issue since the Constitution was adopted. Because House membership is based on population, however, the House grew in size during the nineteenth century. This trend began to pose a serious threat to efficiency as the country's population rose above 100 million. Finally, in 1911, it was decided that the size of the House would be fixed at 435 members. It has remained at this level ever since, with temporary and unimportant exceptions. But the relative populations of the states have changed enormously since 1910, and this fact is the base of a continuing problem about representation. The number of House seats that each state has is determined after each census by a complicated and objective formula worked out by the Bureau of the Census, using its statistics on population trends. This has meant, over the last generation, a slow decrease in the seats of many northeastern, midwestern, and southern states, and a considerable increase for California, Florida, and other fast-growing states.

LEGISLATIVE APPORTIONMENT

Each state is responsible for drawing the district lines for the seats assigned to it. Unlike the objective allocation of the number of seats given to each state, districting has always been an exceptionally political and subjective process. Two kinds of bias are possible in drawing congressional district lines. One is *malapportionment,* in which districts are of unequal population size so that voters in large districts have a smaller share of representation than those in small districts. Shortly after the 1960 census, for example, the twenty smallest House seats represented an average of 227,000 people each while the twenty largest seats represented an average of 697,000. The small seats were usually in rural areas while the large ones were usually urban or suburban. The consequence of this practice was to reduce the political power of cities and suburbs and to increase that of farmers. This problem was ended by a series of Supreme Court decisions in the 1960s that established the principle of *one man–one vote* in all legislative districts. Congressional districts now are of virtually identical size, averaging a bit more than 460,000 people each.

The second type of bias in districting is called *gerrymandering*. The guiding principle in gerrymandering is to take political considerations into account in determining how the lines between districts are drawn. The aim is to achieve the largest number of legislative seats for one's own party and the smallest number for the opposition. This can be accomplished either by concentrating the opposition party's strength in the smallest number of districts or by scattering its voters through many districts. Although congressional districts are supposed to be "compact and contiguous," state legislatures continue to draw lines to the advantage of the majority party. District lines in some cities are drawn so carefully that they wiggle around individual apartment houses or residential blocks as a way of avoiding or including certain social classes or ethnic groups.

Gerrymandering may sound complex, but the basic idea is simple. For example, assume there is a city of 1,000,000 voters, surrounded by a suburban area also consisting of 1,000,000 voters. Assume also that this combined metropolitan area has to send five representatives to Congress and that the city is overwhelmingly Democratic while the suburbs are overwhelmingly Republican. Each party thus has just about equal support. If the Democrats were drawing the lines, they could draw them so that four of the five districts each consisted of 220,000 inner-city residents (Democratic) and 180,000 suburbanites (Republican). The fifth district would contain the remaining 120,000 inner-city voters and 280,000 suburban Republicans, giving the Democrats a margin of four seats to one. Or they might draw lines to put one district entirely in the suburbs. This would concede a seat to the opposition but would mean that the remaining 600,000 suburban votes would be divided among the remaining four districts, again leaving the Republicans with only one seat. Of course, if the Republicans were doing the dividing, they could just as easily do it the other way around.

The problem of fair districting raises some fascinating and complex problems. How should district lines be drawn? Should districts be "compact and contiguous"? Should such natural areas as cities, geographic units, metropolitan areas, and so on be kept together, or should they be divided? Should districts be as socially and economically diverse as possible, or should they be homogeneous? It is difficult to give objective answers to these questions, for it really comes down to a question of which political interests one wants to help. The more diverse the district, the greater freedom its representative is likely to have because he will not be beholden to a particular interest. Yet making districts more diverse reduces the number of minority legislators, thus hurting groups like blacks and Chicanos who have few resources in politics other than their votes.

Should district lines be drawn to make a state's total number of representatives more or less proportionate to the total number of votes that are cast? If the statewide vote averages 55 percent Democratic, should the lines be drawn in order to give the Democrats 55 percent of the seats? Or should they be drawn so that each district contains 55 percent Democrats and 45 percent Republicans? If the latter procedure were followed, the Democrats would have a good chance of winning 100 percent of the seats, but every election would be a close fight. Politicians, though, are no fonder of uncertainty than anyone else, and so they tend to shy away from districting formulas that could produce great payoffs at the cost of great risks. They would rather give themselves as many safe seats as possible and not risk taking chances with close races, even if this means conceding a certain number of safe seats to the opposition.

CONGRESSIONAL ELECTIONS

As we saw in Chapter 5, public knowledge of congressional candidates and issues is very low. Fifty to 60 percent of the population does not know the name of *either* House candidate in their district. Scarcely more than half the population knows which party controls Congress, and only a fifth knows how their representative voted on *any* issue.[3]

Because so many citizens do not know who the candidates are, the vast majority of votes cast in congressional elections are party-line votes. Seventy-five to 80 percent of the votes in House elections are by party identifiers voting for their party's candidate. Since senators and senatorial candidates are better known, the figures are slightly lower for their races; 69 to 79 percent of Senate votes are cast along party lines. Voters who know the name of only their own party's House candidate are almost certain to vote for him. About one out of five who know both candidates' names will cross party lines. And someone who knows only the name of the *other* party's candidate is more likely than not to vote for him. The majority of voters, however, know neither candidate's name. Almost 90 percent of this group votes along party lines. Since few people change their party identification, there is a "standing vote" in each constituency that is cast on the basis of party. This is why the relative strength of the two parties remains so stable over the years. As a result, Democrats have controlled Congress for all but four years since 1932.

The importance and stability of party identification result in a very high probability that incumbents will be re-elected. In the past fifteen years, the tendency for incumbents to win re-election has increased. Even in 1974, which was widely regarded as a disastrous year for Republicans, 89 percent of all incumbent representatives were victorious. This is the *lowest* success rate for incumbents in at least twenty years. In the period 1962–72, 94 percent of incumbent representatives won their general election races. Only thirteen incumbents were defeated in general elections in 1972, twelve were beaten in 1970, and nine in 1968. What is more, most of the sitting congressmen who did lose their seats had been in office only one or two terms. Senators are

---

[3] This last item is from the *Gallup Opinion Index*, October 1970, p. 16. Unless otherwise indicated, findings reported in this section are from our own research or from Robert B. Arseneau and Raymond E. Wolfinger, "Voting Behavior in Congressional Elections," paper presented at the 1973 annual meeting of the American Political Science Association.

almost as secure, with incumbent senators having won re-election almost 90 percent of the time since 1960.[4]

Incumbents have three major advantages:

1. They have access to publicly supplied staffs and free or very cheap services, including postage, stationery, television and radio facilities.
2. As officeholders, they are in a position to do things for people, and this makes it easier to raise campaign funds. Although incumbents need contributions less than challengers, they get more of them. And why not, given the odds? Who wants to contribute to a loser?
3. The most important reason, however, is simply that the incumbent is far more likely to be known to the voters than the candidate challenging him.

In addition to all these factors tending to make life easier for incumbents than for their challengers, incumbents also are aided by the fact that the number of competitive seats has been shrinking. More and more elections are being won by large margins. In 1974, two-thirds of all House seats and two-fifths of all Senate seats were won with at least 60 percent of the vote — a 20 percent margin between winner and loser. (In fifty-eight House districts there was no major party competition at all, the winner having no opposition except perhaps from splinter candidates. All but one of these uncontested seats was won by a Democrat, and thirty-seven of them were in the South.)

The advantages of incumbency are more than merely a reflection of the incumbent's party strength in the district or state. Incumbent senators, for example, are more likely to pull votes across party lines than are non-incumbents.[5] The most interesting illustration of the power of incumbency comes from recent House elections in the South. As we saw in Chapter 6, southerners are finally giving up their traditional monolithic loyalty to the Democratic party. In presidential elections they now vote more heavily Republican than any other region. But Republicans still have less than a third of the South's House seats. This is a vast improvement over the mere half dozen they used to have before the so-called "Solid South" crumbled, but it is far from what one would expect, given the dramatic changes in party loyalty in that part of the country. With rare exceptions, Republicans capture Democratic House seats only when the incumbent no longer runs for re-election. When a Democratic incumbent is the candidate, the Democrats still win 97 to 100 percent of all southern House elections. But when the

[4] Steven J. Rosenstone, unpublished M.A. thesis, University of California, Berkeley, 1974; Warren Lee Kostroski, "Party and Incumbency in Postwar Senate Elections," *American Political Science Review*, 67 (December 1973), 1213–34; and Charles S. Bullock, III, "Redistricting and Congressional Stability, 1962–72," *Journal of Politics*, 37 (May 1975), 569–75.

[5] See the sources cited in note 4; Robert S. Erikson, "Malapportionment, Gerrymandering, and Party Fortunes in Congressional Elections," *American Political Science Review*, 66 (December 1972), 1240; and Andrew T. Cowart, "Electoral Choice in the American States," *American Political Science Review*, 67 (September 1973), 841.

seat is open, the victory levels for the Democratic party have fallen as low as 40 percent.[6]

The Fifth Congressional District in Mississippi dramatically illustrates the power of incumbency. For 40 years the district was represented by William C. Colmer, an ultraconservative Democrat who usually was returned to the House without opposition. When Colmer announced his retirement in 1972, his young assistant switched parties and was elected to Colmer's seat as a Republican. He was re-elected with 83 percent of the vote in 1974, which was not generally a good year for Republican congressional candidates.

PARTY IMAGES AND PRESIDENTIAL COATTAILS

National changes in the fortunes of the two major political parties have a powerful impact on the electoral chances of candidates for the House and Senate. Party images are determined largely by the President and the presidential candidates. Congress is eclipsed by the White House in public attention. Even so simple a fact as which party controls Congress is hard for most people to keep in mind when the President belongs to one party while the other party has a majority on Capitol Hill. During the latter years of the Eisenhower administration, and again during Nixon's presidency, scarcely half the population knew that the Democrats controlled Congress. But in the Johnson administration, when the presidency was in the hands of the Democrats, 70 percent of the population correctly attributed control of Congress to the Democrats. Because most voters do not know which party controls Congress, they do not know which party can be held responsible for what Congress does.

Therefore congressional elections are to some degree referenda on the President and the presidential candidates. When a presidential candidate is very popular, his candidacy helps everyone on his party's "ticket." This is the *coattail effect,* so called because the lesser officeholders on the ticket are said to be carried into office on the President's coattails. Conversely, however, when the presidential candidate is unpopular, he hurts the ticket. This explains why a party's officeholders are so interested in who the presidential candidate is going to be. If he is a popular disaster, they risk going down to defeat also; but if he is popular in their area, they are likely to be assured of success at the polls. Since all candidates for a party's presidential nomination are not equally popular everywhere, people from different states or regions will have different ideas about which candidate will be more helpful to their own races.

In off-year elections, representatives who were carried into office by the coattail effect no longer have this source of added strength at the polls. In addition, the President—and therefore his party—may lose some of the popularity that originally got him into the White House. As a result, the number of seats lost by the President's party in midterm elections has ranged

---

[6] Richard G. Hutcheson, III, "The Inertial Effect of Incumbency and Two-Party Politics: Elections to the House of Representatives from the South, 1952–1974," *American Political Science Review,* 69 (December 1975).

in the last thirty years from five to fifty-three. This enormous range means that newspaper talk about the "average" midterm loss is meaningless.

The importance of presidential coattails—or any other kind of coattails, for that matter—is strongly dependent on the kind of ballot. Some states use the *party column* ballot, on which the voter sees his choices arranged by party. He can vote a "straight ticket"—that is, vote for the same party in every race—merely by pulling a lever or by making a mark across a party line or down a column. In states using the *office block* ballot, he sees a number of groups of choices, one for each office. This arrangement makes it much harder to vote a straight ticket because the voter must make a decision anew for each office rather than taking care of all his choices with one stroke.

These differences may seem trivial, but they have enormous consequences for the careers of many candidates for "lesser" office. Remember that most people do not know who their congressman is. In states where the party column ballot is used, the coattails of the candidate at the head of the ticket are a good deal longer and stronger than in states using the office block ballot, where a voter must stop and think each time for each office. In Connecticut, which has the party column ballot, all six Republican congressional candidates were elected by enormous margins when the very popular President Eisenhower was at the head of the Republican ticket in 1956. In the midterm election two years later, when the popular Governor Abraham Ribicoff led the Democratic ticket, the opposite happened: all six Republican congressmen were unseated. In states like California, where the office block ballot form is used, the power of coattails is considerably weaker and split ballots are more common.

The Connecticut example given above should not lead us to conclude that the effects of a President's popularity necessarily disappear in midterm election years, when his name does not appear at the head of his party's ticket. Even in midterm elections, voters' choices of congressional candidates are affected by the incumbent President's popularity and performance. A study of midterm House elections since 1938 shows that a shift of ten percentage points in the President's Gallup Poll rating produces a corresponding change of 1.3 percentage points in his party's vote in the midterm election.[7]

The 1974 midterm election provided a particularly dramatic illustration of how congressional candidates can suffer for their President's record. Nixon's resignation might have lifted the curse of Watergate from Republican campaigns that year. But President Ford's pardon of Nixon not only dropped his own popularity by 20 percentage points but also blighted his party's campaigners. Together with the country's economic decline, the pardon dashed the hopes of Republican office-seekers. As a result, the Republicans lost forty-nine House seats while the Democrats lost only six.

Although the popularity or unpopularity of a party's presidential candidate affects the success of the rest of the ticket, over the years the performance

[7] A change of fifty dollars in the real personal per capita income results in a change of 1.8 percentage points in the total votes for House candidates of the President's party in midterm elections. See Edward R. Tufte, "Determinants of the Outcomes of Midterm Congressional Elections," *American Political Science Review*, 69 (September 1975), 812–26.

of the two major parties is much more stable and consistent in congressional elections than in presidential voting. As Figure 10-1 shows, since 1952 the Democrats have had as much as 61.1 percent of the votes for President and as small a share as 37.5 percent, a gap of 23.6 percentage points. But their fortunes in congressional voting have been much more stable, from a low of 49.7 percent to a high of 60 percent.

These findings might give the impression that nothing ever changes, except perhaps in those districts and states where the two parties are so evenly balanced that there is perpetual uncertainty about who is going to win. This stereotype has a good deal of truth. But the stereotype is seriously incomplete because of several dynamic factors that do introduce a good deal of change.

One of these factors is the ability of some candidates to establish popular perceptions of themselves independent of party label. There are always a few popular Republicans elected to Congress from Democratic constituencies, and vice versa. Such exceptions usually are liberal Republicans or conservative Democrats, or at least they are people who manage to give the impression of being so.

A second dynamic factor is short-term change in the national fortunes of one party or the other. These usually result from an unpopular presidential candidate (or an unusually popular one), or a war, depression, or other major disaster that affects widespread public images of the parties. When such a shift occurs, candidates belonging to the unlucky party are likely to suffer.

A third factor is perhaps the most important of all in the long run — population change in a district or state. This may be a shift from rural to urban, from middle class to working class, from white to black, or some combination

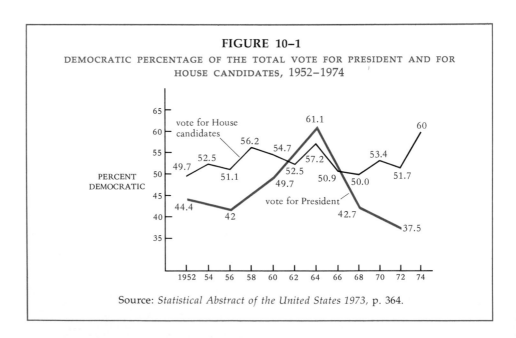

FIGURE 10–1

DEMOCRATIC PERCENTAGE OF THE TOTAL VOTE FOR PRESIDENT AND FOR HOUSE CANDIDATES, 1952–1974

Source: *Statistical Abstract of the United States 1973*, p. 364.

of these. For instance, as the core cities of America have grown increasingly poor and increasingly black, they have become to a much larger degree safe bastions of the Democratic party. This accounts for the considerable growth in the number of safe northern Democratic seats, and also for the dramatic increase in the number of black representatives, from five in 1962 to sixteen after the 1974 elections.

A fourth source of change is a historic shift in party alignment—the only dynamic factor that actually embodies a lasting change in the political outlook of individual voters. The only important example at present is in the South, where the overwhelming loyalty of southerners to the Democratic party has eroded dramatically in recent years.

This last case also reminds us, however, that changes in voters' attitudes and loyalties are muffled by the advantages of incumbency and the large electoral margins in most congressional elections. These considerations are among the reasons why elections are *not* a very sensitive measure of changing public moods. Congressional contests simply do not yield much of a mandate, except perhaps as a rough index of popular discontent with the President's performance.

CONGRESSIONAL NOMINATIONS

Because most general election contests are not competitive, nomination by the majority party in a district is often tantamount to election. If incumbents are a fairly safe bet to win re-election in general elections, they are even more likely to win in primaries. Primary elections attract less attention and about half the turnout of general elections. Moreover, the primary challenger lacks one great advantage that the general election opponent has—the party label. A primary challenger does not start out with an assured bloc of votes by virtue of his party, for he belongs to the same party that the incumbent does. Because voter discontent usually is expressed in party terms—voting for the candidates of the opposition party—the incumbents whose party image is unpopular will not suffer the consequences until the general election. Besides, if the incumbent is so much better known than his general election opponent, it seems reasonable to assume that people who challenge him for renomination within his own party will have even less public visibility. Thus, despite a great deal of talk that Watergate would lead to widespread primary defeats for incumbents in 1974, Republican legislators did not have to fear being ousted by other Republican candidates at the primaries. The general elections were, of course, a different story.

In other words, renomination is an even smaller hazard than re-election. Since World War II, less than 2 percent of incumbent representatives seeking re-election have lost primary elections. The same factors that make senators slightly more vulnerable in general elections also mean that they tend to lose primaries a bit more often; but even here, only 7 percent have lost their bids for renomination.[8] Most primary losers are either very old or are beaten

---

[8] Kostroski, "Party and Incumbency in Postwar Senate Elections," p. 1216n.

by other incumbents when redistricting has thrown two members into the same district. In 1972, incumbents had an unusually bad year, with twelve representatives and two senators denied renomination. Of the twelve representatives, however, four were seventy-four years of age or older and showed their age when vigorous primary challenges forced them to make damaging public appearances. Five more primary victims were beaten by other incumbents. Of the two senators denied renomination in 1972, one was seventy-five years old, had recently undergone an operation for cancer, and died shortly thereafter; the other had been appointed to his seat in 1974 to fill a vacancy. In 1974, presumably a bad year for politicians, only eight representatives and one elected senator lost their primaries.

Clearly, the most crucial nomination contest is the first one, when the House or Senate seat is open. Nomination is a party process, the means by which the two parties select the alternative candidates from whom the voters choose the winner. In discussing this process, we proceed on the assumption that what a legislator has to do to reach and hold office influences his or her behavior once in that office. Thus, our main concerns are the nature and sources of the obligations that may govern a legislator's conduct. As we shall see, there are great variations in the sources of support and, therefore, in the obligations that each member accumulates.

SOURCES OF CAMPAIGN SUPPORT

In most democratic countries, each party's legislative candidates are picked by the national party organization. The ability to deny renomination to a maverick legislator is the foundation of party discipline. This form of control is wholly lacking in the United States, where neither party has anything remotely resembling a national "machine." The closest approach is the influence that the President exerts over his party. He is a national focus, his program is the "party line," he has certain resources that can be used to influence local figures, and he is somebody whom no politician in his party antagonizes lightly.

But the President's powers are ill-suited to intervention in specific congressional primaries and he has little ability to defeat candidates to whom he is opposed. Indeed, not since 1938 has a President openly intervened in his party's congressional primaries. In that year, Franklin Roosevelt attemped to deny renomination to several Democratic senators and representatives who had obstructed his legislative program. But his failure was so complete that Presidents generally have resigned themselves to putting up with hostile members of their own party rather than attempting to prevent their renomination.

Although the President lacks life-and-death power over the campaigns of his party's congressional candidates, he does have some sources of leverage. Presidents can help by making personal appearances at campaign rallies or fund-raising affairs. Some have provided more direct financial help. White House aides have been known to travel around the country giving contributions to friendly candidates. The most extensive effort of this kind was the Nixon Administration's "Operation Townhouse," which distributed $4 million (mostly in cash) to favored Republican candidates in 1970. The subsequent revelation that Operation Townhouse involved several violations of the law probably will discourage this level of presidential involvement in at least the near future.

A more important source of money for congressional candidates is the campaign committee of each party in each house. Republicans have been much more successful than Democrats at national-level campaign financing. In 1968 and 1970 combined, various national Republican party organizations spent a total of $5.3 million on individual congressional races, compared to only $1.8 million spent by Democratic organizations. Somewhat more money was spent for such indirect aid as registration drives, research, and so on. Even these additional funds, however, were not extraordinarily large. In 1972, the House Republican Campaign Committee anticipated being able to spend between $2 and $3 million in contests around the country, both in financial aid directly and in technical advice on campaign organization and strategy. In 1974, the House Democratic Campaign Committee could give more than $2,500 to only thirteen candidates, and its biggest grant was $7,500. Since a Senate campaign can cost as much as $2 million, and a House race $300,000, these figures do not seem so imposing, although they are not negligible either.

The important point to be borne in mind about the congressional campaign committees is that they do *not* use their financial power to enforce party discipline. In 1959, the chairman of the Republican House Campaign Committee publicly advised Republican congressional candidates to express disagreement with President Eisenhower's policies if they indeed disagreed with them. He insisted that his committee would not discriminate against anti-Eisenhower congressmen when it came to disbursing money. More recently, Donald Riegle of Michigan, a conspicuously anti-Nixon Republican, enjoyed the support of the congressional leadership in campaigning, fund raising, and so on.[9]

Because congressional candidates get only a fraction of the support they need from the central national party organization, they must rely on a variety of other sources for campaign aid. Most of the campaign help congressmen get comes from their constituencies. Some money, however, does come from outside private interests. We will look briefly at this source of campaign contributions before concentrating on the local roots of congressional campaigns.

NATIONAL CONTRIBUTIONS. Private campaign contributions at the national level are available mainly to incumbents, who have had a chance to dem-

---

[9] The data for 1968 and 1970 are taken from official reports filed with the Clerk of the House of Representatives and compiled by the Democratic Study Group. For an interesting description of the House Republican leadership's tolerance of Riegle's behavior, see his *O Congress* (Garden City, N.Y.: Doubleday & Company, Inc., 1972). In 1973, Riegle carried his hostility to Nixon to its logical conclusion: he became a Democrat. Like other congressional switchers, he won his new party's nomination and was easily re-elected.

onstrate their potential usefulness in practical terms. Major interest groups give to members of the relevant congressional committees. For example, members of the Agriculture Committees get aid from various farm and commodity organizations; bankers and the building industry give to members of the Banking, Currency, and Housing Committee; and civil rights groups give to members of the Judiciary Committee. Members of almost any committee may get money from labor and organized liberal and conservative groups.

Some contributors are remarkably even-handed, giving to both sides in order to be sure of having friends in the right place. Often recipients of substantial contributions have little in common other than membership on a committee that deals with a particular interest's problems. In other situations, a congressman's strategic position may make him the special favorite of generous contributors. In 1970, the chairman of the House Public Works Committee received 167 donations from highway construction firms in thirty-eight states—but lost the primary anyway.[10]

The most important national source of contributions in congressional campaigns probably is the labor movement—both individual internationals and the AFL-CIO's Committee on Political Education (COPE). Even so, the total amount of money spent in congressional races by national labor interests never exceeds a few million dollars, which is only a small share of the totals spent by campaigning politicians in any year. Labor also can deploy a rarer and perhaps more valuable campaign resource. It has at its command numbers of experienced political organizers who can be sent to a state or district to help plan and execute many phases of a campaign, from position papers on issues to door-to-door electioneering.

Numerous other organizations, firms, and associations disburse money and, occasionally, technical aid to selected House and Senate races in all parts of the country. These range in ideological orientation from ultra-conservative groups to liberal organizations like the National Committee for an Effective Congress (NCEC), which, by its own reporting, gave $826,000 to twenty-one Senate and fifty-eight House candidates in 1970. The scope of these organizations' goals is equally broad, ranging from the wide open reformism of the NCEC to the narrowly focused (and well financed) goals of the national dairy interests, which are concerned almost exclusively with federal regulation of milk prices.

One final category of nationwide givers is the rich individual ideologue. As we saw in Chapter 7, these come in all philosophical varieties, from the late oil billionaire H. L. Hunt on the extreme right to assorted patrons of radical militants on the extreme left. These wealthy contributors seldom make specific legislative demands of their client politicians. Instead, their

[10] *Congressional Quarterly Weekly Report*, September 9, 1972, p. 2281; and May 18, 1974, p. 1295; and Richard Harris, "A Fundamental Hoax," *New Yorker*, July 7, 1971, p. 52. (Congressional Quarterly, Inc., a private firm in Washington, is an invaluable source of information about American politics in general and Congress in particular. Its basic publication, the *CQ Weekly Report*, is available in most college libraries and is an excellent starting place for anyone doing research on Congress.)

interests are likely to be pitched at a "higher" level, where mundane consideration of bills and amendments are subordinated to symbolic politics and contemplation of utopias.

As the foregoing paragraphs suggest, many legislators have national constituencies as well as local ones. To some extent, all members of Congress find that the interest groups relevant to their committee assignments are part of their constituency, no matter where they are located. These interest groups want to stay on the legislator's good side and are willing to spend money to prove it. This generosity is intensified when an interest group finds a legislator who is not only relevant but also sympathetic.

Quite beyond such tangible motivations, some representatives and a good many senators have another kind of nationwide constituency. They are able to gain the support of people with special concerns and political orientations that make them delight in congressmen who express and personify particular points of view. For example, two California congressmen, John Rousselot, a former member of the John Birch Society, and Ronald Dellums, a fiery black radical, each has a national constituency and hence financial support that extends throughout the country. Occasionally, this sort of support is so considerable that a congressional campaign is dominated by out-of-state contributions. In the 1970 North Dakota Senate race, for example, it was estimated that almost 90 percent of the money spent by both sides came from outside the state.[11] But this seems to be an exception. In the vast majority of cases the bulk of aid comes from inside the constituency. Therefore, we now turn from national to local sources of campaign support.

LOCAL PARTY ORGANIZATIONS. Although the national party organizations do not have disciplinary powers over congressmen, what about state and local parties? Are they more helpful to legislators' careers, and therefore more influential over them? Do they decide who gets the nomination in the first place? Blanket answers to these questions are impossible because, as we saw in Chapter 9, there are enormous variations in the style and strength of party organizations in this country. We can reduce this variation to three types of local congressional parties.

The first of these is a tightly held organization that can effectively name the party's nominee. Where such organizations are strong and cohesive, the real decisions in the nominating process may well be made secretly by a few leaders or even a single boss. Organizations of this kind seldom have power that extends far enough to control a senatorial nomination. In Illinois, Pennsylvania, and a few other states, the party regulars sometimes can bestow the nomination on a favorite candidate if the opposition is not united behind a strong alternative. There are still dozens of congressional seats whose incumbents were first picked by the dominant local machine. Such organizations, typically motivated by patronage, generally have continuity from one election to the next. They also are likely to be highly influential in picking city, county, and state candidates.

[11] See David R. Mayhew, *Congress: The Electoral Connection* (New Haven: Yale University Press, 1974), p. 39n.

Indeed, their main concern is with government at these levels rather than at the congressional level. Because congressmen have little patronage power, seats in Congress are not as highly prized by machine politicians as the judgeships and municipal posts which control the spoils of government. Even strong party organizations usually are not greatly interested in congressional elections or in controlling members of Congress. Even so, a congressman may find it difficult to get renominated if he incurs the hostility of the local organization. A few years ago, a Chicago congressman who had deeply offended Mayor Daley rushed up to a House colleague, crying in alarm, "They say I'm through! They say I'm through!" His fellow congressman asked indignantly, "Who says you're through?" When the first man told him who, the second replied sadly, "You're through." Indeed, he was.

Fortunately for congressmen, such cases are rare. Usually, such machines do not have either enough influence or enough interest to discipline their members closely. One political scientist who interviewed dozens of congressmen repeatedly throughout a session to discover who had tried to influence their votes found that less than one member in ten was ever contacted by local party officials about pending legislation.[12] As one representative explained, "The sheriff in my county has seventy or eighty jobs to pass out, and everyone is interested in who is sheriff. No one cares about us." Another congressman observed, "If we depended on the party organization to get elected, none of us would be here."[13]

More common than the tightly controlled party organization is the situation in which a machine is opposed by a reform faction, or several different machines are fighting each other for control of the party. If these warring factions could get together, they could control some initial Senate nominations and a number of House seats. Usually, though, they do not get together, so although there is a good deal of continuity in such organizations, there is very little stability in effectively controlling congressional nominations.

If national party organizations are impotent to affect nominations, and if state and local parties are largely weak, uninterested, or both, there is only one answer for individual members—they must develop their own organizational support. This third situation is by far the most common in congressional constituencies. Most candidates do not inherit their campaign workers, contributors, and precinct workers from the local party. Instead, they develop their own backing. Thus, the most prevalent type of campaign machinery consists of discontinuous, *ad hoc* organizations whose support and membership are activated by a single candidate. He is the focus of organization. It is *his* organization, *his* supporters, *his* campaign contributors. Contributors like to give to an individual candidate rather than to the party as a whole. By doing so, they get credit directly with the beneficiary rather than having the obligation diluted through the intermediary of the party.

[12] John W. Kingdon, *Congressmen's Voting Decisions* (New York: Harper & Row, 1973), p. 34.
[13] Charles L. Clapp, *The Congressman: His Work as He Sees It* (Washington: The Brookings Institution, 1963), pp. 344, 351.

The low visibility and weak party support given to most congressional candidates has the effect of increasing the influence of local interest groups. Such groups are a way for the candidate to establish a basis of communication and relationship with his constituents and are often the most economical way to raise money, aside from the personal connections of the candidate and his immediate supporters.

Our interest in the nominating process comes in part from the possibility that the process can be a source of discipline over congressmen. Once in office, this danger is fairly slight, for incumbents rarely have to fear that they will not be renominated. The gravest threats to a sitting congressman are advanced age, population change, or legislative activity so consistently unpopular that a popular candidate may be tempted to launch a challenge.

POPULAR ACCOUNTABILITY

Elections play a crucial role in democratic theory. Not only are they the method of choosing leaders, but they also provide the threat of defeat in the next election, which supposedly keeps those leaders responsive to the public. At least this is the theory. But if incumbents are seldom defeated and if few elections are even close, how can congressmen be considered answerable to their constituents?

Although the odds favor incumbents, there still are upsets—and even occasional disasters, like 1964 and 1974 for Republicans and 1966 for Democrats. Furthermore, although narrow electoral margins may be the exception rather than the rule, the number of close races adds up to a fairly impressive total in the long run. In 1974, over half the members of the House and 70 percent of the Senate had won by less than 55 percent at least once in the course of their careers. Over three-fourths of the House and 86 percent of the Senate had gone below 60 percent on occasion.[14] Memory of such close calls tends to remind members that the law of averages is cold comfort to someone who has lost when the odds were in his favor. Although the *chances* of defeat may be slight, the *consequences* of defeat are enormous.

Thus, prudence and human nature both lead congressmen to run scared, to be "unrealistically" worried about their re-election prospects. As Richard F. Fenno observed:

> One of the dominant impressions of my travels [with congressmen running for reelection] is the terrific sense of *uncertainty* which animates these congressmen. They perceive electoral troubles where the most imaginative outside observer could not possibly perceive, conjure up or hallucinate them.[15]

The low level of public information about Congress makes it unlikely that anything incumbents may do will have much influence on many voters. But this is beside the point. From the standpoint of popular accountability, the

[14] Mayhew, *Congress: The Electoral Connection*, p. 33.
[15] Quoted in Mayhew, p. 35n.

important thing is what congressmen *believe* about the electoral consequences of their behavior, not the reality. Most congressmen think that
their success in winning elections is strongly influenced by popular reaction
to their voting records in Congress. In other words, they think that their
behavior is far more conspicuous than it really is.[16] Political pollsters commonly find that their congressional clients are reluctant to acknowledge
just how little they figure in the public's perspectives.

Even a congressman who fully accepts his own obscure public image
knows that he *may* be able to change some votes if he works hard at it. He
may also accept the fact that no one really knows what kinds of behavior
will win or lose votes. The rational response to this uncertainty is not to
give up, but to try a variety of tactics, appealing in numerous ways to
various groups and bodies of opinion. Politicians keep trying to find the
right key. Striving to control one's environment is a human characteristic,
and politicians are as human as other people.

Finally, they can be sure that at least some constituents are following
what they are doing in Washington. These well-informed citizens are likely
to be unusually influential, for they include campaign activists and contributors, interest group leaders, journalists, local public officials, and other
people whose opposition or support goes far beyond their own votes. If
a member antagonizes some interest group in his district or state, he may
well stimulate a primary challenge or tempt a more formidable candidate of
the other party to run against him.

We can summarize the important influences on congressional candidate
selection as follows:

The nomination process is determined locally. Individual campaigns
usually are financed and organized locally, although money from outside is
sometimes available. The outcome of the general election is determined by
the local division of party identification, modified on the one hand by the
advantages of incumbency and on the other by the prevailing tides of
national party fortunes.

Congressmen are seldom obligated to national or even local party organizations for their nomination and election. The principal limits on their discretion are predominant sentiment in their constituencies, modified by the
individual coalitions they have built to gain nomination and election. As one
political scientist wrote, "The constituency has a virtually unqualified
power to hire and fire. If the member pleases it, no party leader can fatally
hurt him; if he does not, no national party organ can save him."[17] Although
members of Congress cannot ignore the sentiments of their constituents,
constituency opinion is often confined to vigilant activists and interest
groups. On most issues, congressmen are *not* constrained by public opinion.

---

[16] Warren E. Miller and Donald E. Stokes, "Constituency Influence in Congress," in Angus
Campbell et al., *Elections and the Political Order* (New York: John Wiley & Sons, Inc., 1966),
pp. 351–72.

[17] Ralph K. Huitt, "Democratic Party Leadership in the Senate," in Huitt & Robert L. Peabody,
Congress: Two Decades of Analysis (New York: Harper & Row, 1969), p. 140.

The demographic characteristics of congressmen are a far cry from those of the American electorate. Fully 53 percent of the members of Congress in 1975 were lawyers, a third were businessmen, 13 percent were educators, and 8 percent were farmers. Hardly any were members of the working class, although some had held blue-collar jobs at earlier points in their careers. The educational level of Congress is far above the average, for most members are college graduates. They are also far wealthier than the average citizen. Eighteen women were elected to the House in 1974, and none to the Senate. There was one black senator, 16 black representatives, and about a dozen Spanish-heritage and Asian-American members. Contrary to a popular misconception, congressmen are no more likely to come from rural backgrounds than other Americans of similar age.[18]

One of the most familiar complaints about Congress is that many members are too old and, therefore, presumably out of touch with contemporary forces of change and innovation. In 1975, the average age of senators was fifty-six and of representatives forty-nine. Eighty-seven representatives and three senators were under forty. In 1972, the average citizen of voting age was forty-three. The age difference between the electorate and the Congress, while appreciable, is not enormous.

It is easy enough to describe the obvious personal characteristics of members, but it is a good deal more difficult to figure out what difference they make. Researchers have been unable to find many relationships between the demographic characteristics of legislators and the way they behave. Such factors as occupation, income, and sex may be useful in explaining the attitudes and behavior of citizens in the mass, but they tell us little about how someone with the personality characteristics required of a successful politician will respond to the pressures of big-time politics.

We are not persuaded that a senator must be a woman or a black or a worker in order to understand the views and interests of women, blacks, or workers. It is no more necessary for a congressman to resemble his constituents than it is necessary for a lawyer to have the same education, race, and sex as his clients in order to do a good job of looking after their interests. The most important forces leading to effective advocacy are not parallel demographic categories but the needs of politicians to be re-elected and their own sense of their obligation to serve their constituents.

Whatever their "civilian" backgrounds, most congressmen are dedicated to just one occupation. They are professional politicians. Few are elected without significant political experience at the state and local level, most commonly as state legislators or some kind of district attorney. Nearly half the members of the Senate have served either in the House or as gov-

---

[18] The information on the characteristics of congressmen is from *CQ Weekly Report,* January 18, 1975, pp. 120–30. The occupation figures add up to more than 100 percent because some members have more than one occupation. See also Leroy N. Rieselbach, "Congressmen as 'Small Town Boys': A Research Note," *Midwest Journal of Political Science,* 14 (May 1970), 321–30.

ernor of their state. Freshmen in both houses are vastly outnumbered by veterans, even in 1975 when there was a bumper crop of newcomers. In 1975, there were ninety-two new members of the House, and 170 representatives with ten or more years of service; of these, fifty-two had served at least twenty years. The Senate had twelve newcomers and forty-five members with ten or more years of service, including fourteen who had been in office continuously since 1955 or earlier.

WHAT DO THEY WANT?

In trying to explain the behavior of congressmen, the future is more important than the past. The question, then, is not what they have done, but what they want, what they hope to get out of politics, what aspirations they have for their future careers. Many representatives want to be elected to the Senate and a few hope to be governor of their state. Politicians with statewide ambitions are careful to modify their positions to suit the larger arena. But probably the majority of representatives do not have such ambitions. They want to succeed in the House, to become powerful and influential in that body, to leave their mark on legislation—that is, on history—and to earn the respect and prestige that come with recognition by their colleagues. There are many ways to attain this goal of power and recognition in the House. Although ambitious members of the House can aim their careers toward the Senate or the state house, senators who are not content in that body can look to only one higher office—the presidency. The Senate has become the biggest single source of presidential candidates. Fully 10 percent of all the men and women who served in the Senate from 1936 through 1972 received appreciable popular support for a presidential nomination in the Gallup Polls.[19] Usually at least a dozen senators actively entertain thoughts of moving to the White House. Their behavior in the Senate is directed in part to this goal, principally by seeking publicity and identification with popular issues. As we shall see, the abundance of subcommittees in the Senate is ideal for these activities.

One may be fairly confident that almost all members of Congress have one ambition in common. They want to be re-elected. Here again, there are several roads to success, but the constancy of this desire and the possibility of electoral defeat serve as a fixed point of reference from which one can safely interpret congressional behavior.

If the future is more important than the past, and there are many ways by which future ambitions can be realized, we should turn to the context of these ambitions. First, we will examine working conditions and resources on Capitol Hill. Then we will turn to the structures and procedures Congress has evolved to solve the problem of coherence and organization.

[19] Donald R. Matthews, "Presidential Nominations: Process and Outcomes," in James David Barber, ed., *Choosing the President* (Englewood Cliffs, N.J.: Prentice-Hall, Inc., 1974), p. 45.

The grounds of the Capitol cover 155 acres on a low hill overlooking the Potomac River, northern Virginia, and the Washington Monument. A mile to the west, down Pennsylvania Avenue, lies the White House. In between, along Pennsylvania and Constitution Avenues, are the massive office buildings housing most of the principal executive departments. This is "downtown" — the common Capitol Hill expression for the executive branch.

The Capitol sits on the brow of the hill. Behind it, to the east, are the Supreme Court and the Library of Congress. On the south flank of the Capitol are the three huge House Office Buildings, each taking up a solid block. To the north are the two Senate Office Buildings, and the construction site of a third. Linking these six buildings is a honeycomb maze of tunnels that house the innumerable service facilities required to keep this city-within-a-city operating.

The Capitol is jammed with statuary, portraits, and heroic canvases depicting stirring moments in American history. A popular tourist attraction, it draws as many as 25,000 visitors a day. Few tourists venture into the fascinating underground life of the Capitol, with its subway trains, tunnels, and esoteric offices. The Capitol complex includes a dozen restaurants and cafeterias, at least four barber shops, a beauty parlor, radio and television studios, a bank, a travel agency, several post offices, a picture framing shop, and a facility where a man called "Father Time" repairs the Capitol's several thousand clocks. Two first-aid rooms, an around-the-clock doctor, as well as x-ray, laboratory, pharmacy, and electrocardiographic services are available on the Hill. For members' more routine health needs there are two swimming pools, two gymnasiums, and an indoor paddle tennis court.

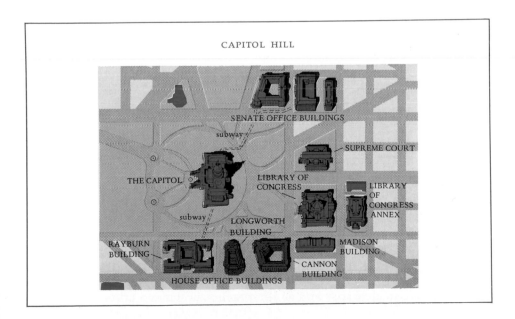

CAPITOL HILL

In addition to the separate chambers of the House and Senate, commonly referred to as *the floor,* the Capitol contains the offices of the leaders of both parties in both bodies, their staffs, a few committee rooms, and several dozen "hideaways"—special offices that senior senators and representatives use to get away from workaday pressures. In the office buildings, each senator has a suite of five rooms and each representative three.

Congressmen spare few expenses in giving themselves a comfortable working environment. The total cost of running the legislative branch was $827.5 million in the 1976 fiscal year, more than three times the amount Congress cost the taxpayers only ten years previously. This lavishness should give us a bit of perspective whenever we hear the common complaint that congressmen do not have enough money for staff experts and other such expensive necessities. When one considers that the newest completed construction project on Capitol Hill, the Rayburn House Office Building, cost anywhere between $80 and $120 million, one can reasonably conclude that if Congress lacks certain things, it is not because Congressmen are unwilling to appropriate money for themselves.

Salaries for members of Congress are relatively low. Representatives and senators alike got $44,625 a year in 1975. This is a modest sum compared either to prevailing rates in higher business and professional circles or to the extraordinary demands on their pocketbooks. Under legislation passed in 1975, congressional salaries henceforth may be pegged to the cost of living and therefore could go up without the politically painful necessity of congressmen voting themselves raises. The pension situation is a somewhat different story. Recent liberalization provides a veteran legislator with as much as $31,000 a year on retirement. (These provisions were designed by liberal Democrats to tempt conservative senior representatives to quit. The changes had the desired effect, since a record number of older members retired in 1972 and 1974.)

In addition to their salaries, many congressmen enjoy the fringe benefit of foreign travel paid for by the government, commonly called *junketing.* The annual cost reached the million dollar mark in 1971 and 1972, when nearly 250 members went abroad at government expense. There is no question that it is desirable for members to visit other countries to gather information and discuss matters of common interest with foreign officials. There is also no question that this privilege is abused by some congressmen, who use it for recreation rather than research. This is particularly blatant in the case of travel by defeated or retiring members in their last months in office.

Representatives can hire as many as eighteen staff assistants to help them in Washington and in their home districts. They get $227,270 a year for this purpose. Senators get between $400,000 and $750,000 a year for staff, depending on the size of their state, and can hire as many people as they like with this money. Staff salaries on Capitol Hill are more generous than the pay in the executive branch. Aides get up to $37,800 a year. Some wealthy senators supplement staff salaries from their own pockets. Although this violates a law forbidding payment of federal employees with private funds, no one seems to have made a fuss and so the practice is winked at.

IN 1909, A BATTERY-POWERED COACH CARRIED SENATORS THROUGH THE TUNNEL FROM THE SENATE OFFICE BUILDING TO THE CAPITOL. IN 1960, AN ELECTRIC SUBWAY SYSTEM WAS PUT INTO OPERATION. *Wide World Photos*

A typical representative will have eight to twelve staff members working on Capitol Hill and anywhere from three to six in his district office. Usually there will be two or three "professional" staff in Washington. The remainder are secretaries and "caseworkers" who settle constituent problems with the government.

A senator's personal staff typically will have six to eight professionals, of whom one will be a press secretary, several other specialists on subject matter of particular concern to the senator, and two or three experts on national and state politics. Many congressmen and senators also draw on the services of committee and subcommittee staff. Because often no real distinction is made between committee staff and personal staff, a senior senator can end up with as many as eighty aides.

Members receive a stationery allowance of $6,600 a year. Their franking privilege allows members of Congress to send mail free and accounts for over 300 million pieces of mail annually. Members also have communications allowances for telephone and telegraph. They get twenty-six round trips a year to their constituencies and six round trips a year for one staff member.

The congressional majority and minority party offices will print, fold, and insert in envelopes a variety of newsletters, questionnaires, and similar items. Another office on Capitol Hill maintains computerized mailing lists for each member. Many of these services are free, and the rest can be paid for from the stationery allowance. Both parties also maintain media consultants of all kinds to advise or provide brochures, billboards, slides, movies, television tapes, and so on. Both houses have television and radio studios where tapes can be produced at extremely low rates—about $20 for a five-minute television film that would cost around $400 at commercial rates.

Most congressmen send newsletters to their constituents. Of course, these "reports" are written for maximum political advantage. In 1975 Congress voted to pay for each member to produce and send two newsletters a year to all constituents. Previously, members often had paid for their newsletters with money from financial backers, usually left over from campaign contributions and kept in special "office funds." Like so many things in politics, this step can be viewed as either a progressive innovation or an outrageous steal. On the one hand, the new measure further increases the electoral advantage enjoyed by incumbents, and at the taxpayers' expense. On the other hand, it is also a step toward relieving elected officials of financial dependence on private interests.

THE INFORMAL SIDE OF LIFE

National politicians are sometimes accused of losing touch with "the real America" as a result of living too long in the special environment of Washington, a town whose one industry is politics. Capital society does indeed run at a hectic pace. Most foreign embassies (there are around 130) give two formal banquets a year, to which most or all congressmen are invited. Innumerable organizations, ranging from trade associations to reform groups, provide an unending round of cocktail parties and dinners. (If

THOUGH FASHIONS
HAVE CHANGED
OVER THE YEARS,
THE RIGORS OF AT-
TENDANCE AT OFFI-
CIAL FUNCTIONS
HAVE NOT.
Wide World Photos

politics is Washington's leading industry, catering must be a close second.) As a result, congressmen are thoroughly immunized against the pettier forms of social influence. A lobbyist has little hope of buying a senator with a free dinner when the senator has more dinner invitations than he wants. Indeed, when a politician goes to the lobbyist's dinner, he is doing the lobbyist a favor, not vice versa.

For much the same reason, no one need worry that congressmen can be won over by women procured for them by vested interests. Although it was a member of the executive branch who observed that "power is the ultimate aphrodisiac," congressmen come to the same conclusion from the profusion of what might be called Capitol Hill groupies. Barbara Howar, who speaks with authority in such matters, has observed, "Political power, like wealth, gives an otherwise ordinary man the sexual attractiveness generally reserved for movie stars, athletes, and playboys. . . . Power is the magic that turns tiny, portly, egocentric, albeit personable, men into dashing, mysterious sex symbols.[20]

The line between social life for pleasure and for business is extraordinarily hard to draw in Washington, where politics is pervasive. Most important politicians seem to work almost all the time, even when engaged in ostensibly sociable activities. For this reason, determination and physical stamina are among the most important qualifications for a successful political career. The demands placed on a prominent congressman are well illustrated in the following comments on Massachusetts Senator Edward Kennedy:

> Successful modern politicians, for better or worse, have a special kind of intelligence—like an oil slick, broad, restless, and only deep enough to make sure everything is covered. . . . [Kennedy] is no scholar, and he is neither reflective nor imaginative—he has people to do all that for him—but on any day he can absorb two twenty-pound briefcases of memos and background papers, take a couple of dozen verbal briefings ranging from 30 seconds to an hour, handle a dozen confrontation situations with senators, reporters, or bureaucrats trying to trap him, juggle the egos of 50 staff members and ex-officio advisers, interrogate the presidents of four drug companies and their counsel about their business, debate . . . about handgun production in the South, read the newspapers, remember 500 faces and names, and be witty at dinner. You try it.[21]

OUTSIDE INCOME

Members of Congress have numerous ways to supplement their salaries, ranging from outright corruption to wholly innocent sidelines. One can

[20] Barbara Howar, *Laughing All the Way* (Greenwich, Conn.: Fawcett Publications, Inc., 1973), pp. 99, 231. Also see Riegle, *O Congress*, pp. 232–33. Riegle, who is far from an admirer of Congress or most of its members, also concedes that there is virtually no bribery by lobbyists.

[21] Richard Reeves, "Teddy or Not," *New York*, April 22, 1974, p. 43.

easily identify examples of the two extremes, but there is also a substantial gray area where the line of moral acceptability is ambiguous.

Some states seem to have more than their share of dishonest legislators. Maryland has had three since 1970: a former senator convicted of accepting an "illegal gratuity"; a former representative jailed for his part in a savings and loan scandal; and an incumbent representative who committed suicide after testimony that he failed to report a $25,000 cash contribution from the Nixon administration's "Operation Townhouse." A former New Jersey congressman was jailed in 1973 for tax evasion. Two New Yorkers were convicted of bribery in 1974. At about the same time a Texan went to jail for taking a $25,000 bribe to block a Department of Justice investigation of a Baltimore home improvement firm. Invariably, these cases do not involve major issues of public policy. They are concerned with such mundane matters as a Capitol garage, a clause in a bill regulating mail-order houses, and similar highly particular measures of concern to a single person or firm.

Other examples are less blatant. For years the chairman of the House Judiciary Committe (which handled private immigration bills) maintained a law partnership in Brooklyn. These law offices had two doors, one of which listed the chairman's name among the firm's partners. The other door, leading to the same offices, did not bear his name. Customers with business with the federal government entered through this second door![22]

Problems of this sort have finally raised public concern about conflicts of interest. The House now requires its members to report annually on: (1) any significant investments in or income from firms that do business with or are regulated by the federal government; (2) income for services (chiefly legal fees) in excess of $5,000; (3) capital gains over $5,000; and (4) the sources of speaking fees amounting to $300 or more annually. In 1974, 267 representatives reported some sort of outside financial interest or income. These reports disclosed only a few instances in which representatives sat on committees that dealt with areas in which they had financial interests. For example, of the sixty-five members who owned stock in major defense contractors, only three were on the Armed Services Committee.

Senators do not have to make this kind of disclosure (although many of them do anyway), but they do have to report any speech, writing, or television appearance for which a fee of $300 or more was paid. Speaking fees are an important source of income to many senators and a few representatives with celebrity status. In 1973, eighteen senators made $20,000 or more apiece. Hubert Humphrey earned $178,236 this way in his first three years back in the Senate after his term as Vice President.[23] Speaking fees of $2,500 are not uncommon. The biggest source of speaking fees is colleges. Often the favorite congressmen of student body officers get handsome fees. In 1973, Senators McGovern and Eagleton earned a total of $48,650 from colleges

[22] Jack Anderson and Carl Kalvelage, *American Government . . . Like It Is* (Morristown, N.J.: General Learning Press, 1972), p. 26.

[23] All figures on outside investments and income are from *CQ Weekly Report,* August 10, 1974, pp. 2127–39.

and universities. The three best paid members of the House, all of whom earned most of their money on college campuses, were Shirley Chisholm, Paul N. McCloskey, and Bella S. Abzug. Colleges, of course, are not the only organizations that pay legislators to talk. Naturally, when large sums of money are paid to members of Congress by people with positions on pending legislation, questions of propriety are bound to be raised. To allay such questions the 1974 Election Finance Reform Act imposed an annual limit of $15,000 for income of this sort.

While a fascinating topic for gossip, it is not clear what significance this subject has for the legislative process. For every example of a congressman voting for his own personal financial interest, there is a counter example of someone voting against. Students of Congress have been unable to find any systematic relationships between congressmen's financial interest and their behavior on Capitol Hill.

THE COMMITTEE SYSTEM

The House consists of 435 highly diverse people; the Senate, of 100. Most of them are intelligent, ambitious, energetic, self-confident, strong-willed, and politically experienced. They represent diverse constituencies. Each is affected by various political, economic, and social interests. Although one interest or another, from dairy farming to rifle shooting, may touch many members, few interests are important to all. Most legislators may be broadly liberal or conservative, but the United States Congress does not have distinct groups of communist, socialist, or Catholic members whose ideological and party identifications produce close-knit blocs of the kind found in many European legislatures. No one member, or even a majority of all members, can do much to help or hinder the electoral future of any other.

In short, organization and discipline for Congress do not emerge from the kinds of people who are elected, the process that elects them, the party structure, the ideological climate, or the character of interest group representation in Congress. Quite the contrary. The diversity of constituencies and personal ambitions, the absence of polarizing ideologies, and the weakness of the national political parties produce a lack of "natural" outside forces from which congressional organization could be devised.

And yet Congress is faced with a staggering workload:

1. Enacting new laws and amending existing ones to govern a highly complicated and interdependent society of 210 million people. Over 25,000 bills are introduced in each two-year Congress, of which nearly 1,000 are enacted into law.
2. Appropriating money to operate the federal government and, through the numerous grant-in-aid programs, much of state and local government. The annual federal budget exceeds $375 billion.
3. Overseeing how the laws are administered by almost 3 million federal employees.

4. Confirming presidential appointees to the courts and high executive posts.

The basic challenge to Congress, then, is how to organize its diverse and autonomous membership in order to get things done. One major response to the challenge is specialization. Each house is divided into standing committees according to subject matter. Each committee has a fairly stable membership and a clearly defined jurisdiction, such as taxes, agriculture, defense, or education. When a bill is introduced, it is referred to the relevant committee, which considers it, probably amends it, and reports on it to the entire membership (or fails to do so, thus killing the bill). The committees are the places where most of the work of Congress is done.

There are twenty-two standing committees in the House and eighteen in the Senate.[24] Each representative is on one or two standing committees, each senator on two or three. Once assigned to a committee, a member remains until he voluntarily moves to another committee or leaves office. The ratio of Democrats and Republicans on each committee is roughly proportionate to the ratio in the parent body as a whole. During the Ninety-fourth Congress (1975–1976), for example, every House committee had twice as many Democrats as Republicans, plus one more Democrat.

Three committees in the House—Appropriations, Rules, and Ways and Means—are *exclusive* committees. This means that a member of one of them may not belong to any other committee, except the Budget Committee. Another group of House committees is *semi-exclusive*, which means that no one may belong to more than one of them. There are no such restrictions on membership on the remaining, *nonexclusive* committees. The Senate recently adopted a somewhat similar classification, but with a "grandfather clause" that exempts existing deviations.

It is essential to understand the simple, but often overlooked, fact that committees differ in several important respects:[25]

1. Some, such as the Committees on Merchant Marine and Fisheries or Post Office and Civil Service, deal with relatively narrow areas. These committees are of little concern to most members. Other committees deal with matters that affect the political interests of all members—for example, the Appropriations Committees, the House Ways and Means and Senate Finance Committees (concerned with taxes, social security, foreign trade), the Public Works Committees.

[24] A standing committee has an indefinite life, generally assumed to be unlimited. Occasionally "select committees" are established to study a particular problem and report on it. Select committees have a fixed life span and generally do not develop legislation. The Senate's committees on Watergate and on intelligence activities are examples of select committees. In addition, each party in each house has several committees that consider only party matters.

[25] Our discussion of differences among committees relies heavily on Richard F. Fenno's brilliant *Congressmen in Committees* (Boston: Little, Brown, 1973), although we differ from Fenno in some respects.

2. Some committees have more prestige than others. The easiest way to discover a committee's appeal is to examine the ratio of voluntary departures to transfers. In the House, the three exclusive committees are clearly the most desirable. In a twenty-year period, no one left any of them, except to switch to another one of the three. On the other hand, the Post Office and Civil Service Committee had fifty-seven departures and only five voluntary transfers. Less than a third of the Democrats assigned to this committee served there more than one term.[26] Although Senate committees also vary considerably in prestige, the issue is less important for individual senators, each of whom serves on several committees.

3. The least prestigious committees nevertheless are much more important to some members than to others. The stepchild Committee on Post Office and Civil Service is attractive to members whose constituents include many government employees or companies that make heavy use of the mails. The members who remain on the Interior Committee are likely to be from western states where public lands, national parks, Indians, mining, and irrigation are major issues.

4. Because some committees affect all members and others touch the interests of only some (except in the relatively unimportant sense that everyone is a taxpayer and consumer), the first type tends to be representative of the membership of the body as a whole with respect to region and ideology. These committees usually enjoy a much higher level of trust than groups like the Agriculture Committees, which are composed largely of legislators from farm areas, or the House Education and Labor Committee, whose members tend to be pro-labor ideologues (if they are Democrats) or pro-management ideologues (if they are Republicans).

5. Some committees are highly centralized in organization and procedure. In others, decisions are made in subcommittees and the full committee meets only to ratify what its subcommittees have worked out. The Appropriations Committees can fulfill their mission of scrutinizing and adjusting the federal budget only by dividing into thirteen subcommittees, each of which specializes in a particular part of the government. The detailed budgets approved by each subcommittee are seldom altered in full committee. At the opposite extreme are those committees that assign only a small portion of their jurisdiction to subcommittees and retain responsibility for the rest in the full committee, where the chairman can maintain greater control. There are about 140 standing subcommittees in the House and almost as many in the Senate.

COMMITTEE ASSIGNMENTS

Republicans are assigned to committees by the Republican committee on committees in each chamber, and Democrats by similar bodies. Committee assignments are a separate matter for each party and are among the most

[26] Charles S. Bullock, III, "Committee Transfers in the United States House of Representatives," *Journal of Politics*, 35 (February 1973), 85–120.

important functions and sources of power for the congressional party organizations. Once elected to Congress, the freshman member's committee assignments are his most important concern. By custom, new senators are given one desirable committee and a couple of less prestigious appointments. Thereafter, senators move to "better" committees partly on the basis of seniority and partly as a result of political maneuvering. New representatives seldom go on one of the exclusive committees, because leaders want to appraise their qualities before entrusting them with such responsibilities.

A number of factors influence members' requests for committee assignments. Perhaps the most important is their desire to be where they can do something for their constituents. This means that they want to be on the committees that concentrate on matters of particular interest to their constituents. They also want to serve on committees that handle the broadest central concerns of government—that is, the Appropriations and Ways and Means Committees. There are two reasons for this. In the first place, because these committees concern themselves with the whole range of government taxing and spending, they are important to every constituency. In the second place, much of what is done in Congress proceeds by exchanges of support between members. A member of any important committee can serve his own particular constituents by offering his aid to other members in return for their support of projects for his constituency.[27] Thus a second consideration in committee assignments is accumulating power in the body as a whole through the ability to do favors for colleagues and build up obligations that can be parlayed into influence.

A third major motive of congressmen in requesting committee assignments is being in a position to influence public policy. Some committees are attractive to members because they provide opportunities to play important roles in central areas of government decision making, like education, regulation of the economy, and social welfare. This opportunity may be valued for its own sake, because helping write laws that deal with major social problems is a rewarding experience for many politicians. It also is valued as a way of getting personal publicity. This latter motivation is more prevalent in the Senate. That body is more open to individual policy initiatives that produce not only mass media exposure but also tangible legislative results. Members of the more workaday House often grumble that "senators make speeches, we make laws."

The party leaders and committees who make committee assignments look at the subject from much the same point of view as the individual members. Each party wants all its legislators to be re-elected and therefore tries to put them on committees that will let them serve their constituents' interests. Since 87 percent of Nevada is owned by the federal government, the single representative from that state is always on the Interior Committee, despite

[27] This process of trading one's vote on a matter of indifference in return for someone else's vote on a matter that he is indifferent to is called *log rolling*. Since most issues are important only to some members, log rolling is an inevitable method of building coalitions for the passage of all but the most important and controversial legislation.

changes in party control of the seat. The "universal" committees, whose work affects every member, are of greatest concern to the party leaders. They want to be sure that the members appointed to the most important committees are competent, hard working, and reasonable—that is, able to compromise and to recognize the importance of considerations other than their own re-election. This is so important a consideration for the House Rules Committee that the Speaker now nominates all Democratic members of that group.

The constituency-oriented committees often are geographically unbalanced. Other House committees are often so geographically balanced that their seats virtually "belong to" state delegations or groups of several states. Thus a new committee member usually will be from the same state or region as the person he replaces. He is expected to look after the interests not only of his own constituency but of his entire state.

COMMITTEES AND CAREERS

In both House and Senate, the committees are the place where all but a few members can make their contributions to governing the country. They are where most legislators do most of their work. The role played by committees in the careers of individual members differs from one body to the other, however.

The best way to see this difference is to consider the committee assignments of Representative Daniel J. Flood (D—Pennsylvania) and Senator Gaylord Nelson (D—Wisconsin). Flood has been in the House since 1955. He is the chairman of the Labor-Health, Education and Welfare Appropriations Subcommittee and also serves on the Defense Appropriations Subcommittee. These are his only assignments; he can concentrate his attention on funding the Departments of Labor and Health, Education and Welfare. Senator Nelson, elected in 1962, has the following committee assignments:

MEMBERS OF THE SENATE FOREIGN RELATIONS COMMITTEE LISTEN TO TESTIMONY. FROM LEFT ARE SENATORS JOHN SPARKMAN, FRANK CHURCH, STUART SYMINGTON, HUBERT HUMPHREY, AND EDMUND MUSKIE.
Wide World Photos

International Trade
Supplemental Security Income
Revenue Sharing
Private Pension Plans (chairman)

Labor and Public Welfare, and these subcommittees:

Aging
Children and Youth
Employment, Poverty, and Migration (chairman)
Health
Labor
Alcoholism and Narcotics
Arts and Humanities (special subcommittee)
Human Resources (special subcommittee)

Select Committee on Nutrition and Human Needs:

(This committee studies and investigates poverty and hunger. It has no standing subcommittees.)

*Select Committee on Small Business, (chairman),
and the following subcommittee:*

Monopoly (chairman)

The contrast between Flood and Nelson illustrates the different role of committees in the two bodies. The Senate has less than a fourth as many members as the House but almost as many committees and subcommittees. Legislation usually gets its most meticulous study in the House for the simple reason that senators seldom can devote the necessary time because there are so many competing claims on their attention. Senators can be specialists — and many of them are — but only by neglecting some committee assignments in favor of concentrating on others.

Because each representative has only two or three subcommittees where he can make his mark on public policy, House committees usually consider legislation more thoroughly. Consequently, the House tends to defer to its committees' decisions more than the Senate does. Each representative expects that *his* committee's work will be respected and therefore is inclined to reciprocate when another committee reports a bill to the floor. Senators, whose committees usually are not so thoroughgoing, are more likely to amend legislation on the floor.

The fact that there are more than two committees and subcommittees for every Democratic senator means that every majority senator is chairman of at least one subcommittee within two years. Nelson, with less seniority than thirty-four other Senate Democrats, already heads three subcommittees and one full committee. As a result, he has access to additional staff, can schedule hearings, and can otherwise use his subcommittees to focus public opinion and help advance the chances of legislation he favors. By the same token, virtually every Republican senator is ranking minority member on one or more committees and subcommittees, which usually gives him control of the minority committee staff.[28] Although some senators have more important chairmanships than others, power is widely distributed in the Senate. Virtually every senator is the dominant legislative figure in some policy area.

Power is more closely concentrated in the House, where scarcely half the Democrats head a committee or subcommittee. Unlike senators, who quickly gain control of *some* bit of jurisdiction, representatives must wait a few years. In the Ninety-first Congress (1969–1970), 75 percent of all House members with four or more years of service were chairmen or ranking minority members of a subcommittee.[29] In 1971, House Democrats decided that no member could be chairman of more than one subcommittee. This important but little noticed reform dispersed power more widely in the House. Because of the shrinking number of senior conservative southern Democrats, it also increased liberal influence.

Many congressmen seek to carve out careers as subject matter specialists. Long service on a committee or subcommittee makes them experts on atomic energy, civil aviation, school lunch programs, or whatever. Within their special areas they become highly influential, for their colleagues who know little about the subject defer to the person who does. This type of long-term, quiet expertise is found in both houses but is more typical of the House of Representatives. A different pattern is more evident in the Senate, where committee service can be a springboard to national prominence and even a chance at the presidency. This prominence often comes from use of a subcommittee or select committee to conduct eye-catching investigations of such sensational topics as hunger, crime, drug prices, Watergate, the CIA, and so on. Senators often exploit their committee and subcommittee positions to become national spokesmen for new policy proposals.

In short, some congressional committee careers are inward-looking, producing prestige within Congress and power in the government through mastery of a specialized policy area. Others are outward-looking, using the committees as platforms to bring ideas and names to the attention of the electorate.

COMMITTEE CHAIRMEN AND THE SENIORITY SYSTEM

No feature of Congress is more criticized and more misunderstood than the *seniority system*. Seniority (length of service) *in Congress* is useful in many ways. For example, offices are assigned on this basis, so that the members with the most service get the most desirable office locations. Such inconsequential uses of the seniority system are not what all the criticism is about, however. As an object of denunciations and reforms, the seniority system is the method by which chairmen of full committees are chosen, *and it is nothing else*. The member of the majority party with the longest continuous service *on a committee* is the chairman of that committee.

---

[28] The majority party has about 75 to 80 percent of all committee staff positions.
[29] Bullock, "Committee Transfers," p. 97.

Although not a formal rule, the seniority system was violated only once between 1946, when the present committee structure was devised, and 1975. It was seldom violated in the previous thirty years.[30] We will consider the 1975 "revolt" against seniority after describing the principle that supposedly was revolted against.

HOW SENIORITY WORKS. Before the seniority system came to dominate the selection of committee chairmen, it was the practice for party leaders to choose the chairmen. This procedure was tolerable when most members served in Congress for relatively brief periods. But as more legislators found long careers on Capitol Hill, they could not so easily accept having their careers subjected to the caprice or calculations of a single leader or group of leaders. A House vote in 1910 stripped the Speaker of his power to appoint chairmen. This was a victory for progressives over forces that had blocked many popular reforms. By the 1920s, seniority was the main criterion in appointing chairmen. It provided a considerable measure of certainty about the rewards of congressional service.

The seniority system is important because the chairman of a committee has considerable power. He hires and fires committee staff, calls and presides over meetings, represents the committee in negotiations, and usually manages on the floor the more important bills reported by his committee. In the Senate, some committee chairmen control the staffs of all their subcommittees, while other Senate chairmen allow their subcommittee chairmen to hire some of their own aides. Technically, most aspects of the chairman's power are subject to the will of his committee's majority, and occasionally a committee has revolted against a chairman who was incompetent or who grasped too much power too often. But a chairman with even moderate political acumen will rarely run into this sort of trouble. House and Senate chairmen unquestionably are second in power only to the party leaders in each chamber.

The seniority system results in several systematic biases. First, chairmanships go disproportionally to older senators and representatives. It is not clear that legislators in their sixties and seventies are necessarily either better or worse at governing than their younger colleagues. There are some cases where advancing age has seriously diminished physical and mental powers, which has led critics to talk about the "senility system." Nevertheless, examples of this sort are neither common nor the real source of opposition to seniority.

A second built-in bias of the seniority system gets us closer to the real issue. Because of seniority, chairmanships go to members from safe seats, for they are the ones who are returned to Congress year in and year out. Having fewer worries about re-election, they are insulated from the tides of electoral change. Are such chairmen "better," because they need not worry so much about their own political survival and can concentrate on legislation?

[30] See Nelson W. Polsby et al., "The Growth of the Seniority System in the U.S. House of Representatives," *American Political Science Review*, 63 (September 1969), 787–807.

Or are they "worse," because they need not be attuned to public opinion for their own re-election?

The strongest criticisms of the seniority system are based on the fact that safe senators and representatives are re-elected *despite* the national popularity or unpopularity of their party. Safe Democratic congressmen are the ones who survive a Republican landslide, and vice versa. Thus, a national congressional victory brings chairmanships to those members who are *least* subject to broadly representative opinion. One byproduct of a presidential victory is usually committee leadership by the most senior members of the President's party in Congress, who may well have opposed him and in any event do not have to agree with his policies.

The seniority system became a major source of controversy because safe congressmen used to come mostly from rural areas and were more conservative than their party's congressional membership as a whole. Although this problem existed in the Republican party, it was far more severe and conspicuous among Democrats for two reasons. In the first place, except for 1947–48 and 1953–54, Democrats have controlled both houses of Congress since 1932. And in the second place, because of the pronounced conservatism of most southern Democratic congressmen, the Democratic party is deeply split along ideological lines. From the late 1930s through 1965, most of the twenty-two senators and one hundred representatives from the South usually voted on the conservative side of controversial domestic issues. They were also unanimously conservative on civil rights. Northern Democrats *never* had a majority in Congress during this period. (See pp. 358–59 for further discussion of this matter.) The corresponding split in the Republican party was relatively trivial, since only a handful of members voted for liberal positions with any consistency.

The southern Democrats, then, are the main reason for attacks on the seniority system by liberals. Because of historical Republican weaknesses in the one-party South, almost all southern congressmen used to be re-elected without significant opposition. But most Democrats in the North, where the bulk of the population lives, faced strong Republican competition. If the Democrats controlled Congress, it was because of their victories in the North. Yet the consequence in Congress of a nationwide Democratic victory was that southerners reaped most of the benefits. Being a majority among the senior Democrats, they headed most of the committees. Democratic Presidents were frustrated by conservative opposition from the Democratic heads of the committees through which liberal legislation had to pass.

The long-standing southern dominance of the congressional Democratic party persisted somewhat into the mid 1970s, even after the 1972 Democratic presidential candidate lost every southern state by an enormous margin. In 1975, the chairmen of six of the sixteen major Senate committees were southerners, as were seven of the eighteen major House committee chairmen.[31] These southern chairmen were considerably more conservative than

---

[31] "Major committees" are all standing committees, with the exception of several unimportant groups in each body. In the House, we excluded the Committees on House Administration, the District of Columbia, Standards of Official Conduct, and Small Business. In the Senate, we excluded the Committees on the District of Columbia and Rules and Administration.

the majority of their party. In the Senate, the southern chairmen had a party unity score of 29, compared to a rating of 63 for all Senate Democrats and 74 for the northern chairmen. (A party unity score of 100 would mean that a Democrat always voted for the position supported by the majority of his party.) The figures for the House are similar. In other words, the southern Democrats heading committees were generally out of step with the majority of congressional Democrats.

This, then, is the indictment against the seniority system. It puts in positions of power congressmen who are unsympathetic to the political views of the majority of their party. Since the majority views are considerably to the left of those held by the chairmen, it is not surprising that the seniority system is a favorite target of attack by liberal reformers. Indeed, it is probably the most commonly criticized feature of Congress.

The conservative bias of the seniority system came about because of historical circumstances that are passing from the scene. It is a result of the fact that the conservative South was a one-party area while the liberal North had few safe Democratic seats. Thus most safe Democratic seats were in the South. But in recent years, Republicans have been winning more and more previously invulnerable Democratic offices in the South. At the same time, the number of safe northern seats has been increasing drastically. As American core cities become more working-class, a generally overlooked consequence is the creation of safe northern constituencies for Democratic congressmen. This trend can be seen most conspicuously in the rapid increase in minority representatives, almost all of whom consistently win re-election by over 70 percent of the vote.

In the Senate, the Democratic landslide of 1958 resulted in the replacement of nine northern Republican senators by Democrats, who then enjoyed the great good fortune of running for re-election in 1964, when Senator Goldwater led his party to a record-breaking defeat. All nine were elected to third terms in 1970.

This combination of historical trends and accidents is bringing about the decline of southern power in both houses. Figure 10–2 shows how the southern share of influential positions in the House fell from 1964 to 1975. In the earlier year, southerners comprised 38 percent of all Democratic congressmen; by 1975, they had dwindled to 28 percent. Their share of major committee chairmanships had also fallen somewhat—to 39 percent in 1975, down from 53 percent in 1964. Their share of subcommittee chairmanships was also 53 percent in 1964, but eleven years later it had fallen to 32 percent, scarcely more than a "fair share." The trend in the Senate follows similar lines.

The declining southern control of subcommittee chairmanships portends the future role of the South in the congressional Democratic party. Instead of holding the dominant position they enjoyed for so many years, southern Democrats are headed for an era where they will be lucky to have a share of committee chairmanships proportionate to their numbers. This new situation is forecast in Figure 10–3, which shows the seniority of northern and southern Democrats in the House and Senate. In the Senate, five northerners and five southerners have twenty or more years of seniority; but only one

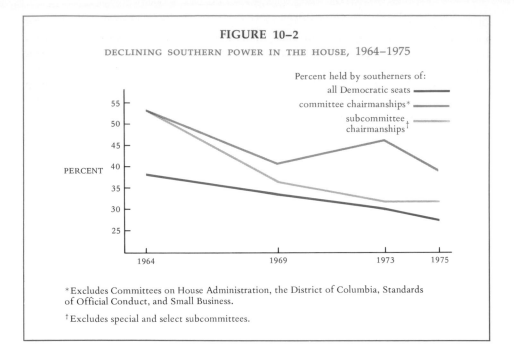

FIGURE 10–2

DECLINING SOUTHERN POWER IN THE HOUSE, 1964–1975

Percent held by southerners of:
all Democratic seats
committee chairmanships*
subcommittee
chairmanships†

*Excludes Committees on House Administration, the District of Columbia, Standards of Official Conduct, and Small Business.

†Excludes special and select subcommittees.

southerner and twenty-three northerners have ten to nineteen years of service. This second group constitutes the heirs apparent to committee power, and many of them are chairmen already. The situation is much the same in the House. The southerners almost hold their own in the most senior group but are outnumbered more than three to one in the next generation of representatives, those with ten to nineteen years of service.

THE REVOLT AGAINST SENIORITY. Criticism of the seniority system had little practical consequence on Capitol Hill until the early 1970s. In 1973, House Democrats adopted a crucial modification of the seniority system. The Democratic Caucus (that is, all Democratic representatives) would vote by *secret ballot* to confirm nominees as chairmen. (Senate Democrats will follow the same procedure beginning in 1977.) Nominations come from a new party group, the Steering and Policy Committee, which itself chooses nominees by secret ballot.

At the beginning of 1975, the Democratic Caucus stunned political observers by deposing three veteran chairmen, all from the South, and replacing them with younger northern liberals. This was widely acclaimed as the death knell of the seniority system. A closer look at the three cases suggests that obituaries for seniority are premature.

One of the victims was the eighty-one-year-old Wright Patman, who had served in the House since 1929 and was the most senior member of Congress. Far from being a conservative obstructionist, Patman was an old-fashioned populist who had been defended by Ralph Nader. But he had lost his ability to control his committee, which had been in a state of near-anarchy for years. The other two deposed chairmen stubbornly adhered to right-wing policies that were increasingly unpopular with the growing liberal majority among Democrats. Both were in their mid-seventies, one ran his committee in a highly arbitrary manner, and the other had a furious, abrasive speaking style.

The Caucus basically followed seniority in replacing the three deposed chairmen. The two conservatives were succeeded by the next senior members of their committees without any question or controversy. Patman was replaced by the fourth-ranking Democrat on his committee, but this was only a slight violation of seniority. The next man in line to Patman was a seventy-eight-year-old machine politician widely known to possess only modest talent, energy, and ambition. The third-ranking member was already chairwoman of another committee.

Although predictions are always risky, we will try one here. The "revolution" in 1975 did not overturn the seniority system but merely applied some controls to it. In the future as in the past, the most senior member of each committee will be its chairman unless he is senile or persistently uses his power to flout the wishes of a strong majority of his party. The threat of being deposed will make chairmen more responsive to majority sentiment. If this happens, reformers will have gotten the substance of their goals without changing the form. This result would be consistent with the merit that most members see in the seniority system—its compatibility with and encouragement of long careers on Capitol Hill. Long careers and expertise contribute to the ability of Congress to maintain its independence of the executive branch and its capacity to deal with the President as an equal partner.

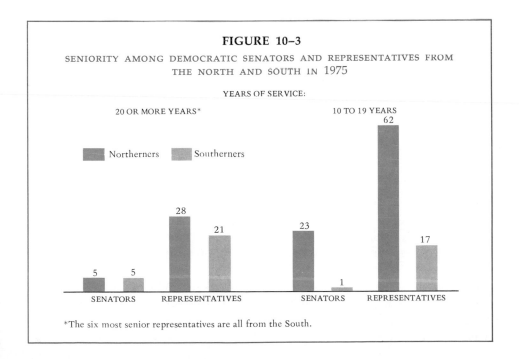

FIGURE 10–3

SENIORITY AMONG DEMOCRATIC SENATORS AND REPRESENTATIVES FROM THE NORTH AND SOUTH IN 1975

YEARS OF SERVICE:

*The six most senior representatives are all from the South.

Seniority has another virtue that should not be overlooked and is becoming increasingly relevant to radical critics: it protects mavericks from party discipline by guaranteeing them their slice of power. Black militants and white segregationists alike stand to benefit from a method of choosing chairmen that works without reference to their political opinions. As liberals begin to inherit the fruits of the system, it will be interesting to see if they continue their attacks on it. Perhaps they will. On the other hand, it is useful to remember this observation:

> Representatives and senators start out their congressional careers resenting the seniority system. But after a while, as one of them once told me, "it sort of grows on you."[32]

Committee seniority is also the guide for appointing subcommittee chairmen in the House, subject to two restrictions: all Democratic members of the full committee must ratify each appointment, and no representative may be chairman of more than one subcommittee. Moreover, the chairmen of the thirteen powerful and nearly autonomous House Appropriations subcommittees must be confirmed by the Democratic Caucus. It did not fail to confirm anyone in 1975, even though some of the chairmen were far to the right of the party's mainstream. In the Senate, subcommittees are more under the control of the full committee chairmen. This usually does not present much of a problem, however, since there are more than enough subcommittees to go around.

PARTIES IN CONGRESS

Committees are one major way to bring order to the legislative process. They are the framework in which work is done. Parties are the second solution to the problem of congressional organization. They guide the decisions that are made about most issues. In Chapter 9 we saw that the word *party* has several different meanings, depending on the context. We also saw that parties usually are quite weak as organizations but strong as frames of reference for individual perceptions of the political world. The same things are true in Congress. Party membership is by far the most important determinant of how members vote; yet the organized parties in Congress have relatively little power to control the behavior of their members.

When talking about individual voters, we used the notion of *reference groups* as a handy way to understand party identification. *Republican* and *Democrat* were important identities for most of the electorate. The same is true of congressmen. Their constituencies, their committees, their areas of expertise, their personal political organizations, and various other factors may guide their behavior. But by far the most important aspect of their identity is their party. With occasional insignificant exceptions, members of

[32] Nelson W. Polsby, "Seniority, What Is It?" in *Political Promises* (New York: Oxford University Press, 1974), p. 112.

Congress are all elected as Democrats or Republicans. Their previous political careers have usually occurred in partisan politics. They have been nominated as the candidate of one party or the other. Together with their party's other nominees, they are the Democratic or Republican ticket. What is good for one of the party's candidates is likely to be good for all of them. Indeed, the limit of most voters' knowledge about them is the party label next to their names. For all these reasons, then, congressmen cannot escape the fact that they have reached Capitol Hill by one of two routes—Republican or Democratic.

Many aspects of Congress reflect this fundamental division. In each chamber, the Republicans sit on one side of the center aisle and the Democrats on the other. They have separate cloakrooms and usually enter the floor through different doors.[33] The same segregation occurs on committees; Republicans sit on one side, Democrats on the other. Each party assigns its members to committees, and once there, elevation to a chairmanship depends on being a member of the majority party. Although it would be an exaggeration to say that social life also is organized along party lines, it is true that legislators are likely to find their friends among members of their own party. The same attitudes are mirrored in congressional aides, whose lunchtime companions, professional connections, and off-duty friends usually are in the same party.

CONGRESSIONAL PARTY ORGANIZATION

Congress has its own party organs and leaders, distinct from the national party organizations and the presidency. Chosen by the party's members in each body, the party leadership reflects the interests and inclinations of the legislators who elected it. (In its special congressional sense, *the leadership* refers to a party's elected leaders in one or the other body. See Table 10–1.) Each party's legislative leaders are among its principal national spokesmen.

The Speaker of the House of Representatives is elected by the majority party and in effect is the head of that party in the House. He is more than a party figure, however; he presides over the House and is next in line of presidential succession after the Vice President. The minority party in the House has no counterpart to the Speaker. Otherwise, the leadership organizations of the two parties are similar. Each party has a *floor leader,* a *whip* (or assistant leader), and a number of assistant whips in charge of floor business. The Speaker joins these officers on the majority side and is actually superordinate to the majority leader in scheduling legislation, acting as a party spokesman, and representing House Democrats (or Republicans) to the President and the public.

Party organization in the Senate takes a similar form. The Vice President is the Senate's presiding officer (technically, he is the "President of the Senate"), but otherwise he has no influence there except to cast the deciding vote in case of a tie and to issue an occasional parliamentary ruling. (In fact,

[33] The cloakrooms are not places to check overcoats, but lounges where members can telephone, nap, hold quick strategy conferences, negotiate, make last-minute notes, and otherwise conduct business literally a step away from the floor.

TABLE 10-1

CONGRESSIONAL PARTY ORGANIZATION IN 1975

DEMOCRATS	REPUBLICANS
HOUSE OF REPRESENTATIVES	
Speaker	Minority Leader
Chairman of the Caucus	Chairman of the Conference*
Majority Leader	Minority Whip
Majority Whip	Regional Whips
Deputy and Assistant Whips	Committee on Committees
Steering and Policy Committee	Policy Committee
Democratic National Congressional Committee	National Republican Congressional Committee
Patronage Committee	
SENATE	
Majority Leader	Minority Leader
Majority Whip	Minority Whip
Chairman of the Conference*	Chairman of the Conference*
Policy Committee	Policy Committee
Steering Committee	Committee on Committees
Senatorial Campaign Committee	Senatorial Campaign Committee
	Personnel Committee

*The conference consists of all members of the respective party.

the job of presiding over the Senate usually is done by junior members unless an important debate or vote brings the Vice President to the chair.) The Senate Democrats put all party organs under the control of their leader, while the Republicans use a system of plural leadership in which each party committee is headed by someone other than the floor leader.

Contrary to popular belief, neither the Speaker nor the rest of the party leaders are chosen by seniority. Speaker Carl Albert was eleventh-ranking Democrat in the House in 1975, and the Senate leader, Mike Mansfield, was the ninth most senior Democrat. (He was a good deal more junior than that when he was first chosen majority leader in 1961.) To be sure, leaders have served long enough to learn their way around and to become widely known among and helpful to their colleagues.

Leaders seldom are committed ideologically to any one wing of their party. Within the context of the issue positions held by their party's members, they tend to be moderates. Their approach to politics is likely to be pragmatic—that is, they are more interested in reaching agreement than in defending any position to the bitter end. Senator Everett Dirksen, the able Republican leader for ten years, once remarked, "I am a man of principle, and one of my basic principles is flexibility."[34]

[34] Quoted in Neil MacNeil, *Dirksen* (New York: The World Publishing Co., 1970), p. 153.

What part do the party leaders play in the legislative process? The majority leadership in each house manages legislation after it comes out of committee. Scheduling the workload is an important power in itself because a bill's chances of passage or escaping major alteration are affected by how and when it comes before the entire membership. For example, many representatives from eastern cities live at home and are in Washington only three days a week. Most members of this "Tuesday to Thursday Club" are Democrats, and therefore Democratic House leaders seldom schedule floor votes for Monday and Friday. Much legislation is interesting to only a few congressmen. The leaders can use their knowledge of members' travel schedules to schedule particular bills when concerned members are present—or absent. This control of the schedule is one reason prudent members try to stay on the good side of the leadership. This is not so hard to do as one might think, for the leadership traditionally prides itself on its broad tolerance and willingness to oblige.

Because the leaders handle all the scheduling, they are at the center of the web of information, adjustment, compromise, and negotiation about pending legislation. They must be consulted on every bill and kept informed of its progress. Thus, they have the power of middlemen or brokers. They know more than their Senate or House colleagues about what is going on, what bargains are possible, and who needs to talk with whom. They can use this knowledge to facilitate members' pet projects. Their power over low-visibility bills gives leaders bargaining "chips" that can be exploited on major issues.

The leadership also plays a role in committee assignments, although the extent of its participation in this process varies over time and from party to party and house to house. After the 1974 election, the House Democrats gave their leadership a greater role in the assignment process. The Speaker can use the Steering and Policy Committee to fill committee vacancies with sympathetic members. This increases his influence by making members who want choice assignments a bit more amenable to his wishes in floor action.

This change was one of several new departures by the House Democratic Caucus. The party *caucuses* (called *conferences* in the Senate and by House Republicans) always have been the ultimate authorities of the parties in Congress. The extent to which they actually assert themselves, or merely rubber stamp the seniority system and the committee chairmen, has changed from one historical era to another. For the half-century after World War I, the caucuses were largely passive ratifiers of decisions made elsewhere. Beginning in the early 1970s, when it passed a rule limiting each member to one subcommittee chairmanship, the House Democratic Caucus has been an increasingly active new element in the struggle for power. We saw one example of its new role in the limits placed on the seniority system in 1975. The Caucus is also starting to play a part in the legislative process, in addition to its organizational and procedural actions. It has exercised its power to permit consideration by the full House of provisions that might otherwise be killed in committee. At the present time it is impossible to foresee how far this trend will go. The Caucus may try to impose binding instructions

HOUSE SPEAKER
CARL ALBERT
(LEFT) AND
MINORITY LEADER
JOHN RHODES
(RIGHT).
Wide World Photos

on all Democrats to vote a certain way. Or, probably, it will limit itself to an occasional procedural intervention. The Caucus probably will not become a way to impose party discipline on Democratic representatives.

Although the leaderships have a considerable amount of influence, the leaders do *not* have the power to give orders to their fellow lawmakers. They cannot tell their members how to vote and expect the members to follow orders. It should already be clear why congressional party leaders do not enjoy this sort of power. Party discipline is weak in Congress because it is weak in the nation at large. Party leaders cannot control who will get congressional nominations or even how much campaign help will go to individual candidates for the House and Senate. To be sure, they can provide some marginal assistance by giving members good committee assignments or helping push pet bills. But because they give only marginal aid in keeping their party members in office, and because they cannot keep them out, they exercise only marginal power over them.

PARTY PROGRAMS

So far we have pointed out that the leadership uses its influence to encourage members to support the party position. But where does the party position come from? Who originates it? The party leaderships themselves certainly are not the people who develop substantive programs. They are specialists in the politics of getting policies adopted rather than in the policies themselves. Their job is to make majorities, not policy.

The answer is relatively simple with regard to the President's party. The President's position *is* his party's position. Once a piece of the President's program emerges from committee, his party's leadership is concerned with getting it passed. Relations between the President and "his" party leadership are not simple, however. The leaders are both the President's main conduits to Congress and Congress' representatives to the White House. This double-facing position puts considerable strain on the legislators involved. They are elected by their colleagues and seldom lose sight of the fact that this is the source of their power. Yet the leaders are also *party* leaders and know that the popular perception of their party is determined largely by the President's popular standing.

A leader who is too subservient to the wishes of the President will lose his credibility with the members who elected him. This will undermine his effectiveness and ultimately cost him his job. On the other hand, a leader who is not willing to work for the President by putting pressure on his colleagues will find that party unity is crumbling, with disastrous results for the President's—and the party's—programs. The leadership thus has a double job. In the first place, they want to re-elect all their members and add to the seats their party already holds. This means getting members in line to assure the success of the party's program. But in the second place, they want to be sure of holding their party together in Congress, and this may mean being careful not to step on too many toes by pressuring members to support party programs they do not like. The President shares both these goals, so there is a sizable community of interest between the two elements.

The strength of the bonds between the President and his party in Congress can be illustrated by examining the behavior of Republican legislators during the last years of the Nixon administration, a period when extraordinary strains were placed on those bonds. Shortly after Nixon's landslide re-election in 1972, the Watergate scandal exploded and the President's popularity dropped to historic lows. Before his resignation in August 1974, Nixon was universally considered a tremendous electoral handicap to his party in the 1974 midterm campaign. In private, few Republican politicians had a good word for Nixon. But in public, the reverse was true. Until the final crisis, relatively few Republican congressmen would criticize their President and *relatively few voted against his legislative positions.* They were particularly reluctant to override his vetoes.

The support given by congressmen to their President's policies is partly a manner of substantive agreement and partly a reflection of the fact that they have a common identity as members of the same party. Normally, a president will not propose legislation unless he thinks that he and his party (the two are inseparable here) will benefit politically from its passage. Some congressional members of his party may not share the President's political assessment; some may not agree with what he proposes; and some may agree but feel that a proposal is unpopular in their own state or district. There is still a strong presumption, however, that if the President gets what he wants from Congress, it will be good for his party because it is good for him. The President and his party will get the credit and, as an astute congressman remarked some years ago, "Politics is 80 percent getting credit."

The position of the opposition party is somewhat more complicated. If a Democratic President wants a bill passed because it would raise his popularity, then it would seem to follow that Republicans should try to defeat the bill and prevent their opponent from strengthening himself. What is good for the Democrats must be bad for the Republicans, and vice versa. During recent Democratic administrations, some Republican congressmen argued that they did not need to offer legislative programs of their own because, in the words of one Republican leader, "The business of the opposition is to oppose." Other Republicans felt that this was an unwise posture—bad for the country because it restricted ideas to only one party, and bad for their party because it gave it a negative image. They tried to develop "constructive alternatives" to Democratic proposals. The "Republican position" on an issue was basically established by the senior Republicans on the relevant committees, who worked out their party's alternatives to presidential proposals. The drawback to this approach was that the Democrats, being in the majority, could appropriate Republican ideas as their own and get the credit.

The situation is even more complicated when one party occupies the White House and the other has a majority in Congress. This was the situation for fourteen of the twenty-two years between 1955 and 1977, when there was a Republican President and Democratic majorities in both houses of Congress. Presidents Eisenhower, Nixon, and Ford often succeeded in rallying *effective* majority coalitions in Congress, thanks mainly to massive defections by southern Democrats. But committee chairmanships and control of floor business were in Democratic hands. Thus, each party could have a program—for the Republicans it was what the President proposed; for the Democrats, what the relevant committee reported.

In these circumstances, the President tends to have the initiative, however. The congressional Democratic leadership was unable to put together an alternative legislative program to that of the President, a package that would stand forth as *the* Democratic program. There are two reasons for this failure. First, there is no mechanism to convert a collection of committee notions into a program. Second, and perhaps more important, conflicting ambitions among individual congressmen make it difficult for Democrats to discipline themselves in this way. Why, for example, should Democrats in both houses decide that Senator Edward Kennedy's plan for national health insurance should be their party's prime legislative interest? Whatever consequences such a decision might have for individual medical care budgets or for the Democratic party, it clearly would be helpful to Kennedy's chances of becoming the Democratic presidential nominee.

We can summarize this discussion of congressional parties with two generalizations. First, a Republican (or Democratic) President and the congressmen of his party are held together not by being parts of a single disciplined organization, but because they share a common identity as Republicans. The voters think of them as Republicans and, for better or worse, they must think of themselves in the same way.

Second, the two main modes of congressional organization—parties and committees—have contradictory influences. The committee system *decentralizes* Congress by delegating decision making to specialized groups, each of which has a vested interest in maintaining its own power. The parties are a *centralizing* impulse that brings national forces to bear on decisions. The balance of influence between committee and party shifts over time. Currently the parties—the centralizing force—seem to be gaining power at the expense of the committees. We will examine the consequences of these fluctuations in the next chapter, which focuses on the dynamics of the legislative process.

SOME OTHER WAYS TO ORGANIZE

Although parties and committees are the two principal instruments for bringing order and coherence to congressional business, there are other types of organization, usually more evident in the House than the Senate.

STATE DELEGATIONS

Delegations—all the members of one party from one state—are one way of dealing with the impersonal size of the House and the fragmentation that results from the committee system. Committee assignments are strongly affected by delegation influence. A member is much more likely to get the assignment he wants if his delegation backs him. Committee seats are often "reserved" for particular delegates or groups of delegations. The committees on committees are themselves organized on a regional basis, with the understanding that each committee member acts for all the colleagues of his party and region. Committee assignments are important to the entire delegation since wide representation on committees extends the delegation's ability to help its members. Covering all committees of interest to the delegation is more important than putting each member on the committee he individually is interested in, because someone else from his delegation will look after his special interests, just as he is expected to look after the special interests of other constituencies in his state. By representing the interests of all the districts in his state, he makes it possible to do a better job of looking after his own district.[35] Thus, a cohesive state delegation helps each member extend his influence beyond the jurisdiction of his own committees.

Although delegation cohesiveness clearly is beneficial, some delegations are a good deal less united than others. The New York Democrats, for example, are notoriously divided and sometimes do not meet for years at a time. Others, like the California or Texas Democrats, get together frequently to trade information and make plans on issues of statewide concern. For example, California has unusually stringent laws on automobile exhaust pollution and its congressmen want to be sure that federal exhaust emission rules do not interfere with state law. They refused to vote for a major air pollution measure some years ago until it was amended to protect their state's stricter approach.

Delegations can use their cohesion to enhance their negotiating position. A bloc of twenty votes is a potent bargaining counter. Sometimes a delegation may vote as a bloc on issues of no particular statewide concern in order to build up obligations that can be cashed in later. The eight Democrats from Chicago are especially well known for this practice. On other occasions a delegation may trade its vote for a particular concession. When the Johnson administration's anti-poverty legislation was being considered in the House in 1965, the North Carolina Democrats told the White House that they would vote for the bill in return for a commitment from Johnson that Adam Yarmolinsky would have no connection with the war on poverty. Because Johnson needed their votes, he agreed to sacrifice Yarmolinsky, a lawyer who had played a prominent part in drafting the legislation and had become *persona non grata* to conservatives because of his liberal views.

IDEOLOGICAL GROUPS

Both parties have liberal and conservative wings, each of which has some degree of organization, ranging from elaborate to casual. The conservative southern Democrats have long had an informal caucus, called (by northerners) the "Boll Weevils." The liberal Democrats have by far the most ambitious

[35] Barbara Deckard, "State Party Delegations in the United States House of Representatives—An Analysis of Group Action," *Polity*, 5 (Spring 1973), 323–24.

organization, the Democratic Study Group. The DSG was founded in 1959 to provide a counterweight to the deference given by the party leadership to senior conservative southerners. Originally composed largely of junior congressmen, the DSG now dominates the mainstream of the party, includes more than two-thirds of all House Democrats, and is a combination goad and partner to the Speaker and majority leader. It has its own whip system, a staff of twelve, and a nationwide fund-raising campaign to help liberal congressional candidates. Despite its name, the DSG's goals are not to study problems, but to reform congressional procedures, enact progressive legislation, and elect liberal Democrats to the House. DSG staff drafted the proposals that created the Democratic Steering and Policy Committee, modified the seniority system, and established the one-subcommittee-chairman limit. Its leaders did the politicking that brought these reforms to fruition. The DSG also prepares fact sheets on bills. At election time, it provides liberal candidates with campaign material as well as money.

Republican counterparts to the Boll Weevils and DSG are far less important. The handful of liberal Republicans band together in the Wednesday Club, which has a small staff and issues occasional position papers, sometimes in conjunction with liberal Republican senators. The more numerous ultraconservatives have the "Republican Study Committee."

The seventy-five freshman Democrats elected in 1974 formed their own caucus immediately after the election to help them exert influence on the Hill. Encouraged by their successful efforts at modifying the seniority system, they formalized this body, hired staff, and hoped to remain in being as a cohesive force. Funds for their organization came from one or two prominent liberal benefactors. This group turned out to have little staying power, however. What the freshmen had in common was the year of their first election to Congress. This bond was weak compared to their diverse committee assignments, constituencies, and problems of re-election. These latter factors quickly came to dominate the freshmen's perspectives.

Two more congressional groups are the Black Caucus and the Members of Congress for Peace through Law. The latter, founded in 1966, is the only bicameral, bipartisan group. That is, it draws members from both parties in both the House and the Senate. It commissions research and tries to work out common positions on peace issues. The Black Caucus is supported by the sixteen black representatives, all of whom are Democrats.[36] It develops positions and strategies on behalf of policies to help blacks. Its spokesmen say that they follow the familiar slogan: "We have no permanent friends or permanent enemies, only permanent interests." Yet they can hardly escape the fact that they are all Democrats.

SUMMARY

We have explained congressional organization as a pattern of responses to the foundation of the institution. Since we assume that the fundamental fact

---

[36] There is a seventeeth member—Walter Fauntroy, the delegate to the House from the District of Columbia. He has an office, a staff, committee assignments, and access to the floor—but no vote on the floor.

about Congress is that its members like being in Congress and try to remain there, our examination of the legislative process started with the basic elements of nomination and election. We have seen that this electoral environment does not impose much structure or discipline on Congress. Once they get to Congress, members must organize themselves to get things done. One major solution to this problem is the committee system, which combines division of labor and delegation of responsibility. The second major solution — the two-party system — counteracts the fragmentation of the committee system and implements the passage of legislation from the committee hearing rooms to the President's desk. In the next chapter we will turn to the dynamic process by which these structural features interact with each other.

CHAPTER ELEVEN
CONGRESS IN ACTION

IN DECEMBER 1972, a rare cold snap struck the San Francisco Bay Area. Every night for a week the temperature fell below freezing, an extraordinary departure from the region's normally mild climate. The cold killed millions of eucalyptus trees in the Berkeley hills to the east of San Francisco Bay, the site of some of the area's most attractive residential neighborhoods. The dead trees were far more than an ecological loss and an eyesore. When they dried out during the long California summer, they would become a fire hazard of staggering proportions. Any ordinary brush fire could trigger a terrifying firestorm that might destroy thousands of houses. Similar conditions in 1926 had produced a fire that devastated much of Berkeley.

Believing that the trees had to be cleared to avert a catastrophe, local interests began to look for a way fo finance the clearance. This is just the sort of situation that leads to an appeal to Congress. But Berkeley's representative was Ronald V. Dellums, a black militant whose verbal enthusiasm for "revolutionary change" was matched by his habit of referring to most of his colleagues as "prostitutes." Would Dellums be either willing or able to get the federal government to assist in eliminating the fire hazard? Ultimately, he failed, but his description of his attempt to make eucalyptus clearance a federal project is a fascinating short account of the legislative process. It illustrates many of the motivations and relationships we describe in Chapter 10 and in this chapter. No "old politics" congressman could have been more assiduous than Dellums in his attempt to advance his district's interests.

In early February, the East Bay Congressional Delegation, Congressmen Jerome Waldie, Pete Stark and I joined with Senator Alan Cranston, Governor Reagan and local officials in asking the Secretary of Agriculture to provide financial assistance to local governments and citizens to meet the fire threat. Projected costs were estimated to be in excess of $50 million.

In late February, the Department of Agriculture told us no money was available. At the same time, representatives of Governor Reagan and local officials met to develop joint local-state plans aimed at substantially reducing the fire danger. These plans emphasized fire suppression, and also included an appeal to President Nixon to declare threatened portions of the East Bay hills a disaster area.

Congressmen Stark and Waldie joined me in contacting the White House and urging action by the President. These appeals brought flowery responses—but no action.

Since it soon became apparent that effective and complete fire suppression efforts were beyond the capability of local governments, and since we had no offer of financial or other assistance from President Nixon, I met again with Senator Cranston and Congressmen Stark and Waldie, this time to develop a legislative response that would furnish predisaster assistance in accordance with the Disaster Relief Act of 1970. As a result of this meeting, we introduced identical bills in both houses of Congress.

We wrote these bills in such a way that the Senate version would be sent to the Small Business Subcommittee of the Senate Committee on Banking, Housing and Urban Affairs, a subcommittee chaired by Senator Cranston. An initial hearing was held on May 9, 1973 during which I testified along with the other East Bay legislators. Cranston's bill (S. 1697) was rapidly approved by his subcommittee, the full committee and finally by a voice vote of the Senate.

In the House, the measure was referred to the Forestry Subcommittee on Agriculture. I brought the issue before the California Democratic Delegation and secured unanimous support. I took this step essentially because the Delegation includes the influential House Majority Whip, John McFall of Manteca, and an important member of both the Agriculture Committee and the Rules Committee, Congressman Bernie Sisk of Fresno.

In response to significant Democratic Leadership support, the Forestry Committee held hearings in June and approved the bill. Unexpectedly, the measure gained the enthusiastic support of the Subcommittee Chairman, Representative John Rarick. "Judge" Rarick from Baton Rouge, Louisiana, is one of the strongest advocates of conservative causes in the Congress. He proved to be an appreciated exception to the many Congressmen, on both sides of the aisle, who oppose all legislation from political opposites. It turned out that Baton Rouge had greatly benefited from federal disaster aid after several Mississippi River floods. Congressman Rarick gave us strong and visible support as the measure moved forward. Also, Congressman Charles Teague, Republican of Santa Barbara, the Ranking Minority Member of the committee, actively entered the struggle for the bill.

Unfortunately, the Agriculture Authorization Bill—which authorizes every program in the Department of Agriculture from food stamps to crop subsidies—got to the full committee before the Eucalyptus Bill. All else stopped, as various agriculture interest groups fought over the main authorization bill.

Finally in July, after a delay of weeks, the full committee got around to consideration of our bill. The hearings were extensive. I, and the other East Bay Congressmen, testified along with representatives and experts from the state and local governments. As a result, the committee re-wrote parts of the bill. The final version authorized the President to make funds available for fire suppression and tree removal activities on both public and private lands in Alameda and Contra Costa counties. Federal aid was to be matched by state funds and the total federal grant was not to exceed $11 million.

Owners or operators of public and private lands could receive reimbursement of up to 75% of the removal expenses.

The House of Representatives has a peculiar legislative process. All bills that pass the committees which actually work on their relevant subject area must go before the Committee on Rules before actually reaching the floor for a vote. This is the Committee that, in earlier years, blocked many progressive measures such as civil rights legislation for a long time. Now, however, with a moderate Chairman and several new members, it is much more responsive to the House Leadership. The Rules Committee decides when and how a bill is scheduled for debate or action. Although more than 20,000 bills are submitted to the House, only some two to three hundred go through the committee process and are approved by the Rules Committee. By the time the Eucalyptus bill came before Rules, the Legislative Calendar was very full. Odds on a bill that benefited only three congressional districts being given favorable treatment were very long.

I contacted Speaker Carl Albert, Majority Leader "Tip" O'Neill and Congressman McFall. Their active support joined with support from Congressman Sisk, all the California Democrats, Representative Teague and Senator Cranston together secured a rule and placed the bill on the House Calendar for debate and a vote.

It was scheduled for just before the August recess. At this time, the House was meeting even on Saturdays and very late into the night. There were many controversial measures before the House being considered under time constraints. Tempers grew hot and careful reflection was not the watch-word. The narrow application of the bill caused it to become a lightning rod for chance frustrations of the moment. Rather than have it defeated on irrelevant emotion, the East Bay Delegation requested that the House Democratic Leadership pull the bill off the Calendar until after the recess. This was done.

During the recess, we worked very hard to contact each Member and carefully explain the purpose of the bill and the nature of the fire danger problem in the East Bay.

At this point in late August, Governor Reagan announced a $800 million state budget surplus. The House naturally began to question why the state couldn't spend some of this money to solve the eucalyptus problem. All our efforts to actively engage the Governor to explain the background and intentions regarding the surplus or to involve him in lining up Republican votes were completely ignored.

When the House reconvened in September, the bill came to the floor with the albatross of Governor Reagan's statement and rebate tossed around its neck.

On September 11th, the House voted "NO" on the rule and refused even to debate the bill, despite solid and active support of the House Leadership and most Democrats.

This has not been a partisan effort. We received invaluable

help from former Republican Senator Bill Knowland as well as Congressman Teague.[1]

This chapter describes the steps by which a bill becomes a law and then analyzes the major features of this process. Our purpose is to provide an account of Congress's place in the national political system and a realistic understanding of what Congress can reasonably be expected to do.

THE COMMITTEE STAGE

HEARINGS

Once a bill is introduced, it is assigned to the committee having jurisdiction over its subject matter. Thousands of bills are introduced each year and most are discarded simply because there is not enough time to consider them. The committees and subcommittees exercise the power of picking out a few hundred bills for real consideration, leaving the remainder in limbo. When a bill is deemed worthy of consideration, either the committee or one of its subcommittees holds hearings on the subject. Witnesses who testify at hearings usually are invited by committee staff and their appearances are orchestrated to make a point. If the bill is controversial, the witnesses probably will repeat arguments that have been heard before about the issue. Most bills are not very controversial; they are designed to help specific interests. Often the only testimony will be from

[1] This narrative is taken from Dellums' December 1973 newsletter to his constituents.

MEMBERS OF A CONGRESSIONAL DELEGATION TO INDOCHINA TESTIFY AT A SENATE FOREIGN RELATIONS SUBCOMMITTEE HEARING. FROM LEFT ARE REP. JOHN MURTHA; SEN. DEWEY BARTLETT, REP. BELLA ABZUG; REP. PAUL MCCLOSKEY; REP. DONALD FRASER; AND REP. MILLICENT FENWICK. *Wide World Photos*

those to be benefited. Only where legislation clearly helps some people at the expense of others is a real conflict of testimony likely.

Although hearings are rarely the occasion for searching pursuit of the truth, they are important for a number of reasons. First, they provide help in polishing the draft of the proposed legislation. Government officials who are experts on the subject and who will have to administer the program envisioned in the bill usually are key witnesses. So are representatives of the private groups that will be affected. Often they can point out the practical consequences of using one wording in the bill rather than another, or of adding or subtracting a detailed provision. They can help Congress get a clearer picture of what consequences will follow from various alternative proposals.

Hearings also help congressmen assess the strength of support and opposition to a particular measure. This kind of information—political rather than substantive—is important both to the sponsor (and opponents) of a measure and to those who are on the fence. The sponsors need to know their chances of success and what amendments they may have to accept to get a majority to support their bill. In other words, they must know how much they will have to compromise in order to win. The uncommitted members will want to know the political hazards of voting yes or no on the measure, which interests are for it and which against it. This is important both for purposes of political survival and because many members base their votes on the opinions of particular groups. Some vote with the oil industry, or the unions, or blacks, or bankers, or conservationists, and so on.

A third purpose of hearings is to provide time to mobilize additional support or opposition. A hearing brings a proposal to greater public attention, so that groups outside of Congress with an interest in the bill are alerted and, in turn, alert their members and allies. Sometimes hearings will provide the time and publicity necessary to build a coalition of sufficient strength to push a bill through. Broad public opinion may be far more favorable (or hostile) than the attitudes of bureaucrats, lobbyists, and politicians. Usually the side that thinks it can get wider public backing will try to raise the level of attention in order to bring public pressure to bear on Congress.

TELEVISED HEARINGS OF THE SENATE WATERGATE COMMITTEE IN 1973 FOCUSED PUBLIC ATTENTION ON THE CRIMES OF THE NIXON ADMINISTRATION.
Wide World Photos

MARK-UP SESSIONS

After hearings, the committee or subcommittee "marks up" the bill. The mark-up session is crucial for any bill. It is the point of final decision for all but the most controversial items. Members go over the bill line by line to fix its wording. Provisions may be struck out and new ones added or features of various proposed bills may be combined. Opponents will offer amendments to delete or "gut" parts of the bill.

The marked up bill is then reported by the committee, along with a committee report that explains and defends the bill. Sometimes, particularly when there is ideological or partisan division, there is also a minority report attacking the legislation. For most bills, the committee has almost

FIGURE 11–1

PART OF THE TABLE OF CONTENTS OF A SINGLE BILL PASSED BY CONGRESS. THE ENTIRE ACT IS 24 PAGES LONG.

Public Law 93–595
93rd Congress, H. R. 5463
January 2, 1975

An Act

To establish rules of evidence for certain courts and proceedings.

Be it enacted by the Senate and House of Representatives of the United States of America in Congress assembled, That the following rules shall take effect on the one hundred and eightieth day beginning after the date of the enactment of this Act. These rules apply to actions, cases, and proceedings brought after the rules take effect. These rules also apply to further procedure in actions, cases, and proceedings then pending, except to the extent that application of the rules would not be feasible, or would work injustice, in which event former evidentiary principles apply.

Federal
Rules of
Evidence.
28 USC App.
Effective
date.

TABLE OF CONTENTS

complete power. What it decides is what is enacted into law. When bills are controversial, partisan, or important, however, the committee stage is only the first hurdle. The next stage — consideration on the floor of the House and Senate — is equally crucial.

THE FLOOR

SCHEDULING

Although the committees reduce the number of bills from thousands to hundreds, the press of legislative business makes scheduling a delicate subject with major strategic implications.

In the Senate, scheduling legislation is formally the responsibility of the Democratic Policy Committee. As a practical matter, it is done by the majority leader. He works closely with the majority whip and the bill's floor manager, who is usually the chairman of the committee that considered it. The floor manager is the expert on substance while the majority leader specializes in tactics. It is the leader's responsibility to schedule the bill so as to accommodate any interested senator of his own party. He also keeps the minority leader informed, for the Senate traditionally disapproves of springing sudden scheduling surprises on the opposition. (The conduct of business in both houses is based on a general recognition that all the people concerned will be dealing with each other for decades. In these circumstances, it would be a foolish politician who would think only of the day's issue.) Both the folkways and the rules of the Senate prescribe ample opportunity for every member to have his say on any issue that comes up.

THE HOUSE RULES COMMITTEE

In the House, the path of major legislation is more complicated. Unless it is non-controversial, a bill must get a "rule" after being reported from the committee that considered it. A *rule* in this sense specifies the conditions under which the bill will be considered. Will amendments from the floor be permitted, or will there be a "closed rule" forcing the House to accept or reject the bill as it stands? Will the House be able to consider amendments that do not concern the substance of the bill, or will it be forced to adhere to its "germaneness rule" that forbids the introduction of irrelevant amendments? These are the sorts of technical but crucial decisions that the Rules Committee makes on every major bill after it leaves the committee where it originated and before it reaches the floor. What is more, at the end of each session, when there are more bills awaiting action than can possibly be considered, the Rules Committee decides which bills will reach the floor and which will die. It is easy to see why the House Democratic Caucus has empowered the Speaker to nominate the Democratic members of this committee.

The first stage in consideration of a bill by the whole House is a vote on the rule. Almost always, the recommendation of the Rules Committee is approved handily. In part, this is because the work of the Rules Committee is not done by the majority party alone, but by members of both parties. Its bipartisan membership increases the Rules Committee's power and gives it the capacity to be a major factor in shaping and stopping legislation.

In the past, coalitions between the Republican and conservative southern Democratic members of the Rules Committee were a potential hazard to many progressive bills backed by a majority of Democrats. The worst thing the Rules Committee can do is to refuse to grant a rule at all, which prevents the House from considering a bill that has been reported from committee.[2] This was the fate of several major bills during the Truman and Eisenhower administrations, when the committee consisted of four Republicans and eight Democrats, two of whom were ultraconservative southerners who often voted with the Republicans to deadlock the committee and deny a rule. At the beginning of the Kennedy administration in 1961, the House narrowly voted to expand the committee to five minority and ten majority members, changing the ideological arithmetic and providing an eight-to-seven advantage for the liberals on most issues. This simple change drastically reduced the likelihood that the Rules Committee would bottle up major bills. The partisan arithmetic of the present Rules Committee means that it is unlikely to return to its familiar—if outdated—role as a device for obstructing liberal majorities.

DEBATE

A bill's supporters worry not only about getting the bill passed but also about turning back amendments that may delete or pervert major provisions. If a sure majority for passage is not in sight, the floor manager may agree to amendments in order to win votes through compromise or to attract the support of members with particular interests. In order to avoid giving away more than is necessary, this requires a reliable *headcount* of those for, opposed, and undecided. Headcounts are one of the leadership's most important activities. (They are also made by the White House and lobbyists.)

The Senate's rules permit unlimited debate. This makes it possible for a small group of determined opponents to *filibuster*—that is, to prevent a bill's passage by literally refusing to stop the debate and permit a vote. A filibuster can be choked off by a procedure called *cloture*, which, until recently, required a two-thirds vote. The effect of this rule was to frustrate majority rule. If the opposition felt strongly enough about a bill to stage a filibuster, the bill's supporters would have to be able to muster a two-to-one majority in order to invoke cloture. This tactic is popularly associated with southern opposition to civil rights legislation. Its importance in this respect has been exaggerated, however, for the evidence shows that only one major civil rights bill that was supported by a majority in both houses was killed

---

[2] A *discharge petition* signed by a majority of the House can remove a bill from the control of the Rules Committee, or any other committee, for that matter. While the threat of being discharged (and thus losing control over the bill) occasionally influenced the Rules Committee in the days when it refused to grant rules, this tactic is too cumbersome and irregular to be a reliable antidote to obstructive committees.

by unlimited debate.[3] Both liberals and conservatives have used filibusters to defeat a wide variety of legislation.

Filibusters are most effective toward the end of the year, when there is a big backlog of pending bills. In these circumstances there is a premium on speedy consideration of all bills, and delay is tantamount to killing a bill, since there are so many other measures to consider. By raising the threshold of success from a simple majority to a two-thirds majority, the filibuster increased the bargaining power of the senators whose votes were needed for passage. It gave a minority the power to win compromise amendments as the price of their support. Filibustering became so common in the 1970s that more than half of all cloture votes in the history of the Senate have occurred since 1971.[4] This trend brought about a predictable reaction. In 1975, the Senate made it easier to cut off debate by lowering the majority required for cloture from two-thirds of all senators voting to a fixed sixty votes.

In the House, which is so much larger than the Senate, unlimited debate would be an unreasonable procedure. It would take over 36 hours for each member of the House to speak for five minutes on a single bill. In view of the complexity of many bills and the need to consider the amendments, the need for control of time in floor debate is obvious. Accordingly, the House requires tight scheduling of floor action. So many hours are allotted for general debate, so many for considering and voting on amendments. In contrast to the Senate, which may debate a bill off and on for weeks or months, the House briskly disposes of even the most important legislation in a day or two, or a week at most.

CONFERENCE COMMITTEES

Although a bill must pass both houses (and be signed by the President) to become law, each house usually goes through the laborious legislative process with minimal concern for what is taking place on the other side of the Capitol. A measure supported by the administration or any major interest group is sure to be introduced as a bill in both houses of Congress. Because representatives and senators are fiercely jealous of their own house's autonomy from "the other body" (the common congressional phrase), the versions of a bill passed by each house almost always are different.[5]

The differences usually are resolved by a *conference committee* composed of the senior Democrats and Republicans on the relevant committee in each house, who meet to work out a compromise between the two versions. The

---

[3] For the evidence, see Raymond E. Wolfinger, "Filibusters," in Wolfinger, ed., *Readings on Congress* (Englewood Cliffs, N. J.: Prentice-Hall, Inc., 1971), pp.286–305.

[4] *Congressional Quarterly Weekly Report,* March 1, 1975, p. 452.

[5] There are two fairly persistent differences between the bills passed by the House and those passed by the Senate. (1) The Senate usually provides more money in appropriations bills. (2) The Senate usually is more liberal on domestic legislation. See Richard F. Fenno, Jr., *The Power of the Purse* (Boston: Little, Brown, 1966); and Sam Kernell, "Is the Senate More Liberal Than the House?" *Journal of Politics,* 35 (May 1973), 332–63.

TABLE 11-1
THE LEGISLATIVE PROCESS

HOUSE	SENATE
1. Bill is introduced by one or more members and referred to committee[a]	1. The same
2. Committee phase	2. The same
a. Bill may be referred to a subcommittee or considered in the full committee	
b. Hearings scheduled	
(1) This is the highest hurdle; the vast majority of bills do not get hearings	
(2) Staff does research, requests information, invites witnesses	
c. Hearings: testimony and publicity; transcript of hearings is printed eventually	
d. The bill is "marked up": (sub) committee goes through bill line by line, voting on amendments proposed by members	
e. The bill is reported, accompanied by the "(sub)committee report"—i.e., the arguments for the bill	
f. If steps *b-e* have been in subcommittee, the process is repeated in the full committee, although hearings may be omitted and the mark-up session may be perfunctory	
3. Rules Committee	3. No equivalent committee. The leadership usually negotiates a unanimous consent agreement governing the length of floor debate
a. Holds hearings	
b. Grants a rule	
4. Leadership schedules bill for floor debate	4. The same
5. Floor debate	5. Floor debate
a. Vote on rule	a. Amendments considered
b. Amendments considered	b. Vote on final passage
c. Motion to recommit bill; this is offered by opposition to bill and effectively kills bill if it passes	
d. Vote on final passage	
6. Appoint members of conference committee if bill is different from Senate version[b]	6. The same
7. Conference committee works out compromise version of bill	
8. Vote to accept report of conferees	8. The same
9. Bill goes to President. If he signs it, it becomes law. If he vetoes it, it goes back to Congress.[c]	
10. Vote to override veto, which requires a two-thirds majority.	10. The same

[a]Identical or similar bills may be introduced in one or both houses, except for tax and appropriations bills, which originate in the House. Bills may be considered simultaneously or in sequence. Each house may amend bills that come to it from the other body. A bill does not last after the end of the two-year Congress in which it was introduced. If not passed, it must be introduced again in the next Congress.

[b]The House and Senate may pass identical bills or one body may vote to accept the other's version, but either of these possibilities is rare on controversial bills.

[c]There is no "item veto"; the President must take the whole bill or veto it.

resulting conference committee report is then voted on by each body. Rejection of a conference committee report is rare, because the members, having passed the measure once, know that there is little reason to expect that the conference committee will do a more acceptable job the second time around. As at every stage of the legislative process, there is a presumption in favor of those legislators who have done the work.

PARTY VOTING

Despite the weakness of party discipline, there is a remarkable degree of party voting in Congress. Democrats vote together not because they are compelled to but because they are likely to share certain opinions about policy, because they rely for support on certain elements in their constituencies (labor, blacks, liberals), and because they have a common orientation to the President (either he is theirs or he is the opposition's). The same factors are likely to make the Republicans coalesce around another position. If none of these factors operates—if the President has not taken a stand, for example—then the issue is less likely to see the two parties pitted against each other, and voting coalitions may form on some basis other than party.

Even when an issue is not explicitly partisan in this sense, however, voting alignments are still likely to follow party lines to some extent. The reason is simple. Congressmen often do not have opinions on the issues on which they must vote; and even if they do have some inclinations, they need the advice of trusted specialists. What better sources of advice than their fellow members? Among all their colleagues, the most trusted sources are members of their own party, who share the same basic orientations, interests, and sources of support. Congressmen report that the most important sources of cues about how to vote come from colleagues of the same party.[6]

For all these reasons, party is the best predictor of voting patterns. If you know what party a member belongs to, you can predict his vote more accurately than with any other characteristic. The extent of party-line voting is shown in Figure 11–2, which is based on the most thoroughgoing scholarly analysis of congressional voting patterns.[7] This graph also demonstrates that party voting is much stronger on some issues than others. It is quite weak on civil rights, for example, because scarcely any southern Democratic representatives voted for civil rights measures while few northern Democrats voted against them. It is relatively weak on foreign policy, because the two parties tend to lack fixed positions on most international questions. But it is quite high on the issue of government intervention in the economy.

The skill of congressional party leaders is shown in their ability to take advantage of the "natural" tendencies of members of the same party to vote together, to add whatever incentives and persuasive power they have, to make best use of their scheduling and informational role, and thus to produce more party-line voting than would occur from natural tendencies alone.

[6] John W. Kingdon, *Congressmen's Voting Decisions* (New York: Harper & Row, 1973), Chap. 3.
[7] Aage R. Clausen, *How Congressmen Decide* (New York: St. Martin's Press, 1973).

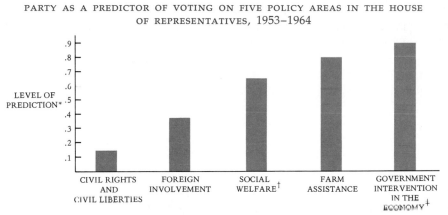

FIGURE 11–2

PARTY AS A PREDICTOR OF VOTING ON FIVE POLICY AREAS IN THE HOUSE OF REPRESENTATIVES, 1953–1964

*A prediction value of 1.0 would mean that every vote could be predicted by knowing only each member's party. A value of 0.0 means that party is no help in predicting votes.

† Includes public housing, federal aid to education, social security, minimum wage laws, and similar measures.

‡ Includes tax reform, regulation of business, conservation, and public works of all kinds.

Source: Aage R. Clausen, *How Congressmen Decide* (New York: St. Martin's Press, 1973), p. 93.

Party leaders are more effective when they can rely on the help of the President, whose techniques for influencing Congress include not only most of those available to the leaderships but also others that only a President can muster, such as the ability to command public attention. We will return to this subject in Chapter 12, when we examine the presidency in detail.

THE CONSERVATIVE COALITION

The Democrats have controlled Congress steadily since 1932, except for 1947–48 and 1953–54. This does not mean, however, that policies supported by most Democrats have been generally successful on Capitol Hill. The reason is the lack of party discipline in general and the major deviation of the southern Democrats in particular. As we observed in Chapter 10, the northern "mainstream" Democrats have never had a majority in Congress since World War II. This can be seen in Table 11–2, which depicts the Republican, northern Democratic, and southern Democratic strength in every Congress from 1947 through 1976. It shows that the southerners have always held the balance of power. A few southern congressmen were fully as liberal as any northern Democrat; others favored particular progressive measures or could be induced to vote for them on grounds of party loyalty or as part of a bargain. The majority of southerners in both houses, however, were conservatives. In any other part of the country, most of them would have been Republicans.

TABLE 11-2
PARTY STRENGTH IN CONGRESS, 1947–1976

	1947–1948	1949–1950	1951–1952	1953–1954	1955–1956	1957–1958	1959–1960	1961–1962
HOUSE OF REPRESENTATIVES								
Republicans	246	171	199	221	203	201	154	174
Southern Democrats	103	103	103	98	99	99	99	99
Northern Democrats	85	160	131	115	133	135	184	164
SENATE								
Republicans	51	42	47	48	47	47	35	36
Southern Democrats	22	22	22	22	22	22	22	21
Northern Democrats	23	32	26	25	26	27	43	43

	1963–1964	1965–1966	1967–1968	1969–1970	1971–1972	1973–1974	1975–1976
HOUSE OF REPRESENTATIVES							
Republicans	176	140	187	192	180	193	144
Southern Democrats	95	89	83	79	79	74	81
Northern Democrats	163	206	165	164	177	168	210
SENATE							
Republicans	32	33	36	42	45	43	38
Southern Democrats	21	20	19	18	17	15	16
Northern Democrats	47	47	45	40	38	42	46

This is why Democratic Presidents have had so much trouble with Congresses that had a nominal Democratic majority. The *real* majority much of the time was the "conservative coalition," an alliance of Republicans and most southern Democrats. Indeed, Republican party leaders confer frequently with leading southern members. The conservative coalition is, as John F. Manley put it, "an informal, bipartisan bloc of conservatives with leaders who jointly discuss strategy and line up votes."[8]

While the coalition often is evident in committee, the easiest way to measure it is in floor voting. The coalition comes into being when a majority of southern Democrats vote with a majority of Republicans against a majority of northern Democrats. By this criterion, the coalition was at work on a

[8] John F. Manley, "The Conservative Coalition in Congress," *American Behavioral Scientist,* 17 (November-December 1973), 235.

quarter of the votes in both houses during the early 1970s. When it did appear, it won about 60 percent of the time.[9]

The conservative coalition often seems "irrational" to observers of American politics, who ask why the two parties do not realign themselves on the basis of ideology—conservatives in one party and liberals in another. Like many such prescriptions for reform, this one overlooks the interests of the politicians involved. Until very recently, few southern conservatives could be elected as Republicans; if they wanted to win, they had to be on the Democratic ticket. Nor could the northern Democrats afford to kick the conservative southerners out of the party. Although they comprise a majority of the party nationwide and control its presidential nominations, they would have been a consistent minority in Congress without the southerners.

The coalition does not seem to have a bright future. Democrats newly elected to Congress from the South are a good deal more liberal than their senior colleagues.[10] As southern voters desert the Democratic party in growing numbers, conservative candidates who want to win will not be restricted to the Democratic ticket. As northern liberals comprise an ever-growing share of the congressional Democratic party, they will have less need of the southerners to reach a majority. Thus, the processes of political change are producing a gradual realignment in the strongest bastion of the old Solid South—the Congress.

VETO POLITICS

We will discuss the President's use of his veto powers more fully in the next chapter. Here we will consider the veto from the congressional viewpoint. Unlike the governors of many states, the President does not have an *item veto*. He cannot veto a specific provision that he dislikes in a bill he finds otherwise satisfactory. The President must accept or reject the entire bill. Thus Congress sometimes attaches provisions that the President dislikes to bills that he either must sign in order to keep the government going (such as appropriations bills), or cannot afford to veto for political reasons. For example, when the dimensions of the depression that began in late 1974 first became evident, there was general agreement that taxes had to be cut to stimulate the economy. President Ford quickly submitted such legislation to Congress. The legislature took advantage of this opportunity by attaching to the tax reduction bill various provisions to reform the tax laws in ways that had nothing much to do with the original goal of providing a quick stimulus to the economy. Ford would have vetoed some of these proposals if they had come across his desk as separate pieces of legislation. But because he felt a tax cut was urgent, he had to swallow the unwelcome amendments.

---

[9] *CQ Weekly Report,* January 25, 1975, pp. 189–94. The coalition is weakest when northern Democrats are almost a majority themselves and thus can win with the aid of the handful of liberal southerners, as in 1965–66 and 1975–76.

[10] *Washington Post,* February 10, 1975.

The lack of an item veto often leads to a game of "chicken" between President and Congress. He vows to veto crucial legislation if Congress attaches certain provisions to it. Are such threats genuine? Sometimes Congress backs down and sometimes it calls his bluff. Calling the bluff may produce a presidential retreat, or a nasty shock for Congress.

Congress can override a veto by a two-thirds vote of each body, with the house in which the legislation originated voting first. The difference between the simple majority required to pass a bill in the first place and the two-thirds needed to override a veto is sufficiently great to make the veto a potent instrument of presidential influence in the legislative process. His ability to veto legislation gives the President considerable leverage in bargaining with Congress over the content of legislation.

OVERVIEW: A BIAS AGAINST ACTION?

The procedures of the United States Congress do not favor rapid decision. The impediments to fast action are apparent from Table 11–1, which summarizes the steps in the lawmaking process. The long series of decision points is a bias not only against speed but also in favor of the status quo. The proponents of any measure must win all along the line to get what they want. They must assemble a majority at every stage from subcommittee mark-up to final passage. The opponents can get their way by winning only once.

Table 11–1 describes the path a bill *normally* takes. Both houses have rules that permit quick action to circumvent many of the potential bottlenecks in this long, tortuous road. For example, discharge petitions or other devices can remove a bill from a committee's control or keep it from going to committee in the first place. But Congress is generally unwilling to clear bottlenecks even for bills desired by a majority. Why? Because what look like bottlenecks to outsiders may look like flood control projects to members. Every year Congress is deluged with thousands of bills, each with its supporters who think that their bill is the most urgent business before Congress. Senators and representatives inevitably become hardened to such pleas. The typical member has seen so many "must" bills come and go that he develops considerable skepticism about whether the Republic will collapse if something—or anything—is not done. Most members are content to let normal procedures work, convinced that occasional abuses are less important than disruption of what they see as time-tested ways of doing business. They trust the committees to get rid of most bills and pass the best ones on for floor consideration.

The easiest power to wield in Congress is the power to say no. Getting things done is not too hard if a member is strategically placed and what he wants has no apparent victims, only beneficiaries. But as proposals become more controversial or promise to help some people at the apparent cost of other interests, they become more and more difficult to achieve. The hurdles a bill must cross grow higher if the measure is conspicuous enough to attract public attention, controversial enough to attract enemies, and important enough to inspire those enemies to exert themselves. These are important qualifications to the simple belief that the cards are stacked against action. (As we saw, Dellums' bill to tap the federal treasury for the benefit of Berkeley homeowners moved to the House floor rather easily.) A great deal of legislation is inconspicuous, uncontroversial, or seems to have specific beneficiaries and diffuse costs. The sum total of congressional action in these areas is a substantial proportion of the laws passed each year.

Thus, it is a little too glib to say simply that congressional procedures are biased against the status quo. Because the committee system means that Congress delegates so much of its authority to quasi-autonomous bodies, it is almost more accurate to speak of Congress as "they" rather than "it." We will turn now to this crucially important feature of Congress —its variability.

MINORITY RULE IN CONGRESS

Organizing congressional business by committees results in a great decentralization of power. Careful attention to most issues can be sustained only at the committee or subcommittee level. The result is that single members acquire great power over particular aspects of public policy. They are powerful because they are the only ones who have done the work and because their colleagues defer to their roles. The other side of the coin, of course, is that every member has his own bit of turf that he hopes will be equally respected.

The direction of federal policy on all but the most important and conspicuous issues depends in large measure on the interests, attitudes, and abilities of individual members in strategic positions. For any particular policy area—aircraft safety, higher education, national parks, soil conservation—the House and Senate each has a legislative subcommittee and an appropriations subcommittee that is decisive. The chairmen and (perhaps) the ranking minority members of these tiny panels are the effective legislative decision makers. We can illustrate how this division of labor works by describing the political environment of the public health field.

For many years, congressional action concerning public health and medical research was determined by two legislators who were extraordinarily sympathetic to expanding federal activity in these areas. The key figure was Senator Lister Hill of Alabama. Raised in a doctor's family and named after Sir Joseph Lister, a famous figure in nineteenth-century medicine, Hill was chairman of three key groups: the Senate Committee on Labor and Public Welfare, its subcommittee on Health, and the Appropriations subcommittee on health. Hill's major ally in the House was John Fogarty of Rhode Island, chairman from 1949 to 1967 of the corresponding Appropriations subcommittee, and equally favorable to more and bigger federal health programs. The year after Hill assumed his Appropriations post, funds for the Public Health Service increased 56 percent. Within ten years, they had multiplied eight times and spending for the National Institutes of Health had gone up more than twelvefold. In contrast to most Appropriations subcommittees, which try to trim the President's budget requests, both Hill and Fogarty would actually increase administration requests for health programs.[11]

The committee system gives great weight to the idiosyncracies of legislators who occupy strategic positions. There was no reason inherent in their constituencies or their committee positions for Hill or Fogarty to be so openhanded about spending on medical research. It was purely a matter of happenstance that for almost twenty years the congressmen concerned with health programs were unusually sympathetic to this area of public policy. This point is illustrated by how drastically the situation changed when Hill and Fogarty left office. A former HEW official who dealt with Congress described the shift this way to one of us:

> They [Hill and Fogarty] criticized John Gardner [Secretary of HEW] for not asking enough, and would add half a billion on top. You didn't even have to go up to the Capitol, you'd just write them a note asking for what you wanted, and they'd add half a billion on top.
>
> Then those fellows retired and their places were taken by very different kinds of men, and it was a whole new ball game. It was like facing Murderers' Row when you sent health legislation up to the Hill.

LIMITS ON MINORITY RULE

Although public health and medical research are important topics, they are not front-page news of the sort that attracts conspicuous and extended public attention. When policies are of concern principally to restricted groups—cherry growers, say, or cancer researchers—a committee's decisions are accepted by Congress almost automatically. The vast majority of members will follow the lead of those who do know and care—the members of the committee. With controversial bills, however, this sort of automatic deference to committee decisions is usually lacking. The more attention and partisan conflict a bill attracts, the less the likelihood that the final decision will rest with the committee. This is because controversial issues provide motivation for members not on the committee to examine the issues in the light of their own opinions and political situations. Even in the most publicized and partisan situations, however, the committee shapes the alternatives and defines the conflicts that will occur when the bill is considered by the whole House or Senate.

A congressional committee is powerful in proportion to the confidence

---

[11] Our discussion of Hill, Fogarty, and the National Institutes of Health is taken from David E. Price, *Who Makes the Laws?* (Cambridge: Schenkman Publishing Co., 1972), pp. 216–21.

that the members of the entire body have in it. Yet, as we saw in Chapter 10, assignment to some committees is attractive primarily to members with certain constituent interests. Members from farm states, for example, want to be on the Agriculture Committee. This seems reasonable, given the nature of the committee system. Big-city representatives seldom can do much for their constituents on this committee. The result, however, reminds one of the fable about the fox guarding the chicken coop. A committee with this image, of course, is likely to have its bills roughly handled on the floor:

> In recent years, as redistricting made the membership of the House more urban, the [Agriculture] committee remained overwhelmingly rural. When it took legislation to the floor, it was perceived increasingly as a single-interest committee that treated agriculture as a client to defend rather than an institution to regulate.[12]

The House Education and Labor Committee is another notoriously mistrusted committee. The reasons begin with the assignment process. The committee is so important to the unions that the leading labor lobbyist, Andrew Biemiller of the AFL-CIO, picks most of the Democrats who are appointed to it. Southern Democrats, who usually do not represent districts with much labor influence, are very reluctant to serve on the committee. In 1975, only two of the 27 Democrats on the committee were southerners. For its part, the Republican leadership wants only orthodox supporters of conservative economic doctrine on the committee.[13]

Because of these pressures, moderates of both parties are scarce on the committee. It thus becomes a cockpit of zealots who seem never to have heard the old proverb that "half a loaf is better than none." As Fenno puts it, "they will prefer a live political issue to a passed compromise."[14] The result is that Education and Labor bills are likely to be defeated or amended beyond recognition on the floor of the House. Over a twelve-year period, only 59 percent of its bills passed the House. In contrast, the Ways and Means Committee, dealing with equally important, partisan, and controversial legislation, had a 94 percent success rate in the same period.[15] In large part this is because the two parties do not assign such contentious legislators to Ways and Means. Its former chairman, Wilbur Mills, was famous for his painstaking pursuit of consensus in his committee before any legislation was reported. A politician who dealt with both committees explained the difference this way:

> When congressmen see Wilbur Mills bringing out a bill, they know . . . Wilbur Mills has done his homework. They know the

[12] *CQ Weekly Report,* February 22, 1975, p. 381.
[13] Richard F. Fenno, Jr., *Congressmen in Committees* (Boston: Little, Brown, 1973), p. 34.
[14] Fenno, *Congressmen in Committees,* p. 234.
[15] Fenno, *Congressmen in Committees,* p. 235.

Ways and Means Committee has worked on the bill. . . . When an Education and Labor Committee bill is on the floor, things are so confused that the Members don't even know who is in charge of the bill. There are amendments coming out of your ears. . . . From the beginning every bill is accompanied by bickering. [The senior Democrats] are all talking at once, vying to see who will get what. And it shakes the confidence of the Members of the House.[16]

The Ways and Means Committee is an exceptionally strong example of minority rule. Its tax bills come to the floor of the House under a "closed rule" from the Rules Committee. A closed rule forbids *any* amendments. No representative who is not on the Ways and Means Committee can have any direct say in writing a tax bill. He is reduced to voting for or against the entire bill. The House generally accepts this restriction for four reasons that provide a key to understanding the power of committees.

First, tax law is extremely technical. Most congressmen feel that members who are not on the committee should not participate because they do not really understand what they are doing.

Second, various tax provisions are related to one another in highly complex ways. Before a bill reaches the floor, the committee has constructed an elaborate package of compromises and adjustments. Interventions by individual congressmen might upset the whole applecart.

Third, many members are under pressure from influential constituents and supporters to obtain special tax treatment. If tax bills could be changed on the floor, they would be "amended out of shape" by special interest provisions. Each member might vote for every other's amendments on a you-scratch-my-back-and-I'll-scratch-yours basis. Indeed, in the Senate, where there is no counterpart to the closed rule and less deference is paid to committee decisions, tax bills are so amended on the floor that they are called "Christmas tree bills" because of the way they are festooned with special tax provisions. When members of the House vote for a closed rule, they are voting to protect themselves from their own worst impulses.

Fourth, the House trusts the Ways and Means Committee to do the job because its members are broadly representative of the House as a whole. This is not to say that the committee is not "stacked" for or against particular interests, but that, despite this, its membership as a whole is respected by the House in a way that some other committees are not.[17]

"SUBGOVERNMENTS"

Deference to specialization in various areas of lawmaking cannot be understood in a purely congressional context. Because the Agriculture Committees

---

[16] Quoted in Fenno, *Congressmen in Committees,* pp. 239–40.

[17] For discussion of the Ways and Means Committee, see John F. Manley, *The Politics of Finance* (Boston: Little, Brown, 1970).

deal with farm problems day after day, they are constantly seeing and talking to farm groups and Department of Agriculture officials. *And they hardly talk to anybody else.* Each of the committees tends to be embedded in a circle of lobbyists, interest groups, and bureaucrats, all of whom specialize in the same set of problems. Ideas for new legislation and suggestions for changes in existing legislation usually come from bureaucrats and lobbyists, who are also the major witnesses at committee hearings. Government officials typically provide the bulk of data about the real world that serves as the background for committee decisions. They and the lobbyists shuttle between House committees and their Senate counterparts seeking to keep the two together. In many issue areas the lawmaking sequence in Congress is dominated by a series of clusters of committees, bureaus, and interest groups, each expert in its own field. Not inaccurately, they have been described as *subgovernments.*

The generous health appropriations in the Hill-Fogarty era were the product of just such a net of informal relationships. The heads of the National Institutes of Health were doctors chosen for their ability and achievements, not on political grounds. Each Institute had an independent advisory council of eminent medical and scientific figures. Some of these were famous "doctor-politicians," the kind of men whose pictures were on the covers of national magazines and who were skilled at using their medical achievements to advance public causes. Working through their advisory councils and sympathetic foundations, the National Institutes of Health could communicate their budgetary needs to Congress, thus circumventing the desire for lower spending of the Department of HEW, the Office of Management and Budget, and the White House.

Subgovernments tend to be limited to issues on which the two parties are not divided sharply and on which the President does not want to take the initiative. With bills involving highly controversial issues of interest to masses of people and important in building party positions for the next election, however, Congress generally does not delegate as much authority to its specialists.

THE APPROPRIATIONS PROCESS

One form of minority rule is so important that it deserves special attention. This is the process by which Congress provides the money needed to run the government. Let us suppose that Congress has enacted and the President has signed a law to control gypsy moths. The law is an *authorization* to the Department of Agriculture to set up a spray program. *But an authorization is not an appropriation.* The Department of Agriculture cannot actually spend money to spray bugs until money has been appropriated for this purpose. So it asks for such an appropriation.

This request does *not* go to the Agriculture Committees. It goes, as one item in a massive annual Department of Agriculture Appropriation Bill, to the Agriculture-Environmental Subcommittee of the House Appropriations

Committee. This is one of thirteen subcommittees on the House Appropriations Committee (HAC). Each HAC subcommittee has its counterpart on the Senate Appropriations Committee.

The President's annual budget request comes to Congress as a series of appropriation bills, each for a different administrative agency. Each bill is assigned to a HAC subcommittee. After preliminary spadework by its staff, the subcommittee holds hearings at which the relevant administrative agency defends its budget requests and justifies its conduct of affairs over the past year. Other witnessses contribute their testimony. Usually, these are clientele groups asking for more money for particular activities that benefit them. For example, the Student Lobby may ask for a higher funding level for scholarships, or the Navy League will argue the case for another nuclear-powered aircraft carrier.

After hearings, the subcommittee goes over the bill item by item in mark-up sessions. Each subcommittee's membership is stable from year to year—indeed, from decade to decade. Thus, the subcommittees have a good deal of accumulated expertise about the operations of the agencies under their jurisdiction. Even so, the limited staff and time as well as the sheer size and diversity of any agency's activities restrict the subcommittee's deliberations. As a general rule, most attention goes to changes from the previous year's budget, on the assumption that the past establishes a precedent of acceptability.

Unlike other committees, which often have the option of deciding not to take any action for the time being, the Appropriations Committees *must* report their annual crop of bills. Moreover, appropriations decisions are not categorical choices between grand alternatives. It is not a question of either accepting or rejecting proposed appropriations bills. By their very nature, appropriations bills are amenable to finely graduated adjustment and compromise. These considerations encourage a nonpartisan, consensual attitude on the Appropriations Committees, particularly on the House side. HAC members are convinced that only the HAC stands in the way of a perpetual wild spending spree by the executive branch, aided and abetted by the extravagant Senate. They are genuinely committed to the ideal of governmental economy. Moreover, if the HAC did not exercise a good deal of independent judgment about the federal budget, it would not be one of the most desirable committee assignments in the House. Therefore, HAC subcommittees cut most budget requests.[18]

It is also true, however, that each subcommittee (and especially its chairman) is likely to look after the interests of its own favorite projects, agencies, and constituencies. Thus the general inclination to cut budget requests is modified by the fact that some agencies have considerably more political influence than others. Generally speaking, agencies with strong domestic clienteles fare better than those with no supporting interests.

The contrasting experiences of the State Department and the FBI illus-

---

[18] Our discussion of the appropriations process is based largely on Fenno, *The Power of the Purse*.

trate this point. Both agencies are in the jurisdiction of the HAC Subcommittee on State, Justice, Commerce, and the Judiciary. Except for two years of Republican control, this subcommittee's chairman for a quarter of a century was John J. Rooney, a conservative machine politician from Brooklyn. Rooney was an enthusiastic supporter of the FBI. His subcommittee always gave the FBI at least as much money as it requested. On the other hand, Rooney was deeply suspicious of the State Department and regularly cut its budget to the bone. The State Department's inability to purchase modern communications equipment for most of its foreign posts—another product of Rooney's attitude—forced it to rely on the Central Intelligence Agency's ultramodern facilities. The result, of course, was to make ambassadors dependent on their nominal subordinates in the CIA.[19]

As this example illustrates, effective control of the budgetary process in the House is centered in the HAC subcommittees. Due to the complexity of the subject matter, the full committee scarcely looks at the reports of each of its thirteen subcommittees, much less tries to change them. It is easy to see why the HAC subcommittee chairmen are widely considered more powerful than the chairmen of most full committees, and why the House Democratic Caucus now confirms them as it does committee chairmen.

There is a good reason for lodging this power in the hands of the Appropriations Committee. Each appropriations bill is a bundle of temptations to the membership of the full House, since each contains innumerable opportunities for the individual member to seek higher federal spending in his district. The HAC must maintain a solid facade of unity in order to defend its bills against floor amendments. Its power is based on its ability to make spending decisions in committee, and this ability depends on unity in the face of "outside" challenges. In order to be able to monopolize decisions about the budget in the House, the HAC must make sure the bills it reports are invulnerable to amendment. Each subcommittee exercises minority rule in the policy areas covered by its jurisdiction. Like other forms of minority rule in Congress, this is accepted by the majority, which, if it chose to, could amend a bill that the HAC reported. But it rarely chooses to do so.

After the House passes each appropriation bill, the bill goes to the relevant Senate Appropriations subcommittee. Senate attention is typically less detailed. Unlike members of the House Appropriations Committee, the Senate subcommittee members have a host of other assignments and cannot devote as much time to careful scrutiny of budget requests. There is no feeling in the Senate corresponding to the special pride the HAC takes in budget cutting. Moreover, because senators have multiple committee assignments, Senate Appropriations subcommittees usually include members from the corresponding legislative committees. They naturally tend to identify with the programs whose budgets are being considered, and their

---

[19] John Franklin Campbell, *The Foreign Affairs Fudge Factory* (New York: Basic Books, 1971), pp. 157–58.

Most of the money spent by the federal government each year is *not* provided by the annual appropriations bills. About 75 percent of all federal expenditures are fixed outlays of various kinds that represent either binding long-term commitments or various accounting devices to get around the Appropriations Committees.

Most of these fixed outlays are money that the government's past decisions commit it to spending. These include such items as social security payments, interest on the national debt, and contracts already signed and in force. Another technique for getting around the Appropriations Committees is called *backdoor spending*. This term refers to techniques such as borrowing money from the Treasury. One consequence of this situation is that the Appropriations Committees, while very important, nevertheless do not have their hands on all federal spending. The second implication, to which we will return in Chapter 15, is that the leeway for new departures in public policy is limited by the extent to which future revenues are mortgaged. Much of what the government will do next year is inescapably determined by fiscal commitments already made that have a prior claim on most of the budget.

sympathy is translated into higher budgets. For all these reasons, the Senate is likely to be more generous than the HAC. In effect, it serves as an "appeals court" to which agencies that have been roughly treated in the House can come for a second chance.

Differences between the House and Senate versions of each bill are compromised by a conference committee. Rather than splitting the difference on each disputed item, the two bodies are more likely to trade concessions. The House version will be accepted on some items, the Senate allocation on others.

MAKING POLICY IN WATERTIGHT COMPARTMENTS

The committee system evolved because of the absence of external sources of discipline and the need to make informed decisions about the issues facing Congress. The system strengthens Congress because it results in subject matter specialists with continuous concern for limited areas of public policy. Congress can be something more than a sounding board and rubber stamp for the executive branch. Congress counters the expertise of the bureaucracy with its own expertise. A legislature that simply considered new legislative proposals in general session or in committees without stable membership, staff, and jurisdiction could not really perform an independent policy-making role.[20] There are so many bills on so many topics that, if there

---

[20] The British House of Commons refers important legislative proposals to *ad hoc* committees. Lacking continuity, staff, or expertise, such committees are little more than microcosms of the parent body and do nothing to give Parliament any independence from the Cabinet, to which it is totally subservient.

were no committees, most of the time a legislator could form an intelligent opinion only by relying on the executive branch. The strength of the committee system is not that it provides specialized knowledge as such, but that it provides *specialists within its own membership* whom the other members can trust.

The committee system heightens reciprocity among congressmen. Many of the bills in which any particular member is interested will not fall within the jurisdiction of his committees. Every representative and senator will often need help from his colleagues. The most natural mode of seeking help is to be willing to give help in return. Although the committee system works on the principle of minority rule, the fragmentation inherent in this situation is somewhat alleviated by the ties of reciprocity and trust among members.

Committee jurisdictions overlap a good deal. Responsibility for broad policy areas like energy, transportation, and conservation is scattered among several committees. While this increases the number of approaches to problems, it also leads to waste motion and piecemeal solutions. In 1973, twenty-six different senate subcommittees considered energy legislation.[21]

Another important consequence of the committee system is a tendency toward *compartmentalization*. Because each committee is supreme in its own bailiwick, it is almost impossible for Congress to gather up a bunch of related bills, compare them with one another, and decide how to devise a coordinated program on the basis of priorities.

The most striking example of this weakness is in fiscal policy. The tax laws are written by the Ways and Means Committee in the House and the Finance Committee in the Senate. Spending is the jurisdiction of the two Appropriations Committees. The committees that decide on spending levels take little notice of the taxing committees' work, and vice versa. It would seem at least that the budget-making process would provide Congress with a chance to weigh priorities. It might consider questions like this: Since there are only X billion dollars to spend, how much should we give to program A — killing gypsy moths in the forests — and how much to program B — killing rats in the slums? But gypsy moth control is done by the Department of Agriculture and is part of its budget, which is reviewed by the Agriculture-Environmental Appropriations Subcommittee. And rat eradication comes under the Department of Housing and Urban Development and is part of its budget, considered by the Appropriations Subcommittee on Housing and Urban Development, Space, Science, and Veterans. Each of the thirteen Appropriations subcommittees in each body is very nearly autonomous; their recommendations are seldom changed by the full committees. The budget passed by Congress, therefore, consists of a number of different specialized appropriations bills that are coordinated neither with the tax outlook nor with each other.

Tax policy displays a similar lack of internal harmony. Tax loopholes or exemptions represent decisions not to tax certain forms of income. Each exemption is justified by the argument that it will provide an incentive for

[21] *CQ Weekly Report,* March 15, 1975, pp. 542–43.

some form of activity that the government should encourage, such as oil exploration, home buying, or charitable contributions. In 1975, tax exemptions totaled about $78 billion. The income lost to the government through exemptions was equal to about one-quarter of the total federal budget.[22] This is a form of federal subsidy of staggering proportions. Despite the cumulative impact of tax exemptions, they are enacted piecemeal. Once in the law, they are not subject to annual scrutiny.

One senator summed up the congressional approach to fiscal policy this way:

> Congress never decides how much total expenditures should be, nor does it go on record as to whether the budget should have a surplus or deficit. The total just seems to happen, without anyone being responsible for it, or knowing with much confidence what it will be.[23]

By failing to adjust spending to income, Congress surrenders control of fiscal policy to the President. Presidents have filled this vacuum by *impounding*—refusing to spend—billions of dollars of appropriated funds. As in so many other areas, President Nixon carried past practices to new extremes. The annual rate of impoundments under Presidents Eisenhower, Kennedy, and Johnson had been between $6 and $7.8 billion.[24] As Nixon's impoundments rose toward $11 billion a year, Congress responded with plans for a revolutionary new approach to fiscal policy designed to restore its slipping grip on the power of the purse.

The 1974 Congressional Budget and Impoundment Control Act established a Congressional Budget Office and a Budget Committee in each house. The goal is to coordinate spending and revenue policy, rather than having it emerge as the incidental by-product of fragmentary appropriations and tax measures. Each spring, Congress is to pass a resolution setting spending targets for each broad area of government activity for the coming fiscal year (which is to begin on October 1, starting in 1976). The budget resolution sets a revenue target and thus determines whether there will be a budget deficit or surplus. This resolution provides guidelines to the appropriations and revenue committees. In the fall, when work has been completed on that year's appropriations bills and any revisions of the tax laws, the Budget Committees review the outcome. If the spring's goals have not been met, the Budget Committees can recommend any combination of raising taxes, reducing spending, or revising the original targets.

Each of the two Budget Committees will have a staff of about thirty-five professionals and will receive help from the brand-new Congressional Budget Office. This new process will be tried for the first time in 1975, but

---

[22] *CQ Weekly Report,* April 20, 1974, pp. 971–75.

[23] Senator Sam J. Ervin, quoted in Joel Havemann, "Pursestrings," *National Journal Reports,* May 18, 1974, p. 734.

[24] Andrew J. Glass, "Budget Battle," *National Journal,* April 14, 1973, p. 527.

will not be considered binding until 1976. If it succeeds, it will be a major change in the age-old congressional habits of committee autonomy. Whether it will succeed or not remains to be seen. "I'd put our chances at about 50-50," the staff director of the Senate Budget Committee observed.[25]

INFORMATION

Any policy-making organization must have ways of gathering information. Without knowing what their constituents and the public want, legislators cannot fulfill their duties as representatives. Without information about problems in the real world and their possible solutions, Congress cannot enact policies that work. We will focus here on the second sort of information and postpone to the next section consideration of how congressmen learn about public opinion.

It is often said that politicians learn by listening, not reading. This is somewhat misleading, for many congressmen have heavy reading loads, ranging from the *New York Times* to research reports, books, and magazines. They do learn a lot by listening, however, and by skimming the written record of what has been said by and to other members. The *Congressional Record* is an almost verbatim record of floor debate.[26] Members either read it themselves or assign this task to an assistant. Hearings and committee reports are quickly printed and distributed. Members also hear a great deal in their daily rounds—on the floor, in committee meetings, the cloakrooms, over lunch, riding home together, and so on.

Government agencies are the most important source of information for Congress. In addition to testifying at hearings and providing official reports, the executive branch responds to thousands of requests for information from committees and individual members. Much of this material comes from nonpolitical experts who try to be objective, but of course this is not always the case. Some subjects are amenable to precise reporting. For example, infant mortality can be described by exact and universally accepted measures. In other areas, the facts may be more elusive, or expertise may be a matter of professional judgment rather than "hard data." Congressmen may accept

---

[25] Quoted in Joel Havemann, "Hill Budgets," *National Journal Reports,* September 28, 1974, p. 1446.

[26] We say "almost" because members and their assistants can look over the stenographers' rough transcripts of floor debate and add, remove, or alter material before that day's issue goes to press. Apart from this commonplace minor tidying up, members insert material in the *Record* to support their arguments, do someone a favor, or make a good impression. The *Record* Appendix is devoted to reprinted newspaper and magazine articles, speeches not made on the floor, and miscellaneous other material.

The *Record,* averaging two hundred pages in length, is delivered to every member's office at 6 A.M. after each day Congress is in session. This remarkable feat helps explain why the Government Printing Office is part of the legislative branch and had an appropriation of $145 million in 1976. Almost 50,000 copies of the *Record* are mailed every day to libraries, the mass media, scholars, and citizens who ask their congressman for a subscription.

without question material from the Bureau of Labor Statistics but be deeply suspicious of a report from the State Department about the condition of our relations with Panama. Much information given to Congress comes from agencies reporting on their own past performance and asking for new programs and more money for the old programs. Few people would be surprised if they did not slant the story in their own behalf.

Congressmen are far from hapless victims of whatever the executive branch tells them. For one thing, outright lies or blatant distortions are rare. The officials involved have to deal with Congress for years, and getting a reputation for lying is not helpful to a bureaucrat who must keep coming back to Capitol Hill for appropriations requests. Keeping things secret in Washington is difficult. Congress gets a constant stream of information leaked by officials on the losing side in factional struggles, employees shocked at their superiors' behavior, and other dissidents. If the President has imposed a policy on an agency against the wishes of its professional heads, they will find a way to let Congress know their side of the story despite injunctions to be loyal to the elected leadership in the White House.

CONGRESSIONAL INFORMATION RESOURCES

Congress maintains several information gathering services of its own. The General Accounting Office (GAO) has a budget of over $135 million for studying how appropriated funds are spent. Originally conceived as a kind of legislative auditor, the GAO has become a major watchdog of the executive branch. It does not provide staff assistance to individual members or committees and is not important as a source of information on problems for which new policies must be devised.

The Library of Congress is, among other things, the largest and most complete general library in the United States. Its Congressional Research Service (until recently called the Legislative Reference Service) has around 360 specialists to do research for members of Congress. This service is nonpartisan and the CRS staff is not supposed to recommend policies. The CRS is not as important a resource as might be thought, however. One problem is its workload. Over 180,000 inquiries a year are made by congressional offices. Most of these are simply questions asked of members by constituents and forwarded for answers to the CRS. It is widely believed on Capitol Hill that many students write to their congressman for help on term papers—and get it in the form of a report from the CRS. The CRS staff includes able scholars in many fields. But the organization as a whole is not a major provider of the information congressmen use in resolving important issues.

Individual CRS staff members sometimes have contributed in important ways to the work of Congress, more through their informal work with committee staff than through official CRS studies. The requirement of political neutrality tends to produce CRS papers that are bland collections of general information rather than pointed, incisive analyses that bring new light to a problem or point the way to solutions. It is difficult to do research on problems of public policy that does not, at least by implication, indicate that some solutions are better than others. Above-the-battle objectivity has inevitable drawbacks in the politicized Washington environment. The heart of the congressional information problem is getting advice from experts whose loyalties are not doubted by the recipient.

Congress's main informational resources are the staffs of committees, and, to a lesser extent, the staffs of the individual members themselves. The Senate Judiciary Committee, with about two hundred people, has the largest single staff complement. The next largest Senate committee has about half this many and most other committees have about fifty. House committees have about the same number, except Appropriations and Ways and Means, with about one hundred each. Because the majority party has absolute control over how many aides will be allocated to each party, the question of minority staffing is always a sore point with Republicans. Currently, House Democrats allow Republicans about one-quarter of the committee staff. Senate Democrats are considerably less generous on most committees. All House and Senate committees combined employ about 2,000 people. Personal staffs of representatives number almost 6,000, and senators' personal aides account for about 2,200 more.

About half of the committee aides are lawyers. The other half consists mostly of subject matter experts in areas relevant to each committee's work, such as irrigation or fisheries. Many are former employees of executive agencies. Some staffs are highly professionalized and almost nonpartisan. Others are equally competent but work only for the chairman or ranking minority member. Some are little more than political operatives for senior committee members.

Congressional staffs are supposed to provide autonomous advice and an expert check on the material provided by outside sources. Although they do increase congressional independence enormously, they do not solve the problem of providing Congress with enough information to do its various jobs. Compared to the mammoth staffs available to the executive agencies and major private interest groups, congressional aides are a tiny handful. They do not provide real experts on all the multitude of issues that Congress decides. No staff member of either Agriculture Committee (or either Agriculture Appropriations Subcommittee) knows half as much about the gypsy moth as the Department of Agriculture entomologists with whom they deal, and yet Congress must pass legislation dealing with gypsy moth control. Some help comes informally from lobbyists, sympathetic bureaucrats, journalists, and policy-oriented members of the academic community.

Most of the informational capability Congress has belongs to it collectively and is not available equally to all members. For example, the House Armed Services Committee staff has considerable access to military information and skill at interpreting that information. They are hired by and loyal to the committee chairman. Some junior members of the committee, who are rather hostile to the Pentagon, often complain that Congress lacks the technical experts to stand up to the administration on defense policy. Strictly speaking, this may not be true. Certainly these junior committee members lack the staff that could help them pursue *their* policy goals. Adequate staff is in fact available to Congress. It is simply unavailable to *them.*

This situation brings home the point that "information" and "experts" are not neutral. If only one side in a dispute can call on specialists for technical advice, it clearly has an enormous advantage over adversaries who lack such resources. The fact that most useful information comes from the executive branch is no hardship to the administration's allies in Congress. The same is true for congressional allies of particular bureaucratic interests. The Air Force, Soil Conservation Service, Office of Education, National Institute of Mental Health—these and hundreds of other agencies have their friends on the Hill whom they supply (openly or covertly) with information and technical advice. The forces in Congress that are at a disadvantage when it comes to expertise are those that cannot call on the White House or the bureaucracy for help and are not senior enough to command the staff resources that come with subcommittee chairmanships.

As we have observed, experts are not useful to congressmen unless the congressmen can count on their political loyalty. This means that Congress needs not *a* body of expert advice, but a number of bodies, to match the variety of political orientations issue by issue. Why, then, does Congress not hire such help? One reason, of course, is that plenty of members have enough already, either through staffs under their command or with the help of allies in the executive branch and private interest groups of all kinds.

We saw in Chapter 10 that Congress is openhanded in spending for creature comforts on Capitol Hill. We think that it is unenthusiastic about vast expansion of its own staff for fear of losing control of them, much as the President loses control of his huge bureaucracy. In fact, most representatives do not hire as many aides as they are entitled to. One congressional staff member remarked in this connection:

> The limiting factor is that there are only 100 Senators and 24 hours to the day. As you multiply staff you just multiply the number of people running around asking the Senators questions, and their answers have to be more and more hurried.[27]

If Congress were to create massive expert staffs to watch the experts in the executive branch, who would watch the congressional experts? If the staffs get much larger, there is always the danger that they will not so much serve the congressmen as capture them. They may become yet another group who want certain things and provide loaded information to help

---

[27] Quoted in Michael J. Malbin, "Senate Study," *National Journal Reports,* May 3, 1975, p. 650.

get them. They often work closely with executive agencies. Instead of providing a counter to bureaucratic power, they may act on the basis of their common expertise to increase the bureaucracy's pressure on Congress. When a generalist sets an expert to watch another expert, he may simply end up with two experts instead of one taking advantage of his ignorance.

This dilemma is inescapable in an independent legislature. Congress deals with it, in part, by sampling. A subcommittee will pick a small area to look at carefully as a sign of an agency's reliability and performance in its entire jurisdiction. The committee system enhances the legislature's ability to deal with problems requiring great expertise, and congressmen learn to be connoisseurs of experts. On issues attracting public attention, congressmen often can draw on the services of experts from the academic and business worlds.

LOBBYISTS

Lobbyists are essential to Congressmen. They provide them with useful information about the merits of proposed legislation. More important, they also provide a political reaction. It is the lobbyist's job to know when the crucial decisions on a bill are being made. With this information, he can organize pressure when it will do the most good — before the politicians have made their deals and formed coalitions among themselves. Important bills are carefully constructed compromise packages designed to give satisfaction to each part of the coalition. Once such a package has been assembled, congressmen are reluctant to disturb it. Each provision is related to the others. Changing one of them may alienate a key faction that has given its consent only because it was given this particular provision in return.

Those lobbyists who are not well informed about the progress of a bill may miss their chance to influence it. In 1963, the Kennedy administration introduced a major bill that became the landmark Civil Rights Act of 1964. When this bill was being considered in the House Judiciary Committee, pressure from labor and civil rights lobbyists resulted in adding to the bill a provision that would, for the first time, establish federal procedures prohibiting racial discrimination in employment. This provision was accepted by both the Kennedy administration and leading Republicans on the Judiciary Committee and was one keystone of the bill's bipartisan majority. The leading business lobbies, the National Association of Manufacturers and the Chamber of Commerce, had always opposed such provisions in the past and had not thought that they had to worry about them in 1963. They did not know about this bipartisan deal until after the bill had been reported out of the Judiciary Committee. By then it was too late to oppose this provision since both parties had accepted it.

In addition to bill-watching, lobbyists sometimes get involved in what might be called *bill management*. There are many bills about which no one congressman may care a great deal. In these cases, lobbyists often supply the energy to keep the bill moving through the mill with minimal damage. They do a great deal of running back and forth at various points in the legislative process, making sure that everyone involved knows what the relevant others are doing. In this way they supplement the efforts of the party leaderships and the executive branch to keep the process moving.

The most effective lobbying approach is through a member's constituents, rather than directly from a Washington office. The reason this is so was perfectly expressed by a representative who asked, "If it doesn't come from my district, why should I care?"[28] By the same token, when individuals and groups want the government to do something, it is only natural for them to turn to their own representatives and senators. Hence it is often difficult to distinguish between "lobbyists" and "interested citizens," or between representing one's constituents and giving in to lobbyists. This leads us inevitably to consideration of the many facets of the problem of representation.

REPRESENTATION

To a congressman, the most important kind of information often concerns not the substance of public policy, but what people think—specifically, what his constituents think. Legislators want to know what their constituents are thinking both because they want to be reelected and because they want to represent them. This seems obvious enough, but the apparently simple notion of representation turns out, on close examination, to be one of the knottiest problems in political thought.[29]

For present purposes we can distinguish three different types of representative. Each of these definitions states an ideal, and each ideal is in conflict with the other two. But all three ideals also are at odds with what we know about the real political world. We will not try to resolve these conflicts or to state our own conception of proper representation, but we do want to focus attention on the conflicts.

1. The *instructed delegate* does in the legislature what his constituents want him to.
   a. In this view, does good representation consist of voting and talking so as to reflect the whole constituency's views? Or to reflect the views of the majority who voted for the congressman? What if most voters do not have an opinion on an issue? Should he express the preferences of those who do have opinions? But if he does this, won't he often be representing "special interests" rather than "the people"? Who has

[28] Kingdon, *Congressmen's Voting Decisions*, p. 144.
[29] For a discussion of the complications and attempts to resolve them, see Hanna F. Pitkin, *The Concept of Representation* (Berkeley: University of California Press, 1967).

an opinion about depletion allowances for oyster beds except oyster farmers?

2. The *trustee* does what he thinks best for his constituents, or for the country as a whole, without concerning himself about public opinion. If the voters dislike his performance, they can always vote him out of office.

   a. If a legislator is re-elected, can we take this as evidence that he is doing a good job of representing his constituents on all issues? Or on those issues of greatest concern to them? Since congressmen usually *are* re-elected, shall we conclude therefore that Congress does a wonderful job of representing the people?

3. The *responsible party legislator* votes for his party's legislative program because he campaigned on the basis of his party's position. He represents the people in the sense that those who voted for him were really choosing his party and thus his party's policies.

   a. People who vote for a candidate on the basis of his party (that is, most of the voters) do not even *know* the party position on many issues, much less agree with it. Does the legislator really represent those who voted for him to the extent that he votes with his party? If so, why do congressmen often vote *against* their party's position because of local considerations?[30]

These views of representation all assume that the voters know a great deal about their congressmen and that congressmen know a great deal about their constituents. We saw in Chapters 5 and 6 that the first set of assumptions is largely unrealistic. What about the second set? How accurately do congressmen perceive what is going on in the minds of their constituents? How do they find out? What difference does it make?

Systematic research on this subject is exceptionally difficult to do and only one such study has been attempted.[31] Its authors report that congressmen try hard to learn what their constituents think about issues confronting Congress. The results of their efforts are mixed, however. They have quite accurate impressions of their constituents' opinions on some issues but not on others. Members of the House were well informed on what their constituents thought about civil rights but were not particularly accurate in their impressions about district sentiment on foreign policy and domestic economic issues. Since race relations are the most emotional issue in much of the country, it seems reasonable that congressmen would be best informed on this subject. Voting in Congress was closely related to constituent opinion on civil rights, but only slightly so on foreign policy. Congressmen were more likely to vote the way their constituents felt about economic issues than they were to perceive those views correctly.

The study also revealed that congressmen vastly overestimate their own visibility to the voters. That is, they are far less widely known and observed

[30] Warren E. Miller and Donald E. Stokes, "Constituency Influence in Congress," in Angus Campbell *et al., Elections and the Political Order* (New York: John Wiley & Sons, 1966), pp. 351–72.

[31] Miller and Stokes, "Constituency Influence in Congress."

by the general public than they think they are. Congressmen exaggerate their position in the public eye for two reasons. One is the perfectly natural tendency of all human beings to have inflated impressions of their own importance to others. The second reason is more political. Although congressmen are largely "invisible" to *most* voters, they are, nevertheless, on the receiving end of a very substantial amount of communication from *some* of their constituents. The constituents they hear from tend to be more articulate and informed. As we saw in Chapter 7, this means that congressmen are more likely to hear from people who are (a) wealthy and well educated, and (b) at the extremes of political belief. Congressmen also are likely to hear from organized interests of any sort.

HOW CONGRESSMEN LEARN WHAT THEIR CONSTITUENTS WANT

Most legislators try to balance the hothouse quality of Washington life by touching base frequently with their constituencies. The average representative makes 35 trips home every year and spends about 40 percent of his time in his constituency.[32] All members of Congress maintain one or more "home offices," which feed them information. Every congressman reads the local newspapers religiously.

Many members conduct "polls" by mailing questionnaires to some or all of their constituents. The results are inserted in the *Congressional Record* and are always good for a press release to the local news media. This is probably the most suspect kind of survey research imaginable. The questions are often slanted, it is impossible to calculate what kinds of people respond, and some members have been known to doctor the answers. In any event, few knowledgeable observers take these polls seriously and their chief purpose is propaganda. Professionally conducted surveys are usually bought for help in campaigning, not legislating.

Mail is an important source of information about what the folks back home are thinking. Some senators routinely get over two thousand letters a day and few congressional offices receive less than hundreds weekly. These figures jump when an issue captures public attention or when a lobby organizes a letter-writing campaign.

Dealing with the mail is an important task. At the very least, all letters from the state or district are answered. No matter how critical or abusive the letter, the general rule is not to argue back. The basic reply thanks the writer, expresses the member's intention to keep his views in mind, and invites further expressions of opinion. The reply may also include information about the issue, but this is secondary to making the writer feel good. The style of much congressional mail is illustrated by the specimen we have reproduced on the next page.

Few members personally read very much of their mail, but they are keenly interested in what it reveals of public opinion. Many offices prepare weekly summaries to give the member an idea of what issues are agitating the

[32] Richard F. Fenno, Jr., "Congressmen in their Constituencies: An Exploration," paper presented at the 1975 annual meeting of the American Political Science Association, p. 11.

Congress of the United States

House of Representatives

Washington, D.C. 20515

July 2, 1975

Dear Friend:

I have received the petition you recently signed as an expression of your support of efforts to set aside the week of July 1 to 2 as National Drum Corps Week.

Thank you for giving me the opportunity to know of your interest in this matter. I sincerely regret the necessity to answer you in this form, for I would much rather write you a personal letter. I am sure you will understand, however, that time prohibits a personal answer to each of you.

I would like to assure you that I am in complete agreement with your position on this and shall do everything I can to bring Congressional approval of this recognition.

I long have been an admirer of such organizations as yours and feel that you are more than deserving of this honor.

Again, thank you for signing this petition. Should you have any additional comments or questions on this or any other matter before Congress, I sincerely hope you will not hesitate to communicate directly with me.

Sincerely yours,

public and what the predominant sentiment is. Very often "the issues around which mass opinion is mobilized are not the crucial ones in the minds of those who frame legislative policy." When this is the case, "the net effect of communication [is] to heighten attention to an issue, rather than to convey specific content about it."[33] At the very least, then, mail alerts the congressman to what the politically aware fraction of his constituency is thinking. This is true even when the member is on the receiving end of organized letter-writing campaigns. In this case it is not the individual messages that count but the fact that some interest group has the capacity to generate hundreds or thousands of letters, and may have the same ability to mobilize workers for or against him at the next election.

Congressmen are more likely to hear from and to pay attention to certain types of constituents—people who are active in local politics, people who

---

[33] Both quotations are from Lewis Anthony Dexter, "The Job of the Congressman," in Wolfinger, ed., *Readings on Congress*, pp. 76, 79.

speak for major social and economic forces, friends and supporters, or any combination of these. The tendency to listen to politically active rather than rank-and-file constituents is reinforced by the fact that congressmen have committee constituencies as well as electoral ones. As we have seen, there is often an overlap between the two, because congressmen seek and receive committee assignments that will help them get re-elected. But the committee constituencies will be even more completely composed of interest groups and political activists than the perceived home constituency. Rank-and-file voters rarely present their views to committees in person. If their views are expressed, it is through an organized group of some kind.

In short, the representativeness of congressmen is not a simple matter. Sometimes they know what their constituents are thinking and sometimes they do not. Sometimes they follow this opinion and sometimes they do not. Generally, they guide themselves by the opinions of the outspoken and organized members of their constituency—and by the opinions of those constituents who know and support them. As Fenno puts it, "Congressmen feel more accountable to some constituents than to others because the support of some constitutents is more important to them than the support of others."[34] Because they overestimate the visibility of their behavior on Capitol Hill, congressmen are often more representative than they have to be for political survival. They play it safe, anticipating more constitutent reactions than in fact exist. But even though they are responsive to public opinion, the "public" to which they are responsive is not a microcosm of their constituency. Instead, it includes a disproportionate number of the organized and articulate—the squeaky wheels who get the grease of congressional response.

LEGISLATIVE CONTROL OF THE EXECUTIVE BRANCH

As the old-fashioned civics textbook saw American government, "Congress makes the laws; the President enforces them." In the real world, of course, there is often no clear line between making a law and enforcing it, between "politics" and "administration." Richard Neustadt provides a realistic picture of relations between the executive and legislative branches when he writes:

> The constitutional convention of 1787 is supposed to have created a government of "separated powers." It did nothing of the sort. Rather, it created a government of separated institutions *sharing* powers. "I am part of the legislative process," Eisenhower often said in 1959 as a reminder of his veto. Congress, the dispenser of authority and funds, is no less part of the administrative process.[35]

[34] Fenno, "Congressmen in their Constituencies," p. 51.
[35] Richard E. Neustadt, *Presidential Power* (New York: John Wiley & Sons, 1960), p. 33.

Congressional *capacity* to intervene in what the executive branch does is considerable. Congressional *willingness* to do so is quite another matter. Considering these two issues, we will look at three major types of congressional power over the executive—legislative oversight, reorganization, and confirmation.

LEGISLATIVE OVERSIGHT

Implicit in the power to make laws is the need to see how the executive branch is administering them. The same is true about the power of the purse. The twenty-six Appropriations subcommittees assess this year's budget requests by trying to find out how the various agencies are spending the money they got last year. Congress includes a number of specialists on various topics who devote part of their time to examining administrative efficiency. Usually they operate from a committee or subcommittee chairmanship that legitimates their interest, gives them a forum and staff, and, through hearings, provides occasions for questioning executive officials.

Congressional investigating committees traditionally have been a means of uncovering shady, unconstitutional, or incompetent behavior in the executive branch. The two Government Operations Committees provide platforms for such inquiry. The Permanent Investigations Subcommittee of the Senate Government Operations Committee has a staff of forty. It can be an important congressional watchdog, although it tends to be a vehicle for the ambitions of its chairman, who can use it to occupy the spotlight on whatever issue is most interesting to the public. The General Accounting Office reports to Congress on the legality and efficiency of the administration's spending practices. It has been one of the few outside forces to penetrate the Defense Department's screen of secrecy and publish useful information on cost overruns, delivery delays, irregular contracting arrangements, and other deplorable news.

For obvious reasons, Presidents and bureaucrats are not well disposed to legislative oversight. They have two reasons for wanting to frustrate it. In the first place, some governmental activities should be kept secret. This is notably true of many aspects of military, diplomatic, and intelligence work. And in the second place, oversight embarrasses the administration and provides ammunition to its political opponents, particularly when Congress is controlled by the other party.

The problem, of course, is that the first reason, which is a worthy one, is often used to justify coverups of incompetence and crimes. The Watergate scandal is the most striking example. President Nixon tried to abort investigations into the crimes of his lieutenants by claiming that further inquiry would jeopardize national security. Revelation of the tape recording of his discussions on this topic was the event that forced him to resign.

In the early 1970s there were several sensational revelations of covert and often unsavory operations by the Central Intelligence Agency and the military, ranging from the secret bombing of Cambodia to attempts to subvert left-wing governments in Latin America. These led to widespread demands for greater congressional supervision of the executive branch. Some critics charged that Congress lacked the will to do a vigorous job of oversight. This accusation is close to the truth. The CIA oversight committees, for example, regarded that agency much the same way that the Agriculture Subcommittees on Cotton looked at cotton growers—as a constituency to be protected.

The CIA is hardly a new issue for Congress. Between 1949 and 1971 almost two hundred bills to make it more accountable were introduced. Only two were reported from committee, and neither came close to passing.[36] It is difficult to escape the conclusion that Congress did not keep its eye on the CIA for the simple reason that most members were not too dissatisfied with the CIA. The congressmen who complained about the lack of energetic oversight were a minority. More important, *they are not on the committees that approve the CIA's budget.* When Congress finally did look into the CIA, it was by creating select committees in each body, not through resolutions requesting investigations by any of the existing committees and subcommittees that had the jurisdiction and expertise.

We think that most examples of feeble or nonexistent legislative oversight have the same explanation. When Congress fails to call the executive branch to account, it is because the relevant congressional committees are not displeased with what the executive branch has been doing, and because members outside those committees are not sufficiently concerned to prod them into action or circumvent them with a select committee.

REORGANIZATION

Constitutionally, it is Congress, not the President, that has the authority to fix the organization of the executive branch. Organization can be a powerful weapon of policy control. Abolishing an agency or redefining its mission or jurisdiction is the ultimate weapon of administrative in-fighting. This is particularly true because in the United States Civil Service, rank goes with the job, not the person. By transferring a program and abolishing an agency, the policy survives but the bureaucrat may find himself unemployed.

Congress has given much of this power to the President, subject to congressional veto. Within certain limits, the President can propose new arrangements of administrative agencies. Such a proposal goes into effect unless Congress votes to disapprove the new organization. By putting the onus on Congress to veto what the President has undertaken, this legislation shifts some power away from Capitol Hill. Congress, though, has not surrendered all control over organization. Ambitious changes in organizational structure, such as the creation, abolition, or merger of existing departments, still require legislation from Congress.

Although Congress has not exercised the power, it can drastically rearrange the administrative structure of the government to achieve certain ends. If it wanted to, it could, for example, shift responsibility for military aid from the Pentagon to the Agency for International Development. Some politicians have argued that by using this power of organization more

[36] *CQ Weekly Report,* August 28, 1971, p. 1840.

vigorously, the legislative branch could exert much more influence over the conduct of policy. Its failure to do so, we believe, indicates the existence of a vested interest in preserving existing agency-congressional committee relationships.

CONFIRMATION

Cabinet officers, ambassadors, federal judges, and thousands of miscellaneous other officials appointed by the President must be confirmed by the Senate before they can take office. The total number of such appointments is really quite staggering. In 1969–71, for example, the Senate confirmed 133,797 presidential appointments.

Judicial appointments below the Supreme Court are largely the prerogative of senators of the President's party from the state in which the appointee will serve. When a vacancy occurs, the relevant senator often will take the initiative in proposing a candidate for the post. Even when the Justice Department has taken the lead in choosing the nominee, his political relations with the senator are crucial. If the senator dislikes the person nominated by the President, he can kill the appointment simply by stating his dislike on the floor of the Senate.

This practice, known as *senatorial courtesy*, is based on wholly informal custom, but is nevertheless an unavoidable fact of life. This unwritten senatorial veto sometimes results in the appointment of federal judges who are quite out of sympathy with the President who appointed them. For example, some of President Kennedy's appointments to the federal bench in Mississippi were notorious racists. This came about because of the power of senatorial courtesy and the inclinations of Senator James Eastland of Mississippi, an unreconstructed segregationist who was chairman of the Judiciary Committee.

Presidents take the initiative in appointments to the Supreme Court. The Senate usually gives the President the benefit of the doubt here, although there are limits to this tolerance. In 1969 and 1970, the Senate refused to confirm two of President Nixon's nominees to the Court. Both men were conservative southerners. One was rejected for apparent conflicts of interest in cases he had decided while serving as a federal district judge. The other was offensive both for the apparent mediocrity of his talents and for his role in attempting to circumvent a desegregation decision in his home town.

The Senate ordinarily approves the President's executive nominations as a matter of routine, on the assumption that he is entitled to choose his own team. In unusual circumstances, however, the Senate may exact concessions from Cabinet nominees before agreeing to their appointments. When this happens, it means that the President's ability to be master in his own house is limited. Indeed, this limitation was fatal to Nixon's presidency. In 1973, early revelations in the Watergate case led to the resignation of Richard Kleindienst, Nixon's second attorney general. Nixon then designated Eliot Richardson to replace Kleindienst. Instead of a speedy routine affair, the Judiciary Committee hearings prior to Richardson's Senate confirmation became a searching inquiry into his commitment to unearthing the truth about Watergate. Since the Justice Department had seemed unwilling to investigate very thoroughly, it was decided to assign the case to a special prosecutor who would be appointed from outside the government and would be given wide latitude and the power to hire a large staff. Although the prosecutor would be formally part of the Justice Department, he would be guaranteed freedom from any control by the Attorney General. Richardson gave this commitment to the Judiciary Committee:

> The attorney general will not countermand or interfere with the special prosecutor's decisions or actions. The special prosecutor will determine whether and to what extent he will inform or consult with the attorney general about the conduct of his duties and responsibilities. The special prosecutor will not be removed from his duties except for extraordinary improprieties on his part.[37]

In the course of his investigations, Archibald Cox, the special prosecutor, subpoenaed documents and tape recordings from the White House. Nixon resisted the subpoenas, and when Cox insisted on obtaining this material, Nixon ordered Richardson to fire him. Unwilling to break his commitment to the Senate, Richardson resigned. Nixon had Cox fired anyway, but he had badly misjudged public opinion. What was widely called a "firestorm of protest" engulfed the White House.

The Judiciary Committee was soon holding confirmation hearings on yet another Nixon designee as attorney general, William Saxbe. With the President's agreement, Saxbe gave the committee assurances that a new special prosecutor would be free to follow the Watergate trail wherever it led and would receive cooperation in his search for relevant evidence. When the new prosecutor, Leon Jaworski, subpoenaed tape recordings of Nixon's secret conferences about Watergate, the President resisted and the case went to the Supreme Court. Nixon argued, among other things, that as a member of the executive branch, Jaworski was his subordinate and therefore had no basis for demanding the tapes. The Court held, however, that the pre-confirmation agreements about Jaworski's independence meant that Nixon had waived his right to give Jaworski orders in this respect. It was these tapes that revealed Nixon's conspiracy to use "national security" as an excuse for covering up Watergate. His resignation followed.

This case shows how the confirmation power can be used to extract from Cabinet members concessions that could cripple the President's authority within the executive branch. But the extreme rarity of the Senate's use of this power demonstrates an even more important feature of American politics—the extent to which each of the major elements in the system respects the boundaries of the other branches. There is a good deal of guerilla warfare along the borders, to be sure. But both Congress and the President shrink from confrontations and blatant usurpations of the other's power.

[37] Aaron Latham, "Seven Days in October," *New York*, December 9, 1973, p. 42.

It is useful to summarize our discussion of Congress by considering what it is reasonable to expect Congress to do, and what sorts of things Congress seems inherently incapable of doing very well.

Congress is good at passing laws that benefit some particular segment of the population by drawing on the revenues and facilities of government without hurting any specific groups (except the taxpayers). In other words, Congress is responsive to policies with specific beneficiaries and diffuse costs. Representatives of the group to be benefited will persistently push their bill along the legislative path. Opposition will seldom be strong. Foot-dragging and opposition by some congressmen can be traded off.

Congress is also good at passing "perfecting legislation"—improvements in existing programs. The close ties between the government agencies that administer the old program and the legislative committee that handles the new changes facilitate such legislation. General congressional respect for expertise and hard work help smooth the path for such bills.

Congress is not good at taking government benefits, services, or favors from a group that has enjoyed them in the past. The potential losers usually can muster enough friends somewhere in Congress to set up one roadblock. Where the attempt is to withdraw benefits from a group in the interests of equity and to save government money, there is no group to fight hard in favor of the withdrawal.

Congress is sometimes successful in passing legislation that benefits the public at large, or some segment of the public, at the expense of another part of the public. Consumer protection and environmental bills are examples of "public interest" legislation that has very wide, almost indeterminate beneficiaries and rather specific "victims." Universal health care and higher minimum wages are bills with more specific beneficiaries, opposed by people who think their interests will be harmed by them. Legislation of these sorts is difficult to pass and usually requires presidential backing and the support of congressmen who seek public recognition by being identified with "good causes."

Congress is not particularly good at coordinating and setting priorities among the many special demands for government services. Congress is good at handling one bill at a time, with the leadership directing the flow of bills from all the committees, one by one, across the floor and onto the President's desk. But the committee system and the general mores of congressmen make it almost impossible for Congress to gather up a bunch of related bills, compare them with one another, and decide how to form a coordinated program on the basis of priorities.

Congress can oversee the bureaucracy to a certain extent through the appropriations process and committee scrutiny of requests for new legislation. It can appropriate new money and create new programs to reward bureaucrats it thinks have been doing well. On the other hand, Congress has neither the staff nor the time to make day-to-day decisions necessary to keep programs going or to spell out the detailed supplementary rules necessary for applying general statutes in particular cases. It must leave these things to administrative agencies and courts. Given its incapacity in these areas, it is not clear whether or not congressional oversight can be sufficiently constant and detailed.

Congress cannot conduct policies that require fast and secret decisions. Its style and organization do not allow for secrecy, speed, or decisiveness. Although the amount of these qualities needed in defense and foreign policy may be exaggerated by advocates of a strong presidency, it is clear that the potential for congressional influence in these areas is limited. Congress cannot easily participate in ongoing operational decisions, but it does provide the executive branch with the resources used in foreign policy, ranging from economic aid to naval task forces.

What is more, past congressional action can limit the options available to the executive officials who are trying to decide how to deal with a particular situation. Certain policies may be limited or precluded altogether by unavailability of the means to carry them out. Congressional responses to presidential requests for defense spending are the most obvious and important example of this opportunity to influence foreign policy. One student of this subject has written:

> Just as struggles within the executive branch over the content and direction of defense policy are manifest as conflicts over weapons systems, Congress may believe that decisions relating to present and future weapons systems, reflected in . . . budget actions, are at the very heart of national security policy, and constitute that part of the budget on which Congressional efforts to influence national security policy are most economically expended. As Charles Hitch, former Pentagon Comptroller, has observed: "These [weapons systems] choices have become the key decisions around which much else of the defense program revolves."[38]

The Vietnam war provided the occasion for an excellent example of this sort of congressional control. During the first years of the war, Congress seldom dealt harshly with presidential budget requests for defense. As disenchantment with the war and defense spending mounted, so did congressional willingness to take a hard look at Pentagon spending proposals. This critical scrutiny was focused on the most strategic point, requests for new weapons systems. Congress began to reduce these significantly by 1970, in some cases deleting all funds for a particular project from the budget. Explaining one such deletion, the chairman of the Senate Appropriations Committee said, "If we build anything like this, we are just going to be handed more and more of this business of fighting everybody's wars everywhere."[39]

[38] Arnold Kanter, "Congress and the Defense Budget: 1960–1970," *American Political Science Review,* 66 (March 1972), 135.

[39] Quoted in Kanter, "Congress and the Defense Budget," p. 137. The relative power of Congress and the President in foreign policy is further discussed in Chapter 12.

By the mid 1970s, its willingness to exercise the power of the purse made Congress a significant source of restraint on the executive branch's foreign and military policy. In 1973, Congress forbade use of appropriated funds for bombing Cambodia. In 1975, it refused more military aid to Cambodia, thus guaranteeing the defeat of the anti-Communist government we had sponsored for five years. In the same year, congressional distaste for further military expenditures in Vietnam hastened the doom of the Saigon regime, for whose survival we had spent so much blood and money. A few months before that Congress had refused all aid to Turkey until its troops pulled back from their invasion of Cyprus. The President and his secretary of state called this a subversion of American efforts to solve the Cyprus crisis through diplomacy. Other observers felt that the cut-off strengthened our hand in this respect. Whoever was right, one thing seemed certain: Congress was having an impact on foreign policy.

From time to time, a formal treaty negotiated with one or more other countries is important to American foreign policy. On such occasions the Senate plays a crucial role because of its constitutional power to ratify treaties. Presidents have been forced to make major changes in treaties already negotiated in order to win the support of two-thirds of the Senate.

The slowness and openness of congressional proceedings make Congress a good public educator. Hearings and floor debate bring issues out in the open and leave them there long enough for special interests to mobilize and make their views known, and for at least part of the general public to learn what the issues are and to express its preferences. (The distinction between *special interest* and the *general public* is very often so indistinct as to be nonexistent. Here we mean by the *general public* those people who learn about a particular issue and respond to it without direct contact with an organized group.) Public access to the lawmaking process is guaranteed by the requirement that the President, the bureaucracy, and interest groups submit their legislative proposals to the publicity and delays of congressional procedures.

Finally, Congress is a good incubator and educator of politicians. It is a large group of policy makers whose numbers include people experienced in any subject that may be important at a given moment. It trains some of them to take broader views of public issues. It provides many of them with a platform for public recognition. Groups ranging from the John Birch Society to the Black Panthers have sympathetic spokesmen in Congress. Closer to the mainstream, the congressional forum creates alternative national spokesmen to the President, potential candidates for his office, and a place where the party that has lost the White House can keep itself poised for the next attempt.

SUMMARY

The law-making process in Congress begins with the assignment of a bill to a committee of either the House or Senate. Each committee elects to hold hearings on some of the bills assigned to it. After hearings, the committee marks up and reports the bills on which it held hearings. The House Rules Committee and the party leadership in both houses determine which of the reported bills get to the floor and in what order. The floor debate stage involves not only trying to win enough votes for passage but the adding and blocking of crucial amendments. Both House and Senate must go through all these stages. If they pass differing versions of a bill, a conference committee will be formed to bring in a single final version.

Despite the weakness of formal party discipline, there is a remarkable amount of party voting in Congress. More often than not most Democrats are to be found on one side of a vote and most Republicans on the other. Party voting is stronger on some issues than others, and the frequent coalition of conservative southern Democrats with Republicans somewhat weakens party lines.

Congress confronts the veto power of the President with a number of tactics designed either to avoid or override the veto or to assign to the President the responsibility for the failure to get needed legislation.

Organizing congressional business by committee results in a great decentralization of power. Thus the direction of federal policy on all but the most important and conspicuous issues depends in large measure on the interests, attitudes, and abilities of individual members in strategic positions. Congressional committees tend to be powerful in proportion to the confidence that the members of the entire body have in their expertise and willingness to work together.

Once a bill authorizing a new government program becomes law, the new program still must get an appropriation of money if it is actually to get underway. Appropriations bills go to the House and Senate Appropriations Committees. These committees see themselves as having a special role in guarding the taxpayers from unnecessary federal expenditure.

The Congressional mode is to assign major responsibility in each area of government concern to a single committee or subcommittee that is relatively independent of other committees. This creates grave problems of coordination, particularly in budgetary and fiscal matters.

Congress has a number of ways of getting information. Lobbyists not only provide information, but may provide continuity in steering a bill toward passage.

Congressmen may represent their constituents either as instructed delegates, trustees, or responsible party legislators. Congressmen use many channels to learn what their constituents want but on most issues no clear, informed, and unified body of constituent opinion exists.

Congress has considerable capacity to control the executive branch through its powers of legislative oversight, reorganization, and confirmation. On the whole, however, Congress has not been anxious to supervise closely the administration of federal programs except for sporadic interventions occasioned by particularly grave discontent with the way an agency has been operating.

Much of the discontent with Congress stems from expecting it to be good at every kind of governmental task. In reality it is good at some of these and bad at others.

CHAPTER TWELVE
THE PRESIDENCY

"T̲HE President of the United States of America is, without question, the most powerful elected executive in the world."[1]

"He'll sit here [in the White House] and he'll say 'Do this, do that.' *And nothing will happen.* Poor Ike—it won't be a bit like the Army. He'll find it very frustrating."[2]

The first of these quotations represents a commonplace assessment of the power of the presidency. The second, Harry Truman's observation on the frustrations that his successor, General Eisenhower, was likely to encounter, also expresses a well-known perspective on the presidency. How can the President be both the most powerful democratic official on earth and so frustrated that when he says, "Do this, do that," nothing will happen? In part, the answer depends on the context. Compared to the other individual performers on the political scene, a modern President is unquestionably more powerful than any other single American political official. But, compared to the size of the tasks before him, not to mention his own goals, the President may not be strong enough.

For some tasks, the President is the *only* feasible actor. If he cannot do the job, no other agency of government is a plausible substitute. For example, Congress is inherently unsuited for fighting a war. Yet often the President is not strong enough. He is blocked by the many other checkpoints and obstacles on the political scene from obtaining policies he desperately desires. Even in the case of wars, his constitutional power as commander-in-chief does not always enable him to get his way automatically.

The limits on the power of even the nation's highest single leader are the most dramatic illustration, in fact as well as in the language of the Constitution, that we have a government of separate institutions sharing powers. Although the Constitution that was framed in 1787 is far from an adequate description of precisely how the modern presidency works, it is the most convenient place to begin.

Political scientists have certain handicaps in studying the presidency. Unlike Congress, which is as open to researchers as it is to tourists, the presidency is located in buildings surrounded by a tall iron fence. The White House and the Old Executive Office Building, where hundreds of presidential staff members are based, is equipped with electric eyes to detect intruders and armed guards who carefully check the identity and purpose of each visitor. These physical barriers symbolize the intellectual screen that makes it difficult for scholars and tourists alike to penetrate the secrets of the White House.

Moreover, it is risky to talk about "Presidents in general" or "the average President" because there have been only fourteen Presidents in this century. The presidency is shaped by each incumbent. Not only is each President

---

[1] William H. Young, *Essentials of American Government*, 9th ed. (New York: Appleton-Century-Crofts, 1964), p. 251.

[2] This assertion President Truman made just before yielding office to General Eisenhower is quoted in Richard E. Neustadt, *Presidential Power: The Politics of Leadership* (New York: John Wiley & Sons, 1960), p. 9.

different from his predecessors, but, his effect on the institution lingers. The office that he passes on to his successor is different, subtly or dramatically, from what he inherited. Indeed, one of the most important things to understand about the American presidency is its susceptibility to personal factors. The American presidency is shaped and reshaped by the personal character of each man who holds the office.

THE PRESIDENT'S CONSTITUTIONAL POWERS

The Founding Fathers were torn between their worry about overbearing executives like the British king and their desire for a government with more power of decision than the legislature-centered system that existed under the Articles of Confederation. They thought the presidency should have rather modest and restrained powers. In their confidence that George Washington would be the first President and would exercise his powers in a responsible fashion, they described the President's duties in a manner so vague as to be subject to vastly expanded interpretations by later Presidents.[3]

The initial clues provided by the Constitution to presidential strength and weakness are largely in Article II. Subject only to congressional power to "raise and support Armies," the President is responsible for the size, equipment, organization, leadership, mission, and deployment of American armed forces. He can send paratroopers to Arkansas to enforce a Supreme Court decision to desegregate a high school. He can send warships into the navigable waters of the world in order to influence, by force or by threat, the behavior of other countries. He must make the split-second decisions about whether to unleash the nuclear defense system. Recent Presidents have exercised their powers as commander-in-chief in very different ways. During World War II, Franklin D. Roosevelt decided only on the most general strategies, picked his generals and admirals, and then left the war to them. Lyndon Johnson, on the other hand, went so far as to *personally* choose individual bombing targets in Vietnam.

Article II authorizes the President to make treaties with other countries, subject to ratification by two-thirds of the Senate. The President also can make *executive agreements* with foreign powers. These are not subject to Senate ratification. Under modern Presidents, use of the executive agreement has dramatically increased to the point where this type of arrangement is now far more common than Senate-approved treaties. Article II also directs that the President will "receive Ambassadors." This is another way of saying that he will conduct relations with other countries. Although he does not have the power to declare war, the President is authorized to engage in relations with other nations that may in fact lead to declared or undeclared wars.

[3] The classic discussion of the constitutional basis of the presidency is Edward S. Corwin, *The President: Office and Powers,* 4th ed. (New York: New York University Press, 1957). For a more up-to-date discussion, see C. Herman Pritchett, "The President's Constitutional Position," in Rexford G. Tugwell and Thomas E. Cronin, eds., *The Presidency Reappraised* (New York: Frederick A. Praeger, 1974).

Taken together, these powers make the President unquestionably supreme—though far from all-powerful—in foreign affairs. Subject only to the congressional power of the purse, the Senate's power to ratify treaties, and the informal realities of political feasibility, the President controls foreign affairs.

The Constitution also directs that the President "shall take Care that the Laws be faithfully executed." On the face of it, this statement may sound like a restriction on the President's behavior, for it seems simply to be a reminder that he has to obey the law. But it also gives the President the power to *administer* legislation. The act of carrying out a general law invariably entails substantive policy choices. Increasingly laws are written so as to leave a great deal to administrative discretion. Together with the constitutional power to appoint officials, this provision puts the President firmly in charge of the federal bureaucracy.

Finally, we should note the sentence with which Article II begins. Sometimes called the "wild card" in the deck of presidential powers, it declares: "The executive Power shall be vested in a President of the United States of America." The meaning of "the executive Power" is vague, vast, and constantly subject to expansion and redefinition. On many occasions this phrase has been used to justify striking acts of presidential autonomy.

The Constitution provides for removal of the President by the Congress through *impeachment* (indictment) by the House of Representatives and a Senate trial requiring a two-thirds vote for conviction. As everyone knows, impeachment proceedings against Abraham Lincoln's successor, Andrew Johnson, led to a Senate trial that ended in acquittal—by one vote. Impeachment was then thought to be a dead letter, but proceedings initiated against President Nixon led him to resign from office when it became clear that otherwise he would be convicted in the Senate for his role in the Watergate scandal.

Whether the President has too much power, as many Americans have argued, not enough, as others believe, or too much of some kinds of power and too little of others, he unquestionably has vastly more power than the Founding Fathers anticipated. This is due, in part, to his performance of

PRESIDENT NIXON
WAS RESPONSIBLE
FOR REOPENING
DIPLOMATIC RE-
LATIONS WITH
CHINA, SYMBOLIZED
BY HIS VISIT TO
CHINA IN 1972.
Wide World Photos

roles not formally recognized in the Constitution. In part, too, it is a result of the inevitable impact on the public perceptions of the President that are generated by the central place he occupies in the real and the symbolic political world. And in part it is simply a product of aspects of twentieth-century national and international politics that have strengthened executives everywhere.

WHAT THE PRESIDENT MEANS TO AMERICANS

We can begin to understand the President's complex and contradictory role by examining his place in public opinion. He is the first political figure children recognize and often the only one. Even among adults, he is the only *political* figure all Americans can identify. Scarcely a quarter of the public can name the Speaker of the House, the Secretary of Defense, or the Secretary of the Treasury. An occasional political celebrity, such as Secretary of State Henry Kissinger, may share this level of visibility, but normally the President tends to dominate public perceptions of national politics.

THE SYMBOLIC PRESIDENCY

Everything about the President seems to be a source of fascination to the mass media—what he has for dinner, whether he makes his own breakfast, how he spends his time, how his children spend their time, how his wife decorates the White House, even his pet animals. The President monopolizes the media. This extremely high level of visibility reflects the fact that two roles are combined in the presidency. He is both the *head of government* and the *symbolic leader of the country*.

The United States differs from parliamentary nations that endow the prime minister and cabinet with political power while the symbolic power of personifying the nation is embodied in royalty or a weak figurehead president. In England, for example, the Queen symbolizes the country; it is her food habits and clothes that attract public attention. The most admired man in England, according to a survey conducted some years ago, was Prince Philip, the Queen's husband. That nation's real political leader, the prime minister, was in third place.

In America, in contrast, both the symbolic and the political roles are combined in one office. In his symbolic capacity, the President heads not just his party but all the people. He is the personal embodiment of the United States of America. When he is photographed every year with a crippled child to publicize the fund-raising campaign for muscular dystrophy, he is above politics, as when he lights the White House Christmas tree or pins medals on heroes. To be sure, he does benefit politically from these ceremonial functions, but they also make him politically vulnerable because, as the embodiment of lofty aspirations, it is he who will be held responsible for national disappointments. As Presidents Truman, Johnson, Nixon (after Watergate) and Ford (after pardoning Nixon) learned, a President can decline

PRESIDENT EISEN-HOWER IN THE ROLE OF CHIEF OF STATE, ENTERTAINING QUEEN ELIZABETH IN 1957.
Wide World Photos

quickly and very far in public esteem. His singular visibility makes him a lightning rod for political discontent.

What is more, the President's high visibility and his role as symbolic head of the country mean that he will be held to account when things go wrong regardless of his actual responsibility for them. An example of a President who became a scapegoat for national ills was Herbert Hoover. Having taken office in March 1929, he could hardly be blamed for the Depression that began that October. Nevertheless, the global economic collapse became "Hoover's Depression" for many Americans. Similarly, the stalemated war in Korea was "Truman's war," Johnson inevitably bore the brunt of the backlash that resulted from a prolonged Vietnam war, and Ford suffered for the economic recession he inherited.

The President so dominates public perceptions of the political world that it does him little good to protest that America is not omnipotent in the world, that the government cannot manipulate the economy, and that he is unable to control Congress, the Supreme Court, mayors, governors, and other political figures whose decisions have a great deal to do with public policy. If there is trouble, he is blamed, no matter how much of the responsibility is his. This vulnerability is a powerful inducement for Presidents to take action, whether symbolic or real, to respond to every public misfortune.

Symbolizing the country itself, as well as his own political program and party, the President occupies a crucial place in the emotions of the public. This is revealed most dramatically when death or illness comes to the President. When news of President Eisenhower's heart attack reached Wall Street in 1955, the stock market fell to its lowest point since the 1929 crash. The widespread mourning into which the country plunged after John Kennedy's assassination resembled bereavement for the death of a loved one. Indeed, psychiatrists reported that patients displayed symptoms similar to those that accompany the death of a father or mother. A survey of responses to President Kennedy's death showed reports of actual psychosomatic distress—headaches, insomnia, loss of appetite, even symptoms such as dizziness. When Presidents Roosevelt and Harding died in office, similar mass sorrow took place. Since such displays do not occur when an ex-President dies, the mourning seems to be for the loss of the leader and whatever is symbolized by his role, not simply for the departure of a revered figure.[4]

Much of the time, many Americans will approve of what the President does *because the President has done it*. For example, although the war in Vietnam eventually became enormously unpopular, at its outset there was strong support for the President's actions. In circumstances of contention with foreign adversaries, there generally is a rally-round-the-flag phenomenon which, at least in the short run, helps the President. In the spring of 1966 when President Johnson refrained from bombing the major cities in North

[4] For a summary of the literature bearing on public images of the President, see Fred I. Greenstein, "What the President Means to Americans: Presidential 'Choice' Between Elections," in James David Barber, ed., *Choosing the President* (Englewood Cliffs, N.J.: Prentice-Hall, Inc., 1974).

Vietnam, most Americans supported this policy. Two months later, when he shifted to bombing Hanoi and Haiphong, there also was substantial support for his action. And two years after that, when he partially halted the bombing of North Vietnam, there was another switch in public opinion—this time back toward bombing halts.[5] As John Mueller observed after extensive study of public opinion toward the Vietnam and Korean conflicts, there is

> an important group of citizens, they can be called "followers," who are inclined to rally to the support of the President no matter what he does. . . . Followers cannot be classified in hawk-dove terms: if the Administration is using force, followers will respond like hawks; if it is seeking peace, they will respond like doves.[6]

Aware of their position as symbolic stewards of the national destiny, Presidents may go to great lengths to present what they consider "appropriate" images. Lyndon Johnson discouraged photographers from taking his picture while he was wearing glasses, or from his right side, which he considered less flattering than the left profile.[7] Ford hired a photographer who specialized in snapshots of the President in informal, relaxed, "non-imperial" activities. This was very much the post-Watergate image Ford tried to convey.

Nevertheless, Presidents are not always able to turn the proper face to the public. When Richard Nixon was forced to reveal the "White House tapes"—the recordings of his conversations about his associates' illegal entry into

[5] John E. Mueller, *War, Presidents and Public Opinion* (New York: John Wiley & Sons, 1973), p. 70.

[6] Mueller, *War, Presidents and Public Opinion*, pp. 69–71.

[7] James David Barber, *The Presidential Character: Predicting Performance in the White House* (Englewood Cliffs, N.J.: Prentice-Hall, Inc., 1972), p. 85.

TRAVELERS AT GRAND CENTRAL STATION WATCHED A LARGE-SCREEN TELEVISION PRESENTATION OF PRESIDENT KENNEDY'S FUNERAL.
Wide World Photos

the offices of the Democratic National Committee—the country was swept by a wave of revulsion at his obscene vocabulary. It is hard to believe that many of the people who were shocked by Nixon's language do not talk that way themselves on occasion. Since this moral outrage was expressed by Republicans as well as Democrats, we do not consider it mere political hypocrisy. Instead, it further reveals how the President is held up to idealized standards of purity out of a desire to feel that the public's fate is in worthy hands.

PRESIDENTIAL POPULARITY

No matter how narrow the electoral margin which brought them to the White House, Presidents take office in a glow of popular approval. This was true of Presidents like Woodrow Wilson and Richard Nixon, who did not even pull a majority of the popular vote. It was true in the first Gallup Poll ratings of Truman, Johnson, and Ford, who succeeded to office via the vice presidency. In the case of Kennedy, there was an extraordinary upward surge in the Gallup Poll between election day, when he won by less than 1 percent of the

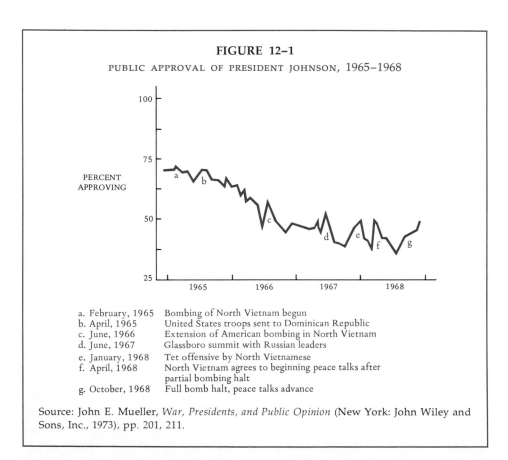

FIGURE 12–1

PUBLIC APPROVAL OF PRESIDENT JOHNSON, 1965–1968

a. February, 1965   Bombing of North Vietnam begun
b. April, 1965   United States troops sent to Dominican Republic
c. June, 1966   Extension of American bombing in North Vietnam
d. June, 1967   Glassboro summit with Russian leaders
e. January, 1968   Tet offensive by North Vietnamese
f. April, 1968   North Vietnam agrees to beginning peace talks after partial bombing halt
g. October, 1968   Full bomb halt, peace talks advance

Source: John E. Mueller, *War, Presidents, and Public Opinion* (New York: John Wiley and Sons, Inc., 1973), pp. 201, 211.

vote, and his inauguration. This first flush of popularity invariably fades somewhat as the "honeymoon period" ends. Popular support for the President then goes up and down in response to the pressure of events, but every modern President except Eisenhower has experienced at least one long-term decline in popularity.

Ever since the Gallup Poll began to make monthly ratings of presidential popularity during Franklin Roosevelt's administration, more than half of the Presidents (Truman, Johnson, Nixon, and Ford) have experienced dramatic declines to the point where more people disapproved than approved of their conduct in office. Does this happen because, as problems are increasingly defined as political, we are asking more and more of government? In other words, is it possible that unreasonable expectations of what the government can do are focused on the President, inevitably leading to a decline in his popularity?

There is no simple answer to this question. In a sense, the remainder of this chapter is devoted to answering it. As our understanding of the American presidency increases, we will be able to compare the actual political institution with the realistic and unrealistic expectations people hold about it.

WHO ARE THE PRESIDENTS?

The Constitution states two qualifications for the presidency. The President must be at least thirty-five years old and a natural-born American citizen. Political reality and American society impose some other qualifications that are almost as ironclad as these formal provisions.

Until Kennedy, no President had been a Catholic, and it was widely believed that Catholicism was an insuperable handicap to a successful candidacy. Kennedy's religion was indeed the most important issue in the 1960 election. But the country's ability to withstand the alleged perils of a Catholic President made this issue vanish without a trace. No one considered Senator Muskie's Catholic faith an issue in his quest for the Democratic nomination in 1972 or a factor in his failure to win the nomination.

Table 12–1 lists twentieth-century American Presidents, the terms they served, their ages at inauguration, their occupations, and the offices they held before entering the White House. As can be seen, most Presidents were in their fifties when they took office. Three of the five exceptions—Theodore Roosevelt, 42, and Truman and Ford, 60 and 61, respectively—succeeded as Vice Presidents.

The occupations shown in Table 12–1 are a bit misleading, because modern Presidents are almost invariably professional politicians, with decades of seasoning in public life before entering the White House. Ford spent scarcely three years in civilian life between his graduation from Yale Law School in 1941 and his election to Congress in 1948. Virtually his entire adult career was in the House of Representatives. Nixon was first elected to Congress in 1946 at the age of thirty-three. He spent all his time in politics including his years out of office, from then until his election to the presi-

TABLE 12-1

TWENTIETH-CENTURY AMERICAN PRESIDENTS

PRESIDENT	TERM IN OFFICE	AGE AT INAUGURATION	OCCUPATION	PREVIOUS PUBLIC OFFICES
William McKinley	1897–1901	54	Lawyer	U.S. Representative Governor
Theodore Roosevelt	1901–05 1905–09	42	Writer	State Assemblyman U.S. Civil Service Commissioner President, New York Police Board Assistant Secretary of the Navy Governor Vice President
William Howard Taft	1909–13	52	Lawyer	Prosecuting Attorney Superior Court Judge U.S. Solicitor General Federal Circuit Judge Governor of Philippines Secretary of War
Woodrow Wilson	1913–17 1917–21	56	Professor College president	Governor
Warren G. Harding	1921–23	55	Newspaper owner	State Senator Lieutenant Governor U.S. Senator
Calvin Coolidge	1923–25 1925–29	51	Lawyer	City Councilman City Solicitor State Representative Mayor State Senator Lieutenant Governor Governor Vice President

dency twenty-two years later.[8] Johnson was elected to the House at the age of twenty-eight and had been exposed to or involved in professional politics since childhood. He served in the House and Senate until he became Vice President and, as a result of Kennedy's assassination, President. After his unexpected decision not to seek re-election in 1968, he restlessly observed the political scene while in retirement, participating in a politicized dedication ceremony of the Johnson Library less than a week before his death. John

[8] Nixon practiced law in New York City for six years, but most of his energies were devoted to presidential politics. See Jules Witcover, *The Resurrection of Richard Nixon* (New York: G. P. Putnam's Sons, 1970), Chaps. 2–9.

PRESIDENT	TERM IN OFFICE	AGE AT INAUGURATION	OCCUPATION	PREVIOUS PUBLIC OFFICES
Herbert Hoover	1929–33	54	Engineer Businessman	War Relief Administrator Secretary of Commerce
Franklin Delano Roosevelt	1933–37 1937–41 1941–45 1945–45	51	Lawyer (briefly)	State Senator Assistant Secretary of the Navy Governor
Harry S. Truman	1945–49 1949–53	60	Farmer Clerk Haberdasher (briefly)	County Administrator U.S. Senator Vice President
Dwight D. Eisenhower	1953–57 1957–61	62	General College president	Supreme Allied Commander, World War II NATO Commander
John F. Kennedy	1961–63	43	Journalist (very briefly)	U.S. Representative U.S. Senator
Lyndon B. Johnson	1963–65 1965–69	55	Teacher (briefly) Congressional aide	U.S. Representative U.S. Senator Vice President
Richard M. Nixon	1969–73 1973–74	56	Lawyer	U.S. Representative U.S. Senator Vice President
Gerald R. Ford	1974–	61	Lawyer (briefly)	U.S. Representative Vice President

Kennedy was elected to Congress at the age of twenty-nine and remained there until he reached the White House. With the exceptions of Wilson and Eisenhower, every President elected in the twentieth century has had at least a dozen years of prior full-time political experience.

There is little in the family backgrounds of the various Presidents to provide obvious clues about the direction their policies will take.[9] Nixon, a conservative, was the son of an unsuccessful grocer whereas Kennedy, who advocated liberal policies, was a multimillionaire's son. Herbert Hoover,

[9] For an interesting and ambitious attempt to find certain of the roots of presidential behavior in the President's childhood *psychological* background, see Barber, *The Presidential Character*.

although wealthy at the time of taking office, was the orphan child of a blacksmith, passed from one relative to the next. Franklin Roosevelt came from an aristocratic family with roots deep in American history. Yet Hoover was a conservative, unable to bring himself to provide direct aid to the poor during the depths of the Depression, whereas Roosevelt molded a major political realignment by championing the poor and underprivileged.

In short, there are too many complications to explain Presidents' behavior on the basis of their socioeconomic backgrounds. Anyone who reaches the White House is far too unusual an individual to be classified according to his outward social and economic characteristics. At any rate, the number of Presidents is too small for statistical analysis.

THE PRESIDENTIAL ROLE

There are several major tasks that any President must carry out. Many political scientists have found it helpful to describe these as *roles*. This term is borrowed from sociologists, who in turn have borrowed it from the theater. In essence, a role is simply a part a person plays whenever he or she behaves more or less in conformity with certain social expectations. In everyday life, each person plays many roles. You are simultaneously a student, a classmate, a co-worker, an employee, a brother or sister, and so on. Each of these roles presupposes different behavior patterns in the way you relate to situations and to the other people involved in your role performance.

In a sense, roles are the "scripts" we follow in going about our business. But as any theatergoer knows, even a well-established role like Hamlet will be performed with enormous differences by different actors. The same is true in everyday life and in the performance of presidential roles. The President has to function as chief of state, as party leader, as chief legislator, as chief executive, and as commander-in-chief of the armed forces. Each of these roles will demand different types of behavior. What is more, each President will play each of the roles with his own unique style which is determined largely by his personality. The role provides only a rough script. To understand the performance, we must understand the personality of the actor.

Here are some of the more or less constant aspects of the script around which various Presidents improvise.

PRIMACY

The recurrence of the word *chief* in listing presidential roles is no accident. Whatever he does, the President is *superordinate*. This is true even in summit conferences with the heads of other major nations, except when he is dealing with one of the other superpowers. George E. Reedy, a veteran aide to President Johnson, describes one of the dangers of this aspect of the modern President's position:

A President moves through his days surrounded by literally hundreds of people whose relationship to him is that of a doting mother to a spoiled child. Whatever he wants is brought to him immediately—food, drink, helicopters, airplanes, people, in fact, everything but relief from his political problems.[10]

GOALS

Each President has different goals and uses different means to achieve them. Nevertheless, we can safely state a few general points that apply to all Presidents. Most important, every first-term President wants to be re-elected. To do this, he must maintain enough popularity and political support to ensure adequate financial contributions and other help.

It should not be thought that the desire for re-election reflects only "unworthy" personal ambition. A President cannot lead without public support. He cannot induce other officials to do what he considers necessary if he is highly unpopular, nor can he influence the general public. The uncertain leadership provided by the Nixon administration on numerous issues, during the Watergate crisis illustrates the costs of presidential unpopularity. In order to lead, a President must persuade others, and a principal resource is his ability to rally public opinion in support of his goals and against his opponents. In other words, in order to do an effective job this term, the President needs the kind of popular support that will help him win re-election next term. This means that the President must maintain his own political position if he is to govern effectively, whether or not he is a candidate for re-election.

In addition to purely political goals, any President also wants to avoid depressions, riots, war, deprivation, and visible loss of American world power. Beyond this, any President will want to improve the condition of Americans at home and of American power abroad, out of commitment to national values and to his place in future history books. As one of President Kennedy's closest aides noted, obviously reflecting Kennedy's own view, "A President knows that his name will be the label for a whole era. Textbooks yet unwritten and schoolchildren yet unborn will hold him responsible for all that happens."[11]

TIME PERSPECTIVE

The President may be the most visible figure on the Washington scene, but he also is the most transient major political actor. We have already discussed the long tenure in office of contemporary members of Congress. Civil servants, judges, and even such informal leaders as interest group representatives and journalists are usually around Washington for many

---

[10] George E. Reedy, *The Twilight of the Presidency* (New York: World Publishing, 1970), p. 24.
[11] Theodore C. Sorensen, *Decision-Making in the White House* (New York: Columbia University Press, 1963), p. 83.

years more than the President. The President is limited by law to only two terms. This creates a divergence in outlook between the President and his close White House advisors on the one hand, and these other leaders. The President is, to paraphrase Shakespeare, but a poor player with a brief time on the stage before exiting. Modern Presidents are in a hurry. None of Washington's other major actors need be.

President Kennedy, frustrated because a tax reduction that he desperately wanted was stalled in the Ways and Means Committee, observed to an assistant, "Wilbur Mills knows that he was chairman of Ways and Means before I got here, and that he'll still be chairman after I'm gone—and he knows I know it. I don't have any hold on him." Mills was only fifty-three years old at the time. Before his tenure as chairman of the Ways and Means Committee ended in the 1970s, five Presidents had come and gone from the White House.

THE NEED TO PERSUADE

This difference in time perspective inevitably complicates the President's central challenge. If he is to make his mark in history, or even to survive politically, he must win the cooperation or consent of officials such as congressmen, bureaucrats, and judges whom he did not choose and cannot get rid of. He can fire high administrative officials if he is willing to bear the political consequences, but as a practical matter no President can afford to discharge too many of his own appointees, whether they are political appointments or career officials whom he has named to the higher levels of the civil service. Because of his lack of coercive power, the President must *persuade* other people if he is to do his job.[12] He must arrange circumstances so that other political actors find it in their interest to do what the President wants them to do.

PERSONALIZATION

One of the most enduring features of the presidency is its openness to change. Since the 1930s, the modern presidency has in some ways become a separate branch of government, comparable to the 535 members of Congress and their staff aides. Yet no other "branch" of government undergoes as complete a change in personnel as the President's. The stability of incumbents makes for a high degree of continuity in Congress. There is lifetime tenure in the judiciary and civil service protection in the bureaucracy. But the President and his chief advisers on the White House staff can change completely on inauguration day. The presidential office responds dramatically to the personal needs and political style of its incumbent.

This personal quality of the presidency is enhanced by our "entrepreneurial" method of presidential selection, in contrast to the "apprenticeship" system typical of parliamentary systems that are not modeled on the

[12] Neustadt, *Presidential Power,* Chaps. 2 and 3.

American pattern.[13] The President takes office at the head of *his* political coalition that *he* has built and led in order to gain *his* nomination and election. He is more like the sole owner of a company than the head of a corporation with a board of directors. There is no permanent party framework to provide continuity from one administration of the same party to the next, as there is, for example, in Great Britain.

In most democratic countries, if one knows that the head of government belongs to a certain party, one can readily predict the names of most of the Cabinet officers. This is not the case in the United States. If Nelson Rockefeller rather than Richard Nixon had been elected President on the Republican ticket in 1968, the Cabinet would have been almost wholly different. Johnson made a number of Cabinet changes when he succeeded Kennedy, as did Truman when he succeeded Roosevelt. For reasons of tact, both Johnson and Truman did not make these changes immediately. They waited for a "decent interval" to pass before replacing the appointees of their deceased predecessors. By the same token, President Ford appointed his own people to most Cabinet posts within a year of taking office after Nixon's resignation.

THE IMPACT OF PRESIDENTIAL PERSONALITY

Because the presidency is such an individual office, it is important to point out some of the ways in which the personal needs and capacities of the President have an impact on public policy.[14] One simple and important variation among White House incumbents is in energy level. Calvin Coolidge often slept eleven hours a night, finished his official day by noon, and napped after lunch. But Coolidge was a pre-modern President. We may assume that almost any modern President works far harder and longer than most men. The only President since World War II who has approximated Coolidge's slow personal pace was Eisenhower, and even he worked a fifty-five hour week, except during the several hundred days of work lost through three major illnesses.

Although the modern presidency demands an active, energetic man, Lyndon Johnson's energy was prodigious even by presidential standards. He habitually began his day with a bedside conference at 7 A.M. and worked until 2 P.M. After lunch and a nap, he was working again by four and kept at it until midnight or later. By this method, he got almost two entire working days out of every twenty-four hours and was fresh during the late afternoon when most people begin to slow down. This was the kind of extra political advantage that Johnson prized. LBJ's constant activity seemed to grow out

[13] Hugh Heclo, "Presidential and Prime Ministerial Selection," in Donald R. Matthews, ed., *Perspectives on Presidential Selection* (Washington: The Brookings Institution, 1973), pp. 28–29.

[14] See in particular Fred I. Greenstein, *Personality and Politics: Problems of Evidence, Inference, and Conceptualization* (New York: W. W. Norton Company, 1975), "Introduction to the Norton Library Edition." Also, Fred I. Greenstein and Michael Lerner, eds., *A Source Book for the Study of Personality and Politics* (Atlantic Highlands, N. J.: Humanities Press, 1971).

of an incapacity for relaxation; attempts at recreation usually turned into political conferences in new settings. When he was persuaded to try swimming, he soon grew so impatient that he had a floating telephone installed in his pool.[15] Johnson made use of his extra working time in a number of ways. For example, he could see career administrators who were too far down the chain of command to expect any direct contact with the President. Flattered and stimulated by personal attention from Johnson, they could be expected to be more loyal and energetic instruments of his policies. Realizing that most congressmen seldom talk with the President and that direct presidential requests are hard to refuse, Johnson often telephoned key legislators about bills he wanted passed.

Yet sheer energy—grinding willingness to work—does not seem to be automatically translatable into results. Herbert Hoover was, in political terms, rather passively unresponsive to the Depression, yet he drove himself from early morning to late at night, rarely sleeping for more than four hours. Indeed, one controversial theory of presidential personality distinguishes between two quite different types of hard-working Presidents. On the one hand, there are those who are able to work hard out of a sense of joy and positive fulfillment, recognizing that they will inevitably make errors and get criticism. On the other hand, there are those who seem driven from within by some inner psychological demon, not only to work hard, but to brood and suffer periodic psychological pain from their work. This theory argues that the latter tend to get into difficulties out of inflexibility and a desire to overachieve, whereas the former are more inclined to self-correcting, pragmatic behavior.[16]

Presidents also seem to differ enormously in their ability to maintain informal give-and-take with their advisers, weigh competing points of view, and tolerate disagreement. Ability to "take the heat" seems to be more a matter of personality than of intellect. Woodrow Wilson probably understood as well as any President the importance of good press relations to his own political position and at times he held frequent press conferences. But he failed in dealing with the press because he could not tolerate skepticism, inconvenient questions, or signs of opposition to his policies. When he talked to reporters, they considered him resentful, lofty, and often angry. Wilson was a striking contrast to Theodore Roosevelt, who began the official practice of making room for the press in the White House. Roosevelt cheerfully held forth to reporters while sitting in the barber's chair for his afternoon shave!

[15] Barber, *The Presidential Character,* p. 52.

[16] James David Barber is the chief proponent of this theory. Franklin Roosevelt, Kennedy, Truman, and Ford are his active positives. Among presidents since the New Deal, Nixon and Johnson are his active negatives, and Eisenhower is more like a pre-1933 President in adopting a passive stance. Barber's thesis is presented in his *The Presidential Character.* For scholarly debate about Barber's position, see Alexander L. George, "Assessing Presidential Character," *World Politics,* 26 (1974), 234–82; Erwin C. Hargrove, "Presidential Personality and Revisionist Views of the Presidency," *American Journal of Political Science,* 18 (1973), 819–35; and Barber's "Strategies for Understanding Politicians," *American Journal of Political Science,* 19, (1974), 443–67.

Differences in personal style from one President to another are visible in even the smallest details of the way they run their offices. The President has enormous flexibility in the way he organizes both his time and his staff. He can arrange matters to suit his own capacities and habits. The ways he chooses to do this can have vast consequences for public policy outcomes. Eisenhower liked a neat hierarchial staff arrangement in which his aides generally reported to his chief of staff, Sherman Adams, who in turn supervised the flow of both paper and advice from assistants to the President. On the other hand, Kennedy and Truman were more like the hub of a wheel. Kennedy often saw his major assistants one at a time, and even assigned the same task to more than one individual. He used this method to avoid the isolation and restriction of information that might occur if a single person stood between him and the outside world. Kennedy liked to hear contending points of view argued out in front of him by members of his administration. He also liked informal contacts with newsmen—often in order to manipulate them. Although criticism annoyed him, he was able to avoid the kind of suspicious "bunker mentality" that plagued Johnson and Nixon when they encountered heavy criticism.

In marked contrast to this approach was Nixon's preference for pondering decisions in solitude and excluding the normal give-and-take of contending viewpoints. He wanted options for choice, but these had to be provided in writing. His staff closely controlled access to him and thus had enormous power both of decision and of information. Nixon disliked reading the newspapers and instead had an aide prepare an elaborately detailed press summary, including television broadcasts. One of his first rearrangements of the Oval Office was to remove the multiple television screens Johnson had controlled from a console on his desk.

There are arguments in favor of both the hierarchical and the more informal systems. In the final analysis, a President will get the advisory system that he thinks best fits his personal needs and preferences. The system he gets will have a good deal to do with the organization of the White House and this, in turn, will have major impact on the way public policy is made and hence on its character.

THE PRESIDENT AS PARTY LEADER

In sharp tension with his ceremonial role as President-of-all-the-people, the President is also his party's chief. What does this mean? Of what is he chief? His party's headquarters, the national committee, is a backwater staffed by a handful of employees. During the frenzy of a presidential campaign it has a bigger staff, but it is still scarcely the nerve center of a powerful and coordinated institution. In spite of some modest growth since the 1920s, when there weren't even party headquarters in Washington, national parties in the United States exist as organizations for the sole purpose of winning a presidential election. They come together only to choose the best candidate to accomplish this goal. Party chairmen can be mildly influential, but they are not major political movers. In the extreme case, represented by the 1972 Nixon re-election campaign, the national party organization was not even used significantly for presidential election purposes.

Since the real organizational strength of the two parties is at the state and local level, the President cannot *order* party leaders to obey him. He cannot command mayors, governors, state legislators, or congressmen of his party to do as he wishes, although he may seek to persuade them.

The President has little control over the nomination of his party's candidates for any elective office, except possibly his own successor when he is not a candidate for re-election. Lacking this power, he is unable to discipline dissidents. Presidential inability to influence the choice of congressional candidates has been well accepted since 1938, when President Roosevelt campaigned in primaries against several Democratic representatives and senators who had opposed his legislative program. With one exception, FDR's targets were renominated. Since then presidential attempts of this kind generally have been considered counterproductive. Occasionally, there have been covert White House interventions in primaries, but these usually have not involved incumbents and therefore did not serve the function of punishing legislators who failed to support the President's policies.

The other major figures in the President's party typically are not part of his administration. They are congressmen, governors, and mayors, whose power bases are independent of him. This decentralization of the parties cuts both ways. Although there is not much of a national organization for the President to be the chief of, by the same token the party is not in a position to impose much control on its winning presidential candidate. The President need not fear that he will be dominated by party leaders. In this sense, the party system reinforces the Constitution's establishment of the President as an independent figure in the national policy-making leadership.

If the President does not command a disciplined party organization, he nevertheless symbolizes his party to the mass electorate. His party's current image is determined primarily by his popularity. What people think of the President tends to be what they think of his party.

Of course, party affiliation does have *some* effect on presidential influence. The mere fact of the President's party affiliation automatically brings him the support of a significant proportion of his party. This is true both of office-holders and party identifiers in the electorate. American politicians generally try to give the impression that they are above party, but Democratic Presidents are more likely than Republicans to emphasize their party ties because there are so many more Democrats than Republicans in the electorate.

In no respect is the President's position as party leader more important than in his formulation of legislation. When Nixon ran for re-election in 1972, he played down his party identification in an attempt to win Independent and Democratic support. Nevertheless, the proposals that he sent to Congress were the Republican program in Congress—not because the Republican party endorsed them but because a Republican President initiated them. The President, then, establishes his party's line. The act of doing so brings support from members of his party and opposition from members of the other party.

THE PRESIDENT AND CONGRESS

In twelve of the twenty years between 1957 and 1977, both houses of Congress were controlled by Democrats while Republicans sat in the White House. For three-fifths of the time, the partisan interests of the congressional majorities did not include a concern for the political well-being of the President. Even during the other eight years, Presidents Kennedy and Johnson found that large Democratic margins in both houses of Congress were no guarantee that their legislative programs would be approved, because the combined forces of the Republicans and the southern Democrats formed an effective opposition coalition.

Congress is a genuinely independent body, unlike most legislatures elsewhere in the world. As we saw in Chapter 10, members of Congress are nominated and elected by their own efforts, not by national party organizations. Each house of Congress, moreover, is independently powerful, controlling its own organization and procedures. Decisions about such matters as who is to lead the party in each house are based on calculations in which the wishes of the President are not very important.

This is not to say that Congress and the President are invariably at odds. What is unusual about the American political system, however, is that, unlike virtually every other democratic government in the world, the executive leadership and the legislature do not *necessarily* work in concert. Many textbooks recite long lists of reasons for conflict between Congress and the President. Boiled down, these lists simply indicate that conflict occurs because the policy views and political interests of the people in these two interdependent institutions are frequently not identical. Needless to say, these interests do coincide in individual cases; or at least they can be made to coincide after careful and extensive political negotiation. Otherwise, the United States Code would not exist, consisting, as it does, of the countless laws passed by both houses of Congress and signed by the President.

THE PRESIDENT AS CHIEF LEGISLATOR

The framers of the Constitution did not anticipate that the President would become the major source of the legislative agenda. Traditionally, it was Congress that proposed laws and the President who disposed of them by signing or vetoing the bills sent to him. It was thought that a President who played too public a role in proposing legislation would be acting in an unseemly manner. From time to time during the nineteenth century, even modest presidential exercise of the constitutional privilege of "recommending measures" to Congress would be greeted with cries of "tyranny" and "Caesarism." As a result, what legislative strength nineteenth-century Presidents had was largely negative. Andrew Jackson first used the veto as an explicit negative means of asserting the theory that the President, as the country's single nationally elected official, should have a major voice in legislative policy. Presidents did occasionally propose legislation, but usually through friendly congressmen. These people carried the burden of influencing public opinion and negotiating the winning legislative coalition. Matters began to change in the twentieth century. Theodore Roosevelt and Woodrow Wilson made suggestions for legislation and played a public role in winning their passage. Wilson was especially active and hard-driving in this respect. But Wilson's three successors once again left legislation largely to the legislators.

When Franklin Roosevelt took office in the depths of the Depression, the country was desperate for governmental remedies to a series of crises. Congress *wanted* Roosevelt to tell it what to do. Banks were failing daily. One out of every four members of the labor force was unemployed, with virtually no welfare programs in force to mitigate their hardships. While Congress rushed through FDR's emergency banking bill in March 1933, the Republican leader of the House urged congressional approval with the famous statement that "The house is burning down, and the President of the United States says this is the way to put out the fire."[17] In the whirlwind "Hundred Days" that initiated his first administration, Roosevelt submitted and Congress quickly approved an impressive list of major laws designed to deal with the Depression. When the immediate emergency was over, Roosevelt continued to propose legislation and urge Congress to pass it. He even made personal radio appeals to rally public opinion in support of his policies.

PRESIDENTIAL AGENCIES: INSTITUTIONALIZATION

With the advent of the Truman administration in 1945, the presidential practice of submitting legislation to Congress became firmly institutionalized. It soon became customary for the State of the Union message, which in the nineteenth century was not even personally delivered by the President, to be accompanied by an official presidential legislative program—including draft bills. Members of the executive branch cannot officially introduce bills, and it is standard practice for senior members of the President's party to introduce items in his legislative program.

[17] Quoted in Pendleton Herring, *Presidential Leadership* (New York: Farrar and Rinehart, 1940), pp. 57–58.

The growth of the presidential role in the legislative process suffered a temporary setback when Eisenhower took office in 1953. Disapproving of presidential legislative initiative, Eisenhower presented no legislative program during his first year in office. This led to substantial congressional confusion, however, for the complexity of national life and government policy had become too great to permit the government to rely on whatever bills just happened to be introduced by various congressmen. By his second year in office, Eisenhower resumed the practice of submitting a legislative package.

The sheer bulk of technical know-how about diverse problems of almost 3 million executive branch employees has contributed to the tendency to think of the President as the country's chief legislator. Every year the numerous executive agencies come forth with new proposals for legislation, both to improve the handling of existing programs and to innovate with new ones. Although the President himself cannot possibly examine all these proposals personally, a presidential legislative program is hammered out of these agency proposals by the Office of Management and Budgeting. Originally named the Bureau of the Budget when it was first formed in 1921, this agency processes budget requests from the other federal agencies. Since the 1930s it also has had the job of clearing and coordinating executive branch legislative proposals.

Occasionally, when a federal agency finds its proposals for legislation rejected by the President, it will attempt an end run to its friends on Capitol Hill. Agencies like the Federal Bureau of Investigation during the heyday of J. Edgar Hoover or the Army Corps of Engineers, which devotes itself to public works which congressmen covet for their districts, are particularly adept at this technique. Such agencies are governed by their horizontal links to key committees or subcommittees of Congress, as well as by their nominal superior, the President. Most agencies, however, are under firmer presidential control. Nevertheless, there are informal ways of circumventing the need for presidential clearance of agency proposals. This can occur because the bureaucrats in the agencies invariably have congressional allies with whom they worked before the incumbent entered the White House and with whom they will continue to work long after he has departed to write his memoirs.

THE PRESIDENT'S POLICY STANCE AND INITIATIVE

For a number of years it was widely thought that Presidents tend to be liberal because they must appeal to voters in large industrial states in order to get elected and because, once in office, the fact that they have a national constituency gives them the perspective to see overarching national problems. Congress, on the other hand, seemed to be more conservative because of the rural overrepresentation that existed for many years and because each individual member represents only "parochial" local interests.[18] But if we look systematically at the period from 1953 to 1977, a different picture emerges. During most of the Eisenhower administration, all of Nixon's tenure, and the Ford administration, Congress was *less* conservative than the President, with respect to almost any particular piece of major legislation.

Thus, one of the main arguments for casting the President in the role of chief legislator—that he wants to innovate whereas Congress wants to stand still—does not hold water. Even during the New Deal, Congress was responsible for major innovative legislation.[19] During the two Democratic administrations of the 1960s, congressmen took the lead in pioneering legislation in consumer protection, conservation, and automobile safety. In these and other areas, important innovative bills were supported by Presidents only after they were prodded into action by enterprising senators and congressmen. It was the legislators who identified problems, proposed solutions, refined those solutions through consultation with interested groups, and stimulated public opinion to a greater awareness of both the problems and the possible solutions. Of course, once the President decides to support a proposal, it is in his interest to put his own brand on it so that the credit will go to him rather than to the congressmen who may have done much of the early spadework in identifying the problem and building support for the proposed solution.

A bill controlling the drug industry, signed into law by Kennedy in 1962, illustrates all of these tendencies—the congressional function of identifying problems, the presidential tendency to steal congressional thunder, and the weakness of the argument that Congress is conservative while Democratic presidents are liberal. During the last days of the Eisenhower administration, a subcommittee of the Senate Judiciary Committee chaired by Senator Estes Kefauver began hearings on pricing, advertising, patent policy, and other aspects of safety and competition in the drug industry. Stretching over several years, Kefauver's hearings sensationally demonstrated that the drug industry was making enormous profits and was spending far more on advertising than on research.

Kefauver drafted a bill to deal with the worst of these abuses but found the opposition so strong that he could not even get his bill considered by the full Judiciary Committee. He sought support from the White House. But reforming the drug industry was not one of Kennedy's priorities. Wary of alienating congressmen whose help he wanted for matters of greater importance to him, Kennedy decided not to support Kefauver's bill. Instead, he sent his own drug message and draft legislation to Congress. It fell far short of what Kefauver had proposed. Without consulting Kefauver, members of the administration met with the very conservative Senator Eastland, Chairman of the Judiciary Committee, to work out a compromise that drastically reduced Kefauver's bill.

[18] See Nelson W. Polsby, *Congress and the Presidency,* 2nd ed. (Englewood Cliffs, N. J.: Prentice-Hall, Inc., 1971), Chap. 2.

[19] Lawrence H. Chamberlain, "The President, Congress, and Legislation," *Political Science Quarterly,* 61 (March 1946), 42–60.

At this point, the thalidomide scandal broke. A worldwide uproar resulted when it was revealed that the sedative thalidomide caused pregnant women to give birth to tragically crippled babies. His hand forced by this publicity, Kennedy made a television speech in favor of a stronger drug bill. Pressed hard by Kefauver, the Kennedy-Eastland coalition strengthened its bill somewhat, although the result still fell short of what Kefauver had originally drafted. [20]

Once he decided to play a legislative advocacy role, Kennedy did his best to gain credit for drug legislation himself and tended to bypass Kefauver both in public recognition and in private decision making. His intervention made the drug bill a party issue and thus rallied to its support many Democratic senators and congressmen who were not fervent believers in the cause but who were loyal Democrats prepared to support their President. Although the President did not initiate the ideas and specific proposals in this major legislation, his support was necessary to make passage of the bill a realistic possibility. As a Kefauver proposal it was doomed, but as a Kennedy proposal it became law.

Often, the question of where ideas originally come from is almost impossible to sort out. Many bureaucrats, congressmen, and lobbyists have pet ideas for dealing with problems that are not generally recognized or arouse no political interest. To the President, Congress is something like a cafeteria — he usually can find what he likes among the innumerable bills that have been introduced by various members. When the time seems ripe, such ideas become more publicized. If their advocates are lucky, the President will seize upon them and lend them his prestige and support. Thus the President's distinctive contributions to legislation include *focus, leverage,* and *party image.* If he does not provide all the major items on the legislative agenda, his proposals at least establish its major outlines.

LEGISLATIVE LIAISON

How does the President get Congress to do what he wants? By far the most important source of presidential influence is the fact that *his program is the program of his party in Congress.* This is not to say, of course, that all members of his party automatically will vote for what he proposes, but only that his program provides a focus for his party's congressional membership.

Once the President advocates a legislative measure, he is assured the strong support of those members of both parties who already were enthusiastic about it. He is unlikely to win over out-and-out opponents from either party, especially if the measure contradicts deeply felt views of theirs or seems not to be in the interest of their districts. But at least some members of the President's party who would otherwise be reluctant to support the bill will do so when the magic words are spoken: "The President is very interested in this bill and really would like to have your help." Presi-

---

[20] Richard Harris, *The Real Voice* (New York: The Macmillan Company, 1964).

dents, even relatively unpopular ones, have both an aura of importance and a wide array of rewards and punishments to dish out.

As Presidents have come to play an increasingly active legislative role, the need has become recognized for specialists in the White House who can deal with Capitol Hill on the President's behalf. This was done on an *ad hoc* basis by Roosevelt and Truman. During the relatively undemanding administration of Eisenhower, a formal legislative liaison staff was organized in the White House, largely at the initiative of Bryce Harlow, an Eisenhower aide who, for the previous several years, had systematically managed the Pentagon's liaison with Capitol Hill. Ike's lack of interest in day-to-day politics encouraged him to expand the White House staff to handle formally much of what had been done informally and on a personal basis by Truman and Roosevelt. Kennedy, who had both a slim majority in Congress and ambitious legislative plans, gave Lawrence O'Brien, one of his most trusted and intimate advisers, responsibility for dealing with Capitol Hill. O'Brien's operation occupied a central place in the White House, and since then legislative liaison has been one of the major formal activities of the President's staff.

As a general rule, White House attempts to build support for the President's program are directed at members of his party whose support of particular bills is uncertain. In many respects, the techniques and perspectives of the White House liaison people resemble those of the congressional party leadership. Like the congressional leaders, the White House aides are less concerned with the substance of policies than with getting them passed or blocking them. Liaison aides devote a good deal of time to head counting, trying to find out who will support a particular measure, who is certain to be against it, who is on the fence, and how many votes can be swayed by particular changes in the bill or other influences. They work in cooperation with the congressional leadership of the President's party.

PRESIDENT FORD HOLDS AN INFORMAL CHAT WITH REP. LESLIE ARENDS
IN THE OVAL OFFICE. *Photo by David Hume Kennerly.*
Wide World Photos

In attempting to exercise influence over congressmen, the President makes use of the following sources of leverage:

PATRONAGE. Although there are fewer patronage jobs in the federal government than in Chicago, New York, Philadelphia, or a number of other cities, counties, and states, it is nevertheless true that many of the available federal appointive jobs are highly desirable. Senators and congressmen are interested in gaining these appointments for their own political supporters. Presidents normally make these appointments with some care in order to get the most political mileage out of them.

PORK BARREL. Every year the federal government makes tens of thousands of decisions to spend money on particular projects. These include dams, beach reclamation programs, small boat marinas, model cities projects, urban renewal projects, highways, airports, hospitals, college dormitories, and numerous other possibilities. Politics plays a greater role in deciding where and when to build a dam than a cancer research facility. Different Presidents have different attitudes about the extent to which political considerations should dictate decisions about local federal expenditures. Nevertheless, even the most fastidious administration will recognize that funding for some categories of projects can be allocated in accordance with political considerations. Because congressmen and senators are always eager to obtain federal projects for their constituents, the White House can use this power—which in some cases is at the sole discretion of the executive branch—to get favorable votes in Congress.

THE PRESIDENT'S PRESENCE. The President is so preeminently the most important person in the country that any sort of connection with him is highly prized—except in such unusual situations as the second Nixon administration, when the President seemed so unpopular that even members of his party sought to disassociate themselves from him. Congressmen value help from the President in fund raising or other campaign activities. Even so simple a thing as a hometown newspaper photograph of a congressman in the President's presence or a presidential appearance in the congressman's district goes a long way toward enhancing the legislator's image as an important person. Any suggestions of access to or influence with the President are considered great boons in Washington and in the home constituency. Even such apparently trivial tokens as matchbooks with the White House seal are highly prized as symbols of presidential intimacy. Congressmen who offend the President may not be able to send their important constituents on uncrowded VIP tours of the White House, thus avoiding throngs of ordinary citizens who crowd through the East Wing after standing in line outside for hours.

USE OF INFLUENTIAL CONSTITUENTS. The federal government can influence the fortunes of a very large number of people who do business with it, are regulated by it, or have ambitions that can be frustrated or satisfied by it.

In many cases, the people who are dependent upon federal agency rulings are important supporters of key congressmen and senators. Presidents can use their powers over executive agencies to orchestrate lobbying campaigns.

THE PRESIDENT AND THE EXECUTIVE BRANCH

In the summer of 1962, President Kennedy ordered the removal of obsolete, unreliable nuclear missiles that the United States had stationed in Turkey. His instructions vanished into the labyrinth of State Department policy making. The fall of that year brought the Cuban Missile Crisis, when the Kennedy administration tried desperately to reverse a Soviet decision to locate nuclear missiles in Cuba. The Russians proposed linking the removal of their secretly installed missiles from Cuba to the removal of American missiles from Turkey. Kennedy was enraged that the American weapons were still in Turkey, and embarrassed because, although he did not want them there, he also felt it would look like a lack of resolve in facing the Soviet Union if he appeared to be removing the missiles as a concession. Kennedy asked one of his aides, "Just to set the record straight, will you find out when was the last time I asked to have those damned missiles taken out of Turkey? Not the first five times I asked for their removal, just the date of the last time." [21]

If Kennedy had had nothing else on his mind that summer, he could readily have had the missiles out of Turkey before they became a complication to American diplomacy. But he had a multitude of other problems and had no time to impose his will on a dilatory Department of State. Sheer time limitations often make it impossible for the President fully to control the massive executive branch, even when he and his agency officials agree on policy and the latter are not simply delaying out of bureaucratic inertia.

Although the President is the individual in whom "the executive Power shall be vested," all modern Presidents have complained bitterly about their difficulties in getting the executive departments to do what they want. In many accounts of recent administrations, it seems that the principal villains are not Russians or members of the other party, but the permanent civil service of the United States. [22] Some of the reasons for this will be explored in the next chapter, which deals with the administrative branch.

Although the President may not have full control of the federal bureau-

---

[21] Quoted in Kenneth P. O'Donnell and David F. Powers, with Joe McCarthy, *Johnny, We Hardly Knew Ye* (New York: Pocket Books, 1973), p. 390.

[22] This perspective is particularly striking in the accounts of the Kennedy administration written by his former assistants. See especially Theodore C. Sorensen, *Kennedy* (New York: Harper & Row, 1965); and Arthur C. Schlesinger, Jr., *A Thousand Days* (Boston: Houghton Mifflin, 1965). Also see Rowland Evans, Jr., and Robert D. Novak, *Nixon in the White House: The Frustration of Power,* Vintage Books ed. (New York: Random House, 1972); and Thomas E. Cronin, "'Everybody Believes in Democracy Until He Gets to the White House . . .': An Examination of White House-Departmental Relations," in *Law and Contemporary Problems,* 35 (Summer 1970), 573–625.

cracy, he does have considerable influence over it. Let us now examine some of the tools of that influence.

PRESIDENTIAL APPOINTMENTS

The permanent civil service of the federal government consists of almost 3 million civilians, plus around 2 million uniformed servicemen. To supervise this multitude of bureaucrats, the President has available only about 6,700 appointive positions. These are "the President's people," the officials through whom he imposes his policies on the vast body of the permanent government. Since he has so few people to help him direct the behavior of so many others, the President must pay a great deal of attention to filling this handful of positions. Judicious use of the appointing power is one of the most pressing tasks facing any newly elected President, not only for the legislative liaison reasons discussed above, but also for purposes of establishing direct presidential mastery of his own branch.

Within days after the election and thus two months before entering office, recent Presidents-elect have established special personnel selection teams which generate long lists of prospects for presidential appointments. The names on these lists come from volunteers, congressional and party leader recommendations, general tips, and sometimes from executive recruiting firms. Presidents lean toward one of two patterns, although all have mixed the two in practice. In one, the President and his advisers concentrate on picking the Cabinet, leaving the Cabinet secretaries free to find their own subordinates—although the White House usually will provide plenty of suggestions. This was Nixon's first-term practice. He later regretted it and, during the pre-Watergate scandal period of his second term, he actively sought to substitute Nixon loyalists for many of the first-term appointees. The other pattern, which was more Kennedy's mode, finds the President active in all levels of political appointment while each Cabinet member negotiates with the President's team about appointments in his own department. Under either pattern, it is rare to find any subordinate appointment imposed on a Cabinet member against his will, although under the second pattern a new Cabinet member may find that several of his subordinates have already been appointed before he himself has been selected. Four factors seem to determine the recruitment of the new presidential team.

TALENT OR EXPERTISE. Each new administration looks hard for truly qualified individuals. Typically, they are in relatively short supply. Most administrations find themselves with far fewer available options than they would like. The problem is often finding someone of sufficient competence who will take the job rather than choosing among eager applicants. The skills prized in high presidential appointees are not specific familiarity with particular issue areas, but more general ability to administer large organizations in political situations. In a career of less than five years in the Nixon administration, Elliot Richardson, a highly respected administrator, served as Undersecretary of State, Secretary of Health, Education, and Welfare, Secretary of Defense, and Attorney General. Shortly after taking office, President Ford appointed Richardson Ambassador to England, and in late 1975 he made him Secretary of Commerce.

POLITICAL CONSIDERATIONS. Party workers are pushed for appointment by those around the President and in Congress who want to reward faithful service. A second sort of political consideration applies most to those agencies strongly oriented to specific clienteles. With departments such as Labor, Agriculture, HEW, and Transportation, the relevant pressure groups want appointments for people who reflect their own points of view. For all practical purposes, these groups can exercise something close to a veto power. Although presidential willingness to respond to such pressure groups is sometimes denounced as a "sellout to the interests," in very practical terms it is necessary and serves a useful purpose. Officials in these agencies have to work with the people in the private sector who make up these clientele groups. Making a faith healer Assistant Secretary for Health in the Department of HEW would not do much to bring government and the medical profession into partnership, nor would it make sense to appoint a pacifist as Secretary of the Army or a professional strikebreaker as Secretary of Labor.

LOYALTY. A third consideration is especially important. Appointees should be supporters of the President's policy positions and of the President himself. Obviously, in many instances these political considerations run at cross purposes. This is particularly the case when the appointment power is delegated downward from the White House. In that case, satisfying interest groups is likely to become more important than personal loyalty to the President. When the President plays an active role in the appointment process, he is liable to weigh loyalty to himself most heavily.

AVAILABILITY. Most people likely to be considered for a presidential appointment would face major financial loss if they were to accept the post. Federal executive salaries may seem high compared to average income levels, but they are dramatically lower than those available to top executives and professionals in the private sector (see Table 12–2). What is more, conflict of interest laws often require newly-appointed public officials to give up investments. In extreme cases, such losses have amounted to millions of dollars. Although young executives have fewer assets than their older colleagues, and therefore face this problem in less acute form, they are often reluctant to go into government service because they are on career ladders and may find their rivals gaining on them if they take a couple of years out in Washington. Another factor that discourages experienced private executives from taking government positions is the realization that the holders of such positions are subject to criticism by Congress, the press, and interest groups.

For all these reasons, the appointment process can turn into a desperate search. It took the Nixon administration a year to fill the political posts

ELLIOT L. RICHARDSON IS REPRESENTATIVE OF
CABINET-LEVEL APPOINTEES. IN THE PAST FIVE
YEARS, RICHARDSON HAS HELD THE FOLLOWING
POSITIONS: SECRETARY OF HEW, 1971 (UPPER LEFT);
SECRETARY OF DEFENSE, 1973 (UPPER RIGHT);
ATTORNEY GENERAL, 1973 (LOWER RIGHT);
AND AMBASSADOR TO GREAT BRITAIN, 1975
(LOWER LEFT). IN LATE 1975 HE WAS NAMED
SECRETARY OF COMMERCE.
Wide World Photos

TABLE 12-2

SALARIES OF FEDERAL OFFICIALS IN 1975*

President	$200,000
Vice President	65,625
Speaker of the House of Representatives	65,625
Chief Justice, Supreme Court	65,625
Associate Justice, Supreme Court	63,000
Cabinet Member	63,000
Congressman	44,625
Court of Appeals Justice	44,625
Undersecretary	42,000
District Court Judge	42,000
Assistant Department Secretary	39,900
Bureau Chief	37,800

*Under legislation passed in 1975, but subject to revision, salaries of high federal officials will be pegged to increases in the cost of living.

Source: Data from the Senate Post Office and Civil Service Committee published in *Congressional Quarterly Weekly Report*, August 16, 1975, p. 1820.

available. The annual turnover rate of executives appointed by the President is about 25 percent. Most appointees turn out to be either people who supported the winning President or people suggested by his supporters and by his personal staff. In recent administrations, about a fifth of the appointees have been businessmen and another fifth lawyers. Most of the rest are already in elective or appointive positions at some level of government.[23]

THE CABINET

The work of the federal government is done by about a dozen departments and a host of nondepartmental agencies. Each department is headed by a secretary, who is appointed by the President and confirmed by the Senate.[24] Together with the Vice President and several other major officials, the secretaries comprise the *Cabinet*. As an organization in its own right, the Cabinet is not particularly important. The very term Cabinet is not men-

[23] Dom Bonafede and Andrew J. Glass, "Nixon Staff Changes," *National Journal Reports*, April 6, 1974, pp. 495–511.

[24] The President's Cabinet nominees usually are confirmed as a matter of course, but if a nominee seems to offer opportunities for political exploitation by the senators, there may be some of this in the confirmation hearings or in floor speeches. When a President is in deep political trouble, as Nixon was during the Watergate crisis, the Senate will not readily confirm his nominees and may do so only if the President gives assurances that limit his normal freedom of action. In late 1973, the Senate confirmed William Saxbe's appointment as Attorney General only after promises that the government's investigation of Watergate and related matters would be wholly free from control by the President—the investigator's nominal superior.

tioned in the Constitution and any comparisons with the British Cabinet, which plays the major leadership role in British political life, would be totally misleading. The American Cabinet is *not* an executive council of the government, a forum for discussion of large questions, or a source of advice to a President pondering major decisions. Cabinet meetings are infrequent, superficial, and brief. Kennedy observed that they were "simply useless." A former member of his Cabinet wrote:

> Decisions on major matters were not made—or even influenced
> at Cabinet sessions and . . . discussion there was a waste of time. . . .
> When members spoke up to suggest or to discuss major administra-
> tion policy, the President would listen with thinly disguised impa-
> tience and then postpone or otherwise bypass the question. . . . [25]

It is customary for each incoming President to announce that his Cabinet will play a major role in his administration. Then, like Kennedy, he usually ignores it. The occasional President (FDR, Eisenhower, and Ford) who calls frequent Cabinet meetings uses them as a general morale-building device rather than a vehicle for making important decisions.

The reasons for the weakness of the Cabinet illuminate why Presidents have so much trouble maintaining control over the executive branch. Traditionally, only one or two members of the President's Cabinet have been close to him politically in his struggle to gain the White House. For the most part, the Cabinet is made up of people whom the President may not even have known before being elected. They are chosen partly to satisfy the claims of various major interests to which the President feels bound to be responsive, and partly to satisfy different factions in his party. For example, the Secretary of Labor generally is someone associated with organized labor or with labor-management relations, and with rare exceptions the Secretary of Commerce is a prominent businessman.

Although Cabinet members are appointed by the President and owe their primary allegiance to him, they also must develop good relations with the departments they head. These departments are composed of career civil servants who remain at their posts from one administration to the next. Quite understandably, they have interests which may be different from those of the President. Often they are fiercely dedicated to the programs they administer. They expect that the secretary who heads their department will be as committed to representing their interests to the President as he is to representing the President's interests to them. The secretary's need for loyalty from his staff gives him commitments and perspectives different from those of the President. The secretary's tendency to be somewhat at cross-purposes with the White House is augmented by the fact that he is responsible only for his part of the government and thus lacks the President's need to balance a wider range of interests. The secretary must build his own alliances in Congress and among his clientele groups if he is to get his job done, for he cannot go running to the White House for help every

[25] Quoted in *National Journal Reports*, October 6, 1973, p. 1473.

time he encounters political trouble. But then these allies become a source of pressure on the secretary, often pushing him in a "parochial" direction that is inconsistent with the President's overall goals.

Presidents, of course, are not totally without ways to deal with the centrifugal tendencies of the Cabinet. One technique which reached remarkable proportions in the 1960s and 1970s involved expanding the White House staff and assigning White House aides to "ride herd" on departments. A variant of this technique involves "colonizing" a department by placing a presidential agent directly in the department at a level normally staffed by a civil servant.

Despite such stratagems, all modern Presidents have complained of their difficulty in gaining control of the very bureaucracy that is one of the bases of their power. The various ploys just described have not been enough to give the President close control of the administrative branch. The major response of the President to this dilemma has been the *institutionalization of the presidency*. Let us now consider this development in more systematic detail.

THE INSTITUTIONALIZATION OF THE PRESIDENCY

When the telephone rang in the McKinley White House, the President himself often answered. Woodrow Wilson typed his own speeches and even some of his own correspondence. Hoover was the first President to have a telephone on his desk. In those more leisurely days, the White House staff consisted largely of gardeners and cooks. For help with governmental affairs, the President needed only a handful of stenographers and clerks and a couple of personal assistants. By Franklin Roosevelt's time, the President's official household had expanded somewhat. But FDR's highly publicized and dedicated aides—the so-called "Brain Trust" of college professors who helped him early in his first term with legislation drafting—were not listed on the payroll as presidential aides. Neither was Harry Hopkins, Roosevelt's key wartime lieutenant who literally lived in the White House. To secure their services, Roosevelt had to employ the mild subterfuge of giving them jobs without duties in other executive agencies. It was not until 1939, after several years of political give-and-take, that legislation was passed creating the Executive Office of the President (EOP). This legislation was accompanied by the executive order moving the Bureau of the Budget (BOB), established in 1921, from the Treasury Department to the new EOP.

The Executive Office of the President now has a staff of over five thousand. More than 220 people are kept busy answering the nearly 3 million letters addressed to the President that arrive at the White House every year. The White House itself is flanked by a constellation of buildings housing staff offices. The building immediately west of the White House, once occupied by several departments, became first "the Executive Office Building" and then "the Old Executive Office Building." The "New Executive Office Building," an inconspicuous red brick structure north of the White House, is set beyond

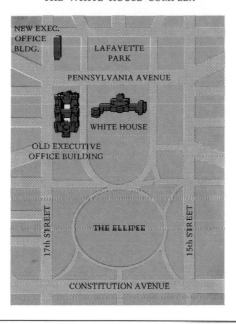

FIGURE 12–2

THE WHITE HOUSE COMPLEX

a facade of renovated early nineteenth-century buildings. As an attempt on Truman's life and Kennedy's assassination made presidential security more vital, both the White House and the Old Executive Office Building were enclosed by a carefully guarded metal fence. The widely photographed Oval Office of the President, facing south to the White House gardens and the Washington Monument, is itself a twentieth-century development. Like the East and West Wings of the White House, the Oval Office (which, incidentally, has two-and-one-half inch bulletproof glass windows) was built in the first decade of this century.

Within the Executive Office of the President, the White House Office has almost six hundred employees officially charged to it. It also borrows extensively from other agencies. Among the employees in the White House are the often highly publicized immediate aides to the President, including the appointment secretary, the press secretary, and the special assistant for foreign affairs, such as Dr. Kissinger in the Nixon administration before he became Secretary of State. Indeed, Kissinger considered his White House role and staff so important that he maintained them throughout the Nixon administration and first year of the Ford administration, even after being made Secretary of State.

In contrast to Cabinet secretaries, members of the White House staff frequently are young and unknown before going to the White House. They are not chosen to please party factions or constituent interest groups and are not subject to confirmation by the Senate. Because their careers depend exclusively on the President, they are undistracted by outside loyalties. Their organization and assignment of tasks can be changed at will by the President.

In the last thirty years, these presidential aides have occupied an increasingly important place in the center of the national government. As the complexity and size of the bureaucracy increase the challenges to presidential control, his staff inevitably grows more influential. A former presidential assistant confided to an interviewer: "I had more power over national affairs in a few years in the White House than I could if I spent the rest of my life in the Senate."[26]

One major function of the White House staff is to protect and advance the President's political interests. This includes legislative liaison, press relations, and control of the President's schedule, travel, and relations with major interest groups and party figures.

Every President also has to have assistants who perform such inevitable but disagreeable tasks as refusing access, discharging officials, and denying requests for special consideration. Such aides do what the President wants; their function is to give the boss the results without the blame. The need for this service is explained in Patrick Anderson's description of Sherman Adams, Eisenhower's chief of staff:

> Eisenhower remained beloved, even by those who were fired or turned away; it was always Adams who was hated. Eisenhower was the most beloved man of his time. . . . The people's affection for him was his strength, and he hoarded it like a miser. On the national scale he saw it as his mission to unite the nation, and on a personal scale it pained him, more than most men, to say "no." . . .[27]

Another group of staff are "policy people," concerned with developing new programs, identifying problems and opportunities, defining issues, reconciling proposals from agencies and interest groups, and overseeing administrative execution of major programs. We noted earlier that the Office of Management and Budget (OMB) coordinates policy proposals flowing upward from the Cabinet departments. The President's own assistants also work out many policy programs directly for the President. They are more attuned to politics than the OMB. In the field of domestic policy, much coordination and background policy research have been done, since the Nixon years, by a group of White House advisers collectively known as the Domestic Council (DC). The Domestic Council is not a group that normally meets on a regular basis to discuss issues collectively. Rather, it is a pool of White House policy advisers, who form more or less ad hoc teams to establish a presidential view on domestic policy. The DC has a jurisdiction that somewhat overlaps that of the OMB. The DC tends to be involved in

[26] Quoted in Patrick Anderson, *The President's Men* (Garden City, N. Y.: Doubleday & Company, Inc., 1969), p. 1.

[27] Anderson, *The President's Men,* p. 184.

bigger issues on which the Administration wants to place a distinctly presidential stamp.

White House aides typically have something of an adversary relationship with career civil servants. The President's men are preoccupied with speed and the presidential perspective, which inevitably grates on bureaucrats accustomed to a specialized and long-term perspective. Anderson described the Kennedy staff's attitude toward the civil service:

> It astounded the New Frontiersmen that the civil servants were disinclined to work until ten at night and all day Saturday, that they were somehow immune to the magic of the moment.[28]

The National Security Council plays a similar role with respect to foreign policy. Headed by a presidential Adviser for National Security, the NSC has a staff of seventy-five. Its original purpose was to coordinate foreign policy by bringing together the views of the numerous major departments that have an important stake in our dealings with other countries. These include the Departments of State, Defense, the Treasury, and Commerce; the Central Intelligence Agency, the Agency for International Development, and the U.S. Information Agency.

The NSC thus helps the President decide among the conflicting positions advocated by different agencies concerned with foreign policy. It has been called the "little State Department in the basement of the White House." Some observers have deplored this development because they believe that it weakens the morale and influence of the State Department's corps of professional diplomats, the Foreign Service. Nevertheless, the development

AS THE PRESIDENCY HAS GROWN, SO HAS THE NEED TO PROTECT THE PRESIDENT. TRUMAN, IN 1947, CROSSES PENNSYLVANIA AVENUE FLANKED BY SECRET SERVICE MEN; JOHNSON, IN 1964, RIDES IN A MOTORCADE, GUARDED BY AGENTS ARMED WITH AUTOMATIC WEAPONS.
Wide World Photos

[28] Anderson, *The President's Men*, p. 242. Such grueling schedules are commonplace in the White House.

of some kind of a shadow State Department in the White House is an inevitable result of changes in the nature and complexity of government we have described. It arose out of the need for a presidential point of view in foreign policy and the inability of the State Department, which is merely one of the interested parties, to impose its will on other competing bureaucracies.

The development of the National Security Council is the most dramatic, but by no means the only example of the emergence in recent years of presidential agencies largely independent of the bureaucratic departments. These include the Domestic Council, Council of Economic Advisers, and Wage and Price Council, plus other EOP agencies contributing to the institutionalization of the presidency.

The expansion of these and other presidential agencies reflects not just a need for coordination and advice, but the President's desire for officials loyal to his goals, not to the interests of the career bureaucracies. As the tasks of government have become more diverse and specialized, the permanent civil servants themselves become increasingly specialized. This trend challenges the President's ability to impose his own direction on the organs of government. All modern presidents have responded to the challenge in the same way, by expanding their personal staffs. Thus the EOP has grown steadily over the past forty years, irrespective of the personal style or ideological commitments of the President. This trend has intensified in recent years. The budget for the White House staff alone grew from $3.6 million in 1970 to $16.9 million just six years later. More than anything else, these figures indicate the tension between the President—the country's elected leader—and the professional civil servants who comprise the permanent part of the executive branch.

ADVISING THE PRESIDENT

It is important to distinguish between those who *act for* the President and those who *advise* him. Advice from members of his official family comes from people who are dependent on him for their jobs and are tempted to tell him what they think he wants to hear. In addition, as one close observer of such matters put it, "the aura of reverence that surrounds the President when he is in the Mansion is so universal that the slightest hint of criticism automatically labels a man as a colossal lout."[29]

In order to free himself from this combination of self-interested caution and overprotectiveness, a President may turn to congressmen, Washington lawyers, journalists, retired elder statesmen, and others who are not dependent on him and are likely to provide more disinterested counsel. Such advisers may not be more "loyal" to the President than Cabinet members and White House aides, but they are less dependent on him for jobs and status than his staff. Only a man without further ambition could speak as frankly to a President as former Secretary of State Dean Acheson, who, when asked by Lyndon Johnson, "Why don't people like me?" replied, "Because, Mr. President, you are not a very likable man."[30]

[29] Reedy, *The Twilight of the Presidency,* p. 80.
[30] Quoted in Barber, *The Presidential Character,* p. 93.

Presidents generally are aware of their advisers' reluctance to express unwelcome opinions. Eisenhower tried to cope with this problem by keeping silent or noncommittal in meetings until everyone else had spoken, knowing that if he expressed his opinion he would prematurely freeze the discussion, inhibiting others from speaking frankly. Similarly, Kennedy sometimes left the room during crisis discussions to avoid stifling dissent.

Recognizing the chilling effect of the President's prestige, Johnson made use of it in the opposite way, to protect himself from after-the-fact criticism of his policies. He would announce a decision at a meeting, and then ask each person in the room if he agreed with the decision. There were seldom any open dissenters. Johnson then could use this coerced agreement to "lock in" people to his policy and keep them loyal to it. This gained him support, but the cost was high. He was kept insulated from advice that might have convinced him to "unwind" a bloody and politically damaging war in Asia.

One sometimes hears about a President: "It's not his fault, he just had bad advice." Indeed, supporters of certain presidential candidates have argued that their lack of substantial mental ability was not crucial, because what is really important is the President's advisers. These arguments have a number of flaws. In the first place, the President picks his advisers, so the nation is dependent upon his ability to choose capable ones. Second, the President organizes his advisers and chooses how he will employ them. And finally, advisers often present opposing views. It is the President alone who must finally choose among them or reconcile them.

IS THE PRESIDENT TOO POWERFUL?

The American political system is based on the assumption that power will be divided among the three branches of government. Each branch will be predominant in certain areas, while in other areas decisions can be taken only if there is some sort of coordination or cooperation between all three branches. In any event, the three branches are supposed to be in a rough kind of equilibrium. This system of checks and balances was designed to avoid undue concentration of power and to provide multiple points of citizen influence over government.

At various times in American political history, each of the three branches has been accused of seeking and exercising excessive power—of disturbing a presumably ideal balance of power among the three institutions. In the mid 1930s, the Supreme Court was widely accused of "judicial tyranny" because it struck down as unconstitutional many major pieces of New Deal legislation that had been passed by overwhelming congressional majorities and signed into law by a popular President. At the same time, another set of critics believed that Roosevelt had so far exceeded traditional presidential powers as to pose the threat of a dictatorship. Needless to say, the Court critics were largely New Deal enthusiasts, while those people who professed fears that Roosevelt would become a tyrant were largely Republicans and conservative Democrats.

During the Truman administration, the conservative coalition so thoroughly dominated Congress that the President was unable to win passage of innovative economic and social legislation he badly wanted. This period, frustrating to the liberal Democrats who comprise the majority of political scientists, soon brought a new theme: The President *lacked* the power he needed to carry out his pledges to the people, the pledges that presumably brought about his election. This became the conventional wisdom of the 1950s and early 1960s.

By the middle 1960s, yet another theme began to emerge with increasing frequency. The President was not too weak, but too strong. He was able to do too much, to impose his will too thoroughly and in too many areas of political life.

Deciding between whether the President has too much power or not enough depends to a large extent on whether one likes what the incumbent is doing. The real question, however, is whether presidential power cuts into the power of the other branches of government—particularly the legislative branch. As we have seen, the President cannot *command* Congress to do his bidding. This is acknowledged by those who believe that his power has grown too great. They argue, instead, that the President does not so much dominate Congress as ignore it, that Congress lacks the will and the capacity to hold its own in dealing with presidential assertions of power.

In the next few pages we will consider the popular contemporary belief that the President's power has become so great as to overshadow the Congress. The principal developments that are customarily cited as evidence are: (1) the undeclared war in Vietnam, (2) presidential vetoes, (3) the use of "executive privilege," and (4) presidential impoundment of appropriated funds.

THE VIETNAM WAR

The war in Vietnam heightened public recognition of the inescapable fact that foreign policy is essentially a presidential rather than a congressional domain. Prior to World War II, America had played a minor role on the world stage, with the exception of our entry into World War I, which was followed by a hasty withdrawal from major foreign policy involvement after the failure to ratify the Treaty of Versailles. Reflecting predominant public opinion, the government followed an essentially isolationist policy toward events outside the Western Hemisphere.

But with the onset of World War II, the United States entered a dramatically different era. The next two decades saw the conclusive rejection of isolationism by the American people and their leaders, the decline of French and British imperial power, the advent of a bipolar world dominated by the two superpowers, Russia and America, the development of an elaborate structure of alliances and bases overseas, the beginnings of a major foreign aid program, and the growth of a complex set of foreign commitments roughly summarized by the phrase "the cold war." America was committed to maintaining military forces as strong as those of the Soviet Union, a far cry from the days before World War II when the United States had the nineteenth largest army in the world.

Foreign and military affairs, therefore, became a larger part of the totality of American public policy. In most of the years between the end of World War II and the end of the war in Vietnam, the largest single category of federal expenditures was for defense and defense-related purposes. (By 1975, social welfare took the largest fraction of the budget. Defense spending had shrunk to less than 7 percent of the country's total income.)

As foreign policy becomes more important, the President inevitably becomes more important, because foreign policy is essentially a presidential field. The President's powers as commander-in-chief, his constitutional authority to deal with other nations, his position as chief executive and as the official who carries out the laws all establish his preeminence in foreign policy. The predominance of the President in the foreign policy area was upheld by the Supreme Court in the *Curtiss-Wright* decision of 1936. Holding that treaties are among the laws that the President is charged with enforcing, the Court went on to describe the "exclusive power of the President as the sole organ of the Federal Government in the field of international relations—a power which does not require as a basis for its exercise an act of Congress."[31] For many years it was customary to justify virtually any unilateral presidential act in the field of foreign or military policy in terms of this decision. Now, however, it is widely argued that the Curtiss-Wright decision was an excessive statement of presidential power in foreign affairs.

Those who feel that the President has become too powerful in foreign affairs cite as evidence for their view the constitutional provision that Congress shall have the power to declare war, and the fact that we were engaged in a long and costly war in Vietnam despite the absence of any declaration of war. The President seems to have war-making powers that the Constitution did not intend him to have.

This criticism is indisputably correct, but it has come to be beside the point. Modern technology provides superpowers with the capacity to destroy an enemy with virtually no warning, through intercontinental nuclear missiles. If an enemy power were to launch a nuclear strike against the United States, a decision on nuclear retaliation would have to be made within minutes of the time our Early Warning System at the Arctic Circle first detected the enemy missiles. If a congressional declaration of war were required before the President could act, such a war would be lost before it could be declared.

Even in terms of conventional weaponry, the President, in his capacity as commander-in-chief, can send units of the armed forces to any place he considers them needed. If their presence then provokes attack by another country, the President could easily rally both public opinion and congressional support for American retaliation. This is just what happened in 1964, when American warships in the Gulf of Tonkin were patrolling in an area where South Vietnamese commandos were staging raids on North Vietnam.

---

[31] *United States* v. *Curtiss-Wright Export Corp.*, 229 U.S. 304 (1936).

Even though the American ships were in international waters, it was not surprising that the North Vietnamese responded with torpedo boat attacks against them. This gave President Johnson what he had been looking for, a congressional resolution that "the Congress approves and supports the determination of the President, as commander-in-chief, to take all necessary measures to repel any armed attack against the forces of the United States and to prevent further aggression." This measure passed with only two dissenting votes in the Senate. In the view of most constitutional scholars, the resolution had no legal effect on the President's authority to wage war in Southeast Asia. It did, however, inhibit congressional criticism of his policies. In short, although only Congress is empowered by the Constitution to declare war, the President, as commander-in-chief, has the power to create situations that are like war in everything but the name.

Anticipating future situations in which the President might exploit his power as commander-in-chief to precipitate military confrontations abroad, Congress adopted the War Powers Act in late 1973. Passed over President Nixon's veto, this measure set a sixty-day limit on presidential commitment of American troops abroad, unless Congress specifically authorized their deployment. A thirty-day extension also was authorized, if necessary, in order to extricate troops safely. In addition, Congress could end such assignments before the sixty-day deadline by passing a concurrent resolution, which does not require presidential consent.

Only time will tell if this measure will trim the President's power in foreign affairs. Can Congress restrict the President's power as commander-in-chief without amending the Constitution? Would such action by Congress be politically feasible? In any situation in which the War Powers Act might be applied, the tendency to rally around the President in foreign affairs probably would guarantee widespread support for whatever he wanted to do. Certainly this was true early in the Ford administration when the President took immediate, decisive military action to recover an American merchant ship and its crew when they were seized by Cambodian Communist forces. Although the view of some professional observers was that Ford had acted precipitously, much approval and virtually no criticism was heard on Capitol Hill. And Ford's Gallup Poll popularity score rose sharply, if temporarily.

Although presidential dominance in foreign affairs undoubtedly will continue, congressional power to influence foreign policy is far from nonexistent. When the President wants to take ventures that require the creation of new institutions or formal alliances, congressional assent is crucial. In the period after World War II, when the United States emerged from its historic isolationism, the Truman Administration had to gain congressional support for the North Atlantic Treaty Organization (NATO), a binding agreement that keeps an American army in Europe; and the Marshall Plan, a scheme to finance postwar economic recovery in Europe. Such recent steps toward peace as the Test Ban Treaty and the Strategic Arms Limitation Talks (SALT) Treaty were modified in response to Senate pressure.

The most important source of congressional power in foreign affairs comes

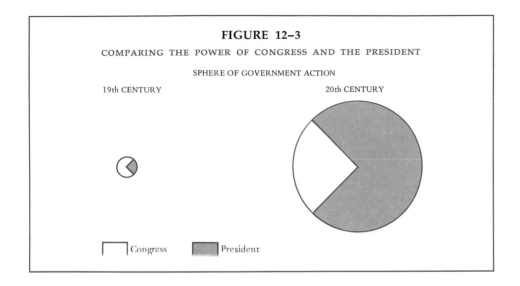

FIGURE 12–3

COMPARING THE POWER OF CONGRESS AND THE PRESIDENT

SPHERE OF GOVERNMENT ACTION

19th CENTURY   20th CENTURY

☐ Congress   ▨ President

from the fact that money cannot be spent for any purpose unless Congress appropriates it. During the long, undeclared, and increasingly unpopular war in Vietnam, Congress continued to appropriate the necessary funds. This was perhaps the crucial test—a test not of power but of will, however. Congress could have cut off the money for American military action in Southeast Asia and brought the war to a conclusion. But it is politically difficult to vote to cut off money and "leave our boys fighting abroad helpless in the face of the enemy." and both the President and Congress know it. Thus Congress continued to fund the war in Southeast Asia until the summer of 1973, when all American troops had been withdrawn from Vietnam. Then it passed a military appropriation bill forbidding the bombing of Cambodia after August 15, 1973.

Finally, Congress provides those who disagree with the President's foreign policy with numerous opportunities for criticism and publicity. During the war in Vietnam, this opportunity was often exploited by opponents of the war. This is important because in foreign affairs the President usually needs or wants to present a united face to the world. The ability to disturb this public posture by threatening open criticism is often a source of congressional influence on foreign policy that is exercised behind the scenes. Essentially, President Ford and his advisers were restrained *politically* in 1975 when the rapid collapse of anti-communist forces in Indochina led to widespread congressional and public response in favor of an end to any military involvement in Southeast Asia.

PRESIDENTIAL VETOES

The veto power is of little use to a President who wants to bring about change, for when Congress refuses to enact legislation the President wants, there is no way for him to veto their inactivity. But the veto is an invaluable tool when a President wants to prevent innovation. It enables him to defeat any legislation that cannot be supported by two-thirds of Congress. The veto power means that a President with negative goals needs to get support of only one-third of one house of Congress in order to get what he wants. A President with affirmative intentions needs to get a majority of both houses of Congress.

This leads to the paradoxical situation that a President who does not want to innovate often *looks* more powerful than a President who does. The power of the veto advantage may be judged by the fact that from the beginning of the Republic through the end of the Nixon administration, Presidents had vetoed 2,293 bills passed by Congress and Congress had been able to muster a two-thirds majority to override the veto only seventy-eight times. Eisenhower faced Democratic majorities in both houses of Congress for six of his eight years in office and chose to veto 181 bills passed by Congress. The difference between one-half and two-thirds is so great that only two of these vetoes were overridden. Kennedy and Johnson, who had more ambitious legislative programs than either Eisenhower or Nixon, vetoed less than a third as many bills as Eisenhower.

Nixon had relatively modest legislative goals and was confronted throughout his administration by Democratic Congresses with far more extensive ambitions. Nixon's ability to veto legislation made him look far stronger than in fact he was, because his goals were negative rather than positive. Ford used the veto power on an even greater proportion of bills passed by Congress than did Nixon. (See Table 12–3.)

TABLE 12-3

VETOES BY TWENTIETH-CENTURY PRESIDENTS

PRESIDENT	BILLS VETOED	VETOES OVERRIDDEN
McKinley	42	0
T. Roosevelt	82	1
Taft	39	1
Wilson	44	6
Harding	6	0
Coolidge	50	4
Hoover	37	3
F. D. Roosevelt	635	9
Truman	250	12
Eisenhower	181	2
Kennedy	21	0
Johnson	30	0
Nixon	43	5
Ford	34 (thru 9/10/75)	6

Source: *CQ Weekly Report*, December 7, 1974, p. 3281; and September 13, 1975, p. 1948.

Nixon's presidency brought about two further developments that led to cries of excessive presidential power: impoundment of funds and claims of executive privilege. In neither case were the Nixon administration's actions unprecedented. Presidents throughout our history have argued successfully that the separation of powers entitled them to receive advice without congressional inquiry into the character of that advice. Consequently, members of the White House staff traditionally have refused to testify before Congress on the grounds that doing so would violate the constitutional prerogatives of the President to receive counsel without congressional scrutiny. This claim, although occasionally challenged, has nevertheless been respected. Cabinet officers, their subordinates, and officials of the regulatory agencies have always been answerable to Congress. But as the powers of the White House staff have grown in recent years, key decisions have been made increasingly in the White House, not in the executive agencies. Congressional ability to question Cabinet officers has been of decreasing utility while congressional inability to question White House personnel has been an increasing source of frustration.

The Nixon administration's attempts to claim total executive privilege for all members of the Executive Office of the President foundered on the rock of possible criminal acts committed by members of the EOP. Public opinion and Congress alike were intolerant of the argument that no one on the President's staff could be required to testify about *anything*, including criminal matters, on grounds that it might be a breach of executive privilege. Thus, the President was forced to retreat from his blanket claim of executive privilege. The most striking instance of this retreat came about when the Supreme Court denied the President's claim to executive privilege over subpoenaed tapes of conversation in his office. After the Court handed down its decision in the landmark case of *United States* v. *Nixon*,[32] evidence was released proving Mr. Nixon's complicity in the cover-up of the Watergate burglary. These revelations resulted in a loss of support among key conservatives that eventually forced Nixon's reluctant resignation from office—the first presidential resignation in American history. But the issue remains a difficult one, sure to cause trouble in the years ahead as the Executive Office of the President gains more and more power and as claims of executive privilege—justified as the principle may be—come to conflict more and more with the congressional right of oversight. Within Ford's first two years in office he was already in disagreement with Congress over questions connected with divulging information about presidential foreign policy negotiations and agreements.

IMPOUNDMENT

Just as the Congress can refuse to appropriate funds for activities of which it disapproves, so the President can refuse to spend money that Congress has

---

[32] *United States* v. *Richard Nixon, President of the United States, et al.*, 418 U.S. 683 (1974).

appropriated. This process is known as *impoundment,* and has been used by many Presidents. One of the most famous examples was Truman's refusal to build an air force as big as Congress wanted. In this case, and in others during the Kennedy Administration, impoundment was based in part on the President's powers as commander-in-chief of the armed forces. As it did in so many areas, the Nixon Administration carried an established practice to unacceptable lengths. Nixon's impoundments were concentrated in areas of domestic spending where Congress provided more money than the President wanted. At one point, more than $10 billion in appropriated funds were impounded and whole programs were in danger of termination because the President did not approve of them.

In a series of decisions beginning in 1973, the courts held that the President's obligation to faithfully execute the laws required him to spend money appropriated by Congress. (Congress echoed this view with legislation in 1974 that forbade impoundment except with its permission.) As the courts saw it, both the bills authorizing the programs and appropriations measures were laws. The courts also have held that the President cannot plead general budgetary considerations as a legitimate ground for impoundment. But the courts have not universally struck down impoundment. Once again, the ultimate resolution of this question is in doubt.[33] In fact, ultimate resolutions of such issues are few and far between in American politics. As we saw with Congress, attempts to carry an advantage too far brought about a severe reaction. Institutional overreaching tends to produce a backlash. The end result of Nixon's enthusiastic use of impoundment seems to be a net loss in the President's power to withhold appropriated funds.

PRESIDENTIAL POWER: AN OVERVIEW

The President tends to be predominant in foreign and military policy not only by virtue of constitutional provisions but also because many aspects of these fields are inherently more suited to executive than legislative action. Legislators are best at deliberation and reflection of the popular will; the results of legislative action are general rules. But general rules are not crucial in foreign policy, which requires quick responses to changing and complicated specific situations.

In recent years, other areas of governmental activity have come to resemble foreign policy in seeming to require rapid, flexible, or complex executive responses. As they have done so, the President's power inevitably has increased. Usually the exercise of such domestic executive powers has been possible only as a result of congressional authorization. For example, early in the Nixon administration, Congress passed a bill giving the President standby power to control prices and wages. Nixon did not want this authority and signed the bill with great reluctance. Nevertheless, in 1971, when the cost of living began to rise at an accelerated pace, he invoked these powers in

[33] On impoundment and a variety of more subtle ways Presidents circumvent congressional intent in allocating funds, see Louis Fisher, *Presidential Spending Power* (Princeton: Princeton University Press, 1975).

a series of attempts to control inflation. In all the various phases of Nixon's anti-inflation program, major restrictions on both prices and wages were imposed and enforced by the President without any specific congressional participation.

Similarly, when a severe energy shortage struck America in 1973, the Senate passed a bill authorizing the President to take steps to deal with the crisis. He was, for example, given power to limit "nonessential recreational activities." Congress did not define "nonessential" and left this decision to the President. Legislation did not suggest whether the President might enforce such limits by rationing, by taxation, by mandatory allocation of fuel, or by other measures. In other words, the Senate specified that the national interest required certain kinds of governmental action, and then left it to the President to decide what to do.

In part, this delegation of power is motivated by the legislature's genuine inability to figure out what to do. In part, also, it is motivated by a desire to avoid the political consequences by making the President bear the burden of responsibility. But probably the major reason for such measures is the unavoidable fact that dealing with the energy crisis, like dealing with inflation, requires many fast decisions adjusted to meet changing conditions, and here, as in warfare, legislatures are inherently ill-suited to perform aedquately.

We can conclude that Presidents have an enormous advantage when they want to prevent rather than bring about innovation. What is more, to the extent that public policy consists of administration rather than the statement of general regulations, Presidents inevitably have increasing power relative to the power of Congress. But, as we shall see in later chapters, these same conditions often give advantages to professional, long-term civil servants. Thus, in some measure, both Congress and the President—the two elected decision-making agencies—may be losing power to the professional bureaucrats.

THE VICE PRESIDENCY

The Constitution says that "the Vice President of the United States shall be President of the Senate, but shall have no Vote, unless they be equally divided." His principal duty is to be available to take office in the event of the President's death, resignation, or removal from office. In this century alone, one President has resigned, two have been assassinated, and two more have died of natural causes. Five of the fourteen twentieth-century presidents first reached the White House by succeeding a man who died in office. Yet the post itself provides no formal powers of any consequence besides that of resolving a tie vote in Congress.

HOW VICE PRESIDENTS ARE CHOSEN

Presidential nominees almost always personally choose their running mates. Occasionally, the vice presidential nomination is a bargaining

LYNDON B. JOHNSON IS SWORN IN AS PRESIDENT, NOVEMBER 22, 1963. *Wide World Photos*

counter needed to clinch the presidential nomination. This was the case in 1932, when Franklin D. Roosevelt had to promise the nomination to John N. Garner, a prominent conservative Democratic congressman, in order to win the support of the Texas and California delegations for himself. Usually, the nominee chooses a running mate who will contribute strength where the presidential candidate considers himself vulnerable, someone with complementary ideological, regional, or ethnic qualities. In 1960, John F. Kennedy, knowing that his Catholicism would be particularly costly in the South, chose as his running mate the leading southern politician, Lyndon Johnson of Texas. Although this decision was unpopular with many northern liberals, it was a masterstroke. Johnson concentrated his campaigning south of the Mason-Dixon line, where he was most appreciated and effective.

Not only are vice presidential candidates picked for reasons other than their suitability as Presidents, but very often the decision is not carefully considered. This is due to concentration on winning the nomination, the desperate fatigue that accompanies high-pressure campaigns, and the short time allowed at national conventions for the vice presidential nomination. In 1972, McGovern assigned very little staff time to investigating possible running mates. He chose Senator Thomas Eagleton of Missouri, who was forced to withdraw a few weeks later when the press revealed that he had been hospitalized three times due to psychological problems.

Similarly, in 1968, Nixon seems not to have looked very deeply into Spiro Agnew's background in Maryland politics when he chose him as his running mate. Five years later, the Nixon administration, already reeling under the Watergate crisis, suffered yet another blow when Agnew (who had nothing to do with Watergate) became implicated in a federal investigation of corruption in Maryland. While serving as a county official and then as governor, Agnew had required county and state contractors to pay him substantial illegal kickbacks, some of which he still received after he became Vice President. Agnew resigned as Vice President in October 1973 as part of an agreement that let him escape a prison term by pleading no contest to a single charge of income tax evasion.

The Eagleton and Agnew fiascos prompted the two parties to consider more rational methods of nominating vice presidential candidates. The most likely improvement is to give the presidential nominee the option of postponing the decision for several weeks. Then the nomination would be made formally by the party's national committee, which doubtless would pick whomever the presidential candidate desired. It was in just such a "mini-convention" that the Democrats picked Sargent Shriver to succeed Senator Eagleton as vice presidential nominee in 1972. This method could be used by either party in 1976.

With the ratification of the Twenty-fifth Amendment in 1967, a new method of choosing a Vice President has been added to the constitutional system. It operates only when the office is vacant. The President nominates an individual who takes office when confirmed by a majority vote of each house of Congress. This procedure was followed in 1973–74 when Nixon picked Ford to replace Agnew, and again in 1974 when Ford, having succeeded Nixon as President, named Nelson Rockefeller as his Vice President. In striking contrast to the hasty convention method, this new procedure results in a painstaking scrutiny of the nominee by House and Senate committees. The FBI investigation preceding Ford's confirmation included more than a thousand interviews. Congressional testimony on Ford covered everything "from his voting record on civil rights to how much paint his family's paint and varnish company had sold to a Michigan furniture maker; from his experience in foreign affairs to how he financed his vacation home in Colorado."[34]

WHAT THE VICE PRESIDENT DOES

The Vice President's duties as President of the Senate are not very time-consuming. Unless the legislative situation calls for an important parliamentary ruling, he actually spends little time presiding over the Senate. Nor does the office carry much congressional influence. When the Senate Majority Leader formally presented Vice President Ford to the Senate, he warned him, "Here, presiding officers are to be seen and not heard, unlike the House where the Speaker's gavel is like a thunderclap."[35]

One of the staple items of political commentary is the suggestion that the Vice President's status be raised so that full use can be made of his talents. Incoming Presidents always promise to do this and then make a great show of doing so. In fact, though, they rarely do anything to upgrade the vice presidency. After the campaign, the Vice President's usefulness to the President is limited. Whatever he does (except presiding over the Senate) is on the President's sufferance. As former Vice President Humphrey observed of the post, "the only authority he has is what the President gives him. He who giveth can taketh away."[36]

Vice Presidents usually perform two ceremonial and rhetorical tasks such as good will tours abroad, political advocacy at home (not always in the spirit of good will), standing in for the President as head of state, and so forth. They often become administration apologists to their particular political constituencies. As Johnson escalated the war in Vietnam, he assigned Humphrey to defend administration policies before the liberals who had been the basis of Humphrey's following. Nixon used Agnew as a spokesman to the conservative Republicans to whom Agnew had extraordinary appeal. Thanks to the power of the mass media, this gives the Vice President visibility that was lacking before the television era. As a result, Vice Presidents since the 1950s have been serious contenders for the presidency.

The Vice President's main responsibility, however, is to wait—which is not much of a job for an energetic, intelligent person accustomed to activity and influence. Yet who else would be desirable in the post but an experi-

AS VICE PRESIDENT, GERALD FORD TOOK TO THE CAMPAIGN TRAIL IN BEHALF OF FELLOW REPUBLICANS. *Wide World Photos*

[34] *Congressional Quarterly Weekly Report,* January 12, 1974, p. 48.
[35] Quoted in Dom Bonafede, "Ford and Staff Tend to Business . . . and Wait," *National Journal Reports,* August 10, 1974, p. 1181.
[36] Quoted in the *San Francisco Chronicle,* December 17, 1973, p. 24.

enced, energetic, intelligent, and ambitious person? This is the paradox of the office.

One political scientist summed up the situation this way:

> There seems, in short, to be no way for a Vice President to avoid the dilemmas built into the office: unless he is scrupulously loyal to the President, he cannot get the access to the President that he needs to discharge his constitutional function; when he is loyal to the President, he is saddled, at least in the short run, with whatever characteristics of the President or his program the President's enemies or his own care to fasten on him. He sits there in the limelight, visible, vulnerable, and for the most part, powerless.[37]

SUMMARY

The President is the focal point of our governmental system and a global leader with immense powers. At the same time, he is also hemmed in and constrained by many persons and institutions. Presidents can engage in highly consequential unilateral actions—especially in foreign affairs. But domestically, and even to some extent in the foreign policy realm, much of what is done in the name of Presidents has been planned by others—administrators, members of the private sector, and members of Congress. Presidential support for major policy innovation often is necessary, but it is sufficient only if other factors—for example, the heavily liberal Congress elected with Johnson in 1964—are lined up with the President.

Further, unpopular Presidents—or even popular Presidents who lack the requisite congressional backing—are frequently stalemated in their policy goals. Even the President's own "house"—the executive branch—is not his to command unilaterally.

Thus, assertions about whether the President is too strong or too weak in general are too vague for assessment. Such judgments partly depend upon the evaluator's personal value stance. What is more, the strength of the presidency varies with the particular qualities of particular Presidents. While the official responsibilities of this globally unique office and its physical resources have expanded massively in the present century, the "presidential branch" is very much a function of the personal and political qualities of the chief executive himself.

[37] Nelson W. Polsby, "Dilemmas of the Vice Presidency," in *Political Promises* (New York: Oxford University Press, 1974), p. 159.

CHAPTER THIRTEEN
THE NATURE AND POLITICS
OF ADMINISTRATION

THE federal government takes about a fifth of our national income in taxes and spends the money on a staggering variety of goods and services. The government is the country's biggest buyer of almost everything and, likewise, is the biggest source of innumerable services. It delivers the mail, patrols the coasts, the high seas and their subterranean depths, and outer space. It operates ferry boats, hospitals, nuclear submarines, museums, and parks. It helps farmers grow better strains of food, pays them not to grow crops, and provides Food Stamps to 20 million people. It pays people money when they are out of work and when they retire. It finances research into the causes of war and heart disease, the consequences of malnutrition and lovesickness, the mating calls of fruitflies and undergraduates. It stockpiles corn and hydrogen bombs.

The people who do all these things are called *civil servants* if one feels sympathetic to them, or *bureaucrats* if one is in a jaundiced mood. Some of the functions they perform are done only by the federal government; others are shared with state and local jurisdictions; and some also are done by private firms, cooperatives, labor unions, churches, and other organizations. There is no inherent reason why many of the functions performed by other agencies cannot be done wholly by the federal government. By the same token, there is no reason why many of the things the federal government does cannot be accomplished privately or by other levels of government. Since this is so, we should expect that many features of the federal bureaucracy also will be found in large private organizations like corporations, universities, cooperatives, and labor unions.

Any big organization has certain characteristics that seem to be universal: (1) *Specialization, or division of labor.* Individual jobs have specific tasks assigned to them, irrespective of the individual who holds the job. (2) *Hierarchy, or fixed lines of command.* Each worker knows who his boss is, and whom, if anyone, he supervises. Decisions from the top are transmitted to the people who carry them out, information flows up from "the field," and responsibility can be fixed. (3) *Incentives to attract people to work for the organization and be loyal to its purposes.* By far the most important incentive is the assurance that once someone has a job, he will keep it unless he commits a gross transgression. Stability of employment helps not only morale, but also efficiency, because efficiency suffers if people change jobs frequently.

Any large organization also has "bureaucratic" characteristics, which are usually understood to mean impersonality, devotion to rules at the cost of individual values, rigidity, too much paperwork, and red tape. And any large organization is staffed mostly by permanent employees who continue on pretty much the same despite the comings and goings of the people at the top.

Although all large organizations are "bureaucratic," it seems nevertheless that elected officials complain about the civil service more than the presidents of corporations or colleges do about their employees. This is not because government workers are inherently more objectionable, but because certain features of American government make *public* administration a more difficult challenge than ordinary administration. Thus to understand how and why the administrative branch is as it is, we must understand the properties common to all large organizations and then realize that this particular organization operates in a very special environment that affects its behavior in a number of important ways.

What differentiates the United States government from, say, the United States Steel Corporation? The most obvious point is that some governmental functions are exclusively public, notably diplomatic and military affairs. Beyond this, the most important factor is the Constitution, which tolerates, encourages, and prescribes conflict within the federal government—checks and balances—and between the federal and other levels of government—separation of powers. This results in a number of specific differences, including these: (1) appeal of many administrative decisions to the courts; (2) Congress as a source of laws, money, publicity, intervention, and oversight; (3) an elected head; (4) a head whose term is considerably shorter than that of most of the other important officials with whom he must work.

In reaction to the heritage of patronage, federal employees have a much higher degree of job security than workers in the private sector. The president of US Steel can fire or reassign his subordinates much more easily than the President of the United States, and without worrying that they will go running to Congress or the newspapers to complain.

Beyond all this is publicity. It is not only legitimate to pry into government affairs far beyond what is tolerated (or legal) in private business, but there is far more public curiosity about government activities. This seems to be a peculiarly American phenomenon, as we noted earlier. In other democratic countries, it is taken for granted that the government makes its decisions confidentially. Officials reveal only what they want the people to know, and the government has formidable legal powers to prevent disclosure and publication of almost any information about policy formation.

Finally, of course, there is partisan politics. There are no parallels in the US Steel Corporation to Democrats and Republicans. Combined with the goldfish bowl atmosphere of government administration, this means that federal civil servants are very conscious of public accountability and of the need to justify what they do. Federal administrators are legally accountable both to their superiors in the executive branch and to Congress. The possibility of litigation often makes them answerable to the courts as well. And they also are accountable, informally but realistically, to relevant private organizations with which they deal.

Let us now see in more detail how the administrative branch of American national government is organized and how it functions. We will also note some of the ways in which nominally private organizations are in effect part of the administrative branch.

THE ORGANIZATION OF THE ADMINISTRATIVE BRANCH

LINE AGENCIES

The oldest, most conventional government organizations are the Cabinet-level *line departments*. The line departments, composed of agencies and

CABINET-LEVEL LINE
DEPARTMENTS ARE
THE FOUNDATION OF
THE ADMINISTRA-
TIVE BRANCH. HERE,
FORMER SECRETARY
OF THE INTERIOR
ROGERS MORTON.
Wide World Photos

bureaus, are responsible directly to the President through the Cabinet secretaries who head them. They are the workhorses of the federal administrative establishment. The basic working segments of most departments have
a variety of names, such as those shown in Figure 13–1, which depicts the
Department of Agriculture's table of organization. These component parts
typically are referred to as *bureaus,* hence the term "bureaucrat." The people
who work in the bureaus are almost exclusively civil servants who stay on
over the years, in contrast to the political executives above them, who come
and go with each changing administration. By and large, bureau heads are
appointed by the President from the ranks of career employees.

It is instructive to see when the line departments were established and
how they have grown and evolved. A core set of these agencies performs
tasks that must be done by some agency in any political system. Others have
grown up over the years in response to the evolving needs of the government
itself and the people it serves. James S. Young has reconstructed the full
roster of federal personnel and agencies as they existed at the turn of the

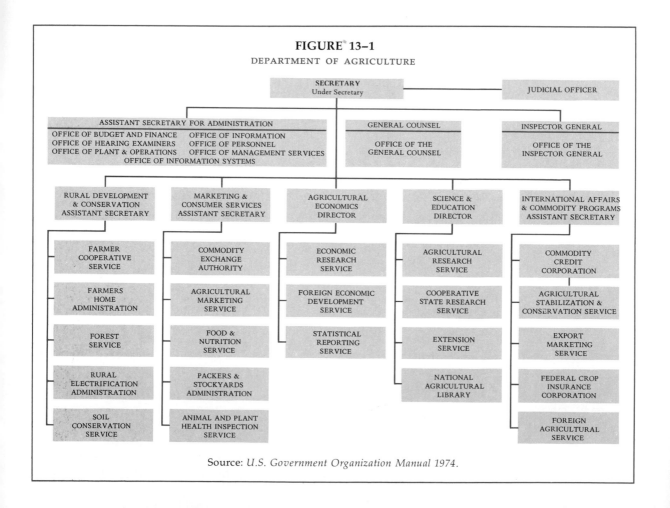

FIGURE 13–1

DEPARTMENT OF AGRICULTURE

Source: *U.S. Government Organization Manual 1974.*

nineteenth century.[1] In 1802, he reports, there were less than ten thousand government employees, of whom roughly three thousand were nonmilitary. The fighting establishment consisted of the War (i.e., Army) and Navy Departments. (The military services were not unified into a single Defense Department until after World War II.) The other departments were concerned with revenue raising (the Treasury Department) and foreign relations (the State Department). The presidential staff consisted of a single clerk.

Certain other governmental functions were carried out but did not yet have Cabinet status. The Attorney General had no staff and operated out of his own home. There were roughly a thousand revenue collectors and a thousand postmasters. Revenue collection was not officially part of the Treasury, and the Post Office had not received Cabinet status. (Recently the Post Office has become a government controlled corporation, rather than a Cabinet department.)

The march of agencies to Cabinet status, plus the growth of some very sizeable agencies outside the Cabinet, continued throughout the nineteenth century. By noting the dates that Cabinet status was acquired, we get some sense of when groups became recognized as quasi-official partners in the process of governing, as well as a notion of when the increasing complexities of administration made new agencies a "functional necessity."

In the next few pages we will take a brief look at the various federal departments (leaving aside the Post Office and those basic departments referred to above which were already in existence by 1802). Detailed examination of their workings is not necessary, but we will note the date when each was established, along with a rough indication of the interests or clientele it serves. All the agencies of the federal government, together with the number of employees that each had in 1974, are listed in Table 13–1.

INTERIOR. The Department of the Interior was established in 1849. At first, it was concerned with the expansion of population into the western states. Even today it is primarily involved with the special requirements of land, mineral, and natural resource development in those states. The congressional committees which oversee and fund this agency are dominated by westerners.

AGRICULTURE. The Department of Agriculture was established in 1862, at a time when the secession of the slave states made the small northern farmers key constituents of the ruling Republican party.

COMMERCE AND LABOR. A Department of Commerce and Labor, established in 1903, served to provide federal recognition of the decades of massive industrial expansion and the rise of labor union organization that followed the Civil War. In 1913, Labor lost its stepchild status with the formation of separate Labor and Commerce Departments.

[1] James S. Young, *The Washington Community: 1800–1828* (New York: Columbia University Press, 1966), p. 29.

THE RANGE OF JOBS DONE BY FEDERAL EMPLOYEES IS INCREDIBLY DIVERSE; IT INCLUDES SUCH WORK AS PATROL OF U.S. BORDERS (DEPT. OF THE TREASURY); MAINTENANCE OF BUOYS AND OTHER NAVIGATIONAL AIDS (DEPT. OF TRANSPORTATION); AND DAILY BURNING OF AROUND $31 MILLION OF WORN-OUT PAPER MONEY (DEPT. OF THE TREASURY).
Wide World Photos

TABLE 13-1

AGENCIES OF THE FEDERAL GOVERNMENT

AGENCY	NUMBER OF EMPLOYEES	AGENCY	NUMBER OF EMPLOYEES
ALL AGENCIES	2,835,348	Army	371,767
Legislative branch	34,696	Department of the Navy	323,359
Judicial branch	9,300	Department of the Air Force	272,828
Executive branch	2,791,352	Other Defense activities	72,119
Percent Dept. of Defense	37.3	Health, Education, and Welfare	139,024
Percent Postal Service	25.3	Housing and Urban Development	16,769
		Interior	69,424
EXECUTIVE OFFICE OF THE PRESIDENT:		Justice	49,285
		Labor	13,572
White House Office	527	State	33,296
Office of Management and Budget	642	Agency for International Development	9,710
Council of Economic Advisers	47	Transportation	70,552
Executive Mansion and Grounds	71	Treasury	126,260
National Security Council	79		
Office of Economic Opportunity	1,143		
Office of Emergency Preparedness	(NA)		
Office of Science and Technology	(NA)	INDEPENDENT AGENCIES	
All other	2,121	ACTION	2,050
		American Battle Monuments Commission	390
EXECUTIVE DEPARTMENTS:		Arms Control and Disarmament Agency	162
Agriculture	103,621	Atomic Energy Commission	7,749
Commerce	35,359	Board of Governors, Federal Reserve System	1,283
Defense	1,042,090		
Office of the Secretary	2,017		
Department of the			

HEALTH, EDUCATION, AND WELFARE. In 1953 President Eisenhower brought the Republicans back to power after twenty years of vast expansion in federal welfare programs under the Democrats. The agencies administering these programs were consolidated and given Cabinet status as the Department of Health, Education, and Welfare (HEW). The new department has been little more than a loose holding company of bureaus, each with its own strong ties to constituency groups and congressional committees and subcommittees. Nevertheless, the creation of the new department symbolized

AGENCY	NUMBER OF EMPLOYEES	AGENCY	NUMBER OF EMPLOYEES
Canal Zone Government	3,539	Nat'l Aero. and Space Administration	26,523
Civil Aeronautics Board	692	Nat'l Credit Union Administration	523
Civil Service Commission	7,752	National Foundation on the Arts and Humanities	535
Commission on Civil Rights	251	National Labor Relations Board	2,433
Environmental Protection Agency	10,302	National Mediation Board	104
Equal Employment Opportunity Commission	1,968	National Science Foundation	1,323
Export-Import Bank, U.S.	401	Panama Canal Company	12,342
Farm Credit Administration	209	Railroad Retirement Board	1,723
Federal Communications Commission	1,869	Renegotiation Board	194
Federal Deposit Insurance Corporation	2,642	Securities and Exchange Commission	1,759
Federal Home Loan Bank Board	1,313	Selective Service System	3,570
Federal Maritime Commission	294	Small Business Administration	4,454
Federal Mediation and Conciliation Service	441	Smithsonian Institution	3,192
Federal Power Commission	1,255	Soldiers' and Airmen's Home	1,157
Federal Trade Commission	1,648	Tariff Commission	335
General Services Administration	38,557	Tennessee Valley Authority	24,726
Information Agency	8,948	U.S. Postal Service	704,744
Interstate Commerce Commission	1,931	Veterans Administration	200,303
		All other	1,884

Source: *Statistical Abstract of the United States 1974.*

the fact that the New Deal would not be wiped out by the Republican return to power.

HOUSING AND URBAN DEVELOPMENT. One of the first of Lyndon Johnson's Great Society acts, following his overwhelming 1964 election, was the founding of a Department of Housing and Urban Development (HUD). This brought together a number of independent agencies concerned with housing, urban renewal, and related issues. As the Great Society produced new programs—such as Model Cities—to deal with urban problems, these were added to HUD's jurisdiction.

TRANSPORTATION. Another of Johnson's Great Society actions was the establishment in 1966 of a Department of Transportation to coordinate the many overlapping jurisdictions of agencies concerned with land, sea, and air transport. This coincided with increasing public awareness of grave problems of transportation management, such as the decline of passenger railroads.

OTHER AGENCIES. In addition to the Cabinet-level departments, there are numerous other agencies that conduct important programs. Among the most prominent of these are the Veterans' Administration, the National Science Foundation, and the Central Intelligence Agency. Some of these are not sharply distinguishable in their activities from agencies enjoying Cabinet status.

Sometimes the responsibility for major new programs is not assigned to an established department but is given instead to a brand new agency. Such new units typically are not placed under the jurisdiction of a line department and may even be attached to the Executive Office of the President. This is done to increase the chances that the new tasks will be attacked without restraint from bureaucrats who are already set in their ways of dealing with the issue. Thus Johnson's "War on Poverty" was conducted largely by the independent Office of Economic Opportunity rather than by the Department of HEW or HUD. (The "poverty agency" faded out of existence during the Nixon administration.) By the same token, when public concern with ecological issues grew in the early 1970s, the newly created Environmental Protection Agency was sheltered under the President's wing.

INDEPENDENT REGULATORY COMMISSIONS

The independent regulatory commission is another major component of the executive branch. This type of agency was invented because the American ideological commitment to free enterprise was coupled with a pragmatic recognition that business is too important to be left entirely to businessmen. Most regulatory bodies deal with industries that are natural monopolies (such as electric power) or with business activities in which wholly unrestrained competition seems undesirable. For example, without some controls, unfair trade practices such as false advertising would be far more severe. Because Americans traditionally abhor "socialism," government regulation rather than government ownership seemed the best substitute for competition where competition did not seem to work or was not feasible.

For similar reasons, it was generally felt that such regulation should be kept free of "politics." The commissions were intended to make general policies in the public interest. Most of their actions would necessarily be an interference with the private property "rights" of the business they regulated. Thus, the invention of the commission form, in which the agency is headed by a board numbering between three and eleven members who are appointed by the President for staggered terms of from three to fourteen years. At any given time, therefore, these boards consist of appointees of two or three Presidents who may have had very different views on the kind of regulation desirable. What is more, they suffer from the general dilution of authority and administrative vigor that occurs when authority is dispersed among a number of individuals rather than concentrated in one.[2]

The commissions are *independent* in the sense that, unlike the conventional departments, they are not in the chain of command leading to the President. He cannot dismiss the commissioners at will, as he can Cabinet members. They are *quasi-legislative* in the sense that they typically operate under very general congressional statutes that empower them to make many supplementary laws of their own. They are *quasi-judicial* in the sense that they must follow courtlike "hearing" procedures in making decisions affecting the specific economic interests of individual firms. Their decisions are often appealable to the federal courts.

For many years, the commissions have been subject to a torrent of criticism for their alleged failure to pursue the public interest vigorously. It must be remembered, however, that the commission form was adopted precisely in those instances where Congress wanted some government intervention in the economy but not very much.

The commissions have done best at two tasks. The first is providing private industries with central services that they would otherwise have had to provide for themselves—such as compiling rates for shipments involving two or more railroads. The second is doing things which private industry could not do for itself without violating the anti-trust laws—for example, allocating the limited number of broadcasting frequencies to individual radio and television stations. The commissions have curbed the most fraudulent, exploitative tendencies of the most piratically inclined businessmen. On the whole, the commissions have served to focus, regularize, and enforce the standard practices and general business ethics of the industries they regulate.[3]

Another set of devices for government intervention in the economy includes the government-owned corporation, the mixed corporation in which both government and private persons hold stock, the corporation established by statute to pursue specified government policies whose stock is nevertheless privately owned, and the agencies which insure or guarantee or provide loans underwriting various business transactions. Figure 13-2 illustrates the diversity of forms and purposes of these governmental corporations.

---

[2] Marver H. Bernstein, *Regulating Business by Independent Commission* (Princeton, N.J.: Princeton University Press, 1955); and Paul W. MacAvoy, ed., *The Crisis of Regulatory Commissions* (New York: W. W. Norton & Company, 1970).

[3] See Henry J. Friendly, *The Federal Administrative Agencies: The Need for Better Definition of Standards* (Cambridge: Harvard University Press, 1962).

FIGURE 13–2
GOVERNMENT CORPORATIONS

WHOLLY-OWNED UNDER EXECUTIVE DEPARTMENTS
St. Lawrence Seaway Development Corporation
Commodity Credit Corporation
Federal Crop Insurance Corporation
Federal Prison Industries, Inc.
Federal Savings and Loan Insurance Corporation
Panama Canal Company

WHOLLY-OWNED INDEPENDENT CORPORATIONS
Federal Deposit Insurance Corp.
Export-Import Bank of Washington
Tennessee Valley Authority

MIXED-OWNERSHIP GOVERNMENT CORPORATIONS
Central Bank for Cooperatives
Regional Banks for Cooperatives
Federal Intermediate Credit Banks

INDEPENDENT NOT-FOR-PROFIT CORPORATIONS*
Aerospace Corp.
Institute for Defense Analysis
Logistics Management Institute
Institute for Urban Studies
Rand Corporation

UNIVERSITY AFFILIATED RESEARCH CENTERS*
Applied Physics Laboratory
Human Relations Research Organization
Brookhaven Laboratory
Lincoln Laboratory
Los Alamos National Laboratory

RESEARCH CENTER OPERATED BY PRIVATE INDUSTRY*
Oak Ridge National Laboratory

*Private institutions organized and initially financed by the federal government to provide contractual services to government

INDIRECT FEDERAL ADMINISTRATION

A conventional treatment of the executive branch of *government* would end here and would leave out some of the most significant developments of government in the years since the New Deal. As we shall see, major developments have taken place *outside* the official organization chart of the central government.

For example, there has been an enormous growth of federal grants-in-aid — that is, payments of federal funds to state and local governments. Most federal grant statutes provide for various formulas of state "matching," such as $25 from the state for every $75 of federal funds. Many provide elaborate "equalizing" formulas so that those states with the greatest needs and the least financial resources of their own receive more favorable ratios of federal-to-state funds than the wealthier states. These grants are distributed and supervised from Washington. They account for much of the activity of the Department of Health, Education, and Welfare, the Department of Housing and Urban Development, and the Department of Transportation. The size of the grant programs means that many state, county, and city agencies are now supported largely by federal funds and devote much of their time to administering federal programs. The level of federal supervision of these programs varies from careful to nonexistent. In effect, thousands of local government agencies serve as part of the federal administration.[1] Many federal programs are carried out largely by state and local agencies operating under their own political officials and their own budgeting, personnel, and policy directives.

[1] See Peter Morris and Martin Rein, *Dilemmas of Social Reform, Poverty and Community Action in the United States* (New York: Atherton, 1967); Gilbert Y. Steiner, *The State of Welfare* (Washington: The Brookings Institution, 1971); and Deil S. Wright, *Federal Grants-in-Aid: Perspectives and Alternatives* (Washington: American Enterprise Institute, 1968).

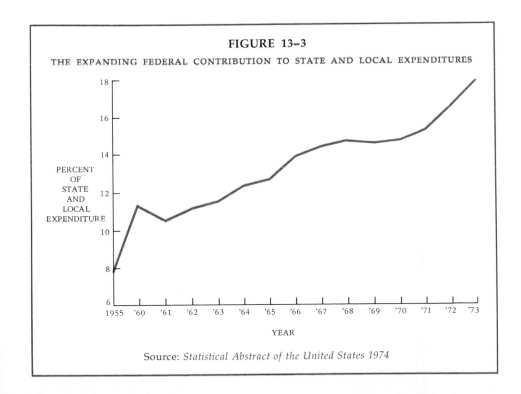

FIGURE 13–3

THE EXPANDING FEDERAL CONTRIBUTION TO STATE AND LOCAL EXPENDITURES

PERCENT OF STATE AND LOCAL EXPENDITURE

YEAR

Source: *Statistical Abstract of the United States 1974*

An even more innovative administrative device was introduced with the "war on poverty" under Presidents Kennedy and Johnson. Many new federal programs provide for grants directly to any local organization, governmental *or private,* which submits a suitable plan. In many cases, local governments were not eager to participate in some of these programs. As a result the bulk of funds under the Economic Opportunity Program was spent by nongovernmental community action groups organized specifically for the purpose.[5] Self-selected representatives of the poor and minority groups are very active in these bodies, which frequently become potent political forces in their communities. Substantial sums of federal money are dispensed today by administrators who are not in any traditional sense bureaucrats, civil servants, or even government employees.

OUTSIDE CONTRACTORS

The practice of "contracting out" is one of the more dramatic developments in the area of nongovernmental government. This practice chiefly involves defense production and defense and scientific research and development. For years, the armed services operated their own arsenals and shipyards, but they also bought substantial quantities of supplies—including food, clothing, and weapons systems—from civilian firms. Often, these purchases were made by contracts that specified quality, design, price and delivery date. The contracts were let after sealed bidding between competing firms, the contract going to the firm providing the best merchandise at the lowest price. These transactions were not substantially different from those between, say, a department store and a pants manufacturer. Indeed, most of the firms involved produced roughly the same goods for the civilian market, devoting only a small part of their production to military supplies. The government was simply one customer among many. A clear line thus could be drawn between the government and its civilian suppliers.

The combination of World War II and the sudden acceleration of the need for aerospace equipment in the postwar years produced a new system of defense production. It has since been supported by the increasing reliance on extremely expensive, incredibly elaborate weapons systems such as intercontinental missiles and supersonic bombers. These systems are useless for any but military purposes. They usually require technological innovations that will only occur in the actual course of developing the weapon.

The acquisition of such new weapons systems follows a typical course. One of the armed services indicates its desire for a new weapon to fulfill a particular mission. If such a weapons system seems worthwhile to the Defense Department, it will authorize a design competition. A number of firms then will be given government contracts to create designs. This operation typically involves several million dollars and the work of hundreds of engineers and scientists. If none of the rival designs seems entirely satisfactory,

---

[5] Daniel P. Moynihan, "What is Community Action?" *Public Interest* (1966), and John C. Donovan, *The Politics of Poverty* (Indianapolis: Pegasus, 1967).

TABLE 13-2

DEPARTMENT OF DEFENSE EXPENDITURES

(IN MILLIONS OF DOLLARS)

YEAR	TOTAL BUDGET	TOTAL MILITARY PROCUREMENT	RESEARCH AND DEVELOPMENT	CONTRACTS WITH EDUCATIONAL AND NON-PROFIT INSTITUTIONS
1965	49,578	27,997	6,236	738
1970	80,295	35,977	7,166	740
1973	76,021	36,920	8,157	740
1974	82,852	40,983	8,396	†
1975*	88,554	42,971	8,833	†
1976*	104,998	53,902	10,608	†

*Estimate   †Not available

Source: *Statistical Abstract of the United States 1974;* and *Budget of the United States Government, Fiscal Year 1976.*

a second and perhaps a third stage of design competition will be financed by the government. Although the government retains the power to choose among the completed designs, it is the private firms and their employees that make the thousands of decisions that go into the two or three completed packages from which the government takes its choice. Thus most of the design decisions on which the nation's security rests are made by private companies. When the Defense Department finally selects a design, it awards a contract for "development"—that is, doing the actual construction of the first prototype. Then, if the prototype is successful, further contracts for quantity production will be awarded.

At no stage does this process involve competitive bidding. Although firms which lost at the design stage may compete in the negotiations for later contracts, the designing firm almost always has such an obvious advantage over other firms in know-how and experience about its own design that it normally will get the subsequent contracts. These usually guarantee the contractor his cost plus some profit. Frequently, the government supplies the contractor with a great deal of production equipment and facilities. Moreover, major weapons systems contracts often are handled by firms which do most of their business with the government. When they get into financial trouble, they request assistance from the government. In this situation, it is not at all clear where government leaves off and private industry begins.[6]

Behind the design and development of new weapons lie the major scientific innovations that are the basis for technological advance. Recognizing this, the Defense Department has financed a great deal of basic scientific research for many years in the expectation of eventual payoffs. But

[6] See Clarence H. Danhof, *Government Contracting and Technological Change* (Washington: The Brookings Institution, 1968).

the government's science business is not confined to defense. Many federal agencies finance scientific research.[7] Some of this is done "in house"—that is, by scientists directly employed by the government and working in government facilities. Most of it, however, is accomplished by grants to outside scientists.

Basic science is very difficult to manage. There is usually no way to tell in advance which scientific leads will pay off in terms of "practical" knowledge. Research for which there seemed to be no practical application has proved to be the foundation for technological breakthroughs a few decades later. Nor is it clear that the government *should* finance only research that has a practical payoff. Indeed, precisely because "pure" science often does not have cash payoffs, it is likely to be neglected by private corporations engaged in scientific research. As a result, the purer the research in which scientists are interested, the more they rely on federal grants.

From the government's standpoint, it seems most sensible to invite scientists to submit research proposals and then to finance as many as possible. Of course, there is never enough money for everything, so the proposals must be comparatively evaluated and the best ones supported. But so long as the government has no policy goals, "best" can only mean soundest and most interesting from a scientific point of view. The best judges of this are the best scientists, but the best scientists are interested in doing science, not in working as scientific managers for the government. Accordingly, most government science agencies have minimal staffs and delegate decisions about what projects to support to advisory panels of distinguished non-government scientists who devote a few days or weeks a year to government service.

The grant system accounts for so much of the financing of university science departments and medical schools that today we get the same tangle in science and education that we have in weapons development. The "private" units become heavily dependent on the federal government. At the same time, so much government decision making has devolved on private parties that it is not clear where the government begins or ends.[8]

It should be obvious by now that it is misleading to speak of civil servants or bureaucrats as if they were a closed and distinct group. The design engineer at General Dynamics and the systems analyst at the RAND Corporation do the work of the national government. So does the Assistant Secretary of State for Near Eastern Affairs. So does the Superintendent of Schools of Schenectady as he works on an HEW grant application. Even within the national government, conceived in the narrowest sense, thousands of secretaries, shipping clerks, auto mechanics, and foremen are doing work that differs not at all from what their counterparts employed by private companies are doing.

---

[7] See Don K. Price, *Government and Science* (New York: New York University Press, 1954).

[8] See Ralph E. Lapp, *The Weapons Culture* (New York: W. W. Norton & Company, 1968); Merton J. Peck and Frederick M. Scherer, *The Weapons Acquisition Process* (Cambridge: Harvard University Press, 1962); and Julius Duscha, *Arms, Money, and Politics* (New York: Ives, Washburn, 1965).

CIVIL SERVICE

The patronage system, in which federal jobs were given as rewards for service to one of the political parties, has been replaced since the passage of the Civil Service Act of 1883 by a *merit system* supervised by the U.S. Civil Service Commission. A job description and an appropriate examination are created for each job in the classified system. Individuals seek out jobs by taking the scheduled examinations.

Although most federal workers do jobs that are in no way distinctively governmental, they are linked by common concerns related to the relatively enlightened, but far from perfect, personnel system that governs their careers. The growth of interest in federal employee unions is a reflection of that concern.[9] This movement had gone quite far in the Postal Service even before the reorganization of the Post Office Department, and presumably it will go further now. Gradually, the government is coming to recognize that its employees have a right to bargain collectively. Nevertheless, normal union-management relations are difficult to introduce into the federal government for three reasons. In the first place, it is not easy to see just how the right to strike can be incorporated into government service or what substitute for it can be devised. Second, although "management" for some purposes consists of the executive heads of the federal agencies, it is Congress that sets wages and the outlines of the hiring, firing, and promotion system. And it is not easy to see how to bargain collectively with Congress. Third, the movement toward unionism is discouraged because of a fear that unions might attempt to influence questions of public policy, in effect trying to assume powers that belong to the President and Congress.

The Civil Service Commission has arrived at a working arrangement with the departments that allows them considerable discretion in hiring and promotion, particularly at management levels. Commission supervision basically has been aimed at preventing arbitrary and unfair decisions and at equalizing promotion and pay policies among the various departments. The Commission also has actively recruited young management talent. Yet there are still many complaints that Commission red tape hampers dynamic personnel management in the departments and that the federal government has failed to compete successfully for professional and executive talent.[10]

To deal with this latter problem, an attempt was made during the Eisenhower administration to put the government in a better competitive position for attracting and holding top executives, professionals, and scientists. The commission established a number of "super-grades" with higher pay

[9] See Maurice E. O'Donnell, "New Dimensions in Employee-Management Relations in the Federal Civil Service" in O'Donnell, ed., *Readings in Public Administration* (Boston: Houghton Mifflin, 1966); and Neal R. Peirce, "Public Employees," *National Journal,* August 23, 1975, pp. 1198–1206.

[10] See Dean E. Mann, "The Selection of Federal Political Executives," *American Political Science Review,* 58 (March 1964), 81–99; W. Lloyd Warner et al., *The American Federal Executive* (New Haven: Yale University Press, 1963); and David T. Stanley et al., *Men Who Govern* (Washington: The Brookings Institution, 1967).

scales for outstanding personnel. While super-grade employees are protected and regulated by the Commission rules for the career service, their
appointment is subject to control by agency heads. Indeed, President Johnson ordered that no super-grade would be appointed without direct approval
from the White House. Even with the super-grades, however, the federal
government cannot offer salaries that are competitive with those in the private sector. In 1975 the top pay grade for career civil servants was just under
$38,000. This is far below the salaries paid highly regarded executives and
professionals outside government.

The civil service system has generated other snags from the management
side. In most modern organizations, personnel management is an important
executive tool in establishing policies and insuring their implementation.
Experts on management increasingly have come to understand that there is
no clear line between policy and administration. Even "lower level" administrators strongly influence what policies are adopted and how they really
turn out. Consequently, elected officials often are frustrated by a merit
system that protects civil servants against arbitrary firing and demotion so
thoroughly that they are often free to thwart or change the policies of their
political superiors.

The Ford administration ran into this problem in 1975 on the issue of
affirmative action in college faculty hiring. In the previous decade, a series
of statutes, presidential executive orders, court decisions, and agency regulations had produced a substantial but imprecise body of law intended to
remedy racial and sexual discrimination. At the same time, several federal
agencies had been created or greatly expanded to enforce these laws. The
bureaucrats in these agencies were predominantly women and members of
minority groups. The believed that bold steps were necessary to end racism
and sexism in all areas of American life. One area singled out for particular
attention was universities, whose faculties were overwhelmingly white
males. In the early 1970s the government required the nation's leading
universities to develop individual affirmative action plans that met federal
approval, or face the loss of all federal funds. Many educators felt that the
plans they were forced to adopt committed their institutions to thinly
disguised employment quotas based on sex and race. Some officials denied
this, others insisted that the schools' alleged past sins could be remedied
only by reverse discrimination. Perhaps the most common assessment of
the situation, however, was that whether "affirmative action" became a
synonym for "reverse discrimination" would depend on the case-by-case
enforcement of the plans by the federal officials in regional field offices of
the various civil rights agencies.

In 1975 President Ford and the relevant members of his Cabinet came to
feel that attempts to eliminate racism and sexism had gone too far with
respect to faculty hiring. In other words, they accepted the accusation that
the government's coercive powers were being used to subordinate merit to
racial and sexual considerations in hiring professors. But having come to
this conclusion, it was not at all clear to the President and his Cabinet
secretaries what they could do about it. The officials who were in day-to-day
contact with the universities did not share their superiors' views. These

bureaucrats were the people who had negotiated the affirmative action plans. They would determine whether each school was "in compliance" with its plan and would investigate and make rulings on specific charges of discrimination by groups and individuals. Having civil service protection, they could not be fired without cause. A well-publicized mass resignation by some of them might be too high a political price for the President to pay to get his way about the policy. The same desire to avoid a confrontation on this issue restrained the President and his appointees from a clear-cut announcement of a change in government policy.

WHO WORKS FOR THE GOVERNMENT?

THE CAREER EXECUTIVES. Excluding scientists, engineers, and lawyers, a picture of the typical career executive can be outlined. More often male than female, he comes from almost any sort of family background, with two exceptions. (1) One exception is what we would expect: blacks and Spanish-heritage people are scarce in the highest levels. (It is also true, however, that minorities encounter much less job discrimination in government employment than in the private sector.) (2) The other exception is more revealing about the character of the American civil service: outside the Foreign Service, very few people from wealthy families work for the government as a career. This is a striking contrast to almost all other industrial countries, where government service does not take second place to a career in business or the professions.

The typical executive is at least forty years of age, with a college degree and perhaps some graduate training. If his bureau's activities are concentrated in particular parts of the country, he is likely to come from one of those regions himself. For example, someone in the Bureau of Land Management probably hails from the West, whereas someone in the Bureau of Family Services doubtless comes from a city. By the same token, his college degree probably matches his bureau. The BLM employee may well have majored in forestry or conservation, and the Bureau of Family Services has more than its share of people with master's degrees in social work.

If our executive had significant work experience in the private sector, it was a long time ago. He has served in no more than two government agencies, and has been in the one where he reached executive status for at least twenty years. He probably joined that bureau early in his adult life and worked his way up from a low-level position to top management. Because most departments have an extensive network of field offices, many executives spend their entire careers outside Washington, and few have worked only in the capital. He is unlikely to move to another bureau or to be promoted to a position at the top of his department. He is dedicated to the affairs of his particular slice of the government's business and probably knows more about it than anyone else.

It is easy enough to see the drawbacks of this personnel system: (1) The absence of an elite career track discourages the very brightest young people. It is not so much that everyone starts at (or near) the bottom, but that for people of great promise there is no recognized "special route" to the top that begins at the bottom. (2) There is little opportunity for "lateral entry" into the highest ranks by outsiders who have not worked their way up, no matter how qualified they may be. (3) As this suggests, in practice qualifications for high-level posts are defined in limited technical terms corresponding to the bureau's special mission, rather than in more general terms that would emphasize broad administrative skills. (4) The result, then, is that the experience of top-level civil servants is intensive rather than extensive. The dominant perspective is that of the bureau in which the individual has spent his career.

THE OFFICER CORPS. There are two major "officer corps" in the government. The distinctive features of such corps are: (1) They have their own personnel systems rather than falling under the Civil Service Commission. (2) The number of people in the corps is relatively small. (3) Admission to the corps is not easy and occurs only at the most junior level. (4) Entry is assumed to be the first step on a ladder to high position, thus all members of the corps share an identity as a self-conscious elite. (5) There is no lateral entry except in unusual circumstances, such as a major war.

The best known of the officer corps is of course the military one. There has been a great deal of speculation and some hard research about the military profession, none of it very conclusive.[11] Military officers do not have a distinctly different philosophy or set of values from the rest of us. Like all professionals, they probably overemphasize the importance of their own responsibilities. But unfortunately, their responsibilities have in fact been almost impossible to overemphasize in recent times.

If "the military mind" creates any problems for American politics, they come from the fact that there is not one mind but three. The separate personnel systems and the separate loyalties that go with each of the three separate branches of the service have done more than anything else to hamper true unification of our military system.[12] As a general rule, the leaders of any administrative agency are committed to their agency as an institution and to what they consider its traditional missions. The closer the missions of different agencies, the greater the potential for conflict between them. Each will try to maintain the broadest possible jurisdiction consistent with its traditions. Thus the Departments of the Interior and Agriculture have squabbled for seventy years about where the Forest Service should be located and which one should properly be in charge of soil conservation. Since all three military services have overlapping missions, they sometimes seem to devote more strategic energies to jurisdictional maneuvers within the American government than to dealing with foreign military forces.

The only other large officer corps is the Foreign Service.[13] The Foreign

THE DEPARTMENT OF
DEFENSE, HEAD-
QUARTERED IN THE
PENTAGON, IN-
CLUDES THE DE-
PARTMENTS OF THE
ARMY, NAVY, AND
AIR FORCE, AS WELL
AS THE ORGANIZA-
TION OF THE JOINT
CHIEFS OF STAFF.
Wide World Photos

[11] For example, Morris Janowitz, *The Professional Soldier* (New York: Free Press, 1961); and Charles C. Moskos, Jr., ed., *The American Enlisted Man* (New York: Russell Sage, 1969).

[12] Ernest J. King and Walter M. Whitehill, *Fleet Admiral King: A Naval Record* (New York: W. W. Norton & Company, 1952), p. 635.

[13] Katherine Crane, *Mr. Carr of State: Forty-Seven Years in the Department of State* (New York: St. Martin's Press, 1960); and Frances Fiedler and Godfrey Harris, *The Quest for Foreign Affairs Officers: Their Recruitment and Selection* (Washington: Carnegie Endowment for International Peace, 1966).

Service is designed to be an elite corps. Entrance is by a special and difficult examination favoring first-class liberal arts students. Traditionally, a disproportionate share of entrants were drawn from the dozen most prestigious colleges and universities. Thereafter, the Foreign Service Officer gradually works up in rank, just as the military officer does, on the basis of seniority and the written evaluations submitted evey year by his superiors. Officers are rotated between various posts approximately once every three years, usually alternating between a job in the State Department in Washington and in an embassy or consulate abroad. Nearly all important jobs in the State Department below the assistant secretary level are held by Foreign Service Officers.

There are three characteristics of all officer corps systems which contribute to the difficulties faced by both the Foreign Service and the military services. First, the aim of an officer corps is to provide each officer with a career-long chain of work and education that is supposed to fit him for one of the top jobs, whether it be general, admiral, or career ambassador. High morale and loyalty to the corps depend upon all officers feeling that they have an equal chance of making high rank. Clearly most officers will not reach the top, but all must be given job assignments as if they were going to. Their careers must be managed so that they develop whatever mystical quality the corps uses to symbolize the capacity to do the top job. In the military services it is called "leadership"; in the State Department it is known as "diplomacy."

These qualities, it is widely felt, can best be generated by exposing an officer to a wide range of the jobs done by the corps and by protecting him from the narrowing influence of specialization. Both the Foreign Service and the military service rotate all officers from place to place and job to job every three or four years. Although an officer's experience usually is concentrated somewhat in particular fields and regions of the world, someone who specializes excessively is doomed to end his career short of the top. As a result, most officers are jacks-of-all-trades and masters of none. Thus the commander of a navy yard may know nothing in particular about ship repair although he has served on lots of ships. Or the Ambassador to Peru may never before have worked in Peru although he has served previously in Brazil and Panama. Specialist assignments are shunned particularly by the best officers with the most potential. This places officer corps at a disadvantage in dealing with the rest of the government, where special expertise is considered essential in dealing with contemporary problems. The State Department in particular has paid dearly for its lack of expertise in such specialized fields as economics, losing much of its influence in such areas to other agencies.

A second weakness of officer corps is the excessive preoccupation of the officers with their career prospects rather than with the job at hand. All job holders in and out of government want to be promoted, but in officer corps the expectation of transfer in a short time and the institutionalized emphasis on permanent rank as the crucial mark of achievement are hardly calculated to inspire undivided commitment to the job at hand.

Finally, promotion in officer corps is often slow and depends on seniority plus the good opinions of one's superiors. This is likely to encourage the conformist organization man and may drive out the brilliant and innovative dissenter. Thus officer corps have a structural bias toward caution. This tendency is offset in the armed forces by the high premium that the military places on personal initiative and aggressiveness as desirable qualities for leaders in combat. The tendency is aggravated in the Foreign Service by the premium placed on harmony, tact, and compromise as "diplomatic" qualities.

MEMBERS OF THE PROFESSIONS AS CIVIL SERVANTS

The Foreign Service and military services present one of the facets of the more general problem of professionalism in government service. The diplomatic and military professions, of course, encompass a variety of more specific skills. And they are limited to a single government department. The only way to be an ambassador or the commander of an armored division is in government service. The other professions used by the federal government are different in two respects: (1) they cut across departmental lines; and (2) they are practiced largely outside government. Their training and sources of identity and achievement are also largely nongovernmental. Professionals are loyal to the ethics, values, standards, and personnel of the profession itself, as well as to those of the government agency where they work. Thus a physicist in the Bureau of Standards thinks of himself as a physicist first. Whether he thinks of himself as a government employee second and a member of the Bureau of Standards third, or vice versa, is not entirely clear. What is clear is that circumstances may arise in which the primary loyalty to the profession may run counter to the demands of public policy and political leaders.

On the positive side, however, is the fact that professional ties outside the government provide an important check upon certain aspects of government power. Loyalty to professional standards may lead civil servants to resist political pressure. The government chemist is unlikely to falsify his experimental findings to satisfy a political superior or even his own policy preferences. Nor is he likely to conceal what he is doing from other chemists who are the peer group to which he looks for professional approval. Thus professionalism encourages a certain openness and permeability in government. Government professionals outraged by political decisions that contradict their professional judgments are a major source of leaks to the press and Congress. We should be quite clear, however, that the price of this openness is insubordination by bureaucrats to the country's elected leaders. What looks like "political pressure" to the government specialist on birth control is the manifestation of democratic opinion to the elected official who overrules the specialist.

CLIENTELISM

As we have seen, there is a twilight zone where government directly overlaps the private sector. Among the inhabitants of this twilight zone are the agencies frequently described as *clientele oriented*, or, for short, *clientele agencies*. A clientele agency seems to place a higher priority on certain speci-

SHIRLEY TEMPLE BLACK, U.S. AMBASSADOR TO GHANA.
Wide World Photos

fic interests or groups than on the general public interest. The reason is that the clientele agency often acts as if its most important contribution to the public interest is to represent the interests of its clientele. The public interest cannot easily be defined and in any event is too vast a concept to be a useful guide to policy makers. But the interests of, say, wheat growers are not too vague, and it is difficult to argue that they should be ignored by the government. The Departments of Agriculture, Labor, and Commerce, for example, were established to be the voices of the farmer, worker, and businessman in the inner circle of the Cabinet.

To be sure, none of the great departments serves simply and exclusively as a benevolent friend of its clients. For the very federal programs that its clients wanted and the department now administers invariably contain controls and limitations on the clients. The clients do not necessarily like all the rules the department enforces, but they have to face the fact that government largesse is almost never unlimited. Congress generally demands some level of accountability from the recipients. At the very minimum, departments often must choose which of their clients gets more and which less. For example, the educational policy makers in the Department of Health, Education, and Welfare could never hope to make both their academic and vocational education clienteles totally happy, because they are in direct competition for the funds available.

The most dedicated of the clientele agencies have been the regulatory commissions.[14] One cause of this phenomenon is the fact that specialization merges so readily with clientelism. The typical official at the Interstate Commerce Commission has spent many years dealing with railroad problems. His whole career revolves about railroads. Most of the people he talks to outside the government are railroad officials. If and when he leaves the ICC, he probably will go to work for a railroad. The government man who eats, breathes, and sleeps railroads—or airlines, or the stock market— would have to have a heart of stone not to develop a special sympathy for "his" industry and the problems of the men who run it.

Of course, the same is true of the officials who watch housing in HUD or forests in Agriculture, but there are special factors that tend to create especially high levels of clientelism in the regulatory commissions. Chief among these is the ambiguity of the concept of "regulation" itself. Regulation is designed to protect the public while preserving the profit motivation and the private ownership of the regulated industries. One of the responsibilities written into the congressional statutes creating each of the commissions is the duty to preserve the health of the industries regulated. This means, in effect, preserving their profits. The regulator thus inevitably walks both sides of the street. The industry side of the street is thickly populated with executives who are articulate exponents of industrial needs, but the public side is only occasionally and sporadically manned by anyone at all. In recent

[14] See William L. Cary, *Politics and the Regulatory Agencies* (New York: McGraw-Hill, 1967); and Robert S. Friedman et al., "Administrative Agencies and the Publics They Serve," *Public Administration Review,* 26 (1966).

years, however, there has been a dramatic rise in the activities of public interest and consumer groups, as we saw in Chapter 8. Through a combination of publicity and lawsuits to compel the commissions to enforce the law, these groups have begun to redress the balance between the interests of clients and consumers.

INTEREST GROUPS AND ADMINISTRATION

We have seen that one of the reasons organized interest groups are able to exert influence in Congress is because they can supply staff work and special expertise which Congress lacks. This source of influence is, of course, sharply reduced in dealing with the bureaucracy, which knows as much about the subject at issue as does the lobbyist. Nevertheless, there is a great deal of formal lobbying of bureaucrats.[15] Interest group representatives make the views and goals of their clients known to the relevant agency. In many instances they actually bring to light some facts or at least interpretations of the facts that are new to the agency.

If an interest group is not satisfied with the response it gets from an agency, it can go over the heads of agency officials, directing its appeals to Congress, the White House, or the department head. When agency officials cannot satisfy the interest groups that come to them, it is often not because they are unwilling to do so, but because their hands are tied by policies and regulations emanating from higher up. In such cases, these officials generally welcome the assistance of lobbyists who can rove across the government and elsewhere in society lining up support.

There is no question that the major access of the "interests" to the bureaucracy comes not through contact by lobbyists or organized groups, but through the day-to-day routine business that government officials do with recipients of government services. The Bureau of Land Management officials who run the grazing program find themselves out on the range talking with cattlemen about cows, grass, water, and beef prices. The Office of Education people who supervise federal grants-in-aid for elementary education find themselves corresponding regularly with the Reading Curriculum Supervisor of the Omaha Public Schools over details of her proposal for a grant to cover the costs of a remedial reading project.

Reinforcing this constant routine contact is the high level of similarity between the bureaucrat and his or her counterpart in the private sector or in local government. Chances are that the government man on the range himself grew up in the West and has a degree in animal husbandry from a state university. The Office of Education executive probably has an advanced degree from the same kind of university as her Omaha counterpart, and they both probably share whatever professional ideology the schools of education have been purveying.

INTEREST GROUPS
OCCASIONALLY
ORGANIZE PROTEST
DEMONSTRATIONS AS
A WAY OF MAKING
THEIR OPINIONS
KNOWN.
Wide World Photos

[15] Lewis A. Dexter, *How Organizations Are Represented in Washington* (Indianapolis: Bobbs-Merrill, 1969).

This convergence not only makes routine contact easier and more harmonious, but also reduces the need for actual lobbying as a means of bringing outside views into the bureaucracy. There is a great deal of "virtual representation" in Washington and the field offices, in the sense that the bureaus tend to be staffed by people who look at things in much the same way as do those with whom they deal. Thus, it should not be assumed that because the bureaucracy is not an elected branch of government, it is an alien presence that must be prodded by a democratic, elected Congress. Various elements in the bureaucracy *do* represent various interests in the world at large. Whether the pattern of bureaucratic representation adequately reflects the pattern of needs in the society as a whole is about as open a question as whether the congressional pattern does.

ADMINISTRATORS AS INDEPENDENT INFLUENCES IN GOVERNMENTAL DECISION MAKING

In the last decade or so, political scientists have overemphasized the impact of clienteles and interest groups on governmental action. Such an emphasis results in a picture of the government official as frantically balancing and compromising conflicting political demands. While this phenomenon is real and is felt by most high-ranking bureaucrats, bureaucrats are not mere conflict mediators. Most of their time is spent in dealing with what they see as the problems of the "real" as opposed to the "political" world. How can minority children be brought to reading grade level most economically? Which line of research is most likely to yield a cure for cancer? Can we get a nuclear reactor design that will produce power at competitive cost without excessive thermal pollution? Which cutting practices will produce maximum long-term timber yield? How can we organize a local poverty office to coordinate the thirty-seven anti-poverty programs Congress has enacted?

This concern of bureaucrats with positive program operation was once emphasized by traditional students of public administration in terms of the distinction between politics and administration. This distinction has been subject to devastating intellectual attack in recent years, as it became clear that administrative decisions inevitably have policy implications.[16] Nevertheless, the attack on the distinction should not be allowed to obscure the high degree to which bureaucrats are devoted to finding technically correct answers, rational and efficient administrative arrangements, and the best solutions to real human problems. It is for this reason that we have placed so much emphasis on the professional training and the specialized expertise to be found in the bureaucracy. What is technically correct, efficient, and rational is usually defined by bureaucrats, not by the political demands on them but by the standards and procedures enshrined in their professional training and identity. The highway engineer in the Department of Transpor-

---

[16] Harold Seidman, *Politics, Position, and Power,* 2nd ed. (New York: Oxford University Press, 1975).

tation does not consult the wishes of the President, the steel industry, or the American Automobile Association in determining whether the right girders have been specified for a bridge. He consults a stress table in an engineering text. For most bureaucrats, the outside world consists primarily of problems to be solved, and only secondarily of political conflicts to be resolved. It is precisely this ordering of priorities that makes the bureaucracy such a potent political force.

Unfortunately, the strengths of the bureaucracy are also its weaknesses. The most important of these arise from the division of labor that is inherent in any bureaucracy. The single-minded concern of many bureaucrats with their own specialized fields leads to problems of internal control and coordination in the bureaucracy as a whole. Each group of specialists tends to develop particular perspectives, in which the value of its own programs and policies naturally tends to be exaggerated. This distortion is aggravated by the fact that each segment of the bureaucracy deals almost exclusively with its own clientele, who also are likely to hold an exaggerated view of the importance of the government services rendered to them. As a result, bureaucrats often find it difficult, if not impossible, to see the programs they administer in the context of a comprehensive view of government policies.

LIMITATIONS ON HIERARCHICAL CONTROL. Presidents and their Cabinet members and other appointees face major difficulties in controlling the bureaucracy. The first is that a department head does not have policy preferences on most of the specific decisions that he or she must make. He does not enter office convinced of how much money should be spent on the school lunch program or whether the Army should have one or three airmobile divisions. By the time policy decisions reach the secretary, the bureaucracy has defined the problem, narrowed the alternative solutions, and marshalled the factual data to support this shaping of the agenda.

This brings us to the secretary's (or President's) second major limitation. It is almost impossible for him to reclaim data or alternatives discarded early in the policy-making process. He will never know of the memorandum to an official in the Food and Nutrition Service of the Department of Agriculture, citing experiments conducted under a federal grant at the University of Kansas showing that school breakfasts would be both cheaper and more beneficial to students than school lunches. Nor is he likely to discover that the allocation of major artillery components to corps level in a three-year-old reorganization scheme makes the three airmobile divisions the Army is asking for really equivalent to only one division because the necessary artillery support for them is now assigned to corps headquarters. We cannot expect that the President or the relevant department secretary will just happen of their own knowledge to know enough about childhood metabolism or artillery support plans to even ask the right questions at the right time. The people who do know enough, of course, are the bureaucrats—nutritionists in the Department of Agriculture and career officers in the Army. (Both of these examples are imaginary.)

The President's third major limitation is his limited follow-up capacity. Even if he firmly makes his own policy decision, it is difficult for him (and his Cabinet appointees) to insure that the intention of the decision is not altered or even reversed after it is passed back to the bureaucracy for execution. The President may clearly choose school lunches because he wants to improve learning conditions for poor children. Two years later, he may find that a combination of diligence by suburban school authorities, inefficiency by administrators in large city schools, and inattention by Department of Agriculture officials have totally defeated his purpose. The Department of Agriculture has supplied food to every school district that qualified for aid by submitting a complicated application. The Department's officials may not have known or cared that most poor school districts were not applying, and most wealthier ones were, so most of the food went not to the poor, but to the middle class.

There are, of course, various organizational devices that the President and his Cabinet members can use to deal with these three problems, as we saw in Chapter 12. We should not conclude that political officials are helpless before the bureaucrats. But we also should remember that there are less than 7,000 political appointees and almost 3 million civil servants. The former are in government for a short time, whereas the latter spend their careers there. The bureaucrats are experts at their particular fields, whereas the political appointees probably are not.

AGENCY OVERLAP AND COMPETITION

Many government programs overlap any single bureau or other sub-unit of the government. For example, the Office of Contract Compliance in the Department of Labor, the Civil Rights Division of the Department of Justice, the Office of Civil Rights in the Department of Health, Education, and Welfare, and the Equal Employment Opportunity Commission, which is independent of any department, all are concerned with the problem of sex and race discrimination in universities. Sometimes a university can painstakingly work out an affirmative action program after years of negotiation with one agency, only to find that the agreement doesn't satisfy another one. This happened in early 1975 to the University of California's Berkeley campus, when the Department of Labor refused to approve an agreement hammered out with the Department of HEW.

Because problems overlap, but federal agencies and personnel do not, inter-agency coordination is a crucial challenge for the executive branch. A number of devices are available to attack this problem. The most obvious and common is the *hierarchical* pattern of organization. Bureaus operating in similar areas and thus likely to encounter overlaps are grouped together under an assistant secretary who presumably can coordinate their activities from above. In turn, the assistant secretaries are grouped under a secretary who also undertakes coordination. Coordination between agencies of two different departments can be achieved through the two secretaries concerned.

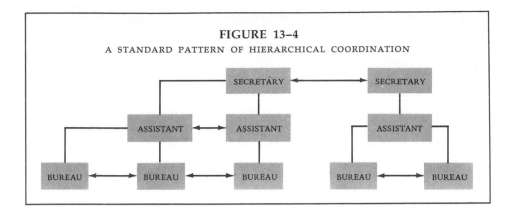

FIGURE 13–4

A STANDARD PATTERN OF HIERARCHICAL COORDINATION

And if the secretaries cannot coordinate their two departments, the President can.

Subordinates who come into conflict are thus highly motivated to solve the problem themselves in order to avoid the imposition of solutions from above. As a result, the hierarchical system is responsible, both directly and indirectly, for a great deal of coordination. Indeed, if the hierarchical system did *not* work, it is unlikely that the government could be run at all. But if hierarchy worked perfectly, Washington would be far different from the way it actually is. As we have seen, career officials sometimes appeal the unfavorable decisions of their political superiors by making "end runs" to Congress with the backing of friendly interest groups. This is a risky strategy, but it is not uncommon or unsuccessful when done with skill and subtlety.

Moreover, hierarchy is unsuitable when coordination must be attained between two or more equal and independent agencies, like the Departments of Defense and State. In such circumstances, two methods of *lateral coordination* are widely used in the federal government to supplement hierarchical methods. The first is the much denounced but quite unavoidable *committee system*. Hundreds of committees composed of officials of roughly equal status from different agencies meet constantly to work out differences and concert mutual plans. The membership and jurisdiction of some of these committees are established by statute, but most are temporary arrangements that come and go as new problems arise and are settled. Generally, an assistant secretary in one department who encounters overlapping concerns with an assistant secretary in another will avoid referring his coordination needs upward to his own secretary. Instead, he will discuss the problem with his fellow assistant secretary in a committee where they both sit as equals.

Committees are often criticized for reaching "lowest common denominator" solutions. Differences between agencies are compromised, unresolved conflicts are papered over by vague generalizations, and a facade of harmony is established behind which each agency continues to go its own way. To some extent this criticism is valid, for committees of equals can hardly be expected to resolve implacable agency quarrels. Fortunately, however, the areas of mutual concern with which committees must deal rarely involve such quarrels. Most inter-agency committees operate as good media for the exchange of information and viewpoints among officials who are concerned with similar or overlapping problems but who are not normally in face-to-face contact with one another. More often than not, these officials can find common, mutually beneficial courses of action.

A second and similar lateral coordination mechanism is the *clearance system* in which a report, evaluation, or policy recommendation drawn up by one agency must be "cleared" by other agencies involved in the same area before being sent on to higher authority. At the minimum, clearance insures that each agency is kept informed of relevant actions by its fellows. Clearance does not usually involve a veto power, but it does give the agency receiving the report an opportunity to file a dissent. Because agencies do not want their reports passed on with dissenting opinions attached, the initiating agency usually is willing to modify its proposals or at least its language to meet the objections. Thus, clearance provides the same opportunity for genuine interchange and cooperation, and the same risk of papering over differences, as the committee device. The clearance system is most widely used in international affairs, in which it is obviously important that whatever the United States says, it must speak with one voice.

The most general complaint about lateral coordination is its dampening effect on innovation. An agency with a new idea immediately finds itself confronted by a half dozen other agencies anxious to preserve the status quo. Innovations are compromised to death. Bureaucrats become less concerned with changing the real world and more concerned with getting the fourteen necessary signatures. By the time the State Department's Italian desk officer has gotten the clearance of the Bureau of Near Eastern and South Asian Affairs, the Commerce Department's Bureau of International Commerce, the Assistant Secretary of Treasury for International Affairs, and an Assistant Secretary of Defense for a proposal to encourage a particular program of Italian technical aid to Lebanon, the Lebanese may not want aid any more. Despite these drawbacks, however, lateral coordination seems to be necessary. Unconstrained agency initiatives would have the government charging off in all directions at once.

THE POLITICS OF ADMINISTRATIVE REORGANIZATION

It is often felt that many of the problems of both hierarchical and lateral coordination could be eased or eliminated if only the government were correctly organized. Since the 1930s, the United States government has been subjected to a series of reorganization studies, proposals, and actions, all purportedly designed to improve "management," which for the most part meant improved coordination of disparate government programs. The would-be reorganizers argued that if all the like activities of government could be put in the same organizational box, or at least in neighboring boxes, it would be easier to insure that their activities reinforced one another.

In fact, however, closer scrutiny of most reorganization proposals reveals that they are more concerned with bringing certain policies to the fore and suppressing others than with coordination.[17] Although occasional bureaucratic overlaps and other irrationalities can be organized out of existence, most reorganization schemes merely substitute one coordination problem for another. For instance, when the Office of Education had a Division of Vocational Education, a Mental Retardation Branch, and a Technical Education Branch, all three were concerned with elementary schools, secondary schools, and higher education. Interbureau coordination of their programs was required for each level. When the Office was reorganized into Elementary, Secondary, and Higher Education Bureaus, each had vocational, technical, and remedial programs which had to be coordinated with similar programs in the other bureaus.

Congress has delegated much of its reorganization power to the President. He can use it to create new and more hospitable organizational settings for programs that might not appeal to the agency to which they normally would have been assigned. Or he can create new positions in old agencies that can be filled with new men energetically dedicated to the program while agency deadwood is shunted aside.[18] Nevertheless, as President Nixon learned when he attempted a major consolidation of departments, the politics of administrative reorganization is sticky and complex. Interest groups and Capitol Hill allies of the agencies involved frequently are able to block efforts at reorganization. But even without reorganization, the glamor and smell of success which surround programs specially anointed by the President may inspire increased administrative morale and support. Everybody wants to be part of a winner.

THE BUDGET: A KEY TOOL OF POLICY COORDINATION

Today, perhaps the most important tool of coordination is the budget. The budget provides the President with a method of controlling the bureaucracy. Presidential leadership is largely a matter of setting priorities. The best measure of priorities is money, and the budget is the government's instrument for allocating money. Certainly the budgetary process is central to presidential control. The budgetary process and the format of the budget are rather complex. Figure 13–5, which shows the timing of the budgetary process, should help the reader grasp this process more easily.

The President's overall budget target is a crucial aspect of presidential control over the bureaucracy. In setting a target figure, the President announces roughly what the bureaucratic units can expect and what is reasonable to ask for. Of course, agency heads in all departments routinely put in requests exceeding the target. Nevertheless, their general budgetary ambitions, their own receptiveness to new programs, and their bargaining power are deeply affected by the reactions they anticipate from "above." Whether the presidential target figure looks tight or generous determines much of their anticipations.[19]

[17] Seidman, *Politics, Position, and Power.*
[18] Seidman, *Politics, Position, and Power.*
[19] Aaron Wildavsky, *The Politics of the Budgetary Process,* 2nd ed. (Boston: Little, Brown, 1974).

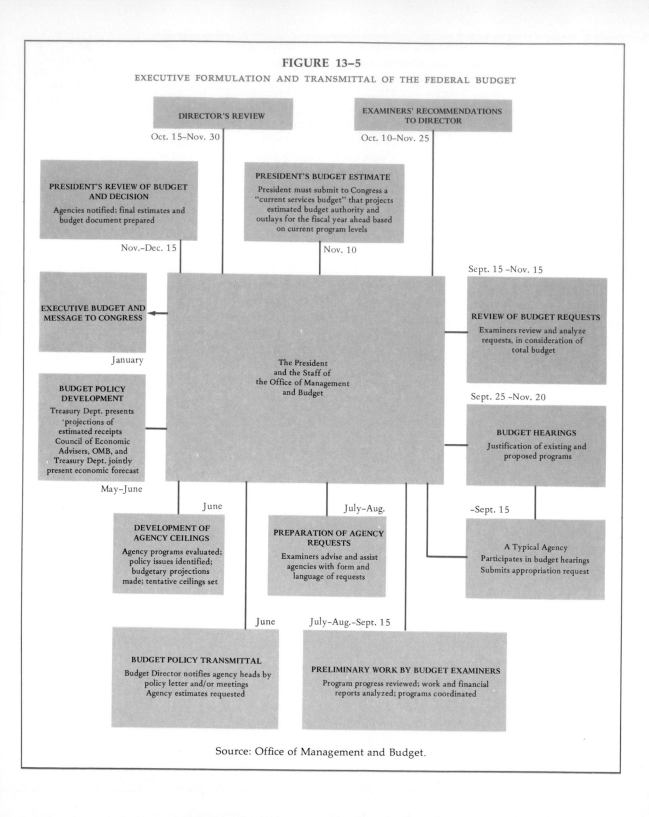

FIGURE 13–5

EXECUTIVE FORMULATION AND TRANSMITTAL OF THE FEDERAL BUDGET

DIRECTOR'S REVIEW

Oct. 15–Nov. 30

EXAMINERS' RECOMMENDATIONS TO DIRECTOR

Oct. 10–Nov. 25

PRESIDENT'S REVIEW OF BUDGET AND DECISION

Agencies notified; final estimates and budget document prepared

Nov.–Dec. 15

PRESIDENT'S BUDGET ESTIMATE

President must submit to Congress a "current services budget" that projects estimated budget authority and outlays for the fiscal year ahead based on current program levels

Nov. 10

Sept. 15–Nov. 15

EXECUTIVE BUDGET AND MESSAGE TO CONGRESS

January

REVIEW OF BUDGET REQUESTS

Examiners review and analyze requests, in consideration of total budget

The President and the Staff of the Office of Management and Budget

BUDGET POLICY DEVELOPMENT

Treasury Dept. presents projections of estimated receipts Council of Economic Advisers, OMB, and Treasury Dept. jointly present economic forecast

May–June

Sept. 25–Nov. 20

BUDGET HEARINGS

Justification of existing and proposed programs

June

DEVELOPMENT OF AGENCY CEILINGS

Agency programs evaluated; policy issues identified; budgetary projections made; tentative ceilings set

July–Aug.

PREPARATION OF AGENCY REQUESTS

Examiners advise and assist agencies with form and language of requests

–Sept. 15

A Typical Agency Participates in budget hearings Submits appropriation request

June

BUDGET POLICY TRANSMITTAL

Budget Director notifies agency heads by policy letter and/or meetings Agency estimates requested

July–Aug.–Sept. 15

PRELIMINARY WORK BY BUDGET EXAMINERS

Program progress reviewed; work and financial reports analyzed; programs coordinated

Source: Office of Management and Budget.

Each department's own internal budget examination is potentially an instrument for exercising political control by the secretary over the bureaucracy. The budget requests submitted to the department by its various bureaus always substantially exceed any realistic hopes about what the department will be able to get for them. It is clear to all his bureaucratic subordinates that the secretary and his budget officer will have to make some choices between bureaus within the department. Whether or not those choices become tools for insuring that the bureaucracy responds to the policy desires of the administration varies widely from department to department. In some departments, for example, a number of the sub-units operate very popular programs. They enjoy strong support from public and congressional constituencies, so that the secretary may not feel he is in a position to shift budgetary favor from them to other sub-units. What the secretary takes away, Congress might well restore in the appropriations process. Needless to say, the more popular a sub-unit's programs, the more friends that agency will have on Capitol Hill. In addition, there are always some departments in which the secretary simply does not know enough about the affairs of the department to apply the budgetary carrot and stick as a means of determining policy. If he cannot penetrate his subordinates' budget figures to grasp the relative merit of various programs, his theoretical power to alter those figures will be of no use to him.

The Office of Management and Budget serves a critical coordinating staff function in connecting the President with the numerous agencies of the administrative branch. The core of the OMB is a group of about sixty budget examiners. Although there is some rotation and reassignment, most examiners work on the budgets of the same set of bureaus for a number of years. They typically are expert in the substantive concerns and the past history of the organizations they examine. Viewed from the standpoint of presidential control, the basic purpose of the Office of Management and Budget is to get one group of career government experts—the examiners—to watch another group—the bureaucrats. The risk is, of course, that the experts who have been set to watch the experts will have policy views of their own which differ from those of the President. The OMB staff has had a very good record of loyalty to the President—at least when they could discern what the President wanted.

The style adopted in most budget negotiations is known as *incrementalism*. Since most government programs are ongoing, the program operator is able to construct next year's proposed budget by taking this year's figures as a base.[20] He then asks for a little more—an incremental addition—for some programs, the same for others, and a little less for others, depending on current experience with each. Using such an approach, it is natural for the department budget officer and later the budget examiners to focus on the changes proposed for next year.

Under such a system, most programs pass through a rather similar budgetary life cycle. First, a very small sum is requested for research and/or pre-

[20] Otto A. Davis et al., "A Theory of the Budgetary Process," *American Political Science Review,* 60 (September 1966), 529–47.

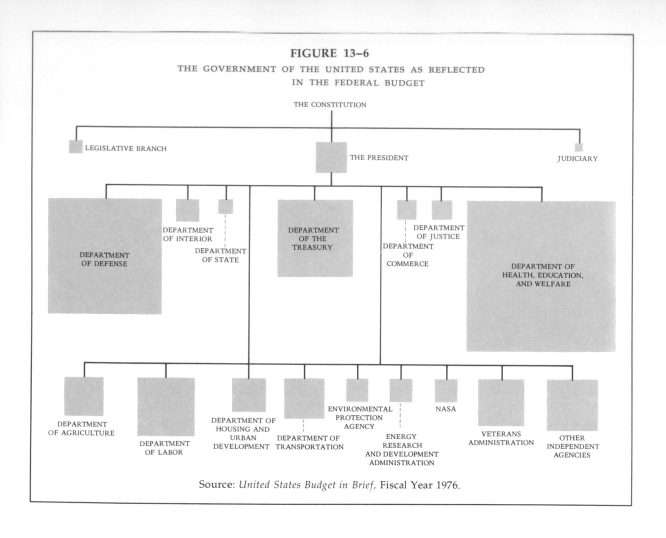

FIGURE 13-6

THE GOVERNMENT OF THE UNITED STATES AS REFLECTED
IN THE FEDERAL BUDGET

THE CONSTITUTION

LEGISLATIVE BRANCH

THE PRESIDENT

JUDICIARY

DEPARTMENT
OF DEFENSE

DEPARTMENT
OF INTERIOR

DEPARTMENT
OF STATE

DEPARTMENT
OF THE
TREASURY

DEPARTMENT
OF
COMMERCE

DEPARTMENT
OF JUSTICE

DEPARTMENT OF
HEALTH, EDUCATION,
AND WELFARE

DEPARTMENT
OF AGRICULTURE

DEPARTMENT
OF LABOR

DEPARTMENT OF
HOUSING AND
URBAN
DEVELOPMENT

DEPARTMENT OF
TRANSPORTATION

ENVIRONMENTAL
PROTECTION
AGENCY

ENERGY
RESEARCH
AND DEVELOPMENT
ADMINISTRATION

NASA

VETERANS
ADMINISTRATION

OTHER
INDEPENDENT
AGENCIES

Source: *United States Budget in Brief,* Fiscal Year 1976.

liminary planning for a new program. It is not easy for a department to get a new "line" put in its budget. Usually a recent congressional authorization for a new program serves as the agency's justification. Once the new line is born, it is carefully nurtured each year by a request for somewhat larger funding. A "pilot program" is usually the next step after research and planning have been completed. This is followed by an attempt at nationwide application of the successful pilot, which in turn is followed by a concentrated effort to "really get on top of the problem," and then by a vigilant effort to "maintain the advances" already made. Using this approach, most programs continue from year to year at a gradually rising budgetary level once they have been accepted as a routine and normal part of government service.

Perhaps the chief reason for the widespread use of the incremental approach is simple necessity. In the first place, the budget contains an extremely large number of lines. It would be quite impossible to start from scratch and reexamine the basic validity of each line or progam each year. Focusing only on the changes saves the most precious of all governmental commodities, decision-making time. Secondly, of necessity budgets must be based on predictions about future needs and demands that cannot be known with great certainty. In such circumstances, it seems more reasonable to take small steps out from what we are currently experiencing than great leaps into the unknown. Thirdly, ongoing government programs generate large-scale human expectations among government workers, political leaders, and segments of the public. Many government programs—for instance, farm subsidies and weapons development—involve massive, complex, and long-term arrangements of men and resources. Extremely rapid changes in such programs would lead to confusion and demoralization in government, and severe hardship or alienation in the private sector. The price in pain and confusion of abrupt change is greater than we are usually willing to pay.

As necessary as budgetary incrementalism is, however, it does have a major drawback in that it robs the budgetary process of much of its value to political leadership as a mode of bureaucratic control. Even with the Office of Management and Budget and the secretaries working hard to move the government in the directions the President wants it to go, the budget has a sticky, molasses-like quality. It is extremely difficult to achieve rapid redirections of funds from some programs to others or even radical change in overall levels of expenditure. The incremental technique is not well suited to asking such questions as: Why do we have this program at all? Does it work at cross-purposes to other programs we have funded? Would some other program do more for less money? Under current practices, it would not be at all unusual for the Bureau of Sport Fisheries and Wildlife to get $300,000 more this year for a program boosting the growth of the deer population, while the Agricultural Research Service got an extra $100,000 for its research on reducing crop damage by wild animals, including deer. Both programs may in fact be justifiable, but current procedures make it difficult even to spot the potential conflict. Nevertheless, the President's budget is a way to enforce the principle that a proposed expenditure that looks all-important from one perspective is merely one rival among thousands for limited public funds.

After budgetary requests have passed through the departments and the Office of Management and Budget, the President has one round in which to invoke his will. In the final budget meetings held in November and December each year, the President, with an eye to his fiscal and monetary policies, is likely to take a strong line on the gross budget figures. For many a bureaucrat, these final sessions determine whether he will live in pleasure or pain over the next year. Of course, this power of the President is largely of the meat-axe rather than the scalpel variety. He can do much more about the total figures than about which programs go ahead and which slow down. Even when the President delivers his budget message, his role in the budget is not finished, but at this point the main arena shifts to Congress. The power of Congress to raise or lower any figure in the President's budget allows bureaucrats who are dissatisfied with what they got from the President to appeal to their friends on Capitol Hill.

TABLE 13–3
BUDGET OUTLAYS BY AGENCY
(IN MILLIONS OF DOLLARS)

DEPARTMENT OR OTHER UNIT	1974 ACTUAL	1975 ESTIMATE	1976 ESTIMATE
Legislative branch	625	744	882
Judiciary	205	308	342
Executive Office of the President	66	109	76
Funds approp. to the President	3,329	4,607	6,610
Agriculture	9,767	8,756	9,662
Commerce	1,455	1,644	1,789
Defense—Military*	77,625	83,493	90,775
Defense—Civil	1,682	1,928	2,005
Health, Education, & Welfare	93,735	109,932	118,377
Housing & Urban Development	4,786	5,517	7,055
Interior	1,779	2,236	2,503
Justice	1,797	2,061	2,221
Labor	8,966	18,966	22,617
State	735	871	950
Transportation	8,104	9,142	9,991
Treasury	35,993	39,665	43,453
Energy Research & Development Admin.†	2,308	3.090	3,815
Environmental Protection Agency	2,030	2,937	3,080
General Services Admin.	−276	−1,008	−476
Nat'l Aero. & Space Admin.	3,252	3,207	3,498
Veterans Administration	13,337	15,445	15,576
Other independent agencies	13,742	15,935	16,712
Allowances‡	———	700	8,050
Undistributed offsetting receipts:			
Employer share, employee retirement	−3,319	−4,070	−3,888
Interest received by trust funds	−6,583	−7,769	−8,305
Rents and royalties on the Outer Continental Shelf lands	−6,748	−5,000	−8,000
Total budget authority and outlays	268,392	313,446	349,372

*Includes allowances for civilian and military pay raises for Department of Defense.
†This agency assumed on Jan. 19, 1975, the energy research and development activities previously performed by the Atomic Energy Commission and several other agencies.
‡Includes allowances for energy tax equalization payments, civilian agency pay raises, and contingencies.

Source: *The Budget of the United States Government, Fiscal Year 1976*, p. 323.

AN OVERVIEW OF ADMINISTRATION AND POLICY

The bureaucracy is clearly a major participant in policy making. It might be convenient briefly to summarize here the various facets of bureaucratic policy making we have already encountered. First, the bureaucracy (or, more correctly, the many and often competing groups and individuals in the executive branch) is probably the major initiator of public policy. Many proposals for new legislation come from the bureaucracy, which thus helps set the agenda of alternatives for other policy makers. It is true that the crucial initiative for the most important new legislation comes from the President and Congress. But even here the bureaucracy usually provides much of the background information and analysis and frequently does the actual bill drafting as well.

Second, the bureaucracy provides a significant share of the continuity and flow of information necessary to pass legislation. The agencies join forces with pressure groups, presidential staff, and congressional leaders in shepherding their bills through the maze of Congress. Some of the agencies' congressional work is done by their political appointees, but a great deal is done by bureau chiefs and other career people. And much of what the political appointees say to Congress has been composed by their career staffs.

Third, the bureaucracy does an enormous amount of supplementary lawmaking after statutes are passed. In many instances, Congress deliberately delegates very broad discretion to the agencies. But even when it does not intend such delegation, Congress necessarily writes legislation in relatively general language. It is the bureaucracy that "interprets" this language in each specific instance.

For example, Congress may pass a law calling for "maximum feasible participation" by the poor in poverty programs. But when HEW turns down the grant application of Dry Forks, Wyoming, because its community council plan does not provide for separate representation for Indians and Mexican-Americans, then it is HEW, not Congress, that has made the policy of ethnic representation for the poor. Similarly, if the anti-trust division of the Justice Department invariably decides not to fight mergers in industries threatened by foreign competition, then the division has made a major anti-trust policy. The pattern of its decisions will have precisely the same effect as if Congress had passed a bill granting exemption from the anti-trust law for certain industries.

Closely related to this factor is another that also derives from the bureaucracy's responsibility for the thousands of "routine" decisions that comprise the day-to-day business of government. The federal government is a very large buyer of goods and services. In some cases it is the largest buyer, or the only one. It is a major builder and an even more important building inspector. Most dam, reservoir, flood control, harbor, bridge, highway, school, home, military, and ship construction is done either by or for the federal government or under federally approved codes and standards. For instance, Federal Housing Administration standards have been the most important single determinant of the style and quality of the homes owned by most Americans. The millions of decisions about what the government will or will not buy, or provide its money for, are made by career civil servants subject to very general supervision and guidelines. The collective impact of these decisions *is* the government's policy.

Processing Area

Accounting Branch	
Computer Branch	
Data Conversion Branch	
Examination Branch	
Input Perfection Branch	
Receipt & Control Branch	
Rest Rooms	

Administration Area-Health Unit	
Dining Area	
Receiving Area	
Taxpayer Service Area	

THE INTERNAL REVENUE SERVICE IS THE GOVERNMENT AGENCY WHOSE
WORK AND POLICIES ARE BEST KNOWN BY AMERICANS.
John Veltri, Photo Researchers, Rapho Division

473

THE NATURE AND
POLITICS OF
ADMINISTRATION

The bureaucracy makes thousands and thousands of such decisions. Its patterns of interpretation may be as important a determinant of public policy as the language and intention of Congress. The bureaucracy is involved in every stage of the policy-making process. It drafts the bills that eventually become laws and it creates the patterns of detailed applications that determine what those laws eventually mean in practice. The less important or salient or controversial a policy decision, the larger part the bureaucracy is likely to play in it. The President and Congress play greater roles in what appear to be the major decisions. But many decisions that seem small at the time can be seen in retrospect as the first step either up to the heights or down the slippery slope. What is more, the sum of many small decisions may have an impact rivaling that of the few big ones.

It is for these reasons that some of the grander problems of bureaucracy continue to trouble us. These problems can be shaped into three overlapping paradoxes. The first involves *client orientation versus problem solving.* There are real problems in the real world. Most people believe that some solutions to these problems are objectively better than others, and that scientific and technical knowledge rather than self-interest is a sound basis for deciding which are best. Therefore, most of us would desire an expert, independent bureaucracy which seeks the best solutions to such problems as smog and high infant mortality. Something strikes us as wrong with a Food and Drug Administration that is too intimate with the drug industry or a Public Health Service that is closely associated with the American Medical Association.

On the other hand, most of us fear that bureaucrats are likely to be arbitrary when they intervene in private affairs. An independent and isolated bureaucracy may develop a high level of inertia and indifference to pressing human needs. We want a responsive and sensitive bureaucracy which "really understands" our problems.

The second paradox involves *generalization versus specialization.* Our society solves its problems by specialization, by division of labor among experts, each trained and interested in a specific set of problems. We want a bureaucracy that can solve problems. Thus, we want a specialized bureaucracy. But we also want a bureaucracy that pursues the public interest, that has some sense of perspective and priorities, that realizes that government is there to achieve the general good. Experts and specialists are notorious for lacking perspective and pursuing their own particular problems and solutions at the expense of others. Thus, we also need a generalist component in bureaucracy. But can generalists rotated from one job to another learn enough to deal with many technical problems?

The third paradox involves *representativeness versus elitism.* Both the British and French have developed elite corps of civil servants drawn from the best graduates of the best universities. The government is assured some share of the best young brains in the country in this way. The prestige, sense of mission, and social status of these elites helps keep them in government by compensating them for their low pay compared to those in business and the professions. But such an elite corps may become highly unrepresentative of the people it is supposed to serve. Eventually it may come to feel that *it* is the government, that it knows best, and that it is responsible for giving the bumbling politicians and the ignorant masses what is good for them, not what they want. But without such an elite corps (as the American government is), are we not in danger of being governed by leftovers and people who cannot succeed in the private sector?

Because "the bureaucracy" is so vast and complex, and because the term covers so many phenomena, it is difficult to make any authoritative closing remarks on the subject. Certainly citizens are unwarranted in their easy use of the term "bureaucrat" as a mere negative stereotype. They *are* warranted in their desire to evaluate the public service. Although little hard evidence for such an evaluation exists, it does seem that we would be justified in concluding that the federal service today is a relatively competent, moderately responsive, and modestly creative organization.

SUMMARY

The federal bureaucracy is sufficiently large and independent of presidential control to constitute a fourth branch of government. Its basic units are the cabinet-level departments, each of which is subdivided into bureaus. In addition there are many important non-cabinet agencies such as the Veterans Administration, Postal Service, and independent regulatory commissions. Much federal administration is done indirectly through grants and contracts. Thus federal administration involves not only the federal bureaucracy but millions of state and local administrators and employees of private firms.

The civil service system has supplanted the previous patronage methods of filling federal jobs, but that system is not entirely successful in making the career bureaucracy responsive to its political superiors. The career executives come from a wide range of backgrounds, but have spent most of their adult lives working for one or two agencies of the federal government. The Foreign Service and military officer corps constitute separate sets of federal executives with special characteristics and problems, as do the members of various professions who fill executive positions in government.

Federal agencies develop special ties with the particular segments of the society they are designed to assist and regulate. Interest groups lobby the administrative branch as well as Congress. Administrators, too, become representatives of various segments of public opinion. Nevertheless bureaucrats basically see themselves as seeking to provide workable solutions to real world problems rather than simply reflecting the political desires of others.

Because agencies are highly specialized but operate overlapping programs, the federal administration employs both hierarchical and lateral methods of coordination. Although administrative reorganization frequently purports to be aimed at solving problems of coordination, in reality it is usually more concerned with encouraging or suppressing specific government programs or policies. The budget is a key tool of policy coordination because it presents a relatively clear picture of all government programs in relation to one another. The incremental style of budgeting, however, makes it difficult to raise fundamental questions about which government programs are most worthwhile and which might be dropped altogether.

The bureaucracy is a major participant in policy-making, makes a major contribution to the law making and budgetary processes, and does a good deal of supplementary law making. The bureaucracy presents three overlapping paradoxes: (1) client orientation vs. problem solving; (2) generalization vs. specialization; and (3) representativeness vs. elitism. On the whole, American bureaucracy tends to be clientele-oriented, specialized, and representative.

CHAPTER FOURTEEN
THE COURTS

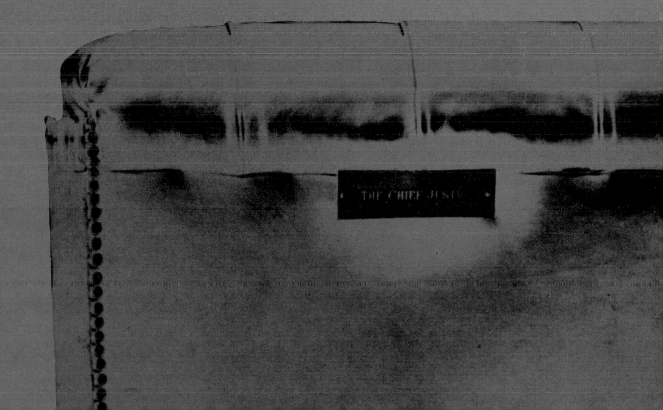

I N 1795, a group of land speculators bribed the Georgia legislature to give them a large part of what later became Alabama. The Supreme Court eventually ordered them to give it back. President Andrew Jackson reportedly said, "John Marshall [the Chief Justice] has made his order. Now let him enforce it"[1]

• In 1960, the Internal Revenue Service asked the Court to state a set of rules that would define a "gift" as opposed to "income" for tax purposes. The Court refused.

• In 1964, the Court told the Interstate Commerce Commission what factors to consider before allowing a railroad to abandon passenger service. The Court also decided that the Santa Fe Railroad could run a truck line between Fresno and Los Angeles.

• In 1952, the U.S. Patent Office was so fed up with the Court's refusal to acknowledge the validity of the patents it issued that it pushed a new patent law through Congress. Almost no congressmen realized that the law was intended to force the Court to agree with the Patent Office. Fourteen years later, the Court said that the law really had been intended to force the Patent Office to agree with the Court. The Patent Office continues to issue thousands of patents knowing that they would be invalidated if they ever got to the court. They seldom do.[2]

• In 1949, a major Supreme Court decision held that the Court should not decide political questions. In 1963, the Court held that litigation (that is, suing someone in court) was a form of political activity protected by the First Amendment.[3]

In order to see a pattern in all the diversity—and seeming perversity—of the Supreme Court, let us briefly outline its general powers and its impact. First, the Supreme Court wields the power of *judicial review*. In the American context, *judicial review* is the power to declare that statutes and the actions of administrative officers are unconstitutional and thus legally null and void. The power of review extends over local, state, and federal governments. Besides the special American meaning of judicial review, the term more generally refers to the power of courts to examine the actions of administrative officers to see if they are in accord with the statutes governing those officers. The Supreme Court does this to federal administrative officers. Second, the Court has *appellate jurisdiction*. This is the power of a higher court to correct legal errors made by a lower court. The Supreme Court has appellate jurisdiction over lower federal courts on all matters of law and over state courts on legal issues arising under the federal Constitution.

In exercising judicial review and appellate jurisdiction, the Supreme Court has had a major impact on American life. In recent years, its decisions have

---

[1] C. Peter McGrath, *Yazoo* (Providence: Brown University Press, 1966).

[2] Martin Shapiro, *The Supreme Court and Administrative Agencies* (New York: Free Press, 1968), Chap. 3.

[3] *Luther* v. *Borden,* 7 How. 1 (1849); *NAACP* v. *Button,* U.S. 415 (1963).

been at the center of the rapid and not always peaceful changes in race relations and have led to a major national controversy over the practice of busing children to achieve school integration. Its decisions have radically changed the composition of many state legislatures that were forced to equalize the populations of the districts from which their members were elected. Other decisions have overturned state laws against birth control and abortion, and have fundamentally changed the system of criminal justice by providing lawyers for indigent defendants and abolishing the death penalty. Its obscenity decisions now permit explicit sexual expression in books, magazines, films, and on the stage that was undreamed of twenty-five years ago. And Court decisions have blocked numerous proposals to provide state aid to parochial schools, one of the most fundamental bread-and-butter issues in many communities.

Yet this very list indicates the limits of the Court's political intervention. All its actions combined have not succeeded in bringing blacks to full educational equality in many parts of the country and have not integrated the schools. In thousands of communities the police and the courts have made no appreciable changes in their methods despite the long string of Court decisions designed to foster better treatment of suspects.

Perhaps most important, there are large areas of government activity about which the Court has virtually no say. It has always been extremely timid in challenging the war and foreign affairs powers of the presidency. It has no direct way of dictating priorities to legislatures, of forcing them to spend more on hospitals and less on highways. It can intervene sporadically to assure that the bureaucracy has followed proper procedures or obeyed specific statutory commands, but most of the planning and operation of federal programs remain beyond its reach. In short, the Court can alter the real world in some areas, but in many other areas it is powerless.

The web of relationships between the Supreme Court and the rest of American government and politics is extremely complex. There are a great many facts to be presented and organized. The central fact, however, and the one that needs the most explanation, is that we accept this most peculiar Court as a central and integral part of our political process.

THE COURTNESS OF THE SUPREME COURT
THE THIRD PERSON

When two people quarrel, it is so logical for them to find a third person to help them resolve their dispute that nearly every society uses some form of this third-person device. The universal appeal of the third person explains the social magic of courts, the special something that earns them popular favor and support. The third person can be a mediator, voluntarily chosen by the two disputants themselves, who proposes one compromise solution after another until one is found that makes both parties happy. The picture is universally appealing because it means that a quarrel will be ended to everyone's satisfaction, with no one being forced to do anything he or she does not want to do.

We still use voluntary mediation to settle disputes in some areas, such as labor-management relations. But for many kinds of quarrels most modern societies have introduced a system based on law and judicial office. The society creates the office of judge and the government chooses the third person to fill it. The two disputants are now told that if either or both of them wants their quarrel settled by a third person, they must use the official, pre-selected person. And they are told that they will both have to accept whatever solution to their quarrel is provided by the law. Thus, all modern courts of law are at least one step away from the fundamental appeal of thirdness. In place of pure consent, they have substituted an imposed system for settling disputes.

The judge, moreover, is an officer of the government. The laws he applies are passed by the government, and they reflect the general interests present in the society. When the two disputants come to court, they no longer face a third person whose sole concern is their particular interests, but a person who is concerned with the interests of each of them *plus* a third set of interests—those of the government and the society. To the extent that the solutions the court imposes seem to reflect the interests of the government rather than a simple compromise between the interests of the disputants, courts lose some of their universal appeal. All modern courts suffer from this loss of social magic, but the Supreme Court has suffered more than most other American courts because it often seems to represent the interests of a central government very far away and very unsympathetic to the interests of the disputants.

COURTS AS LAWMAKERS

Legislators have neither the time nor the imagination to write laws that explicitly dictate the solution to every specific quarrel that might arise in the society. They therefore content themselves with writing more or less general statutes in broad language. A statute forbidding "assault" is an example. Such general statutes must be interpreted—the details filled in—to provide solutions to specific quarrels. The job of bringing the general words of the law down to specific cases falls to the courts. If the courts decide that "assault" includes hitting a man with a cleaver but not with wet spaghetti, they have made the law mean that hurting a man's body is forbidden, but not hurting his dignity. If they decide that assault does include spaghetti, then they have made the assault law protect dignity as well as body. Either way, they have made part of the law of assault. In interpreting the meaning of law, the courts inevitably and inescapably *make* law. In this respect their ostensibly neutral decisions are like the statutory interpretations made by administrators, as described in the previous chapter. Courts, like administrators, *make* public policy.

Two factors push some courts very far into lawmaking. Courts that apply the most generally and vaguely worded laws must fill in more meaning than do other courts that apply relatively specific, detailed, and precise laws. As we shall see shortly, one of the laws that the Supreme Court applies is the

Constitution, and the Constitution is our most generally and vaguely worded law. Thus, the Supreme Court is pushed far from the universally beloved role of a dispute-settling third person and deeply into the role of lawmaker.

Besides the vagueness or specificity of the law, a second factor moves some courts deeper than others into lawmaking. Consider what would happen if one trial court decided that spaghetti-hurling is assault and another court decided that it is not. We do not want the law to mean one thing in one court-room and something different in another. For this reason, we have a system of appeals courts that review trial court decisions under their jurisdiction and make sure that all trial courts are interpreting the laws in the same way. An appeals court does this by taking a specific appeal in a specific case from one of its trial courts. In the course of deciding the specific appeal, it announces the one single correct interpretation of the law that all its trial courts must follow in the future.

In such cases, the main energies of the appellate court are likely to be devoted to formulating a legal interpretation—that is, making a law—that will work well for all its trial courts. It is less concerned with satisfying the interests of the two disputants and more concerned with making a law that will best serve the interest of society in future quarrels. As the highest appellate court in the nation, the Supreme Court spends more of its energies making legal interpretations for the guidance of lower courts and less on the settlement of specific quarrels than does any other American court.

COURTS AS INSTRUMENTS OF GOVERNMENT

We have used courts in disputes not only between two individuals but between an individual and his government. Court cases often read not *Smith* v. *Jones* but *United States* v. *Jones* or *Connecticut* v. *Jones.* The judge him-self is a government official, the laws he applies were made by government, and the government is one of the litigants. We have a situation that looks more like two-against-one than one-against-one with an independent mediator deciding between them. To guard against this impression of unfairness, we have taken steps to insure the relative neutrality and im-partiality of judges when their own government is one of the parties before them. For example, federal judges hold office for life, so that their govern-ment cannot fire them if they decide against it. Or the judiciary may be set up as a very separate part of government which has almost no contact with and little dependency on the rest of government. Nevertheless, a litigant who loses a case to the government is likely to have some suspicions about the true impartiality of the judge. A very high proportion of the Supreme Court's cases involve the federal government as one of the parties. So here again the Supreme Court looks less like an impartial third person than most other courts.[4]

---

[4] The general discussion of courts on the preceding pages is drawn from Martin Shapiro, "Courts," in Fred I. Greenstein and Nelson W. Polsby, eds., *Handbook of Political Science,* Vol. 5 (Reading, Mass.: Addison-Wesley, 1975).

THE SUPREMENESS OF THE SUPREME COURT
COURT AND CONSTITUTION

The existence of the Supreme Court is commanded by Article III of the Constitution: "The judicial power of the United States shall be vested in one Supreme Court. . . ." More important than this bare constitutional authorization, however, has been our historical experience of intimate linkage between the Court and the Constitution. As we have seen, our intellectual tradition identifies the Constitution both with the notion of "higher law" and with the notion of a "contract of government." Considered as a legally binding contract, the Constitution contains five basic kinds of provisions:

1. Specification of the structure of the central government and boundaries between the various parts of that structure.
2. Limited grants of power to the central government, authorizing it to do certain specific things.
3. Open-ended clauses giving the central government those powers "necessary and proper" for carrying out its specific powers and making it "supreme" over the states in the exercise of the powers granted to it.
4. Specific prohibitions against certain activities by the central government.
5. Specific prohibitions against certain activities by the states.

Our cultural inclination to view such provisions as legally binding made it seem normal and natural that when disputes arose over their meaning in the first decades of the Constitution's operation, a court should decide such disputes. John Marshall, the first great Chief Justice, took advantage of what seemed "natural," and established the Court's role as the arbiter of constitutional quarrels in a series of historic decisions.[5]

In *Marbury* v. *Madison* (1803), the Court held unconstitutional a congressional law giving additional powers to the Supreme Court itself, arguing that those powers belonged to another part of the government—the lower federal courts.[6] In denying *itself* additional powers in the particular case at issue, the Court asserted its general authority to police the boundary lines between the various branches of the central government. Although the Constitution did not confer the power of judicial review on the Court, Marshall reasoned that since the Constitution was law, and judges interpret the law, it followed inescapably that judges should be the ones to interpret the Constitution. Americans always have tended to restate their political quarrels as constitutional quarrels. From the time of the Marshall Court, they became accustomed to restating their constitutional quarrels as legal quarrels to be settled by the Court.

FORMER CHIEF
JUSTICE JOHN
MARSHALL.
Wide World Photos

[5] Martin Shapiro and Rocco J. Tresolini, *American Constitutional Law,* 4th ed. (New York: The Macmillan Company, 1975).
[6] 1 Cr. 137 (1803).

The decisions of the Marshall Court went a long way toward confirming the natural association of Court and Constitution. In subsequent periods, the Supreme Court built on Marshall's foundation with varying degrees of success. A rather simple-minded historical view pictures the great heyday of the Supreme Court as roughly the period from 1890 to 1930. It is to these four decades that the tag "judicial supremacy" has often been applied.[7] The Court, it is charged, wielded the Constitution right and left to strike down government actions regulating business and aiding the poor that were not in harmony with the conservative economic and social philosophies of the Justices.

The actual historical pattern is not as cut and dried as this superficial summary makes it appear. It is not really clear that the Justices differed very much from other men in government in their political sentiments. Indeed, their decisions went both ways, with a strong preference for free enterprise but occasional bows toward governmental intervention to correct the incidental malfunctions in what they saw as a fundamentally sound system. About the same mixture is to be found in the legislative and executive branches. It should be remembered that for every liberal statute "vetoed" — that is, declared unconstitutional — by the Supreme Court, state governors and Presidents vetoed dozens.

Despite complaints about "judicial supremacy" and "judicial tyranny," the history of the Court does not show a single instance in which the Court succeeded over time in preventing a determined people from doing what it wanted to do. Even its defense of free enterprise during the 1890–1930 period reflected rather than opposed the general political sentiment of the day. The Court was, as it always is, one source of political influence and point of access for interest groups. From the 1890s to the late 1930s, it was often most hospitable to businessmen and their sympathizers. In this period its weight was cast, more often than not, onto the conservative side of the struggle for economic regulation. The Court may have delayed, modified, and occasionally deflected social policies, but this was no more than what other government agencies had done. In short, the Court did not stand alone between "the people" and what they allegedly wanted. This is not to say that the Court played no major role in shaping public policy during the era of "judicial supremacy." It is simply an acknowledgement that there is little evidence to show that the Court subverted government by the people.[8]

---

[7] Charles G. Haines, *The American Doctrine of Judicial Supremacy*, 2nd ed. (Berkeley: University of California Press, 1959).

[8] Two good general histories of the Supreme Court are C. Herman Pritchett, *The American Constitutional System* (New York: McGraw-Hill Book Company, 1971); and Alfred Kelley and Winfred Harbison, *The American Constitution*, 4th ed. (New York. W.W. Norton & Company, 1970). On the relationship between judicial review and democratic government, see also Robert A. Dahl, *Pluralist Democracy in the United States* (Chicago: Rand McNally, 1967), pp. 150–70.

The tendency to exaggerate the supremacy of the contemporary Court and its predecessors is in large part due to our traditional constitutional belief that the federal government is divided into three great and presumably equal branches—the Congress, which makes the laws; the Executive, which administers them; and the Supreme Court, which decides individual cases arising under them. The problem is that this standard textbook account of the three equal branches is incorrect in a number of fundamental ways.

First of all, as earlier chapters on Congress, the President, and the bureaucracy have shown, lawmaking is not the exclusive prerogative of the legislative branch. The American lawmaking process is complex. It involves many different participants from each of the branches and many others from outside the government. The mix and the relative contributions of these participants vary from statute to statute. If we began from the reality of the lawmaking process instead of the frozen vision of three great branches, we would quickly see that the Supreme Court participates either very little or not at all in the making of most laws and very much in the making of only a few.[9]

One brief example will show how small a part the Supreme Court often plays even when it makes a major constitutional pronouncement. Welfare programs had for many years been almost exclusively the business of the states. State legislatures had passed thousands of laws on relief, aid to dependent children, and so on. Beginning in the 1930s, the federal government gradually entered the field, setting standards, making grants to the states, and establishing social security programs. Congress passed dozens of detailed laws. By the 1960s there were increasing demands that the whole welfare program be federalized, with a single, national minimum income guaranteed to every family, the cost of which was to be borne by the federal treasury.

In 170 years of welfare legislation, the Supreme Court had intervened significantly only once. This was in 1937, when the Court upheld the constitutionality of the Social Security Act. Then, in 1969, the Court struck down state residency requirements for welfare.[10] This was a sweeping decision, which in effect declared that portions of the welfare laws of nearly every state were unconstitutional. It was just the sort of decision that evokes cries of judicial supremacy. The practical effect was to hasten the movement toward uniform national standards. But the Court decision came only after the movement for national standards was well under way. The movement would have continued even without the Court decision, which at most gave national standards a boost along the way. The Court did not and could not determine what kind of welfare program we should have, how much each family should get, which old programs should be phased out, or how new programs should be financed. A major constitutional intervention by the Supreme Court thus becomes a minor event in the history of welfare law-

[9] Martin Shapiro, *Law and Politics in the Supreme Court* (New York: Free Press, 1964).
[10] *Shapiro* v. *Thompson,* 394 U.S. 618 (1969).

making. The decision may mean much less to the future shape of welfare programs than a key vote in a House committee or a few paragraphs in a presidential message.

Later in this chapter, we shall see that the Supreme Court does exercise more power in some areas than it does in the welfare area. But the problem is always one of discovering how much the Court does in each area. We cannot make blanket statements about *the* power of the Supreme Court.

The temptation often arises to think of the Court as one of those three large and equal squares on the organization chart of American government. This temptation should be met by remembering that the Court's square contains nine men with a few dozen assistants making a few thousand decisions a year, while the other two squares, those of Congress and the President, contain thousands or millions of people making hundreds of thousands of decisions. If the proverbial man from Mars were to descend on Washington and wander around looking at what goes on in the federal government, it might be weeks before he stumbled upon the Supreme Court. The Supreme Court can play a major and even occasionally decisive role in American politics. But nothing about our political system requires or insures that it ever will play such a role, let alone play it continuously and across all fields of public policy.

OUGHT THE SUPREME COURT TO ACT?
THE COURT AND DEMOCRACY

It has been necessary to say many general things about the nature of the Supreme Court, rather than simply to describe what it does, because the central fact of its political existence has been the continuing debate over whether the Court ought to do anything at all. One side in this debate has been labeled *judicial activism,* the other *judicial self-restraint* or *judicial modesty.*[11] The arguments for and against judicial activism rest largely on the nature of American democracy. The Supreme Court consists of nine men appointed by the President, confirmed by the Senate, and serving for life rather than submitting themselves to periodic reappointment or election. As Table 14–1 shows, Supreme Court Justices do indeed serve for long terms, well beyond the tenure of the Presidents who appoint them. The average Justice sits on the Court for 15 years. Their decisions are not subject to formal veto or change by anyone else. Except for subsequent reversal or modification by the Court itself, their decisions are final. In order to preserve their virtues as a Court, they must remain isolated from the normal play of political pressures that make other parts of government responsible and responsive to the people. In other words, the very qualities that establish the Court's independence from "political pressure" also make it "undemocratic."

[11] The debate over judicial activism and judicial self-restraint is summarized in Alexander M Bickel, *The Least Dangerous Branch: The Supreme Court at the Bar of Politics* (Indianapolis: Bobbs-Merrill, 1962); Wallace Mendelson, *Justices Black and Frankfurter: Conflict in the Court* (Chicago: University of Chicago Press, 1961); and Martin Shapiro, *Freedom of Speech: The Supreme Court and Judicial Review* (Englewood Cliffs, N.J.: Prentice-Hall, Inc., 1966), Chap. 1.

TABLE 14-1

YEARS OF SERVICE OF
SUPREME COURT JUSTICES

NUMBER OF YEARS ON THE COURT	NUMBER OF JUSTICES	PERCENT OF JUSTICES
Less than 4	7	7%
4–8	25	26
9–16	27	28
17–24	18	19
25+	18	19
Total	95	99%

Source: Congressional Quarterly Service, *Congress and the Nation*, Vol. I-III.

The argument that the Court should not interfere with the other branches of government focuses on the difference between an institution whose members are appointed for life and a President and Congress who are elected for fixed terms and can stay in office only through re-election. Because they must win a majority of votes to gain and hold their positions, the elected branches are assumed to embody the popular will. As we have seen, it is unrealistic to believe that elected officials necessarily do what the majority of the public wants, or that they are undemocratic if they do not. A more sophisticated outlook defines democracy as popular choice of leaders, not policies. Thus the crux of the argument against judicial review is that it permits non-elected Justices to frustrate democratic government by overruling elected officials.

The standard response of those favoring Supreme Court activism has been that "we the people" who established the Constitution and continue to support it never wanted pure democratic government. They insist that the Constitution itself and the role of the Court in its enforcement are beneficial, popularly approved checks on majorities who might otherwise destroy individual rights and freedoms.

This argument can be put in a clearer perspective by looking at the cases where the Court has invalidated laws passed by Congress and signed by the President. As we saw earlier, the Court seldom frustrated a determined majority in the other branches of government. When it did, it rarely was at odds with them for very long. The Court changed its position, the other branches changed theirs, or they tacitly accepted what the Court had done. Some of the most striking confrontations have involved a Court whose members were appointed by past Presidents, reflecting obsolete political doctrines that were no longer accepted by contemporary elected officials. Time supplies an inevitable corrective to this sort of conflict. The chances are about five out of six that a President will get an opportunity to make at least one Supreme Court appointment during his first four-year term. Given the fact that the Court decides most controversial questions by five-to-four or six-to-three votes, we can see that it does not take long for the Court to react to at least those changes in public sentiment that are reflected in the outcome of presidential elections. Table 14–2 illustrates this point by depicting the interval between individual appointments to the Supreme Court. It shows that it is unusual for more than two years to go by without the President having an opportunity to fill a vacancy on the Court. Nixon, for example, appointed four Justices (who were confirmed by the Senate) in less than three years. Ford named his first Justice after 18 months in office.

The table also shows that occasionally a long period goes by when the membership of the Court is "frozen" and the President has no chance to make his imprint on it. Franklin Roosevelt had to wait four years before he could make his first appointment. This period coincided with the sweeping innovations of the New Deal. A Court reflecting the old commitment to *laissez-faire* overturned much of FDR's legislative accomplishments, thus precipitating the strongest challenge to judicial review in American history. The crisis dissipated as a quick series of retirements gave Roosevelt the chance to alter the balance on the Court.

In another sense, too, the Supreme Court does seem to follow the election returns. The Justices depend upon the cooperation of others to have their decisions enforced. The Court's major weapon is the fact that most Americans have a firm ideological commitment to the rule of law. Any official who will not obey an order of the Court is stigmatized as a lawbreaker. Of course, other public sentiments may balance or even overwhelm the long-term ideological commitment to the rule of law at various times. After the Court's ban on prayers in the public schools, for example, some school boards, faced with what they conceived as a choice between God and the Court-enunciated law, chose God. They went right on praying. This illustrates an impor-

---

TABLE 14-2

THE INTERVAL BETWEEN APPOINTMENTS TO THE SUPREME COURT, 1789–1975

INTERVAL IN YEARS	NUMBER OF APPOINTMENTS	PERCENTAGE OF TOTAL	CUMULATIVE PERCENTAGE
Less than 1 year	40	41%	41%
1	23	23	64
2	12	12	76
3	10	10	86
4	6	6	92
5	6	6	98
12	1	1	99
Total	98	99%	99%

The table excludes six Justices appointed in 1789. It includes only Justices who were appointed and confirmed and served on the Court.

Source: Robert A. Dahl, *Pluralist Democracy in the United States*, p. 157; and Congressional Quarterly Service, *Congress and the Nation*, Vol. I-III.

tant fact of life for the Court. The more unpopular the policy embodied in the Court's command, the less the Court can use the principal weapon in its arsenal to get its policy enforced. The Justices have always been aware of this phenomenon and rarely have been willing to invite massive resistance to their commands by prolonged adherence to policies opposed by the public.

The Court must call on the executive branch to force compliance with its orders. If, however, those orders encounter nationwide opposition or even indifference, the executive may not cooperate. Thus, at the crucial point of enforcement, the Court is intimately connected to the mainstream of democratic politics.

FINALITY OF SUPREME COURT DECISIONS

There has been much confusion about the finality of Court decisions. This confusion arises from failure to distinguish between the Court's role as resolver of disputes between two litigants and its role as a policy-making branch of the government. Let us consider a hypothetical antitrust suit brought by the Baxter Button Company against Superglomerate, Inc. Baxter, a little firm, is trying to force the big corporation to sell a button company that it has recently bought in order to gain 90 percent of the button market. A Supreme Court decision that Superglomerate has violated the antitrust laws and must divest itself of the Bikini Button Company is final and binding on Superglomerate. No other agency of government may block it, change it, or reverse it. As a resolution of the dispute between the two litigants, the Court's decision absolutely and forever determines that Baxter won and Superglomerate lost.

Behind the Court's condemnation of Superglomerate, however, undoubtedly lies a set of policy preferences held by the Justices. Let us say, in this instance, they prefer an economy in which there are many small producers and no single giant. The Court's decision does *not* fix this preference for small firms as the final policy of the government. It may encourage some other small firms like Baxter Button to sue some other large firms like Superglomerate, but that is about all. If other branches of the government do not share the Court's economic preference, the Court can do almost nothing to bring about the type of economy it desires. For example, the Justice Department may be reluctant to prosecute giant firms for antitrust violations and the Defense Department may actually favor industrial giants in its procurement policies.

The point is not only that the Supreme Court is not so supreme as it sometimes looks. Just as important is the fact that, in order to achieve their policy goals, the Justices need to enlist the cooperation of the whole machinery of politics—machinery in which they themselves are one cog rather than the final governor. Thus, at the very point at which the Court seems most gravely to threaten the democratic political process, it becomes most subordinated to that process. Even in the highest constitutional spheres, and even leaving problems of enforcement aside, it is difficult to discover any Supreme Court policy pronouncement so final that its goals can be obtained without a great deal of complicated cooperation by other political actors. The power of those actors to withhold that cooperation, to blunt or redirect the thrust of the Court's policy when it does not enjoy sufficient popular support, is a decisive democratic check on the Court's activity.

THE COURT AND INTEREST GROUPS

Lobbyists for special interests do not drop into the offices of Supreme Court Justices or take them on duck-hunting trips. The Court ought to be and is separated from the hurly-burly of everyday political demands. To assure that neither party to a case gets ahead of the other, judicial ethics, unlike those for legislators or administrators, prevent judges from talking privately to the representatives of either party. But this difference in procedure does not mean that the quantity or quality of the information received by judges is lower than that obtained by elected officials and administrators, nor that they will be less sensitive to public needs.

Let us say a truck line sues a railroad to prevent it from starting its own truck line. Most of the facts and arguments the Supreme Court hears from the lawyers for the two litigants are precisely the same ones a congressional committee gets from the lobbyists for the Association of American Railroads and the American Trucking Association about the general desirability of railroads running truck lines. Thus, when the Court reaches a decision in this individual case that has broad policy implications for the transportation industry as a whole, there is no reason to believe that the Court was unqualified to make such a determination because it did not get a chance to hear from the interest groups involved.

Indeed, a convincing case can be made for the proposition that courts frequently are more open to interest groups and individuals than are other public agencies. There are many instances in which particular groups or widely held but unorganized interests do not have adequate access to, or representation in, legislative and executive bodies. Classic instances are unpopular minorities like Jehovah's Witnesses or Communists, disfranchised minorities like blacks, and diffuse interests like those favoring freedom of speech or consumers' rights. Such elements may find it easier to get a test case to the Supreme Court than a favorable hearing elsewhere. To the extent that the Court helps those interests that have been denied a hearing by the rest of the system, it furthers the openness and responsiveness of the system as a whole.

Thus, as we noted in Chapter 8, litigation is itself a form of political activity through which individuals and groups "lobby" the Supreme Court. This lobbying involves not only the lawsuits themselves but the writing of law review articles and the filing of *amicus* briefs designed to influence the thinking of the Justices about current cases.[12]

[12] An amicus or "friend of the court" brief is a legal argument filed with the court by someone not actually a party to the litigation. It is designed to aid the judge in reaching his decision. On the litigational tactics of interest groups in general, see Clement Vose, *Constitutional Change* (Lexington, Mass.: D.C. Heath, 1972).

A major portion of this chapter has been devoted to whether or not the Supreme Court ought to intervene in the political policy-making process. Such prolonged introductory discussions were not necessary in the chapters on Congress or the presidency. It seems obvious that they ought to engage in politics and to make policy. That the Court does and ought to, however, remains as far from obvious and as controversial today as it has been since 1789. The remainder of this chapter presents data about the Court. It assumes that, like the Congress and the President, the Court is and ought to be political, that the Justices do and ought to make conscious political choices, and that the primary criterion for judging the Court is whether it is politically successful—that is, whether it maintains its own powers and makes desirable policy.

THE SUPREME COURT IN 1975.
FROM LEFT, FRONT ROW: ASSOCIATE JUSTICES POTTER STEWART (1958);
WILLIAM O. DOUGLAS (1939); CHIEF JUSTICE WARREN E. BURGER (1969); ASSOCIATE
JUSTICES WILLIAM J. BRENNAN, JR. (1956); AND BYRON R. WHITE (1962). BACK ROW:
ASSOCIATE JUSTICES LEWIS F. POWELL, JR. (1972); THURGOOD MARSHALL (1967);
HARRY A. BLACKMUN (1970); AND WILLIAM H. REHNQUIST (1972). THE DATE
FOLLOWING EACH JUSTICE'S NAME IS THE YEAR IN WHICH HE TOOK HIS SEAT
ON THE BENCH. JUSTICE DOUGLAS RETIRED IN NOVEMBER 1975 AND WAS
REPLACED BY JOHN PAUL STEVENS.
Wide World Photos

BACKGROUND

So far, we have dealt with the Court as if it were a unit. It is time now to recall that it is composed of nine human beings. Detailed examination of the personal characteristics of the Justices who have served in the past half century reveals little that is surprising. As one might expect, some substantial differences can be seen between the backgrounds of the Justices and those of other political actors, particularly bureaucrats. The Justices are drawn from a wealthier, better educated, more socially prominent stratum of society than most other governmental officials. Obviously, this is not a result of some secret elite conspiracy. Given the propensity of our economic system for rewarding professional services, most distinguished lawyers, even those who have served the underdog, are likely to have had high incomes before reaching the Court. Justices Brandeis, Goldberg, and Marshall, for instance, were themselves members of minority groups. Each had been heavily engaged in legal battles against corporate wealth and governmental power before his elevation to the bench. Yet all were "well off," ranging from a modest personal fortune in the case of Brandeis to a very comfortable annual salary for Marshall.

Although only about a quarter of all appointees to the Court had much judicial experience before being named, almost all of them had held some kind of political position. They were not necessarily "professional politicians," but it is clear that practice at being a judge counts for far less than exposure to the world of practical politics. The actual work of the Court is so far removed from the preoccupations of other judges that this lack of judicial experience is of little consequence. It is often observed that few of the Court's most distinguished members have been judges of any kind before their appointments.

Considerable ingenuity has been spent attempting to relate the Justices' backgrounds to their behavior on the bench. About all that has emerged so far is the obvious—but very important—fact that the shared educational and professional experiences of the Justices leave them with a common language, relatively strong allegiance to certain ways of doing business, and some sense of community with other lawyers and judges. We do not know the relative weight of these professional norms compared to the individual political, social, and economic views of the Justices.[13]

JUDICIAL ATTITUDES

Glendon Schubert and his school have made the major scholarly effort to link personal factors to actual Court decisions. Without stopping to explain their elaborate methods or the serious criticisms that have been made of them, we can say that their analysis strongly suggests that most of the Justices have well developed political outlooks which are expressed in their

---

[13] John R. Schmidhauser, *The Supreme Court* (New York: Holt, Rinehart & Winston, 1960).

decisions.[14] These attitudes seem to be basically arranged along two dimensions. The first concerns the issue of *individual freedom versus the power of government*. When cases involve a conflict between the two, some Justices seem to side fairly consistently with the government, others with the individual. The second dimension concerns the issues of *business versus government* and *business versus labor*. Some Justices are consistently pro-business and some consistently anti-business. In general, the Justices stay well within the limits set by the American ideologies described in Chapter 4 and exhibit about the same mixtures of liberalism and conservatism.

APPOINTMENT OF THE JUSTICES

Supreme Court Justices are appointed by the President with the advice and consent of the Senate. Most Presidents have viewed this as one of their major prerogatives. When a vacancy is created on the Court through death, retirement, or resignation, the President will be flooded with suggestions from congressmen, party leaders, and political associates. Normally, the President will delegate to members of the White House staff and/or the Attorney General the initial chore of making up a list of candidates. They will conduct a further canvass for names and then begin to shorten the list. Prospective candidates will be investigated by the FBI and evaluations will be solicited from many sources. At this stage, almost any prominent individual, political organization, or interest group that is not absolutely out of favor with the President may participate. The American Bar Association has sought to assert a right to rate prospective candidates as "qualified" or "not qualified" before their names are submitted to the Senate. Since the Eisenhower administration, however, Presidents have been careful to reject such a right, although Justice Department officials may consult the Bar Association informally.

Among the characteristics that may mark a particular lawyer as "eligible" for a Supreme Court appointment are leadership in the party of the President, distinguished prior judicial service, high status in the legal profession, personal friendship with the President or special service to him, or identification with a politically powerful interest group. Traditionally, some effort has been made to achieve a degree of geographic and religious balance on the Court. Typically, there has been some care to maintain western, southern, Catholic, and Jewish representation. President Nixon explicitly rejected this tradition, however, and it remains to be seen whether it will be revived. As of this writing, for example, there is no Jewish member of the Court. There is, however, one black on the Court and increasing pressure to appoint a woman.

No generalization can be made about the degree of presidential involvement in the final selection. Some Presidents have personally selected their nominees while others have delegated virtually the whole appointment

---

[14] Their work is extended and summarized in Glendon Schubert, *The Judicial Mind: Attitudes and Ideologies of Supreme Court Justices* (Evanston, Ill.: Northwestern University Press, 1965).

power to the Attorney General or other aides.[15] President Nixon and many of his predecessors sought quite deliberately to choose Justices whose political values matched their own in the hope of shaping the future policies of the Court.

When the President has determined who his official nominee will be, the name is sent to the Senate Judiciary Committee for hearings, to be followed by general debate on the floor of the Senate and a vote. The Judiciary Committee hearing usually provides a public forum for those opposing an appointment. At this stage, the American Bar Association and other interest groups present their evaluation of the appointee. In general, the Senate has taken the position that the President is entitled to appoint whomever he feels best reflects his own views. However, as President Nixon's experiences with the unsuccessful nominations of Clement Haynesworth and Harrold Carswell indicated, the Senate may respond unfavorably. This seems particularly probable when the President is of the opposite party, the appointee's policy views are distasteful to a majority of the senators, and substantial evidence of past incapacity or impropriety can be presented.

By his appointments, a President may materially shift the direction of Supreme Court policies, yet his power is severely limited by a number of factors. First, the office of Supreme Court Justice entails a different set of values, expectations, and powers than anything the appointees have encountered in their earlier careers as politicians, lawyers, or even lower court judges. It is not easy to predict from past behavior how a person will act as a Supreme Court Justice. Many a "safe" Justice has turned his vote against the policies of the President responsible for his appointment. Second, it is difficult for a President to find plausible candidates who agree exactly with all his policy views. A Justice appointed because he agrees with the President on "law and order" may differ from the President on race questions or abortion. Third, and perhaps most important, the Court's policies are determined by the interaction of judicial attitudes and existing legal doctrine, not by attitudes alone. The President cannot expect a new appointee to roll back radically or to move ahead rapidly on legal positions firmly established by his predecessors.

Although it is true that a President's Supreme Court appointments are among his most important decisions, they are also likely to have unpredictable consequences. Earl Warren, who gave his name and leadership to the most activist Court in memory, was the first appointment of President Eisenhower, an advocate of political tranquility. President Nixon campaigned against abortions, yet his appointees joined the Court's seven-to-two majority in striking down state anti-abortion laws. The members of the Court may be the President's appointees, but they are seldom "his" Justices.

FORMER CHIEF
JUSTICE
EARL WARREN.
Wide World Photos

---

[15] A revealing case study of the appointment of one Justice is presented in David Danelski, *A Supreme Court Justice Is Appointed* (New York: Random House, 1964). A systematic treatment of the whole subject is to be found in Henry J. Abraham, *Justices and Presidents* (New York: Oxford University Press, 1974).

THE WORK OF THE COURT

We have treated the Supreme Court almost as if it lived all alone in its marble palace quite apart from other courts. It is important, however, to have some general understanding of the place of the Supreme Court in the American judicial system. (See Figure 14–1.)

The bulk of criminal prosecutions and lawsuits between individuals take place in state courts. Only in the relatively rare instance that a question of federal constitutionality arises in one of these cases is there any chance of its moving along the line from state supreme court to United States Supreme Court. When a case arises under a federal statute, it will begin in the lower federal courts. And when residents of different states become involved in a legal conflict, they may take their case to a federal district court rather than to the courts of either of their states. The Supreme Court has appellate jurisdiction over all cases, including military courts-martial, that first arise in lower federal courts. Congress, however, has the authority to create or abolish the lower federal courts and to determine what classes of appeals from them the Supreme Court may or may not hear. In short, subject to congressional limitations, the Supreme Court supervises all the work of the federal courts

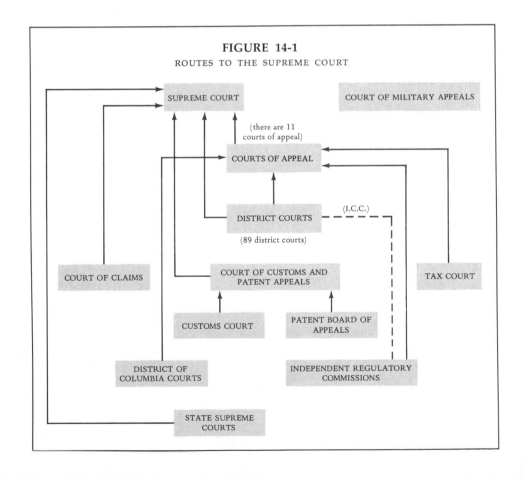

FIGURE 14-1

ROUTES TO THE SUPREME COURT

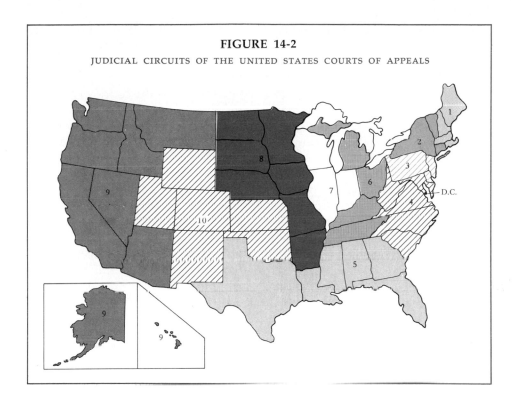

FIGURE 14-2

JUDICIAL CIRCUITS OF THE UNITED STATES COURTS OF APPEALS

but only those state court decisions that involve national constitutional issues.

THE SUPREME COURT AND THE LOWER FEDERAL COURTS

Figure 14–2 depicts the geography of the federal courts. The district courts are the basic trial courts of the federal judicial system. There are eighty-eight judicial districts in the fifty states, and one each in the District of Columbia and Puerto Rico. Each state has at least one district, and some larger states are divided into as many as four districts. There are from one to twenty-four judges in each district, each of whom normally holds court by himself. In 1975, there was a total of 400 federal district judges. This number increases from time to time with the growth of court business. The fact that at present there are more than 80,000 cases pending before the federal district courts, some of them more than two years old, seems to indicate that the time has come to increase the number of district judges. But a Democratic Congress is reluctant to authorize more judges for a Republican President to appoint, and vice versa. Thus, in periods of divided government, Congress holds back from passing the necessary legislation, and the backlog of cases grows.

The job of prosecuting cases in the district courts is done by the United States Attorney for each district and his staff of assistants. U.S. Attorneys are appointed to four-year terms by the President, with the advice and consent of the Senate. These are choice patronage posts, with a good deal of power and status. Senators of the President's party play a considerable part in filling these jobs.

Above the district courts in the judicial hierarchy are the courts of appeals. Each of the eleven courts of appeals hears appeals from the district courts within its circuit. Court of appeals decisions normally are rendered by three-judge panels designated by the chief judge of the circuit. Cases of unusual importance, however, may be decided by all the court of appeals judges of a given circuit sitting together (sitting *en banc*). District court cases normally reach the Supreme Court only after having been reviewed by a court of appeals. But if crucial constitutional issues are involved, a three-judge panel of federal district court judges may be appointed to hear it. Such cases may move directly from the three-judge district court panel directly to the Supreme Court. Another major job of the courts of appeals is to hear appeals from the legal decisions of federal administative agencies and regulatory commissions.

The Supreme Court supervises the lower federal courts in a number of ways, apart from its powers of constitutional interpretation. First of all, it prescribes most of the procedural rules governing the form and manner in which the lower federal courts conduct their business. In addition, its Chief Justice has become the principal spokesman before Congress and the public for the administrative needs of the whole federal court system. But undoubtedly its most important supervisory function derives from the fact that the Supreme Court is ultimately responsible for national uniformity in interpreting federal law. In the course of deciding thousands of cases each year, the lower federal courts must declare what many different federal statutes mean — that is, how their relatively general words relate to specific cases. Although the courts of appeals try to eliminate conflicts among their own district courts, inevitably some courts of appeal will interpret a given statute one way and others another. The Suprene Court must settle these differences, for it would be absurd if the same federal statute meant one thing in Dallas and another in Miami. As a result, much of the Supreme Court's own lawmaking is done in the process of settling conflicts between lower federal courts regarding the meaning of a particular statute.

In Chapter 13 we saw that department heads rarely have much say in the hiring or firing of their subordinates. The Supreme Court is in almost the same position in regard to its judicial subordinates. Appointments to the lower federal courts are made for life by the President with the advice and consent of the Senate. When one or both of the senators from the state where a district court appointment is to be made are of the same party as the President, they will submit a short list of prospective candidates to the Justice Department. At the same time, the Justice Department may make its own list of candidates, although it knows it has little hope of gaining Senate confirmation of its choice if the senator involved is opposed. The final presidential nomination usually goes to one of the candidates suggested by the senator whom the Justice Department likes best. When neither senator from the state is of the President's party or when an appointment is being made to court of appeal, each of which covers at least three states, the role of the Justice Department is much greater.

In appointing judges to the lower courts, the President does occasionally choose nominees from the other party, but the overwhelming majority come from his own. When Franklin Roosevelt took office after a long period of Republican rule, he found that over 90 percent of all federal judges were Republicans. Roosevelt appointed 203 Democrats and eight Republicans to federal judgeships. His successor, Harry Truman, continued with 129 Democrats and thirteen Republicans. President Eisenhower appointed eleven Democrats and 176 Republicans. Kennedy, Johnson, and Nixon continued the same pattern of partisan choice. Federal judges usually have rendered important services to their parties, as candidates, campaign managers, convention delegates, and the like, before their appointments.

The tendency of Presidents to appoint only members of their own party exercises a powerful influence over the inclinations of judges, but this fact does not allow one to conclude much about judicial behavior. Because judges sit for life, they tend to be genuinely independent. Although they see cases from their own political perspective, they are also men of the law, and like members of any profession, they apply professional criteria. John Sirica, the judge whose determined prodding of the Watergate burglars finally resulted in the resignation of President Nixon, was named to the bench by President Eisenhower, a Republican. The federal judge in New York who refused to halt publication of the Pentagon Papers as demanded by the Nixon administration had been named to his post by President Nixon only a few days earlier.[16]

ROUTES TO THE SUPREME COURT

There is no need for beginning students to master the many complex ways a case may reach the Supreme Court from the lower courts. We will content ourselves here with mentioning some of the typical routes. The Supreme Court does not issue general or advisory opinions. It acts only where a genuine legal case or controversy exists. Because some kinds of public policy simply cannot be made into issues for litigation, there are areas in which the Supreme Court is not a suitable forum for settling the issues.

There are four typical categories of trial cases that eventually can reach the Court. The first involves a private individual or corporation and a government agency in dispute over the meaning of a federal statute that the agency is applying to the individual. The second involves two private parties in a dispute that turns on the meaning of a federal statute and the legality of a federal agency's decisions under that statute. For instance, the defendant in a patent case may argue that the patent he is accused of infringing was not really a valid one because the U.S. Patent Office's grant of the patent rested

---

[16] Harold Chase, *Federal Judges: The Appointing Process* (Minneapolis: University of Minnesota Press, 1972).

on misinterpretation of the patent laws. These two categories account for the vast bulk of statutory interpretation done by the Supreme Court. Too often, we tend to think of the Supreme Court as engaged exclusively in the task of deciding whether laws are or are not constitutional. It is important to remember that a substantial share of its work lies in deciding what the language of a particular statute means, rather than whether it is constitutional. As we have seen, deciding what the words of a statute mean is a form of lawmaking. The Supreme Court shares this form of lawmaking with the bureaucracy and the lower courts.

The third category consists of both state and federal criminal prosecutions in which the defendant claims that the statute is unconstitutional or that the investigation, arrest, or trial procedures surrounding his prosecution are unconstitutional.[17]

The fourth category consists of suits requesting a court to order a public official to stop doing something unconstitutional or to do something required by the Constitution. It is in this area that the rule limiting the Court to actual cases and controversies causes difficulties. If a person feels, for example, that a certain law infringes on his constitutional rights, he cannot ask the Court to overturn it unless he can show that the law has personally and directly harmed him. And he cannot show this unless he has violated the law and been prosecuted for it. Until the state takes action to prosecute an offender, the alleged harm done by the law is only hypothetical. For example, when states had laws against abortion, doctors could not ask the Court to overturn them simply on the grounds that they infringed on their right to practice medicine. Until a doctor actually performs an abortion and is prosecuted for it, the state has not interfered with him at all. As we can see, this rule of Court procedure can create some difficult situations. As long as the law against abortions stood, doctors were unwilling to perform them. And the laws did stand until a doctor came along who was willing to risk prosecution — and jail — in order to test the law in court.

WORKLOAD OF THE COURT

Although the bulk of the Supreme Court's business involves appeals from lower courts, the Supreme Court was also granted some *original jurisdiction* by the Constitution. There are a few kinds of cases in which litigation begins in the Supreme Court itself. Of these, suits between two states or between a state and the United States are about the only important categories.

Even if a case does fall in one of the four appellate categories listed in the preceding section, and even if appeals are persistently pushed up the ladder to the Supreme Court, one final hurdle still must be faced. This is the scarcity of the Court's time. We have recurrently encountered this hurdle in

---

[17] Those who do not promptly seek to appeal their convictions on constitutional grounds may later do so by filing writs of habeas corpus in federal district courts. Such writs may allege that a prisoner is being illegally held because his conviction was unconstitutional. Many cases involving the rights of accused persons reach the Supreme Court on appeal from district court decisions on these habeas corpus proceedings rather than from the original criminal trial.

dealing with Congress, the President, and the federal bureaucracy. We have seen how elaborate practices have been developed in these parts of government to winnow down all the claims for attention to a number small enough to be handled by the human beings involved.

The Judiciary Act of 1921 provides the Court with an opportunity for similar winnowing. The act, in effect, provides that the Justices may choose the cases they wish to hear and the ones they wish to take no action on. When the Court refuses to review a case, the decision of the next lower court stands.

Despite this discretionary control of their own time, the workload of the Justices is enormous, as Table 14–3 reveals. The data on petitions dismissed or denied clearly shows that just deciding which cases to decide would absorb most of the Justices' time if they did not adopt further timesaving measures. The Court currently has an administrative staff barely large enough to keep its paperwork straight. It has no research staff, no enforcement personnel, and no one on whom it may devolve any of its formal tasks of judging. Each Justice does have from one to three law clerks, who are recent law school graduates. Customarily, as student editors of their school's law review, they have experience in legal research and writing. The clerks play a major role in selecting from the thousands of petitions those that the Court will finally consider. The Court has developed a set of "cues" for rapidly sorting out which cases it wants to hear. For instance, the Court will almost

TABLE 14-3
FINAL DISPOSITION OF CASES BY THE SUPREME COURT

	1969 TERM	1970 TERM	1971 TERM	1972 TERM	1973 TERM
By written opinion or per curiam decision	220	341	449	443	527
By dismissal, denial, or withdrawal, or appeals, petitions for certiori, or other application	3137	2977	3196	3305	3349
Total disposed	3357	3318	3645	3748	3876
Remaining on docket for disposal in the next term	793	894	888	892	1203

always hear a case in which a court of appeals has reversed the decision of a regulatory commission.[18]

Even after the selection process is completed, the workload is large. The Court does have a number of major labor-saving devices, however. The most important is the adversary proceeding itself. Each of the lawyers for the two litigants submits a written brief, and each makes oral arguments summarizing the factual and legal arguments for his side and rebutting those of the other. The Court also frequently permits *amicus curiae* (friend of the court) briefs to be filed by other interested groups or government agencies that are not actually litigants. Instead of doing research itself, the Court forces the litigants to finance extensive research out of their own pockets as each competes with the other to make a better case for its position and then to present the results in a form readily comprehensible by the Justices. (The word *brief*, however, is misleading. Such briefs, with their supporting appendices, frequently run into hundreds of pages.)

Because the Justices depend so heavily on others for information, providing that information is itself of major political significance. Briefs and *amicus* briefs are the principal means of access to the Court for individuals, interest groups, and government agencies. Litigants work hard to establish in the trial court the kind of factual record that will move the Supreme Court to judge in their favor. Many of the articles published in law reviews by law school professors are more or less open attempts to convert the Supreme Court on a particular legal point.

The Court's decisions take the form of an order to a lower court or a government agency to carry out the mandate of the Court. If any follow-up work has to be done, such as preparing detailed plans in school desegregation suits or spelling out the detailed rules to be followed for the registration of stock certificates, one of the Court's "subordinates" becomes responsible for it.

In view of all this, it is not clear that the Court actually is any more seriously overburdened than Congress or the President. Proposals to create subinstitutions to take over part of the load have been made for the Court, as for the presidency, but nothing has come of them yet. And a number of the Justices have vigorously denied that the workload has gotten beyond them.

THE DECISION-MAKING PROCESS

We have referred to the Court's discretionary power in selecting cases. If any four Justices wish to accept a case, it is placed on the calendar for oral argument. After their written briefs have been submitted, the attorneys in each case present the main points of their arguments orally to the Court. Sitting together on the bench, the Justices listen carefully to these arguments and often interrupt with questions. Each Friday they customarily discuss the cases they have heard that week. As each case is taken up, each Justice

[18] Joseph Tanenhaus et al., "The Supreme Court's Certiorari Jurisdiction: Cue Theory," in Glendon Schubert, ed., *Judicial Decision Making* (New York: Free Press, 1963).

speaks in turn, the Chief Justice first and then the others in order of their seniority. Here the Chief can exercise leadership through his opening remarks, which can set the tone for the discussion that follows. The Justices then take a tentative voice vote, in reverse order of their speaking—juniors first. When the vote is likely to be close, this procedure may also give the Chief some room to maneuver. After voting is completed, if the Chief Justice is in the majority, he assigns the writing of a draft "opinion of the court" to one of the majority. If the Chief Justice is in the minority, the senior Justice of the majority assigns the opinion.

These opinions are then circulated among all the Justices, who append suggestions for changes and improvements. Justices use this device to indicate what they object to, what is most important, and what will have to be modified in order to gain their votes. Although these marginal notes are kept confidential, we know enough about them to conclude that this procedure for circulating opinions is the principal vehicle for internal bargaining on the Court. The extent to which the final opinion reflects the comments of the other Justices depends partly on their rational power—and partly on the internal politics of the Court on that case. Thus even if the final opinion of the Court carries the signatures of five or more Justices, it may be less a tightly reasoned statement of policy and more the kind of vague, internally contradictory compromise that so often emerges from committees. We have repeatedly seen bargaining in connection with parties, Congress, and the executive branch. It is hardly surprising to find it on the Court, where the same policy issues are presented and many of the same attitudes, values, and ideologies are involved.

Since the 1950s, few of the major constitutional decisions of the Supreme Court have been unanimous or even nearly so. The Justices are clearly not working very hard at internal bargaining. Or at least they don't go much beyond the level of bargaining necessary to get a simple majority behind one outcome or the other. Yet there are a few instances in which the Justices clearly do seek to put up a united front. From 1954, when *Brown* v. *Board of Education* was decided, until 1970, all of the Court's school desegregation decisions were unanimous. The Court was also unanimous in *United States* v. *Nixon* (1974). Nixon's own appointee, Chief Justice Burger, wrote the opinion ordering the President to turn over the Watergate tapes to a federal district court. The release of the tapes then provided such damning evidence of presidential involvement in the Watergate coverup that Mr. Nixon was forced to resign.

SUPREME COURT OPINIONS

All the behavior of the Supreme Court is verbal behavior. About the only visible traces of the Court's activities are its opinions, printed in the official and commercial reports.[19] The Court's fellow political actors interact with the

CHIEF JUSTICE WARREN E. BURGER. *Wide World Photos*

[19] The reports are published in three forms: *United States Reports,* which is the official version from the Government Printing Office; and *The Supreme Court Reporter* and *United States Supreme Court, Lawyers' Edition,* both from commercial publishers. *United States Law Week* and the *Supreme Court Bulletin* print the opinions in a loose-leaf format a week or so after they have been issued by the Court.

Court by reading and interpreting those opinions and trying to get the Court to change them. Opinions must be written *to* somebody; they are messages, not simply the embalmed record which scholars later resurrect for study of what the Court did. To whom are these messages sent? We can distinguish seven distinct audiences for the Court's opinions.

1. *The two litigants.* An opinion is an explanation and justification of why the Court decided for one and not the other.
2. *Other similarly situated persons and their lawyers.* By explaining why the Court decided as it did in a particular case, the opinion is supposed to help others predict how it would decide similar cases in the future so that they can conduct their future affairs legally — that is, in such a way as to avoid losing in future litigation.
3. *Lower courts and administrators.* The opinion gives directions to those officials supervised by the Court as to how they are to decide similar matters in the future.
4. *Law teachers and other Court watchers.* The opinion is supposed to demonstrate that the Court has followed the canons of legal craftsmanship taught in the law schools, thus preserving and perpetuating legal standards.
5. *The other participants in the lawmaking process.* The opinion registers the Court's policy position and seeks to recruit support and to disarm opposition.
6. *The publics.* We deliberately used the plural publics because all the data we have on public reaction to the Supreme Court suggests that it is confronted with a number of separate special issue publics rather than a single body of public opinion. For example, the law teachers and court watchers mentioned above constitute one issue public, concerned with the issue of the Court's craftsmanship — with whether it makes good legal arguments. Other publics focus on specific policy issues. There is a patent public, a labor relations public, a criminal justice public, and so on, composed both of lawyers who specialize in those areas and laymen whose interests are immediately concerned. Yet most lawyers do not read the Court's opinions at all, and even the most specifically concerned laymen hear about them from their lawyers rather than reading them themselves. As is the case with most other political actors, the Court reaches the more general levels of the public through a series of intermediaries, including the press. Thus, the general level of public response seems to be determined less by the Court's specific words and deeds than by the general evolution of events and states of the world with which the Court is identified.
7. *The Justices themselves.* As we have seen, the drafting and redrafting of opinions is a major vehicle for reaching agreement on the Court. In this sense, the various paragraphs of many opinions are quite literally written for one Justice or another in order to gain his vote.

Once the multiple audience to which opinions are necessarily directed is understood, it is easier to see why the Court's opinions are criticized so frequently and so bitterly, even by those who admire it as an institution. In theory, at least, it would seem best in addressing audiences 1 through 4 to write very clear, precise, complete opinions that define and take a firm stand on the legal issues. The loser (in audience 1) will then be satisfied that the law—not the Court's partiality—made him lose. Other potential litigants (audience 2) will be able to predict the Court's future decisions. Clear and precise commands give bureaucratic subordinates less room to evade and maneuver. Therefore, to the extent that lower courts and administrators (audience 3) are subordinate to the Supreme Court, clear opinions mean better discipline. The law professors and other Court watchers (audience 4) will give the Court high grades for professionalism.

For audiences 5, 6, and 7, however, vaguely worded, incomplete opinions that fall short of deciding all the issues will frequently be desirable. The need to gain the cooperation, or at least the neutrality, of his fellows frequently makes it desirable for the American politician to avoid premature commitments, dramatic confrontations, and rigid insistence on all-or-nothing positions. For this reason, the Supreme Court frequently must avoid issuing opinions that unnecessarily antagonize its fellow lawmakers (audience 5).[20] Like other political actors, the Court often wants to keep its options open, and this frequently requires opinions that do not neatly answer all the questions raised by the case. Much the same can be said for the Court's relations with the publics (audience 6). Like any other political actor faced with multiple publics, the Court must seek to issue messages that appeal to more than one. As a result, it often gets accused, sometimes rightly, of resorting to double talk. For instance, it may seek to placate church goers by declaring that ours is a religious nation, while appealing to the libertarian by saying that school prayers violate the Constitution. Finally, the Court's vagueness often results from demands placed on it by audience 7—itself. The bargaining process used by the Court to reach a decision sometimes means that only an equivocal compromise decision is possible.

It is no wonder, then, that along with the endless debate about how much the Court should do, there has been continuous complaining about the quality of the Court's opinions. Those opinions cannot possibly satisfy all the contradictory demands made on them.

THE ROLES OF THE COURT

It is no more possible to catalogue all the Supreme Court's contributions to public policy than it is to catalogue the contributions of Congress or the President. In the discussion that follows, each area of the Court's concern will be briefly indicated and a specific example or two offered. The examples are chosen not only to illustrate the substance of the Court's work but to indicate the extremely wide variety of political contexts in which the Court acts and the various weights its acts may have in the political process.

[20] On this and other problems of judicial strategy, see Walter Murphy, *Elements of Judicial Strategy* (Chicago: University of Chicago Press, 1973).

Even those who are most reluctant to have the Court do anything have usually conceded its authority to police the boundaries between the central government and the states, and between President, Congress, and Supreme Court. In a way, this is odd because it is precisely in these areas that the Court is likely to arrive at the most dramatic face-to-face confrontations with other major political actors. The potential for head-on conflict can be seen in the Steel Seizure Case. During the Korean war, President Truman seized control of a steel mill whose workers were on strike. After examining the President's constitutional powers as commander-in-chief and those granted to him by congressional statute, the Court held the seizure invalid. The President chose to obey the Court, but it is not at all clear what would have happened if he had refused to do so.

DEFENDER OF PERSONAL LIBERTIES

FREEDOM OF SPEECH. The First Amendment to the Constitution says that "Congress shall make no law . . . abridging the freedom of speech, or of the press. . . ." The Court is now so identified with the defense of various personal liberties that one has to stop and remind oneself that it really did not get into that business in a major way until the 1930s.[21] Indeed, the major contemporary controversy about Supreme Court activism has centered on whether it should protect such personal rights as freedom of speech. The concept of speech itself has been expanded to include not only the right to speak and write but also the right to organize and join political groups, the right not to disclose membership in such a group, the right to refuse to answer questions put by legislative investigating committees about the activities of such groups, the right to bring test cases in Court, to present movies and other artistic performances, to picket and demonstrate, to travel abroad, to refuse to take various kinds of loyalty oaths, to make comments about public officials that would be libelous if made about private citizens, and to engage in various kinds of symbolic expression. It even has been argued that freedom of speech includes the right to violate valid laws deliberately as an expression of political protest, but the Court has rejected this argument.

At the conceptual level, the protections offered by the freedom of speech provisions of the First Amendment might seem sweeping. The Constitution simply says, "Congress shall make *no* law. . . ." But in terms of actual Supreme Court decisions, the issue is not as simple as it may at first appear. The Court has found only one congressional statute unconstitutional under the First Amendment — a minor one controlling the flow of foreign Communist propaganda through the mails. Its intervention against state

---

[21] On the Court's role in the individual rights area, see Henry J. Abraham, *Freedom and the Court* (New York: Oxford University Press, 1967); and Samuel Krislov, *The Supreme Court and Political Freedom* (New York: The Free Press, 1968).

invasions of free speech has been sporadic and incomplete, with the highest level of activity occurring in the sideshow area of obscenity. The Court consistently has ruled that the states may constitutionally enforce obscenity statutes without having to prove that the depiction of sexual acts has any harmful social effects.

Perhaps the quality of the Court's actions can best be represented by a sort of box score of its achievements in the area of law that most often involves infringements upon free speech — controlling "subversive" activities.

Government action	*Court disposition*
Federal statutes forbidding membership in the Communist party.	Upheld, but made extremely difficult to enforce.
Federal statutes forbidding advocacy of overthrow of the government by force and violence.	Upheld, but somewhat weakened.
Federal statute requiring Communist party to register and file membership lists.	Upheld as to First Amendment, but eventually rendered unenforceable on Fifth Amendment (self-incrimination) grounds.
Congressional investigations of subversive activities.	Upheld, subject to certain trivial procedural limitations. However, during the Communist scare of the 1950s, the Court managed to free on procedural grounds a substantial number of those jailed for refusing to answer committees' questions.
State investigations of subversion.	Some flatly overturned as violating the First Amendment; others knocked out on procedural grounds. The Court has severely limited the power of the states to pierce the anonymity of nonsubversive groups, but has refused to commit itself to a substantial general limitation when subversion is alleged.
State statutes directed at overthrow of the government, anarchism, and so forth.	Where the states openly have sought to enforce such laws, the Court has overturned them.

Government action	Court disposition
Federal security programs designed to keep Communists out of government, labor union leadership, defense industries, and so forth.	Generally upheld, but with the imposition of relatively severe procedural safeguards to insure due process to those accused; and with very grudging interpretation of the statutes to limit executive action under them to the narrowest possible scope that Congress might have authorized—probably far narrower than Congress actually intended.
State loyalty oaths and loyalty-security programs.	Upheld in principle; many oaths and programs specifically upheld. Others subjected to procedural safeguards. Some eventually struck down on such secondary grounds as vagueness.
Statutes prohibiting travel abroad by subversives.	Narrowly interpreted by Court to deprive Secretary of State of most enforcement powers.

From this box score, it is clear that the Court has not always been an outspoken champion of the First Amendment in all areas. When the rest of the government was seized with a passion for infringing political freedom, the Court did not always resist defiantly. During the "Red Scare" of the 1950s, it temporized and sought to limit the damage. At the same time, it was extremely careful to avoid the dramatic confrontation with Congress that would have resulted from a full and direct defense of freedom of speech. In the end, it was the action of Congress, the executive branch, the press, and the public, as well as the Court, that stopped the anti-Communist hysteria.

RELIGION. The First Amendment states that "Congress shall make no law respecting an establishment of religion, or prohibiting the free exercise thereof. . . ." Although the religion clauses of the First Amendment have led the Court to make many controversial decisions, undoubtedly its greatest problems in this area have involved the question of religion in the public schools. We have a clear well-documented record of the impact of Supreme Court decisions in this field.[22]

The Supreme Court has forbidden religious instruction, prayers, and Bible reading in the schools. It has permitted released-time programs in

---

[22] See Theodore L. Becker and Malcolm M. Feeley, eds., *The Impact of Supreme Court Decisions,* 2nd ed. (New York: Oxford University Press, 1973); and Stephen L. Wasby, *The Impact of the United States Supreme Court* (Homewood, Ill.: Dorsey Press, 1970).

which children are excused from school to attend religious classes at their own churches. Ten years after the decision banning religious instruction in schools, about half of the districts that had previously conducted such instruction continued to do so in flagrant disobedience of the Court. After the Court approved released time, it might have been assumed that many of the resisting districts anxious both to serve God *and* to obey the law might have switched to this compromise. In fact, very few did. The decision banning school prayers inspired an extremely loud reaction from religious spokesmen. The reaction to the Bible reading decision was somewhat quieter, partly because in the interval between the two decisions many people got used to the Court's new position and partly because almost as many religious groups supported as opposed the Court's judgments. As the noise died down, substantial numbers of districts continued their religious exercises.

Detailed investigations of the patterns of compliance to these decisions indicate the following:

1. Relatively few of the local officials involved, including lawyers, actually read the opinions.
2. Disobedience, however, was not the result of ignorance of the Court's decisions. Noncompliers knew at least as much about the decisions as compliers did.
3. The attitudes and policy goals of individual school officials, teachers, and the attorneys counseling them were an important factor influencing compliance.
4. Compliance was greatest in those sections of the country where religious instruction was a traditional requirement embodied in old state statutes. It was weakest in areas, particularly in the Midwest, where such programs were optional to the local districts.

In other words, the Court was most successful where its ruling swept away a practice that had been preserved simply by the existence of an old law rather than by active community interest. It seems safe to conclude that the Court's opinions did not operate as overwhelming orders. They were simply an additional element interjected into the community scene that altered the balance of pro- and anti-religion forces without necessarily being decisive in their own right.

NEW CONSTITUTIONAL RIGHTS: TRAVEL, CITIZENSHIP, WELFARE, PRIVACY

In recent years, the Court has been actively engaged in creating new rights. For instance, it recognizes a sort of constitutional *right to travel abroad.* But, mindful of the fact that letting any American go anywhere he wants may pose dangers to our foreign policy, it has not pressed this right very far. On the other hand, the Court has created such an absolute *right to citizenship* that it has forbidden Congress to denaturalize even those Americans who fight in foreign armies. In the 1880s and 1890s, it used the equal protection

ALTHOUGH THE SUPREME COURT HAS FORBIDDEN IT, SOME LOCAL SCHOOL DISTRICTS HAVE REQUIRED TEACHERS TO READ "NON-DENOMINATIONAL" PRAYERS OR BIBLE PASSAGES THAT DO NOT CONFLICT WITH ANY CHILD'S BELIEF. *Wide World Photos*

and due process clauses of the Constitution (Fourteenth and Fifth Amend-ments) to protect business against what was deemed unreasonable govern-ment regulation. Recently, it has used the same clauses to enter the field of *welfare rights,* insisting that the welfare applicant is entitled to certain fun-damental standards of equity and fairness. The Court's entry into welfare is like its earlier interventions in the area of business regulation in that it recognizes some economic rights as fundamental.

The newest officially declared constitutional freedom is the *right to privacy.*[23] Although the Court has not found a single constitutional pro-vision from which the right derives, it supports the right to privacy by whatever odds and ends in the Constitution seem available at any given moment. This right already has been used to strike down state laws against birth control and abortion. In the future, it may serve as a weapon against some sorts of government snooping, particularly wiretapping and electronic surveillance.

THE RIGHT TO VOTE

Enough has been said about elections to make clear our belief that there is no single, ideal electoral mechanism, and that every alteration in the mechanism favors some interests and harms others. In a series of cases in the 1960s, the Court came to grips with the electoral process and imposed a constitutional requirement that legislative districts be of equal population.[24]

Several points are dramatically illustrated by the reapportionment cases. First, the Court is in a position to make special contributions to the demo-cratic process that the popularly elected branches are incapable of making. It was absurd to expect state legislators, who owed their own seats to mal-apportionment, to reform themselves out of office. But because the Court is not elected, it had no self-interested motives to keep it from acting. Although its reapportionment decisions raised a storm of political protests, the Court met those protests effectively under the banner of "one-man—one-vote." The opposition to the Court eventually was silenced because most Americans saw one-man—one-vote as an obviously correct principle of democratic government.

RIGHTS OF ACCUSED PERSONS

TABLE OF RIGHTS OF ACCUSED

Fourth Amendment	*Fifth Amendment*
The right of the people to be secure in their persons, houses, papers, and effects, against *unreasonable*	No person shall be held to answer for a capital, or otherwise infamous crime, unless on a presentment or

[23] Alan Westin, *Privacy and Freedom* (New York: Atheneum, 1967).
[24] Robert G. Dixon, Jr., *Democratic Representation: Reapportionment in Law and Politics* (New York: Oxford University Press, 1969).

searches *and seizures,* shall not be violated, and no Warrants shall issue, but upon probable cause, supported by Oath or affirmation, and particularly describing the place to be searched, and the persons or things to be seized.

Sixth Amendment

In all criminal prosecutions, the accused shall enjoy the right to a speedy and public *trial, by* an impartial *jury* of the State and district wherein the crime shall have been committed, which district shall have been previously ascertained by law, and to be informed of the nature and cause of the accusation; to be confronted with the witnesses against him; to have compulsory process for obtaining witnesses in his favor, and to have the *Assistance of Counsel* for his defence.

Fourteenth Amendment

Section 1. All persons born or naturalized in the United States, and subject to the jurisdiction thereof, are citizens of the United States and of the State wherein they reside. No State shall make or enforce any law which shall abridge the privileges or immunities of citizens of the United States; *nor shall any State deprive any person of life, liberty or property, without due process of law;* nor deny to any person within its jurisdiction the equal protection of the laws.

indictment of a Grand Jury, except in cases arising in the land or naval forces, or in the Militia, when in actual service in time of War or public danger; *nor* shall any person be subject for the same offence to be *twice put in jeopardy* of life or limb; *nor* shall be *compelled* in any criminal case *to be a witness against himself,* nor be deprived of life, liberty, or property, without due process of law; nor shall private property be taken for public use, without just compensation.

Eighth Amendment

Excessive bail shall not be required, nor excessive fines imposed, nor *cruel and unusual punishments* inflicted.

Closely related to other individual freedoms are the parcel of rights associated with the criminal law process. These include the right to grand jury indictment and trial by jury, the rights against self-incrimination and illegal search, and the right to counsel. This area is particularly appropriate for examining the Court's ability to maneuver and to institute positive governmental programs.

From the 1880s until well into the 1960s, the Supreme Court used two legal doctrines to allow itself to experiment freely with the processes of federal criminal law enforcement while leaving the states largely free to develop their own experience. On the one hand, the Supreme Court has a general supervisory power over the lower federal courts. This power does not derive from any provisions of the Bill of Rights but from the Court's position as the highest court in the federal court system. On the other hand, the specific provisions of the Bill of Rights traditionally were held by the Court to apply directly only to the federal government, and not to the state governments. Add these two together, and it becomes possible for the Court to enforce the most rigorous standards on its own federal subordinates while disclaiming responsibility for the states.

This tactic allowed the Supreme Court to institute a pilot program of federal reform that was protected from the storm of resistance that it would have encountered had the Justices attempted to impose their standards on state criminal law procedures. Inasmuch as the great mass of criminal law enforcement was handled by the states, even those most opposed to "coddling criminals" could not get too excited about experiments conducted in the federal sideshow.

Confining itself to the federal sphere, the Court slowly progressed with such "revolutionary" reforms as guaranteeing defense counsel to those who could not afford it, refusing to admit illegally seized evidence at trial, and insisting that prisoners be promptly arraigned rather than held secretly for days and even weeks by the police. It seems to have hoped to influence state courts by its example—which in fact it did. By the late 1930s, many state criminal law systems were substantially reformed. As a result, very great disparities existed between the way accused persons were treated by the federal courts and the most advanced of the state courts on the one hand, and the worst of the state courts on the other. Quite naturally, this situation led to the feeling that something unconstitutional must be going on somewhere.

In the early 1940s, the Court sought to combine this feeling with its tactical decision to avoid the massive reform of state practices. It invented something called the *fair trial rule,* which declared that although the Court would not impose detailed regulations on the states, it would invalidate state convictions resulting from trials that violated "our fundamental concepts of ordered liberties." The fair trial rule kept the Court out of most state business, and at the same time gave it latitude to nudge and nibble at state injustices. The idea was to avoid imposing rules on the states while educating them into cleaning up their own problems.

Unfortunately, a large number of the states refused to learn. By the 1950s, the disparities between the federal system and the worst state practices were very great. In response to this problem, the Court slowly shifted from the fair trial rule to the much stronger doctrine of *selective incorporation*.[25] As early as 1925, the Court had suggested that although the freedom of speech provisions of the First Amendment did not apply directly to the states, they might be "incorporated" into the due process clause of the Fourteenth Amendment, thus making them binding upon the states. Now, one after another, the Court incorporated most of the criminal law guarantees of the Bill of Rights.[26] In this way the Supreme Court federalized the state criminal law processes. So we have here not only an instance of the Court's role in protecting liberties but also of its role in adjusting federal relationships—in this instance, giving the whole pie to the federal side and indeed to itself.

This is a good example of the Court's using its negative powers to initiate positive programs. By invalidating all convictions in which indigent defendants have not been offered legal counsel, the Court forced many communities to create and finance public defender offices. It has done this as effectively as would a state legislature that passed a statute requiring the establishment of such offices. Nevertheless, as with most other programs, it is clear that the Court cannot do the whole job. The thoroughgoing reform of the criminal law process the Justices desire can be obtained only through a wide range of initiatives, from better police training through more efficient criminal court procedures to vastly improved correctional programs. Only a fraction of these needed reforms are amenable to direct Supreme Court control.

RACE RELATIONS

The Court's activities in behalf of black Americans are surely the central phenomena of its post-World War II existence. The decision in the famous case of *Brown* v. *Board of Education,* which required the end of legal segregation in southern schools, raises quite acutely a number of key problems in evaluating the work of the Court.[27] The major issue we would like to examine here revolves around what Charles Black calls the *legitimating role* of the Court.[28] Too many discussions of the Supreme Court focus on its power to declare laws *un*constitutional. The Court rarely exercises that power. Most of the time it finds that the laws before it *are* constitutional. This is not simply a neutral act but the addition of some margin of legitimacy, a kind of constitutional blessing added to the legitimacy the statute has already acquired in its passage through the legislature.

[25] For the pressures on the Court during this period, see Jonathan D. Casper, *Lawyers Before the Warren Court* (Urbana, Ill.: University of Illinois Press, 1972).

[26] For a summary of the constitutional rights of accused persons, see Shapiro and Tresolini, *American Constitutional Law,* Chap. 15.

[27] 347 U.S. 483 (1954).

[28] Charles L. Black, Jr., *The People and the Court* (New York: The Macmillan Company, 1960).

This legitimating role was particularly important in the segregation problem. Although the Supreme Court did not invent the southern practice of legally enforced segregation, it had given it constitutional legitimacy in 1896 when it declared that "separate but equal" facilities met the equal protection requirements of the Fourteenth Amendment.[29] Thus, if the Court had sidestepped the issue in the *Brown* case, it would have been continuing to legitimate most segregation. The NAACP had mounted a vigorous litigational campaign to bring the issue of primary and secondary school segregation directly before the Court. It had tried in every way possible to limit the Court's choices to a simple yes or no on the constitutionality of segregation. Those who have criticized the boldness of the *Brown* decision rarely face up to the problem of just how the Justices could have legitimated segregation in 1954 and still lived with their consciences as judges and as political leaders.

In the last analysis, the crucial issue may indeed be the question of political leadership. By 1954, the majority of Americans were surely opposed in principle to legally enforced segregation. But this principled sentiment was not focused in ways that would move Congress or the President. The Court could and did focus it. Perhaps even more important, the *Brown* decision gave tremendous impetus to the process through which racial minorities trained themselves to make the kinds of self-conscious, specific demands on the political process that lead to legislative and executive action. It was only in the aftermath of *Brown* that Congress finally began to pass significant civil rights legislation and the executive began to take major steps toward the goal of racial equality.

This is a good point at which to note the Court's special relation not only to racial equality but also to equality in a much more general sense. Equality has always been a part of the American ideology. In the past it has been

[29] *Plessey* v. *Ferguson,* 163 U.S. 537 (1896).

TO ENFORCE THE LAW, IN 1956 PRESIDENT EISENHOWER SENT TROOPS TO ESCORT BLACK STUDENTS INTO LITTLE ROCK CENTRAL HIGH SCHOOL, PAST THE NATIONAL GUARD POSTED BY THE GOVERNOR OF ARKANSAS.
Wide World Photos

balanced by other important American values, but in recent years Americans seem to have become particularly sensitive to issues involving equality. The Supreme Court has been a principal spokesman for this sentiment. In the three major areas in which it has intervened—legislative apportionment, equal criminal justice, and desegregation—it has done so under the banner of equality. Here we have concentrated on school desegregation, but the Court also has moved against racial discrimination in voting, jury selection, and other important areas of government activity.

THE COURT AND ECONOMIC RIGHTS

The standard historical cliché about the Court is that it served as the principal protector of the interests of business against government from the 1890s until 1937, but then turned to the defense of personal liberties. The trouble with this cliché is that it gives the Court too much credit or blame, depending upon one's point of view. Actually, in the decades preceding the New Deal, the Court was not particularly more or less liberal than other branches of the government on the issue of state interference with the free economy. The historical record tends to get distorted on this score, because Court decisions striking down new legislation are far more memorable than Court decisions upholding it. For example, when the Court struck down laws governing child labor, history books duly recorded its role as a defender of business interests. But when the Court upheld antibusiness legislation, the credit for the legislation went not to the Court but to the legislatures that passed it. In fact, though, the legislatures do not deserve their reputation as champions of economic liberalism who were often frustrated by a conservative Court. In the early decades of this century, there was a fairly steady stream of demands for legislation to deal with specific problems that the free economy did not seem to be solving on its own. Federal and state legislatures turned down thousands of these demands, and governors and Presidents vetoed hundreds, but the Supreme Court ruled only a few dozen unconstitutional.[30]

Occasionally, one hears the argument that the Court should not interfere with the economy at all. If we condemn the Court for protecting business freedoms in the past, it seems that in consistency we should condemn it now for protecting personal economic freedoms. This line of reasoning, though, seems to be based on an essentially false disjunction between economic and civil rights. Economic rights are about eating—the rights to material well-being. If you cannot eat, the right to speak and to vote are meaningless and soon disappear. The right to a living is therefore a fundamental personal right, not merely a matter of abstract economic theory. In defending businessmen against government regulation, many Justices thought they were defending this fundamental personal right. Today the Court has begun to defend the rights of welfare recipients. From time to

[30] See Arthur Selwyn Miller, *The Supreme Court and American Capitalism* (New York: Free Press, 1968).

time, our views may change regarding whose right to eat is in need of protection, but it is not easy to argue that the Court has acted illegitimately in defending the economic rights upon which all other rights ultimately depend.

THE COURT TODAY: AN OVERVIEW

During the early years of the 1970s, the federal courts, and the Supreme Court in particular, became dramatically visible to the American people in new ways. The Environmental Protection Act, the civil rights statutes calling for nondiscrimination in employment, and a number of other recently enacted federal laws enable many individuals and whole classes of persons to sue in federal courts. Almost every time a new bridge or dam or building is proposed, old housing torn down, a woman fired, a white male hired, a television station's license renewed, a new town incorporated, or any one of thousands of other decisions taken that affect the environment or the status of minority persons, someone has a right to sue. And someone very often does.[31] It is alleged that the proposed new dam will have an adverse effect on the ecology of a wild river, or that a company is discriminating against women in its hiring, or that incorporation of a new town will create racial imbalance in the schools. As a result, the federal courts find themselves looking into thousands and thousands of routine governmental and private decisions about investment, hiring, construction, advertising, pricing, procurement, personnel management, education, and school admissions that would have seemed totally outside their jurisdiction a few years ago. To

[31] See, for instance, Frederick R. Anderson, *The National Environment Protection Act in the Courts* (Washington, D. C.: Resources for the Future, 1973).

SCHOOL BUSING HAS BECOME A NATIONAL ISSUE OF INCREASING INTEREST TO LOCALITIES AND LEGISLATORS AS WELL AS TO THE COURTS.
Wide World Photos

many executives in business, education, labor, and government, it now seems that whatever decisions they make, they will almost routinely be sued by somebody.

So far, much of this new judicial activity has occurred in the lower federal courts. But as appeals build up, the Supreme Court is increasingly entering the new areas. Within the last few years it has handled cases involving admissions to law schools, job qualifications for factory workers, the routing of highways through parks, and the location of hiking trails.

Quite apart from this explosion of judicial activity in the environment and job equality fields, the Supreme Court recently has become involved in a number of major public controversies. Supreme Court decisions led the way to great liberalization of the abortion laws in most states. In the Pentagon Papers incident, in which the Nixon administration sought to prevent the publication of classified information about the Vietnam war, and then in the Watergate case, the Court has made historic decisions about the extent of presidential powers. And it continues to be embroiled in the school busing controversy. Under Chief Justice Burger, the Court has pretty clearly been trying to avoid the extreme integrationist position. It has stressed that exact mathematical integration in which each school has exactly the same proportion of majority to minority students is not required. It has hinted that one-race schools caused by residential patterns rather than by conscious government policy are not unconstitutional. It has cautioned that the means chosen for desegregation should not be so costly and disruptive as to determine the quality of education. It has blocked lower court attempts to create huge new school districts in which suburban white students would be made available for integration with central city blacks. Yet the Court has not abandoned its basic commitment to the dismantling of school segregation.

Here, as in so many other areas of public policy, the Supreme Court seems to be in the same boat as most other political actors. For the rest of this decade, questions of racial integration undoubtedly will continue to trouble not only the Court but the President, Congress, the political parties, and many state and local governments.

SUMMARY

The Supreme Court makes many large and small policy decisions over a wide range of issues. It wields the power of judicial review — the power to declare acts of government unconstitutional. Courts derive their basic legitimacy from their position as a neutral third person resolving conflicts between two opponents. But courts also act as lawmakers and instruments of government. The lawmaking and governing aspects of the Supreme Court's work tend to overshadow its basic legitimacy as a conflict-resolving agency. The Supreme Court is supreme in the sense of its close linkage to the Constitution, but it is only one agency among the many that govern the country. How much or how little the Supreme Court ought to engage in policy making in a democracy has been a traditional subject of political debate. In evaluating that debate it must be borne in mind that Supreme Court decisions are rarely final, that interest groups have considerable access to the Court, and that by his appointments, a President may materially shift the direction of Supreme Court policies.

Each state has its own judicial hierarchy which handles most cases. Only a limited variety of cases can enter the federal judicial hierarchy headed by the Supreme Court. The Supreme Court does not issue general or advisory opinions. It acts only where a legal case or controversy exists. Even though the routes to the Supreme Court are few, its case load is heavy.

The Court's decision-making process allows each Justice to reach his own independent decision or act with his colleagues to reach collective decisions. Its written opinions are the mode by which the Court issues policy messages to various audiences.

The Court has many roles. It seeks to set constitutional boundaries, defend personal liberties, regulate race relations, and deal with economic problems. In its role of announcing uniform national interpretations of federal statutes for lower federal courts, it participates in the lawmaking process in nearly every area of national policymaking from labor relations to home financing. During the last three decades the federal courts have become increasingly visible to most Americans as they have become more actively involved in a wider range of public policy making.

PART FOUR
PRODUCTS AND CONSEQUENCES OF AMERICAN NATIONAL POLITICS

CHAPTER FIFTEEN
PUBLIC POLICY MAKING
CHAPTER SIXTEEN
CHANGE AND VIOLENCE
IN AMERICAN POLITICS
CHAPTER SEVENTEEN
EVALUATING
THE AMERICAN
POLITICAL SYSTEM

CHAPTER FIFTEEN
PUBLIC POLICY MAKING

FFERSON

Poughkeepsie
URBAN RENEWAL AGENCY

is administrating the Redevelopment of this
Urban Renewal Project Area under Title I of the
Housing Act of 1949 as amended with Financial
Assistance from the

CITY OF POUGHKEEPSIE

NY DIVISION of HOUSING & COMMUNITY RENEWAL
U.S. DEPARTMENT of HOUSING & URBAN DEVELOPMENT

IN Part Three we examined the major government institutions one by one. We analyzed the procedures through which each of them makes decisions, the ways they interact with each other, and how their institutional interests clash and harmonize. These institutions—Congress, the presidency, the bureaucracy, and the courts—have distinctive resources and powers that affect how each of them operates. Discussing each institution separately, we naturally are inclined to emphasize their characteristic features, that is, what distinguishes them from one another. This approach should not leave the impression that officials in one institution make decisions in ways completely different from people in the other institutions. In fact, certain common features of policy making are found in all our national governmental institutions. These common features of the policy-making process are discussed in this chapter, as we examine American politics from the standpoint of how issues are decided rather than who makes the decisions.

Public policy is a very broad term. It covers the tax rate on capital gains, a loan for a farmer in Kansas or a dictator in Africa, relocation of a federal office building, and innumerable other acts. Our second purpose in this chapter, therefore, is to analyze certain recurring patterns in how problems are approached and decided. Once again, these differences concern not the institutions that make a policy, but the nature of the policy area itself.

POLICY

SCARCITY OF RESOURCES

Policy involves *resources, alternatives,* and *goals.* The policy maker has certain material and human resources available to him. By definition, these resources are limited. Policy decisions must take into account how many dollars, how many tons of steel, how many engineers, teachers, typists, or social workers will be available for putting the policy into effect. The first fact of policy, therefore, is *scarcity.*

Scarcity of physical resources is the most obvious form of scarcity, but it is not necessarily the most important one. For instance, a large number of the world's nations have the physical and capital resources necessary for producing a moon rocket, but most of them have too limited a pool of scientists to afford diverting so much brainpower to such a nonproductive program. Thus, an important element in policy decisions is the relative scarcity of creative, managerial, and intellectual resources. This is why we often hear complaints about the shortage of new ideas. The scarcity of ideas in government is as real a limitation on policy as shortages of oil or weapons or money.

Scarcity of time in which to make policy decisions is yet another crucial scarcity that affects policy makers. The President simply does not have enough time to decide every policy issue that faces his administration. There are hundreds of thousands of such issues, ranging from a proposed new treaty with China to a proposed new Department of Agriculture field office in Des Moines. He must ration his time and set priorities for what he can think about and what he must leave to others to think about. Along another dimension, too, time may be scarce. A crisis may occur which must be responded to immediately or not at all. For instance, the army of a small democracy may suddenly rise against the civilian government, which immediately asks for U.S. assistance. If it doesn't come within a few hours, the capital will fall to the rebels. Policy makers may have only a few minutes to make a decision that they would like to think about for months.

CHOOSING ALTERNATIVES

Because resources are scarce, the number of *alternatives* open to policy makers is necessarily limited. The Japanese government, for instance, cannot choose between the alternative policies of using its own oil or importing oil from abroad, because it has almost no oil of its own. It could choose between the policies of relying entirely on homegrown food and importing food from abroad, because it still does seem barely possible to grow enough food in Japan to feed all the Japanese. But in order to do so, Japan would have to throw so much of her total resources into the growing of food that she could do almost nothing else. Although the alternative of total independence of outside food sources is theoretically available, the scarcity of agricultural land in Japan is sufficiently great to eliminate this alternative for practical purposes. As this example illustrates, scarcity is usually not an absolute but a relative matter. Given the relatively scarce quantity of any resource, certain alternatives become prohibitively expensive.

GOALS AND PRIORITIES

Although resources are scarce and the number of alternatives is therefore limited, political goals or values are infinitely expansible. As we noted in Chapter 4, there is a strong utopian element in political ideology. Few of us could specify exactly what the ideal society would be, but most of us can imagine one much better than the one we have. At any given moment, the policy maker is likely to face goal demands far in excess of what he can reasonably hope to achieve. Thus, from a policy perspective, the crucial task in dealing with political values or goals is the *ordering of priorities*. Which of the many good things we want to achieve should we pursue first and which ones should we leave for later?

Frequently, we use the word *policy* to refer simply to a choice among various alternatives. When we say "the U.S. policy on the recognition of Red China," or "the policy of the Department of Agriculture on school lunches," we mean the choice between the alternatives of recognizing or not recognizing the People's Republic of China or of providing or not providing surplus food for children's lunches. Yet for the policy maker, the most difficult task may not be the choice between alternative programs but the choice of which goals he is going to pursue at the cost of ignoring or even undermining others. For instance, should the Department of Agriculture pursue the goal of national security by disposing of its surpluses in the Third World in the hope of preventing Communist takeovers? Or should it pursue the goal of child welfare at home by disposing of its surpluses in such a way as to improve the nutrition of American schoolchildren? And even assuming we wish to pursue both goals, which one do we want more, and how much more? Should we split the available surplus in half, or should foreign aid get twice as much food as school lunches? There are not enough resources to fuel enough alternatives to achieve every goal of every member of society simultaneously. Policy makers must make some judgments of which goals have first claim on how much of their resources.

One of the greatest problems in choosing priorities—that is, choosing which goals to pursue first—is that of comparing *utilities*. The term *utility* refers to the use or benefit people derive from various objects or activities. It may be a practical benefit, such as a nutritious meal provides, or a psychological benefit, such as one gets from a gourmet dinner. Economists tell us there is no correct way of comparing one person's utilities with those of another. That is, we cannot say that the satisfaction one man gets from ice cream is worth more or less than the pleasure another derives from apples. Nor can we simply count noses and say that the more people a policy benefits, the better the policy. This is because utility has a qualitative dimension as well as a quantitative one. Many people would agree that a kidney machine that keeps twelve people alive represents a better use of funds than a fresh-air program that sends a hundred city children to the country for two weeks. But most issues are not this simple. For example, some people may want the preservation of unspoiled wilderness. Others may want to turn the same area into a park with roads, campsites, and swimming pools. In a sense, they both have the same long-term goal—the enjoyment of nature. But they want to enjoy it in different ways. Is it better for a few backpackers to enjoy an underdeveloped wilderness or for thousands of weekend campers to drive their families over paved roads to campsites with showers? Our instinctive answer tends to be that it is best to have both wilderness and parks. But our answer is instinctive precisely because we cannot estimate how much good either would do. More importantly, policy makers often must choose one or the other because they don't have the resources to do both.

MEANS AND ENDS

Any discussion of policy must deal with the perennial issue of *means and ends*. It is not easy to differentiate sharply between means and ends. Most policies are links in a chain that runs in this manner: If the government adopts a free school lunch policy that feeds poor schoolchildren better, then they will learn more in school. If they learn more in school, then they will get better jobs. If they get better jobs, then they will be able to achieve higher social and economic status later in life. If they achieve higher status, then disparities in status will be reduced in our society. If greater equality is achieved, then the nation will be more democratic. We tend rather arbitrarily to call the early links in this continuous chain means, and the late links ends. In this case, a school lunch program is seen as a means of achieving an end labeled equality. The major difficulty is that, starting from the earliest link it usually is possible to construct numerous contradictory chains.[1] If the government feeds schoolchildren, then they will learn to depend upon the government for their daily bread. If they learn dependence on government, then they will not become free, self-supporting citizens. If they are not truly free, then there can be no real democracy. The guesses each man makes about which chain will come out where will undoubtedly affect his policy preferences. Notice, however, that simply agreeing that democracy is our ultimate goal will not solve the dispute over school lunches. The problem does *not* arise from a lack of agreement on ultimate values. It arises from different predictions about how current practice ultimately will affect those values. Even if we simplify our goals, put aside the "big" issues such as democracy and freedom, and concentrate on the immediate benefits, policy decisions do not necessarily become simpler. We may all agree on the goal of achieving better education for the poor. This still leaves us with the question of whether a school lunch policy is the best available means for achieving this end.

In short, policy makers may disagree about the means to be used even when they are in fundamental agreement about the ends they are pursuing. Obviously, it goes without saying that they are even more likely to differ about the means when they differ about the ends. The materials presented earlier in this book on political participation and interest groups show that differing values *do* play a part in American politics. The policy maker lives at the overlap between problem solving and ideology. He cannot decide only what the most efficient government program for feeding children would be. He also must decide if it is a good idea for government to feed children in the first place. He makes this decision in the light of his own and other people's vision of what the ideal relation between the government and its citizens ought to be.

TYPES OF POLICIES

Frequently, we use the terms *policy* and *decision*, or *policy making* and *decision making*, interchangeably. When the President *decides* to withhold future arms shipments to the People's Republic of Swat, the *policy* of the United States becomes not to ship arms to Swat. On the other hand, the President may announce that his *decision* to stop the shipments was taken in pursuance of our long-standing *policy* against providing aid to regimes formed by military coups against democratic governments. According to this usage, a policy is something larger than a decision. It is the pattern or principle that policy makers use to give shape and consistency to their individual decisions. Thus, when we speak of "the President's economic policy," we may not be referring to any one policy in particular, but to the general direction in which all his individual policies point.

[1] See Herbert A. Simon, *Administrative Behavior: A Study of Decision Processes in Administrative Organizations*, 2nd ed. (New York: The Macmillan Company, 1957).

A number of analysts have suggested general typologies for dividing policies into broad categories. These various systems for classifying policies help us to understand the differences between policies by giving us meaningful ways of contrasting the various alternatives. In the next few pages, we will be examining five such typologies. Each focuses on a different facet of policy making and implementation. Obviously, there is no one right way of classifying policies, just as there would be no one right way of classifying sports. One classification might distinguish between board games (such as checkers and chess), card games (poker and bridge), and ball games (baseball, football, soccer, and golf). Another might distinguish between team games (bridge, baseball, football, and soccer) and individual games (checkers, chess, poker, and golf). Yet a third might distinguish between indoor sports (checkers, chess, bridge, and poker) and outdoor sports (baseball, football, soccer, and golf). In some of these typologies, games A and B fall in the same class and are contrasted with game C; in others, games A and C are in the same class, in contrast with game B. Neither classification is right or wrong. They simply tell us different things about the games, depending upon

what we want to know. The same is true of these typologies for classifying political policies.

DISTRIBUTIVE, REGULATORY, AND REDISTRIBUTIVE POLICIES

Our first typology divides policies into those that are aimed at *distribution*, those that are aimed at *regulation*, and those that are aimed at *redistribution*.

DISTRIBUTIVE POLICIES. Many government programs *distribute* government services and resources to specific segments of the population. Farm subsidies are an obvious example because they involve the transfer of money from the Treasury to a small and special group of people. Far more typical, however, is the provision of free public education or the building of irrigation projects. Here the government is providing an important service to particular citizens with children of school age or to those who own land in the area to be irrigated.[2]

[2] Theodore J. Lowi, "American Business, Public Policy, Case Studies, and Political Theory," *World Politics,* 16 (July 1964), 677–715.

THE WORKS PROG-
RESS ADMINISTRA-
TION (WPA), A NEW
DEAL PROGRAM THAT
PROVIDED JOBS
FOR OVER 2½ MIL-
LION AMERICANS,
WAS A LARGE-SCALE
GOVERNMENT DIS-
TRIBUTIVE POLICY.
OVER $10 BIL-
LION IN FEDERAL
FUNDS FLOWED
THROUGH THE WPA
AND INTO THE NA-
TIONAL ECONOMY.
Wide World Photos

The most important thing about distributive policies is that they usually create many winners but no losers. Typically, they involve expenditures of public funds to aid particular groups. The groups of course gain. In a sense, every taxpayer loses a little bit because the money spent on the group is tax money. But no particular taxpayer or group of taxpayers especially feels the pinch. If a million dollars of federal money is spent to build a new dam in Arizona, some construction workers get jobs, some farmers get irrigation water, some businessmen get increased business. But less than a penny of each individual taxpayer's dollars is lost.

Distributive policy making often seems to operate on the "take turns" principle. The various groups within our society line up and each gets a turn at asking for something that will help it and hurt no one in particular. Public works legislation is like this. Each year, Congress passes out hundreds of dam-building, harbor-dredging, and similar projects for hundreds of places in the United States. Los Angeles gets a new flood control channel. A rural county in Kentucky gets a new levee. And so on. This is often called *pork-barrel* legislation because every part of the country sooner or later gets a chance to dip into the barrel and pull out a fat piece of pork. The congressional representatives from Los Angeles and Kentucky do not fight each other for the money. In fact, the representative from Kentucky will vote for the Los Angeles flood control project even though it doesn't do his constituents in Kentucky one bit of good. But he knows that soon he will be needing votes for his levee. There may not be enough money for everyone to have every federal project he wants. But there is enough so that everyone can have some projects if he will just wait his turn.[3]

Meanwhile, there are few opponents to the federal public works bill. No congressman or congressional district is hurt by the bill. Only those governmental institutions, like the Appropriations Committees, which are generally concerned with keeping down taxes and government spending, are likely to be in any way negative. And they will be concerned with keeping the total figure for all construction down, rather than with fighting any particular project. Indeed, one of the major causes of the continuous growth of the federal budget is congressional generosity with distributive programs such as health research, aid to education, and the like. These programs have very specific friends but no specific enemies, since each one is only a tiny bite of the entire tax bill.

REGULATORY POLICIES. Regulatory policy in the United States takes many forms. The bulk of regulation is actually done by the states rather than the federal government. Probably the most widely known form of regulation is embodied in the criminal law statutes, which are a set of policies regulating how one individual may and may not conduct himself toward another. In addition, the states have an even larger body of laws governing property, contracts, personal injury, commercial transactions, health, and safety. On the federal level, the regulatory policies with which we are most familiar are associated with the numerous *independent regulatory commissions.* Bodies

[3] John A. Ferejohn, *Pork Barrel Politics* (Stanford: Stanford University Press, 1974).

such as the Interstate Commerce Commission, the Federal Trade Commission, and the Federal Communications Commission regulate rates, routes, safety, and business practices of railroads, airlines, radio and television stations, and utilities. Such regulatory agencies are a typically American halfway house between pure private enterprise and public ownership.

The regulatory commissions do not tell the whole story of federal regulatory policies. In addition, we also must classify as regulatory policy all civil rights laws and most of the federal policy directed at labor unions. Farm subsidies, which are such a good example of distribution policy, also can be classified as regulatory when they contain provisions for acreage limitation, storage rates, and minimum prices.

REDISTRIBUTIVE POLICIES. Redistributive policies are aimed at changing the existing pattern of wealth and social prestige in the nation. In theory, the progressive income tax is a redistributive measure because it was designed to take more tax money from the rich than the poor and so reduce traditional disparities in wealth. Minimum wage laws have a redistributive effect since they result in higher expenditures by employers on wages for unskilled workers. Welfare laws designed to help the needy are usually redistributive.

Classifying government policies as either distributive, regulative, or redistributive is a useful way of describing the major thrust or intention behind a policy. It has often been pointed out that in the United States it is easier for political policy makers to reach agreement on distributive policies, more difficult on regulative policies, and most difficult on redistributive policies. This may only be another way of saying that we are dominated by the liberal ideology described in Chapter 4. As you will recall, a major tenet of this ideology is that government justifies its existence by providing its citizens with certain goods and services. This is essentially a distributive view of government. But Americans have not been terribly receptive to the idea of the government telling a person how he must behave with his own property. They are even less sympathetic to policies obviously designed to take property from one person and give it to another. As a result, it seems fair to say that by and large American policy has concentrated on providing a wide range of services, facilities, and regulations for specific groups and places. The government gave land to railroad builders, homesteaders, and state colleges. It controls competition among airlines, shippers, and railroads. It grants money to states, cities, and private organizations in more than a thousand programs to support local projects. It guarantees loans to

IN 1975, NINE PERCENT OF AMERICANS RECEIVED FOOD STAMPS, A GOVERNMENT MEASURE THAT IS LARGELY REDISTRIBUTIVE. *Wide World Photos*

successful farmers and unsuccessful aerospace firms. It subsidizes ship-builders, cotton growers, rapid transit districts, and neighborhood medical clinics. Such policies are likely to have a limited or indirect impact on the distribution of wealth. All in all, they do not make the rich much poorer or the poor much richer. They do reward people who organize to press on the government a claim that can be met without obviously hurting some identifiable other people. As a general rule, American politicians are most responsive to groups that can point to a specific demand, a limited remedy, and no particular opponents.[4]

PUBLIC AND DIVISIBLE GOODS

Our second typology is based on the distinction economists make between *public* and *divisible* goods. All citizens presumably share equally in the national security benefits derived from the operation of the armed forces, in the health benefits of clean air and cancer research, and in the enjoyment of the Grand Canyon and the National Gallery of Art. At least, there is no easy way of calculating which citizens are benefiting more than others. For this reason, such benefits are called *public goods*. In contrast, only farmers benefit from farm subsidies, only war veterans benefit from veterans' aid programs, and so on. These benefits are said to be *divisible goods*. It is possible to divide government policies into those that provide public goods and those that provide divisible goods. This approach gives us a somewhat different perspective than the distinction between distributive and redistributive policies.

Some government policies have both public and divisible aspects. Although the public schools provide direct and distinct benefits to the children who attend them and their parents, in fact the whole population benefits from the skilled workers and professionals created by the educational system. Some goods that look very public—highways and bridges, for instance—are in fact largely divisible. The number of miles per year each person travels on roads or bridges can be determined fairly easily. Some government programs deal almost exclusively in divisible goods—the provision of irrigation water to individual farms through government-constructed water projects, for instance.[5]

The distinction between public and divisible goods is often significant in determining how government policies should be funded. The more divisible the benefit, the more reasonable is the demand that the user, rather than the general taxpayer, should pay for it, and pay according to how much he uses. This is the rationale behind bridge tolls and gasoline taxes, which are funneled directly to highway construction and maintenance funds. It is also the rationale behind the policy of demanding payment for irrigation. By the same logic, federal loans for college dormitories are required to be self-liquidating

CLEAN AIR IS A
PUBLIC GOOD THAT
GOVERNMENT
POLICIES ATTEMPT
TO PROVIDE.
Wide World Photos

---

[4] See Daniel P. Moynihan, *The Politics of a Guaranteed Income: The Nixon Administration and the Family Assistance Plan* (New York: Vintage Books, 1973).

[5] See Robert A. Dahl and Charles E. Lindblom, *Politics, Economics, and Welfare* (New York: Harper & Row, 1953).

but grants for college laboratories are not. It seems reasonable to make those who live in the dorms pay enough rent to pay for the building eventually and not reasonable to demand the same of those who work in the laboratory. This is because we have come to think of scientific education as a public good from which the whole population derives benefits, but we still think of adequate living quarters as basically a private matter.

One way of looking at American policy is in terms of changing views on where the boundaries should be drawn between public and divisible goods. Because many Americans believe that illiteracy, ill health, or poverty are social evils that adversely affect the whole society, they tend to see government policies aimed at eradicating these evils as matters involving public goods chargeable to the general population. On the other hand, the continuous demands for higher tuition in state universities indicates that many Americans still subscribe to the notion that those who benefit from a government service most directly should pay a higher proportion of its costs than those who benefit indirectly.

PARTISAN AND NONPARTISAN POLICIES

A third way of classifying policies is to distinguish between *partisan* and *nonpartisan* policies. It is sometimes said that there is no Republican or Democratic way to pave a street. There are many policies of which the same can be said. Such policies can be described as *nonpartisan*. Sometimes the distinction between partisan and nonpartisan policies is unclear. Many policies that were once partisan come to be so universally accepted that they become nonpartisan, at least for a time. Social security is an obvious example. Free public education is another. But federal aid to education is only now moving out of the partisan realm. How much of that aid should go to whom is still a hotly partisan issue.

In many instances, nonpartisan policies may involve a crucial partisan dimension. There may be no Republican or Democratic way to pave a street, but rival Republican or Democratic contractors may be anxious for the job of paving it. Similarly, we may all share in the protection offered by the latest missile, but who gets the contract to build it may be very important for the citizens who live near rival defense contractors. Even when general policies are agreed upon, determining who is to carry out the policies may be so important a policy question that it overshadows the more general agreement.

SUBSTANTIVE AND PROCEDURAL POLICIES

Our fourth typology distinguishes between *substantive* and *procedural* (or *organizational*) policy issues. In this instance we are distinguishing between those policies that determine *what* is to be done and those that determine *who* is to do it. Often, however, the two tend to merge in real life, no matter how clearly we separate them analytically. As we saw in our discussion of the bureaucracy in Chapter 13, organizational issues are frequently substantive issues in disguise. Who is going to manage a program often determines what the program will really be like. An air pollution program run by the Department of Commerce, with its traditional association with business, will be different from one run by the Department of Health, Education, and Welfare, which is sensitive to health issues and relatively indifferent to the problems of industry.

EASE OF ADMINISTRATION

A final dimension along which policies may be classified is *ease of administration.* Some policies are designed to be almost entirely self-enforcing. The President may ask every family to voluntarily turn down its thermostat two degrees to save energy. No elaborate administrative mechanisms are created to enforce the policy. Other policies entail only marginal changes in administration and few if any additional administrative costs. Congress asks the states to lower speed limits to fifty-five miles per hour and they do so. Special ticket drives and publicity releases may be necessary to inform motorists that they really will get a ticket if they go over fifty-five. But state and local police have been enforcing some speed limit all along. They don't have to do anything about changing their organization or procedures in order to write speeding tickets for cars going over fifty-five instead of those going over sixty or sixty-five.

In contrast, if the government were to institute a federal policy of gas rationing, administrative and enforcement costs might be very high. Millions of ration books would have to be printed, stored, and distributed. Elaborate bookkeeping systems would have to be imposed to keep track of the gas. The oil firms and gas stations must be monitored by federal officials. Boards of appeal must be established to grant some people with special needs more gas than others.

Some policies cannot be efficiently administered no matter how much we are willing to spend on administration. We simply may not know how to do a particular job. A policy of rehabilitating federal prisoners may fail because no one knows how to administer a prison in such a way as to turn dishonest people into honest ones. Or the administrators may simply refuse to do the job they are asked to do. During the Nixon presidency, the FBI and the CIA often refused to carry out the domestic intelligence and surveillance policies desired by the President. They recognized that if implicated in such illegal actions their agencies would suffer congressional retribution. Or a policy may inspire such massive resistance and evasion as to be unworkable. Prohibition of production and consumption of alcoholic beverages in the 1920s was a classic example of a policy that simply could not be administered effectively.

POLICY AND INTEREST

The notion of interest is almost inseparable from that of policy, for if policy is about outputs and goals, it must be tested by whether it gives those it is

THIS 1942 POSTER
EXPLAINED THE
GOVERNMENT'S GAS
RATIONING SYSTEM
TO MOTORISTS.
Wide World Photos

designed to benefit what they want. Insofar as this is the case, the criterion for measuring the success of any policy is likely to be: Are the groups that are most immediately affected by it satisfied with it?

If we visualize public policy primarily as providing various interests in the society what they want, a number of key questions arise for policy makers. How large does a particular group have to be for it to qualify as a legitimate interest? Does it involve dozens, or thousands, or millions of people? How intense is their need? To what extent does one group's interest reinforce or conflict with other interests? Congressmen, for instance, spend a great deal of their time seeking political information about who wants what. One dimension of this approach involves assessing not only the wants of various interest groups but also their political resources. To what extent can a given interest reward a policy maker for giving it more of what it wants? To what extent can it punish him for giving it less?

Evaluating policies in terms of the interests they affect is a relatively straightforward matter with regard to distributive policies. If the government is doing things for people, a good test of the quality of its programs is surely whether the people like what is being done for them. Making an inventory of which interests the government is serving and which it is neglecting does provide a helpful way of assessing distributive policies.

Greater problems arise when we try to evaluate regulatory policies in terms of interests. For instance, a major criticism of the regulatory commissions is that their policies have too often been in the interest of those most immediately affected—the industries they were set up to regulate. Somehow, we feel that the Interstate Commerce Commission ought not to serve only the interests of the railroads and truckers. It ought to control their conduct in the interests of their customers. But how can we assess whether it is doing this or not? The transportation industry has spokesmen who can say whether or not they are satisfied with the government's policies. But the users of transportation are unorganized and politically inarticulate. There is no way to ask them whether or not they like what the government is doing in this area.

When we get to redistribution, the test of whether the groups most affected are satisfied seems least applicable. Among the interests most directly affected will be those from whom the government is taking something in order to give it to someone else. We can hardly expect the losing interest to be happy. About all we can ask for is that more interests gain than lose.

The major drawback of the multiple interest approach is that it can tell us little about which interests *ought* to gain and to lose, which *ought* to be regulated in favor of which others, and which *ought* to receive more and which less of whatever is being distributed. There is no obvious way of ranking the interests. Therefore the "best" policy often becomes simply a matter of greasing the squeakiest wheel. The government's policy program is then judged on the basis of whether it gives enough to each interest to keep it quiet. Naturally, the result is that those with the biggest mouth and the most persuasive skill get the most.

532

PRODUCTS AND
CONSEQUENCES OF
AMERICAN NATIONAL
POLITICS

THE PUBLIC INTEREST

Another way of assessing public policy is to ask whether a given policy serves the public interest as opposed to some special interest.[6] The phrase *public interest* has something compelling about it. Even the most cynical among us believes deep down that there ought to be something more to politics than splitting up the take. We may be reluctant to say that a given policy necessarily *is* in the public interest, but most of us can clearly identify policies that are *against* the public interests.

It is easiest to tell what the public interest is in the area of public as opposed to divisible goods. Most of us know that cancer research or the maintenance of national parks is in the public interest. Even here, of course, the problem of priorities arises. If we had to choose between the two, it would not be easy to say which is more in the public interest.

When divisible goods are involved, or when we are dealing basically with distribution or regulation, it is often quite difficult to discern where the public interest lies. Usually, about all we can say is that a given policy favors certain interests and disfavors others. For example, setting a high freight rate· favors the railroads and disfavors the shippers. But where does the public interest lie? It may be in the public interest to keep freight rates low, but it is also in the public interest to maintain a financially strong railroad system.

Even though we can't define the public interest, the notion of public interest nevertheless serves as a guide and a check on policy makers. When someone is promoting a program to help some particular group, it may be useful to stop long enough to ask, "Yes, it helps you — but is it in the public interest? Is there a good reason why this particular group should benefit? Will other groups be hurt? Will the taxpayers be hurt? Is this the best way to spend this money?" If the answer to all of these questions is "Yes," then the policy is probably in the public interest.

THE POLICY-MAKING PROCESS

An important part of political analysis is not concerned with evaluating the substance of the policy decisions the government makes. Rather, it is concerned with evaluating *how* the government makes its decisions. In one sense, this may seem like a gigantic evasion. After all, one is likely to assume, it doesn't matter so much through which procedure the government decides whether or not it will recognize Communist China or whether or not it will build an atomic power plant. The important thing is that it makes the *right* decision. This point has a certain validity. But it should not obscure the fact that, in the long run, the way decisions are made may be more important than any particular decision that is made. Indeed, the American commitment to democracy is not a commitment to political decisions of any particular kind. It is a commitment to a *method* of making political decisions.

[6] See Carl J. Friedrich, ed., *The Public Interest* (New York: Atherton Press, 1962); Richard E. Flathman, *The Public Interest* (New York: John Wiley & Sons, 1966); and Glendon Schubert, *The Public Interest: A Critique of the Theory of a Political Concept* (New York: The Free Press, 1960).

THE SYNOPTIC APPROACH. A little earlier we saw that policy making consisted of identifying goals, thinking of alternative ways of reaching those goals, and then choosing the alternative that is most likely to achieve the stated goals in the light of the available resources. That alternative becomes the decision-maker's policy. Such an approach to policy making is called *synoptic.*

THE INCREMENTAL APPROACH. Another kind of policy-making procedure is called *incremental.*[7] The incremental policy maker does not search for the best or ideal policy. Instead he adheres to the *status quo* unless or until it becomes obvious that the *status quo* policy is not working. Even then, he is content to identify what has gone wrong and try to move away from it, rather than precisely stating particular goals or objectives. The incrementalist considers only a few alternatives that often are not much different from the one he has been following. He anticipates only the immediate consequences of each of the alternatives that are of particular interest to him.

The incrementalist does not attempt to do these rather modest things all at once. He tends to spread his work over a considerable period of time, making series of small decisions that he keeps revising. Instead of choosing the alternative that will best achieve a long-range goal, the incrementalist often will adjust his goals to match what he thinks the best available alternative actually can achieve. The gradual process of incremental decision allows him to set less ambitious goals if necessary. It also allows him to revise his picture of the facts and change his list of alternatives as his first steps yield new information or *feedback.* Instead of announcing a definite rule for decision among the alternatives, he works in terms of *themes* and rules of thumb. That is, he announces he will consider a number of factors (or themes) in reaching a decision: "We must carefully weigh the interest of the public, the financial health of the industry, and the needs of national defense." (But he does not specify how much weight to give to each.) Or he announces a rule of thumb: "Certainly no rate of return under 5 percent could be considered fair." (But he does not specify exactly what rate he does consider fair.) Table 15-1 compares the synoptic to the incremental approach.

An incremental policy-making process is likely to be especially common where decisions must be made by a group of people. The synoptic approach assumes unity of decision—either that one person is making the decisions or that all the decision-makers agree on objectives, estimates of facts and probabilities, and choice of feasible alternatives. The incremental approach allows for multiple decision-makers with different views of the whole problem. The incrementalist is likely to (1) search for an alternative that partially satisfies the various goals and assessments of each of the decision-makers, although no one may believe it is the best or optimal so-

[7] Charles E. Lindblom, "The Science of 'Muddling Through'," *Public Administration Review*, 19 (1959), 79–88; and Richard M. Cyert and James G. March, *A Behavioral Theory of the Firm* (Englewood Cliffs, N.J.: Prentice-Hall, 1963).

TABLE 15-1
TWO STRATEGIES OF DECISION FOR A CORN FARMER PLANNING NEXT YEAR'S CROP

SYNOPTIC	INCREMENTAL
1. Obtain soil analysis; study costs of growing every possible crop; predict future prices on each crop; get real estate analysis of probable future development of the area (likelihood of selling land for housing, industrial, and/or commercial development).	1. Continue to grow corn unless profits decline sharply.
2. Specify priorities for the following: a. profit b. remaining in farming, becoming businessman, builder, and so on c. aesthetic beauty of the area d. economic development of the area e. interest of neighbors, and so on.	2. If profits decline, estimate whether increased fertilizer will increase yield and whether profit might be made from changing to beans or rye for the coming year.
3. Consider the likelihood that over the next 20 or more years, each of the following will yield the desired outcome under Step 2 on the basis of facts in Step 1: a. plant corn again b. plant oats, beans, marijuana, or peas c. leave empty d. sell it e. build houses on it.	3. If it seems likely that fertilizer or other crops may increase profit, then plant part of the field in corn and partially fertilize, and plant the rest in another crop. If the fertilizer seems to be working, add more.
4. Choose one from Step 3.	4. If these steps are only partially successful, settle for a lower profit than previously made.
5. Await harvest and then return to Step 1.	5. Now study local real estate market and consider selling off a small part of the field as house lots.
	6. If future profits go below a specified minimum, then consider yield, market conditions, and desire to stay in farming when deciding whether to sell more lots.

lution; (2) accept the first proposed alternative to which none of the decision-makers strongly objects; (3) avoid pressing the search for facts or optimal solutions so vigorously that the internal cohesion, morale, and mutual loyalty of the group of decision-makers is threatened. Thus, in reaching decisions, the incrementalist considers the smooth working of the organization along with other goals.

In the next few pages we will be examining the policy-making process. Our description, as well as much of the material presented earlier in the book, shows that American policy making mixes synoptic and incremental approaches with a strong emphasis on the latter. The policy-making process in any political system is composed of a number of steps or stages. These have been split up and labeled in various ways by various students of policy making.

Let us begin by dividing policy making into four stages. In the first, the policy makers *receive information* on who wants what and on the resources and alternatives available to meet those wants. They also *invent* proposed policy solutions. In the second, they *make an official policy*. The third stage involves *applying or administering the policy*—actually going out and building the dam, or making the social security payments, or integrating the schools. The fourth stage involves *evaluating* how the policy actually worked out so we can decide what to do about it next.

THE LAWMAKING PROCESS

By far the most important policy-making process in domestic American politics is the lawmaking process. Various aspects of the lawmaking process have been described in earlier chapters of this book. Here we want to put all the pieces together in one detailed account of the way in which laws are made, taking note of what occurs at each of the four policy making stages.

INFORMATION AND INVENTION STAGE

Readers of this book are already well aware that the legislative process extends far beyond the boundaries of Congress. The first stage—*the information and invention stage*—often begins when some portion of the citizenry voices a complaint or makes a plea for some services or other benefit. The electoral mechanism plays a significant role in bringing such information to the fore. As election time approaches, campaigning candidates seek out live issues, the parties draft platforms, and at least some of the voters try to use their voting potential and their votes to express their policy desires. (In the case of an incumbent President running for re-election, the Office of Management and Budget actually may index the President's campaign promises, preparing draft legislation and messages to Congress for use if he is re-elected.) In Chapter 9 we pointed out that the parties try to "hunt where the ducks are"—that is, they attempt to pitch their appeals to the mass of the voters. One way to attract ducks is to discover what they are looking for and offer it to them.

We need hardly press the point that interest groups are a major channel for voicing the needs and desires of portions of the citizenry. It is important, however, to remind the reader that the bureaucrats who operate governmental programs are also a principal source of information about people's needs. Much of the initiative for new legislation comes from the felt deficiencies of existing programs. It is the operators of those programs who are likely to be the first and continuous targets of those who feel these deficiencies. Elected officials are a natural alternative target for such complaints, but if you are dissatisfied with the way the local Agriculture Department substation is handling a hybrid cotton program, you complain to the Agriculture Department first and your congressman only after that.

Of course, some participants in the legislative process actively seek out public needs instead of waiting for complaints. A congressman, President, or bureaucrat may start planning for a change well in advance of any widespread public outcry.

In any case, once a need has been identified, the process of inventing a solution goes on in a number of places simultaneously. In the legislative process, these inventions take the form of drafts for new bills. Most new legislation is written in the bureaucracy, although interest groups also propose bills. Major items of the President's program may be designed by special task forces composed of White House staff, other presidential appointees, career bureaucrats, and private experts. Even in such instances, final, detailed drafting is likely to be done through normal bureaucratic channels. Congressmen and their staffs also do some of their own bill drafting, and party platforms sometimes contain at least the first rough outline of new legislation. Typically, we find career executives, interest group representatives, and congressmen cooperating to propose new legislation. Congressional committees are often major participants, even at this early stage, either through individual members or through committee staff.

If a bill is written in the administrative branch, it moves through the legislative clearance machinery of the Office of Management and Budget. Bills then are introduced in the House and Senate. Most bills go routinely to the appropriate legislative committee. Occasionally a bill's chances may be crucially affected by which of two or more committees gets it.

At first drafting, a bill is a matter of invention or innovation, of adding a new idea or a suggestion for improving an existing program. Soon, however, the drafting process becomes a matter of assessing how likely the new idea is to get the job done. By the time a bill reaches committee, it is likely to be a combination of a number of different proposals. It will have undergone endless additions and subtractions as the relative merits and strengths of various ideas have been weighed and compared. The internal mechanisms for coordination and clearance within the executive branch probably will have drawn a number of agencies into the proposals. If the proposals were initiated by the President, or if they have drawn his attention, one of his assistants is likely to be on the scene from the earliest stages. Agency clients and other affected interest groups often make proposals also.

It is at the committee stage that this sort of multiple participation usually reaches a climax. As we saw in Chapter 11, the committee is where cooperating forces meet to concert a final version. Committee hearings typically involve a fairly wide representative sample of witnesses. Thus, the task of writing up the bill after committee hearings involves a good deal of *perfecting*—that is, of ironing out differences that have become clearer to the participants in the course of detailed negotiation over the specifics of the bill.

Most bills do not survive this committee process. An enormous number of bills is introduced in any session, often mainly to publicize an issue. Thus serious attention is given only to a fraction of the legislation referred to committee. Successful legislation only has had forerunners, which bounced around administrative agencies and congressional committees for years before eventually making it all the way. In any given Congress, the whole process can be viewed as a vast funnel into which a great many bills are poured at the drafting mouth, of which few come out the enactment spout.

FORMAL ENACTMENT STAGE

A bill reaching the floor of the House or Senate contains a number of clues that tell members how to react to it. First is the committee vote, which may be unanimous or split. If it is split, it may be along party lines or in some other way. Accompanying the bill is a committee report, either with or without a minority report. Some bills have presidential endorsement or opposition. Some will have strong interest group endorsement or opposition. A substantial share, however, carry no sign other than a favorable committee report. Congressmen will use any of these various kinds of information to guide them in making their votes on the vast bulk of bills in which they have no particular interest or expertise. With bills that are of particular interest to their constituents, however, they are likely to vote the way their constituents want them to. This part of the legislative process goes on twice once in each house. A conference committee generally is needed to harmonize the legislative products of the two houses. Further, most bills also require appropriation of funds.

Once a piece of legislation is passed by both houses of Congress, it is subject to presidential veto. If it is not vetoed, or if the veto is overriden, it becomes law. At this point it passes to the administrative stage, where it begins to be transformed from a collection of printed sentences into the concrete output of the American governmental process.

THE ADMINISTRATIVE STAGE

After the President signs a bill, the new legislation goes to the bureau charged with enforcing it. The process of administration then begins. Administration involves not only routine technical program operation but also supplementary lawmaking. Administrators must fill in and modify the policy of the legislation via executive orders that have the force of law. Less formally they communicate guidelines for enforcement to relevant publics. Sometimes, in fact, modifications occur at this stage that fundamentally change the impact of the legislation from what was expected by some of those who voted for it. We also saw, in Chapter 14, the role of the courts as supplementary lawmakers.

Only after a policy has been implemented for some period of time does the fourth stage of the policy-making process begin. This is the stage of *evaluation*. Bureaucratic implementation of the new policy is likely to generate new complaints, new suggestions for improvement, and new demands for more resources or expanded programs. In this stage, both Congress and the bureaucracy may conduct more or less elaborate evaluations of the policy and its results. On the basis of complaints, suggestions, and their own evaluations, the policy makers come full circle and begin again the bill drafting stage for new legislation to modify, correct, or replace the old policy.

ANALYSIS OF THE LAWMAKING PROCESS

By examining the four stages in the lawmaking process one at a time, it is possible to make some evaluative generalizations about each.

INFORMATION AND INVENTION STAGE

On the whole, the information gathering capacities of those engaged in the lawmaking process are relatively good. The census, elections, public opinion polls, interest group lobbying, the efforts of the parties to estimate public sentiment, the contacts of congressmen with their constituencies, and the press, radio, and television provide policy makers with a great deal of information about prevailing views in the various publics that make up the American population. In addition, bureaucrats acquire and scan vast amounts of technical data relevant to their own specialized programs and public response to these programs. Even the Supreme Court, which has only a tiny staff, nevertheless manages to have access to an enormous reservoir of information because the adversary process forces the litigants in each case to present to the Court all the facts that seem to support their side of the case. Although Congress has not developed a large information-gathering capacity of its own, the committee system has created a corps of expert congressmen, aides, and committee staff members who are skilled at evaluating the floods of information directed at them by the bureaucracy, interest groups, and individual citizens. In sum, each of the branches of government seems well equipped for receiving the information needed in the first stage of the lawmaking process.

After information is gathered, policy alternatives must be invented. Here, too, our political system seems to do quite well. The lawmaking process in the United States is marked by a high degree of receptivity to new ideas. Our bureaucracy, like all bureaucracies, views innovation as a normal part of administration. The composition of the American bureaucracy, with its vast spectrum of technical specializations, professions, regional and educational backgrounds, and links to various facets of the private sector, ensures a very wide range of new ideas.[8] Somewhere in this vast, multi-faceted government there is usually someone who is receptive to nearly any new proposal or has invented a similar one himself.

Interest groups often develop new proposals. All governmental institutions—and especially Congress—are accessible to suggestions from private citizens and organizations. Congressmen are often on the lookout for new ideas, in part because they want to improve public policy, and in part because they want to publicize themselves. Either motivation leads to the same result: receptivity to new ideas. Most innovations are not purely congressional creations. But Congress does provide those who have new ideas with 535 routes to the lawmaking process.

When it comes to major advances in government policy, the President is the most important figure. The public expectation that the President is the chief lawmaker has moved Presidents and presidential candidates to devote increasing energies to both the reality and rhetoric of new ideas. Each President feels he must contribute new programs of his own to ensure his place in the history books. The executive branch gives the President vast staff resources to draft legislation.

Thus, as far as the first stage of the lawmaking process is concerned, our system seems to deserve high marks for its ability to gather information and formulate policy alternatives. Nevertheless, the information and invention stage of the lawmaking process does encounter some very serious problems. These problems arise because our policy-making system devotes remarkably few resources to putting what it has into packages that make sense. Somewhere in the government, one person knows everything about the shells of bird eggs. Someplace another expert knows all about mosquito abatement. But they do not begin to put their knowledge together until someone finds that the birds have disappeared downstream from where the mosquitoes have been sprayed with DDT.

Thus, although the system works well once it is pointed in the right direction, often it does not work at all until it must react to emergencies like the dead birds. Another way to describe this inadequacy in our system is to say that the government sometimes does not use its command over data to define problems for itself. Where problems exist in the boundaries between jurisdictions, action waits until the complaints of citizens or bureaucrats reveal that a certain arrangement of facts constitutes a problem. In these cases, the government does not *act* so much as it *reacts*. It is this fact, more than anything else, that often makes our lawmaking process seem so agonizingly slow.

THE FORMAL ENACTMENT STAGE:
SETTING PRIORITIES AND BARGAINING

PRIORITY SETTING. The setting of priorities is, in a sense, what the political process is all about. Priority setting is what determines who gets what, how,

[8] See Bruce L. R. Smith, *The Rand Corporation: Case Study of a Non-Profit Advisory Corporation* (Cambridge: Harvard University Press, 1966).

when, and why. This being the case, let us begin our examination of priority setting by asking who does it. Here, for once, the answer is relatively simple. Overwhelmingly, the bulk of the priority setting in our political system is done by the President, or at any rate by executive branch proposals, collated in the Executive Office of the President and advanced in the President's name. Modern Presidents are supposed to have a coherent and relevant legislative program that establishes an overarching set of national priorities. This is what the American people expect of them. It is also what Congress has come to expect even though such presidential legislative initiatives were rare and roundly criticized in the nineteenth century. Indeed, it is precisely because we think of priority setting as a presidential task that we tend to identify political events with Presidents. Credit for the New Deal is given to the "Roosevelt administration," not the various Congresses that passed the legislation. Similarly, the space program is identified with the Kennedy and Johnson administrations, the Cold War with the Truman and Eisenhower administrations, and the energy crisis with the Nixon and Ford administrations.

Although the Executive Office of the President is the only institution that effectively establishes *overall* priorities, most parts of the government do have mechanisms for ranking their own goals. Until 1976, Congress was an exception. The new Budget Committees are an attempt to parallel the President's priority-setting function. They are too new for a verdict on whether they will alter the normal congressional pattern. Each committee in the Senate, paired with its counterpart in the House, goes its own way with minimal attention to other committees' output or to an overall sense of what the government should be doing. The piecemeal approach fostered by the committee system discourages efforts to compare one item with another and establish rankings among them. The whole legislative process is structured so that the participants ask, "Is this a good bill on its own merits?" rather than, "Should this bill have a higher priority than those being considered in other committees?"

Until 1975, congressmen often passed legislation without much concern about what future claim a law would make on the treasury. The vast growth in social welfare policies that began in the Johnson administration was soon reflected in the federal budget. Within a dozen fiscal years, from 1965 to 1977, the budget exploded from under $100 billion to over $400 billion.

By the mid-1970s observers began to realize that neither Congress nor the President could do very much about this increased federal spending in the short run. About 75 percent of the 1976 budget represents *uncontrollable spending,* money that the government must spend because of previous commitments. By far the biggest share of this amount, almost half the total federal budget, is payments to individuals that are guaranteed by the government and authorized into the indefinite future. These include social security, federal employees' pensions, unemployment and welfare benefits, medicare and medicaid payments, and veterans' benefits. Individual entitlements of this sort are often tied to the cost of living and go up automatically.

A second kind of inescapable federal commitment comes from previously-agreed-to contracts. These accounted for $54 billion in 1976, of which less than half was for defense spending. The third ironclad claim on the treasury is for interest on the national debt—$26 billion in 1976.

President Nixon's unsuccessful attempts to impound appropriated funds were one response to the growth in uncontrollable spending. By trying to have more influence in the area of controllable expenditures, Nixon hoped to impose his priorities where short-term changes in spending were possible. It remains to be seen whether Congress will be able to establish priorities that effectively regulate individual legislative policy decisions bearing on federal spending. If this attempt fails, the government's policy flexibility will continue to be limited by the astonishing fact that, out of a budget of almost $400 billion, less than $10 billion can be cut or reallocated to new programs. The rest of the budget is "locked in," committed by previous decisions to older programs.[9]

Although the lack of clear priorities in the thousands of small bills that make up the bulk of Congress's business does lead to a somewhat irrational situation, nevertheless there are certain advantages to this arrangement. In a large and complex government and society, the enforcement of a priority-setting requirement among the thousands of matters considered each year would be wasteful and paralyzing. Enormous amounts of time, energy, and money would have to be spent in demonstrating not only that a program was worthwhile but that it merited spot 267 rather than 481 on the priority list. Given the number of participants and interests, disagreements about priorities would be constant and would tend to block action on everything. Moreover, as long as official priorities are not assigned, informal priorities can be constantly shifted to take advantage of opportunities of the moment. A committee waiting for support on one bill to crystallize can put it to the side and take up another without bothering about which has the higher priority.

Perhaps most important, the failure of the system to assign priorities encourages greater initiative and innovation from all the participants. Imagine the lethargy that would set in when a bureau found that its six current programs had all been ranked in the bottom 10 percent of the list. But because there is no such list, everyone feels he has some chance of getting a turn at bat, and thus each has an incentive for trying for new legislation. In short, totally rational priority setting would reduce the number of ideas or alternatives that get consideration.

BARGAINING. As the preceding discussion suggests, the principal mode of priority setting in the legislative process does not depend on systematic efforts to compare programs. Rather, it depends on *bargaining*. One typical

---

[9] Joel Havemann, "Uncontrollable Spending," *National Journal*, November 29, 1975, pp. 1619–26.

legislative bargain is in the form, "You vote for my bill and I'll vote for yours" or "If you'll accept my provision on ducks, I'll support your proposal on chickens." This sort of bargaining is called *logrolling*. It is possible because the politician who wants the provision on chickens does not care about ducks. He can trade his vote on ducks, which has no value to him, for a vote on something he wants.

Another, and more important, form of bargaining is compromise. One group of policy makers may wish to end the farm subsidy program; another may wish to continue it at current levels. They compromise by continuing the program at a reduced level of spending. Such bargaining involves setting comparative priorities, at least among those alternatives that interest the bargainers. It raises the issues very clearly. How much more do you want A than B? Are you willing to take C in order to get D? This sort of bargaining forces decision makers to assess the strength of their own preferences and those of others. In this sense, the collection of bargains that constitute the output of Congress may be viewed as a complex mechanism for giving every member some of what he wants.

THE ADMINISTRATIVE STAGE

Unlike the first two stages of policy making in which parties, interest groups, Congress, President, courts, and bureaucracy all play important parts, the administration and implementation stage is largely focused in one place—the bureaucracy. Therefore, rather than having to tie together here things said in a number of earlier chapters, we can simply refer the student to Chapter 13. Our discussion of the bureaucracy in effect describes the third stage of the policy-making process. The important point to be borne in mind is that although the bureaucracy engages in more systematic priority setting than any other branch of government, it too, relies heavily on the *incremental* or *piecemeal* method of setting priorities.

This is nowhere clearer than in the budget process through which the bureaucracy does much of its priority setting. The best predictor of next year's budget figure for any agency, program, or activity is this year's budget allocation. Chances are it will be only slightly higher or lower next time than it was this time. In other words, officials base their future plans on their present activities. They make only small changes in existing programs and in any given year abolish few old ones and start few new ones.

THE EVALUATION STAGE: POST-AUDITING

BUREAUCRATIC EVALUATION. A similar picture emerges when we turn to the last stage of the lawmaking process—the evaluation stage. One of the most important forms of evaluation is called *post-auditing*. Strictly speaking, post-auditing involves checking financial accounts to ensure that no funds have been dispensed mistakenly or dishonestly. The federal departments have their own auditors and accountants whose work is checked by the General Accounting Office (GAO). This congressionally controlled agency serves as an overall supervisor of bureaucratic bookkeeping. It has recently acquired more active investigative functions for Congress, including sub-poena powers.

But post-auditing includes more than merely keeping the books straight. The post-auditing process allows the auditors to assess just how successful the alternatives chosen have been in achieving an agency's goals. How well has the agency been doing at assessing the facts, creating alternatives, doing cost-benefit analyses, predicting the outcomes of the available alternatives, and choosing the most promising? In short, what has it been getting for its money?

In this realm, there has been no assessor of overall government performance comparable to the GAO. Like the congressional budget committees, the new role of the GAO as more than a simple bookkeeping operation has yet to be tested. Individual agency performance varies widely. Some agencies issue annual reports that purport to be reviews of their last year's performance. Some agencies run either continuous or sporadic internal re-evaluations of their own past performance. And sometimes Appropriations Committee hearings for the new year become rather elaborate congressional inquiries as to how well last year's funds were spent. But there is no universal pattern, so generalization is extremely difficult. What is more, the accomplishments of some programs of some agencies can be assessed in quantitative terms whereas other programs cannot be so easily measured.

Where quantitative assessment of costs and benefits cannot be made, post-auditing becomes difficult. This often gives rise to a phenomenon known as *goal displacement.* Agencies that cannot assess results in dollars and cents terms will seek some other way to measure their success. The Park Service, for instance, may point with pride an annual increase of 217,000 visitors to national parks. The Corps of Engineers will emphasize the number of miles of levees built. The Department of Health, Education, and Welfare can show that 627,000 pupils were enrolled in one of its summer education programs. Such figures do not necessarily provide a good measure of past performance. The extra 217,000 visitors may have so overcrowded the parks as to reduce substantially the enjoyment of each visitor. The levees may have been built in the wrong place or may have cost far more than the value of the property they were designed to protect. The pupils may not have learned anything. We speak of *goal displacement* if the Park Service begins to concentrate on packing in more visitors rather than on the quantity and quality of actual recreational benefits from the parks, or if the Engineers count cubic feet of earth moved instead of real navigational and flood control benefits, or if the Office of Education focuses on the number of students enrolled instead of the education they receive. In other words, agencies may concentrate their energies on achieving what can be easily counted and post-audited rather than on the real goals whose achievement is difficult to demonstrate and is reflected only in a distorted or false way by the numbers.[10] Under such circumstances, post-auditing is largely meaningless.

---

[10] See Peter M. Blau, *The Dynamics of Bureaucracy,* 2nd rev. ed. (Chicago: University of Chicago Press, 1963).

Most post-auditing in the policy-making process occurs informally and on a piecemeal basis as the groups affected by new programs and the bureaucrats who administer them gain day-to-day experience. Systematic research and reassessment are rare in domestic programs.[11] For the most part, we rely on the maxim, "If the shoe pinches." As complaints and plaudits come in, the policy makers decide what to do next. It is generally assumed that once a program begins, it will simply be continued until the complaints mount up. At no point in the policy-making process does anyone ask, Has this policy done well enough to justify its continuation?

To some extent, this situation may be changing. In recent years, Congress and the President have begun to insist on more careful and realistic post-auditing. Some new legislation—for example, the Education Act of 1965— contains rigorous testing and reporting provisions designed to give a clear picture of whether the programs instituted do in fact achieve their purpose. The Education Act requires the gathering of data to determine whether new programs are achieving rapid improvement in the educational performance of children from lower income families.[12] The most famous post-audits initiated by a government agency was the exhaustive study of our involvement in the Vietnam war ordered by Secretary of Defense McNamara that resulted in *The Pentagon Papers*.[13]

COORDINATION AND NON-CONSCIOUS FACTORS IN DECISION MAKING

With post-auditing, we complete the policy-making cycle that began with the gathering of information and the generation of alternatives. But there are two other aspects of policy making that may operate throughout the policy cycle. One is *coordination,* which we will examine in the next few pages. The other can best be described as *non-conscious decision making.* This will be the subject of the next section.

COORDINATION

In our discussion of policy making, we often spoke as though a single or unified decision maker were involved. Of course, this is an oversimplification. It is clear that even the most centralized government necessarily involves substantial numbers of decision makers. Thus, policy makers cannot simply carry out the four stages outlined in the preceding discussion. They

---

[11] Theodore J. Lowi, *The End of Liberalism: Ideology, Policy, and the Crisis of Public Authority* (New York: W. W. Norton & Company, 1969).

[12] See Stephen K. Bailey, *ESEA: The Office of Education Administers a Law* (Syracuse: Syracuse University Press, 1968).

[13] See U.S. Department of Defense, *The Pentagon Papers,* with commentary by Neil Sheehan et al. (New York: Bantam Books, 1971).

also must take steps to assure that careful and complete coordination occurs between all the policy makers involved at every stage of the process. American policy making is so crammed with coordinating mechanisms, and they are discussed in so many places in this book, that a chart summarizing the most important of them should suffice here.

COORDINATION THROUGH LEGAL HIERARCHY. We often tend to ignore the most obvious and traditional mode of coordination—coordination through law. The Constitution establishes certain legal interrelations between the three great branches. In addition, the federal bureaucracy is structured in a hierarchical pattern. This pattern is based on a set of legally defined relations of superiors and subordinates. Each superior coordinates the work of a number of subordinates and then reports to *his* superior, who coordinates the work of his subordinates. In theory, this structure ensures the complete coordination of everyone within the hierarchy. Because the theory works far from perfectly in practice, a great deal of attention is necessarily devoted to the various lapses and anomalies in hierarchical discipline. But it should be remembered that hierarchy remains the basic tool of coordination in almost all large organizations. Congress and the political parties are two major exceptions to this generalization. As we have seen repeatedly in earlier chapters, neither the parties nor the Congress is hierarchically organized. The national party apparatus does not control and dominate the local parties. Congressional committees and individual members are not subject to discipline or control by any centralized leader. This absence of effective hierarchy is undoubtedly the major reason these branches of the policy-making system find the task of coordination so difficult.

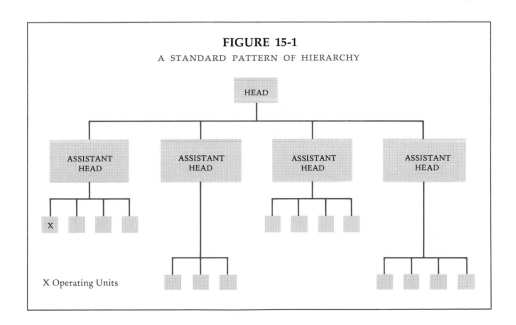

FIGURE 15-1

A STANDARD PATTERN OF HIERARCHY

COORDINATION THROUGH BARGAINING. We already have spoken of bargaining as the principal mode of legislative priority setting. It is also, of course, the principal coordinating mechanism of the process of making policy by passing laws. So much has already been said about bargaining that little more need be said here. We will simply take this opportunity to underline once again the role that bargaining plays in moderating conflict within our political system.

The job of conflict moderation is basically a problem in policy coordination. Americans generally place a good deal of faith in political bargaining to do this job. In order to bargain successfully, the bargainers must have a great many small "counters" or "side payments" available. If we imagine two people, each of whom owned one extremely precious gem, we can readily see that they might not be able to negotiate a trade. Now imagine instead two other people, one of whom has two horses, a mule, and three hundred dollars, while the other has twelve cows and four gallons of whisky. In this situation, a lot of horse-trading can go on.

The lawmaking process in the United States depends on social demands being broken up into small and diverse enough bits to allow easy and continuous bargaining. Our examination of the American people, interest groups, and parties indicates that the potential is there for endless horse-trading. But the extent to which demands are fragmented so that bargaining is possible depends on how these demands are perceived. For example, let us suppose that every policy proposal aimed at distributing government services to the poor, unemployed, and uneducated was defined as a redistribution of wealth from whites to blacks. Once every issue was defined in this way, bargaining might become impossible. Why should the white majority give anything away to the black minority? In such a situation, violence or the threat of violence might be the only bargaining tactic available to the blacks (see Chapter 16).

Another way of putting the point, then, is to say that a major function of the political process is to obscure rather than expose clashes between majorities and minorities. As long as social demands are broken up into little pieces, each identified with a relatively small segment of the population, bargaining over distribution is relatively easy. Everyone can be given a little something and no one appears to lose much. The more sharply issues are defined as majority versus minority, the more apt the majority will be to abandon bargaining and simply impose its will. Indeed, one of the greatest challenges facing our political system in the years ahead will be whether or not the demands of its black citizens can be broken up into small, piecemeal interests that permit the kind of bargaining our policy-making process is accustomed to handling. Only if this happens will we be able to satisfy enough of these demands to prevent the sort of polarization in which there is a black position and an opposite white one on every policy question.

NON-CONSCIOUS FACTORS IN DECISION MAKING

In the preceding discussion, we separated the policy-making process into four stages—information gathering, formal enactment, administration, and

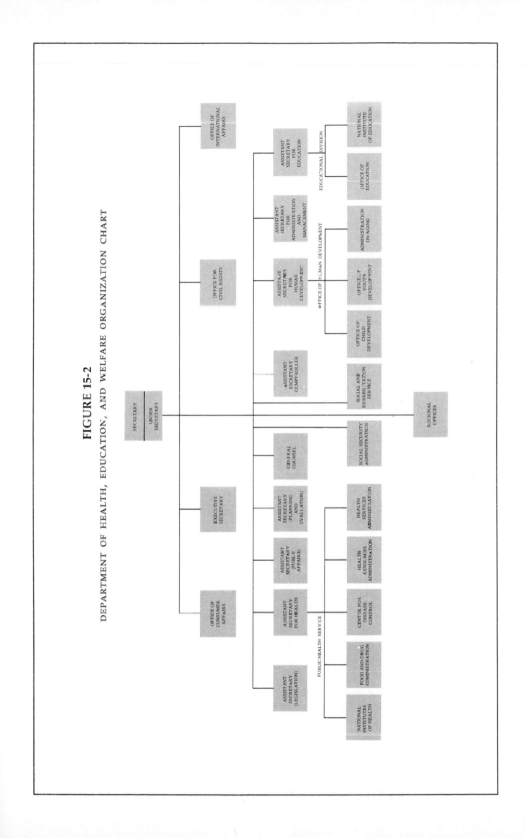

FIGURE 15-2

DEPARTMENT OF HEALTH, EDUCATION, AND WELFARE ORGANIZATION CHART

evaluation. In addition, coordination goes on at all stages in the process. We described the various factors that policy makers must take into account at each stage. Now let us briefly examine another important set of factors —the ones policy makers do *not* take into account when they make their decisions. In this category we include factors such as lack of knowledge, inertia, and the emotional biases of policy makers. These are among the most important *non-conscious* factors in *decision making.*

LACK OF KNOWLEDGE. Perhaps the most overwhelming non-conscious aspect of domestic policy making is our *lack of knowledge* about human beings and social processes. For instance, although we can roughly guess that poverty breeds crime, we do not know why some poor people become criminals and others do not. And we do not know how to treat those who have committed crimes so that they will not do so again. We can talk about prison reform, but we have not yet discovered a truly successful alternative to imprisonment or a way to run prisons so that they will have the effect we want. The fact is that we do not know how to reform criminals, so all we can do at the moment is take them out of circulation for a while. It is simply foolish to attempt to analyze our policies toward "crime in the streets" or "law and order" without taking into account this fundamental failure in social research and technology.[14] We do what we are doing less because we choose to do it that way than because we don't know what else to do.

What is true of prison reform is true of many other areas as well. Government fiscal and monetary policy is an excellent example. For all the advances in the science of economics, we still do not know precisely what policies of the government under what circumstances will produce just what set of actions by business, labor, lenders, and consumers. Nor do we know which of these actions will lead to full employment and economic growth without excessive inflation. A major share of federal economic policy is in reality not much more than a shot in the dark. Thus, policy making often results from a commitment of faith to one economic theory or another in a world in which no economic theory has ever proven really adequate for policy guidance.

INERTIA. Closely related to our high level of ignorance about how and why people think and act as they do is the inertia found in most large organizations. Inertia, of course, refers to the tendency of a body at rest to remain at rest and to the tendency of a body in motion to keep moving in the same direction at the same speed. Many of the policies of the federal government will exist tomorrow because they exist today, just as they exist today because they existed yesterday. In part, the reason for this is that any program produces vested interests—the private citizens who receive government goods or services and the particular officials who provide them. The interests that benefit from a program and the agencies that run it will be far more anxious to keep it going than anyone else is to terminate it.

[14] James Q. Wilson, *Thinking About Crime* (New York: Basic Books, 1975).

In part, too, inertia results from the commitment of all bureaucracies to continuity. In any large organization, change is painful. It requires many people to learn to do things in new ways. It disturbs existing compromises, working relations, and career plans. The easiest way to avoid such disturbances is to avoid change. This is why bureaucrats often reply to the question, "Why do you do it that way?" by answering in effect, "Because we have always done it that way." The safest procedure is to maintain the *status quo* until trouble occurs. As a result, the *status quo* is frequently maintained—and in the most stubborn way—long after the trouble has begun.

For example, tobacco growers still receive subsidies from the Agriculture Department although other government agencies are spending considerable sums of money to discourage cigarette smoking. As this example illustrates, political inertia does not result simply in a failure to innovate. It also results in the persistent implementation of policies that are not working or are downright harmful.

EMOTION. The personal traits of officials affect the whole of the policy making process. We made this point extensively in discussing the presidency and need not elaborate it here. It is enough to point out that policy making cannot be grasped entirely in terms of organizations, roles, and decision-making procedures. If we are to be truthful, we must sometimes say that a decision was made because the President hates Senator X, or that a particular policy lacks coordination because B's prep school mannerisms repel bureau chief A. Strange as it may sound, sometimes affection is the key explanatory variable. Many politicians are experts at giving and receiving the personal attachment that makes for loyalty to them and support of their efforts. Love, hate, fear, greed, ambition, heroism, self-sacrifice, and sadism are a part of policy making that tends to slip away in the descriptive generalizations of policy analysis. A few examples are in order. Senator Edmund Muskie's prospects for gaining the Democratic presidential nomination in 1972 seemed to have been damaged decisively when he broke down in tears of sorrow and anger before a large crowd because a New Hampshire newspaper had published remarks that he regarded as personal insults to his wife. The 1965 Civil Rights Act was helped toward passage by the outrage of constituents and congressmen who had witnessed in person or on television brutal assaults on peaceful civil rights demonstrators by policemen in the South.

THE FOREIGN POLICY-MAKING PROCESS

The lawmaking process serves as an adequate focus for an analysis of domestic policy making. In the realm of defense and foreign policy, however, such a focus is inadequate. Legislation plays only a limited—though occasionally crucial—role in defense and foreign policy. The major share of foreign policy is made by administrative decision within the foreign and defense bureaucracies, or by the President acting alone or with the support of his advisors, rather than through the passage of laws.[15] It is, therefore, necessary to sketch briefly a separate analysis of the foreign policy-making process.

INTELLIGENCE

Foreign and defense intelligence is the one area of American policy making that has consciously and consistently aimed at a totally systematic approach. It is widely felt that we should know every fact relevant to our security about every nation on earth. In the twentieth century, national security must be concerned even with outer space. By the late 1960s, this goal had led to an annual expenditure of over $5 billion and the assignment of about 200,000 government employees in the foreign intelligence fields.[16]

The main problem is one of interpretation. Raw intelligence consists of millions of separate factual bits. Most of this data is culled from newspapers, magazines, and books. Some of it is gathered by direct or photographic observation and the monitoring of radio transmissions. An unknown but relatively small fraction comes from espionage. The central core of intelligence is evaluation. This means both determining the reliability of each report and interpreting information so as to fit it into meaningful patterns that can be used by policy makers. "What does it mean?" is just as crucial a question as "Is it true?" The evaluation process culminates in the National Intelligence Estimate that is handed daily to the President.

Like intelligence agencies everywhere, we have done much better at collection than evaluation, particularly in the realm of political intelligence. Frequently, we know the names and positions of all the players in some struggling new nation. But we may be unable to figure out in advance whether the game they are going to play is waiting or revolution. Even more important, we often do not know who is going to win—the old government, the new generals, or the communists. More often than not, this is because there is *too much information,* much of it contradictory or ambiguous. Somebody on our side "knew" that the generals were going to try a coup on March 16th. But somebody else "knew" equally well that they wouldn't. Confronted with this phenomenon, the crucial analytical question is not what data exist somewhere in the intelligence net, but what quality and quantity of data are accepted by the policy makers as the basis of their decisions.

INVENTION OF ALTERNATIVES

In examining the invention of alternatives, let us separate defense from foreign policy. The Defense Department and its research and development

---

[15] See Burton M. Sapin, *The Making of United States Foreign Policy* (Washington: The Brookings Institution, 1966).
[16] See Harry Howe Ransom, *The Intelligence Establishment* (Cambridge: Harvard University Press, 1970).

contractors have been extremely fertile in the invention of new weapons systems alternatives.[17] After a period of relying primarily on our advantage in atomic bombs and strategic bombers, the Defense Department has shifted to a constant and aggressive search for new and better systems of many different kinds. The number and variety of science fiction weapons considered, selected, and discarded has been incredible.

Yet the armed services do tend to cling to traditional weapons such as the bomber and the aircraft carrier when such weapons are viewed as essential to maintaining their independent missions. If the Navy had no ships and the Air Force no planes, but both used rockets, questions might arise as to why a separate Navy and Air Force should continue.

In one sense, our defense policy has done particularly badly at proposing new policies. It has been almost totally absorbed in the grand strategy of deterrence. This policy is based on creating a balance of terror based on the atomic might of the superpowers. In recent years, however, there has been increased attention to technological and diplomatic moves leading to arms reduction (see Table 15–2).

Turning from military planning to foreign policy, we can see that the immediate aftermath of World War II was a period of enormous innovation. It was during this period that America broke decisively away from its isolationist tradition. We took the lead in creating the United Nations, gave

[17] See S. Enke, *Defense Management* (Englewood Cliffs, N.J.: Prentice-Hall, Inc., 1963).

CRUCIAL FOREIGN POLICY DECISIONS ARE OFTEN MADE IN INFORMAL MEETINGS. HERE, PRESIDENT KENNEDY CONFERS WITH CHAIRMAN OF THE JOINT CHIEFS OF STAFF, GENERAL MAXWELL TAYLOR, AND WITH DEFENSE SECRETARY ROBERT MCNAMARA.
Wide World Photos

enormous economic aid to war-ravaged Europe, and for the first time pledged to defend nations that were attacked. These were all major efforts of political creativity—the inventing of new policies. *Containment* was the overarching policy of this period. It became the policy of the United States to intervene actively throughout the world to "contain" the expansion of Soviet power by military, diplomatic, and other methods. Fittingly enough, this policy was first announced in an academic article in the journal *Foreign Affairs*—an article written by one of the few certified intellectuals in the Foreign Service, George Kennan.[18]

In the three decades since the end of World War II, our economic and military aid and our troop commitments abroad have fluctuated with events overseas and with our domestic political situation. Only in the aftermath of Vietnam have fundamental questions been raised about containment. This reexamination reflects the fact that our relative position in the world has fallen as other countries have approached our level of productivity.

CONTINUITY AND CRISIS

Many outsiders and a number of Presidents have voiced the complaint that the State Department never has any new ideas. The Department's response has been to insist that diplomacy thrives on continuity. Certainly the Department has not been a major generator of new policy alternatives. Most of the alternatives that could plausibly be regarded as new have come from the White House and from the Pentagon. When new foreign policy has been made, it has been made in response to a crisis rather than as a result of an ongoing effort to generate many alternatives and choose the best of them.

This is so largely because in foreign affairs it is difficult to estimate cost and effectiveness. The costs and effectiveness of most alternatives in foreign policy depend upon the decisions and actions other nations would take in reaction to them. In foreign policy analysis, cost-effectiveness studies are in fact attempts to predict what other nations will do in the future. Such predictions are very hard to make and often prove wrong. So there is a tendency to proceed one step at a time, pausing after each move to see how the other side reacts.

For this reason, foreign policy making has a peculiar profile. The State Department devotes most of its energies to keeping abreast of developments, essentially a matter of gathering intelligence and maintaining diplomatic contacts with foreign leaders. Much of the time, our foreign policy relating to most of the countries of the world consists of treading water. This is not to say that the large foreign policy bureaucracies in the State Department, the Agency for International Development, the United States Information Agency, and the Defense Department *never* propose or evaluate new alternatives or choose new priorities. It is to say that the initiation of new policy and the setting of new priorities are not a major portion of their day-to-day business. For the most part, they are content

[18] George Kennan, "The Sources of Soviet Conduct," *Foreign Affairs,* July 1947, pp. 566–82.

TABLE 15–2
RECENT ARMS REDUCTION ALTERNATIVES

GOVERNMENTAL ORGANIZATIONS WITH ARMS CONTROL RESPONSIBILITIES

Arms Control and Disarmament Agency—
  prepares for and leads discussions and negotiations with Soviet Union on
  disarmament
National Security Council
The Bureau of Politico-Military Affairs in Department of State
The Verification Panel (interdepartmental committee, part of NSC system)—
  charged with technical analysis of arms control issues, including verification requirements and capabilities of weapons whose limitation is
  being considered

PROGRAMS AND NEGOTIATIONS

Efforts to control the international traffic in conventional arms
Strategic Arms Limitation Talks (SALT)
MBFR—Mutual and Balanced Force Reductions in Europe
International convention banning biological weapons and discussions on
  banning of chemical weapons
Geneva Disarmament Conference (Conference of the Committee on Disarma-
  ment of U.N.)

ACCOMPLISHMENTS

ABM treaty and interim agreement on strategic arms limitation with USSR
  (1972)
Nuclear weapons non-proliferation treaty
Treaties banning nuclear weapons from outer space and the seabeds
Atmospheric nuclear test ban treaty
Vladivostock agreement (1974)

to keep doing whatever they have been doing as long as things are tolerably
quiet.

When things are not tolerably quiet, the whole picture changes. In a crisis,
choices must be made even if the policy makers cannot predict the eventual
outcome with great confidence. This is why the period immediately after
World War II was so rich in policy initiatives. The whole traditional international system had collapsed and crises existed everywhere. As the world
has gradually stabilized itself, the pace of new American policy making
has slowed. We interpreted Fidel Castro's triumph in Cuba as a crisis that
stimulated a new round of policy making toward Latin America. This sub-
sided as we saw that Castro could not duplicate his success elsewhere.
Vietnam similarly inspired a reassessment of our Asian policies and some
effort to readjust our relations with China and Japan.

Even in a crisis, however, decision makers tend to concentrate on finding
whatever makeshift solution will see them through. Unless the crisis is

global in its scope—as it was after World War II—our foreign policy makers are unlikely to use it as an occasion for full-scale re-evaluation of policy. This is precisely what one would expect. In a crisis, one is usually racing against time. In the middle of such a race, policy makers tend to be willing to pull in for a pit stop and make minor adjustments, but they feel this would hardly be the time to overhaul the whole engine. In sum, when things are going quietly there is no need for a major reevaluation of foreign policy, and when they are not going quietly there is no time for one.

That such decisions as are made are usually made during crises tends to shift the center of policy making from the bureaucracy to the White House. International crises are, after all, preeminently the President's responsibility.[19] This leads to one of the perennial paradoxes of American politics. Presidents consistently complain that they are nearly powerless to control the State Department or even to inspire it to new initiatives. At the same time, foreign service officers constantly claim that no one ever listens to them and that policy is made by the White House gang. Both complaints are essentially correct. In non-crisis periods, the President, given his limited time and resources, can do little more than vocalize piously about the need for dynamic policy while the State Department imperturbably goes on with its daily work. In times of crisis, the President moves in. Naturally, he relies on those people around him whom he trusts the most, and these are rarely career State Department officers.

The real question here is how much conscious priority setting actually gets done by the presidency in times of crisis. In one sense a crisis is, almost by definition, a setting of priorities. Some particular problem or situation—Russian missiles to Cuba, a fall in the international price of the dollar, a Mideast war—is seen as far more important than anything else at the moment and requiring immediate attention. But in another sense a crisis may simply mean that in one particular area something terrible is happening at the moment or will happen soon unless we act quickly. In other words, a crisis may command attention not because this particular matter is especially important in comparison with all other problems facing the United States, but only because it is something to which we must respond immediately if we are to respond at all. There is always the danger that the President and his advisers, shifting from one crisis of this sort to the next, will never get time to shape policy for the most important long-term problems of the nation.

POST–AUDITING

In general, there is a remarkable lack of post-auditing in the foreign and defense policy sphere. When old weapons systems are replaced by new ones, it is simply assumed that technological progress has occurred. Although the Defense Department does engage in some internal post-auditing, it

---

[19] See Graham T. Allison, *Essence of Decision: Explaining the Cuban Crisis* (Boston: Little, Brown, 1971).

carefully hides its mistakes from the outside world. Neither the Presidents nor Congress has been very anxious to uncover them. The General Accounting Office uncovers and publicizes really horrendous tales of waste and inefficiency in defense procurement. Congressional committees sometimes do engage in intensive investigation of the past performance of the defense and intelligence establishments, but such investigations occur only sporadically. Their impact is substantial, but fleeting.

As far as we can determine, the State Department has no systematic devices for auditing the success and failure of past foreign policies. No doubt the Department would argue that its constant surveillance of our relations with other nations constitutes a very detailed form of continuous post-auditing. It is not clear, however, that those who conduct these surveillances consistently and deliberately put the question: Have we been successful or not? Besides, the very people who have been proposing and executing the policies are the ones who are reporting on their own past success or failure.

CONFIDENTIALITY, SECRECY, AND DEMOCRACY

Foreign policy making involves a paradox created by the intersection of three factors. First, because of the great uncertainties and high stakes, the President needs the truest and frankest advice he can get from those he trusts. But if the advice given him were made public, his advisers could not speak frankly. Second, given the world as it exists today, many of the decisions made in foreign policy, the reasons behind them, and the information on which they were based must be kept secret. It would hardly do to have the *New York Times* announce that we have begun secret talks with China that we don't want the Russians to know about. Much of foreign policy is conducted in a situation in which we cannot tell the other side what we are doing. Therefore, we cannot tell our own side either, because there is no way of telling one without telling the other.

The third factor is that the United States is supposed to be a democracy, with some sort of popular sovereignty and some sort of political equality. Foreign policy is crucial to the public well-being. But by its very nature, foreign policy must be made in secret by a small and closed circle of men. How can this be squared with democracy? It does little good to say that the people can rule through the post-audit process of election, for even at election time they may not know which official advised what or whether what he did advise is working or not. Thus it is not at all clear that the foreign policy making process in any country is or can be democratic in any meaningful sense.

DEMOCRATIC ELEMENTS IN FOREIGN POLICY MAKING

There are, however, certain democratic elements that occasionally play a decisive role in the foreign policy process. First, the information media—press, television, and so forth—are sufficiently free and energetic that most Americans eventually can acquire at least a rough, general sense of major events and changes in the world scene.[20] Second, there are numerous relatively independent foreign policy experts and opinion leaders who can provide the public with evaluations of the President's policies. As a result of these two factors, citizens can and do use public advocacy and presidential elections roughly to blame or reward the President and his party for the general shape the world is in. These are not very precise or sophisticated tools of democracy, but their presence does make Presidents consider public opinion when making foreign policy.

Finally, because the President engages in both domestic and foreign policy, it is possible to exercise some popular control over his foreign policy by holding his domestic program hostage. In order to achieve his domestic program, the President must build and constantly juggle many complex alliances, bargains, and compromises. The more congressmen, party leaders, interest groups, and opinion leaders his foreign policies antagonize, the more trouble he is likely to have getting his domestic programs through. Thus, he may trim his foreign policies to satisfy various segments of the population on whom he depends for approval of policies. One source of the President's power is the general expectation that he will take the lead in dealing with the nation's problems. But the same condition also increases his vulnerability. Because there are many things he cannot do without help, he is subject to outside control in some areas where he might otherwise have a free hand.

COORDINATION

Coordination is a crucial problem of foreign policy. As in the domestic bureaucracy, the principal mode of coordination is the legal hierarchy. The Defense Department seeks to coordinate the three armed services through the civilian Secretary of Defense and military leaders who constitute the Joint Chiefs of Staff. The State Department is organized into geographic desk offices (see Figure 15-3). Each group of desk offices is supervised by a regional assistant secretary. The assistant secretaries report to the Secretary. In this way, State seeks to coordinate all American foreign relations.

Both Defense and State also make an attempt to coordinate in the field. Defense is organized into regional field commands coordinating all army, navy, and air force units in a particular area. The State Department uses "country teams" under the leadership of the ambassador. These teams coordinate the work of all American government representatives in each country (see Figure 15-4).

The most important foreign policy coordination is not done by either the State Department or the Defense Department, however. It is done by the National Security Council Staff. Most Presidents have used small formal and informal advisory groups on important foreign policy issues. These groups have various names, but in every instance they consist of a small cluster of

[20] See Martin Shapiro, *The Pentagon Papers and the Courts: A Study in Foreign Policy-Making and Freedom of the Press* (San Francisco: Chandler Publishing Co., 1971).

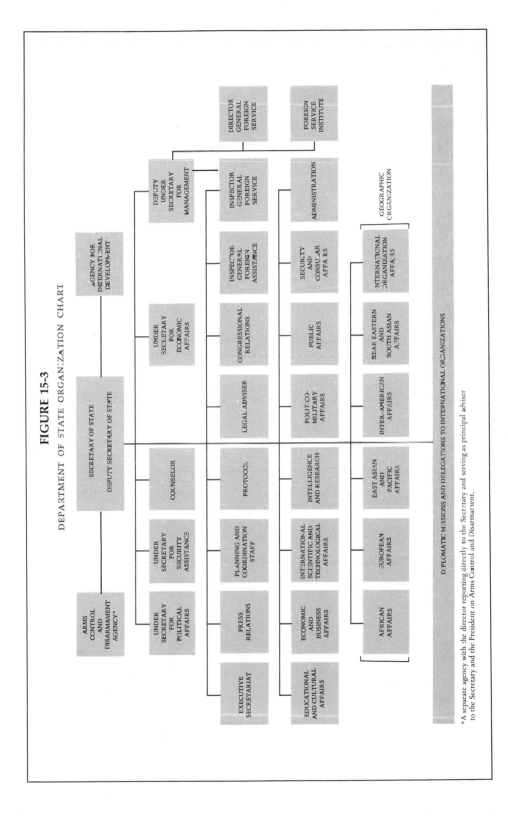

FIGURE 15-3

DEPARTMENT OF STATE ORGANIZATION CHART

*A separate agency with the director reporting directly to the Secretary and serving as principal adviser to the Secretary and the President on Arms Control and Disarmament.

presidential assistants and Cabinet and sub-cabinet members. They meet, usually weekly, to advise the President and to make sure that the various parts of the foreign and defense policy establishment are pulling together and moving in the direction desired by the President. In the last analysis, the major foreign policy decisions of the United States are made by the President in consultation with a handful of his personal advisors who meet with him both singly and in small groups. Because these groups typically draw their members from a number of different agencies, they function as coordinating bodies even if they were not particularly designed for that purpose.

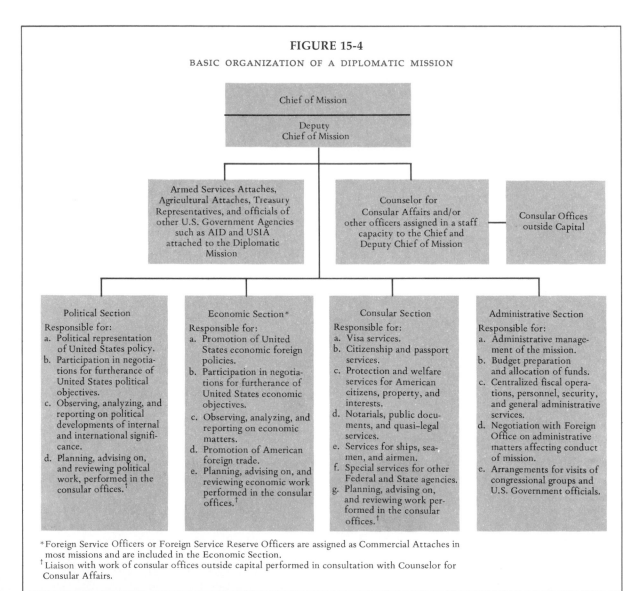

FIGURE 15-4

BASIC ORGANIZATION OF A DIPLOMATIC MISSION

Chief of Mission

Deputy Chief of Mission

Armed Services Attaches, Agricultural Attaches, Treasury Representatives, and officials of other U.S. Government Agencies such as AID and USIA attached to the Diplomatic Mission

Counselor for Consular Affairs and/or other officers assigned in a staff capacity to the Chief and Deputy Chief of Mission

Consular Offices outside Capital

Political Section
Responsible for:
a. Political representation of United States policy.
b. Participation in negotiations for furtherance of United States political objectives.
c. Observing, analyzing, and reporting on political developments of internal and international significance.
d. Planning, advising on, and reviewing political work, performed in the consular offices.[†]

Economic Section[*]
Responsible for:
a. Promotion of United States economic foreign policies.
b. Participation in negotiations for furtherance of United States economic objectives.
c. Observing, analyzing, and reporting on economic matters.
d. Promotion of American foreign trade.
e. Planning, advising on, and reviewing economic work performed in the consular offices.[†]

Consular Section
Responsible for:
a. Visa services.
b. Citizenship and passport services.
c. Protection and welfare services for American citizens, property, and interests.
d. Notarials, public documents, and quasi-legal services.
e. Services for ships, seamen, and airmen.
f. Special services for other Federal and State agencies.
g. Planning, advising on, and reviewing work performed in the consular offices.[†]

Administrative Section
Responsible for:
a. Administrative management of the mission.
b. Budget preparation and allocation of funds.
c. Centralized fiscal operations, personnel, security, and general administrative services.
d. Negotiation with Foreign Office on administrative matters affecting conduct of mission.
e. Arrangements for visits of congressional groups and U.S. Government officials.

[*]Foreign Service Officers or Foreign Service Reserve Officers are assigned as Commercial Attaches in most missions and are included in the Economic Section.
[†]Liaison with work of consular offices outside capital performed in consultation with Counselor for Consular Affairs.

Nevertheless, the fact remains that major foreign policy coordination is almost exclusively the province of the presidency. This has certain dangers. Relying on one very harried and tired man does not seem a perfect way to introduce greater rationality into foreign policy. Because of the President's role as political leader, he tends to be more alert to short-term (specfically, four-year term) than long-term developments. How often must our Presidents have awakened with the thought, "God, I know it's going to happen, but please, please let it happen after the next election."

SUMMARY

Having sketched the lawmaking and foreign policy-making processes and attempted some critical evaluation of them, we must repeat that no one yet has developed a generally accepted set of criteria for what constitutes a good versus a bad policy-making process.[21] The synoptic model, which we tend to apply unconsciously in evaluating such processes, is not a completely satisfactory evaluative tool. The incremental model tends to excuse nearly any amount of confusion, ignorance, and fragmentation in policy making. We must acknowledge that as long as humans make decisions, the particular qualities and limitations of their minds, psyches, and environments will play some part in policy making. But we are not at all sure whether more humanness in policy making is good or bad, or what human qualities we would like to see there. Because the policy-making process is, in a way, the culmination of the whole political system, evaluations of policy making ultimately blend into evaluations of American politics as a whole. We will turn to such evaluations in the last chapter of this book.

[21] See Yehezkel Dror, *Design for Policy Sciences* (New York: American Elsevier, 1971).

CHAPTER SIXTEEN
CHANGE AND VIOLENCE
IN AMERICAN POLITICS

I N preceding chapters, we have presented the components of American politics dynamically rather than statically, showing what each component does and how they interact. In order to simplify our account for purposes of clear exposition, we focused on short-run or "typical" activity of the sort that is repeated constantly. Such a treatment of the complex world of politics is often labeled *equilibrium analysis*. Equilibrium analysis rests on the assumption that the phenomena being studied make up a *system* — that is, a cluster of interacting parts. The behavior of each part affects all the others. If any of the parts or the relationships between them is disturbed or broken, the system repairs itself so as to return to its original condition or to a new stable pattern.[1] For this reason, the system is said to be in equilibrium.

EQUILIBRIUM ANALYSIS

The two-party system in America, for example, can be usefully studied as a system in equilibrium. If one of the two parties moves very far toward either ideological extreme, it may lose an election so badly that its leaders worry about fading out of existence (as American parties have done in the past). When this happens, the losing party moves back toward the middle of the road, thus restoring the two-party equilibrium. Similarly, if a policy issue of importance to many voters is not being satisfactorily handled by the two major parties, a dissident leader in one party is likely to appeal to these voters. He may do this by trying to get his party's presidential nomination, as Eugene McCarthy did in 1968 to provide an alternative to support for the war in Vietnam. Or the challenger may run for President on a third-party ticket, as George Wallace did in 1968 and threatened, at least, to do in 1976. If such a candidacy attracts much support, thus jeopardizing one major party's chances of winning, that party's leaders will adjust their stand to appeal to the dissatisfied voters. This is the sort of ideological opportunism we discussed in Chapter 9. Robbed of its reason for existence, the third party then disappears and the two-party equilibrium is restored.

PROBLEMS OF EQUILIBRIUM ANALYSIS

Equilibrium analysis does not deny the existence of change, but it does treat politics as a system that tends to return to normal conditions or a new balance following disturbances.

There are a number of major difficulties with equilibrium analysis. First of all, it is not clear that politics is, strictly speaking, a system. Some parts of it may be entirely unaffected by the actions of others. Moreover, some parts may be more affected by influences outside of the conventional boundaries of politics — for instance, the economy — than by anything within them.

Nevertheless, equilibrium analysis remains the central core of most political analysis for a number of reasons. In the first place, it enables the

[1] See David Easton, *The Political System* (New York: Alfred A. Knopf, 1953); Easton, *A Systems Analysis of Political Life* (New York: John Wiley & Sons, 1965); and Talcott Parsons, *The Social System* (New York: The Free Press, 1951).

political scientist to concentrate on those things that tend to happen over and over in the short run. Some of these are important even if they do not continue to exist permanently. Secondly, many political phenomena *do* appear to be interrelated and to persist over long periods of time. Again, the dominance of two major parties in the United States over a long period of time is an excellent example. Thirdly, the United States itself has persisted over a relatively long period of time as a relatively unified political entity.

One need not make the empirical assumptions of systems analysis to build one's analysis on the premise that stability is a political goal prized by almost all humanity. Nevertheless, it is possible to argue that much of American political science has consciously or unconsciously emphasized stability over change. Not enough attention has been paid to those modes of political action that threaten to disrupt the "normal" or repetitive patterns of political behavior. To correct this imbalance, in this chapter we will treat both routine and violent change as central features of American politics.

Since change is so often thought of as valuable in its own right, we will begin by defending the viewpoint that political stability is a good thing. Stability secures for the individual some continuity of expectations about his or her personal safety, security, autonomy, material well-being, and intellectual and moral development. Quite obviously, the policies and goals of a stable political apparatus may be crucial to the quality of life an individual enjoys. To be sure, even a stable state *may* treat its citizens badly, but an unstable state is almost certain to. High and continuous levels of political instability are likely to affect most humans adversely.[2] Few of us live from day to day. It is difficult to make plans if one does not know what laws and rulers will be in force next week or next month. If a farmer's crops are likely to be stolen by a marauding band of soldiers/guerrillas/bandits, why should he plant more than he needs for his family? It is hard to be a great painter if your studio is being shelled by the insurgents one day and the government forces the next. Nearly every culture or society has devoted a major portion of its resources to attaining security of expectations. At the very least, both material prosperity and psychological well-being require that most people have some assurance that they can go on tomorrow doing what they have done today.

Political stability, however, does not mean the absence of change. Economic, technological, and social systems have a life of their own. As they develop, they may force a static political regime to change accordingly, or be replaced by a regime more capable of dealing with new conditions. In this sense, even political stability requires a capacity on the part of the political system to respond to changes in the rest of the world, lest the tension between an old system of government and a new world mount until the breaking point we call revolution. Thus even the notion of political stability implies the capacity for change as a means of preserving the basic continuity of human expectations about how the political system is going to operate.

NORMAL POLITICAL CHANGE

American politics has a number of "normal" modes of political change. That is, it has recurrent patterns of short-term change. These patterns are themselves a part of the political equilibrium.

PERSONNEL CHANGE

ELECTIONS. One obvious form of this sort of change is the constant circulation in political officials that results from our system of elections. An enormous range of party and government officials is elected, and elections occur with great frequency. (See Table 16–1.)

In the first 75 years of the twentieth century, the United States had 14 presidents, an average of one every 5.4 years. Some presidential transitions produced quite striking changes in policy, as from Wilson to Harding, Hoover to Roosevelt, and Johnson to Nixon.

TABLE 16–1

SOME ELECTED OFFICIALS AND THEIR TERMS OF OFFICE

OFFICIALS	TERMS
1. President	4 years
2. Vice president	4 years
3. U. S. senators	6 years
4. U. S. representatives	2 years
5. State governors	2 or 4 years
6. Members of state legislatures	2 to 10 years*
7. Other statewide elected officials (lieutenant governor, attorney general, treasurer, etc.)	2 or 4 years
8. Other officials chosen by statewide elections (public service commissioners, Board of Education, Tax Commission, University Regents, Insurance Commissioners, etc.)	2 to 10 years
9. County officials	1 to 7 years
10. State and local judges and court officers	1 year to life
11. Local executives (mayors, city councilmen, aldermen, selectmen, etc.)	1 to 7 years
12. Local functional officers (highway surveyors, school board members, tax collectors, water commissioners, etc.)	1 to 12 years

*Beginning in 1972, members of the Idaho state senate are elected for 10-year terms.

The impact of elections on Congress is more complex. There is a fair amount of turnover on Capitol Hill. In 1975, a quarter of the Senate and 36 percent of the House had been in office less than three years. This is an abnormally high proportion of newcomers. Most of them did not defeat their predecessors but replaced incumbents who had retired, died in office, or run for another office. We have seen, moreover, that newcomers to Congress are vastly outnumbered by the veterans.

Still, new faces often do mean new laws, particularly when the opposing forces on Capitol Hill have been evenly matched. In these circumstances, a moderate shift in party strength may tilt the balance of forces in the other direction. The greatest impact of elections, however, lies in the threat they pose to congressional careers. As we have seen, congressmen exaggerate their electoral vulnerability, seeing dangers where none exists. Thus the possibility of defeat exerts a greater effect than the actuality of personnel change, and congressmen are more open to new policies than they have to be. During some historical periods, even normal electoral procedures lead to substantial changes in governmental personnel. Thus, for example, after the "critical" or "realigning" elections of 1860 and 1932, whole new groups of political leaders appeared in Washington with new policies and new ways of doing things.

APPOINTMENTS. The second major mode of change in political personnel is through the process of appointment. Because federal judges are appointed for life, the composition of the judiciary is least responsive to political change. The actual rate of turnover on the Supreme Court varies considerably, however, depending on how the law of averages interacts with the health and activity levels of the nine Justices. President Nixon's rapid and major reorientation of the Court testifies to the potential for change via this route. The same is true of the lower federal courts. Furthermore, periodic increases in the number of judges present another opportunity for change by the appointment process. Here, too, Nixon exercised influence that will long survive his term in office. In his five-and-a-half years in the White House, Nixon appointed 4 of 9 Supreme Court Justices, 45 of 97 circuit court justices, and 171 of 400 federal district judges.

The statutory terms of regulatory commissioners deliberately have been made longer than presidential terms in order to build resistance to personnel change. Nevertheless, most Presidents make enough appointments to alter the balance of power on each commission. If in fact the commissions have been resistant to real policy change, it is less because of long terms of office than because Presidents have failed to use their appointing powers as a conscious instrument of change.

The major constraint on the appointment process as a mechanism for personnel change has been the gradual extension of the civil service system. Although various loopholes allow Presidents some flexibility in bureaucratic personnel matters, a substantial proportion of federal bureaucrats with policy-making responsibilities are locked into their jobs. On the other hand, the growing use of grants and increased use of outside contractors

PUBLIC OPINION CAN INFLUENCE PERSONNEL CHANGE, AS IT DID IN MARCH 1968 WHEN OPINION AGAINST HIS HANDLING OF THE WAR IN VIET-NAM FORCED LYN-DON JOHNSON TO BOW OUT AS A CANDIDATE FOR RE-ELECTION.
Wide World Photos

to do government work have augmented the potential for personnel change. Private contractors can hire and fire more freely than the government. What is more, the very choice of awarding the contract or grant to one outside firm, agency, or institution rather than another is a choice of what personnel are to do the job. This is a choice that can be changed each time a new contract or grant is to be awarded.

ORGANIZATIONAL CHANGE

Instead of or in addition to changing the personnel of political bodies, change is also made by altering the constitutuencies, procedures, organization, and powers of various government bodies in relation to other bodies. Because the Constitution sets the basic pattern of our government, constitutional amendment is a major mechanism for change in this area. The Fourteenth Amendment, for instance, as interpreted by the Supreme Court, resulted in a major shift of responsibilities from the states to the federal government. Within the federal government, reorganization and changes of procedure are largely accomplished through new legislation. Often this legislation is based on presidential recommendations and is then carried into effect by detailed executive orders. Thousands of lesser, but often crucial, changes in jurisdiction, organization, and procedure result from decisions made by the bureaucrats themselves.[3] Moreover, the federal courts, in exercising their power of judicial review over administrative decisions, sometimes impose changes on bureaucratic ways of doing business.

Changes in congressional procedure can be made by the Congress itself in the form of new or amended rules of the House and Senate. Most of the congressional reforms we discussed in Chapters 10 and 11, however, were the result of changes by the majority party in its internal rules. Changes in the procedures of the national parties are made by the parties themselves in the form of resolutions passed at national party conventions. Even more crucial changes occur in such profusion at state and local party conventions and by other party mechanisms that it would be impossible to describe them fully. Local party machines are often thought to be institutions that perpetuate the dominance of a small clique. But the machines are only one aspect of local party organization, and by no means the most important one for national politics. The rise of ideologically motivated party activists, the political activities of labor unions, and minority group community organizations all have introduced even more change. As a result, many of the local bases of the national political parties are now in a state of great organizational flux.

It is obvious that changes in political personnel—in *who* governs—are important political changes. The significance of changes in *organization and procedures* is not always so obvious, but it is very real. In a sense, organizational and procedural changes *are* changes in who governs. For example,

---

[3] Kenneth Culp Davis, *Discretionary Justice* (Louisiana State University Press, 1969); Martin Shapiro, *The Supreme Court and Administrative Agencies* (New York: The Free Press, 1968); and Peter Woll, *Administrative Law: The Informal Process* (Berkeley: University of California Press, 1963).

reorganization in the federal bureaucracy often means taking a policy problem from administrators who do not want to do anything about it and giving it to others who do, or vice versa.

THE PACE OF CHANGE

The American political system uses organizational and procedural changes to generate the continuous alterations necessary to adjust existing programs to the needs of formally organized or otherwise politically salient groups. The system is, however, sluggish in the initiation of major new programs, particularly those involving benefits to unorganized and socially diffuse groups, as was long the case of migrant workers in the first instance and consumers in the second. This sluggishness is especially evident if the change involves redistribution of benefits that will be paid for by specific, identifiable groups.[4] One dramatic failure of this type has been in the realm of medical care. The government has been able to support major programs of medical research and education. But the United States lags behind almost every other industrial nation in the provision of low-cost or free health care to all its citizens.

Most observers would probably list transportation and preservation of natural resources as areas in which the government has been slow to respond to new conditions. It would probably be universally agreed, however, that the most important, longest term failure to make sufficient policy change has been in the area of race relations. This failure is so serious that it is frequently used as an indictment of the entire policy-making process. Yet it is not clear that the American political system has done a notably worse job of dealing with race relations than political systems elsewhere. Throughout the world, the history of large racial, linguistic, or religious minorities has been tortured and troubled at best.

Whether faster or slower change is more desirable in such policy areas is a matter of one's own political principles. For example, federal urban renewal programs now look to many observers like a foolish and destructive tampering with natural urban development. Whether the rate of change seems to be satisfactory or unsatisfactory is almost always dependent on whether or not we approve of the *substance* and *direction* of change. Change itself, and the rate of change, are not really the issue.

This observation leads to an extremely important point about routine or normal change in American politics. The principal means of obtaining such change, be it in personnel, procedures, or policy itself, is through a combination of education, persuasion, bargaining, and moral leadership. That is, American politics—at least domestic American politics—is essentially consensual politics. Most of the smaller political changes occur because someone can convince others that the change will benefit them or those with whom they sympathize and will cause no significant harm. *Larger* changes are achieved by convincing others that the policy is good for some group *and*

---

[4] See Theodore J. Lowi, *The End of Liberalism* (New York: W. W. Norton & Company, 1969).

good for the general public as well. Campaigns for major change typically are conducted by seeking to show the uncommitted that the proposed program is good for the nation, that it provides a feasible means of achieving widely held values and goals. Often, such an attempt at persuasion will take the form of an effort to build a coalition through bargaining. The reservations of the uncommitted are accommodated by concessions offered by the advocates of a new departure. To this is likely to be added a good bit more far-reaching and abstract political rhetoric about the public interest.

Impatience with the slowness of policy change frequently results from failure to appreciate the educational, persuasive, and bargaining campaigns that must go on behind the scenes before change can come about. Why can't new policies be proposed and a vote be taken? If 51 percent say yes, the policy will be put into effect immediately. What takes so much time? Why all the milling about? The answer is fairly simple. If you were to march up to any group of politicians and announce, "I want you to pass a law protecting soft-shell crabs. All those in favor raise your right hand," their response would not be to start flinging their arms in the air. Instead they would begin asking: "Why do you want to protect soft-shell crabs? Will the law you are proposing actually protect them? Is the protection of soft-shell crabs good for the country? Is it good for me? Who is it bad for? If I help you with your law to protect soft-shell crabs, will you help me with the law I want to eliminate electric eels? How much will this cost, and who will pay the costs?" The crucial, final question in policy change often comes down to the brutally clear question, *"Have you got the votes?"* The answers to all the other questions we have just listed will determine whether you *do* have the votes. And these questions often take a long time to answer.

Major policy change is complex, costly in far more than a financial sense, highly disposed to stir controversy, and bristling with unresolved questions of fact, value, and prediction. Because of the way our political system is organized, such change requires the support—or at least the neutrality—of many political actors. Most of them are initially uncommitted one way or the other and know little if anything about the problem. Thus change by persuasion and bargaining is likely to take a long time, precisely because the participants are in fact seeking good solutions to real problems and are genuinely concerned for the interests of both the majority and minorities in the society.

Those who seek significant change therefore may grow impatient or even infuriated with the slow-moving way our system responds to pressure for change. When this happens, they can have recourse to a number of techniques for accelerating change through direct action. Physical coercion and varying degrees of violence, the threat of such methods, and other "nonstandard" modes of seeking influence can be employed to hasten (or resist) change within a stable political system. Indeed, there are a number of options between politics as usual and revolution. In the next few pages we shall explore some of them, beginning with those that involve the least threat to stability and ending with those that come closest to revolution.

CONFRONTATION STRATEGIES

RITUALIZED DEPARTURES FROM NORMAL CHANGE STRATEGIES

Over time, American politics has developed several forms of controlled, ritualized, and legalized confrontation. Among the most common are the peaceful protest demonstration, the strike, the boycott, and the test case. The first three are so familiar that only the last requires some brief explanation. Often a group desiring change feels blocked by the prevailing interpretation of existing law. One response is to attempt to persuade legislatures to amend the law or the Constitution, or administrators to change their interpretation of it. If this approach fails, or if it does not seem likely to succeed, one can try to get judges to change the law or the prevailing interpretation of it.[5] But judges do not give decisions in hypothetical cases; to have a trial, there must be an alleged crime. Therefore, people who want the judges' help must at least nominally violate the law. Then, when they are prosecuted, they can argue against the constitutionality of the law, its consistency with more fundamental laws (e.g., with federal laws in the case of a state or local law), or against the current interpretation of it. Winners get the change they want; losers are declared law breakers.

Protest demonstrations, strikes, boycotts, and test cases are usually undertaken to achieve limited political objectives without basically upsetting the normal functioning of government and society. These methods are *ritualized* in that the passionately held sentiments of quite large masses of people are represented in rather orderly ways, often through the use of symbols. For example, a strike by thousands of dock workers who are bitterly contemptuous of their employers' wage offers may tie up the nation's whole export trade. Yet the only visible sign of this ferocious encounter may be a few dozen cheerful, neatly dressed, middle-aged men who can be seen drinking coffee as they prop their picket signs against their cars, which they are passing the time by washing in the dock parking lots. When, during the Korean

[5] See, for example, Maurice G. Barton, *The Steamboat Monopoly: Gibbons v. Ogden, 1824* (New York: Alfred A. Knopf, 1972); and Anthony Lewis, *Gideon's Trumpet* (New York: Random House, 1964).

STEEL WORKERS ON
STRIKE, 1952.
Wide World Photos

conflict, President Truman interpreted the prevailing laws as permitting the government to take control of the nation's steel industry to prevent a strike, the only visible change was the raising of the American flag over factories operated by the same industry executives and the same union-member plant workers. The ritualization is clearest in the test case, when no external physical change occurs and even very passionate demands are expressed by the solemn, almost silent filing of long, written court briefs.

These ritualized methods generally are recognized and protected by the law. Those who use them generally perceive themselves, and are perceived by others, as acting legally. The protest march, or rally, is protected by the First Amendment. It occurs within a web of counterbalancing freedom of speech rights and valid police regulations for controlling traffic and maintaining order. Labor union strikes are legalized and minutely governed by federal and state regulations, court injunctions, and labor management contracts. Boycotts also are protected by law and subject to considerable legal regulation. The consumer boycott is firmly based in the legal right of the individual not to buy for any reason he or she pleases.

All these methods can be used to resist change as well as to initiate it. White parents have used the school boycott to resist integration of their schools just as black parents have used it to achieve integration. In both cases, boycotts are employed by those who have not found the normal processes of political persuasion and bargaining effective in achieving the results they desire from the political system.

Most of these methods require a fairly wide base of support and a high level of organization among those employing them. Strikes and boycotts cannot be effective unless substantial numbers of persons refuse to work or to buy. Protest demonstrations attended by a few dozen demonstrators may be less effective than no demonstration at all. In contrast, the test case is a valuable technique precisely because it can be brought by a very small group surrounded by a large, hostile army of opponents. The test case takes matters out of the streets and the legislatures, where numbers are likely to count for a good deal, and puts them in a courtroom. There, in the case of *Smith* v. *Jones,* or even *Smith* v. *The United States,* each party counts for one, in terms of the time and attention it gets.

CONSUMERS FROM
CALIFORNIA TO NEW
YORK HAVE JOINED
IN BOYCOTTS
AGAINST GRAPES
AND LETTUCE NOT
PICKED BY MEMBERS
OF THE UNITED FARM-
WORKERS UNION.
Wide World Photos

A particular advantage of the test case is that the appellate mechanism allows a minority badly outnumbered on the local scene to escape into the bigger world. The brave little band of Hare Krishna sectarians, jailed in Flower Patch for challenging an anti-noise ordinance, may lose in the municipal court and even on appeal to the Alfalfa County Superior Court. But its appeal to the state supreme court may tap the more enlightened sentiments of the broader community. The test case can allow weak groups or even individuals to gain backing from more powerful organizations which have greater skill at litigation or which enjoy broader support, since a litigant may be joined by co-litigants, such as the civil liberties and public interest law groups discussed earlier in the book. If our sect wins an appeal, it will go back to Flower Patch flourishing its Supreme Court opinion along with its tambourines. It will depend on that opinion to keep it out of jail.

In this sense, it is gaining support for its activities from the organizational discipline of the judiciary and the police machinery and, more important, the widespread public support for law.

The peaceful protest demonstration works in a rather different way. It is designed to show that a substantial number of persons feels very strongly about some social change, even though their voices have been ignored in the normal process of persuasion and bargaining. Unlike the strike, boycott, and test case, which are often attempts to induce change without the help of the formal governmental policy-making apparatus, the demonstration is typically designed to stimulate formal changes in policy. It is a mode of showing officials the extent and intensity of public sentiment so that they will respond through the normal governmental channels of change.

THE LOGIC OF SMALL-SCALE VIOLENCE, QUASI-VIOLENCE, AND DISOBEDIENCE

So far we have confined ourselves to the peaceful and legal forms of direct action and confrontation. About as far into illegality as we have ventured is the deliberately isolated, single violation of a law in order to provide the standing for a test case. To be sure, demonstrations, strikes, and boycotts may be mounted in the face of valid laws or court orders forbidding them. What is more, relatively high levels of social and physical coercion and violence may be mixed in with all these methods. We often read of fights breaking out between strikers and those who do not honor the picket line, of rock-throwing incidents at protest demonstrations, of the occasional vandalism of businesses that refuse to stop selling boycotted goods. This sort of scattered, almost accidental violence often occurs in the context of massive movements aimed at bringing about change. When this happens, what began as a controlled, ritualized, and legalized confrontation escalates to a more intense level of direct action. And yet, there is no sharply defined legal or moral line separating the legal confrontation from the confrontation that is mixed with some degree of violence.

THE QUESTION OF NONVIOLENCE. Many Americans try to draw a rather unrealistic but highly moralistic line between violent and nonviolent confrontation. The difficulty, of course, arises when we try to define what we mean by "nonviolent" physical coercion. Shouting a speaker down just as effectively deprives him of his right to speak as does shooting him, although it does him less physical harm. A barrier of massed bodies just as effectively deprives others of their right to come in and hear the speaker as would turning them away at bayonet point. If a group of strikers outside a factory indicate by their presence that they will not permit anyone to enter the factory, can their action be classed as nonviolent simply because no would-be strike-breakers come forth to call their bluff? It certainly can be argued that the implicit *threat* of violence is itself a form of violence.

Nonviolent techniques raise some difficult paradoxes. What is the political or moral justification of awarding victory to whichever group manages to get the biggest bunch of bodies into the street first or keep them there longest? The logic of nonviolent physical coercion is that whoever gets their bunch into the doorway first decides who gets to enter and leave, even if there are only 25 people blocking the door and 200 waiting to get in or out. The 200 would then presumably be justified in forming a human chain around the 25, preventing anyone else from reaching them until they were sufficiently uncomfortable to go away. Why should either the 25 or the 200 be the winner depending on who can sit it out longer?

Thus it is difficult to see how certain forms of direct action can be defended as "nonviolent" when they rest on the physical or psychological coercion of others, even though actual force is not used. On the other hand, however, it must be pointed out that techniques such as mass picketing, the sit-down strike, the sit-in, and various forms of harassment usually have been used to *minimize* rather than maximize confrontation with the rights of others. For instance, the sit-down strikes of the 1930s, which involved the peaceful occupation of factories by employees protesting management's refusal to recognize the workers' collective bargaining organizations. gained wide sympathy for the workers. In these strikes, the workers simply refused to leave the plant at the end of the working day. The physical coercion involved was directed against a rather abstract property right of a corporation to have its premises empty when it wanted them empty. Such strikes served to prevent the operation of the factory by "scab" labor, but since no men would be hired until the plant was cleared of strikers, no individual worker was deprived of a job by the strike. The same point can be made about the "sit-in" demonstrations against segregation in the South in the early 1960s. In these demonstrations blacks occupied the seats at "whites only" lunch counters, fully prepared to buy lunches. The only right with which such action seemed to interfere was the rather dubious right of the proprietors to practice racial discrimination.

THE EXPRESSIVE ELEMENT IN CONFRONTATION. These examples serve to remind us that the essential purpose of most non-ritualized, illegal, and actually or potentially violent conduct aimed at achieving change is actually *expressive* rather than directly instrumental. (In fact, even the scattered acts of violence by left- and right-wing "underground" protest groups of the past half-dozen years—e.g., the Minutemen and the Weather people—were expressive attempts at what turn-of-the-century anarchists called "propaganda of the deed" rather than specific attempts at concrete policy changes.) Typically, the "in system" forms of expressive confrontational politics have been preliminary or auxiliary to the routine politics of bargaining and negotiation. It is in this context that civil disobedience as employed in the United States is to be understood. American practitioners of civil disobedience have rarely hoped to attain anything like what Gandhi hoped for in India. He aimed at generating such massive levels of popular disobedience that the British imperial government would collapse because it simply would not have enough jails and police to deal with the offenders.

In this country, in contrast, civil disobedience basically has been a means for minorities to deal with a key fault in the electoral mechanism. Voting registers only numbers. It cannot measure the intensity of feeling of each of the voters. A minority that feels intensely may be overborne by an almost indifferent majority. By deliberately violating the law, such a minority can express the intensity of its policy sentiment. This is why the classical (as opposed to the radical) theory of civil disobedience stresses the open, deliberate violation of the law and the willingness to be punished for the violation. The willingness to go to jail for the offense is important because it testifies to the intensity of the sentiment at issue and to the protester's desire to be protected by the rules of the political system rather than to wipe out the system itself.[6]

The classic American form of civil disobedience, recently revived by a number of celebrities, is the tax strike. Refusal to pay all or some portion of one's taxes can be an expression of intense disapproval or moral condemnation of certain government policies. Such an act is illegal. It is in principle subject to severe penalties. It is done openly and defiantly. And it hurts no other individual. For that matter, it does not even hurt the government in any serious way, especially if the government chooses simply to place a lien on the assets of the tax refuser. Such protests are almost a purely expressive rather than an instrumental act of illegality.

The forms of illegal political conduct that have drawn so much public attention in recent years seem to involve a subtle combination of expressive and coercive elements. The mass protest march may or may not turn into a riot. The occupation of a computer facility may or may not wreck millions of dollars' worth of equipment. The destruction of card catalogues may or may not be a preliminary to burning down the library and at any rate drastically impedes the capacity of the library to perform its services to the academic community. Thus the expressive element is mixed with a coercive threat as the demonstrators seem to be saying, "Look, you can see how strongly we feel about these things, how much moral fervor and dedication we have. If you don't give us what we want, we may smash everything."

THE LEGALITY OF DIRECT ACTION. Other elements in our political system further complicate the issue of the legality or illegality of various forms of direct action. As we saw in Chapter 3, our constitutional traditions encourage the belief that an unconstitutional law is not really a law; hence, violating such a law is not really illegal. Thus, whether a particular march or demonstration is ultimately legal or illegal depends upon court decisions that may occur months or even years after the event. Many of the activities of Martin Luther King, Jr., and other southern black leaders have fallen into this ambiguous category, as do all instances in which a person breaks the law in order to bring a test case to court. By breaking the local law of the moment, the demonstrators express the intensity of their needs and beliefs. By asserting that their actions are protected by the Constitution, they clothe their

[6] See Henry David Thoreau, *Civil Disobedience* (1849; many editions); Abe Fortas, *Concerning Dissent and Civil Disobedience* (New York: New American Library, 1968); and Martin Luther King, Jr., "Letter from Birmingham Jail," in Staughton Lynd, ed., *Nonviolence in America: A Documentary History* (Indianapolis: Bobbs-Merrill, 1966).

immediate law-breaking in a higher legality and morality. And if the courts uphold their view of the law, they will escape actual punishment even while demonstrating their willingness to go to jail for their beliefs.

STRATEGIC ASPECTS OF USING AND RESTRICTING VIOLENCE

TIME LIMITS

So far, we have examined various types of direct action, most of which contain a mixture of legal and illegal, violent and nonviolent, expressive and coercive elements. Almost all of these tactics are practiced as a means of pursuing change within the political system rather than as a means of overthrowing the system. To be effective, such action must necessarily be limited in time and must serve as a preliminary to bargaining and persuasion of the more routine sort. This is true for a number of reasons.

First, long continued use of illegal or seemingly illegal action tends to lose its look of civil disobedience and to be transformed in the eyes of the outside population into simple criminality. Thus a rent strike initially may show the moral fervor or desperation of the tenants, but if continued too long it may appear to the rest of the world as just a marvelous excuse for not paying the rent.

Second, where violence or coercion, whether physical or psychological, is directed against the rights of others, it cannot be expected that the remainder of society will tolerate such a condition indefinitely. Eventually, the police or the soldiers show up. This has proved equally true when students physically coerced college administrators illegally and also when southern political leaders coerced black people. The basic reasons for this reaction are moral distaste for civil violence and at least implicit public recognition that lawlessness is not easily confinable to a single "good" cause. Once one group is allowed to coerce and assault others, additional groups inevitably avail themselves of the same opportunity. Very few Americans are willing to return to the land "West of the Pecos" where there is no law and power goes to the fastest gun or the biggest mob, even if they do enjoy television romanticizations of such practices.

Third, direct action tactics persisted in for long periods are wearing on the participants and their sympathizers. A prolonged strike impoverishes the strikers and in many instances the entire community. Few men and women can muster the courage or the resources to participate in protest marches day after day and year after year. Even the bulk of those college students who are highly sympathetic to radical causes have experienced the war weariness that sets in after too many bombs, too much tear gas, and too long a distraction from other affairs of life.

THE INGREDIENTS OF SUCCESS

What factors determine the success or failure of physical coercion mixed with violence or the threat of violence?

CAPACITY FOR VIOLENCE. Obviously, the first determining factor is the *distribution of the capacity for coercion and violence.* How strong is our side? How strong is their side? This calculation is not static. For instance, an uninformed outsider, observing twenty demonstrators on one side and two hundred policemen on the other, might hastily conclude that the police will win. The movement of the police against the demonstrators, however, may bring a thousand previously idle bystanders over to the demonstrators' side. The relative capacity of the various participants may fluctuate wildly according to time, place, and the skill of the participants in marshaling their forces and employing them effectively. The sudden upsurge of violent tactics in the 1960s meant that the police and their leaders were repeatedly confronted with situations for which they had little past experience or training. As a result, their capacity to employ effectively the men and equipment at their disposal was quite limited, but a further result was the acquisition of new police technologies to deal with such circumstances.

WILLINGNESS TO USE VIOLENCE. A second factor is the *willingness* to employ coercion and violence, a factor intimately related to capacity.[7] The Cold War has made this factor dramatically clear on the international scene, where the crucial question often is not whether one side has the capacity for destruction of the other in a war, but whether it has the will to make the decision to do so. In the 1950s it became clear that just because the United States had the enormous capacity for violence represented by the atomic bomb, it did not necessarily follow that the United States could successfully dominate nonatomic powers, since American leaders clearly were unwilling to use the bomb in any situation short of an all-out war with the Soviet Union.

Simular calculations are evident in domestic conflict. The police have the capacity to clear any street in a few minutes with guns. Such blood baths have occurred in human history, and not merely in the remote past. Yet illegal street demonstrations frequently operate with impunity because those who control the police are unwilling to resort to firepower. The authorities repeatedly face a fundamental paradox. Ten policemen with guns may have a greater capacity for violence than a thousand demonstrators. Yet if they do not use their guns, this capacity for violence is meaningless. In terms of sheer force, the *effective* superiority passes to the side of the demonstrators.

The single most significant factor in most instances where the tactics of coercion and violence have worked successfully to achieve change has been the unwillingness of the defenders of the status quo to employ the capacity for violence at their disposal. *Thus we encounter the paradox that the more*

AT THE 1968 DEM-
OCRATIC NATIONAL
CONVENTION IN
CHICAGO, BOTH
DEMONSTRATORS
AND POLICE
SHOWED A CA-
PACITY FOR
VIOLENCE THAT RE-
SULTED IN SEVERAL
NIGHTS OF BLOODY
CONFRONTATIONS.
Wide World Photos

[7] H. L. Nieburg, *Political Violence* (New York: St. Martin's Press, 1969); Richard Hofstadter, ed., *American Violence* (New York: Alfred A. Knopf, 1960); Michael Lipsky, "Protest as a Political Resource," *American Political Science Review,* 62 (December 1968), 1144–58; Hugh Davis Graham and Ted Robert Gurr, eds., *The History of Violence in America: A Report to the National Commission on the Causes and Prevention of Violence* (New York: Bantam Books, 1969); and Thomas Perry Thornton, "Terror as a Weapon of Political Agitation," in Harry Eckstein, ed., *Internal War* (New York: The Free Press, 1964).

committed the society and the regime are to the normal politics of persuasion and bargaining, the more vulnerable they are to short-term, tactically skillful employment of violent or otherwise coercive direct action.

Particularly important in this respect is the secret police mechanism. The survival of ultraradical militants in the United States depends on the government's unwillingness to remove them from society illegally. They can carry on, confident that the secret police will not come in the night and that tomorrow they will not be un-persons hidden away in a labor camp or mental hospital. Much radical rhetoric and threats of violence depend on the radicals' supreme confidence that "the system" will continue to protect even those who express contempt for it. In other words, the personal costs of their conduct are low. Of course, the costs to the political system of suppressing dissidents, in the style of the Soviet Union, would be very high.

THE RELATIVE COSTS OF VIOLENCE. Among the factors that determine whether change can be achieved through violence or the threat of violence are the relative costs of violence to each side and perception of these costs by each side. The militant may quickly reach a plateau of threat and sporadic violence beyond which he cannot move without risking massive breakdown in the system of law, order, legal rights, and legitimacy on which he depends for his political freedom and physical security. He may wish to preserve the fundamentals of this system. Although systematic research could not easily be done on the small groups or single individuals who are prepared to engage in explosively violent protest (even assassination) without regard for preserving "the system," impressionistic evidence suggests that only a few individuals fall in this category, when considered in terms of the size of the American population. Such individuals and tiny "outlaw" groups often are most readily explicable in terms of individual emotional needs based on inner psychic unrest. They are wholly expressive rather than instrumental in any remotely practical sense.

The defender of the status quo or of change via more or less "mainstream" political procedures must guard against responding to threats and violence with any more than the minimal counterviolence that may be necessary to subdue a potential bomber, revolutionary bank robber, or assassin. Even if such counterviolence is legal—for example, the shooting of looters under marshal law—it may lead to widespread popular revulsion against the political system, and thus would tend to destroy the very thing such a person is trying to defend. And this is precisely the goal of those proponents of extreme theories of revolutionary political action.

AVAILABILITY OF ALTERNATIVES. Finally, the effectiveness of using violence as a mode of achieving changes within a given political system depends on the availability of other means of achieving the same goals. The costs and risks of violence are so great, and violence runs so much against the main currents of American ideology, that it is very difficult to recruit sufficient supporters for a sustained campaign of violence if they are conscious of alternative peaceful means. Those who resort to violence where nonviolent means for change are available are likely to encounter increased willingness on the part of authorities to employ counterviolence. Moreover, the very psychological instability that seems to induce a small fraction of individuals to take an interest in radical violent activities, whether in the interest of right- or left-wing or simply ill-defined causes, makes it difficult for such people to work together successfully in any stable organization.

On the whole, then, we can describe an optimal situation for achieving change through coercion, violence, or the threat of violence within a relatively stable political system. Those desiring change must have:

1. a high capacity for violence;
2. a high willingness to use that capacity;
3. an intense commitment to change;
4. a low estimate of the costs of violence or a high level of indifference to them;
5. few alternative peaceful means for achieving change.

In addition, the forces committed to defending the status quo should have:

1. a low capacity for violence and/or
2. a low willingness to use that capacity;
3. at least a latent commitment to the same goals desired by those employing violence;
4. a high estimate of the costs to the system of their opponents' behavior or of the counterviolence that would be necessary to repress it;
5. an awareness that peaceful channels for change are not available.

In any actual situation, the mixture of these basic ingredients is likely to be very unstable. A regime with low willingness or even capacity to employ violence one day may call in the National Guard the next. Two thousand roaring demonstrators on a sunny spring day may quickly become two hundred drenched teenagers only a few hours and one thunderstorm later. A band of "martyrs" may be transformed into a gang of "irresponsible kids" or "sick misfits" if it refuses a sudden offer of the other side to negotiate fully and peacefully. *Timing* — the ability to deliver just enough threat, or coercion, or actual violence at just the right moment — is the ultimate factor in the use of violence as an effective tool for achieving change.

It is precisely the difficulty of mastering the art of this sort of strategic timing that so severely limits the potential usefulness of violence as either a tool for change or a tool for resisting change in American society, particularly under twentieth-century conditions. We have long since discovered that violence in a mob — or, for that matter, in the police or the military — cannot be turned on and off at will or modulated to achieve just the effect desired by those who initiated it. If any political actor were sure he could wield violence with the deft precision of the surgeon wielding his scalpel, then violence might be a very popular tool of democratic politics. But in the

THE SHELLS OF
APARTMENTS AND
SHOPS WERE
ALL THAT RE-
MAINED AFTER FIRES
SET BY RIOTERS IN
DETROIT IN 1967
FINALLY WERE
EXTINGUISHED.
Wide World Photos

real world, violence is too unwieldy and undisciplined. It rarely catches the optimal moment or finds just the right shading.

FULL-SCALE VIOLENCE

TYPES OF VIOLENT OVERTHROW

Let us now briefly examine some of the various ways in which full-scale violence can be used in an attempt to overthrow the existing political structure. Our treatment of this matter will be brief because this book is concerned primarily with the dynamics of the working political system, rather than with ways to get it to stop working or with alternatives to it. (If we were writing in 1775 or 1858, the entire emphasis of our book would have to be different with respect to analyzing internal, revolutionary, large-scale violence.) We will see that five basically different but somewhat overlapping types of violent overthrow of governments are discernible in the contemporary world.

MILITARY CONQUEST. The simplest type of violent overthrow results from military conquest by another state. This is called either aggression or liberation, depending on who is on what side. The contemporary governments of Germany, Japan, Korea, Italy, and all of the eastern European states except Albania and Yugoslavia, many of the Southeast Asian nations, and portions of Israel and Cyprus have been established by military conquest. Many countries in the Middle East owe their basic boundaries and political structure to the defeat of the Turkish empire by Britain and France in World War I. In many other instances, such as that of the nations occupied by Germany in World War II, the current political structure is a restoration by one set of conquerors of what another set had destroyed.

MILITARY COUP. The second type is the simple coup, the quick overthrow of the regime by a clique of military personnel. This pattern is common in contemporary Latin American, African, Asian, and Middle Eastern politics. In a curious way, such coups function much like elections. They change the governing personnel without any major direct change in political procedures or policies, although substantial policy change in the type of political system that changes leaders via coups may eventually follow from changes in personnel.

CLASSICAL REVOLUTION. Revolutions in France late in the eighteenth century and in Russia in the second decade of the twentieth century are examples of the third type of violent overthrow. Whole libraries are devoted to the causes and stages of these gigantic historical phenomena. Revolutions of this sort are marked by the sudden breakdown of the government's coercive powers and the seizure of central governing authority by new political groups representing a different ideology and different social interests. Such classical revolutions have been rare. It is not at all clear how one could go about consciously creating one. The dominant formula of modern times has been the Leninist one of creating a tightly disciplined, secret revolutionary party that spreads the new ideology and builds its organization so that it will be able to seize power when the revolution comes. This strategy rests on the comforting assumption that impersonal historical forces are pushing the society toward inevitable revolution. Although party activities give "historical forces" a helping hand, most party activities are not aimed at making a revolution but at seizing power from rival factions at the moment when the breakdown of traditional authority occurs.

REGIONAL REVOLUTION. The fourth type of violent overthrow is sometimes called *peasant revolution,* but might be more clearly designated as *regional revolution.*[8] The most telling example is the Communist revolution in China. This type of revolution occurs if the central government is not strong enough to maintain its dominance throughout its whole territory, thus permitting a group bent on its overthrow to gain control of outlying regions. Once it does so, it may proceed with a war of conquest. Indeed, for years the Kuomintang party of Chiang Kai-shek and the Communist party of Mao Tse-tung were separate territorial states engaged in a rather conventional war against each other. The Communists eventually gained total victory and imposed their rule on almost the whole of the territory once claimed by Chiang Kai-shek's forces. This history is not without resemblance to the successful war the American colonies fought against Britain in the eighteenth century, leading to General Cornwallis's surrender to George Washington at Yorktown.

In some cases, the territorial base of a revolutionary party has been in a foreign country that is sympathetic to the revolutionary cause. Revolutionary forces in Greece, South Vietnam, Malaysia, East Pakistan, and many other countries operated, sometimes successfully and sometimes not, from bases in bordering or nearby states.

MAOIST REVOLUTION. The fifth type of violent overthrow, combining terrorism, subversion and guerrilla warfare, gained widespread attention in recent years and is frequently identified with Mao Tse-tung.[9] As we have just noted, Mao's major success was not due primarily to terrorism and guerrilla warfare. Instead, he engaged in economic, social, and political organization in order to develop a territorial base capable of supporting conventional military field operations. Some use was made of subversive, terroristic, and guerrilla techniques in acquiring this territorial base. But perhaps the main

[8] See Che Guevara, *Guerrilla Warfare* (Baltimore: Penguin Books, 1969); Eric R. Wolf, *Peasants* (Englewood Cliffs, N.J.: Prentice-Hall, Inc., 1966); and Wolf, *Peasant Wars of the Twentieth Century* (New York: Harper & Row, 1969).

[9] See Mao Tse-tung, *Chinese Communist Revolutionary Strategy, 1945–1949* (Princeton University Press, 1961); Mao Tse-tung, *On Guerrilla Warfare* (New York: Frederick A. Praeger, 1962); see also Tim Pat Coogan, *The IRA* (London: Pall Mall, 1970); and Edgar O'Ballance, *The Algerian Insurrection* (London: Faber & Faber, 1967).

reason this approach is identified with Mao has less to do with his use of it in his own struggle for power and more to do with the fact that in his writings Mao has identified himself with it, arguing that it is the proper form of revolution in so-called Third World countries.

The Maoist type of revolution requires the organization of a tightly disciplined, secret party along Leninist lines. Where the central government maintains an efficient army and police, has good control of the countryside, and enjoys strong popular support, such a secret party may remain a Leninist party waiting for natural historical forces to create the right moment. Or it may evolve into a left-wing party of nearly conventional type — such as the Communist parties of France, Italy, and Scandinavia. Under certain conditions, however, it may be possible for such a party to play an active role in making the revolution. If the central government has a weak army and police force which are not capable of controlling the far reaches of the countryside, or if it is so chronically unable to solve the problems of the society that it loses popular support, or if it lacks legitimacy — as often happens when an imperialist power rules over subject peoples of a different racial, religious, linguistic, or tribal group — under any or all of these conditions, Maoist revolution is possible.

THE PROSPECT OF REVOLUTION IN THE UNITED STATES

Much of the rather loose talk of revolution in contemporary America is confusing because the speakers rarely specify what kind of revolution they are talking about. During the height of Senator Joseph McCarthy's virulent anti-Communist campaign in the 1950s, many Americans warned of the dangers of Communist subversion. They seemed to believe that if the Communist Party of the United States continued the spread of its secret organization, one day we would wake up and find that it had "taken over." As we have seen, however, Leninist parties do not take over simply because they are organized. They can take over only if fundamental social conflicts create revolutions. No such conflicts existed in America in the 1950s. At the time, the fate of Eastern Europe seemed to give some credence to American fears, but in fact those nations had experienced revolution by invasion. The Russian army, rather than the local Communist party, was the decisive instrument of political change. Short of atomic cataclysm, revolution by invasion seems unlikely in the United States.

The great American coup has been the subject of a good bit of popular fiction, some of it in the radical press. But nothing in American historical experience suggests that we are about to experience this kind of violent change. In most of the world, coups depend upon a professional military establishment accustomed to political intervention and highly alienated from a weak and discredited civilian political leadership. We do not have such a military establishment in the United States. Indeed, one objection to the all-volunteer army was precisely that it might produce a professional army, whereas the draft insured that the rank-and-file in the military were largely civilians, temporarily in uniform. A professional army, particularly if it was recruited from the poorest or most discriminated-against segments of society, might show greater potential for military takeover.[10]

As to classical revolution, the portents are easy to dramatize precisely because we are so uncertain what they are. Nothing could be simpler than seizing upon any failure or contradiction in the system and, by the exercise of a daring imagination, exaggerating it into an early tumble onto the slippery slope leading to classical revolution. Those who commit themselves to the cause of classic revolution in the United States, however, are likely to have a long wait. In the meantime, the commitment to such a revolution, together with the discipline, self-sacrifice, secret planning, rhetoric, and imagined martyrdom that accompany such a commitment, no doubt provide certain psychological satisfactions for some members of American society. American Communist parties of various kinds—Stalinist, Trotskyite, Maoist, and groups like the tiny New Left fringe "underground movements" of recent years—have always had some following, but never a very big one.[11]

The fourth and fifth types of revolution involving terrorism, guerrilla warfare, and conquest from a territorial base have been more fashionable in recent years. Even so, no more than a few thousand people altogether have given any indication of active interest in these activities. Quite apart from the lack of willing personnel, the other requisites of successful insurrection seem to be lacking. No satisfactory territorial base is available. The black ghettoes of big cities have been suggested.[12] But the dispersion of blacks in these slums, separated by hundreds of miles of intervening white territory, make them implausible military bases. For the same reasons, it is unlikely that sufficient military resources could be gathered in these areas, even if their populations were interested in revolutions, which they do not seem to be.

Radical white movements are even more handicapped in these respects. Scattered throughout the general population, the potential revolutionaries are without a base from which they could conduct any sort of sustained operation. The hippie youth culture gives at least a series of safe havens if not a territorial base. There may be places where they could take to the hills. If they did, they would face inhospitable terrain and a surrounding population far more hostile than is healthy for guerrillas, who must rely on the local populace for food, information, and silence.

American society today contains a glint of the prerequisites for guerrilla warfare that have made it occasionally successful in other parts of the world.

[10] See Morris Janowitz, "Toward an All-Volunteer Military," *The Public Interest*, Spring 1972; and Richard F. Rosser, "American Civil-Military Relations in the 1980's," in Richard G. Head and Ervin J. Rokke, eds., *American Defense Policy* (Baltimore: Johns Hopkins University Press, 1973).

[11] See Earl Browder, *Communism in the United States* (New York: International Publishers, 1935); Theodore Draper, *The Roots of American Communism* (New York: Viking Press, 1957); and Nathan Glazer, *The Social Basis of American Communism* (New York: Harcourt Brace Jovanovich, 1961).

[12] See Robert Moss, "Urban Guerrilla Warfare," in Head and Rokke, *American Defense Policy;* Harold Jacobs, ed., *Weatherman* (New York: Ramparts, 1970); Max Stanford, "Black Guerrilla Warfare: Strategy and Tactics," *The Black Scholar* (1970); and Martin Oppenheimer, *Urban Guerrilla* (Baltimore: Penguin Books, 1970).

That glint is sufficient to make talk of revolution a heady brew for student bull sessions, the radical press, right-wing alarmists, and liberal masochists. It may also be sufficient to allow the tactical use of revolutionary rhetoric in order to achieve non-revolutionary goals. In recent years, a few terrorist organizations, such as the Symbionese Liberation Army, have been able to maintain a tenuous existence. At least for the immediate future, however, it seems unlikely that any radical movement could recruit large enough numbers or find a sufficiently secure operating base to do more than engage in sporadic acts of terrorism. Such acts of terrorism are more often a confession of lack of popular support than the first steps on the road toward revolution.

RESPONSES TO VIOLENCE

In discussing change outside the conventional channels of bargaining and persuasion, we essentially have taken the viewpoint of those who choose to employ confrontation, coercion, and/or violence. It is not difficult, however, to turn the picture around and specify what those who wish to keep politics as much as possible within conventional boundaries ought to do when facing confrontation.

A Chart of General Rules

1. Seek to maintain conventional channels of politics even during confrontations (for example, keep bargaining during strikes).
2. Maintain a high capacity for violence, but troops and police must be trained and equipped so that precisely the right amount of counterviolence can be employed to stop violence without falling into vicious cycles where terrorism breeds counter-terrorism, which in turn further encourages terrorism.
3. Be willing to use the capacity for violence to protect the normal political mechanisms and individual rights, but employ the absolute *minimum* level necessary for success.
4. Use the conventional channels of politics quickly to grant those changes which enjoy broad popular support; do not freeze or become stubborn under threats and refuse to make desirable changes simply because their proponents have become abusive or violent.

These rules are easier to state in the abstract than to follow in the real world. We have noted repeatedly that timing and control are often the crucial stumbling block of those who employ unconventional political means. The same is true for those who must respond to such tactics. Just as a "peaceful demonstration" may become a violent riot at the wrong time, "crowd control" by the police may turn into incidents that have sometimes been described as "police riots."

One of the major problems encountered in the wave of domestic violence that began in the 1960s was that, in almost every instance, the political authorities were faced with a brand new problem about which they had little or no preparation or experience. Even those who conscientiously tried to follow the rules we have just listed frequently made errors of judgment, applying too much counter-force too soon or too little too late.

SUMMARY

The American political system—like most others—accommodates a good deal of change. Indeed, responsiveness to new social, economic, and political development is the price of the system's survival. Political change normally occurs through the electoral process. Elections replace old officials with new ones, or the threat of defeat causes incumbents to change their policies. Electoral changes also are reflected in the kinds of people appointed to non-elected positions.

The pace of change in American politics is uneven. Ordinarily, it is rather slow. Sometimes major alterations occur quickly in a number of fields, as in the New Deal, the Great Society of the mid 1960s, or the Supreme Court from 1954 through 1968. Some apparent departures from conventional political strategies are so ritualized and familiar that they are really part of normal politics. Demonstrations, strikes, boycotts, and test cases are in this category. All these tactics are legal. All but the last are useful primarily for their symbolic impact and are generally most effective when used sparingly.

Symbolism is also the hallmark of illegal behavior like civil disobedience and small-scale violence. These forms of direct action are designed to influence the political system, not to overturn it. They have the capacity both to produce change and to provoke excessive reactions. The success of such tactics depends, therefore, on the restraint with which they are used and on the relative tolerance of the authorities.

Full-scale violence that aims at the destruction of existing political institutions is rare and currently unimportant in American politics. None of its various forms is likely to be effective in the foreseeable future, since none of the conditions for their successful employment exists at present.

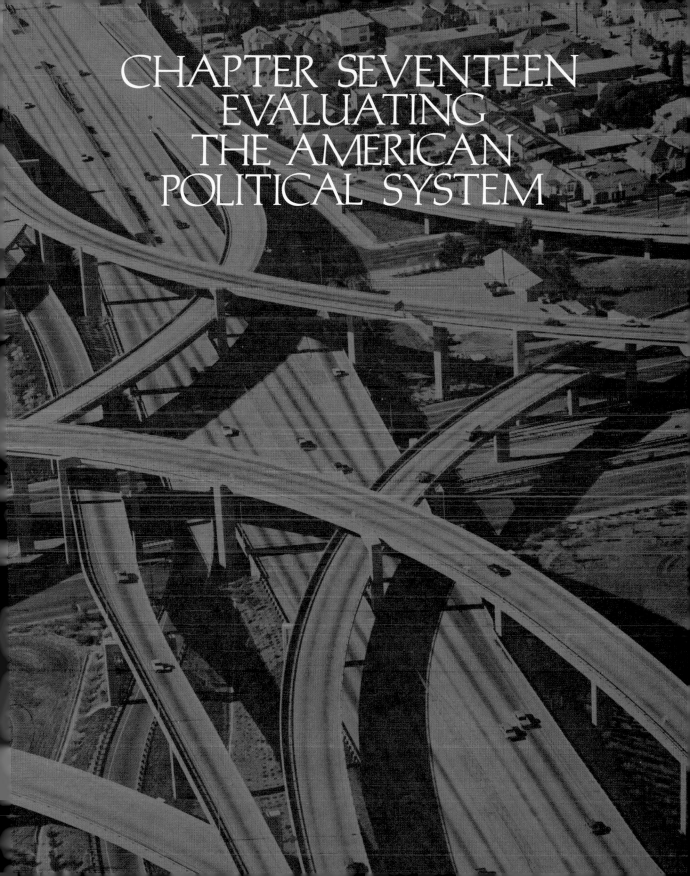

CHAPTER SEVENTEEN
EVALUATING
THE AMERICAN
POLITICAL SYSTEM

Throughout this book we have described and analyzed politics and government in the United States in terms of political institutions and processes. We have tried to avoid making judgments as to the "goodness" or "badness" of the American political system. We leave that to you.

But the task of evaluating a political system is by no means easy or straightforward. What criteria should be used? What constitutes a "good" political system as opposed to a "bad" one? By what standards does one judge the system and its policy outputs? These are questions to which there are a number of answers. And they are questions which must be understood and answered before one can begin to evaluate a political system. In this concluding chapter, we will examine the factors one should consider and the perspectives one can take in evaluating the American system of government.

STANDARD IDEOLOGICAL CRITICISMS OF AMERICAN POLITICS

It is easy to catalogue the most prominent ideological criticisms of American politics. Essentially they fall into four groups.

1. *The right-wing perspective.* Conservatives see the expansion of the government into more and more aspects of people's lives as a threat to individual freedom.[1] Big government, no matter how benevolent it may be in its intentions, is viewed by the conservatives as necessarily antithetical to individual initiative, self-development, and political liberty. From the perspective of the political right, the best government is that which governs least.

2. *The traditional left-wing, or socialist, perspective.* Here the major criticism of the American political system is that government allows economic power to remain for the most part in private hands where it is used to benefit selfish interests rather than the people as a whole.[2] The left contends that because the government does not directly control the means of production, it inevitably supports the exploitation of the poor by the rich. Leftists believe that the American political system preserves grave disparities in wealth, power, education, and social status. They are therefore suspicious of the claim that such a system can be democratic or can offer political equality in any meaningful way.

3. Between these two extremes lies *the liberal-pragmatic perspective.* Those who subscribe to this view reject the criticisms of both the right and the left. They do not believe that all government is bad government, nor do they believe that total government is necessarily the route to utopia. Rather, they tend to criticize specific failures or omissions of government in the context of immediate problems. The right denounces liberal-pragmatism as a form of "creeping socialism" because its proposals seem constantly to lead to new increments in governmental authority. The left denounces

TO WHAT EXTENT SHOULD GOVERNMENT CONCERN ITSELF WITH CONSUMER PROTECTION? *Wide World Photos*

[1] See, for example, Milton Friedman, *Capitalism and Freedom,* (Chicago: The University of Chicago Press, 1962).

[2] See, for example, James R. O'Connor, *The Fiscal Crisis of the State* (New York: St. Martin's Press, 1973).

it on the grounds that it naively or manipulatively invents palliatives that will not eliminate the fundamental social and economic injustices of capitalism, but merely will make them less painful for those who suffer the most.

4. In recent decades there has arisen a mixed bag of social critics commonly called the *New Left*.[3] The New Left is a curious and not fully articulated mixture of each of the three critical perspectives outlined above. The core of the New Left doctrine is the belief that equality can co-exist with individual freedom. The New Left asserts that political and social equality and rule by the people can be combined with free, spontaneous, individual life styles. Thus, the New Left rejects the conservative belief that equality can be purchased only at the price of total individual conformity to whatever the majority defines as right and proper. But since the New Left views big government as a dehumanizing, bureaucratized establishment, its partisans reject the traditional left's solution of governmental control of the means of production. In the New Left, then, we see combinations of the right's criticism of government as a threat to individual freedom and the left's criticisms of the inequalities in American society.

POLITICAL EVALUATION

Evaluation of American government and its policies from the perspectives of the conservative, leftist, or New Left ideologies tend to be holistic and non-specific. They lump all of government and politics together and then view the whole thing from a distance as if we were looking at American society from the outside.

Fortunately, an alternative mode of evaluation is available. It is possible for us to establish our critical viewpoint from *within* the society. We can roughly accept as "givens" the general contours of the society's values and institutions. Such a perspective need not accept everything within the society as good. But instead of lauding or condemning the *whole* system as "bourgeois," "capitalist," "materialistic," "socialistic," or whatever, it evaluates how well *each* element within the society works in the context of other aspects which we accept as given. Using this mode of evaluation, we would not conclude that "A society that tolerates poverty is unjust." Instead, we would ask, "How well does the welfare program work in breaking the poverty cycle?" Similarly, we would not conclude that "Congress is the champion of democracy and freedom." Rather, we would ask, "Does the House Rules Committee have too much power to block legislation?" Terms like *pragmatism* are commonly used to describe this mode of evaluation.

[3] See, for example, Priscilla Long, ed., *The New Left* (Boston: Extending Horizons Books, 1969); Robert P. Wolff, Barrington Moore, Jr., and Herbert Marcuse, *A Critique of Pure Tolerance* (Boston: Beacon Press, 1965); and William E. Connolly, *The Bias of Pluralism* (New York: Atherton Press, 1969).

At this level, evaluation parallels conventional social science. It consists of "if . . . then . . ." statements. *"If* you want Congress to be able to pass legislation more quickly, *then* the powers of the House Rules Committee should be reduced." Or put another way, "We predict that a reduction in the powers of the House Rules Committee will lead to the more rapid passage of legislation." In this form of evaluation, the social scientist actually engages only in empirical prediction, leaving "you" to choose whether or not it is a good thing to pass legislation more quickly.

This is not to suggest, however, that the "if . . . then" approach is free from all ideological bias. As one moves along the if . . . then chain from smaller to larger questions, empiricism tends to shade into ideology. For example, "If you want freedom, then you must avoid central economic planning," has the correct grammatical structure. It may represent a sincere effort to make an unbiased prediction. But it is obviously more an ideological statement of faith than an empirical prediction. For the most part, we have the greatest certainty in the smaller and shorter-term predictions. The more grandiose and long-term predictions a social scientist makes, the more he or she is guessing. And the more he or she is guessing, the more his or her personal values and ideology are likely to color the predictions. There is a considerable difference between "Does the Chevrolet have a more effective emission control system than the Dodge?" and "Has the internal combustion engine been a net benefit to American society?"

ILLUSTRATIONS OF POLITICAL EVALUATION

For these reasons, the easiest and most accurate evaluations are those which assume as a given the political system as a whole, and question the relationship between its various parts. For instance, it is not difficult to provide a framework for evaluating the electoral college. The student himself can use this framework on the basis of the knowledge gained from this book. (See Table 17–1.)

More difficult, however, is an evaluation of the effect these procedural changes would have on the larger segments of the political process. For instance, considering the process of selecting the President, do the procedural changes suggested yield "better" results? (We will leave the question of what is "better" to you.) We can have far less confidence in the evaluations made in Table 17–2 than we can have in those suggested in Table 17–1.

Most procedural evaluation rests on a quick, almost instinctive guess about who is going to get what if things are done one way rather than another. Those who want to weaken the House Rules Committee in order to speed up legislation are not interested in deriving some aesthetic pleasure from watching legislation move faster than a speeding bullet. They want legislation to move faster because they believe that at this particular time their side will benefit more from a fast legislative process than from a slow one. It is difficult to evaluate the intrinsic merits of fast versus slow legislative processes on a purely abstract basis. This means that in order to evaluate a proposal for speeding the legislative process, one must identify who is likely to benefit from this procedural change.

TABLE 17–1

If the existing electoral college method of choosing the President is retained . . .	*Then* the voters in the seven largest states have an advantage. (Because even a marginal victory in a state harvests *all* its electoral votes, so candidates are especially responsive to large states.)
If the electoral votes of each state are assigned to the candidates in proportion to the popular vote they receive in that state . . .	*Then* the voters in the fourteen smallest states have an advantage. (Because small states have a proportion of electoral votes somewhat in excess of their proportion of citizens in the population.)
If the President is chosen on the basis of who receives the most popular votes . . .	*Then* the voters of no particular state have an advantage.

THE GOOD OF THE PEOPLE
VERSUS THE PEOPLE'S VIEW OF THE GOOD

Procedural analysis can tell us only, "If you want policy A, then choose procedure X." But how can we analyze whether we want policy A in the first place? Here we encounter several related problems: should policies be evaluated on the basis of whether *the people* like or want them, should they be evaluated on the basis of whether *the evaluator* likes or wants them, or should they be evaluated on the basis of whether *experts* believe that they are good for the people?

TABLE 17–2

If you want to maintain the power of urban constituencies in the selection of the President . . .	*Then* retain the electoral college method of choosing the President.
If you want to increase the power of farmers in the selection of the President . . .	*Then* the electoral votes of each state should be assigned to the candidates in proportion to the popular vote they receive in that state.
If you want to increase equality and popular sovereignty . . .	*Then* the President should be chosen on the basis of who receives the most popular votes.

At first glance, it might seem that if one were committed to a democratic ideology, the answer inevitably would be that what the people want is the alternative that should be selected. However, even for the purest democrat, this answer is not always a satisfactory one. Certainly every one of us has felt at some time that a policy which does not enjoy popular support *now* would be of such great benefit to the people that they would certainly approve of it once it was in effect. Much of the talk of creative democratic leadership is a polite way of saying that the people must be pulled and hauled into things that they don't really want now but will like once they get them.

Consider the following example. If we know that contour plowing will reduce erosion and increase production, and if the farmer resists contour plowing out of sheer rural backwardness and suspicion, we may choose to "educate," "demonstrate," and "provide incentives" to the farmer to contour plow. In short, we may push him into what is "really" good for him rather than letting him go on doing what he wants. We can justify our action in terms of our democratic values by saying that after all, deep down, what he truly wants is to live better and we are helping him do that. Or we may say that his current desires are a product of ignorance. Once he is properly educated he will want the better policy.

It is this type of problem that is dealt with regularly in American politics. The survey data reported earlier in this book show that in day-to-day politics "the people" usually do not have any firm view of what they want. (See especially Chapter 5.) Even the most committed democratic leader must make decisions on the basis of what *he* thinks the public would want if they were aware of and understood the alternatives.

THE ROLE OF EXPERTS IN EVALUATION AND POLICY MAKING

At one time, many people were confident that rule by scientific experts promised a correct, impartial, scientific substitute for politics. Why should political actors bargain, struggle, and negotiate about what should be done, when experts could settle the matter in the best way for all concerned? Today, however, most observers no longer express this sort of confidence in the idea of handing over policy evaluation and decision making to the "experts."[4] In part, we are suspicious of experts because of our adherence to the notion of majority rule. Rule by experts means rule by the few over the many. Second, our suspicion of experts arises from awareness of the possibility that "expert" recommendations are translations of the expert's own personal political preferences into scientific language. This is one reason that one expert is very often contradicted by another. Conflicts among experts also reflect the fact that even in the hard sciences specialists may disagree for reasons that have nothing to do with politics. And as one progresses from, say, physics to biology to economics to social relations, the range of phenomena that is truly subject to expertise shrinks dramatically. The unhappy

[4] Guy Benveniste, *The Politics of Expertise* (Berkeley: Glendessary Press, 1972); Adam Yarmolinsky, "Ideas into Programs," *The Public Interest* (Winter 1966), pp. 70–79; Francis E. Rourke, *Bureaucracy, Politics, and Public Policy* (Boston: Little, Brown and Co., 1969).

truth is that expert knowledge is insufficient to deal with many of our most intractable problems because, with all the good will in the world, the experts often cannot offer much more than educated guesses. A sensible politician would rely on experts much more fully when deciding about bridge building than when worrying about the problems of rural slums, because construction engineers really do know a lot about how to build bridges, whereas sociologists have not yet demonstrated much impressive skill in dealing with slums. Finally, in large part our disillusion with experts has resulted from our discovery that science and technology have created almost as many serious problems as they have solved.

Despite the prevalent distrust of experts, most readers of this book probably still have a strong commitment to science and technology. Few believe that such questions as the safety of a new drug should be decided by majority vote. Rather, we think a drug should be permitted on the market only after the scientists in the Food and Drug Administration laboratories have confirmed its safety.

Frequently, conflicts in evaluation are conflicts over *which* set of experts should make the decisions rather than over *whether* experts or "the people" should make the decision. This conflict usually rests on the belief that one set of experts will make good decisions and another will make bad ones. For instance, someone may criticize current defense budgeting practices on the grounds that too much power is given to the civilian budget and management experts in the Office of the Secretary of Defense. This critic probably is saying two things. First, he is saying that the military experts representing the fighting branches are more qualified to make correct defense decisions than are the civilians. Second, he is saying that the military experts are likely to opt for higher expenditures, which he sees as a desirable policy. To offer another example, what a forest will look like ten years from now will be significantly different depending on whether control of the forest is left to an expert on timber management or an expert on wildlife preservation.

In sum, whether to use experts for making policy evaluations really raises two questions. First, should the decision be made by experts at all, or should it be made by "the people"? And second, if experts are to make the decision, *which* set of experts should be chosen to deal with the particular policy?

THE LIMITS OF GOVERNMENTAL ACTION

So far our discussion of evaluation has proceeded on the assumption that there are no bounds to political action. We have tacitly assumed that government can and should do anything and everything that seems to contribute to achieving a particular set of goals. Yet this assumption itself must be evaluated. Let us suppose that we place a high premium on eliminating crime in our society. Let us further suppose that we are reasonably sure that we can achieve this goal by implanting in the skull of every citizen an electronic device which continuously monitors his or her movements on a central locater, and by creating a sufficiently large police force, communica-

FEW AMERICANS WOULD FAVOR ELIMINATING POVERTY AT THE
EXPENSE OF INDIVIDUAL RIGHTS. OUR SENSE OF WHAT CONSTITUTES
LEGITIMATE EXERCISE OF GOVERNMENT AUTHORITY DEFINES
LIMITS ON GOVERNMENT ACTION.
Don Getsug, Photo Researchers, Rapho Division

593

EVALUATING
THE AMERICAN
POLITICAL SYSTEM

tion system, and computer facility to constantly monitor all the individual signals and intervene almost instantly when a person is in an unauthorized place. If we could do this, and if it would accomplish our goal, does this mean that we *should* do it?

Or let us suppose that we wish to eliminate poverty in Appalachia. Because of the absence of natural resources, the difficulty of the terrain, the scarcity of trained manpower, and the sparseness of educational and cultural resources, we conclude that the economic future of the southern Appalachian region is not promising. Given these conditions, the only government policy that would eliminate poverty in this region would be the following.

1. Classify as surplus 60 percent of the population of the region below the age of forty-five.
2. Require all surplus persons to move to industrial centers in the North, West, and urban South.
3. Provide surplus persons housing, education, and guaranteed family incomes for two generations at a level high enough to ensure their movement into the middle class.
4. For all Appalachian residents over forty-five, provide a guaranteed annual income slightly above the poverty level.
5. All those under forty-five who remain in Appalachia will be declared surplus if their income sinks below the level set for those over forty-five; such people will be subject to the provisions of points 2 and 3 above.
6. Those persons declared surplus but refusing relocation will be subject to imprisonment.

Assuming for the moment that these two imaginary programs would give the best promise of achieving our goals, would we want the government to undertake them? We can answer confidently that most Americans would unhesitatingly reject such proposals. But why? Because for most people, the goodness or badness of public policy is not simply or exclusively a matter of achieving specific goals. It may well be that both of our hypothetical policies will achieve the desired goals. But both involve endowing the government with enormous power over the lives and fortunes of individuals. Some people would fear that the power given the government to fight crime or poverty would also come to be used for some purpose of which they deeply disapprove, such as supressing political dissent. Others might feel that, even if they were operated with absolute benevolence, these two hypothetical programs go too far in the direction of governmental manipulation of the individual. In short, achieving particular goals is only one of the criteria used in evaluating the policy. *How* they are achieved is another criterion we cannot afford to ignore. Our sense of what constitutes fitting exercises of governmental authority is one of the most important factors limiting government action.

Another factor limiting governmental action is the sheer lack of capacity. No one may know how to solve a given problem. At the moment, for example, even a massive program of federal expenditure on improving prisons would probably do little to break the cycle of imprisonment, release, and reimprisonment that so many convicts go through. This is simply because no one really knows how to reform prisoners effectively. In other instances, the capacity may exist somewhere in the society, but it may be impossible to vest it in the government. Perhaps we believe that talented artists should be subsidized so they can devote all of their time to creative work. But *untalented* artists probably should not be subsidized. Yet is it possible to create a federal art commission that we would trust to make decisions as to which aspiring artists are talented enough to receive a subsidy and which are not?

In addition to our desire to limit the government's power and its lack of capacity, a third factor tends to restrict further the scope of government. As we have seen, one of the principal tasks of government is the resolution, amelioration, and/or channeling of conflict.[5] Even when a governmental solution to a social problem seems possible, it may generate so much political conflict that it cannot be undertaken. It is in this sense that politics is sometimes defined as *the art of the possible.* One of the first things that surprises novice social and political reformers is how often their "obviously right" solutions appear to be "obviously wrong" to others who will fight against them.

Whether conflict over policies arises from the clash of selfish interests or from genuine differences of opinion over what would best serve the public interest, the presence of conflict itself becomes a limiting factor. It is not enough to demonstrate that a problem exists and that a workable government solution is available. It is also necessary to achieve at least some minimum level of consent for the solution. This need for consent is not only one of the pragmatic needs of our particular processes—the need to get votes in Congress and elsewhere. It is also a response to a broader social need to minimize political conflict. If "good" policies threaten to create so much social conflict that the society may break apart in ways that would drastically diminish the quality of day-to-day life, then only an unusually intense ideologue would believe the policies are worth having, no matter how well they solve some particular social problem.

In an open society like ours, such imposed solutions are not even likely to accomplish the purpose for which they were intended. Prohibition of alcoholic beverages—"the noble experiment"—is the best known example of a

---

[5] See Robert A. Dahl, *Pluralist Democracy in the United States: Conflict and Consent* (Chicago: Rand McNally and Company, 1967), Chaps. 11 and 13; and *Modern Political Analysis,* 2nd ed. (Englewood Cliffs, N.J.: Prentice-Hall, Inc., 1970), Chap. 6.

policy that failed because it could not be enforced short of a police state. More recently, the collapse of police efforts to enforce the laws against marijuana testifies to the need for a minimal level of consent.

THE ROLE OF POWER, CAPACITY, AND CONSENT IN POLICY EVALUATION

Frequently power, capacity, and consent are closely interlocking factors in the evaluation of governmental performance. There is a vast difference between whether a government program is "best" in some ultimate utopian sense and whether it is good given the need to gain consent, the limits of human capacity, and the desire to limit governmental power.

Let us reconsider the earlier example of prison reform. Sociologists or psychologists might determine that prisons are hopeless as places for achieving social reform. More genuine rehabilitation might occur simply by turning all convicted criminals back onto the street with $200 a week in their pockets. Alternatively, the same experts might conclude that if imprisonment were going to continue, then all sentences should be for indefinite periods. The prisoner would stay in jail until professionals decided he was ready for release.

At this point we may confront the brute fact that most citizens simply will not consent to turning dope peddlers, rapists, and murderers loose as fast as the police catch them. Proposals to abolish incarceration completely have little chance of popular acceptance. This immediately eliminates the first of our "best" solutions to the problem.

So we now turn to our next "best" alternative—indefinite sentencing. This "reform" has been introduced in a number of states. However, some prisoners complain that under indefinite sentencing they become absolutely helpless pawns in the hands of prison counselors and psychologists, parole boards, and probation officers. A person serving four years for armed robbery is in a curious way independent. He is a criminal, but he serves the allotted time and leaves as an ex-criminal. But a person who is incarcerated under the rationale that he is sick and will be released only when he is well becomes totally dependent on those who make the judgment as to when he is well. Often these judgments are based on whether a prisoner is docile or surly, cooperative or uncooperative. Thus, an armed robber who is a docile inmate may be released after two years while a surly and uncooperative armed robber may not be paroled for eight years. In effect, the second inmate is being sentenced to six years in prison for being surly, which is certainly not a crime. Because of this possibility, many people now feel that indeterminate sentencing is a "reform" that gives officials too much power over convicts. The uncertainty of indeterminate sentences tends to make prisoners more restless.

To these factors of consent and power, we now add capacity. No one knows how to reform criminals. We know that big prisons do not work, and we are not sure that anything else will help. Turning prisoners back onto the street works for some and not for others. Most people imprisoned for serious crimes already have been turned back on the streets previously. We simply do not know how to solve this problem.

Adding all these factors together, we might come up with the following evaluative analysis. In an absolute sense, prisons are absurd. They are expensive and cruel ways of holding people who will be in no better (and probably worse) shape to face life when they are released. But simply releasing criminals as fast as we catch them is unacceptable to non-criminals. On the other hand, it is desirable to protect some of the convict's rights from prison officials. Accordingly, the "best" policy for the moment might be a compromise involving the creation of many small local prisons (to satisfy the general public), the institution of halfway house programs (to save as many criminals as possible from imprisonment), and the use of fixed sentences of moderate length (to protect the rights of criminals).

"POLITICS" AS A CORRECTIVE IN POLITICAL EVALUATION

As the example of prison reform indicates, there is often a huge gap between the sweeping proposals put forward to achieve racial equality, the end of poverty, the reduction of crime, the restoration of urban centers, or the preservation of the natural environment, and the actual performance of the government. Most grand solutions will adversely affect the interests of some groups, who will understandably demand modification and compensation. A policy issue may appear to be simple in a news release or in a magazine article. It becomes much more complicated as it is subjected to genuine differences of opinion about specific details and the bargaining that is necessary to deal with those differences of opinion.

The promoters of great plans are often willing to give government practically unlimited powers in their own field, while such powers in another field would terrify them. For example, the very persons who condemn the "military-industrial complex" or see signs of police repression everywhere often blithely propose government ecological programs which would give bureaucrats enormous power to control how individuals can use air, land, and water. Naturally, they feel that environmental bureaucrats will be good bureaucrats, as opposed to the bad bureaucrats in the Defense Department. Others who are not so passionately concerned with saving every last tree — for instance, people who earn a living as loggers — may have their doubts about the total benevolence of the environmental bureaucrats.

The simple and obvious solution to many problems often is to give the government vast powers to "totally fix" things immediately. Yet an evaluation of any new program that stops with the "plan" is hopelessly incomplete. Very often a sweeping solution may look good on paper. But its implementation may raise so many problems of conflict, power, and capacity that it is not really a good solution. Sometimes we may conclude that political considerations prevent a good policy from being implemented. But just as frequently we will discover that a proposal that cannot survive the give-and-take of politics is not such a good proposal after all. For politics often consists of bringing many evaluations from many different viewpoints together and asking just how the grand plan will work out on a day to day basis for the many different people involved. This kind of detailed evaluation by those persons most directly concerned may prove to be a better evaluation than has been done by whoever first proposed a new policy.

COMPARATIVE ANALYSIS AS A MODE OF POLITICAL EVALUATION

One aid to the evaluation of the relative merits of various practical and attainable policies and procedures is comparative analysis.[6] For example, some light—although there are differing opinions on how much—is shed on the comparative value of capitalism and communism by comparing the United States and the Soviet Union. Similarly, we can learn something about the level of welfare and economic regulation that is compatible with a basically capitalistic system by comparing the United States and Sweden. Such evaluations run well beyond the scope of this book, but they are suggested as a way of gaining some perspective on the American political system.

In recent years, some people have concluded that the United States is a sick society. The use of comparative analysis gives more meaning to this evaluation by helping us either corroborate or discredit it. In an attempt to understand this evaluation, Benjamin F. Wright offers the following comparisons:

> Is today's society less well—or sicker—than that of 40 years ago, when unemployment was far beyond anything this generation has known? Or sick as compared with 140 years ago, when slavery existed in about a third of the country, when labor unions were conspiracies in the eyes of the law, when men, women, and children worked 14 hour days in mills and factories—until laid off or discarded? Where would one find a well country? In the Communist bloc? In Africa, the Middle East, or South America? Even the small homogeneous countries of Western Europe have critical problems.[7]

The more specific a comparison is, the more immediate value it has. For instance, proponents and opponents of active government involvement in the provision of health care frequently compare the British health plan with the system of private medical care in the United States. Some data suggest that the British manage to provide a higher level of care to a broader range of the population than we do. The United States ranks twentieth out of more than one hundred nations in the world in its rate of infant mortality.

[6] Dahl, *Modern Political Analysis*, Chaps. 4 and 5.
[7] Benjamin F. Wright, review of *The Idea of Fraternity in America*, by Wilson Carey McWilliams, *Journal of Politics*, 36 (August 1974), 824–25.

The United Kingdom ranks eleventh. It is also important to note that the infant mortality rates in the two countries are not very far apart, and in no sense compare with the very high levels in Asia, Africa, and most of Latin America. Although the British system may give more people better medical attention than does the American system, only about 5,000 out of every million Britons are enrolled in colleges or universities. In the United States the ratio is about 28,000 per million.[8] Comparison, then, allows us to look at various priority and distribution mixes. The British mix a lot of medicine with a little higher education. We mix less medicine with a great deal of education. The comparison, of course, does not tell us which mix is better, but it does permit us to evaluate the system in an informed and meaningful way.

Comparative evaluation also can serve as a check on our propensities toward absolute or utopian evaluation. Before we conclude that any feature of American politics is good or bad, it is useful to see if any other nation has been doing better or worse, and at what costs. For instance, the often heard call for a more disciplined and centralized two-party system that will give American voters a real choice between alternative policies may be tested against the British experience of strongly disciplined parties. It is clear that this British party discipline has reduced the independent lawmaking power of Parliament nearly to zero. It is not clear, however, that it has given the British voter any greater control over his own destiny than the American voter has had. Nor is it clear that it has contributed to effective leadership geared to solving Britain's social and economic problems.[9]

WHAT IS THE OPTIMUM BALANCE BETWEEN PROVISION OF EDUCATION AND OF HEALTH CARE IN THE UNITED STATES? *Bruce Roberts, Photo Researchers, Rapho Division*

Turning to another example, we note that many people have made blithely optimistic proposals for a multi-linguistic American society in which Mexican-American and Puerto Rican citizens would be encouraged to continue speaking Spanish in addition to learning English. These proposals must be checked against the startling failure of similiar systems in most countries that have tried to maintain two or more national languages. Even such stable, prosperous, and democratic nations as Canada and Belgium continue to be wracked by language conflicts. Around the world, official minority languages seem to be highly correlated with low economic status and political discontent. This casts grave doubts on what appears to be the liberal and benevolent policy of encouraging bilingualism. Only in Switzerland has the linguistic problem been solved with relative satisfaction. But the situation in Switzerland is so historically and geographically peculiar that it can hardly be used as a model for the United States.

This last point raises the greatest difficulty of comparative evaluation. Nations are, of course, very different from one another. Each is so much a

[8] Charles L. Taylor and Michael C. Hudson, *World Handbook of Social Indicators,* 2nd ed. (New Haven: Yale University Press, 1972), pp. 253, 229.

[9] Committee on Political Parties of the American Political Science Association, "Toward a More Responsible Two-Party System," *American Political Science Review,* 44, Supplement (September 1950); Austin Ranney, *The Doctrine of Responsible Party Government* (Urbana: University of Illinois Press, 1962); and Kenneth N. Waltz, *Foreign Policy and Democratic Politics* (Boston: Little, Brown and Co., 1967).

product of its own peculiar history and culture that one can never be certain if a procedure or policy which is successful in one country will work in another. A proposal will not necessarily be successful in America because it worked in Australia. Conversely, it will not necessarily be unsuccessful here because it did not work in France. The secret ballot, which is a device originally imported into this country from Australia, has turned out to be an important electoral improvement in the United States. The use of proportional representation, in contrast to the winner-take-all procedure used in most American elections, is frequently blamed for many of the persistent ills of the French body politic. Yet proportional representation seems to have worked moderately well in the few American municipalities that have tried it. These examples illustrate the difficulty of drawing unambiguous conclusions from comparative analysis.

Because we have a federal system in which many local governments enjoy some degree of autonomy, comparison need not be confined to foreign countries. We may conclude that the state of Washington manages its forests better than the U.S. Forest Service manages its forests. This conclusion can be tested by comparing two forests in the state of Washington, one run by the federal government and the other by the state government. The overlapping and parallelism of federal and state activities often provide fertile ground for comparative evaluations. Many federal programs have been modeled on earlier state or local experience, and vice versa. Certainly if we notice that the city of Omaha collects garbage once a week at a cost of 75¢ per house per week while Kansas City provides the same service at a cost of $3.50, our critical senses are likely to perk up.

As an evaluative tool, comparative analysis has both its radical and conservative sides. Comparison sometimes reveals that everyone has about the same problem (for example, air pollution) and that no one seems to be doing much better at solving it than we are. Or if they are solving the problem, it may be because they are paying more attention to *its* solution, while giving less attention to some other important problems on which we are doing better. Thus, sometimes comparison deflates abstract, utopian criticism. On the other hand, comparison can be a dynamic technique that fuels demands for change and provides information about how to do a better job. If a British small businessman is not driven into bankruptcy by his hospital bills, why should an American be? If the courts in Minneapolis are trying cases within six months, why should people have to wait two-and-a-half years in Memphis? Why shouldn't the infant mortality rate in the United States be lower than that of any other countries? Comparison frequently will reveal that something actually *can* be done because someone else has done it.

EVALUATION IN TERMS OF LEGITIMACY

In the last analysis, political evaluation may come down to the question of whether or not a political system enjoys the support of the people. Central to the analysis of any government is the question, "To what extent do the people voluntarily obey the decisions of the government because they believe they ought to obey them?'' In other words, *to what extent do the people believe their government is acting legitimately?*

As in the other areas of evaluation, we need to distinguish between procedures and policies. Does government act legitimately when it follows accepted procedures in reaching and carrying out a policy, or when the policy itself is acceptable? Let us suppose the governor of Alaska and the chairman of the Interstate Commerce Commission secretly met in a San Diego hotel room and passed a law limiting aircraft noise. No one would obey such a law because this is not the procedure that we accept for making laws. On the other hand, if the President and Congress followed to the letter every accepted procedural rule, and passed a law ordering the immediate execution of all redheaded women, we still would not voluntarily obey. We would deny the legitimacy of the first law on procedural grounds and of the second law because the substance of the policy offended us.

Judgments about legitimacy are somewhat different than judgments about the goodness or badness of a policy. For example, President Ford's decision to pardon former President Nixon for any crimes committed while in office was generally accepted as a legitimate exercise of presidential power. But most Americans also disputed the wisdom, merit, and morality of Ford's action. Similarly, congressional procedures for handling legislation may leave much to be desired, but most of us would still consider the laws passed under the current rules as legitimate. Admittedly, this is all a question of degree. The more intensely we dislike a policy, the less likely we are to acknowledge its legitimacy.

So far we have considered the legitimacy of a single act or policy. What if the question is, "Is the government itself or the entire political system legitimate?" A government that commits a single illegitimate act does not necessarily lose its legitimacy. (Otherwise, there would be no legitimate governments!) A few Americans who saw our involvement in Vietnam as a war crime concluded from this that the political system as a whole was beyond redemption. Many others, however, while denying the legitimacy— or the wisdom—of the government's Vietnam policy, nevertheless continued to recognize it as the legitimate government of the United States, worthy of their support on most issues. We generally assume that the more a government's actions are judged illegitimate by more of its citizens, the greater the likelihood that both the government and the political system it embodies will themselves be viewed as illegitimate.

MOST AMERICANS
WERE PLEASED TO
SEE THE END OF U.S.
COMMITMENT IN
SOUTHEAST ASIA.
Wide World Photos

One test of legitimacy—though admittedly a very crude one—is the degree of coercion the government must employ to achieve obedience. The more coercion, the less legitimacy. The extreme case is government by an occupation army. The citizens of the occupied country may feel no other motivation to obey than the risk of a firing squad. At the other extreme one can conceive of a state in which all of the citizens voluntarily obey all of the government's directives all of the time. Human experience never has come close to the second extreme. All too often, unfortunately, we have seen examples of the first extreme.

How can one distinguish between an act that challenges the government's legitimacy and an act which is simply criminal? Disobeying a law is not necessarily the same thing as denying its legitimacy. Most professional burglars do not deny the legitimacy of the institution of private property and the laws which maintain it. Indeed, most of the people we call criminals recognize the legitimacy of the laws they break. There are, however, some striking exceptions. Self-proclaimed revolutionaries who rob banks often claim that they engage in such activities both as a fund-raising device and as a challenge to the legitimacy of our legal system based on the institution of private property. If caught, they will be defined as ordinary criminals by the courts, which try them for bank robbery, although they define themselves as revolutionaries whose "criminal" act was part and parcel of their denial of the government's legitimacy.

When crime is concentrated in certain ethnic neighborhoods, it is tempting to attribute the crime rate to the community's denial of the government's legitimacy. It also is tempting for criminals to promote themselves to the more respected status of revolutionaries, particularly after the fact, if they are caught. They prefer to portray themselves as "political prisoners" in revolt against "capitalist law" rather than as unlucky bank robbers. Nearly every body of folklore has its bandit promoted to political crusader beginning with Robin Hood.

It is not easy to unravel these claims and determine when crime in fact represents a withdrawal of legitimacy. When one black man hits another black man over the head and takes twelve dollars from his wallet, it seems more probable that he is expressing his desire for a quick twelve dollars than his contempt for the white man's law. But when we observe that crime rates in black ghetto neighborhoods are twice the level of those in white neighborhoods, we certainly seem to be seeing a breakdown in voluntary obedience to law beyond anything that can be accounted for simply in terms of individual pathology. It simply may be that the depressed economic levels of black ghettos make crime necessary for survival. But suppose ghetto crime levels remain dramatically above average levels even when black ghettos are compared with non-black areas that are socially and economically the same? One begins to suspect that the ghetto residents in fact reject the legitimacy of the laws and those who make and enforce them. In short, there seems to be a point at which the level of crime becomes so high as to denote some loss of legitimacy for the government.[10] However, we do not know what that point is.

EVALUATING THE LEGITIMACY OF THE AMERICAN POLITICAL SYSTEM

How can we go about discovering to what extent the American people see their government as legitimate? Two approaches have been taken. The

[10] David O. Sears and John B. McConahay, *The Politics of Violence* (Boston: Houghton Mifflin Company, 1973).

first is a superficial one and measures the level of citizens' political disaffection, not whether they view the *political system* as illegitimate. Evidence of growing disaffection toward the government since 1964 is quite dramatic. The data are summarized in Table 17–3.

Over the course of the eight years from 1964 to 1972 there were significant increases in the percentage of the population that distrusted the government, saw its leaders as dishonest and incompetent, and viewed the government as wasting money and working for the benefit of a few big interests. In 1972, approximately 33 percent of the population could be classified as cynical, compared to 16 percent in 1964. In 1972, 33 percent could be defined as "trusting," compared to 57 percent in 1964. The remaining people were neutral.

There are a number of reasons for this disaffection. As one might expect, socio economic factors influence the level of disaffection. Blacks are more cynical than whites, the poor more cynical than middle and high income groups, the young more cynical than the old, and those with a grade school or high school education more cynical than those with some college or a college degree. The only substantial difference, however, is between blacks and whites.[11]

Several specific sources of increased disaffection can be identified. One is the war in Vietnam. Those people who favored *either* withdrawal *or* escalation were more cynical than those who liked the policy being pursued at the time—limited military operations combined with negotiations for a settlement. Race relations are a second source of cynicism. As with the Vietnam war, those at the two extremes in their policy preferences were the most cynical, whereas people who favored moderate policies were the least. Both those who wanted much more government help for minority groups and those who said that minorities should look out for themselves were far more hostile to the government and to politicians. Similarly, people who thought that the civil rights movement was pushing too fast *and* those who thought that it was not going fast enough were more cynical than those who thought that the movement's pace was about right.[12]

Another explanation for rising disaffection seems to be an increase in expectations. Americans want more from their government than they used to. New needs and standards of comfort are developed. The more new social policies the government enacts, the more social policies people expect. This explains why, as Aaron Wildavsky puts it, "We are all, in fact, doing better and feeling worse." The reason, he argues, is that we have generated "policy demands that impose burdens on government which no government can meet."[13] Those Americans who look to the government for solutions to their

"MY CONFIDENCE IN THE SYSTEM IS RESTORED. I REALLY WAS GUILTY."
Drawing by Joseph Farris © 1975 The New Yorker Magazine, Inc.

[11] The findings on political dissatisfaction presented here are from Jack Citrin, *Political Disaffection in America* (Englewood Cliffs, N.J.: Prentice-Hall, Inc., 1976), Chap. 3.

[12] Arthur H. Miller, "Political Issues and Trust in Government: 1964–1970," *American Political Science Review,* 68 (September 1974), 951-72.

[13] Aaron Wildavsky, "Government and the People," *Commentary,* August 1973, p. 25. See also Ben J. Wattenberg, *The Real America* (Garden City, N.Y.: Doubleday & Company, Inc., 1974).

TABLE 17-3

INCREASING POLITICAL DISAFFECTION

	PERCENT AGREEING	
	1964	1972
Quite a few political leaders are crooked	29	35
The government wastes a lot of money	46	62
The government is run by a few big interests	29	58
Quite a few political leaders are incompetent	27	47
The government can be trusted to do what is right only some of the time	22	51

Source: Jack Citrin, *Political Disaffection in America* (Englewood Cliffs, N.J.: Prentice-Hall, Inc., 1976), Chapter 3.

problems are more cynical than are those who do not believe that the solutions for all of society's ills lie in government action.[14]

Although expressions of dissatisfaction with the government are widespread and have increased since 1964, does this mean that the legitimacy of the American government is in jeopardy? Probably not. There is a lot of evidence indicating widespread *satisfaction* with American political institutions. In 1972, 86 percent of the adult population said they were "proud of many things about our form of government," and only 15 percent said "big changes" were needed in it. Even of those whom we have described as cynical, 75 percent were proud of many things about our form of government, and only 25 percent thought "big changes" were needed. What is more, those who were cynical were nearly as active in politics as those who were not.[15] These data are incompatible with any conclusion that there has been a drastic decline in the loyalty of Americans to the existing political system.

Other evidence reveals broad satisfaction with life in America, both in general and with respect to the specific major aspects of personal experience. In 1974, only 4 percent of the American adult population, when surveyed by the Gallup Poll, gave the United States an unfavorable rating. In 1973, 71 percent said they were satisfied with their standard of living, 61 percent were satisfied with their children's education, and 74 percent were satisfied with their housing situation. Among those who worked, 90 percent were satisfied with their jobs. This general acceptance of American life is also reflected in the fact that only 11 percent of the adult population said that if they were free to do so, they would like to settle in another country. And of these 11 percent, most would settle in Australia, Canada, and Great Britain—

---

[14] Richard A. Brody and Paul M. Sniderman, "Personal Problems and Public Support," unpublished paper prepared for the Conference on Political Alienation, Iowa City, Iowa, 1975.
[15] Citrin, *Political Disaffection in America*, Chap. 3.

countries with political systems very similar to that of the United States. A comparative analysis of the responses by citizens in other countries reveals the relatively high level of satisfaction among Americans. Forty-one percent of British respondents said they would like to settle in another country; in West Germany, 27 percent, and 18 percent in Finland. All in all, the general level of satisfaction with American life is high, particularly when compared with the levels in other western nations.[16]

A number of political scientists are currently wrestling with the problem of devising indicators which will measure alienation from the political system.[17] At present, such measures are not available. We can infer from existing data, however, that despite widespread expressions of dissatisfaction with the American government and its leaders, the American political system remains legitimate to the vast majority of its citizens.

EVALUATION IN TERMS OF CONFLICT AND ITS RESOLUTION

In our discussion of legitimacy, we were concerned with the attitudes of individuals toward government. A second major way of evaluating a political system is by ascertaining the extent to which the system succeeds in ameliorating or resolving conflict between individuals and groups in the society. In every society, most conflict is handled by face-to-face, individual negotiation, or through the family, school, church, or the thousands of other formal and informal groups to which individuals belong.

The government provides important additional channels for resolving conflict. Perhaps the simplest are the civil courts. If two people find themselves in a dispute over property or money, they may sue one another and use the court's decision as a means of resolving and terminating their dispute. Administrative agencies also play a major role in dispute settlement. When one person wishes to build a twenty-story apartment house on his land while a neighbor claims that such a construction will block his view, a zoning board may have the final say in their quarrel.

In this book we often have treated legislation as a problem-solving activity—a search by the government for the best solutions to social problems. But it is also possible to look at legislation in terms of conflict resolution. When the railroad and trucking industries find themselves in conflict, a new national transportation law may be passed to settle their differences. Much of the legislation enacted each year is designed to resolve the conflicting interests of various social and economic groups—lumbermen and conservationists, management and labor, manufacturer and consumer. The complete list would be very long.

Although legislation and other government policies are a means for

---

[16] *Gallup Opinion Index,* February, 1974, pp. 11–13; *The Gallup Poll* release, December 6, 1973; Graham L. Staines et al., "Is Worker Discontent Rising?" *Economic Outlook U.S.A.,* 1 (Summer 1974), 11; and *Gallup Opinion Index,* May 1971, pp. 24–26.

[17] Jack Citrin et al., "Personal and Political Sources of Political Alienation," *British Journal of Political Science,* 5 (1975), 1–31.

resolving conflict, they also can generate conflict. Often conflict arises over what the government's policy should be. A proposal for new legislation to reduce labor-management tensions may touch off a political battle between unions and industry about what the new law should look like. Very frequently politicians conclude that trying to pass and enforce a new law will create more conflict than existed before. Thus, in evaluating whether a political system has done too little, too much, or just the right amount in solving society's problems, one must ask whether it has held conflict to tolerable levels. As we emphasized in our discussion of consent earlier, often we must ask whether the ideal solution to some problem has been avoided out of sheer stupidity and selfishness, or because the contemplated change would generate intolerably high levels of conflict. For instance, is the busing of school children a good solution to the problem of segregation if opposition to busing is so intense that the end result is an increase in racial conflicts?

It would be a mistake, however, to assume that the government that rules over the society exhibiting the least conflict is necessarily the best government. Disagreement is inherent in human nature. It arises from individual differences in occupation, wealth, location, religion, ability, taste, temperament, race, opinion, and other unavoidable human characteristics. Moreover, a certain level of dynamism, creativity, and change is beneficial, and when a society is changing there is bound to be conflict. Indeed, we may suspect that a society with a very low level of conflict is suffering from stagnation or oppression.

The crucial question, then, concerns the political system's record in accommodating disagreements without stifling them. Does it facilitate the expression and resolution of conflict rather than imposing a lockstep conformity or fanning the flames of domestic violence and hatred? The world has seen many societies torn apart by relentless conflict between factions that could not find peaceful means of resolving their differences. And we have had all too many political systems where every aspect of personal life is organized in government-controlled groups, where disputes are defined as sabotage or treason, and the secret police make sure that conflict never surfaces.

The final complication involves the question of how much and what kinds of conflict should be handled through political channels. Traditional China, for instance, had a great many laws about the relation of children to their parents. But Mandarin courts were so expensive and handed out such stiff penalties that family conflicts were almost always settled in the family or in the village; they were almost never brought to the government. For many centuries, this approach seemed to provide successful resolution of family quarrels. In the American Southwest, conflicts over water and grazing land sometimes erupted into range wars. The coming of "law and order" and the transfer of such disputes into the court were a major part of the "growing up" of the Southwest.

In different areas we want conflict politicized to different degrees. For example, the National Labor Relations Board was created as a governmental means of resolving labor-management conflicts. The NLRB is an independent regulatory commission, partially insulated from day-to-day political influence. It presides over labor-management bargaining without imposing agreements on the bargainers. In this way, labor-management disputes are brought part way, but not all the way, into governmental channels. On the other hand, there are some areas where it seems best *not* to handle conflict through political channels. Religion is one of these areas. The "no establishment clause" of the Constitution was in part intended as a guarantee of religious freedom. But more important, it was grounded in the Founding Fathers' desire to avoid the sort of politicization of religious conflict that had led to the bloody European religious wars of the seventeenth century. Recent experiences in Ireland, the Middle East, and the Indian subcontinent continue to indicate that religion and politics are likely to be a dangerous mixture.

Here we can offer a very obvious example of evaluation in terms of conflict and its resolution. Parochial schools in America are in desperate need of money. If the 7 percent of American children who attend parochial schools were transferred into the public schools, enormous new burdens on public education would result, particularly in some of our most hard-pressed eastern and midwestern urban centers. Obviously, it is not in the national interest for the educational quality of schools handling a substantial portion of our children to deteriorate further.

Seen simply from the problem-solving perspective, the best solution would be federal aid to parochial schools. From the point of view of conflict resolution, however, it is not so easy to endorse general federal aid to parochial schools. There has been little explicit conflict between Catholics and Protestants in this country, because religious issues that divide Catholics and Protestants have been rare and indirect. Unrestricted government aid to parochial schools would bring religious conflicts out into the open, and into the electoral arena. Catholic versus Protestant electoral confrontations are a sight that most of us wish to avoid. Thus, while recognizing the plight of Catholic education, many political leaders—Protestant and Catholic alike—have sought to sidetrack parochial school aid proposals or to package them with other aid provisions (such as proposals to provide more science labs to all schools). In this way the religious question is camouflaged in order to prevent the politicization of religious conflict.

In sum, any thorough evaluation of political performance must take into account how well the political system works in ameliorating or resolving social conflict. Such an evaluation should analyze the society's potential for disunity, including examination of its social, ethnic, and economic diversity. To what extent are disputes among different blocs contained and controlled? Are different socioeconomic groups at each others' throats? Are societal conflicts settled peacefully, or by violence?

EVALUATION IN TERMS OF EQUALITY

As we saw in Chapter 4, there is significant ideological disagreement over the meaning of equality. At one extreme, there are those for whom equality means nothing more than that people with equal amounts of talent, property, wisdom, or inherited status should be treated equally. This definition of equality carries with it the recognition that these qualities are not equally distributed among the population as a whole. At the other extreme are the absolute egalitarians who see equality as a system in which each person has and does exactly what the next person has and does. In between there is an infinite number of intermediate ideological positions. Some wave the banner of "equality of opportunity."

Another approach emphasizes the difference between equality in different areas of life: economic, social, and political. Some people taking this tack think that if one form of equality is assured—say, economic equality—the other forms of equality naturally will follow. Others argue that the only form of equality that should be guaranteed is political rights like voting and free speech. The rest, they argue, should be left to individual ability, initiative, and taste. The government's role should be limited to providing an absolute minimum level of subsistence to people who literally cannot care for themselves and their children.

Probably the greatest ideological split with regard to equality concerns the relationship between diversity and equality. Even the most extreme egalitarian does not call for a world in which every person is the same as every other in thought, action, appearance, and feelings. The egalitarian tends to believe that people can be equal and still be spontaneous, creative, and thus different from one another. Those who are suspicious of equality are likely to believe that it can be attained only by imposing a flat uniformity on all individuals. They argue that whatever the biological or social causes, inequalities of talent, taste, skill, ambition, and energy are so deeply embedded in *all* societies that meaningful levels of equality could be achieved only by the repressive leveling of all individuals to a lowest common denominator. The anti-egalitarian is likely to feel that equality and mediocrity go hand in hand.

In a related argument, the anti-egalitarian is likely to point out that superior technical, economic, and cultural attainments can be achieved only through the division of labor, and that such a division necessarily entails inequality. Some people can specialize in brain surgery only if others specialize in mopping up the operating room. Inequalities of all sorts inevitably will arise between the surgeon and the orderly. To all this, the egalitarian might reply that we are too much the prisoners of past social structures. Why should the surgeon make more money than the orderly? Like most creative people, the brilliant surgeon undoubtedly finds his work challenging, exciting, and intrinsically rewarding. The best surgeons would probably want to be surgeons even if they didn't get paid for it, just as many artists now struggle at their craft through their whole lives without ever making a living at it. But the orderly probably does not get this kind of intrinsic reward from his work. Perhaps he should be compensated for the drudgery of his work by getting *more* money. This argument may sound perverse, but it should indicate that the question of equality and inequality is far more complex than is commonly supposed.

In evaluating any existing political system, the result will necessarily

WHAT KINDS OF
EQUALITY — POLITI-
CAL, ECONOMIC,
SOCIAL — SHOULD
GOVERNMENT AT-
TEMPT TO ENSURE?
*Nancy M. Hamilton,
Photo Researchers; Ray
Ellis, Photo Researchers,
Rapho Division*

depend in part upon where the evaluator falls along this ideological spec-trum. What is "equal enough" or "as equal as can be expected" to one per-son may appear grossly unequal to another. Even strictly in terms of politi-cal equality, the American picture is mixed. We have achieved equality in voting. But money still plays an extremely important role in politics. Some-times movements toward greater equality in one area may undercut equality in another. For example, the growth of presidential primaries has increased the influence of rank-and-file voters on presidential nominations. Primary campaigns require additional contributions, however. Prospective candi-dates can rarely throw their hats in the primary ring unless they have first found some financial backing. Attempts to reduce the influence of such backers by limiting campaign contributions help well-known incumbent candidates at the expense of aspiring rivals.

Over and above all other pressures toward inequality in American politics is the division of political labor. As long as some people are willing to spend twenty-four hours a day on politics while most are unwilling to devote twenty-four minutes a month, the system is bound to produce great dis-parities in political power. Whether a sufficient number of factors have been built into the political system to reduce this inequality to acceptable levels is a central question of political evaluation.

At this point many critics, particularly on the left, would argue that the separation we have been making between political and socio economic equality is naive. They would insist that any society with great disparities of wealth and social status inevitably will reflect those disparities in the distribution of political power. If it is indeed true that economic and social inequality necessarily breed political inequality, two evaluative conclusions may follow. Those who see considerable economic and social inequality as either inevitable, necessary, or desirable will be more willing to accept greater political inequality. Those who seek social and economic equality will see political inequality as one of the evils of a hierarchical society.

The mainstream of American thought has always insisted, however, that egalitarian, democratic politics can exist side by side with great disparities in wealth. Indeed, many would maintain that it is precisely because we have economic inequality that we need political equality to protect the majority from the abuse of the wealthy. (This is a highly abstract argument, of course. As we have seen in Chapters 5 and 7, rich people are no more united on political issues than anyone else, and their campaign contributions are given to candidates of all political persuasions.) The melange of democracy, cap-italism, individualism, socialism, and welfare which is America's current working ideology is certainly built on this view. We seek to preserve in-dividual freedom and creativity by severely limiting the intervention of government in the economy and society. At the same time, the exploitation, suffering, and abuse of power that might arise from disparities in wealth are to be ameliorated or eliminated by a relatively egalitarian political system. Anti-trust laws, regulatory commissions, and free public education are examples of governmental policies designed to curb economic power and help equalize opportunity.

Thus, the evaluator who has reached a conclusion about how egalitarian our political system is has not finished. He or she is left with the question: Has the political system intervened sufficiently to ensure the *right degree* of limitation on economic and social inequality? The controversy that typically erupts over "redistribution" policies is a question of just this sort of evaluation. What should the government do to ensure that the poor get richer and the rich get poorer? Do we care how much the rich get as long as the poorest people have an adequate standard of living? But what is "adequate"? Who is to decide if that means a color TV set or only black-and-white? Does the 2.56 billion dollars in taxes paid by General Motors in 1971 (more than twice the amount it paid out to its stockholders) promote economic equality? Should more taxation be required? Should more than 34.7 billion dollars be given to the poor each year?[18] Should the nation's tax structure be made more progressive? These are all questions of evaluation which focus on the degree to which the political system has intervened in redistributing economic resources.

EQUALITY AND THE PUBLIC AND PRIVATE SECTORS

Another way of dealing with the question of egalitarianism is to look at the distribution of resources in the public sector compared to those in the private sector. A nation may achieve various mixes of equality, depending

---

[18] The figures cited here are from John O'Riley, "Whose Eye is Being Punched?" *This World,* Supplement to the *San Francisco Sunday Chronicle and Examiner,* May 14, 1972, p. 21 (reprinted from the *Wall Street Journal*); and Benjamin A. Okner, *Transfer Payments: Their Distribution and Role in Reducing Poverty* (Washington, D.C.: The Brookings, Institution, 1973), p. 64.

"I GUESS WE SHOULD COUNT OUR BLESSINGS."
Drawing by Dana Fradon; © *1974 The New Yorker Magazine, Inc.*

upon the allocations it chooses. For instance, a capitalist nation may accept large disparities in income in the private sector in order to provide incentives to people to produce and to invest.

Simply determining the proportion of the nation's resources in the public and private sectors tells us very little, however. For instance, a society that devotes 90 percent of its total resources to military expenditures would show a 90–10 public-private split. But it still might be marked by the gravest social, economic, and political inequalities. Although in theory the millionaire in his mansion and the migrant worker in his hut share equally in the security given by tanks and planes, it is difficult to take this theory seriously.

Nevertheless, once the basic outlines of a society are established, distribution between the public and private sectors may be of central evaluative concern. A principal complaint of critics from the left is that the United States allows far too large a share of its resources to remain in the private sphere. In America in 1972, over eighteen times as much money was spent on alcoholic beverages and tobacco as on *all* medical research. In 1967, twenty-five times more was spent on alcohol and tobacco than on symphony orchestras.[19]

Much of the underlying concern of this criticism is focused on equality. Should a poor man die because there are not enough kidney machines to go around, while at the same time a rich man can buy a new Mercedes sports car? But to some extent, criticism of what is viewed as excessive American devotion to the private sector is not based on a commitment to equality so much as on one or another of the visions of the good life discussed in Chapter 4. Wouldn't even the rich man be better off with an Opel and a decent symphony orchestra for his city? This isn't a question about equality — it is a question about values.

It is easy to answer that sports cars are abundant while symphonies flounder because people want cars, not music. Thus, transferring resources from the private to the public sector would just be a way of imposing on people what someone else thinks they should want rather than what they would buy for themselves. In some ways this is a naive response. The same man who would not voluntarily give money out of his own pocket to the symphony may be in favor of government subsidies for the arts even at the cost of higher taxes to himself. Such a person is willing to transfer resources to the public sphere as a way of expressing his "better self" while buying more chrome and tinsel with "his own money."

THE TENSION BETWEEN FREEDOM AND EQUALITY

So far our discussion of political evaluation has focused on conflict resolution, legitimacy, and equality. For many people, however, individual freedom rather than any of these criteria is the guidepost for political evaluation. As we saw in Chapter 4, freedom is a tricky conception. If we define freedom

[19] *Statistical Abstract of the United States,* 1974 and 1971 (data for 1972 and 1967, respectively).

by saying that the free man is the one who has his fair say in making the laws that govern him, then we can see that freedom and equality are closely related. The greater the inequalities in political power, the less freedom exists.

On the other hand, we can define freedom simply as individual autonomy. In this case, freedom means being free from coercion and having the chance to develop one's own personality and destiny without outside interference. From this point of view, how closely freedom and equality are related is an open question. Different answers are supplied by different schools of political thought.

For those of us who remain roughly within the lines of traditional American ideology, the potential clash between equality and individual freedom from governmental coercion presents a difficult problem of political evaluation. As we noted earlier, our society is marked by considerable economic inequalities. Many actual and proposed government policies are aimed at reducing these inequalities. A large proportion of these policies involve some form of coercion. They reduce freedom in an effort to increase equality. Should doctors and patients be forced to use only those medicines on a government prescription list in order to achieve greater equality in medical care? Should an employer be forced to discriminate against whites now because he used to discriminate against blacks? Many governmental programs involve increasing the coercive power of government over individuals in order to correct social and economic inequalities.

Here we encounter the final difficulty in employing freedom as an evaluative criterion. In Chapter 4 we made the distinction between the positive sense of freedom as *freedom to* participate in government and the negative sense of freedom as *freedom from* government interference. With this distinction in mind, one may argue that people who are sick, hungry, ignorant, or poor are not free to develop their own personalities. To say that an illiterate share-cropper with a family of six and a cash income of a thousand dollars a year is free because the government leaves him alone is a rather odd view of the human condition or an extremely narrow use of the word freedom. A government program which compels each of us, through taxation, to help buy that man a farm, and then regulates in detail how he must farm it, increases the level of government power over individuals. But while it decreases freedom from government coercion, it can easily be argued that it increases the former share-cropper's freedom to develop as a human being. Put another way, governmental coercion may be used as a counterbalance to the social and economic coercions of poverty. On the whole, such coercion may result in an increase in overall freedom. Yet here again, it can be argued that the drawback of the government program is that it puts our individual freedoms more and more at the mercy of the government.

Anyone seeking to evaluate American politics will have to calculate for himself the trade-offs between freedom and equality. Indeed, every one of us does exactly this, even if unconsciously, each time we say we are for or against some proposed policy or government action. In this sense, evaluation is a continuous part of the dynamics of the American political system which this book has attempted to describe.

This chapter discusses the principle dimensions to keep in mind when passing judgment on a political system. Political diagnosis is very different from medical diagnosis. Almost everyone agrees on what physical health is, but there is widespread disagreement about what to consider when evaluating a political system. Should it be political procedures, such as how the nation's rulers are chosen and what civil liberties the people enjoy? Or should we ignore the procedures and concentrate on the results? Does this mean that the level of popular satisfaction determines the system's success? Or should we consider objective conditions, like infant mortality rates, the distribution of income, and the availability of creature comforts? If so, which measures of performance are most important? Is every aspect of a society's existence a valid measure of its government's performance?

Asking these questions raises the problem of what areas of life governments *should* regulate. This is related to the growing problem of governmental capacity: how much *can* a democratic government do successfully?

Public acceptance or legitimacy is a basic evaluative dimension. Here there are findings to suit any preconception about public approval of the political system. A second fundamental dimension is the extent to which potentially severe conflicts in society are peacefully resolved or managed. Our political systems seems to do fairly well on this score. A third dimension is equality. The problem is widespread disagreement about the areas of life in which equality should be guaranteed, and also about how to define "equal enough." Moreover, it is difficult to provide equality without limiting freedom. How much of one should be sacrificed in order to achieve how much of the other?

Clearly, how people answer these dillemmas depends in large measure on their own ideological preferences. Experts sometimes may be able to foretell the consequences of alternative policies, but they cannot provide answers to the question of how much each alternative should be valued. That is a problem for individual judgment, for the lifetime of each reader of this book.

SELECT
BIBLIOGRAPHY

THERE are vast resources available to the student of American government. The purpose of this bibliography is *not* to provide a complete compilation of all the relevant books and articles. Rather, we have identified those sources that we think are the important readings in each area of study. In addition, we have described where to find data and other information on American government. General resources that are useful in all areas of study are discussed in the beginning of the bibliography, and sources of a more specific nature are discussed under the appropriate chapter headings.

Much of what is written on American politics and government is published in periodicals. The *Reader's Guide to Periodical Literature* indexes mass circulation magazines such as *Time* or *Newsweek*. The *Public Affairs Information Service* covers many scholarly journals (e.g. *The American Political Science Review*), selected books, government publications, and certain important background articles (such as *Wall Street Journal* feature stories). The *Social Science and Humanities Index* also indexes scholarly journals and some historical journals not in other indexes. The *Index to Legal Periodicals* contains references to many law journals that cannot be found elsewhere. Also of use are the *Business Periodicals Index* and *Wall Street Journal Index*. The *New York Times Index* is an excellent place to find out when something happened and the basic facts of the event. For each year it is organized by topic and then chronologically. In addition to the citation, a short synopsis of the article is given in the index itself. *Facts on File* is also useful in this respect.

All major political science journals in the world are indexed in the *International Political Science Abstracts*. Other indexes include *Political Science: A Bibliographical Guide to Literature* (1965) with supplements (1968, 1971, and 1973); *Guide to Reference Materials in Political Science*, vol. 1 (1967) and vol. 2 (1968); *The ABS Guide to Recent Publications in the Social Behavioral Sciences* (1965), with annual supplements; *Political Science Bibliographies* (1973) by Robert Harmon; and *ABC Poli. Sci., Advanced Bibliography of Contents: Political Science and Government*, which is a monthly publication of contents from periodicals in political science.

The leading scholarly journals in the field of political science also have their own indexes. These are: *The American Political Science Review; Public Opinion Quarterly; Journal of Politics; American Journal of Political Science;* and *Polity.*

Biographical information can be found in the *Dictionary of National Biography* and the *Dictionary of American Biography*. More recent biographies are found in *Current Biography,* and the very recent biographies not yet in *Current Biography* can be found in *Biography Index*. Other biographical sources include *Who's Who in American Politics; Who's Who in Government; Who's Who in America;* and regional publications of *Who's Who* (e.g. *Who's Who in The West*).

United States government publications are described in L. F. Schmeckebier and R. B. Eastin, *Government Publications and Their Use,* 2nd rev. ed. (1969). Therein you can learn of the various catalogues that list government publications from 1774 to the present. Most useful is the *United States Government Publications Monthly Catalogue,* which covers 1940 to the present. A useful unofficial source covering more than government publications is John Brown Mason, *Research Resources: Annotated Guide to the Social Sciences,* vol. 2.

The *American Statistical Index* is a complete index of all statistical publications of the United States government. The best place to begin, however, is with the *Statistical Abstract of the United States,* published annually. Other statistical compilations include *Historical Statistics of the United States* and the *City and County Data Book.*

General review articles on specific topics in political science can be found in three sources: the *Encyclopedia of the Social Sciences* (1930), edited by Edwin R. A. Segilman and Alvin Johnson; the *International Encyclopedia of the Social Sciences* (1968), edited by David L. Sills; and *The Handbook of Political Science* (1975), edited by Fred I. Greenstein and Nelson W. Polsby. *The Handbook* contains eight volumes of articles summarizing nearly every field of political science. The articles particularly relevant to American politics and government are cited in this bibliography.

The most valuable sources for following current American politics are the *Washington Post,* the *New York Times, Congressional Quarterly Weekly Report,* and the *National Journal* (also published weekly).

CHAPTER 1: INTRODUCTION

DAHL, ROBERT A., *Modern Political Analysis,* 3rd ed. (1976). An introductory discussion of basic concepts in the study of politics.

CHAPTER 2: THE SOCIAL CONTEXT OF AMERICAN POLITICS

The *Statistical Abstract of the United States* is the best place to begin looking for basic economic, social, and governmental data. It is published annually and its footnotes will lead you to more specialized and current sources of information. Historical data can be found in back issues of the *Statistical Abstract* and in *Historical Statistics of the United States, Colonial Times to 1957.*

BRYCE, JAMES B., *The American Commonwealth,* 2 vols. (1888). An Englishman's view in the 1880s of the institutions of government, the political party system, and American politics. Still valuable particularly for Bryce's insights into the roots of American institutions.

GREELY, ANDREW M., *Ethnicity in the United States: A Preliminary Reconnaissance* (1974).

TOCQUEVILLE, ALEXIS DE, *Democracy in America,* 2 vols. (1835). The most famous, enduring, and influential portrait of American society by a foreign visitor. A comprehensive overview of the political, social, and economic culture.

WATTENBERG, BEN J., *The Real America: A Surprising Examination of the State of the Union* (1974). A handy, easy-to-read demographic analysis of American society with emphasis on the changes that took place between 1960 and 1970.

WOLFINGER, RAYMOND E., *The Politics of Progress* (1974), "Ethnic Politics," chapter 3.

CHAPTER 3: THE CONSTITUTIONAL CONTEXT OF AMERICAN POLITICS
CHAPTER 4: THE IDEOLOGICAL CONTEXT OF AMERICAN POLITICS

A useful reference published by the Library of Congress is *The Constitution of the United States: Analysis and Interpretation,* an extensively annotated (over 1500 pages) presentation of the Constitution with references to cases decided by the Supreme Court through June 1964.

An extensive bibliographical volume (approximately 1200 pages) also published by the Library of Congress is *A Guide to the Study of the United States of America: Representative Books Reflecting the Development of American Life and Thought* (1960).

BEARD, CHARLES A., *The Supreme Court and the Constitution* (1972). A classic work on the development of constitutional law.

CHAFFEE, ZECHARIAH, *Free Speech in the United States* (1954). Traces the history of American ideas about free speech.

COMMAGER, HENRY STEELE, *The American Mind* (1959). A standard work in American intellectual history.

CORWIN, EDWARD S., *The Constitution and What it Means Today* (1974). A periodically revised guide to current interpretations of the Constitution.

———, ed., *The Constitution of the United States of America: Analysis and Interpretation* (1953). The most exhaustive and authoritative commentary on the Constitution.

DAHL, ROBERT A., *A Preface to Democratic Theory* (1956). A rigorous analysis of the meaning of democracy in light of the reality of political behavior by citizens and leaders.

FARRAND, MAX, *The Framing of the Constitution of the United States* (1965). Based on the journals of the Constitutional Convention.

GABRIEL, RALPH, *The Course of American Democratic Thought* (1956). A history of American ideas about politics.

HAMILTON, ALEXANDER, JOHN JAY, and JAMES MADISON, *The Federalist* (1788). Originally published as newspaper articles in support of ratification of the Constitution, these papers are a primary source for understanding the ideas of the men who wrote the Constitution.

HAND, LEARNED, *The Bill of Rights* (1958).

HARTZ, LOUIS, *The Liberal Tradition in America: An Interpretation of American Political Thought Since the Revolution* (1955). Traces the origins of the liberal ideology in America.

HOFSTADTER, RICHARD, *The American Political Tradition and the Men Who Made It* (1954).

LIPSET, SEYMOUR MARTIN, *The First New Nation* (1967). Argues that Americans take a distinctive view of politics because of their experience in building a new nation.

MANNHEIM, KARL, *Ideology and Utopia* (1966). The classic work on the nature of political ideology.

PITKIN, HANNA, *The Concept of Representation* (1967).

POLLACK, LOUIS, *The Constitution and the Supreme Court: A Documentary History,* 2 vols. (1966).

POUND, ROSCOE, *The Development of Constitutional Guarantees of Liberty* (1957).

SABINE, GEORGE, *A History of Political Theory* (1973). An overview of the history of political ideas.

Shapiro, Martin, and Rocco Tresolini, *American Constitutional Law*, 4th ed. (1975). An overview of materials on the political aspects of the Constitution and on constitutional law.

Sutherland, Arthur, *Constitutionalism in America* (1965).

Thoreau, Henry David, *Civil Disobedience* (1854). The classic work from which most modern theories of civil disobedience are drawn.

Wheeler, Harvey, "Constitutionalism," in *The Handbook of Political Science*, vol. 5, eds. Fred I. Greenstein and Nelson W. Polsby (1975).

CHAPTER 5: PUBLIC OPINION
CHAPTER 6: VOTING BEHAVIOR

Data on public opinion and voting behavior can be found in a number of sources. *The Gallup Poll* (1972) is a three-volume compendium of *all* the American Institute of Public Opinion poll findings from 1935 to 1971. Polls on everything from attitudes toward new fashions to presidential popularity are included. More recent polls can be found in *The Gallup Opinion Index*, published monthly.

Historical election data are in S. Peterson, *A Statistical History of American Presidential Elections* and in Congressional Quarterly Service, *Presidential Elections Since 1789*. Data on election results for the last twenty years are found in the *America Votes* series edited by Richard Scammon. These are published every two years and contain election results for all major races and the presidential primaries. Additional source information can be found in J. H. Runyon et al., *Source Book of Presidential Campaign and Election Statistics: 1948–1968;* and in Edward R. Tufte, "Political Statistics for the United States: Observations on Some Major Data Sources," *The American Political Science Review* (December 1976).

Berelson, Bernard, and Morris Janowitz, eds., *Reader in Public Opinion and Communication*, 2nd ed. (1966).

Berelson, Bernard, Paul F. Lazarsfeld, and William N. McPhee, *Voting: A Study of Opinion Formation in a Presidential Campaign* (1954). A study conducted between June and November 1948 in Elmira, New York. This is the second election study employing the methods of survey research. Findings focus on electorates' perceptions of the candidates, effect of organizations on the voter, the decision-making process, and the role of the campaign and the mass media.

Campbell, Angus, et al., *The American Voter* (1960). The first comprehensive national study of the American electorate using survey research. Although somewhat dated (the data are primarily from 1952 and 1956), many of the core theories of voting behavior are found here.

———, *Elections and the Political Order* (1966). A set of key essays on public opinion, voting behavior, and elections in America.

Converse, Philip E., "Change in the American Electorate," in *The Human Meaning of Social Change*, eds. Angus Campbell and Philip E. Converse (1972). An analysis of the effect that institutional changes at the turn of the century, particularly registration requirements, had on voter turnout. There also is discussion of recent change in the composition of the American electorate.

———, "The Nature of Belief Systems in Mass Publics," in *Ideology and Discontent*, ed. David Apter (1964). Landmark essay on the ideological capacity of the American Public.

———, "Public Opinion and Voting Behavior," in *The Handbook of Political Science*, vol. 4., eds. Fred I. Greenstein and Nelson W. Polsby (1975).

Converse, Philip E., et al., "Continuity and Change in American Politics: Parties and Issues in the 1968 Election," *American Political Science Review* (December 1969).

———, "Electoral Myth and Reality: The 1964 Election," *American Political Science Review* (June 1965).

Gallup, George, *The Sophisticated Poll Watcher's Guide* (1972).

Greenstein, Fred I., "Personality and Politics," in *The Handbook of Political Science*, vol. 2, eds. Fred I. Greenstein and Nelson W. Polsby (1975).

Jennings, M. Kent, and Richard G. Niemi, *The Political Character of Adolescence* (1975). A study of the development of political perspectives from high school through young adulthood, and of parental influence on children's political views.

Key, V. O., Jr., *Public Opinion and American Democracy* (1961).

Lane, Robert E., and David O. Sears, *Public Opinion* (1964). A brief, comprehensive introductory textbook on opinions and perception of public issues.

McClosky, Herbert, et al., "Issue Conflict and Consensus Among Party Leaders and Followers," *American Political Science Review* (June 1960). A study of attitudes on political issues of party leaders and ordinary citizens.

Miller, Arthur H., et al., "A Majority Party in Disarray: Political Polarization in the 1972 Election," *American Political Science Review* (March 1976).

Mueller, John E., *War, Presidents and Public Opinion* (1973).

Popkin, Samuel L., et al., "Comment: What Have You Done for Me Lately? Toward an Investment Theory of Voting," *American Political Science Review* (March 1976). A critique of the Miller et al. study of the 1972 presidential election and a discussion of alternative theories for voting decisions.

Sears, David O., "Political Socialization," in *The Hand-*

book of *Political Science,* vol. 2, eds. Fred I. Greenstein and Nelson W. Polsby (1975).

STOKES, DONALD E., "Some Dynamic Elements of Contests for the Presidency," *American Political Science Review* (March 1966).

CHAPTER 7: POLITICAL PARTICIPATION

ADAMANY, DAVID, *Campaign Financing in America* (1972).

ALEXANDER, HERBERT E., *Money in Politics* (1972).

Congressional Quarterly Service, *Dollar Politics,* vol. 2 (1974). An analysis of political campaign financing. Topics include: the 1971 Campaign Spending Law, campaign abuses in the 1972 election, and large contributors. It does not, however, include the post-Watergate changes in the laws regarding campaign financing.

NIE, NORMAN H., and SIDNEY VERBA, "Political Participation," in *The Handbook of Political Science,* vol. 4, eds. Fred I. Greenstein and Nelson W. Polsby (1975).

TOLCHIN, MARTIN, and SUSAN TOLCHIN, *To the Victor.... Political Patronage from the Clubhouse to the White House* (1971).

VERBA, SIDNEY, and NORMAN H. NIE, *Participation in America: Political Democracy and Social Equality* (1972). A comprehensive analysis of individual participation and its consequences for the political system.

WOLFINGER, RAYMOND E., *The Politics of Progress* (1974), "Machine Politics," chapter 4.

CHAPTER 8: INTEREST GROUPS

By far the most up-to-date, detailed, and sophisticated accounts of Washington-based interest groups are the background articles on individual groups that appear from time to time in the weekly periodical *The National Journal.*

BAUER, RAYMOND A., ITHIEL DE SOLA POOL, and LEWIS A. DEXTER, *American Business and Public Policy: The Politics of Foreign Trade,* 2nd ed. (1972). A detailed study of the process by which foreign trade legislation was written and passed between 1953 and 1962, with emphasis on the role of American business in the legislative process.

Congressional Quarterly Service, *The Washington Lobby,* 2nd ed. (1974). Includes current federal lobby laws and proposed reforms, descriptions of various lobbies, and a number of case studies.

DEXTER, LEWIS A., *How Organizations Are Represented in Washington* (1969).

GREENSTONE, J. DAVID, "Group Theories," in *The Handbook of Political Science,* vol. 2, eds. Fred I. Greenstein and Nelson W. Polsby (1975).

———, *Labor in American Politics* (1970).

OLSON, MANCUR, JR., *The Logic of Collective Action: Public Goods and the Theory of Groups* (1965). A critical examination, using economic theory, of individual motivations touching on the formation, membership, influence, and tactics of interest groups.

SALISBURY, ROBERT H., ed., *Interest Group Politics in America* (1970).

———, "Interest Groups," in *The Handbook of Political Science,* vol. 4, eds. Fred I. Greenstein, and Nelson W. Polsby (1975).

SMITH, JUDITH G., ed., *Political Brokers: People, Organizations, Money and Power* (1972). Ten studies of interest groups and campaign committees.

TRUMAN, DAVID B., *The Governmental Process: Political Interests and Public Opinion* (1951). A basic text on the group theory of politics with many illustrations of how interest groups participate in the formation of government policy.

WILSON, JAMES Q., *Political Organizations* (1973). An examination of forces leading to the survival, growth, tactics, and appeal of private organizations that engage in political activity.

CHAPTER 9: POLITICAL PARTIES

The complete *Proceedings*—platforms, votes, reports, debates, etc.—of all major and many minor United States party conventions from 1832 to 1972 are published on Microfilm by Micro Publications, Inc., Wilton, Conn. A summary of the major parties' conventions as well as a compendium of voting records can be found in Richard C. Bain and Judith H. Parris, *Convention Decisions and Voting Records* (1973). The text of party platforms can also be found in Kirk H. Porter and Donald B. Johnson, *National Party Platforms, 1840–1964* (1966).

Developments regarding current party politics can be followed in the *New York Times,* the *Washington Post,* and *Congressional Quarterly Weekly Report.*

Barber, James David, ed., *Choosing the President* (1974). Essays on the process by which presidents are selected. Topics discussed include primaries, conventions, public opinion, and the media.

Chambers, William N., and Walter Dean Burnham, eds., *The American Party Systems: Stages of Political Development*, 2nd ed. (1975).

Downs, Anthony, *An Economic Theory of Democracy* (1957). A formal economic model of the role of parties and elections in democracies with emphasis on the "inevitable" character of party competition resulting from the existence of only two parties.

Epstein, Leon D., "Political Parties," in *The Handbook of Political Science*, vol. 4, eds. Fred I. Greenstein and Nelson W. Polsby (1975).

Herring, Pendleton, *The Politics of Democracy: American Parties in Action* (1968). Emphasizes consensus and stability as political goals and argues that the American party system serves to maintain unity among a diverse population.

Key, V. O., Jr., *Politics, Parties and Pressure Groups*, 5th ed. (1964).

Parris, Judith H., *The Convention Problem: Issues in Reform of Presidential Nominating Procedures* (1972).

Polsby, Nelson W., and Aaron B. Wildavsky, *Presidential Elections*, 4th ed. (1976).

Ranney, Austin, *Curing the Mischiefs of Faction: Party Reform in America* (1975).

Sayre, Wallace S., and Judith H. Parris, *Voting for President: The Electoral College and the American Party System* (1970).

Schattschneider, E. E., *Party Government* (1942). A critical examination of the American party system calling for stronger and more centralized political parties.

Sorauf, Frank J., *Party Politics in America*, 2nd ed. (1972).

Sundquist, James L., *Dynamics of the Party System: Alignment and Realignment of Political Parties in the United States* (1973).

White, Theodore H., *The Making of the President* (1960, 1964, 1968, 1972).

CHAPTER 10: HOW CONGRESS IS ELECTED AND ORGANIZED
CHAPTER 11: CONGRESS IN ACTION

The most useful source on Congress is *Congressional Quarterly Weekly Report*. Its quarterly and annual indexes are the best starting point for anyone looking for information about Congress. The *Congressional Quarterly Almanac* is an annual publication summarizing the major legislative action of each session. The *Congressional Record* is published each day that either the House or the Senate is in session. In addition to containing a transcript of the previous day's action on the floor of both houses, additional articles and remarks submitted by members of Congress are published in the *Record*. At the end of each session, the *Record* is bound and indexed. In addition to the *Record*, a *Daily Digest* is published which summarizes the events that took place the previous day on the floor of both houses and in committees. Current information on members of Congress, committee assignments, and on some congressional staff is in the *Congressional Directory*, published annually. The *Almanac of American Politics* contains additional information about members of Congress. Election returns and information on congressional districts are in the *Almanac of American Politics*, the *Congressional District Data Book*, and in a volume published by the Congressional Quarterly Service entitled *Congressional Districts in the 1970s*, 2nd ed. Committee reports and hearings are published by the Government Printing Office and are found in over 1,100 government depository libraries.

Historical information on Congress can be found in back issues of the *Congressional Record*. The *Congress and the Nation* series published by Congressional Quarterly Service covers the period from 1945 to the present.

Bibby, John F., and Roger H. Davidson, *On Capital Hill: Studies in the Legislative Process*, 2nd ed. (1972). A series of case studies illustrating most major aspects of Congress.

Fenno, Richard F., Jr., *Congressmen in Committees* (1973). A study of six House committees, discussion of the organization of the committees, their relationship to the House, the goals of the committees, and the needs they serve for their members.

———, *The Power of the Purse: Appropriations Politics in Congress* (1966).

Ferejohn, John A., *Pork Barrel Politics: Rivers and Harbors Legislation, 1947–68* (1974).

Froman, Lewis A., Jr., *The Congressional Process: Strategies, Rules and Procedures* (1967).

Huitt, Ralph K., and Robert L. Peabody, *Congress: Two Decades of Analysis* (1969). Five articles on the Senate by Huitt and a bibliographic essay by Peabody.

Kingdom, John W., *Congressmen's Voting Decisions* (1973). Study based on interviews with Representatives about the factors influencing how they voted.

Manley, John F., *The Politics of Finance: The House Committee on Ways and Means* (1970).

Mayhew, David R., *Congress: The Electoral Connection* (1974). An analysis of how Congressmen's activities in the House further their goal of re-election.

Miller, Clem, *Member of the House*, ed. John W. Baker (1962). Informative letters written by Congressman Clem Miller to his constituents about the operation of Congress.

POLSBY, NELSON W., "Legislatures," in *The Handbook of Political Science*, vol. 5, eds. Fred I. Greenstein and Nelson W. Polsby (1975).

———, ed., *Congressional Behavior* (1971).

PRICE, DAVID E., *Who Makes the Laws? Creativity and Power in Senate Committees* (1972).

REDMAN, ERIC, *The Dance of Legislation* (1973). A personal account by a 22-year-old student intern of one bill's route to passage.

WOLFINGER, RAYMOND E., ed., *Readings on Congress* (1971).

CHAPTER 12: THE PRESIDENCY

An extensive bibliography compiled by the Library of Congress entitled *The Presidents of the United States: 1789–1962* is a rich compendium of sources on the presidency. Published annually are the *Public Papers of the President*. Current public addresses, executive orders, and other documents are published in the *Weekly Compilation of Presidential Documents* and in the *Federal Register*.

ANDERSON, PATRICK, *The Presidents' Men: White House Assistants of Franklin D. Roosevelt, Harry S. Truman, Dwight D. Eisenhower, John F. Kennedy and Lyndon Johnson* (1968).

BARBER, JAMES DAVID, *The Presidential Character: Predicting Performance in the White House* (1972). A psychobiographical study of Presidents Taft through Nixon with many illuminating anecdotes.

BURNS, JAMES MACGREGOR, *Roosevelt: The Lion and the Fox* (1956). A political biography of Franklin D. Roosevelt's first two terms.

Congressional Quarterly Service, *Watergate: Chronology of a Crisis*, 2 vols. (1973, 1974). A comprehensive review of the events and issues.

EVANS, ROWLAND, JR., and ROBERT D. NOVAK, *Nixon in the White House: The Frustration of Power* (1972). Emphasizes problems of staff coordination in the White House and Nixon's difficulty in trying to control the permanent bureaucracy.

———, *Lyndon B. Johnson: The Exercise of Power* (1968). A political biography useful for Johnson's career as Senate leader as well as his White House years.

GEORGE, ALEXANDER, and JULIETTE L. GEORGE, *Woodrow Wilson and Colonel House: A Personality Study* (1964). The best application of psychological insights to the study of political leadership.

KING, ANTHONY, "Executives," in *The Handbook of Political Science*, vol. 5, eds. Fred I. Greenstein and Nelson W. Polsby (1975).

KOENIG, LOUIS W., *The Chief Executive*, 3rd ed. (1975).

NEUSTADT, RICHARD E., *Presidential Power: The Politics of Leadership* (1960). Influential analysis of the President's ability to impose his will on other politicians.

POLSBY, NELSON W., *The Modern Presidency* (1973). A reader rich in details on recent Presidents and presidencies.

REEDY, GEORGE E., *The Twilight of the Presidency* (1970). An account of presidential isolation and power by a former aide to Lyndon Johnson.

WILDAVSKY, AARON, ed., *Perspectives on the Presidency* (1975).

CHAPTER 13: THE NATURE AND POLITICS OF ADMINISTRATION

The most useful source is the *United States Government Organization Manual*, published annually. It provides a complete picture of the organization and staffing of the federal bureaucracy. Regulations and orders of the federal agencies can be found in the *Code of Federal Regulations*. More current orders are in the *Federal Register*.

The *Budget in Brief* provides an overview of spending by each agency. A more detailed accounting of government expenditures can be found in *The Budget of the United States*. Most federal agencies publish annual reports and many other documents that provide voluminous information about their activities. *Congressional Quarterly Weekly Report* and the *National Journal* contain a good deal of current material on administrative developments.

ALTSHULER, ALAN A., ed., *Politics of the Federal Bureaucracy* (1968).

BERNSTEIN, MARVER H., *The Job of the Federal Executive* (1964).

BRAYBROOKE, DAVID, and CHARLES E. LINDBLOM, *A Strategy of Decision: Policy Evaluation as a Social Process* (1963).

CAMPBELL, JOHN FRANKLIN, *The Foreign Affairs Fudge Factory* (1971). A critical study of the political and organizational troubles of the State Department.

ELAZAR, DANIEL J., *American Federalism: A View From the States*, 2nd ed. (1972).

GRODZINS, MORTON, and DANIEL J. ELAZAR, eds., *The American System* (1966). A comprehensive examination of the relationship between federal, state, and local governments in the planning and administration of public policies.

HALPERIN, MORTON H., *Bureaucratic Politics and Foreign Policy* (1974).

HILSMAN, ROGER, *To Move a Nation: The Politics of Foreign Policy in the Administration of John F. Kennedy* (1967).

KAUFMAN, HERBERT, "Emerging Conflicts in the Doctrines of Public Administration," *American Political Science Review* (December 1956). Brief analysis of three different standards by which to judge bureaucratic performance.

MAASS, ARTHUR, *Muddy Waters* (1951). Describes the politics surrounding the policy decisions of an important federal agency, the Corps of Engineers.

NADEL, MARK, and FRANCIS ROURKE, "Bureaucracies," in *The Handbook of Political Science*, vol. 5, eds. Fred I. Greenstein and Nelson W. Polsby (1975).

McCONNELL, GRANT, *Private Power and American Democracy* (1966). Discussion of the influence of corporations over the government agencies that are supposed to regulate them.

PRICE, DON K., *The Scientific Estate* (1965). Describes the growth of scientific agencies within the federal bureaucracy.

RIKER, WILLIAM H., "Federalism," in *The Handbook of Political Science*, vol. 5, eds. Fred I. Greenstein and Nelson W. Polsby (1975).

ROURKE, FRANCIS, *Bureaucracy, Politics and Public Policy* (1969).

SEIDMAN, HAROLD, *Politics, Position and Power: The Dynamics of Federal Organization* (1970).

SIMON, HERBERT A., *Administrative Behavior: A Study of Decision Making in Administrative Organization*, 2nd ed. (1957).

SMITH, BRUCE L. R., *The Rand Corporation: Case Study of a Non-Profit Advisory Corporation* (1966).

STANLEY, DAVID T., and JAMESON W. DOIG, *Men Who Govern* (1967). A biographical profile of federal executives.

WEBER, MAX, "Bureaucracy," in *From Max Weber*, eds. Hans Gerth and C. Wright Mills (1946). A classic essay on the theory of bureaucracies.

WILDAVSKY, AARON, *The Politics of the Budgetary Process*, 2nd ed. (1974).

CHAPTER 14: THE COURTS

General information about the operation of the federal courts can be obtained from various reports and studies prepared by the Administrative Office of the U. S. Courts. Supreme Court opinions are published in three forms: (1) *United States Reports;* (2) *Supreme Court Reporter,* and (3) *United States Supreme Court, Lawyers' Edition.* Many libraries get only the bound volumes of one of these services, but law libraries and larger general libraries also receive the paperback supplements (called advance sheets) that appear only a few weeks after decisions are rendered. *United States Law Week* and *Supreme Court Bulletin* print opinions even before the advance sheets appear.

Decisions of lower federal courts are found in *The Federal Reporter* and *Federal Supplement.* The *Index to Legal Periodicals* indexes the articles that are published in law reviews. The *United States Code* contains an annotated list of all federal statutes. A wide range of legal dictionaries, encyclopedias, and digests are also available for tracing legal doctrines from case to case.

ABRAHAM, HENRY, *Justices and Presidents* (1974). An examination of the politics surrounding Supreme Court appointments.

BIKEL, ALEXANDER M., *The Least Dangerous Branch: The Supreme Court at the Bar of Politics* (1962).

CHASE, HAROLD W., *Federal Judges: The Appointing Process* (1972).

KRISLOV, SAMUEL, *The Supreme Court and Political Freedom* (1968).

McCLOSKEY, ROBERT G., *The Modern Supreme Court* (1972).

MURPHY, WALTER F., and C. HERMAN PRITCHETT, eds., *Courts, Judges and Politics: An Introduction to the Judicial Process*, 2nd ed. (1974).

SHAPIRO, MARTIN, "Courts," in *The Handbook of Political Science*, vol. 5, eds. Fred I. Greenstein and Nelson W. Polsby (1975).

———, *Freedom of Speech: The Supreme Court and Judicial Review* (1966).

———, *Law and Politics in the Supreme Court* (1964). An analysis of the role of the Supreme Court outside the area of constitutional law.

———, *The Supreme Court and Administrative Agencies* (1968).

———, ed., *The Supreme Court and Public Policy* (1968).

SCHMIDHAUSER, JOHN R., and LARRY L. BERG, *The Supreme Court and Congress* (1972).

SCHUBERT, GLENDON, *Judicial Policy-Making* (1965).

VOSE, CLEMENT E., *Constitutional Change* (1972). Describes the tactics that individuals and groups use in seeking changes in public policy through constitutional litigation.

WASBY, STEPHEN L., *The Impact of the U. S. Supreme Court* (1970). Describes the influence of Supreme Court decisions on the behavior of other government officials and the public.

CHAPTER 15: PUBLIC POLICY MAKING

The volumes published by the Congressional Quarterly Service are useful for the study of public policy. See *Congress and the Nation*, vols. I–III and the *Congressional Quarterly Almanac*. Also, the *United States Code* and the *Federal Register* list the actual rules emanating from the federal government.

DROR, YEHEZKEL, *Public Policy Making Reexamined* (1968).

HALBERSTAM, DAVID, *The Best and the Brightest* (1972). An analysis of the decisions escalating United States involvement in Vietnam.

HITCH, CHARLES, *Decision Making for Defense* (1965). Describes program budgeting.

JONES, CHARLES O., *An Introduction to the Study of Public Policy* (1970).

LINDBLOM, CHARLES E., *The Intelligence of Democracy: Decision Making Through Mutual Adjustment* (1965).

——, *The Policy-Making Process* (1968).

LOWI, THEODORE J., "Distribution, Regulation, Redistribution: The Functions of Government," in *Public Policies and Their Politics*, ed. Randall B. Ripley (1966). An analysis of different types of policy outputs and the politics involved in the attainment of each.

MOYNIHAN, DANIEL P., *The Politics of Guaranteed Income* (1973).

PRESSMAN, JEFFREY L., and AARON WILDAVSKY, *Implementation: How Great Expectations in Washington Are Dashed in Oakland* (1973). "Or, why it's amazing that federal programs work at all, this being a saga of the Economic Development Administration as told by two sympathetic observers who seek to build morals on a foundation of ruined hopes."

SCHNEIER, EDWARD V., ed., *Policy-Making in American Government* (1969).

SINDLER, ALLAN P., ed., *Policy and Politics in America: Six Case Studies* (1973). The case studies examine the Family Assistance Plan, the proposal for the direct popular election of the President, public school financing, the Model Cities Program, the politics of Title I of ESEA, and Congressman John Brademas' bid for reelection in 1968.

SUNDQUIST, JAMES L., *Politics and Policy: The Eisenhower, Kennedy and Johnson Years* (1968).

TALBOT, ROSS B., and DON F. HADWIGER, *The Policy Process in American Agriculture* (1968).

CHAPTER 16: CHANGE AND VIOLENCE IN THE AMERICAN POLITICAL SYSTEM

DAHL, ROBERT A., "The American Oppositions: Affirmation and Denial," in *Political Oppositions in Western Democracies*, ed. Robert A. Dahl (1966). An analysis of cleavages, political oppositions, and political conflict in American society.

——, *Democracy in the United States: Promise and Performance*, 2nd ed. (1972). A textbook on American politics which stresses conflict and its resolution.

——, "Governments and Political Oppositions," in *The Handbook of Political Science*, vol. 3, eds. Fred I. Greenstein and Nelson W. Polsby (1975).

GRAHAM, HUGH DAVIS, and TED ROBERT GURR, *Violence in America: Historical and Comparative Perspectives*, 2 vols. (1969).

GURR, TED ROBERT, *Why Men Rebel* (1970).

LIPSET, SEYMOUR MARTIN, and EARL RAAB, *The Politics of Unreason: Right-Wing Extremism in America, 1790–1970* (1970).

OBERSCHALL, ANTHONY, *Social Conflict and Social Movements* (1973).

SEARS, DAVID O., and JOHN B. MCCONAHAY, *The Politics of Violence: The New Urban Blacks and the Watts Riot* (1973).

SKOLNICK, JEROME, *The Politics of Protest: Violent Aspects of Protest and Confrontation* (1969).

TILLY, CHARLES, "Revolution and Collective Violence," in *The Handbook of Political Science*, vol. 3, eds. Fred I. Greenstein and Nelson W. Polsby (1975).

CHAPTER 17: EVALUATING THE AMERICAN POLITICAL SYSTEM

BARRY, BRIAN, and DOUGLAS W. RAE, "Political Evaluation," in *The Handbook of Political Science*, vol. 1, eds. Fred I. Greenstein and Nelson W. Polsby (1975).

BLACKMAN, BARRY M., ET AL., *Setting National Priorities: The 1975 Budget* (1974).

DAHL, ROBERT A., *After the Revolution: Authority in a Good Society* (1970). An analysis of the principal issues in political philosophy raised by the New Left.

GRUMM, JOHN G., "The Analysis of Policy Impact," in *The Handbook of Political Science*, vol. 6, eds. Fred I. Greenstein and Nelson W. Polsby (1975).

LOWI, THEODORE J., *The End of Liberalism: Ideology, Policy and Crisis of Public Authority* (1969). A controversial critique of the ability of liberal ideology and programs to solve social and economic problems.

MOON, J. DONALD, "The Logic of Political Inquiry: A Synthesis of Opposed Perspectives," in *The Handbook of Political Science,* vol. 1, eds. Fred I. Greenstein and Nelson W. Polsby (1975).

PECHMAN, JOSEPH A., and BENJAMIN A. OKNER, *Who Bears the Tax Burden?* (1974).

WATTS, WILLIAM, and LLOYD A. FREE, *State of the Nation* (1973). How the American public sees itself and the country's condition.

THE CONSTITUTION
OF THE
UNITED STATES

W E the People of the United States, In Order to form a more perfect Union, establish Justice, insure domestic Tranquility, provide for the common defence, promote the general Welfare, and secure the Blessings of Liberty to ourselves and our Posterity, do ordain and establish this Constitution for the United States of America.

ARTICLE I

Section 1. All legislative Powers herein granted shall be vested in a Congress of the United States, which shall consist of a Senate and House of Representatives.

Section 2. The House of Representatives shall be composed of members chosen every second Year by the People of the several States, and the Electors in each State shall have the Qualifications requisite for Electors of the most numerous Branch of the State Legislature.

No Person shall be a representative who shall not have attained to the Age of twenty five Years, and been seven Years a Citizen of the United States, and who shall not, when elected, be an Inhabitant of that State in which he shall be chosen.

Representatives and direct Taxes shall be apportioned among the several States which may be included within this union, according to their respective Numbers, which shall be determined by adding to the whole Number of free Persons, including those bound to Service for a Term of Years, and excluding Indians not taxed, three fifths of all other Persons. The actual Enumeration shall be made within three Years after the first Meeting of the Congress of the United States, and within every subsequent Term of ten Years, in such Manner as they shall by Law direct. The Number of Representatives shall not exceed one for every thirty Thousand, but each State shall have at Least one Representative; and until such enumeration shall be made, the State of New Hampshire shall be entitled to chuse three, Massachusetts eight, Rhode-Island and Provi-dence Plantations one, Connecticut five, New-York six, New Jersey four, Pennsylvania eight, Delcaware one, Maryland six, Virginia ten, North Carolina five, South Carolina five, and Georgia three.

When vacancies happen in the Representation from any State, the Executive Authority thereof shall issue Writs of Election to fill such Vacancies.

The House of Representatives shall chuse their speaker and other Officers; and shall have the sole Power of Impeachment.

Section 3. The Senate of the United States shall be composed of two Senators from each State, chosen by the Legislature thereof, for six Years; and each Senator shall have one Vote.

Immediately after they shall be assembled in Consequence of the first Election, they shall be divided as equally as may be into three Classes. The Seats of the Senators of the first Class shall be vacated at the Expiration of the second Year, of the second Class at the Expiration of the fourth Year, and of the third Class at the Expiration of the sixth Year, so that one third may be chosen every second Year; and if Vacancies happen by Resignation, or otherwise, during the Recess of the Legislature of any State, the Executive thereof may make temporary Appointments until the next Meeting of the Legislature, which shall then fill such Vacancies.

No Person shall be a Senator who shall not have attained to the Age of thirty Years, and been nine Years a Citizen of the United States, and who shall not, when elected, be an Inhabitant of that State for which he shall be chosen.

The Vice President of the United States shall be President of the Senate, but shall have no Vote, unless they be equally divided.

The Senate shall chuse their other Officers, and also a President pro tempore, in the Absence of the Vice President, or when he shall exercise the Office of the President of the United States.

The Senate shall have the sole Power to try all Impeachments. When sitting for that Purpose, they shall be on Oath or Affirmation. When the President of the United States is tried, the Chief Justice shall preside: And no Person shall be convicted without the Concurrence of two thirds of the Members present.

Judgment in Cases of Impeachment shall not extend further than to removal from Office, and disqualification to hold and enjoy any Office of honor, Trust or Profit under the United States: but the Party convicted shall nevertheless be liable and subject to Indictment, Trial, Judgment and Punishment, according to law.

Section 4. The Times, Places and Manner of holding Elections for Senators and Representatives, shall be prescribed in each State by the Legislature thereof; but the Congress may at any time by Law make or alter such Regulations, except as to the Places of chusing Senators.

The Congress shall assemble at least once in every Year, and such Meeting shall be on the first Monday in December, unless they shall by Law appoint a different Day.

Section 5. Each House shall be the Judge of the Elections, Returns and Qualifications of its own Members, and a Majority of each shall constitute a Quorum to do Business; but a smaller Number may adjourn from day to day, and may be authorized to compel the Attendance of absent Members, in such Manner, and under such Penalties as each House may provide.

Each House may determine the Rules of its Proceedings, punish its Members for disorderly Behaviour, and, with the Concurrence of two thirds, expel a Member.

Each House shall keep a Journal of its Proceedings, and from time to time publish the same, excepting such Parts as may in their Judgment require Secrecy; and the Yeas and Nays of the Members of either House on any question shall, at the Desire of one fifth of those Present, be entered on the Journal.

Neither House, during the Session of Congress, shall, without the Consent of the other, adjourn for more than three days, nor to any other Place than that in which the two Houses shall be sitting.

Section 6. The Senators and Representatives shall receive a Compensation for their Services, to be ascertained by Law, and paid out of the Treasury of the United States. They shall in all Cases, except Treason, Felony and Breach of the Peace, be privileged from Arrest during their Attendance at the Session of their respective Houses, and in going to and returning from the same; and for any Speech or Debate in either House, they shall not be questioned in any other Place.

No Senator or Representative shall, during the Time for which he was elected, be appointed to any civil Office under the Authority of the United States, which shall have been created, or the Emoluments whereof shall have been encreased during such time; and no Person holding any Office under the United States, shall be a Member of either House during his Continuance in Office.

Section 7. All Bills for raising Revenue shall originate in the House of Representatives; but the Senate may propose or concur with Amendments as on other Bills.

Every Bill which shall have passed the House of Representatives and the Senate, shall, before it become a Law, be presented to the President of the United States; If he approve he shall sign it, but if not he shall return it, with his Objections to that House in which it shall have originated, who shall enter the Objections at large on their Journal, and proceed to reconsider it. If after such Reconsideration two thirds of that House shall agree to pass the Bill, it shall be sent, together with the Objections, to the other House, by which it shall likewise be reconsidered, and if approved by two thirds of that House, it shall become a Law. But in all such Cases the Votes of both Houses shall be determined by Yeas and Nays, and the Names of the Persons voting for and against the Bill shall be entered on the Journal of each House respectively. If any Bill shall not be returned by the President within ten Days (Sundays excepted) after it shall have been presented to him, the Same shall be a Law, in like Manner as if he had signed it, unless the Congress by their Adjournment prevent its Return, in which Case it shall not be a Law.

Every Order, Resolution, or Vote to which the Concurrence of the Senate and House of Representatives may be necessary (except on a question of Adjournment) shall be presented to the President of the United States; and before the Same shall take Effect, shall be approved by him, or being disapproved by him, shall be repassed by two thirds of the Senate and House of Representatives, according to the Rules and Limitations prescribed in the Case of a Bill.

Section 8. The Congress shall have Power To lay and collect Taxes, Duties, Imposts and Excises, to pay the Debts and provide for the common Defence and general Welfare of the United States; but all Duties, Imposts and Excises shall be uniform throughout the United States;

To borrow Money on the credit of the United States;

To regulate Commerce with foreign Nations, and among the several States, and with the Indian Tribes;

To establish an uniform Rule of Naturalization, and uniform Laws on the subject of Bankruptcies throughout the United States;

To coin Money, regulate the Value thereof, and of foreign Coin, and fix the Standard of Weights and Measures;

To provide for the Punishment of counterfeiting the Securities and current Coin of the United States;

To establish Post Offices and post Roads;

To promote the Progress of Science and useful Arts, by securing for limited Times to Authors and Inventors the exclusive Right to their respective Writings and Discoveries;

To constitute Tribunals inferior to the supreme Court;

To define and punish Piracies and Felonies committed on the high Seas, and Offences against the Law of Nations;

To declare War, grant Letters of Marque and Reprisal, and make Rules concerning Captures on Land and Water;

To raise and support Armies, but no Appropriation of Money to that Use shall be for a longer Term than two Years;

To provide and maintain a Navy;

To make Rules for the Government and Regulation of the land and naval Forces;

To provide for calling forth the Militia to execute the Laws of the Union, suppress Insurrections and repel Invasions;

To provide for organizing, arming, and disciplining, the Militia, and for governing such Part of them as may be employed in the Service of the United States, reserving to the States respectively, the Appointment of the Officers, and the Authority of training the Militia according to the discipline prescribed by Congress;

To exercise exclusive Legislation in all Cases whatsoever, over such District (not exceeding ten Miles square) as may, by Cession of particular States, and the Acceptance of Congress, become the Seat of the Government of the United States, and to exercise like Authority over all Places purchased by the Consent of the Legislature of the State in which the Same shall be for the Erection of Forts, Magazines, Arsenals, dock-Yards, and other needful Buildings;- And

To make all Laws which shall be necessary and proper for carrying into Execution the foregoing Powers, and all other Powers vested by this Constitution in the Government of the United States, or in any Department or Officer thereof.

Section 9. The Migration or Importation of such Persons as any of the States now existing shall think proper to admit, shall not be prohibited by the Congress prior to the Year one thousand eight hundred and eight, but a Tax or duty may be imposed on such Importation, not exceeding ten dollars for each Person.

The Privilege of the Writ of Habeas Corpus shall not be suspended, unless when in Cases of Rebellion or Invasion the public Safety may require it.

No Bill of Attainder or ex post facto Law shall be passed.

No Capitation, or other direct, Tax shall be laid, unless in Proportion to the Census or Enumeration herein before directed to be taken.

No Tax or Duty shall be laid on Articles exported from any State.

No Preference shall be given by any Regulation of Commerce or Revenue to the Ports of one State over those of another: nor shall Vessels bound to, or from, one State be obliged to enter, clear, or pay Duties in another.

No Money shall be drawn from the Treasury, but in Consequence of Appropriations made by Law; and a regular Statement and Account of the Receipts and Expenditures of all public Money shall be published from time to time.

No Title of Nobility shall be granted by the United States: And no Person holding any office of Profit or Trust under them, shall, without the Consent of the Congress, accept of any present, Emolument, Office, or Title, of any kind whatever, from any King, Prince, or foreign States.

Section 10. No State shall enter into any Treaty, Alliance, or Confederation; grant Letters of Marque and Reprisal; coin Money; emit Bills of Credit; make any Thing but gold and silver Coin a Tender in Payment of Debts; pass any Bill of Attainder, ex post facto Law, or Law impairing the Obligation of Contracts, or grant any Title of Nobility.

No State shall, without the Consent of the Congress, lay any Imposts or Duties on Imports or Exports, except what may be absolutely necessary for executing its inspection Laws: and the net Produce of all Duties and Imposts, laid by any State on Imports or Exports, shall be for the Use of the Treasury of the United States; and all such Laws shall be subject to the Revision and Controul of the Congress.

No State shall, without the Consent of Congress, lay any Duty of Tonnage, keep Troops, or Ships of War in time of Peace, enter into any Agreement or Compact with another State, or with a foreign Power, or engage in War, unless actually invaded, or in such imminent Danger as will not admit of delay.

ARTICLE II

Section 1. The executive Power shall be vested in a President of the United States of America. He shall hold his Office during the Term of four Years, and, together with the Vice President, chosen for the same term, be elected, as follows

Each State shall appoint, in such Manner as the Legislature thereof may direct, a Number of Electors, equal to the whole Number of Senators and Representatives to which the State may be entitled in the Congress: but no Senator or Representative, or Person holding an office of Trust or Profit under the United States, shall be appointed an Elector.

The Electors shall meet in their respective States, and vote by Ballot for two Persons, of whom one at least shall not be an Inhabitant of the same State with themselves. And they shall make a List of all the Persons voted for, and of the Number of Votes for each; which List they shall sign and certify, and transmit sealed to the Seat of the Government of the United States, directed to the President of the Senate. The President of the Senate shall, in the Presence of the Senate and House of Representatives, open all the Certificates, and the Votes shall then be counted. The Person having the greatest Number of Votes shall be the President, if such Number be a Majority of the whole Number of Electors appointed; and if there be more than one who have such Majority, and have an equal Number of Votes, then the House of Representatives shall immediately chuse by Ballot one of them for President: and if no Person have a Majority, then from the five highest on the List the said House shall in like Manner chuse the

President. But in chusing the President, the Votes shall be taken by States, the Representation from each State having one Vote; A quorum for this Purpose shall consist of a Member or Members from two thirds of the States, and a Majority of all the States shall be necessary to a Choice. In every Case, after the Choice of the President, the Person having the greatest Number of Votes of the Electors shall be the Vice President. But if there should remain two or more who have equal Votes, the Senate shall chuse from them by Ballot the Vice President.

The Congress may determine the Time of chusing the Electors and the Day on which they shall give their Votes; which Day shall be the same throughout the United States.

No Person except a natural born Citizen, or a Citizen of the United States, at the time of the Adoption of this Constitution, shall be eligible to the Office of President; neither shall any Person be eligible to that Office who shall not have attained to the Age of thirty five Years, and been fourteen Years a Resident within the United States.

In Case of the Removal of the President from Office, or of his Death, Resignation, or Inability to discharge the Powers and Duties of the said Office, the Same shall devolve on the Vice President, and the Congress may by Law provide for the Case of Removal, Death, Resignation or Inability, both of the President and Vice President, declaring what Officer shall then act as President, and such Officer shall act accordingly, until the Disability be removed, or a President shall be elected.

The President shall, at stated Times, receive for his Services a Compensation, which shall neither be encreased nor diminished during the Period for which he shall have been elected, and he shall not receive within that Period any other Emolument from the United States, or any of them.

Before he enter on the Execution of his Office, he shall take the following Oath or Affirmation:- "I do solemnly swear (or affirm) that I will faithfully execute the Office of President of the United States, and will to the best of my Ability, preserve, protect and defend the Constitution of the United States."

Section 2. The President shall be Commander in Chief of the Army and Navy of the United States, and of the Militia of the several States, when called into the actual Service of the United States; he may require the Opinion, in writing, of the principal Officer in each of the executive Departments, upon any Subject relating to the Duties of their respective Offices, and he shall have power to grant Reprieves and Pardons for Offences against the United States, except in Cases of Impeachment.

He shall have Power, by and with the Advice and Consent of the Senate, to make Treaties, provided two thirds of the Senators present concur; and he shall nominate, and by and with the Advice and Consent of the Senate, shall appoint Ambassadors, other public Ministers and Consuls, Judges of the supreme Court, and all other Officers of the United States, whose Appointments are not herein otherwise provided for, and which shall be established by Law;

but the Congress may by Law vest the Appointment of such inferior Officers, as they think proper, in the President alone, in the Courts of Law, or in the Heads of Departments.

The President shall have Power to fill up all Vacancies that may happen during the Recess of the Senate, by granting Commissions which shall expire at the End of their next Session.

Section 3. He shall from time to time give to the Congress Information of the State of the Union, and recommend to their Consideration such Measures as he shall judge necessary and expedient; he may, on extraordinary Occasions, convene both Houses, or either of them, and in Case of Disagreement between them, with Respect to the Time of Adjournment, he may adjourn them to such Time as he shall think proper; he shall receive Ambassadors and other public Ministers; he shall take Care that the Laws be faithfully executed, and shall Commission all the officers of the United States.

Section 4. The President, Vice President and all civil Officers of the United States, shall be removed from Office on Impeachment for, and Conviction of, Treason, Bribery, or other High Crimes and Misdemeanors.

ARTICLE III

Section 1. The judicial Power of the United States, shall be vested in one supreme Court, and in such inferior Courts as the Congress may from time to time ordain and establish. The Judges, both of the supreme and inferior Courts, shall hold their Offices during good Behaviour, and shall, at stated Times, receive for their Services, a Compensation, which shall not be diminished during their Continuance in Office.

Section 2. The judicial Power shall extend to all Cases, in Law and Equity, arising under this Constitution, the Laws of the United States, and Treaties made, or which shall be made, under their Authority;-to all Cases affecting Ambassadors, other public Ministers and Consuls;-to all Cases of admiralty and maritime Jurisdiction;-to Controversies to which the United States shall be a Party;-to Controversies between two or more States; between a State and Citizens of another State;-between Citizens of different States;-between Citizens of the same State claiming Lands under Grants of different States, and between a State, or the Citizens thereof, and foreign States, Citizens or Subjects.

In all Cases affecting Ambassadors, other public Ministers and Consuls, and those in which a State shall be Party, the supreme Court shall have original Jurisdiction. In all the other Cases before mentioned, the supreme Court shall have appellate Jurisdiction, both as to Law and Fact, with such Exceptions, and under such Regulations as the Congress shall make.

The Trial of all Crimes, except in Cases of Impeachment, shall be by Jury; and such Trial shall be held in the State where the said Crimes shall have been committed; but when not committed within any State, the Trial shall be at such Place or Places as the Congress may by Law have directed.

Section 3. Treason against the United States, shall consist only in levying War against them, or in adhering to their Enemies, giving them Aid and Comfort. No Person shall be convicted of Treason unless on the Testimony of two Witnesses to the same overt Act, or on Confession in open Court.

The Congress shall have Power to declare the Punishment of Treason, but no Attainder of Treason shall work Corruption of Blood, or Forfeiture except during the Life of the Person attainted.

ARTICLE IV

Section 1. Full Faith and Credit shall be given in each State to the public Acts, Records, and judicial Proceedings of every other State. And the Congress may by general Laws prescribe the Manner in which such Acts, Records and Proceedings shall be proved, and the Effect thereof.

Section 2. The Citizens of each State shall be entitled to all Privileges and Immunities of Citizens in the several States.

A Person charged in any State with Treason, Felony, or other Crime, who shall flee from Justice, and be found in another State, shall on Demand of the executive Authority of the State from which he fled, be delivered up, to be removed to the State having Jurisdiction of the Crime.

No Person held to Service or Labour in one State, under the Laws thereof, escaping into another, shall, in Consequence of any Law or Regulation therein, be discharged from such Service or Labour, but shall be delivered up on Claim of the Party to whom such Service or Labour may be due.

Section 3. New States may be admitted by the Congress into this Union; but no new State shall be formed or erected within the Jurisdiction of any other State; nor any State be formed by the Junction of two or more States, or Parts of States, without the Consent of the Legislatures of the States concerned as well as of the Congress.

The Congress shall have Power to dispose of and make all needful Rules and Regulations respecting the Territory or other Property belonging to the United States; and nothing in this Constitution shall be so construed as to Prejudice any Claims of the United States, or of any particular State.

Section 4. The United States shall guarantee to every State in this Union a Republican Form of Government, and shall protect each of them against Invasion; and on Application of the Legislature, or of the Executive (when the Legislature cannot be convened) against domestic Violence.

ARTICLE V

The Congress, whenever two thirds of both Houses shall deem it necessary, shall propose Amendments to this Constitution, or, on the Application of the Legislatures of two thirds of the several States, shall call a Convention for proposing Amendments, which, in either Case, shall be valid to all Intents and Purposes, as Part of this Constitution, when ratified by the Legislatures of three fourths of the several States, or by Conventions in three fourths thereof, as the one or the other Mode of Ratification may be proposed by the Congress; Provided that no Amendment which may be made prior to the Year One thousand eight hundred and eight shall in any Manner affect the first and fourth Clauses in the Ninth Section of the first Article; and that no State, without its Consent, shall be deprived of its equal Suffrage in the Senate.

ARTICLE VI

All Debts contracted and Engagements entered into, before the Adoption of this Constitution, shall be as valid against the United States under this Constitution, as under the Confederation.

This Constitution, and the Laws of the United States which shall be made in Pursuance thereof; and all Treaties made, or which shall be made, under the Authority of the United States, shall be the supreme Law of the Land, and the Judges in every State shall be bound thereby, any Thing in the Constitution or Laws of any State to the Contrary notwithstanding.

The Senators and Representatives before mentioned, and the Members of the several State Legislatures, and all executive and judicial Officers, both of the United States and of the several States, shall be bound by Oath or Affirmation, to support this Constitution; but no religious Test shall ever be required as a Qualification to any Office or public Trust under the United States.

ARTICLE VII

The Ratification of the Conventions of nine States, shall be sufficient for the Establishment of this Constitution between the States so ratifying the Same.

Done in Convention by the Unanimous Consent of the States present the Seventeenth Day of September in the Year of our Lord one thousand seven hundred and Eighty seven and of the Independence of the United States of America the Twelfth. In witness whereof We have hereunto subscribed our Names.

[The first 10 Amendments were ratified December 15, 1791, and form what is known as the Bill of Rights]

AMENDMENT 1

Congress shall make no law respecting an establishment of religion, or prohibiting the free exercise thereof; or abridging the freedom of speech, or of the press; or the right of the people peaceably to assemble, and to petition the Government for a redress of grievances.

AMENDMENT 2

A well regulated Militia, being necessary to the security of a free State, the right of the people to keep and bear Arms, shall not be infringed.

AMENDMENT 3

No Soldier shall, in time of peace be quartered in any house, without the consent of the Owner, nor in time of war, but in a manner to be prescribed by law.

AMENDMENT 4

The right of the people to be secure in their persons, houses, papers, and effects, against unreasonable searches and seizures, shall not be violated, and no Warrants shall issue, but upon probable cause, supported by Oath or affirmation, and particularly describing the place to be searched and the persons or things to be seized.

AMENDMENT 5

No person shall be held to answer for a capital, or otherwise infamous crime, unless on a presentment or indictment of a Grand Jury, except in cases arising in the land or naval forces, or in the Militia, when in actual service in time of War or public danger; nor shall any person be subject for the same offence to be twice put in jeopardy of life or limb; nor shall be compelled in any criminal case to be a witness against himself, nor be deprived of life, liberty, or property, without due process of law; nor shall private property be taken for public use, without just compensation.

AMENDMENT 6

In all criminal prosecutions, the accused shall enjoy the right to a speedy and public trial, by an impartial jury of the State and district wherein the crime shall have been committed, which district shall have been previously ascertained by law, and to be informed of the nature and cause of the accusation; to be confronted with the witnesses against him; to have compulsory process for obtaining witnesses in his favor, and to have the Assistance of Counsel for his defence.

AMENDMENT 7

In Suits at common law, where the value in controversy shall exceed twenty dollars, the right of trial by jury shall be preserved, and no fact tried by a jury, shall be otherwise reexamined in any Court of the United States, than according to the rules of the common law.

AMENDMENT 8

Excessive bail shall not be required, nor excessive fines imposed, nor cruel and unusual punishments inflicted.

AMENDMENT 9

The enumeration in the Constitution, of certain rights, shall not be construed to deny or disparage others retained by the people.

AMENDMENT 10

The powers not delegated to the United States by the Constitution, nor prohibited by it to the States, are reserved to the States respectively, or to the people.

AMENDMENT 11

[Ratified February 7, 1795]

The Judicial power of the United States shall not be construed to extend to any suit in law or equity, commenced or prosecuted against one of the United States by Citizens of another State, or by Citizens or Subjects of any Foreign State.

AMENDMENT 12

[Ratified July 27, 1804]

The Electors shall meet in their respective states and vote by ballot for President and Vice-President, one of whom, at least, shall not be an inhabitant of the same state with themselves; they shall name in their ballots the person voted for as President, and in distinct ballots the person voted for as Vice-President, and they shall make distinct lists of all persons voted for as President, and of all persons voted for as Vice-President, and of the number of votes for each, which lists they shall sign and certify, and transmit sealed to the seat of the government of the United States, directed to the President of the Senate;-The President of the Senate shall, in the presence of the Senate and House of Representatives, open all the certificates and the votes shall then be counted;-The person having the greatest number of votes for President, shall be the President, if such number be a majority of the whole number of Electors appointed; and if no person have such majority, then from the persons having the highest numbers not exceeding three on the list of those voted for as President, the House of Representatives shall choose immediately, by ballot, the President. But in choosing the President, the votes shall be taken by states, the representation from each state having one vote; a quorum for this purpose shall consist of a member or members from two-thirds of the states, and a majority of all the states shall be necessary to a choice. And if the House of Representatives shall not choose a President whenever the right of choice shall devolve upon them, before the fourth day of March next following, then the Vice-President shall act as President, as in the case of the death or other constitutional disability of the President.-The person having the greatest number of votes as Vice-President, shall be the the Vice-President, if such number be a majority of the whole number of Electors appointed, and if no person have a majority, then from the two highest numbers on the list, the Senate shall choose the Vice-President; a quorum for the purpose shall consist of two-thirds of the whole number of Senators, and a majority of the whole number shall be necessary to a choice. But no person constitutionally ineligible to the office of President shall be eligible to that of Vice-President of the United States.

AMENDMENT 13

[Ratified December 6, 1865]

Section 1. Neither slavery nor involuntary servitude, except as a punishment for crime whereof the party shall have been duly convicted, shall exist within the United States, or any place subject to their jurisdiction.

Section 2. Congress shall have power to enforce this article by appropriate legislation.

AMENDMENT 14

[Ratified July 9, 1868]

Section 1. All persons born or naturalized in the United States, and subject to the jurisdiction thereof, are citizens of the United States and of the State wherein they reside. No State shall make or enforce any law which shall abridge the privileges or immunities of citizens of the United States; nor shall any State deprive any person of life, liberty, or property, without due process of law; nor deny to any person within its jurisdiction the equal protection of the laws.

Section 2. Representatives shall be apportioned among the several States according to their respective numbers, counting the whole number of persons in each State, excluding Indians not taxed. But when the right to vote at any election for the choice of electors for President and Vice President of the United States, Representatives in Congress, the Executive and Judicial Officers of a State, or

the members of the Legislature thereof, is denied to any of the male inhabitants of such State, being twenty-one years of age, and citizens of the United States, or in any way abridged, except for participation in rebellion, or other crime, the basis of representation therein shall be reduced in the proportion which the number of such male citizens shall bear to the whole number of male citizens twenty-one years of age in such State.

Section 3. No person shall be a Senator or Representative in Congress, or elector of President and Vice President, or hold any office, civil or military, under the United States, or under any State, who, having previously taken an oath, as a member of Congress, or as an officer of the United States, or as a member of any State legislature, or as an executive or judicial officer of any State, to support the Constitution of the United States, shall have engaged in insurrection or rebellion against the same, or given aid or comfort to the enemies thereof. But Congress may by a vote of two-thirds of each House, remove such disability.

Section 4. The validity of the public debt of the United States, authorized by law, including debts incurred for payment of pensions and bounties for services in suppressing insurrection or rebellion, shall not be questioned. But neither the United States nor any State shall assume or pay any debt or obligation incurred in aid of insurrection or rebellion against the United States, or any claim for the loss or emancipation of any slave; but all such debts, obligations and claims shall be held illegal and void.

Section 5. The Congress shall have power to enforce, by appropriate legislation, the provisions of this article.

AMENDMENT 15

[Ratified February 3, 1870]

Section 1. The right of citizens of the United States to vote shall not be denied or abridged by the United States or by any State on account of race, color, or previous condition of servitude.

Section 2. The Congress shall have power to enforce this article by appropriate legislation.

AMENDMENT 16

[Ratified February 3, 1913]

The Congress shall have power to lay and collect taxes on incomes, from whatever source derived, without apportionment among the several States, and without regard to any census or enumeration.

AMENDMENT 17

[Ratified April 8, 1913]

The Senate of the United States shall be composed of two Senators from each State, elected by the people thereof for six years; and each Senator shall have one vote. The electors in each State shall have the qualifications requisite for electors of the most numerous branch of the State legislatures.

When vacancies happen in the representation of any State in the Senate, the executive authority of such State shall issue writs of election to fill such vacancies: *Provided,* That the legislature of any State may empower the executive thereof to make temporary appointments until the people fill the vacancies by election as the legislature may direct.

This amendment shall not be so construed as to affect the election or term of any Senator chosen before it becomes valid as part of the Constitution.

AMENDMENT 18

[Ratified January 16, 1919]

Section 1. After one year from the ratification of this article the manufacture, sale, or transportation of intoxicating liquors within, the importation thereof into, or the exportation thereof from the United States and all territory subject to the jurisdiction thereof for beverage purposes is hereby prohibited.

Section 2. The Congress and the several States shall have concurrent power to enforce this article by appropriate legislation.

Section 3. This article shall be inoperative unless it shall have been ratified as an amendment to the Constitution by the legislatures of the several States, as provided in the Constitution, within seven years from the date of the submission hereof to the States by the Congress.

AMENDMENT 19

[Ratified August 18, 1920]

The right of citizens of the United States to vote shall not be denied or abridged by the United States or by any State on account of sex. Congress shall have power to enforce this article by appropriate legislation.

AMENDMENT 20

[Ratified January 23, 1933]

Section 1. The terms of the President and Vice President shall end at noon on the 20th day of January, and the terms of Senators and Representatives at noon on the 3d day of January, of the years in which such terms would have ended if this article had not been ratified; and the terms of their successors shall then begin.

Section 2. The Congress shall assemble at least once in every year, and such meeting shall begin at noon on the 3d day of January, unless they shall by law appoint a different day.

Section 3. If, at the time fixed for the beginning of the term of the President, the President elect shall have died, the Vice President elect shall become President. If a President shall not have been chosen before the time fixed for the beginning of his term, or if the President elect shall have failed to qualify, then the Vice President elect shall act as President until a President shall have qualified; and the Congress may by law provide for the case wherein neither a President elect nor a Vice President elect shall have qualified, declaring who shall then act as President, or the manner in which one who is to act shall be selected, and such person shall act accordingly until a President or Vice President shall have qualified.

Section 4. The Congress may by law provide for the case of the death of any of the persons from whom the House of Representatives may choose a President whenever the right of choice shall have devolved upon them, and for the case of the death of any of the persons from whom the Senate may choose a Vice President whenever the right of choice shall have devolved upon them.

Section 5. Sections 1 and 2 shall take effect on the 15th day of October following the ratification of this article.

Section 6. This article shall be inoperative unless it shall have been ratified as an amendment to the Constitution by the legislatures of three-fourths of the several States within seven years from the date of its submission.

AMENDMENT 21

[Ratified December 5, 1933]

Section 1. The eighteenth article of amendment to the Constitution of the United States is hereby repealed.

Section 2. The transportation or importation into any State, Territory, or possession of the United States for delivery or use therein of intoxicating liquors, in violation of the laws thereof, is hereby prohibited.

Section 3. This article shall be inoperative unless it shall have been ratified as an amendment to the Constitution by conventions in the several States, as provided in the Constitution, within seven years from the date of the submission hereof to the States by the Congress.

AMENDMENT 22

[Ratified February 27, 1951]

Section 1. No person shall be elected to the office of the President more than twice, and no person who has held the office of President, or acted as President, for more than two years of a term to which some other person was elected President shall be elected to the office of the President more than once. But this Article shall not apply to any person holding the office of President when this Article was proposed by the Congress, and shall not prevent any person who may be holding the office of President, or acting as President, during the term within which this Article becomes operative from holding the office of President or acting as President during the remainder of such term.

Section 2. This article shall be inoperative unless it shall have been ratified as an amendment to the Constitution by the legislatures of three-fourths of the several States within seven years from the date of its submission to the States by the Congress.

AMENDMENT 23

[Ratified March 29, 1961]

Section 1. The District constituting the seat of Government of the United States shall appoint in such manner as the Congress may direct:

A number of electors of President and Vice President equal to the whole number of Senators and Representatives in Congress to which the District would be entitled if it were a State, but in no event more than the least populous State; they shall be in addition to those appointed by the States, but they shall be considered, for the purposes of the election of President and Vice President, to be electors appointed by a State; and they shall meet in the District and perform such duties as provided by the twelfth article of amendment.

Section 2. The Congress shall have power to enforce this article by appropriate legislation.

AMENDMENT 24

[Ratified January 23, 1964]

Section 1. The right of citizens of the United States to vote in any primary or other election for President or Vice President, for electors for President or Vice President, or for Senator or Representative in Congress, shall not be denied or abridged by the United States or any State by reason of failure to pay any poll tax or other tax.

Section 2. The Congress shall have power to enforce this article by appropriate legislation.

AMENDMENT 25

[Ratified February 10, 1967]

Section 1. In case of the removal of the President from office or of his death or resignation, the Vice President shall become President.

Section 2. Whenever there is a vacancy in the office of the Vice President, the President shall nominate a Vice President who shall take office upon confirmation by a majority vote of both Houses of Congress.

Section 3. Whenever the President transmits to the President pro tempore of the Senate and the Speaker of the House of Representatives his written declaration that he is unable to discharge the powers and duties of his office,

and until he transmits to them a written declaration to the contrary, such powers and duties shall be discharged by the Vice President as Acting President.

Section 4. Whenever the Vice President and a majority of either the principal officers of the executive departments or of such other body as Congress may by law provide, transmit to the President pro tempore of the Senate and the Speaker of the House of Representatives their written declaration that the President is unable to discharge the powers and duties of his office, the Vice President shall immediately assume the powers and duties of the office as Acting President.

Thereafter, when the President transmits to the President pro tempore of the Senate and the Speaker of the House of Representatives his written declaration that no inability exists, he shall resume the powers and duties of his office unless the Vice President and a majority of either the principal officers of the executive department or of such other body as Congress may by law provide, transmit within four days to the President pro tempore of the Senate and the Speaker of the House of Representatives their written declaration that the President is unable to discharge the powers and duties of his office. Thereupon Congress shall decide the issue, assembling within forty-eight hours for that purpose if not in session. If the Congress, within twenty-one days after receipt of the latter written declaration, or, if Congress is not in session, within twenty-one days after Congress is required to assemble, determines by two-thirds vote of both Houses that the President is unable to discharge the powers and duties of his office, the Vice President shall continue to discharge the same as Acting President; otherwise, the President shall resume the powers and duties of his office.

AMENDMENT 26

[Ratified June 30, 1971]

Section 1. The right of citizens of the United States, who are eighteen years of age or older, to vote shall not be denied or abridged by the United States or by any State on account of age.

Section 2. The Congress shall have the power to enforce this article by appropriate legislation.

PROPOSED AMENDMENT 27

[Proposed March 22, 1972)

Section 1. Equality of rights under the law shall not be denied or abridged by the United States or by any State on account of sex.

Section 2. The Congress shall have power to enforce, by appropriate legislation, the provisions of this article.

Section 3. This amendment shall take effect two years after date of ratification.

INDEX

ventions), 208–10
See also Presidential nominating conventions
Converse, Philip E., 101*n*, 127*n*, 134*n*, 137*n*, 148*n*, 155*n*, 164*n*, 210*n*
Conway, Jack T., 233
Coogan, Tim Pat, 579*n*
Coolidge, Calvin, 403
Coordination
  of foreign policy, 558–59
  hierarchical and lateral, 462–64
  of public policy making, 545–48
COPE (Committee on Political Education), 189, 225
Corcoran, Thomas, 420
Corporations, government-owned, 445–46
Corrupt Practices Act, 189
Corwin, Edward S., 39*n*, 41*n*
Cotter, Cornelius P., 259*n*
Coup, military, 578
Courts (court system)
  federal, 48–49
    appeals, courts of, 495–97
    district courts, 495–97
    Supreme Court and lower federal courts, relationship between, 495–97
  as instruments of government, 481
  interest groups' use of, 238–39
  as lawmakers, 480–81
  See also Supreme Court, U.S.
Courts of appeals, U.S., 495–97
  judicial circuits of, 495
Cowart, Andrew T., 303*n*
Cox, Archibald, 384
CPS. *See* Center for Political Studies
Crane, Katherine, 454*n*
Cranston, Alan, 192, 346–48
Creditors, rights of, 49
Crisis and continuity, in foreign policy-making, 552–55
Cronin, Thomas E., 414*n*
Cummings, Milton C., Jr., 159*n*, 194*n*
Curtiss-Wright decision (1936), 427
Cyert, Richard M., 533*n*
Cyprus crisis (1975), 387

D
Dahl, Robert A., 28*n*, 169*n*, 173, 483*n*, 487*n*, 528*n*, 594*n*, 597*n*
Daley, Richard, 175, 176
Danelski, David, 493*n*
Danhof, Clarence H., 449*n*
Davis, Kenneth Culp, 566*n*
Davis, Otto A., 467*n*
Debate, legislative process and, 353–54
Decision making by government
  administrators as independent influences on, 460–62
  non-conscious, in policy-making

process, 548–50
See also Public policy
Deckard, Barbara, 341*n*
Declaration of Independence, 66, 68, 76, 77
Dees, Morris, 196
Defectors, voting behavior of, 134–35
  weakening party ties and, 151–52
Defense, Department of, 381
  contractors and, 448–49
  coordination of policy by, 558, 559
  invention of new weapons systems alternatives by, 551–52
Defense spending (defense budget), Congressional control of, 386
Delegates, to conventions of parties. *See* Presidential nominating conventions — delegate selection for
Delegations in Congress, 340
Dellums, Ronald, 311, 346–49, 361
Demagogue, 65
Democracy, 58–66
  American thoughts on, 66
  consent of the governed and, 59–61
  direct, 61, 63, 64, 88, 89
  efficiency and, 64
  equality and, 609
  foreign policy making and, 555–56
  of interest groups, internal, 234–36
  Jacksonian, 63–64
  majority rule and, 65–66
  political evaluation and, 590
  political participation and, 65
  popular sovereignty and, 61
  representative, 42–43, 59–61
Democratic Caucus, 352, 367
  seniority system in Congress and, 333, 337
Democratic National Committee (DNC), 260, 262–63
Democratic party (Democrats), 34, 52
  activists in, 206–11
  black loyalty to, 143–44
  campaign contributions and, 190–92
  convention delegates of (1972), 208–9
  differences and similarities between Republican party and, 287–92
  ideological groups of, in Congress, 341–42
  ideology of, 145–49
  issue voting and, 160–63
  Jews and, 229–30
  labor unions and, 224, 225
  presidential primaries and, 265–68
  prospects for party system and, 149–52
  reforms of, 277–79
  social and economic bases for identification with, 137–45

in South, 140, 141, 150, 303–4
See also Southern Democrats
voting behavior and identification with, 133–35, 137
Democratic Steering Policy Committee, 333, 342
Democratic Study Group, 342
Demonstrations, protest
  peaceful, 569, 571
  violence and, 571–73
Dennis, Jack, 249*n*
Description, 11
Dewey, Thomas E., 269
Dexter, Lewis Anthony, 379*n*, 459*n*
Diplomatic mission, basic organization of, 558
Direct action
  legality of, 573–74
  See also Violent change
Direct democracy, 61, 63, 64, 88, 89
Direct mail advertising, fund raising by
  by political parties, 194–97
  by public interest groups, 232–34, 236
Direct participation, 168
Dirksen, Everett, 238, 336
Disaffection, political, 602–4
Discharge petition, 353*n*
Discrimination, sexual, Civil Rights Act of 1964 and, 237–38
Dissonance reduction, 98–100
Distribution of income, 22
Distributive policies, 525–26
District courts, 495–97
Districts, Congressional, 300–302
Divine Law, 67
Divisible goods, public goods and, 528–29
"Dixiecrats," 149–50
Dixon, Robert G., Jr., 508*n*
Domestic Council, 422–23
Donovan, John C., 448*n*
Draper, Theodore, 581*n*
Drug industry, 410–11
Duscha, Julius, 450
Dynamic approach to politics, 10–11

E
Eagleton, Thomas, 155, 321–22, 434
Ease of administration, public policy and, 530
Eastland, James, 383, 410, 411
Easton, David, 562*n*
Eckstein, Harry, 575*n*
Economic differences, party affiliation and, 138–40
Economic interests, *laissez faire* and, 69–70
Economic Opportunity Program, 448
Economic rights, Supreme Court and, 513–14

Foreign Service, 423, 454–56
Fortas, Abe, 573n
Fortune (magazine), 178
Fourteenth Amendment, 55, 69, 509, 511, 512
Fourth Amendment, 508–9
Fowlkes, Frank V., 222n
Fradon, Dana, 610
Fraser, Donald, 349
Freedom
  equality and, tension between, 611–13
  of speech (free speech)
    Campaign Finance Reform Act of 1974, 203–4
    educational levels and attitudes toward, 108–9
    Supreme Court decisions, 504–6
Frick, Henry C., 199
Friedman, Milton, 586n
Friedman, Robert S., 458
Friedrich, Carl J., 79n, 532n
Friendly, Henry J., 445n
Fund raising. *See* Campaign contributors; Direct mail advertising, fund-raising by

G
Gabriel, Ralph, 75n
Gallup, George, 117, 119
Gallup Opinion Index, 90n
Gallup polls, 396–97
Gardner, John, 233, 362
Garner, John N., 434
General Accounting Office (GAO), 372, 381, 543
General Motors Corporation, 222, 231
General public, 387
General will, 66
Generalization, specialization versus, 473
Geographical diversity
  factions and, 73
  See also Regional differences
Geography, 20–21
George, Alexander L., 404
Gerberding, William P., 81n
Gerrymandering, 301
Glass, Andrew J., 119n, 370n, 418n
Glazer, Nathan, 581n
Glenn, John, 302
Glenn, Norval D., 145n
Goal displacement, 544
Goals, public policy and, 521
Goldwater, Barry, 103, 143, 147–48, 192, 276, 291
  activists' support of, 210, 211
  direct mail fund raising by, 194–96
  as ideological candidate, 181, 182
  personal image of, 153–55, 159, 170
Gompers, Samuel, 223
Government, 15–16

collective effort and, 7–8
fear of big, 61, 63
local, 63
mixed, 41
See also specific topics
Government employees, 30–31, 451–59
  See also Civil service system
Government Operations Committees, 381
Government-owned corporations, 445–46
Graham, Hugh Davis, 575n
Grants-in-aid, federal, 447–48
Great Depression, 144
Great Society programs, 443–44
Greek-Americans, 230
Greeley, Andrew M., 26, 105n
Greenstein, Fred I., 130n, 134n, 394n, 403n, 481n
Grocery Manufacturers of America, Inc. (GMA), 221
Gross national product (GNP), 21
Groups. *See* Organizations; *specific types of groups*
Guerrilla warfare, 579, 581–82
Guevara, Ernesto "Che," 579n
Gurr, Ted Robert, 575n

H
Habeas corpus, writ of, 44
Hahn, Harlan, 273n
Haines, Charles G., 483n
Hamilton, Alexander, 72n, 299n
Harbison, Winfred, 483n
Hargrove, Erwin C., 404n
Harlow, Bryce, 412
Harris, Geoffrey, 454n
Harris, Louis, 119
Harris, Richard, 310n, 411n
Hartz, Louis, 66n
Haveman, Joel, 370n, 371n
Haveman, Robert, 541n
Hayden, Carl, 298
Haynesworth, Clement, 493
Head, Richard G., 581n
Headcounts, 353
Health, Education, and Welfare, Department of (HEW), 442, 443
Health care. *See* Medical care; Public health
Hearings, Congressional, 349–50
Heclo, Hugh, 403n
Hefner, Ted, 145n
Hennessy, Bernard C., 259n
Herblock, 178, 305, 359
Herring, Pendleton, 408n
Hierarchical control, limitations on, 461–62
Hierarchical coordination, 462–63
Hierarchy, 438
  standard pattern of, 546

Highway Safety Act, 231
Hill, Lister, 362
Himmelfarb, Milton, 142n
Hofstadter, Richard, 69, 575n
Holcombe, Arthur, 75n
Hoover, Herbert, 144, 394, 400, 404
Horowitz, Irving Louis, 563n
House Appropriations Committee (HAC), 366–68
House Democratic Campaign Committee, 309
House of Commons (Great Britain), 369n
House of Representatives, U.S., 41–42, 73–74
  basis for representation in, 299, 300
  district lines for seats in, 300–302
  election of members of. *See* Congressional elections
  number of seats in, 300
  party organization in, 335–36
  presidential elections and, 282, 286
  Speaker of, 335–37, 352
  See also Congress, U.S.; *and specific committees*
House Republican Campaign Committee, 309
Housing and Urban Development, Department of (HUD), 443–44, 547
Howar, Barbara, 320
Hudson, Michael C., 598n
Huitt, Ralph K., 314n
Humphrey, Hubert H., 120–21, 142, 171, 183–84, 197–98, 291–92, 321, 326
  1972 primaries and, 266, 267
  as Vice President, 435
  Vietnam issue and, 158, 160–63, 249
Hunt, H. L., 183
Hutcheson, Richard G., III, 304n
Hyman, Herbert H., 153n

I
Identification with party. *See* Party identification
Ideological conflict, 5–6
Ideological criticisms of American politics, 586–87
Ideological groups in Congress, 341–42
Ideological interest groups, 230
Ideological opportunism of parties, 254
Ideology, 5–6
  of activists vs. general public, 206–9
  American, 58–84
    consensus, 82–83
    Constitution, ideas of the, 71–76
    democracy, 58–66
    equality, 76–79

376n
Kissinger, Henry, 116, 421
Kleindienst, Richard, 383
Knowland, William, 349
Korean war, 160
Kostroski, Warren Lee, 303n, 307n
Krislov, Samuel, 50n, 504n

L
Labor, Department of, 441
Labor force, occupational distribution
    of, 29–31
Labor unions, 31
    campaign contributions by, 172,
        189–90, 225, 310
    Congressional campaigns and, 310
    Democratic party and, 224, 225
    federal employee, 451
    as interest groups, 223–26
    political participation by, 172, 189–
        90
La Follette, Robert, 149
Laissez faire doctrine, 67–70
Lakoff, Sanford A., 76n
Lapp, Ralph E., 450n
Lateral coordination, 463, 464
Latham, Aaron, 384n
Law
    coordination of public policy
        through, 545
    natural, idea of, 38, 67
    rule of, 79–80
Lawmaking process, 535–45
    administrative stage of, 538, 542–43
    evaluation stage of, 538
        post-auditing, 543–45
    formal enactment stage of, 537
        setting priorities and bargaining,
            540–42
    information and invention stage of,
        535–40
    See also Congress, U.S.—legisla-
        tive process in
Lawson, Edwin D., 95n
Leach, Richard H., 52n
Leadership, congressional, 335–38
Leaks to the press, 114–16
Left-wing criticisms of American pol-
    itics, 586
Legislative branch. *See* Congress, U.S.
Legislative oversight, 381–82
Legislative process. *See* Congress,
    U.S.—legislative process in;
    Lawmaking process
Legislative role of courts, 480–81
Legitimacy
    Constitutional, 50–51
    political evaluation in terms of,
        599–604
Lengle, James I., 265–67n
Leninist parties, 580
Lerner, Michael, 403n

Letter-writing campaigns, 379
Levitin, Teresa E., 106n
Lewis, Anthony, 569n
Liberal philosophy, 66–67
Liberal-pragmatic criticisms of Amer-
    ican politics, 586–87
Liberals
    as ideological label, 80–81, 100
    interrelation of opinions of, 103–6
    self-identification as, 101–2
Library of Congress, 372
Lindblom, Charles E., 528n, 533n
Lindsay, John V., 176
Line agencies, 439–44
Line departments, 439–40
Lipsky, Michael, 575n
Literary Digest (magazine), 117
Litigation by interest groups, 238–39
Lobbyists, 240–45, 320
    as information sources for congress-
        men, 375–76
    regulation of, 243–45
    Supreme Court and, 489
    See also Interest groups
Locke, John, 38, 41
Log rolling, 325n
Long, Priscilla, 587n
Longley, Lawrence D., 282n
Lorenz (cartoonist), 154
Los Angeles Times (newspaper), 113
Lowi, Theodore J., 525n, 544n, 567n
Loyalty, national, 95
Loyalty oaths, 506
Lynd, Staughton, 573n

M
MacAvoy, Paul W., 445n
McCarthy, Eugene, 163–64, 180–83,
    193–94, 276
McCarthy, Joe, 414n
McCloskey, Paul N., 187, 322, 349
McCloskey, Robert, 68n
McClosky, Herbert, 83n, 108n, 147n,
    206n
McConahay, John B., 601n
McDonald, Forrest, 49n
McFall, John, 347, 348
McGovern, George, 142, 143, 145, 149,
    182, 192, 196, 292, 321–22
    activists' support of, 211
    Eagleton and, 434
    labor unions and, 225
    1972 campaign of, 280
    1972 primaries and nomination of,
        266–68, 270–73, 276
    personal image of, 155–56, 158–59
McGovern Commission, 277–79
McGrath, C. Peter, 478n
Machine politics, 179–80, 260–62
    Congressional elections and, 311–
        12
McNamara, Robert, 545

MacNeil, Neil, 336n
McWilliams, Wilson Carey, 597n
Madison, James, 72, 73
Magazines, 112
Majorities of the moment, 75–76
Majority rule in American ideology,
    65–66, 71–76
    factions and, 72–74
    minority rights and, 72
Malapportionment, legislative, 300
Malbin, Michael J., 241n, 374n
Mandates, elections as, 163–65
Manley, John F., 359, 365n
Mann, Dean E., 451n
Mansfield, Mike, 336
Mao Tse-tung, 579
Marbury v. *Madison,* 482
March, James G., 533n
Marcuse, Herbert, 587n
Margolis, Julius, 541
Marine Engineers Union, 224
Mark-up sessions, 350, 352
Marshall, John, 478, 482, 483
Marshall Plan, 428
Marxist ideologies, 69
Mass media, public opinion and, 111–
    16
Matthews, Donald R., 264n, 273n, 276n,
    316n, 403n
Mayhew, David R., 311n, 313n
Means and ends, public policy and,
    522–23
Meany, George, 224
Median family income, 21–22
Medical care, 104, 146, 148
"Melting pot" notion, 24, 25n
Members of Congress for Peace
    through Law, 342
Mendelson, Wallace, 485n
Meyerson, Martine, 180n
Michels, Robert, 235
Middle class, 28, 31, 32
Mikva, Abner, 192
Milbrath, Lester W., 459n
Military conquest, 578
Military coup, 578
Military officers, 454
Mill, John Stuart, 60
Miller, Arthur, 257
Miller, Arthur H., 103n, 106n, 134n,
    142n, 145n, 152n, 155n, 602n
Miller, Arthur Selwyn, 513n
Miller, Herman P., 27n
Miller, Warren E., 103n, 106n, 314n,
    378n
Mills, Wilbur, 364, 402
Minorities, majorities of the moment
    and, 75–76
Minority rights, 72, 74–75
Minority rule in Congress, 361–71
    appropriations process and, 365–68
    compartmentalization and special-
        ization and, 368–71

in Congress, 334–40
conventions of. *See* Conventions, party
differences and similarities between, 287–92
early American, 251, 253
electoral college's effects on, 286–87
federalism and, 52–53
functions of, 249–50
identification with. *See* Party identification
ideological opportunism of, 254
irrelevance of, 151–52
Leninist, 580
membership in, 254–58
organization of, 258–63
  national party structures, 259–60, 262–63
  state and local parties, 260–63
platforms of, 287–89
presidential campaigns and, 279–82
presidential nominating conventions of. *See* Conventions, party
primaries of. *See* Primaries
procedural changes in, 566
realignment of, 150–51
reforms of, 277–79
registration by, 255–56
regulars and purists in, 256–57
spending on campaigns by, limits, 201
third. *See* Third parties
voting behavior and identification with, 132–37
See also Factions; Party system, . American
Partisan policies, 529
Partisans, 99
Party activists. *See* Activists
Party caucuses, 337–38
Party chairmen, national, 259–60
Party column ballot, 305
Party identification, 133–37
attitudes on issues and, 146, 147
ideology and, 145–49
relevance of parties and, 151–52
roots of, 137
social and economic bases of. *See* Factions—social and economic bases of
Party membership, 254–58
psychological. *See* Party identification
Party platforms, 287–89
Party programs in Congress, 338–40
Party purists, 182, 256–57
Party regulars (professionals), 256–57
Party system, American (two-party system), 251–54
prospects for, 149–52
Patent Office, U.S., 478

Patman, Wright, 333
Patriotism of children, 95–97
Patronage
definition of, 174
machine politics and, 179–80, 260–62
political participation motivated by, 173–81
President and, 413
Peabody, Robert L., 314*n*
Peasant revolution, 579
Peck, Merton J., 450*n*
Peirce, Neal R., 125*n*
Pell, Claiborne, 226
Pennsylvania, presidential primaries in, 266
Pentagon Papers, 545
Permanent Investigations Subcommittee, Senate, 381
Personal appeal, candidates', 152–57
Personal contact with voters, 280–81
Personnel change, 564–66
Philip (Prince of England), 393
Physical coercion
nonviolence and, 571–72
strategic aspects of using, 574–78
Pierce, John G., 101*n*
Pitkin, Hanna F., 60*n*, 376*n*
Platforms, party, 287–89
Pocket veto, 46
Policy, public. *See* Public policy
Policy-making, 16–17
administraion and, overview of, 470–74
Supreme Court and, 490
See also Public policy
Policy-oriented political participation, 172–73
Polish-Americans, 26
Political action
collective, 14–15
individual, 14
as interest-group tactic, 239–40
See also Political participation
Political activists. *See* Activists
Political change. *See* Change
Political disaffection, 602–4
Political equality, 76–77
Political evaluation, 11–12, 17, 586–613
comparative analysis as mode of, 597–99
conflict resolution and, 604–6
equality and, 606–11
by experts, 589–91
ideological criticisms of American politics and, 586–87
illustrations of, 588–89
legitimacy and, 599–604
limits of governmental action and, 591, 593–95
by the people, 589–90

"politics" as a corrective in, 596–97
power, capacity, and consent and, 595–96
Political influence, money and, 199
Political opinions or attitudes
determinants of, 107–9
interrelation of, 103–7
shaping of, 97–100
See also Public opinion
Political participation, 65, 168–212
active, 169
by activists, 204–11
  education and wealth of activists, 204–6
  ideology gap between activists and general public, 206–9
  implications and consequences, 209–11
  letter writers, 210
  regulars vs. purists, 256–57
by blacks, 205
by contributors to campaigns. *See* Campaign contributors
direct, 168
motives for, 171–87
  ideology, 180–84
  patronage, 173–80
  policy, 172–73
  sociability, prestige, and friendship, 184–87
patronage-based, 173–80
policy oriented, 172–73
rates of, 169–71
See also Political action
Political parties. *See* Parties, political
Political skills, 8–9
Political socialization, 91–97
Political stability, equilibrium analysis and, 563–64
Politics
context of American, 12–13
dynamic approach to, 10–11
ideological, 58
machine, 179–80, 260–62
  Congressional elections, 311–12
national, 9–10
negative connotations of, 8
participation in. *See* Political participation
pragmatic or interest-group, 58
as source of conflict, 6–7
See also specific topics
Polls, public opinion, 116–21
method of conducting, 117–19
politicians' use of, 119–21
Polsby, Nelson W., 134*n*, 182*n*, 329*n*, 334*n*, 410*n*, 481*n*
Pomper, Gerald M., 148*n*, 149*n*, 288*n*
Popular accountability of congressmen, 313–14
Popular sovereignty, 61
Population changes, 33–34

650

EXECUTIVE

THE PRESIDENT

Executive Office of the President

The White House Office	Office of Telecommunications Policy
Office of Management and Budget	Special Action Office for Drug Abuse Prevention
Council of Economic Advisers	Federal Property Council
National Security Council	Council on Wage and Price Stability
Office of the Special Representative for Trade Negotiations	Presidential Clemency Board
Council on International Economic Policy	Energy Resources Council
Council on Environmental Quality	Office of the Vice President of the United States
Domestic Council	

DEPARTMENT OF STATE	DEPARTMENT OF THE TREASURY	DEPARTMENT OF DEFENSE	DEPARTMENT OF JUSTICE
DEPARTMENT OF COMMERCE	**DEPARTMENT OF THE INTERIOR**	**DEPARTMENT OF AGRICULTURE**	**DEPARTMENT OF LABOR**

DEPARTMENT OF HEALTH, EDUCATION, AND WELFARE	DEPARTMENT OF HOUSING AND URBAN DEVELOPMENT	DEPARTMENT OF TRANSPORTATION

INDEPENDENT AGENCIES AND OFFICES

ACTION	Indian Claims Commission
Administrative Conference of the United States	Inter-American Foundation
American Battle Monuments Commission	Interstate Commerce Commission
American Revolution Bicentennial Administration	National Aeronautics and Space Administration
Appalachian Regional Commission	National Credit Union Administration
Canal Zone Government	National Foundation on the Arts and the Humanities
Civil Aeronautics Board	National Labor Relations Board
Commission on Civil Rights	National Mediation Board
Commission of Fine Arts	National Science Foundation
Commodity Futures Trading Commission	National Transportation Safety Board
Community Services Administration	Nuclear Regulatory Commission
Consumer Product Safety Commission	Occupational Safety and Health Review Commission
District of Columbia	Overseas Private Investment Corporation
Energy Research and Development Administration	Panama Canal Company
Environmental Protection Agency	Pension Benefit Guaranty Corporation
Equal Employment Opportunity Commission	Postal Rate Commission
Export-Import Bank of the United States	Railroad Retirement Board
Farm Credit Administration	Renegotiation Board
Federal Communications Commission	Securities and Exchange Commission
Federal Deposit Insurance Corporation	Selective Service System
Federal Election Commission	National Selective Service Appeal Board
Federal Energy Administration	Small Business Administration
Federal Home Loan Bank Board	Smithsonian Institution
Federal Maritime Commission	Tennessee Valley Authority
Federal Mediation and Conciliation Service	United States Arms Control and Disarmament Agency
Federal Power Commission	United States Civil Service Commission
Federal Reserve System (Board of Governors of the)	United States Information Agency
Federal Trade Commission	United States International Trade Commission
Foreign Claims Settlement Commission of the United States	United States Postal Service
General Services Administration	Veterans Administration